Maryland and America, 1940–1980

Maryland & America

1940 TO 1980

GEORGE H. CALLCOTT

The Johns Hopkins University Press   Baltimore and London

This book has been brought to publication with the generous
assistance of the Andrew W. Mellon Foundation.

The Johns Hopkins University Press, 701 West 40th Street,
Baltimore, Maryland 21211
The Johns Hopkins University Press Ltd, London

The paper in this book is acid-free and meets the guidelines for permanence
and durability of the Committee on Production Guidelines for Book
Longevity of the Council on Library Resources.

Library of Congress Cataloging in Publication Data

Callcott, George H., 1929–
    Maryland and America, 1940–1980.

    Bibliography: p.
    Includes index.
    1. Maryland—Politics and government—1865–1950. 2. Maryland—
Politics and government—1951–   . I. Title.
F186.C34   1985   975.2′04   85-166
ISBN 0-8018-2492-3 (alk. paper)

Contents

Tables

Figures

Much of the finest historical writing nowadays is local history—accounts of a single medieval village, a seventeenth-century parish, a nineteenth-century factory town—with local detail providing the insight and authenticity that lights an entire age. I began this study in hopes of applying this principle to recent history, and I imagined that Maryland's experience during recent years might contribute to an understanding of our times. Such a concept may be too ambitious. I have sometimes wavered: Maryland is too large, these forty years too long and near, my ability too modest for such grand uses of the past. Still, the questions in my mind have remained large, and I have tried to understand all of our society during these decades through the manageable context of one state. The theme of this book, then, is American history working itself out in the moods and problems of Maryland. More specifically, the theme is the suburbanization, bureaucratization, and modernizaton of America as it occurs in Maryland, transforming politics, culture, and way of life.

Even more than I imagined, Maryland does reflect certain national trends. The parallels are extraordinary, for example, between the concerns of national and state administrations—President Harry Truman and Governor William P. Lane in the late 1940s; President Dwight D. Eisenhower and Governor Theodore R. McKeldin in the happy 1950s; Presidents John F. Kennedy and Lyndon B. Johnson and Governor J. Millard Tawes in the soaring 1960s; President Richard M. Nixon and Governors Spiro T. Agnew and Marvin Mandel, who anticipated and characterized the troubled 1970s; and President Gerald Ford and Governor Blair Lee, who served as caretakers when scandal drove out their predecessors, and Presidents Jimmy Carter and Ronald Regan and Governor Harry Hughes, who reflected a new direction as the 1980s began. Each decade possessed a distinct character, so much alike in Maryland and the rest of America. This parallel, which has gone mostly unnoticed, suggests the existence of a political zeitgeist that is much larger than administrations and that deserves more explanation than historians have provided.

More important than administrations are the dominating events of our times: World War II, postwar affluence, shifting populations, the Cold War, Vietnam, the rise of bureaucracy, the emergence of blacks and women. Each event issues from the grass roots or has an impact there in a way that explicates the event itself. The events, then, along with the evolving public temper, shape our response to the continuing social challenges of our century: poverty, education, health, environment, consumer protection, and the rest. As often as not, events and problems express themselves more intensely, and their outcomes are more clear, in a single state than in a national compromise that results when all states act collectively. As a rule, Maryland between 1940 and 1980 was a little ahead of the national temper in timing, a bit more intense in its response.

Maryland likes to call itself America in miniature, and there is something to the claim. The state's affluent suburbs, its simultaneously decaying and sparkling city, its traditional small town and rural culture, together tend to exemplify, exaggerate, and anticipate the nation. Other places—England, New York, California—anticipate in different ways, but Maryland remains an unusual blend of the mellow and the fresh, things lagging and things advanced. Many places, no doubt, reflect America. The important point is that state history is a useful avenue toward understanding the world.

To be sure, state history also has obvious limitations. Foreign affairs and economic changes, for example, have mostly worldwide or national origins, so that state history cannot examine causes so much as results. Cultural and intellectual history assume a new dimension in local history. The presence of John Barth or Katherine Anne Porter in Maryland was largely fortuitous. For social history, both national and state perspectives are too large, because living styles are best examined at the level of neighborhood or individual. State history, in other words, is sometimes too small or too large to allow total understanding, but it helps us to realize how the pieces fit together.

The study of our times is open ended, largely uncontained at the near end of the continuum, so that knowledge of things in which we are still involved remains less complete than eventually it will become. History provides perspective but not solutions to present concerns. We shall be confident of our judgments only when they matter less.

I believe that state history can be useful in a large context, but it also retains its old-fashioned value in helping us, as Marylanders, to discover our particular identity. This discovery comes not in sentiment or in boasts of achievements or in tributes to the prominent, but in the full and honest knowledge of ourselves. Our faults and virtues, our failures and successes, our diversity and modernity—all are points of pride. A grand heritage of many dimensions embraces us from the past.

Maryland and America, 1940–1980

In heritage and culture one of the smallest states was one of the most divided. This diversity was the main explanation for whatever was unique about Maryland and provided the state with a certain microcosmic significance. Like the nation, it had a powerful but declining cities of ethnic complexity and organization politics. It had Eastern Shore and southern counties dominated by community elites and steeped in conservatism. In the western counties, commercial, industrial, labor, farming, and professional groups stood in protracted conflict that found expression in a politics of personality. Finally, there were the booming suburbs, which threatened to overwhelm the other sections with an antiparty, middle-class ideology. The state, like the nation, was not just an average of all its parts, but a mosaic of particulars. Figures 1. 1 through 1. 7, scattered through this chapter, demonstrate the sharp differences within the state. Before we consider the ways in which the parts of Maryland made common cause within the state's narrow confines, let us consider the separate cultures, especially the political cultures, in which the sections found their distinct identities.

The Four Cultures of Maryland

The City and the Organization

From the late nineteenth century until the 1940s Baltimore was not only the most powerful section of Maryland but so much the most powerful that it almost persuaded the provinces of their backwardness. It comprised 51 percent of the state's population in 1920 and 47 percent in 1940, and its portion of the state's power was overwhelmingly larger than its portion of the state's population. Almost everyone of great wealth lived or worked in the city, and, despite dreadful slums, Baltimore's standard of living was higher than that of any Maryland county. It was the state's hub for railways, manufacturing, banking, insurance, law, medicine, and education. The crossroads clerk, if he was ambitious, migrated to the county seat, and if he made good and retained ambition, he moved on to Baltimore.

The city's newspapers covered the state, except for the fringes. The city's social register, its downtown gentlemen's clubs, its outlying country clubs, and its rich churches dominated fashion if not opinion. Its cultural institutions—the Johns Hopkins University, Walters Art Gallery, Baltimore Museum of Art, Maryland Art Institute, Peabody Institute, Maryland Historical Society, Enoch Pratt Free Library, and, to be sure, the athletic teams and nightclubs—overwhelmed everything the counties had to offer. The late nineteenth and early twentieth centuries were the age of the city.

All was not wealth, of course. More than most American cities, and unlike the smaller towns of the state, Baltimore was a city of ethnic neighborhoods. These were mostly made up of distinctive two- and three-story row houses with clean white marble steps, and of neighborhood bars which were located at almost every intersection. Blacks crowded into two dilapidated enclaves on the east and west sides of the business district, enclaves that swelled after 1945 to embrace almost half of the city. The WASP elite lived in the wedge to the north, from Mt. Vernon Square to beyond Guilford and Roland Park. Jews occupied the large wedge to the northwest and moved farther and

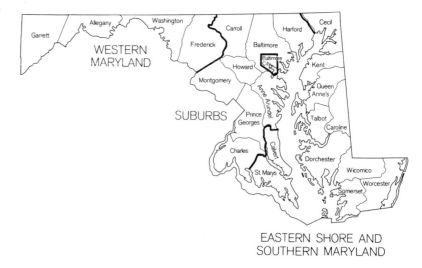

farther out as the blacks encroached. In the west was an Italian wedge;
a German wedge to the southwest; pockets of Germans, Greeks, and
Irish in the south; Poles and Czechs in the southeast; Poles and Greeks
in the east; Germans and Italians in the northeast.[1]

The city, more than the countryside, was in constant flux. Its population was more mobile, its economy more volatile, its response to
technological change more sharp. Following depression was wartime
boom, but then, as the middle class began leaving, came the long
decline. Politicians and boosters denied the decline through the 1950s,
but with the riots of the 1960s denial became impossible. From 1945
to 1980 the city's population dropped from 950,000 to 787,000, from
47 percent to 19 percent of the state's total population (see table 1.1);
the white proportion of the city's population dropped from 81 percent
to 44 percent; and the city's proportion of the state's assessed property
dropped from 56 percent to 11 percent.[2]

Table 1.1. The Four Cultures of Maryland

Area	Percentage of State Population		
	1920	1940	1980
Baltimore City	51	47	19
Eastern Shore and southern Maryland (including Anne Arundel and Prince George's counties to 1939; Charles County to 1979)	22	16	11
Western Maryland (including Baltimore and Montgomery counties to 1939; Carroll and Howard counties to 1959; Harford County to 1969)	27	18	10
Suburbs (including Anne Arundel, Baltimore, Montgomery, and Prince George's counties in 1940; Carroll and Howard counties in 1960; Harford County in 1970; and Charles County in 1980)	0	19	61

Source: U.S. Bureau of the Census.

The row houses of East Baltimore. The machine politics of William Curran in the 1940s evolved into the neighborhood politics of William Schaefer in the 1980s. Courtesy of M. E. Warren.

The city's politics was also more intense than politics in the countryside. Politics was the mirror of the city: its privilege and democracy, its demand for preferment and then for survival. Politics in the city revolved around the organization—"the machine," to its enemies—that lived, at least in a modified form, into the 1970s. Boss Tweed's New York machine of the 1870s and Richard J. Daley's Chicago organization of the 1960s were more publicized, but for at least a century, Baltimore, with characteristic anonymity, maintained a political organization that ranked with the best.

The Baltimore organization, like those in other cities, originated in the time of Andrew Jackson. It grew with the specialization of urban life and with the withdrawal of major economic entrepreneurs from office, and it grew with the professionalization of politics and with the spoils system, in which the livelihood of both government and party workers depended on election victories. As immigrants poured into the port cities, especially from the 1840s to the 1920s, party organizations were a democratizing influence. Party workers helped the newcomers through customs and naturalization, found them jobs, provided food and coal in time of need, offered fellowship, and helped them get into a hospital or out of jail—all in exchange for loyalty and votes. Often, as in Baltimore, there was an ethnic division among the political organizations, as the German newcomers before the Civil War were usually Whig, and the Irish, Democrats. In the 1850s Baltimore was mobtown, the most violent city in America, chiefly as a result of the annual election riots between political organizations, but by the early 1870s the Democrats emerged under a single boss who was powerful enough to incorporate all factions and brook no rivals.[3]

From the 1870s until his death in 1907, with minor interruptions, Isaac Freeman Rasin was boss in the classic sense: the only office he ever held was court clerk, but he was the chief source of order and authority in the city. He supervised the Democratic clubs and party workers in each ward, approved the party nominees for every position, supervised the campaign collections from those who did business with the city, and dictated which city contracts went to which contributors. Rasin was replaced by his tough Irish lieutenants, John J. "Sonny" Mahon and John S. "Frank" Kelley, and then, from 1928 to 1946, by the last of the citywide bosses, and the most brilliant, William Curran.

The son of poor Irish immigrants, Curran grew up running errands for the ward chiefs. The system encouraged the able to leapfrog ahead, and Rasin obtained a scholarship for Curran at the University of Maryland Law School. He finished near the top of his class, married the daughter of an East Baltimore precinct leader, and served briefly in the state senate and city council, but then withdrew, as bosses tended to do, to devote full time to the city's Democratic Central Committee, where he wrested power from his predecessors. Only incidentally did he earn a handsome living as Baltimore's most brilliant criminal lawyer; his greatest genius was running the party and its retainers—often including a governor, a mayor, several congressmen, judges, delegates, and councilmen, along with scores of ward bosses and thousands of city employees.

Curran chewed a cigar as a kind of symbol of boss authority, but he wore the most fashionable clothes and elegant pince-nez spectacles, and he defended bossism in philosophical language. "The organization stands between demagoguery and conservatism," he noted; "organization politics is the anchor against radicalism." He was a manipulator of men, aware, said a lieutenant, of the secret corners of each individual's motivation. He was a master of detail who was concerned with perfect loyalty in the least important office and unforgiving of defectors. It was for him to supervise the favors and the jobs, to balance the tickets that guaranteed victory, and to see that the city obtained its full share in Annapolis and Washington. Curran was above the law, but he was not corrupt. Wealthy enough on his own, and enjoying the greater wealth of power, he was contemptuous of personal payoffs. At the Christmas party each year at City Hall, Curran sat smoking his cigar in regal splendor, his armchair like a throne amidst the milling crowd, as the party faithful waited to thank him for favors or, occasionally, to introduce a son who had been named for him.

It was a world of power and intrigue, of favors and backstabbing, and even Curran counted losses among the triumphs. Coalition reform tickets, independent candidates, and ambitious neighborhood bosses constantly worked out alliances to challenge the organization. Citywide control from the top ended when Curran retired about 1946, and control fell back to the level of district or ward leaders who bargained with one another for votes and power. Organization remained the basis for politics, but the city boss gave way to a multitude of area bosses.[4]

The strongest of the several district bosses from the 1930s to the 1960s was James H. (Jack) Pollack, who managed the Jewish vote of the northwest. He never pretended to influence personally the votes outside his area, but he exercised his firm control of 20 percent of the city's votes as leverage for legislation, jobs, and favors. Pollack was born in Baltimore in 1899, the son of Polish-Jewish immigrants. He barely attended school, was a teen-age prizefighter and prohibition gangster, and was arrested at least thirteen times for a variety of offenses including pornography, assault, hijacking, and murder—but he served only one sentence of thirty days. Curran employed him in the 1920s to tear down opposition signs, and politics became his métier.

As executive director for the Trenton Democratic Club of the Fourth Legislative District, Pollack served as treasurer for local candidates, collecting contributions and dispensing favors. The club got people jobs, gave Christmas baskets to the needy, provided for burials, got potholes filled, persuaded the city bureaucracy to build playgrounds and firehouses where the Democrats wanted them. Trenton Club workers covered the district, and by 1945 Pollack was known as the man who could deliver the votes. His people were in the courthouses and the legislature, on election boards and the city council. Pollack regularly attended city council meetings and major legislative hearings, always debonaire, saying little, taking notes. He had power because the voters knew they benefited from his guidance and because the candidates knew they depended on his support. Pollack provided the core of Millard Tawes's support in his race for governor in 1960, and Pollack obtained a large share of Tawes's patronage appointments during Tawes's first year as governor. Marvin Mandel was a local Pollack protégé until 1962, when he joined Tawes in rebellion.

Pollack was eventually overthrown by population change. Even with partially black tickets he was not able to control the black voters who were moving into his district in the 1950s, and in the 1960s his Jewish voters grew independent. He followed the Jewish vote from the Fourth to the Fifth District and then to the suburbs, establishing new headquarters in the Town and Country Club, but by the 1960s even suburban candidates were avoiding his support.[5]

By the 1970s bosses existed chiefly at the ward level; of these, the best known was Dominic (Mimi) DiPietro, who was headquartered in the middle of Baltimore's Little Italy. He had spent sixty years as a ward worker, presiding over the Twenty-Sixth Ward Democratic Club, doing favors, making deals. He had two indictments for political excesses, one conviction, one pardon. He controlled almost 540 of the ward's 600 votes, to the extent that he could switch or trade them within a few hours' notice. He loved his neighbors, attended almost every christening, wedding, and burial, did favors for everybody, and promoted Little Italy. His votes made him a key to the precinct, a core of support for powerful figures like Mayors Thomas D'Alesandro, Jr. (1947–1959), and Thomas D'Alesandro III (1967–1971) and state senator Joseph Staszak (1967–1974). He parlayed his votes for a seat on the city council which he held for almost twenty years. Most of his neighbors were convinced he was the neighborhood's greatest supporter. DiPietro was one of the stongest ward leaders, but there were others like him around the city.[6]

As characteristic of Baltimore political organization as the boss was the political club. Originally these clubs were gentlemen's retreats, such as Isaac Freeman Rasin's Crescent Club, considered the grandest in the nation, which met in a four-story building with gilt ballrooms and billiard parlors and possessed a large portfolio of investments to be used for political purposes.[7] More often the clubs met in a room or two, often above a store; men came there to drink and talk politics, and sometimes women came for dances and bingo. The club was a social center, sponsored by the party, dedicated to neighborhood interests and neighborhood power. Members of the Eighteenth Ward Club, for example, brought their families to the club's famous "Vacant Chair" ceremony every year. A spotlight shone on an empty chair in an otherwise dark room as one clerk in the back of the room read the names of members who had recently died, including honorary members such as John F. Kennedy, while another clerk intoned, "Absent."[8]

Men like Pollack headed rich clubs, and DiPietro headed a humble one. They were always Democratic and pictures of Democratic officeholders hung on the walls of the meeting place, although from time to time the club found it in its interest to support an independent or a Republican candidate. Loyalty to club decisions was expected. Before elections, the ward boss, who was the club executive, consulted with party officials, candidates, and members of the club. Together club members decided whom to support, what resources to spend or assessments to levy, and who would be assigned to put up signs, to get out invalid voters, and to watch the polls. In the 1940s there were about sixty such clubs in Baltimore, almost one for each ward. In the 1970s nearly twenty were listed in the telephone books, with about that many more unlisted. Some of the clubs in the 1970s became inactive between elections and were revived in election years by a candidate desirous of a personal campaign organization.[9]

Money for the system came, not crudely from bribes or misappropriated tax funds, but from the freely given campaign contributions of everyone who did business with the city. This included contractors who wanted public jobs; banks that held city revenues and sold city bonds; shipping firms that used city port facilities; transportation lines that were regulated by city ordinances; real estate developers who were concerned with zoning; businessmen who were concerned with assessments; bar and restaurant owners who were concerned with inspections; vendors who were concerned with licenses; lawyers who were concerned with coming before local judges; city employees or candidates who were interested in keeping their jobs; unions, service clubs, and neighborhood or ethnic groups that were in need of favors; or even reform groups that were in pursuit of a particular program that might include restrictions on the organization itself.

The money, then traveled in a circle—from the contributors to the party workers, the clubs, and the candidates, and then back as wages and gifts to the contributors. The most blatant organization expenditure kept alive Baltimore's unique tradition of "walking around money"—$40 or $50 given at election time to each of hundreds of party workers who brought in reluctant voters by providing free transportation for invalids or free drinks for barroom drunks. But, like the machine itself, the system of walking around money began to decline by the second half of this century. Observers calculated that $80,000 went into the system for each election in the 1900s, about one-half of the total that was raised and spent in a citywide campaign; $60,000 was available for this direct election-day expense in the 1940s, down to one-third of the total; and about $50,000 in walking around money flowed during the 1960s, less than one-fourth of the total that was raised and spent in a citywide campaign. In 1977 suburban reformers in the General Assembly were successful in their attempt to ban the direct payments, although "expenses" for party workers largely made up for the defunct walking around money.[10]

The organization functioned successfully insofar as it collected contributions effectively, delivered on its promises, and, especially, kept the payoff system within bounds that were acceptable to the public. There were too many hands out for any one person to get rich. The more powerful the boss, the more he depended on broad support for his authority. None of the bosses, large or small, died with a fortune approaching the magnitude of his power.

The bosses and clubs continued to cast a distinctive shadow over city politics, but after 1940 they both began to weaken. New Deal social services and wartime prosperity reduced the bosses' power to dispense welfare and jobs. The geographical and social mobility of the war, and then the postwar rush to the suburbs, diluted party loyalty. Television by the 1960s competed with the social function of the political clubs, gave voters a better understanding of rival candidates, and thus made it easier for independents to challenge the party tickets.

In a larger way the decline of organization politics stemmed from the continuing rise of the middle class. Even as early as the 1870s, middle-class people had fought the alliance of wealthy party contributors and lower-class voters, and by the 1950s the numbers and values of the middle class were beginning to prevail. Charles J. Bonaparte, Severn Teackle Wallis, Frank R. Kent, and H. L. Mencken all tilted against the machine, but the most effective was Marie Bauernschmidt. A socialite, the wife of a local beer baron, she was the conscience of the women's clubs, buying radio time before each primary and general election to fight Curran, Pollack, or whomever she deemed the organization-favored candidate of the moment.[11]

From 1940 to 1980 the anti-organization Democrats usually carried the Second Legislative District around Roland Park, and frequently they joined the Republicans in state and national elections. The Republicans were a tiny band in the city, something of an organization themselves, and they were kept alive largely by patronage from Washington and by patient waiting for divisions to open up among the Democratic bosses. From 1940 to 1980 the Republicans and their independent allies won 2 of 10 elections for mayor; but only 6 of 450 elections to the General Assembly and 1 of 194 elections to the city council. But their continued press for curbs on organization practices, especially for limits on patronage, provided steady erosion to the system of organization politics.

The decline of the organization came not only from the growth of the middle class and the limited successes of Republican candidates, but also from the growth of the black population and an increase in black voter turnout, from about 20 percent of the total vote in 1940 to 50 percent in 1980. Immigrants had supported the machine in proportion to their helplessness, but blacks were less subject to party discipline. Pollack tried to absorb blacks as they moved into his Fourth District, and a black entrepreneur, W. L. (Little Willie) Adams, established a political club in the 1950s and made deals with the organization to deliver the black vote, but Pollack and Adams—both would-be bosses—discovered that their greatest power lay simply in their financial contributions to the campaigns of particular black candidates.[12]

Black voters looked to a different sort of leadership. First were the black ministers, who advised their followers far more bluntly than white ministers, making each church into a kind of political club. Second was the Baltimore *Afro-American,* probably the best black newspaper in the country, which was filled with astute political guidance. Third was the NAACP, guided through the 1950s by the powerful Lillie May Jackson and her daughters, supplemented in the 1960s by CORE and the Community Action Centers. Most important of all were the black candidates themselves, who developed personal followings. In 1954 two black delegates and a senator were elected to the General Assembly, largely with black votes. They were the first blacks ever elected to the legislature. The following year, two blacks were elected to the city council. Within a few years politicians like Verda Welcome and Parren Mitchell had passionate local followings, but successful black politicians were often more jealous of each other than cooperative. The divided black vote meant blacks were never as strong as their numbers dictated, but a common black concern for black interests gave city politics a tilt to the left.

Until the mid-1950s blacks were gerrymandered and largely ignored by the Democratic organization, but growing numbers and increased political participation eventually gained increased attention. The power of elected blacks promoted more power, and by the 1970s blacks occupied about 30 percent of the seats on the city council and in the city's delegation to Annapolis. Overwhelmingly they were Democratic, but, along with anti-organization whites, they provided the margin of victory for Republican Theodore McKeldin when, in 1942 and 1962, he was elected mayor and, in 1950 and 1954, governor. After the mid-1950s, black voter turnout averaged about 35 percent of the eligible black electorate, compared to 43 percent for whites.[13]

Despite the decline of the bosses and clubs, despite the growing importance of television, and despite the antiparty sentiment of the middle class and blacks, the party organization remained the distinctive feature of urban politics into the 1970s. The Democratic Central Committee for the city, which was made up of elected party professionals from each district, still established tickets, filled vacancies, largely controlled the party purse, and advised the city council, the mayor, the General Assembly, and the governor, especially on matters of patronage. The Central Committee remained a government within a government, balancing the interests of ethnic and economic groups, of various contributors, of differing ideologies, and of city and state. Factions, pressure groups, and ambitious young candidates all influenced the party, but the party remained at the center, the agency to be influenced. The party system generally worked because it was responsive to its constituency and to the changes brought by time. Its excesses checked by occasional defeat, it was a source of order and consensus in the volatile city.

At least after Curran's time, the mayor was the most powerful figure in the city, wielding primary control over budget and patronage, as well as three votes, counting his own and two appointees, on the city council. The mayoral administrations provide the framework for city history:

Howard W. Jackson (Dem.), 3 terms	1931–1943
Theodore R. McKeldin (Rep.)	1943–1947
Thomas D'Alesandro, Jr. (Dem.), 3 terms	1947–1959
Harold Grady (Dem.), part-term, resigned	1959–1962
Philip H. Goodman (Dem.), part-term	1962–1963
Theodore R. McKeldin (Rep.)	1963–1967
Thomas D'Alesandro, III (Dem.)	1967–1971
William Donald Schaefer (Dem.), 3 terms	1971–

Through the 1930s Boss Curran and Mayor Howard W. Jackson ruled together. Jackson drank too much and was the brunt of Bauernschmidt's unrelenting attack, but he was an able and popular administrator who was skillful in surrounding organization support with respectability and keeping taxes especially low in the prosperous wards to retain support of the *Sunpapers* and the establishment. He was also generally supportive of the New Deal and somewhat ahead of the state in expanding social and welfare services during the depression. McKeldin came in as a fresh voice after three Jackson terms, taking advantage of Jackson's strained relationship with Curran and promising a nonpartisan mayoralty. Although he was even more liberal than Jackson, especially on matters of race, McKeldin's term was unhappy, for he could hardly control the unanimously Democratic city council, and politics stalemated policy.

From 1947 to 1967 the pattern was repeated, as the organization won three times with an able, old-fashioned Italian pol, Thomas D'Alesandro, Jr. and then a fourth time with his lieutenant, J. Harold Grady, to be defeated again by McKeldin. D'Alesandro was the postwar building mayor, promoting new schools, firehouses, and street repairs, and pretending not to notice that people were moving out. Again McKeldin represented liberal reform, calling for major downtown renewal, public housing, and civil rights. He may have accomplished something with rhetoric, but, as in the past, the city council ignored him, and the record of change was slim.

Thomas D'Alesandro III replaced McKeldin in 1967, the year the deluge began. The next four years were the city's nadir, as riots broke out and crime soared, the tax base collapsed, and bonds from past rebuilding came due. D'Alesandro left office in despair, and people discussed the death of American cities. From 1971 into the 1980s William Donald Schaefer served with striking success by combining strong organizational support, a dynamic television personality, and an aggressive program of urban rebuilding that brought liberals and conservatives together. His popularity and his success in obtaining federal funds made him a national symbol for urban renaissance.[14]

Baltimore's congressmen, legislative leaders, and council members were, like the bosses and mayors, much of a type: generally politicians by profession, and organization loyalists, they were largely ethnic, uniformly able, and increasingly liberal. From 1940 to 1960 nonmayoral city leaders included Congressmen Edward A. Garmatz, George H. Fallon, and Samuel N. Friedel, and Delegates Thomas E. Conlon, John C. Luber, and George W. Della. From 1960 to 1980 leaders included Congressman Parren Mitchell, Congresswoman Barbara Mikulski, Senator Paul S. Sarbanes, and Delegates Marvin Mandel, Harry J. McGuirk, Paul E. Weisengoff, Julian L. Lapides, Benjamin L. Cardin, and Clarence W. Blount. Although the Baltimore delegations no longer intimidated the state, as they often had from the 1870s to the 1940s, their organization and calibre gave them their full share of power in Annapolis. The city had been hurt more than any part of Maryland by mid-twentieth-century change, but people in Baltimore welcomed more change: things had to get better.

Eastern Shore, Southern Maryland, and the Community Elites

The Eastern Shore and southern Maryland, like the southern part of the United States, was the most self-consciously separate of the sections within Maryland. For generations people jested in song, "We don't give a damn for the whole state of Maryland. We're from the Eastern Shore." Hardly a year went by that an editor or orator did not imagine secession from the state, and occasionally meetings were convened to discuss it seriously.

For many years the Eastern Shore and southern Maryland each imagined itself to be separate from the other, as well; there was little contact between the two, and little knowledge of one by the other. The Eastern Shore had divided loyalties in the Civil War, and as a result it remained as neutral as possible, while the southern counties were strongly Confederate. After 1940 truck farming and grain dominated the Eastern Shore economy, while the 1950s saw the establishment of a large poultry industry. Small tobacco farms dominated southern Maryland, along with important military establishments after 1940 and spillover from the Washington suburbs after 1960.[15]

Still, the nine counties of the Eastern Shore (Cecil, Kent, Queen Anne's, Talbot, Caroline, Dorchester, Wicomico, Worcester, Somerset) and the three counties of southern Maryland (Calvert, Charles, St. Mary's) were more alike than not, united by a common English and African heritage, an eighteenth-century golden age of tobacco prosperity, a sense of family and history, a rural and small-town economy, and proximity to the Chesapeake Bay. In the 1870s the refrigerated railroad car created for both areas a booming oyster and crabbing industry and a common folklore of the watermen, as they were deri-

Chestertown on the Eastern Shore was largely dominated by a politics of the local elite. Courtesy of the Maryland Department of Economic and Community Development.

sively called because they owned no land. The military and poultry industries gave each a hint of prosperity in the 1940s and 1950s. Retired businessmen drifted in to restore the eighteenth-century manor houses. Small farmers, watermen, poultrymen, military personnel, and retired rich—all confirmed the area's common conservative ways.

The past haunted the area. From the decline of tobacco prices after the Revolutionary War until the mid-twentieth century, the population changed little. In 1940 three of the twelve counties had a smaller population than they did in 1790, and seven had a smaller population than they did in 1900. Although only Somerset declined from 1940 to 1980, all twelve of the Eastern Shore and southern Maryland counties lagged behind the natural population increase and far behind the state's growth rate (see figure 1.2). In 1940 they comprised 16 percent of the state's population, and in 1980 they comprised 11 percent and were still losing ground, although part of this relative decline in 1980 came when the census bureau changed Charles County from a southern Maryland to "suburban county" designation.

By census definitions the quality of life for people of the Eastern Shore and southern Maryland counties—measured by such standards as income, housing, occupation, and social mobility—lagged behind the quality of life in most of the state (see figure 1.3). Growth and power are the American mythology, but for many areas generations of decline have been an overlooked countervailing theme of American history.

From 1790 to 1980 the chief export of the Eastern Shore and southern counties was their ambitious young men—not primarily the poor, or the women, but the enterprising males. As other historians have shown (and contrary to the theory of Frederick Jackson Turner, who argued that the poor escaped from old areas), the outward bound migrants were the vigorous young people who were seeking opportu-

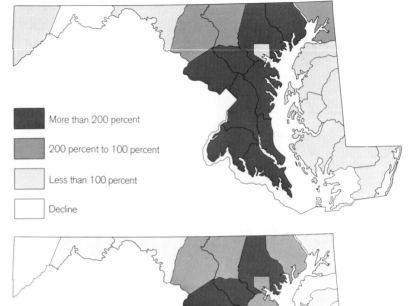

Figure 1.2   Population Growth, 1940–1980
Source: U.S. Bureau of the Census, *Population of the United States* (1940, 1980).

More than 200 percent

200 percent to 100 percent

Less than 100 percent

Decline

Figure 1.3.   Economic and Social Well-Being, 1970
Source: U.S. Bureau of the Census data adapted by Department of Economic and Community Development, *Economic and Social Atlas of Maryland: Statistical Supplement* (1974), p. 148. The "well-being" index is calculated from four measures of income, four of housing conditions, four of employment conditions, four of education, and four of social mobility.

Excellent

Good

Average

Poor

nities in the cities and suburbs. Out-migration curtailed industries like construction, which depended largely on growth, and it also curtailed property owners' expectations for capital gains. It left behind a dependent population of the young and the old, thus further lowering per capita productivity and income. It tended to strengthen class lines, as the rich bought up abandoned lands and grew more powerful. It created an uneven sex distribution, with women outnumbering men. Most of all, it left a *sense* of backwardness, a fear of change, a resentment of criticism, a racism, a basic conservatism that was often shrill and bitter.[16]

A critical measure of the area's decline was its long-cherished political power. Decline intensified the concern with politics, both as a career opportunity and as a means for the society to protect itself. Politics had been the glory of the Chesapeake counties, the field in which they had always excelled. From 1776 to 1920, 65 percent of Maryland's governors were natives of the Eastern Shore or southern counties, but from 1920 to 1980, 20 percent were from the area. The loss of power came from population shifts and from changes in the area's boundaries, as Anne Arundel was lost in the 1960s to suburbanization, but especially from constitutional change, as the courts in the same period ordered voting strength reduced to population levels. So the Eastern Shore and southern counties which in the 1940s occupied 30 percent of the seats in the General Assembly and in the 1950s occupied 24 percent of the seats, with reapportionment in 1966 held only 11 percent of the seats. The twelve counties averaged less than 1 percent each of the state's total vote in statewide elections. In congressional representation, the area had two of the state's six seats through the 1940s, and only one of eight after reapportionment. Their consolidation into a single congressional district after 1966, along with common political interests and the need for the 11 percent remaining in Annapolis to stick together, promoted considerable unity among the mostly rural Chesapeake counties.

The distinctive feature of Eastern Shore and southern Maryland politics—a feature comparable to the organization in Baltimore—was the dominance in the area of the local community elites. Other factors—candidate personality, party organization, ideology, special interest groups, occupation, and race—counted also, but nothing was quite so important as the alliances and rivalries of the people of power. Again history cast a shadow, for the system bore a resemblance to the eighteenth-century government in which the proprietor had incorporated the ten or twenty largest landowners to serve for life as a county court that had the power to make laws and settle disputes and that was able to admit new members into its company whenever men of sufficient distinction and congeniality arose. By the late nineteenth century this system had spawned courthouse gangs of professional pols who were in alliance with the wealthy. The courthouse machines were similar to machines in the city, except that the property owners controlled their employees and tenants more through instruction than through favors. Democracy brought fluidity to the system by the mid-twentieth century, but the structure remained.

The system depended on a small-town environment where people knew one another and, especially, where people of prominence associated together naturally for business, lunch, golf, and church. Membership in the county leadership was largely self-selecting, including those people who particularly *wanted* to be involved in community decision making and who made themselves acceptable to their peers. Major political figures, of course, belonged to the group—it was their business to belong—but they did not dominate in the way that politicians in other parts of the state dominated, for politicians were no more than equals. The local judges always belonged, and they were often the most powerful local decision makers. Successful bankers and businessmen belonged, major investors, developers, contractors, partners of the major law firms, the local publisher belonged. Family counted, but less than money and influence. Membership graded off infinitely, as in any informal group of associates, to physicians, ministers, colonels, school superintendents, farmers, even to black leaders and women's club activists. Membership was vague, but any political leader could name the leaders of his county, the twenty or so. The names on every list would be about the same.

Community leaders, sometimes only half-recognizing that they were doing so, established political tickets, provided money for candidates

Figure 1.4. Blacks in Population, 1940
Source: U.S. Bureau of the Census, *Population of the United States* (1940).

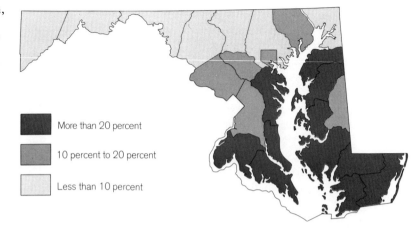

Figure 1.5. Blacks in Population, 1980
Source: U.S. Bureau of the Census, *Population of the United States* (1980).

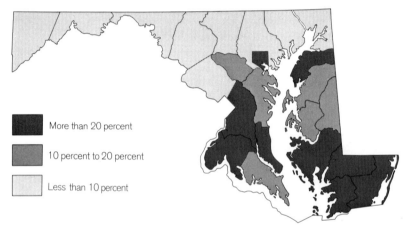

and encouraged family and employees to contribute, filled vacancies, tolerated challenge or crushed it, and mostly established the community consensus on issues and thus established the policies of office-holders. Their occasional deliberate avoidance of a stand, as happened often in national elections, was as important as their positive decisions in local matters. Anne Arundel and Prince George's counties (originally part of southern Maryland) demonstrated the system's limitations, for when these counties in the 1920s grew too large for elite consensus, a tighter, machinelike, organization developed.

The elites were mostly county based and they seldom associated with leaders in neighboring counties. Area congressmen reflected common views, and county delegates to Annapolis established alliances, but there was no effective area political organization. The Tri-County Council for southern Maryland and the Delmarva Advisory Council for the Eastern Shore promoted economic development, but they were largely apolitical. Statewide political candidates negotiated with each county separately, and each county expected the governor to satisfy it separately in his patronage appointments. Although the Republican and Democratic parties were almost equal in size, they tended to be seen as labels that voters accepted indifferently rather than organizations that provided discipline. Talbot, Charles, and Somerset, for example, were usually Republican, while the others were usually

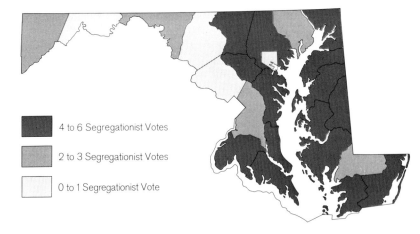

Figure 1.6. Segregation Votes, 1954–1972
Source: *Maryland Manual* (1954–1972). Segregation votes are calculated from votes for H. C. Byrd (governor), 1954; George Wallace (Democratic presidential primary), 1964 and 1972; George P. Mahoney (governor), 1966, and (U.S. Senate), 1970; Public Accommodations Referendum, 1964.

4 to 6 Segregationist Votes

2 to 3 Segregationist Votes

0 to 1 Segregationist Vote

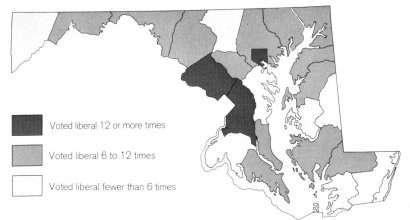

Figure 1.7. Support for Welfare State Liberalism, 1938–1980
Source: Voting returns in *Maryland Manual* (1940–1980). This includes presidential elections of 1940, 1944, 1948, 1960, 1968, 1972, 1980; Democratic primary for governor, 1946, 1950; general election for governor, 1950, 1966; U.S. Senate, 1938, 1946, 1950, 1958, 1970, 1976; U.S. Congress (at large), 1962; Democratic primary for president, 1964.

Voted liberal 12 or more times

Voted liberal 6 to 12 times

Voted liberal fewer than 6 times

Democratic. In Dorchester and Calvert the significant choices among candidates usually came in the primaries, while in Charles and Somerset they came in the general elections. Neither party, however, offered a reliable base for particular constituencies, ideologies, or candidate support.

Blacks had little voice in the direction of affairs in the Eastern Shore and southern counties. They comprised about 29 percent of the area's population in 1940 and 21 percent in 1980 (see figures 1.4 and 1.5)— not as a large a proportion nor as large a decline as in the states of the Deep South. They often obtained a token representative in the town councils of Cambridge or Salisbury, but they seldom influenced a larger election except to confirm the racist views and the general conservatism of the majority. The community leaders who arranged tickets almost never allowed black voters to hold the balance of power. The racist view did not follow the areas of black concentration, for it was especially virulent in Carroll, Cecil, and Baltimore counties, where there were few blacks, and it was weakest in Baltimore City and in Wicomico and Prince George's counties, where there were many (see figure 1.6).

Only once, in the New Deal period, did the poorer classes in the Chesapeake counties, as they did in the Deep South, challenge the local leadership and flirt with liberalism. In 1936 tenant farmers seek-

ing escape from sharecropping, town laborers benefiting from the
minimum wage, and blacks leaving the Republican party overwhelmed conservatives, carrying every county except Calvert and
Somerset, and in 1940 they carried every county except Charles and
Talbot. The area's representatives to Washington in the period—
United States Senator George L. Radcliffe (1935–1947), Congressman Lansdale Sasscer (1939–1951), and Congressman Edward T.
Miller (1947–1957)—although they were establishment figures, supported New Deal and Fair Deal programs. Later leaders, like Governor Millard Tawes and State Senator and then Comptroller Louis
Goldstein, endorsed moderately liberal programs at the national and
state levels.

Conservatism prevailed, however, especially at the local level, and
especially after 1946 (see figure 1.7). Mostly conservatism meant
localism; after that it meant opposition to integration, to labor, to
communism, to government reforms (the merit system, reapportionment, a centralized judiciary, centralized state bureaus, lowered voting
age, campaign disclosure laws), to taxes and services (school expansion, welfare, health facilities, public housing, juvenile bureaus, alcohol and drug abuse programs), to consumer legislation (savings and
loan regulation, auto repair licensing, gun control, utilities control),
to new facilities (throughways, airports, port authority, city transit),
and, often, but less consistently, to environmental legislation (control
of wetlands and oyster beds, strip-mining control, open-spaces bills,
noise and air and water pollution control). Probably this definition
was attitude more than ideology, the product of population decline
and elitism.

The politicians serving the Chesapeake counties were among the
ablest of the state's leaders, carrying weight beyond their numbers.
They tended to come to politics after success in other careers and after
self-earned membership in the leadership club. Starting at an older age
and entering politics near the top, however, they also tended to accept
public service as a profession, and they held office longer than politicians elsewhere. The area leaders of the 1950s, 1960s, and 1970s
included Congressmen Rogers C. Morton (1963–1971) and Robert E.
Bauman (1973–1980) and long-termed state legislators like Senators
Frederick L. Malkus (1947–), Homer E. White, (1947–1978), and
Harry T. Phoebus (1964–1976), and Delegates Thomas Hunter Lowe
(1959–1972), and John Hanson Briscoe (1972–1978). Possibly there
was about them an old-fashioned air, perhaps they were a little
haughty and patrician, as though their service to the people was a
public duty. They were proud of the past and of themselves, but they
did not welcome change.

*The West and the
Politics of Conflict*

The seven western countries (Garrett, Allegany, Washington, Frederick, Carroll, Howard, Harford) that composed 18 percent of the
state population in 1940 and the five counties (excluding Howard and
Harford) that composed 10 percent in 1960 were settled by
Englishmen sailing up the Potomac, Virginia frontiersmen seeping
through the back country, pious German farmers arriving from Penn-

Idyllic countryside belied the economic and political tensions of central and Western Maryland. Courtesy of M. E. Warren.

sylvania, and ambitious Scotch-Irish pushing in from Baltimore and Philadelphia. Each group tended to remain distinct, with separate churches and individual farming patterns. The hardscrabble subsistence farms of Appalachia had little in common with the beautiful dairy farms and orchards of Washington, Frederick, and Carroll counties. After 1850, great railroad and mining industries arrived and with them German and Irish workers, but these ethnic laborers did not feel very close to each other or to the small craft industries in the towns or to the farmers.

Industry continued to grow, but erratically, resulting in a precarious economy. In the 1930s the coal and railroad industries began a precipitous decline, and in the 1940s and 1950s many of the local craft industries—tanning, brewing, metals, dyes, glass, musical instruments—either collapsed or were taken over by giant national corporations. A huge Celanese textile firm employed 13,000 workers in the 1940s, almost one-half of the industrial labor force of western Maryland, but by the 1970s the firm had almost disappeared. Other big corporations—Kelly-Springfield Tire, Mack Truck, Fairchild Aircraft, Hercules rocket components, and Black and Decker tools—alternated between feast and famine. Mostly they were run by out-of-state managers who had little stake in the area. The big firms demanded tax, labor, and environmental legislation as the price of coming or remaining, and the local businessmen and farmers who were affected by the legislation sensed that they had been blackmailed.

Besides farming, business, and manufacturing interests, western Maryland developed a distinct labor class and a proletarian consciousness. The early canal, railroad, and mining companies brought labor from abroad into feudal company towns. From the 1870s to the 1940s the area cast one of the nation's largest socialist votes. In 1910 Maryland passed the nation's first workmen's compensation law, the brilliant achievement of David J. Lewis, who rose from the mines of Allegany County. From 1940 to 1980 approximately 40 percent of the labor force was classified as blue collar, the largest proportion of any area of the state. Labor was only partially unionized, however, and struggles between unions and between union and nonunion labor were as fierce as those between labor and capital.[17]

Western Maryland, like Baltimore City and the Eastern Shore and southern counties, became preoccupied after 1945 with the problems of unemployment and out-migration and the sense of falling behind. The three areas hardly recognized the problems as common, for each felt alone against the booming suburbs. In the western counties, unemployment rose to 25 percent in the 1950s and declined only slightly in the 1960s and 1970s. This rate was the highest in the state with the exception of Baltimore City. Agriculture, railroading, mining, and heavy industry all declined. Harry M. Caudill, a journalist on the other side of the mountains, in Kentucky, said that night came to the Cumberlands.[18] From 1940 to 1980 the growth rate in Garrett, Washington, Frederick, and Carroll counties fell far behind that of the state, and Allegany County had fewer people in 1980 than it had forty years before.

Divisions in the area were reflected in politics: a conflict of class, ideology, and party resolved itself not so much in alliances as in the personalities of particular candidates. The west was the only area of Maryland with a fully developed two-party system, and the parties balanced or checkmated each other. Democratic roots ran back to the gentry in southern Frederick County, to Catholic labor on the canals and railroads, to modern labor unions, and to poor farmers. Republican roots ran back to the antislave tradition of the western counties, in German labor, in large farmers, and, especially, in businessmen. Neither party allowed itself to fall captive to a particular class or ideology, however, and neither was able to sustain a machine except through the personality of its candidates.

Town councils in Cumberland, Frostburg, Hagerstown, Frederick, and Westminster usually maintained a balance between the parties, and even when one party dominated in a town that party was likely to break into factions. Harmony was not in the nature of things. Democrats maintained a margin of about 10 percent of the voter registrations from 1940 to 1980, and they maintained a margin in local elections, but in state and national elections the Republicans benefited from the generally conservative bias of an area that felt itself in decline. From 1940 to 1980 Republicans won 61 percent of the five county seats to the General Assembly, 66 percent of the congressional elections, and 72 percent of the presidential elections. Both Democrats and Republicans were conservative on most matters when they went to Annapolis and Washington, but on labor and racial matters occasionally they were liberal.

With interests and parties stalemated, personality politics became a major factor in elections. In western Maryland it was usually the candidate who sought out party and financial support rather than the other way around. A disproportionate share of campaign financing came from the candidates themselves. Elected officials tended to be young, their political careers short. Of the 206 elections to the General Assembly from 1942 to 1978, incumbents won 52 percent and newcomers won 48 percent. There were few notable leaders after 1940 to whom the western counties looked for continuing leadership, and after 1910 the western counties did not elect a senate president or house Speaker. Probably the western delegates to Annapolis were even less powerful than their relatively small numbers warranted. At a higher level, however, western county politicians were more successful, often benefiting from recognition of their prominent family names. William Preston Lane, who became governor in the 1940s, and Charles McC. Mathias, who was a United States senator in the 1970s, had well-known forebears. J. Glenn Beall was a congressman and senator in the 1940s and 1950s, to be succeeded in the 1960s and 1970s by his son, J. Glenn Beall, Jr. William D. Byron was a Democratic congressman in the 1930s whose wife, Katherine, replaced him in Congress when he died; his son Goodloe Byron was Democratic congressman in the 1970s; and when he died, his wife, Beverly, was elected.

Western Maryland was not as conservative as it thought it was, or its conservatism was often more theoretical than particular. A clear majority denounced the New Deal, communist infiltration, the welfare state, bureaucracy, and the city; but, issue by issue, the western delegates supported many changes. They usually supported such government reforms as the merit system, centralized state bureaus, a nonpolitical judiciary, and progressive tax reforms; they accepted integration; they supported generous expenditures for roads, schools, and public health facilities; they were usually in favor of consumer controls on banking, savings and loan organizations, and utilities. On labor legislation, strip-mining controls, and tax exemptions for industry, the area was divided within itself. All of western Maryland strongly supported federal initiatives in Appalachian regional development.

Western Maryland, then, shared a sense of distress with the Eastern Shore and a common fear of the city, the suburbs, and the future. Its interests, however, frequently coincided with the interests of the forces it feared. Internal division and personality politics produced textbook two-party democracy, but they also reflected frustration.[19]

The Suburbs and the Middle-Class Ethic

Until the 1920s Baltimore and Montgomery counties were part of western Maryland, not much larger in area and population than the other western counties, sharing the west's conflicting agrarian and industrial economy, its two-party system, and its fear of Baltimore City. Prince George's and Anne Arundel counties, meanwhile, were plainly part of southern Maryland, with a tobacco and slavery heritage and dominance by community elites. Even by the 1920s, however, the automobile and the sprawl of the cities were creating a new suburban culture that, within a few decades, largely dominated America.

Back in the eighteenth century, Baltimore was noted more than most American cities for the tendency of its rich merchants to live on the outskirts of town, where they pretended to be country gentry. By the 1890s the outward movement extended from the very rich to the merely affluent as the electric trolley came and as large real estate developers opened country club developments. Two of the first and finest suburbs anywhere were Roland Park, located just inside the Baltimore City limits and designed by the famous landscape architect Frederick Law Olmsted, and Chevy Chase, located mostly inside the Washington, D.C., limits. Somewhat later, somewhat more modest, came Towson, Pikesville, and Catonsville, on the trolley lines out of Baltimore, and Takoma Park, Kensington, and Riverdale, on the trolleys out of Washington. Not until the 1920s, with the coming of the automobile, was the outward flow substantial enough to alter normal county growth rates. During that decade the four suburban counties (Baltimore, Anne Arundel, Montgomery, and Prince George's) grew by 19 percent, exceeding the state's growth rate for the first time.[20]

A further stimulus to suburbanization, almost equal to those of the trolley and the automobile, came in the depression with the New Deal's Federal Housing Authority and Home Owners Loan Corporation. The agencies were designed primarily to stimulate the construction industry and, incidentally, to promote the ideal of private home ownership by offering insured loans at a rate at least one percentage point below prevailing mortgage rates. Almost no one speculated on the impact of this on suburbanization, but by encouraging those with substantial incomes to invest in new housing, the New Deal promoted housing primarily in the suburbs. For all the hard times of depression, Maryland's four suburban counties grew in the 1930s by a striking 38 percent.[21]

By 1940 most people thought of suburbanites as rich commuters—officers of manufacturing companies, insurance executives, department store managers, bankers, and brokers—people who lived on the fringes to enjoy weekends of gardening and golf. From 1917 to 1940 the proportion of Baltimore social register families who lived beyond the Johns Hopkins University grew from 8 percent to 60 percent.[22] The suburbanites were still urban oriented, however, the men traveling into the city each day as their maids traveled out, and on weekends the families went to the city for shopping, entertainment, and church.

The suburban political system clearly reflected the demographic and cultural changes that were underway, first with the rise of political machines in the 1920s, and then with their displacement between 1945 and 1965 by a middle-class bureaucratic ideal that pretended it was not political at all. The machines emerged, as they had in the city, when county populations outgrew the personal controls of community elites and justified the profession of full-time political manager. The machines died when the middle class grew sufficiently powerful to defy being managed.

The Baltimore County organization of Harrison Rider and his successors, from 1918 to the 1960s, was classic among machines. "Rolling Thunder" Rider, "the Corpulent Gorilla," was a shaggy, roaring

Harundale in Anne Arundel County was established in 1946. It was one of the largest prefabricated developments in America, heralding a new kind of suburb, a new style of living, and a new politics. Courtesy of the *Baltimore Sun.*

giant who held court from 1918 to 1934 in the back room of a ramshackle law office across the street from the Towson Court House, establishing every Democratic ticket, approving every county job down to garbageman, collecting a campaign contribution from every agency expecting a county contract, and usually collecting a fixed 2 percent of county employee wages to promote the organization. He was displaced by a rival, H. Streett Baldwin, who ran under the banner of reform and who in turn was displaced by an alliance of Christian H. Kahl and Michael Birmingham, who ruled from 1938 to 1962. The organization required that all county elections be held at large to prevent rivals from securing a power base, and it provided that the county's diverse interests of rich suburbanites, farmers, and industrial workers all be moderately satisfied through a careful balancing of favors.

The organizations knew and reflected the county's mood, even to the point of embracing a civil services system in 1955 that weakened the organization. Politics was rough, requests to contributors and county employees approached shakedown, and favors flowed freely to developers and contractors in the rapidly developing suburbs, but the old bosses were mostly satisfied with power; there was little evidence before the 1960s of personal profiteering. When the reformers—Spiro Agnew and Dale Anderson—came to power, they reduced the rake-offs, but they were too naive to distinguish between campaign contributions and personal bribes.[23]

A similar pattern emerged in Anne Arundel County as population grew and boss Louis N. Phipps developed a centralized Democratic machine. Howard and Harford counties mostly avoided the boss stage of development, evolving almost directly from the political culture of community elites to that of middle-class suburbia.[24]

Montgomery and Prince George's counties, so different and so alike, each followed almost exactly the Baltimore County tradition. In the nineteenth century Montgomery County identified with the west and cultivated small German craft industries, and Prince George's County attracted the rich Washington merchants who wanted to identify with its southern gentry tradition. After 1920 suburban country club developers mostly found their way to the rolling wooded lots of Montgomery, while factory industries and their workers followed the rail lines that ran across the flat sandy soil of Prince George's. By the 1930s both counties were too large for politics based on personal acquaintance, and two powerful political organizations emerged, that of E. Brooke Lee in Montgomery, and that of Lansdale T. Sasscer in Prince George's.

E. Brooke Lee, a handsome aristocrat, one of the country's most acclaimed heroes of World War I, was always "the Colonel." His forebears founded the Republican party in Maryland, his Democratic father was a United States senator, and his son was to become acting governor. The Colonel went to the Maryland House of Delegates, became Speaker, and then served as Governor Ritchie's secretary of state. Mostly, however, his interests centered in Montgomery County as a land developer, especially around the family estates in Silver Spring; as promoter and spokesman for the new suburbanites coming into the county; and, from 1919 to 1946, as the county's political boss.

Lee was a "progressive" in the language of the 1920s, combining the interests of civic organizations and women's clubs with landowners like himself, all in the interests of controlled growth, strict zoning, public parks, good roads, public water and sewer services, good police, and good schools—and ever-enhanced land values. The Lee forces represented a section of the county, a class, and an ideology, but they succeeded as a machine organization, dominating the government, the school board, the road building, and the jobs associated with all of them. Critics complained that the new East-West Highway of 1928 followed exactly the contours of Lee's own property and, naturally, enhanced its value, and that similar roads followed the contours of other landowners who employed workers and influenced votes. Small farmers of the north and west protested the costs of new suburban services, complaining that services raised land taxes and forced them to sell out to developers. In the 1930s Lee faced bankruptcy when his expensive homes went unsold, and the organization suffered occasional setbacks. Reformers included small farmers, the advocates of unrestricted growth, Republicans, and middle-class opponents of machine rule. Occasionally the organization tossed meat to the wolves, such as tax reductions for the farmers in 1932 and a system of merit appointments in 1937, but mostly through World War II the Lee organization prevailed.[25]

Lee's counterpart in Prince George's County was another courtly patrician, Lansdale Sasscer, who ruled from 1934 until his death in 1964. He was a state senator in the 1920s, the president of the state senate in the 1930s, and a congressman from 1938 to 1950, but mostly he was the man to whom all the interests offered their party contributions and to whom ambitious young men came to ask if they might run for public office. The economic mainstay of the organization was T. Howard Duckett, founder of the Suburban Trust Company, which advised its major borrowers—the developers, contractors, and industrialists—on local political matters. The organization was based on favoritism; Sasscer supported the bank and its borrowers, and they supported him. It seemed, to all of those on the inside, to be in the county's welfare, and it was reasonably aboveboard. As in Montgomery County, respectability was the basis of the organization's power. Rich and poor regarded Sasscer as the embodiment of generosity and gentility. The $700,000 estate he left when he died was not substantially larger than his inheritance.[26]

Much of Sasscer's power lay in the political indifference of the unconcerned. Politics was for insiders, in the southern tradition, too serious to be left to the ignorant, who were responsive to demagogues. Voter registration was difficult, voting was intended only for long-time residents, polling places were widely scattered, employers discouraged time off for election day, and, in any case, there was not much choice among the candidates. Roughly 44 percent of the eligible voters cast ballots statewide, but in Prince George's County from 1934 to 1980, only 34 percent of the electorate voted, the lowest turnout in Maryland. Organization based on low voter turnout was the rural machine tradition of Virginia, the opposite of the city machine, which sought maximum participation.[27]

The capstone of the Lee-Sasscer organizations was their alliance in Maryland's most extensive intercounty cooperation. The first joint enterprise was the Washington Suburban Sanitary Commission, originally created in 1916 by Lee-Sasscer predecessors to investigate a typhoid epidemic and to secure a pure water supply for the area. Lee and Sasscer represented their counties on the three-man commission, and the third man was appointed by the governor on their advice. This agency then, came to control the water supply, the sewer hookups, and the patronage for development in both counties. The water and sewer mains of WSSC marked the major streets that were built from the 1920s onward.

The second joint enterprise was the Maryland-National Capital Park and Planning Commission, which was created in 1927 to develop a master plan for area zoning and subdivisions and to acquire land in each county for public parks. MNCPPC obtained state authority to collect up to 10 percent of the property tax in each county. The governors' appointments to the commission, recommended by the county delegations, were mostly developers. T. Howard Duckett of Suburban Trust represented Prince George's; Colonel Lee's brother, then the Colonel, then his son, served from Montgomery.[28]

WSSC and MNCPPC emerged because the two countries comple-
mented each other in their desire for area development. For Colonel
Lee and his country club suburbanites, living quality and thus long-
term capital gains were best served by large residential lots. For Sasscer and Suburban Trust, almost any business was good business,
although rapid property turnover and cash flow mattered most, and
they promoted industry, wholesaling, and blue-collar villages like Mt.
Rainier, Brentwood, Queenstown, Suitland, and Oxon Hill. Each
county obtained what it wanted, dividing the suburban pie, and the
more they tilted in a particular direction the more they became confirmed in the different kind of development they had embraced.

In every one of the suburban counties, however, the story after 1940
was of organizational collapse in the face of middle-class reform. The
new suburbanites, especially the unpretentious ones who arrived after
1940, had different interests from those of the organizations, and they
were not easily controlled. Led by nonpartisan neighborhood
improvement associations, good government leagues, service clubs,
and groups such as the League of Women Voters, the new suburbanites triumphed, and their triumph could be dated with considerable
precision. Lee's organization fell in 1946, Phipps in Anne Arundel
stumbled in 1958, and Birmingham in Baltimore County and Sasscer
in Prince George's collapsed in 1962. In every case the story was
similar. The reformers felt excluded, eventually the machine was
divided, the reformers made common cause with the Republican
opposition, and, finally, the reformers reorganized themselves as
Democrats again.

In Montgomery County the fatal stress began in 1940, when Lee
and the developers began calling for shopping centers and apartments
and the rich homeowners held out for single-family zoning. Homeowners attacked Lee as "the machine" and allied themselves with
farmers in the Republican party. The Lee forces attempted to buy off
their opponents in 1945 with a nonpartisan county manager and a
full-scale merit system to replace patronage, but this only encouraged
them. In 1946 the anti-organization Republicans swept the county,
and two years later they adopted a "home-rule" charter government
that severed the political unity of the county by separating local government from the influence of the county delegation to Annapolis and
by dividing the county into separate election districts. The organization never recovered. The developers who had clung to it found that
the reformers were easier to deal with, anyway.

The Baltimore suburban organizations crumbled between 1958 and
1967, as Anne Arundel, Baltimore, Howard, and Harford counties
successively turned out the old Democratic party establishment. First
Anne Arundel County in 1958 adopted a home-rule charter that provided for a county executive and county councilmen who were to be
elected by districts and freed county lawmaking from veto by the
county's legislative delegation, and thus from control by the Democratic party. The new county executive, Joseph W. Alton, called himself a "nonpartisan Republican" and a professional manager rather
than a politician. In Baltimore County in 1962 an ambitious PTA
president, Spiro Agnew, billing himself as a liberal anti-organization

Republican, swept the entrenched organization at least from the county executive's office. Home-rule charters and the new politics also appeared in Harford and Howard counties.

Finally, the story repeated itself in Prince George's County. Civic federations demanded greater government accountability, the bankers and developers in the organization fell out among themselves, grand juries exposed inefficiencies, and anti-organization Democrats defeated the organization in the primaries. Two years later Sasscer died, and in 1966 court-ordered reapportionment resulted in the creation of election districts, which delivered the final blow to organization candidates. Finally, in 1970, Prince George's adopted a home-rule charter, fragmenting the Democratic party and resulting in the election of Republican William W. Gullett as its first county executive.

In every county the reformers came in like knights in shining armor, and soon the tarnish showed. They were an idea, or at most a group, dedicated to destroying party machinery and strong leadership. From 1946 to 1970 Montgomery County had no executive leadership at all, only a council with rapid turnover, and a president of the council who held office, on average, for only two years, plus an appointed bureaucracy that conducted the real business of the county. Anne Arundel and Prince George's went through shorter periods of non-leadership. Eventually, of course, the suburban counties, all of which had populations that were larger than some states, turned to an elected county executive. The chief qualification for office, however, remained nonpartisanship. Middle-class manners were essential, and inexperience was a virtue:

Anne Arundel County	
Joseph W. Alton	1966–1974
Robert A. Pascal	1974–1982
Baltimore County	
Spiro T. Agnew	1962–1966
Dale Anderson	1966–1974
Theodore Venetoulis	1974–1978
Donald P. Hutchinson	1978–1986
Montgomery County	
James P. Gleason	1970–1978
Charles W. Gilchrist	1978–1986
Prince George's County	
William W. Gullett	1970–1974
Winfield M. Kelly	1974–1978
Lawrence J. Hogan	1978–1982[29]

As if to emphasize nonpartisanship, five of the nine suburban county executives (Alton, Pascal, Agnew, Gullett, and Hogan) were Republicans in otherwise Democratic counties. The county executives were competent managers, but they had little authority to make policy, and their terms were short. All of them were elected as symbols of clean government, but Alton, Agnew, and Anderson were guilty of accepting bribes. Partly their convictions reflected the higher standards of public service demanded by the suburbs, and partly they reflected the naïveté of nonpolitical politicians who wanted the rewards of their predecessors and failed to understand that the rewards lay in power rather than in cash.

Suburban representatives to the General Assembly also tended to be young, to serve short terms and to be nonprofessional in their approach to politics. Many were seeking publicity to launch a law practice or business, and many were homemakers seeking to reenter the world outside the home. Between 1940 and 1980 some 66 percent (235 of 357) of the delegates to the assembly from the three largest suburban counties were newcomers rather than incumbents, far the largest turnover of any area. Suburban delegates tended to lack party or even county cohesion, for many found vote trading or bargaining for their area to be somehow dishonorable. Montgomery County was especially maverick, lacking a single representative from 1940 to 1980 who rose to major leadership position in either Annapolis or Washington, except for Blair Lee III, who was elected lieutenant governor. The Baltimore suburbs had several able and long-termed leaders, including Congressman George H. Fallon (who served from 1944 to 1970), Congressman Clarence D. Long (1962–1984), and state Senators William S. James (1946–1975), Roy N. Staten (1953–1978), James A. Pine (1959–1974), and James Clark (1959–1986).

Prince George's County had the strongest suburban delegation, especially in the 1960s and 1970s, when it experimented with an alliance of the in-group which bore resemblances to a revived organization. The incumbents met, usually at a weekly breakfast, persuaded themselves of the need for unity, pointedly excluded from membership the mavericks and incompetents, and agreed on future tickets that protected the majority. The group had a central fixer, an energetic young attorney, Peter F. O'Malley, who presided over and brokered the compromises. The breakfast club usually took in election victors, even when they replaced incumbents. The system gave the county unusual power in Annapolis, equal to that of Baltimore City and the Eastern Shore. Members included state Senator, President of the senate, and Congressman Steny H. Hoyer (1967–), Congresswoman Gladys N. Spellman (1974–1980), state Senator Meyer Emanuel (1963–1978), and county Councilman Francis B. Francois (1962–1980). Still, the in-group alliance faltered in the late 1970s as Republican Larry Hogan became county executive on an antialliance platform and Peter O'Malley tired of his role. Even Prince George's fell back into the nonpartisan mode, with each office holder independent and often ineffective.

The triumph of middle-class suburbanites, besides replacing politics with bureaucracy, also gave the suburban counties and thus the state a distinctive and mostly liberal tilt. Prince George's County was consistently liberal since the days of Sasscer, who embraced the New Deal out of personal conviction and as an appeal to the county's blue-collar workers. In the 1950s lower-middle-class economic interests coincided with upper-middle-class idealism. During the 1960s the county referendums on racial questions revealed extraordinary liberalism, and the O'Malley alliance pretended to welcome the black migration of the 1960s and 1970s from Washington.

Montgomery County's liberalism was more significant because it marked a shift of power in the 1950s from the country club conservatives to the government bureaucrats who lived in the county, and thus a shift of one of the state's largest counties from the right to the left. The county's influence in Annapolis, and in state and presidential elections, was consistently in favor of civil rights, welfare, consumer, and environmentalist legislation. Its people boasted that the county was usually the first to adopt progressive ordinances and that its schools and libraries were the best in the state.

In Baltimore and Anne Arundel counties the drift to the left was slower, chiefly because of a lingering racism, but also because of a gentry tradition in Baltimore County, a military tradition in Anne Arundel County, and the tendency of blue-collar workers in large industries of both counties to identify with their employers on matters of zoning, environmentalism, and military spending. Baltimore County suburbanites, especially, thought of themselves as refugees from the blackening city, and they sought to maintain a wall of protection. Through the 1960s segregationist candidates like George Wallace and George Mahoney obtained larger majorities in the Baltimore suburbs than in the Eastern Shore and southern counties. Fear of blacks spilled over into opposition to public housing, welfare programs, and public transportation. Not until the 1970s did leaders like Theodore Venetoulis, Robert Pascal, William S. James, and James Clark reflect the triumph of middle-class ideology over business and blue-collar values. The new suburban leadership was never as strong as the numbers it represented, but the leaders had a sense of being in the forefront of change. The counties of the east and west clung with more fear than nostalgia to the past, and the city embraced change with desperation, but the suburbs embraced change with confidence.

Each of the cultures of Maryland—of America—was more distinct in the telling than in reality, a memory or an ideal more than a fact. The city, besides reflecting population change and organization politics, represented threatening slums and sparkling renewal, ethnic neighborhoods and urban vibrance, power and decay. The Eastern Shore and southern Maryland, in addition to history and community elites, were also tidal marshes and geese, crabbing and watermen folklore, Georgian estates and saltbox shanties, lonely roads and sleepy southern towns. The west, in addition to conflict and tension, was weedy coalmining villages and rusting railway yards, rich farmland and stone barns, German crafts, northern towns with narrow streets and drugstores with marble soda fountains. The suburbs were not only growth and reform, but also country clubs and tract houses, neat lawns and monotony, cloverleafs and shopping malls.

All of this was also much of America. In twenty of the twenty-three presidential elections from 1888 to 1980 the state voted for the national presidential winner—a far more accurate gauge than proverbial Maine. In most statistics, however, Maryland was more than average, for it was more prosperous and progressive than most states, and usually, even in negative statistics like crime rates, it ranked among the top one-third of the nation (see table 1.2). It continued,

Table 1.2. Maryland's Rank among Other States

	1940	1980
Population	28th	20th
Percentage urban	9th	7th
Percentage foreign born	26th	21st
Population mobility	—	15th
Percentage white-collar workers	—	2d
Personal income	14th	9th
Scientists and engineers per capita	—	7th
Physicians per capita	—	3d
Percentage above poverty level	18th	5th
Spending for state-local services	21st	10th
Literacy	28th	22d
Per pupil school expenditure	12th	8th
Consumption of alcohol	—	10th
Crime rate	19th	15th

Source: U.S. Bureau of Census, *Statistical Abstracts* (1942, 1982); Council of State Governments, *Book of the States* (1942, 1982); U.S. Department of Justice, *Federal Bureau of Investigation Uniform Crime Reports* (1940, 1980).

during the period, to move further toward the front. Both its stable qualities and its changes were typical but slightly exaggerated expressions of the nation.

For all the differences among the cultures of Maryland, the larger theme was what they had in common. For all the differences between Maryland and the rest of the nation, the larger significance is the way each contributed to an understanding of the other. The cultures and communities felt distinct in many ways, but they were marked by common institutions, tensions, and responses to the changing times.

World War II, like the American Revolution and the Civil War, was one of the watersheds of American history, not so much for what happened on the battlefield, but for the change the war signaled in the kind of life Americans led. For all the disruption and losses the war brought, and for all the tensions that followed it, the change for most people was for the better. During the next forty years Americans experienced an unprecedented material and social well-being, and the gain for Marylanders was considerably greater than the national average.[1]

Maryland's World War II

The Fervor of Mobilization

The depression had been gray and discouraging, but then the war arrived, with drums and sunshine. Marylanders, like Americans everywhere, were mostly neutral when Adolf Hitler invaded Poland in September 1939; but they marched rapidly toward involvement during the following two years. People felt the inexorable drift and from the start called the conflict World War II. The years 1940 and 1941 were good and exciting, years when people were warmed by patriotism and prosperity. Events from outside led the way, and Americans responded with fervor but without hysteria. Memories of World War I eased the way to mobilization and helped the nation avoid some of its earlier anti-German excesses. Fervor and resolution surged again after the Japanese attacked Pearl Harbor in December 1941, and for most people the next year was even better.

At first, in 1940 and 1941, national policy and international events more than local leadership pushed opinion toward preparedness and war. Advocates of preparedness included liberals who were alarmed by totalitarianism and Jews who knew well enough what was happening in Germany, but their warnings were offset by the stances of the skeptics. The Baltimore weekly *Jewish Times,* one of the best Jewish journals in the United States, offered detailed and thorough analyses of nazism, but few people noticed, and some, like Baltimore's famous author H. L. Mencken, explicitly discounted the accounts.[2]

Opponents of rearmament were easier to define than advocates. They included many Catholics who feared Stalin more than Hitler, and many Protestants who leaned toward pacifism. Liberal intellectuals, including many editorial writers, tempered their distaste for totalitarianism with a fear of manipulation by the arms merchants and a relativist tolerance for the fascist experiment. Businessmen, brokers, farmers, and labor provided a harder core to the inertia of nonpreparedness, if not to neutrality. The Baltimore Association of Commerce, Alex. Brown and Sons brokerage house, the Maryland Farm Bureau, and the Baltimore Federation of Labor feared wartime disruption of trade more than they anticipated profits from preparedness. All of these groups supported the United States Neutrality Acts of 1935 and 1937, and they maintained their neutral stand well into 1940.[3] The Dow Jones industrial averages, reflecting investor pessimism as war approached this country, dropped from 190 in 1937, to 150 following the German invasion of Poland, to 120 following the 1940 announcement of lend-lease, and to 101 following Pearl Harbor. Although real profits soared, investor confidence did not reapproach its 1937 peak until after the war ended in 1945.

Maryland's largest arms merchant, Glenn L. Martin, reflected this curious neutralism. His huge plant was dedicated almost entirely to the manufacture of military aircraft. He went beyond his business colleagues in supporting preparedness in the 1930s, but when war actually came he expressed genuine distress, convinced that requisite changeovers and government controls would cause a setback for the company.[4] In short, business and labor in Maryland defied Marxist predictions that they would advocate war. Perhaps they were too shortsighted to recognize that it was in their interest to do so.

As the war began, the drama of the events from abroad quickened the local pulse: the dismemberment of Poland (September 1939), the Russo-Finnish war (October 1939 to March 1940), the invasion of Norway (April 1940), the fall of Holland, Belgium, and France (June 1940), the Battle of Britain and the start of the American draft (September 1940), lend-lease (March 1941), the invasion of Russia (June 1941), American warfare against German submarines (September 1941), and Pearl Harbor (December 1941). These events provided excitement that fed on itself and fed Americans' sense of inexorability. In local communities, people responded with patriotic dedication to nation and democracy, with enthusiasm for a great adventure, with total confidence. Local concerns faded from Maryland newspapers. Americans were united in the national cause.

The trigger for statewide mobilization came from Washington, but mobilization soon took on a life of its own. In May 1940, following the fall of Norway, President Franklin D. Roosevelt created the National Defense Advisory Board to awaken the country to the need for preparedness. The board wrote to the state governors, encouraging them to assume the initiative for preparedness in a manner that assumed responsibility for protecting Western civilization. Some governors hesitated, but Governor Herbert R. O'Conor of Maryland promptly created a Council of Defense that was worthy of the task. Its members were, in the governor's judgment, the twenty-six most powerful and representative citizens of the state: the governor himself as chairman, W. Frank Roberts of the Baltimore Association of Commerce as deputy chairman, and the heads or leading representatives of Bethlehem Steel, the Baltimore and Ohio Railroad, Glenn L. Martin, Pepco, Chesapeake and Potomac Telephone, two major banks, the American Federation of Labor, the Farm Bureau, the *Afro-American,* the Catholic church, the Maryland Federation of Women's Clubs, the firemen's association, the bar association, the medical society, the state police, the state roads commission, the attorney general, the Johns Hopkins University, the University of Maryland, the National Guard, and the Third Army.[5]

The Maryland Council of Defense took its task very seriously, gathered a professional staff, and plunged ahead, avoiding questions of whether or why. Heads of organizations that were pledged to neutrality assumed the responsibility for mobilization. "Leadership in the program for defense will inevitably fall upon the business man," acknowledged the president of the Baltimore Association of Commerce, and other groups assumed the burden as willingly.[6]

The Maryland Council of Defense named eight committees, which anticipated the entire process of mobilization, and for some time they were better organized than Washington. They were: (1) an industrial production committee, which studied the state's industrial capacity and developed plans for converting plants and allocating resources to maximize production; (2) a manpower committee, which considered means of educating labor in higher skills, of bringing women into the labor force, of using prison and foreign labor, of promoting integration to increase the labor pools, of promoting vocational training in the public schools, and of assigning citizens to needed jobs; (3) an agriculture committee, which promoted cooperative use of farm labor and machinery, the control of farm prices, and the supervision of marketing and food processing; (4) a welfare committee, which worried about price controls, physical fitness, public health, and first aid; (5) a housing committee, which considered rent controls and the means of providing emergency housing around military bases and war plants; (6) a public information committee, which published pamphlets on defense, held conventions of media people to promote preparedness, sponsored poster competitions, and organized thousands of volunteers to support various war programs; (7) a defense committee, which worried about sabotage, enemy aliens, blackouts, the training of air raid wardens, and coordination of a home guard to resist invasion; and (8) a legislative committee, which drafted emergency legislation for the General Assembly's consideration.[7] Although the federal government took over many of these activities during the next few years, the program proved exhaustive. The war came because of outside forces, but mobilization came from local enthusiasm. Maryland stood ready to defend itself.

When the Maryland legislature convened in January 1941 it was prepared to dedicate itself to the war, which, by then, was the paramount public concern. The assembly met only biennially, so this was its first opportunity to address the war. Following the lead of the Legislative Committee of the Council of Defense, the assembly wrote the Council of Defense into law and extended its reach, instructing it to create five subcouncils (for Baltimore City, central Maryland, western Maryland, southern Maryland, and the Eastern Shore), and they in turn created sub-sub-councils for each county. Now the state leaders who were responsible for preparedness were joined by several hundred area and county leaders.[8]

The assembly was more extreme in its war fevor than almost any group in the state. It rewrote the antisabotage laws from World War I, strengthening penalties for interfering with war work and making it an act of sabotage to strike or picket plants that were engaged in war production. In 1943 it passed a work-or-fight law, providing that any adult male either work at the prevailing wage or be subject to draft or jail. When the labor unions in western Maryland objected, the legislature made the law a local option that was subject to county approval. The Eastern Shore and southern counties approved it and sent a few recalcitrants to jail. Finally, the assembly passed a war powers act, giving the governor, in consultation with the Council of Defense, authority to suspend civil law, seize property, and issue commands to all state, county, and city employees. Maryland was one of six states to adopt such a law. It was never exercised and expired with the war.[9]

War comes ultimately to matters military, and Governor Herbert R. O'Conor and the General Assembly determined to create the state's own fighting forces. O'Conor, fearful that the state's national guard would be called to federal service, floated the suggestion of a home guard of unpaid volunteers who would be available to defend war plants, railroads, and public property. Professional army officers opposed the idea, but the American Legion and the National Rifle Association mobilized support, and the General Assembly agreed, authorizing ten battalions of two hundred men each and appropriating money for handsome designer-created uniforms and a command staff. There was a unit for cavalrymen (who brought their own horses), a unit for motorcycle troops (their own motorcycles), and a special unit for blacks. The men drilled weekly in local armories, and when news of Pearl Harbor came, over twenty-five hundred responded to the governor's mobilization. After two weeks of patrolling railroad bridges and water reservoirs, the men began to drift away and the governor ordered demobilization, but he also moved to glamorize and expand the volunteer program.[10]

O'Conor authorized the home guard to be supplemented with the all-volunteer reserve guard, soon dubbed the Minute Men, who were limited to providing service within their own county and charged with protecting their county against forays and sabotage. The national secretary of the National Rifle Association urged all Maryland members to "welcome this opportunity to assist in the formation of combat units" and "all rifle clubs . . . to communicate immediately with the Governor, offering their services as complete units ready to take training and serve under their established officers." By the end of 1942 more than twelve thousand citizens had volunteered and were taking weekend or summer training as their schedules allowed. Carrying shotguns, deer rifles, pistols, and bowie knives, they played war games over golf courses, rode in airplanes, took part in mock invasions aboard "real" naval landing craft, and patrolled the streets during practice air raids. Occasionally there was criticism of their zealousness, and at least three people were killed in the exercises. Generally, however, the Minute Men probably strengthened wartime morale, and maybe their existence stayed more excesses than they committed.[11]

Increasingly, local enthusiasm came from above. Maryland's volunteer fervor grew through 1940 and 1941, reached a peak about 1942, and slowly waned in favor of monetary rewards and compulsion. The membership and enthusiasm of the Minute Men had dissipated by 1943. The war was a story of local volunteer enthusiasm that was gradually replaced by the efficiency of centralized management. The Maryland Council of Defense with its regional and county branches gave up its notions of guiding the economy and became a support agency for federal bureaus. Instead of supervising industrial production, the council fed information to the federal Office of Production Management. Instead of controlling prices, it nominated the hundreds of local citizens who served the federal Office of Price Administration by distributing ration coupons and fixing local prices and rents. Instead of supervising manpower, it nominated hundreds of citizens to supervise the federal selective service. Not only did volunteers give way to professionals, but local leadership gave way to national control, as well.

Of Marylanders in the armed forces, roughly 40 percent volunteered, and the rest were drafted (see table 2.1).[12] About 14 percent of Maryland's 1940 population served in uniform, a proportion that was probably slightly above the national average, although comparable figures for the states have not been adequately compiled. Most of those who served were scattered through the services, but almost one-fifth of the Marylanders who served in the army were assigned to the famous Twenty-Ninth Division, which spearheaded much of the Normandy invasion. Roughly 3,560 Maryland servicemen died in action, and another 1,877 died nonbattle-related deaths. Two percent of Maryland servicemen did not return from the war, a significantly higher proportion than the national average. Deaths from war numbered one-half the Maryland wartime civilian deaths from cancer and four times the deaths from automobile accidents. Eighty-four Marylanders were generals or admirals, and three men received the Congressional Medal of Honor, again, significantly ahead of the national average. There are no figures for service by areas or by ethnic groups in Maryland, but more servicepeople were from the Eastern Shore and southern Maryland counties than from any other area in Maryland. Almost all wartime volunteer programs were most successful in the southern-oriented counties, as they were in the southern states of the United States.[13]

By mid-1941 the Maryland Council of Defense and its branches had developed primarily into a civilian defense program that was encouraged by Washington to supervise the thousands of volunteers who served as air raid wardens, aircraft spotters, and auxiliary police, firemen, and medical aides. The civilian defense volunteers overlapped with the game-playing Minute Men, but they were far more

Table 2.1.   Maryland in the Armed Services, World War II

Volunteers, including reserves, state guard, merchant marine, and Red Cross:		
	Male	120,700
	Female	3,499
Draft:		
	Army	128,000
	Navy	26,000
	Marines	3,800
	Coast Guard	300
	Total	264,100

Source: War Records Division–Maryland Historical Society, *Maryland in World War II,* 3 vols. (1950), 1:258-63.

Note: The compilation of these numbers comprised a major part of the work of the War Records Division of the Maryland Historical Society. Unfortunately, the numbers are estimated, for they include both those born in Maryland who enlisted elsewhere and those born elsewhere who enlisted in Maryland. Thus, no reliable figures exist nationally on enlistments by state.

Patriotic navy recruits in Baltimore salute after taking the oath in the wake of Pearl Harbor. Note the man in the foreground using the Boy Scout salute. Courtesy of the *Baltimore Sun.*

significant, numbering more than 165,000 volunteers at the 1942 peak, some 12 percent of the state's population. The largest participation came from the Eastern Shore (especially Dorchester, Kent, Queen Anne's, Wicomico, and Worcester counties), where people often felt otherwise left out of the war effort. The smallest volunteer rates were in St. Mary's and Anne Arundel counties, where large concentrations of troops at the Naval Air Station and Fort Meade made paramilitary activity appear superfluous.

Roughly one-half of the civilian defense volunteers were air raid wardens, one for every urban block or two. They supervised air raid drills and enforced blackout regulations. This was a fairly undemanding job that required a minimum of training, and its volunteers stuck with their duties faithfully through the war years. Aircraft spotting, on the other hand, was an amusement of the Boy Scouts and the American Legion which reached its peak in the weeks after Pearl Harbor, when more than three hundred posts were manned on a twenty-four-hour basis. The excitement of watching the skies from abandoned farmhouses quickly palled, however, and by the fall of 1943 the activity was entirely "deactivated." Occasionally, too, submarine spotter groups patrolled the beaches, especially in the summer. The police, fire, and medical auxiliary jobs were rigorous, involving extensive training and often meaningful assignments in replacing occasionally depleted professional ranks.[14]

The Red Cross experienced particular success in enlisting female support for the war. Every year each of the 270,000 volunteers (15 percent of the Maryland population) contributed an average of thirty-one hours in visiting hospitals, packing bandages, promoting blood donor drives, knitting garments, distributing soldier kits, serving as hospital aides, staffing base canteens, teaching first aid and nutrition classes, and driving ambulances. The Red Cross volunteers raised about $10 million in statewide contributions, approximately $5.59 per capita. The organization was especially active in the affluent Washington and Baltimore suburbs.[15]

One of the most successful volunteer programs was the United Service Organizations (USOs), which were promoted by Washington but mostly funded and staffed by local volunteers to provide social contacts, recreation, and, often, meals and overnight accommodations to troops and war workers whose lives were disrupted by the war. About forty centers operated in Maryland as USOs, and another forty centers for servicepersons were run by churches or service clubs under other names. The government found the organizations useful in promoting troop morale, and Washington subsidized them as necessary with buildings or supervision. Local people found volunteer work in the USOs to be a way of sharing the glamor of war.[16]

Another program that depended almost entirely on patriotic fervor was war bonds. Voluntary loans provided over one-half of the cost of waging war and also served to dampen consumer demands and inflation. This was a carefully orchestrated program of hard sell through local volunteers, including blue-ribbon state and county committees; cooperation of the advertising and entertainment industries; promotion through schools and churches; appeals to patriotism and guilt; semivoluntary payroll deductions; and endless gimmicks such as film previews, kisses from movie stars, and rides on bombers and submarines. Seven bond drives over five years were generally successful, although more than half of the bonds were purchased by banks, thus increasing credit and inflation in a way not intended. Surprisingly, the volume of bond sales grew as the war progressed, probably reflecting a growing conviction about their profitability more than a growing willingness to sacrifice for the war. Marylanders purchased $2.6 billion worth of bonds, an average of $1,445 for every person in the state, compared with a national average of $1,335 (see table 2.2).[17]

Table 2.2.   War Bond Purchases, 1941–1945

Year	Title of Bond	Amount Purchased ($ millions)
1941–1942	"Keep 'Em Flying"	108
1943	"They Give Their Lives, You Give Your Money"	521
1944	"Back the Attack"	1,120
1945	"Finish the Job"	883

Source: War Records Division–Maryland Historical Society, *Maryland in World War II*, 3 vols. (1958), 3:1–18.

The spirit of wartime sacrifice extended to charity for scores of foreign and domestic causes. There were special relief drives for war-ravaged people, especially for children, in England and Russia (each received about one million dollars plus tons of clothing and food from Maryland), in Greece and China (half a million dollars plus clothing and food), and in Poland, Holland, Norway, and Italy. There were many stories of local people, especially Chinese and Greeks, suffering deprivation to help relatives in the old country. There were special drives for the Red Cross and the USOs, as well as regular charity drives for the needy at home. By 1943 most counties had consolidated the appeals (except the Red Cross) into a single War and Community Fund campaign. These campaigns raised annually about $1.50 per capita for foreign and military charity and about $1.00 per capita for local charity, amounts that were considerably ahead of prewar rates of giving.

The measurable volunteer efforts, such as enlistments and contributions of time and money, constituted only the beginning of the local support, both willing and conscripted, on behalf of the national cause. The war also meant scrap drives and victory gardens, curtailed consumer needs, rationing of most items of food and clothing, restricted travel, often difficult living conditions, delayed education, exhausting overtime, and disrupted lives. For all the dissatisfaction and occasional cheating, the war also brought a largely voluntary self-mobilization of the nation and the local communities, especially at the beginning, and an enthusiasm for the national cause of which we would later find it hard to believe ourselves capable.

The Boom Towns

The war did not come to all communities equally, and the average story of what happened from 1940 to 1945 was not the complete story. This is one of the lessons of local history. The majority of Maryland communities actually lost population during the war, and, especially on the Eastern Shore and in the western counties, a remarkable monotony in daily life prevailed. Other communities in the state, meanwhile, throbbed with crowds and change.

The war stimulated two types of extreme activity, one industrial and the other military. The major industrial complex, often overlapping with military activity, extended forty miles along the Chesapeake shore in Cecil, Harford, and Baltimore counties. By 1943 the population in the forty-mile strip was five times what it had been in 1940. The military bases were more widely scattered throughout central and southern Maryland. In both industry and the military, the volunteer enthusiasm that gripped civilians elsewhere was almost irrelevant. Centralized federal leadership—not a welfare-oriented New Deal bureaucracy, but a tough, semimilitary command—was necessary. In a time of stress, neither traditional democracy nor popular fervor sufficed.

At the northeastern tip of the industrial strip was the little Cecil County town of Elkton. Its 1940 population totaled 3,518, and its

largest employer was Triumph Industries, which employed 211 workers making Chinese firecrackers. Early in 1940 the company filled a
small order for signal flares for Finland, and later in the year it sold
powder to England. With lend-lease it converted to detonators and
land mines, and with Pearl Harbor it obtained its first navy contract
for antiaircraft shells and incendiary bombs. Navy auditors quickly
discovered that Triumph's management was corrupt and inefficient,
obviously better suited to fireworks; closing the plant, however, was
out of the question. In April 1942 President Roosevelt confiscated the
plant by executive order, placed all company shares in receivership,
and contracted the management to a group of Pittsburgh steel and
banking executives who had never seen the plant. With that, the company burgeoned. The new managers received $4 million in federal funds
for construction, built close to one thousand small buildings in order
to contain accidents, and launched a vast campaign for employees.

Management was particularly interested in hiring women, whom
they imagined to be best suited to the painstaking and low-paying job
of packing shells. Guided by the Federal Manpower Commission, it
concentrated its search in West Virginia, placing hundreds of ads in
weekly rural newspapers and using airplanes to distribute fifty thousand recruiting leaflets over selected West Virginian counties. Recruiters sought black workers in the Carolinas, and other recruiters
combed ethnic enclaves in southern Pennsylvania. Soon hundreds of
females, many in their teens, arrived at the Elkton bus station every
day. By the end of 1942, in the town of 3,500 long-term residents,
another 11,500 people, 80 percent of them women, were working for
Triumph Industries. Another 6,000 people drifted in as family members, construction workers, or camp followers looking for profits
from the influx. The worst problem was turnover, for tension and
resignations were frequent at munitions plants. Hair turned red and
skin, yellow, and there were accidents. A major blow in May 1943
killed 15 workers and injured 100, and smaller accidents occurred
almost every month. Worker turnover exceeded 100 percent annually;
the company estimated that it employed 85,000 different people over
a six-year period.

The biggest problem in the town, as the newcomers poured in, was
that no one felt responsible. The old residents and the town and
county governments were frightened and unfriendly. Triumph Industries was run by outsiders who were concerned with production. Federal agencies and private entrepreneurs constructed temporary
barracks and cheap housing, and other agencies covered vast areas
with rented trailers. Water and sewerage disposal, police and hospitals, were all inadequate. People stood in lines to get into restaurants,
laundries, grocery stores. Local businesses and churches sometimes
refused to serve the newcomers. There was little for employees to do
in their off hours but walk the streets. Compounding the chaos was
Bainbridge Naval Station, just fifteen miles west, where thirty thousand navy draftees were undergoing basic training. So wild was the
town late in 1942 that a local naval commander sent in military police
to establish a kind of martial law.[18]

Recruited by leaflets dropped by airplanes over Appalachia, thousands of young women sought work in the munitions factories of Elkton. Hundreds of small buildings limited casualties from accidents, yet other dangers were still present. After several months of work, skin often turned yellow and hair fell out. Courtesy of the *Baltimore Sun.*

The unlikely catalyst for order was the Elkton USO. Created in July 1942 by the National Security Agency, local clergymen, and the Cecil County Council of Defense, the Elkton USO became the unofficial mediator between national agencies, Triumph Industries, and the community. Soon its staff almost constituted an area government; supervision of leisure activities, it turned out, was the key to controlling society. The USO kept records of newcomers, who needed staff approval to obtain housing or jobs. It acquired federal funds for public housing, and then for town water and sewer facilities, and it approved water-sewer hookups to private builders who met its demands. It worked with the town council to establish playgrounds, and it saw that cooperative businessmen and churches obtained government-restricted building supplies for expansion. The USO employed its own police, particularly to curtail juvenile crime, and established its own town curfew regulations.

With its federal money and federal connections, the Elkton USO transformed near-chaos into community. Besides its three-building headquarters in town, the USO maintained five branches, including one for blacks and one in the plant. In addition to jobs and housing, it provided counseling, classes, snacks or meals, dances and other entertainment, even free marriage ceremonies. When workers began to be laid off in 1945, the USO helped them pay their bills in Elkton and find new jobs back in West Virginia or in California. By that time Elkton, Triumph Industries, and the USO were almost indistinguishable. The town had grown up to meet the influx, and many of the newcomers had settled down to stay.[19]

Just twenty miles south of Elkton, in the middle of the Cecil-Harford-Baltimore industrial war strip, lay the Aberdeen-Edgewood research and testing complex, which was far larger than Triumph Industries and, for those who thought about such things, even more terrible as a symbol of war. Founded by the army in 1917, Aberdeen Proving Ground was twelve miles long and six miles wide. The facility's population had declined to 914 in 1940, but by 1943 Aberdeen employed 5,700 civilians and 30,000 military personnel. Most employees had families, whose members more than doubled the population in the area. Manufacturers of ordnance and vehicles shipped their materials to Aberdeen, where they were tested or "proved," often modified, and then stored and shipped, as needed. The Aberdeen engineers developed many new weapons, including proximity fuses, new rocket-launching bazookas, mine detonators, and a 914 mm mortar with a 3,750-pound shell, the largest gun ever built.

Adjacent to Aberdeen was Edgewood Arsenal, the Army Chemical Center, whose population of 1,097 in 1940 grew to 3,400 military and 10,700 civilian employees by 1943. Its employees, even more than at Aberdeen, were an unusual combination of civilians and military personnel, including many scientists and skilled technicians, who were involved with both research and manufacture. Its specialty was poison gases, but scientists there also developed the flame thrower, new manganese and jellied gasoline bombs, phosphorous bombs that spewed a flame over hundreds of yards, and new kinds of smoke screens. At least fifteen people were killed at Aberdeen, and many more than that were killed at Edgewood, although exact figures were never provided.

Edgewood also supervised about one thousand employees at Fort Detrick, located forty miles away, in Frederick County. People at Fort Detrick performed research in biological warfare, including viruses, funguses, epidemics, and defoliants. Talk of possible medical benefits helped employees who were sensitive to the morality of their work retain their balance.

The population growth around Aberdeen and Edgewood was huge, but the area was well controlled by a strict military command, usually a major general at Aberdeen and a brigadier general at Edgewood. Approximately one-half of the new personnel lived on the military bases in barracks or apartments. The remainder were scattered over the fifteen miles adjacent to the bases, in apartments and homes constructed by the army or by private builders who enjoyed high priorities for obtaining materials. The army provided base exchanges, schools, chaplains, and recreational facilities, and most people, both military and civilian, considered Aberdeen-Edgewood a desirable wartime assignment.

The small towns of the area—Havre de Grace, Aberdeen, Abingdon, Edgewood, Joppatowne—were generally absorbed by the newcomers. The towns became crowded with cheap restaurants and secondhand automobile dealerships, but old-time residents were placated by rising land values. The rest of Harford County largely turned its back on the wartime strip. The boom towns established their own police and managed their own affairs, while the county collected minimum taxes and provided minimum services. The strip declined only slightly in the late 1940s, then grew again as its tawdry impermanence slowly upgraded to normal unzoned suburbia.[20]

Of all the centers along the new industrial strip the most extraordinary was located another ten miles south, at Middle River in Baltimore

County, where the Glenn L. Martin aircraft plant employed 53,000 people. Within four years, from 1939 to 1943, the population of Middle River grew from almost nothing to 125,000 people, the second largest population center in Maryland. Middle River was an area rather than a city, merging almost indistinguishably into suburban East Baltimore and Essex. Instead of assuming direct control, as they did in Aberdeen-Edgewood, the federal agencies guiding this area's development pushed local government jurisdictions to assume responsibility.

Glenn L. Martin was one of the personal romantic success stories of modern industry. He grew up in Iowa tinkering with kites and bicycles, and then in 1912 he went to California, where he and his mother built airplanes and barnstormed together. Minta Martin, his remarkable mother, shared his entire career as pilot, inventor, and corporation manager. The Martins briefly formed the Orville Wright–Martin Aircraft Corporation, but the Wrights were too cautious for them. Martin and his mother broke away to build a larger plant in Omaha, and in 1929 they moved their headquarters to Middle River, building planes mostly for the navy. In 1939 the Netherlands placed an order for 117 bombers, the next year the French wanted 215, and, with Pearl Harbor, the American army and navy needed thousands. The B-10, the B-26, the B-29 Superfortress, and the PBY Mariner were primarily Martin developments. Martin used hundreds of subcontractors, many of whom were located in the Baltimore area. In turn, the company provided parts, notably power turrets, to manufacturers throughout the country. From 1939 on, the construction, enlargement, and replacement of plants was continuous. As the government let contracts, Martin borrowed from the government on the basis of these contracts and then paid off the costs of construction when the contracts were filled.

The chief recruiting device at Martin was high wages—$40 to $65 a week—which were remarkably uniform across jobs and about 25 percent above prevailing industrial wages. Wage costs were written into the government contract, and Martin was willing to pay whatever wage the government approved. Martin contracted with the Johns Hopkins University, the University of Maryland, and the Baltimore public schools to provide training for company workers in subjects ranging from engineering and management to welding and adjustment to urban living. For this education, Martin spent (and passed on in its contracts) an average of $700 for each of 40,000 workers. Education reduced turnover and promoted the uniform wages. Martin encouraged the use of female workers, who composed 35 percent of the work force. Local people thought "Rosie the Riveter" was a Martin employee. Workers came from Baltimore, from the farms of Maryland and nearby Pennsylvania, from rural areas of Virginia and the Carolinas, and from the ethnic towns of Pennsylvania and New York. Newspapers recounted stories of rural people arriving in jalopies with their chickens and goats, people who were hired to build airplanes but who were not yet accustomed to using indoor plumbing.[21]

The person who kept order in Middle River was James E. Cody, a former Boston developer who had been recruited for the duration as an official of the Federal Public Housing Authority. Cody obtained funds from the federal Lanham Act, which was designed to provide emergency war housing, and with the funds he obtained four thousand government-owned trailers, one thousand one-bedroom duplexes, and four huge barrackslike dormitories. He organized these as Trailertown, Victory Villa, and Glenmar Gardens. Victory Villa was notable for its street names: Fuselage, Compass, Radial, Aileron, Manifold, Strut, Gyro, Cowl. Cody worked with Martin to build two permanent developments of one thousand units each, Aero Acres and Stansbury Manor, whose costs were written into government airplane contracts. He persuaded his own agency, the FPHA, to match the effort of Martin and build Armisted Gardens and Burkleigh Manor. Wisely, Cody used funds intended for housing to develop a commercial center and to subsidize ministers and doctors, a newspaper, a library, day-care centers, and the essential USO.

Cody's greatest triumph was in working with the overlapping government jurisdictions of Baltimore County, Baltimore City, and Essex. He appealed to their hope for permanent rather than temporary development as a means of persuading them to provide schools, playgrounds, and a police force. Even the state contributed funds, after Cody found most of the money from federal sources, to build access roads. Cody's efforts were particularly successful in retrospect, for his promise of permanence was realized. Although the Martin Corporation cut back on its production in 1946 and finally left Middle River in 1973, it was replaced by other industries, which were attracted in part by the above-average working-class neighborhood that never declined.[22]

There were, of course, many other industrial war centers, especially around Baltimore (see table 2.3). Bethelehem Steel and its subsidiary shipyard just a few miles from Middle River grew from 2,000 to 60,000 employees, and Bendix Radio in Towson grew from 700 to 8,600. In Allegany County, Kelly-Springfield Tire grew from 1,000 to 7,000, and in Washington County, Fairchild Aircraft grew from 200 to 8,000. All of these were remarkable corporate stories, but they took place in areas that could accommodate the influx.[23]

The other extraordinary wartime community development was the military camps that burgeoned suddenly and, for the most part, altered the countryside permanently. One consequence, much like the effect of industrialization in Elkton or Middle River, was the physical dominance of large camps in isolated areas. Probably the most traditional and remote corner of the state was St. Mary's County, a forty-mile drive from Washington. Its 1940 population of 24,620 was smaller than its population had been in 1790. Then suddenly the bulldozers began to arrive to build the Patuxent Naval Air Station, the major eastern center for testing naval aircraft, flying instruments, and aircraft weapons. By 1942, 7,000 construction workers crawled over the site, and in 1944, 14,000 civilian and military workers and their families lived in an isolated village of mud, trailers, barracks, shacks, honky-tonks, and brothels.

Table 2.3.   Industries Employing Two Thousand or More, 1940–1945

Area	Company	Employment 1940	Employment Peak 1943–1945
Baltimore City	Baltimore and Ohio Railroad	47,000	64,000
	Baltimore Transit	3,000	3,700
	Consolidated Engineering Construction	10,000	40,000
	Consolidated Gas and Electric	4,700	6,100
	Continental Can	1,000	2,000
	Crown Cork	2,600	5,600
	Davidson Chemical	1,500	3,800
	General Motors	1,000	4,500
	Koppers Metal Products	850	6,500
	Maryland Drydock	1,000	9,400
	Mt. Vernon-Woodbury Mills	3,200	6,100
	Pennsylvania Railroad	9,000	11,000
	Revere Copper	1,000	2,400
	Riggs Distler Construction	5,000	27,000
	S. Rosenbloom Garments	2,500	3,000
	Rustless Iron	1,600	2,800
	Western Electric	2,500	9,000
	Western Maryland Railroad	5,000	5,000
	Westinghouse Electric	1,000	6,300
Allegany County	Celanese Textiles	10,500	12,000
	Kelly-Springfield Tire	1,000	6,500
Baltimore County	Bendix Radio	700	8,600
	Bethlehem Steel	3,500	11,000
	Bethlehem-Fairfield Shipyards	1,350	46,700
	Friez Instruments	300	2,300
	Glenn L. Martin Aircraft	3,500	53,000
Cecil County	Triumph Industries	211	11,500
Dorchester County	Phillips Packing	1,000	4,000
Prince George's County	Engineering and Research Corporation	500	3,800
Washington County	Fairchild Aircraft	200	8,000

Source: War Records Division–Maryland Historical Society, *Maryland in World War II*, 3 vols. (1951), 2:18–519.

Note: These figures, supplied by the companies, were occasionally exaggerated.

The problem for the transient community, as it had been in the industrial boom towns, was one of civilization and order. In one nine-month period there were 2,204 arrests (a figure equaling 10 percent of the population) for gambling, fighting, prostitution, and robbery. The conservative county establishment, pushed aside from the start, refused to have much to do with the Patuxent area, largely ignoring pleas for law, police, courts, schools, and zoning. The navy built a railroad and a highway to Washington so workers could go elsewhere for recreation. Finally, the base commander, Captain A. P. Storrs, offered the Maryland State Planning Commission federal funds to design a town and bring order to it. The challenge appealed to the planners, headed by Alvin Pasarew, who gained grudging county approval to proceed. The result, Lexington Park, was a well-planned and prosperous community, the largest town in the county. It remained an island in the county, federally financed, state designed, and self-governing. Its military population was far more liberal in outlook than were the civilians surrounding it. Similar honky-tonk chaos, isolation, and self-government developed at Fort Meade in Anne Arundel County and Andrews Field in Prince George's County.[24]

There were other, less measurable, consequences of the military presence in Maryland. Military activity in the area tended to consist of research, intelligence, and command operations, which attracted a highly educated and affluent military population that was often quite congenial with the social establishment of Montgomery and Baltimore counties. The Office of Strategic Services, the wartime original of the Civilian Intelligence Agency, maintained five of its leading training centers in Montgomery, Prince George's, Charles, Frederick, and Baltimore counties, where elite volunteers underwent rigorous secret training in espionage, sabotage, forgery, blackmail, and assassination. Personnel in the office were required to establish false identities, break into area war plants to steal designs, and demonstrate their ability to disrupt social undertakings.[25] Maybe these things, like war itself, contributed to the realism and sophistication of society; maybe they also contributed to its corruption. A review of the military activities in Maryland from 1940 to 1945 is presented in table 2.4.

For the people of Maryland the greatest single impact of the war was prosperity: prosperity for almost everyone, especially for once-unemployed workers, prosperity that endured almost continuously for forty years. Prosperity constitutes the transformation of life that made the war a dividing line between the era past and a period dawning. The per capita income in Maryland increased from $634 a year in 1939, 15 percent above the national average, to $1,272 just six years later, 7 percent higher than the national average. Adjusting for an inflation rate of about 25 percent, real income for every person in Maryland increased by almost 50 percent. But prosperity was even greater than this, because the 14 percent of Maryland residents who were in the military service were normally the top wage earners—and they were pegged at an artificially low income. The per capita savings of more than $1,400 in war bonds was also unprecedented.

Even more striking was the disproportionate distribution of the new prosperity to the working classes, whose net wages and salaries increased by 140 percent. Upper-class income from profits, interest, and rents, meanwhile, declined by 20 percent. The war saved the Soviet Union but it weakened the rationale for Marxism insofar as the gap between the poor and the rich narrowed in the capitalist countries. Figures for changes in income distribution are not available by states, but nationally the change from 1939 to 1945 showed the gain in family income for those at the bottom of the income scale to be far ahead of the gain for those at the top: the richest fifth of the population experienced a 20 percent gain in family income; the second fifth gained by 30 percent; the third fifth, by 36 percent; and the fourth fifth, by 59 percent. But the poorest fifth of the population gained by 68 percent.[26]

The War as Watershed

Table 2.4.   Major Military Activities in Maryland, 1940–1945

Location	Installation	Peak Population		Activities
		Military	Civilian	
Anne Arundel County	Fort George G. Meade	70,000	3,800	Training infantry and artillery troops; serving as an induction and separation center
	Annapolis Naval Command	6,000	3,000	Naval Academy for training officers; Engineers Station for testing engines; Radio Station for contacting ships; Hospital
Baltimore Area	Fort Holabird	4,400	3,300	Testing and shipping vehicles and tanks; training in literacy
	Curtis Bay Ordnance	100	1,800	Manufacturing small arms and ammunition
	Army (other)	1,800	1,100	Supervising port loading; construction; supervising area National Guard; undertaking loyalty checks for defense employers
	Coast Guard	2,100	3,600	Undertaking security checks of port employees; repairing ships; supervising private ships on submarine patrol
	Navy	800	100	Inspecting ship and aircraft construction; arming merchant ships
Calvert County	Amphibious Training Base	10,000	100	Providing invasion training
	Mine Warfare Test Station	1,500	300	Testing mines and torpedoes
Cecil County	Bainbridge Naval Training Center	30,000	5,000	Providing basic naval training; serving as induction and separation center; Hospital
Charles County	Naval Ordnance Station	100	900	Research, testing, manufacture of gunpowder, rocket propellants
Frederick County	Fort Detrick	800	200	Undertaking research in biological warfare: viruses, funguses, epidemics, defoliants
Harford County	Aberdeen Proving Ground	30,000	5,700	Developing and shipping ordnance and vehicles
	Edgewood Arsenal	3,400	10,700	Manufacturing war chemicals
Montgomery County	Army Map Service	1,000	2,500	Manufacturing military maps
	Naval Medical Center	900	700	Undertaking medical research; Hospital
	David D. Taylor Model Basin	500	500	Undertaking naval research
Prince George's County	Andrews Air Force Base	2,000	600	Providing advanced air training; protecting Washington area
	Hydrographic Office	400	1,200	Developing ocean maps
St. Mary's County	Patuxent Naval Air Station	7,000	7,000	Testing aircraft
	Torpedo Testing Station	200	100	Testing torpedoes
Washington County	Fort Albert C. Ritchie	1,000	100	Performing military intelligence; interrogating prisoners; training interpreters
Statewide	Office of Strategic Services	1,500	500	Conducting espionage, sabotage; promoting insurrection in enemy countries
Total Peak Employment		176,000	51,600	

Source: War Records Division–Maryland Historical Society, *Maryland in World War II,* 3 vols. (1950), 1:1–252.

This new prosperity explained many of the changes that occurred within specific groups and institutions. It lay behind the high morale, even exuberance, of war, and also behind the impatience with restrictions on consumer goods which grew so noticeably toward the end. The disruption of the old order, and the growing disquiet, especially among conservatives, over it, was also related to the new prosperity.

One principal reason for the prosperity was the entry of two large groups, blacks and women, into the labor force. As workers they began at the bottom of the economic pile, and they enjoyed the greatest rise, a kind of second emancipation. When war broke out, blacks worked mostly as farm tenants and in cities as domestics or common labor, although a sizeable unnoticed middle class of ministers and merchants served the segregated black community. At first change was slow. Even after Pearl Harbor, the Maryland Red Cross refused to accept blood from black donors, and industry employed few blacks. Early in 1942 a survey of the ten largest firms in Baltimore showed that not a single black was employed above the unskilled level, and only a few had jobs above the janitorial level.[27]

Employers, however, were beginning to feel the pinch of a smaller white male labor force. In 1940 the Baltimore Department of Public Works was forced to replace its white male street cleaners with black males, and in 1943 it hired black females. It helped that the wages could be reduced with each step—and service improved. Even greater was the pinch from the federal government.[28] In 1941 President Roosevelt, fearing a disruptive black march on Washington, ordered integration of plants holding war contracts, and by the middle of 1942 various federal agencies, headed by socially conscious bureaucrats, were vigorously pushing integration. The War Manpower Commission made black employment a condition for renewing federal contracts at Triumph Industries, Glenn L. Martin, and Bethelehem Steel. The United States Employment Service approached employers with a black-employee-or-nothing policy. The National Security Administration established USO facilities for black workers. The Federal Public Housing Authority forced Baltimore to accept two thousand black housing units. Even the Federal Office of Civilian Defense, which had been established to supervise the elite Maryland Council of Defense, was required to maintain an integrated staff. There were occasional flare-ups—brief walkouts at Western Electric and then at Maryland Drydock over integrated cafeterias and restrooms, and scuffles at the USOs in Elkton and Middle River—but relative harmony prevailed.

The federal wartime initiative in civil rights has generally gone unnoticed by historians, for Roosevelt was concerned with southern support, and except for his 1941 proclamation little official effort was made to promote integration. The initiatives seemed to come from local federal bureaucrats, many of whom were idealistic recruits to the New Deal and were now in the field exercising power that transcended Washington policy. The war curtailed policies of social reform, but it enhanced the power of the reformer. The people who were pressured by the federal bureaucrats found it harder to oppose field office initiatives than a central policy, and their resentment of federal encroachments smoldered.

For the new, mostly urban, jobs, blacks poured into Baltimore from the rural counties. Black industrial employment in the city grew from 7 percent of total industrial employment in 1940 to 17 percent in 1945, a proportion that never declined. From 1940 to 1950 the proportion of the black population of Maryland living in Baltimore grew from 59 percent to 75 percent. Blacks composed 19 percent of the city's total population in 1940; by 1950 that figure was 24 percent. The proportion of blacks in every Maryland county declined. Few people comprehended the scope of the civil rights movement that was underway.[29]

Women, including black women, composed an even larger portion of the work force, and the emancipation of women was almost as great as that of blacks. Women composed 29 percent of the total Maryland labor force in 1940 (compared to 25 percent nationally, a figure that had not changed since 1910) and 39 percent in 1945 (37 percent nationally). Their absolute numbers increased from 120,000 to 230,000. The increase came not in the service industries and textiles, which had traditionally employed women, but in the expanding war industries, particularly munitions, aircraft manufacture, and shipbuilding. In many plants women for the first time worked at what had once been considered the most masculine of jobs: welding, riveting, and operating drill presses and cranes.

The initiative for women in industry, as for blacks, came from the federal government, especially the War Manpower Commission, which viewed industrial employment of women primarily as a solution to the labor shortage. Management tended to go along because women's wages were lower, although the wage differential shrank during the war. Women entering the labor force during the war were considerably older than prewar female workers had been, and far more of them were married. About two-thirds of the women who first entered the labor force at this time were longtime residents of Maryland, and about one-third were migrants who came to the state for war jobs. The war, in other words, brought family women into the work force, and it promoted a new mobility for women as well as for men.

Female employment dropped in the two years following the war (to 36 percent of the Maryland labor force), but it still remained far above the prewar level. Of the 55,000 women who lost their jobs, about 35,000 rejoined husbands returning from service or returned to their families. For them, work had been a wartime sacrifice. The other 20,000 women were out of work involuntarily, and they eventually rejoined the 180,000 women who retained their jobs. For the majority of women, the war had provided an opportunity.[30]

Labor during the war—black and white, male and female—was both well aware of its prosperity and pleased with its progress. From 1940 on, labor had been one of the most fervently patriotic groups in Maryland, and the fervor lasted until the end. In 1941 the unions offered a no-strike pledge in war industries, and the annual conventions of the AFL and CIO vied with the American Legion in flags and patriotic oratory. The Maryland CIO even promoted a union speedup and employed a production committee to urge workers to greater effort. Union leadership, in a spirit of patriotism, faced down its membership by promoting the employment of women (who joined the unions in large numbers) and, especially, of blacks (who usually declined to join). Protest by local unions to the state's anti-union work-or-fight law was muted, and protest against the federal Little Steel Formula, which limited wage increases to inflation, was almost nonexistent.

The only significant wartime strike in Maryland was a nonunion walkout by Baltimore transit workers who protested the company's eight-hour pay for ten- and twelve-hour workdays. Despite the extreme hostility of the Baltimore *Sunpapers,* which probably represented middle-class opinion, federal arbitration resulted in a victory for the workers.[31]

Business was never very happy during World War II, as the stock market showed. Businessmen were filled with patriotism and talked of cooperation with government and labor, but their fear of dislocation, of shortages, of control, and of eventual reconversion was greater than their pleasure in corporation profits. Business association meetings and annual reports were a litany of complaints about labor's greed and government's bungling. Profits increased approximately 50 percent during the war, but the real gain was in plant capitalization, which more than doubled. From 1940 to 1944 private capital contributed $108 million to Maryland manufacturing facilities, and public capital, primarily in the form of loans from the Reconstruction Finance Corporation, contributed $207 million (see table 2.5).[32]

The number of private firms engaged in manufacturing was actually declining. The government preferred big contracts to small ones, accelerating the trend that had been evident since the late nineteenth century of the big getting bigger. Business dyspepsia, first over the New Deal and then over wartime controls, may have reflected a sense of failure of the weak to compete in an increasingly complex economic environment. One-third of the manufacturing establishments in Maryland shrank during the war, and many of them closed (see table 2.6).

One of the biggest changes of the war, comparable to the change in the conditions of blacks and women, was the transformation of agriculture. This was the story of plunging farm populations as day labor-

Table 2.5. Capital Added to Manufacturing, 1940–1944

Industry	Capital Added ($ millions)
Ordnance and munitions	75
Aircraft	67
Steel	57
Shipping	56
Nonferrous metals	19
Chemicals and oil	19
Machinery	12
Food processing	12

Source: War Records Division–Maryland Historical Society, *Maryland in World War II,* 3 vols. (1951), 2:15–17.

Table 2.6. Manufacturing Establishments, 1939 and 1949

Size of Establishments	Number of Establishments		
	1939	1949	Change (%)
1–19 workers	1,839	1,628	−11
20–99 workers	649	848	+23
100+ workers	253	349	+28

Source: State Planning Commission, *Growth of Manufactures in Maryland, 1921–1947* (1951).

ers faded nearly away, of mechanizing to make up for the loss of labor, and, finally, of soaring farm profits. Since the colonial era, farm tenancy had been a resort of people who could find no other job, the people left behind. The cheap labor of sharecroppers or day laborers was the margin of the farm owner's superiority over them, but it also assured the overpopulation of the farm and the consequent lag in farm profits. To the farm owner, the war seemed to be yet another periodic calamity, as the war industries drained off farming's cheap labor. Farmers blamed organized labor for the seductive wartime wages that attracted away their tenants, and many farmers turned against the New Deal to protest its alliance with the hated unions. In another sense, however, the departure of the tenants was the beginning of the farmer's salvation, for the value of his own labor was enhanced in proportion to the departure of the day laborers and tenants who were in fact his competitors.

The Maryland farm population fell from eighty thousand workers in 1939 to sixty-two thousand in 1945, and wages rose from two dollars to five dollars a day. Farmers clamoring for labor, preferably at the old price, forced the state to create a Farm Emergency Labor Program that promoted draft exemption for farm laborers and at various times recruited three thousand Jamaican migrants, three thousand German prisoners of war, and twelve thousand high school students to work during crucial seasons. The state Extension Service established farm cooperatives where farmers could share or rent farm machinery, and the federal Department of Agriculture created a State Agricultural War Board to supervise labor practices, establish crop goals, and promote maximum farm prices. Low-profit margin production—horses, sheep, potatoes, corn, oysters, and crabs—declined, and new produce—especially chickens, soybeans, pigs, and vegetables—soared. Farm production increased 40 percent during the war, the value of land and buildings, 52 percent, farm machinery, 95 percent, and farm income, 138 percent. The farm was evolving from the residue of those left behind to an occupation of capitalist managers.[33]

Social changes were discomfiting, and frustration erupted in the next decade, especially as people looked for radicals to blame for unwelcome change. During the war, however, most people retained a remarkable equanimity. The antiforeign hysteria of World War I was largely absent, and crime, family, health, and education statistics reflected social stability. The sense of community in a common cause faded as the war went on, but social cohesion remained notably stronger than it had been before the war and than it would be after it.

Sympathy for the enemy powers, or sabotage, was almost nonexistent, and after a brief flurry of concern following Pearl Harbor, the fear of sabotage also subsided. In 1935 about two hundred German-American militarists paraded in Baltimore, apparently thinking that Hitler stood for German pride rather than for totalitarian racism, but they never surfaced again. Baltimore's German-language newspaper, *Taeglicher Correspondent,* was extremely hostile to nazism, and German groups, as if to prove their American patriotism, tried desperately to drive out any hint of disloyalty. Scrutiny by the FBI and by the German-Americans themselves revealed that in Maryland there were never more than half a dozen outspoken Hitler sympathizers, most of them adolescents, during the war. The Maryland police and the FBI made only forty-one arrests under the stringent state and national antisabotage laws. One case involved a self-proclaimed Nazi who fabricated faulty guns in a Martin plant, one involved a man who wrote letters signed "Heil Hitler," and the remaining thirty-nine arrests were judged to be horseplay, thievery, or efforts to embarrass co-workers.

People cultivated the melting-pot theory, pretending not to notice the foreign backgrounds of their neighbors. There were ten Japanese in Maryland in 1940, too few to be a focus of resentment, and there were seventeen thousand first- or second-generation Italians and seventy-three thousand Germans—too many to resent. The seventy-six German clubs that existed before the war remained unobtrusive during the war, but most of them continued to exist. Germans and Italians later reported occasional insults and occasional job discrimination, but there were no reports of physical abuse or destruction of property. The courts reported more name changes among Jews during the war than among Germans or Italians. The state was much amused when someone suggested that Berlin, Maryland, should change its name. A religious group in Baltimore accepted fifty Japanese-Americans who had been deported from the West Coast.[34]

The number of interned aliens was relatively small. After Pearl Harbor the FBI arrested ninety-eight aliens in Maryland—fifty-four Germans, forty-two Italians, one Hungarian, and one Japanese—but only sixteen of them were held for the duration of the war. Subsequently a group of Finns and a Chilean were seized and released. In addition, about five hundred Maryland conscientious objectors were interned during the war, and about five hundred (not necessarily the same ones) were assigned to twenty-three camps over the state, mostly as hospital or prison orderlies. Several conscientious objector groups published newsletters during their internment, describing a life that was hard but not desperate. By far the most popular prisoners in Maryland were the nearly 48,000 German prisoners of war. Farmers pleaded for them, and army officials were disturbed because they thought the local newspapers lionized them to the detriment of the war effort.[35]

Social health was evident in the decline of crime. Police records showed a 95 percent rise in arrests from 1933 to Pearl Harbor, then a 30 percent decline in arrests to V-J Day, and a sharp rise again thereafter. Contrary to expectations, the wartime strains of family separations, consumer shortages, and civilian and military movement were evidently not inducements to crime. The same pattern appeared for rural communities and crowded boom towns and for almost every category of crime, from murder and assault to burglary and drunkenness. Part of the explanation lay in the fact that men of crime-prone age were in service, and part in the availability of jobs. There were wartime rackets, such as selling worthless devices guaranteed to ward off bombs, and there was much publicity about black marketing and cheating on ration systems, but generally public outrage at the excesses exceeded the excesses themselves. The remarkable fact was that the public complied with restrictions. The prison population declined even more than the crime rate, as prisoners were released to the armed services or paroled to meet the demand for labor.[36]

Some people during the war became greatly concerned over what they considered to be juvenile deliquency and sexual promiscuity, but these were matters of social change rather than social disintegration. Teenagers had jobs, money, and freedom as never before, and thousands of them left home without permission. Girls, especially, wandered the streets smoking cigarettes, which the older generation thought was a crime. Married women, who were supposed to be guardians of the home, were going to work, and divorce rates grew, although very slightly by later standards. The armed services for the first time gave domestic troops contraceptives and talked to them about venereal disease. Probably all these things were natural extentions of trends dating at least from the 1920s, but conservatives were disturbed, and "juvenile delinquency" became a code phrase to decry change.

The middle-class service clubs, not the police, discovered juvenile delinquency in Maryland. In Aberdeen the Lions Club's alarm about girls walking the streets became the issue that finally brought the local establishment into common cause with the federal government. Probably concern over juvenile delinquency was the major motive, besides patriotism, which led the middle class to support the USOs so ardently. In Baltimore the Rotary Club demanded action, and in Montgomery County the League of Women Voters took the initiative. Governor O'Conor appointed a committee, including several service club presidents, which in 1943 issued a 298-page report that led to the establishment of a state Bureau of Child Welfare. Police hardly understood the excitement, but they dutifully established a police boys' club, picked up hundreds of teenagers for vagrancy, and established juvenile delinquency as a new category of crime.[37]

Easy morality grew easier during the war, but Maryland's reputation for laxity preceded and followed the war years. Prince George's County prospered as the gambling and girlie club mecca of booming Washington, and Baltimore enjoyed its reputation as the bawdy capital of the East Coast. Many people thought B-girl meant Baltimore girl, although it probably meant bar-girl; and there were claims that "hookers" got their name from Fell's Hook or Fells Point, a sailor hangout on the Baltimore waterfront. Baltimore, Anne Arundel, and St. Mary's counties all resisted efforts by the FBI and the army to clamp down on prostitution around the war camps.[38]

People were generally healthy during the war. The birth rate, the standard by which biologists measure social welfare, soared in Maryland by 37 percent, from 15.8 per 1,000 population in 1939 to 21.6 in the peak year of 1943. The civilian death rate declined slightly, even though many doctors were out of the country. There was a significant decline in deaths from infant mortality, tuberculosis, pneumonia, syphilis, and suicide; and an increase in deaths from heart disease, cancer, and industrial accidents.[39]

Maryland schools were a particular source of social health and stability, promoting democratic values and actively combatting hysteria. School officials held conventions and published dozens of pamphlets such as "Redirecting the School Program in Wartime," but their efforts were usually tilted in a liberal rather than a conservative direction, opposing Hitler as a totalitarian rather than as a German, stressing the dangers of nationalism and militarism rather than glorifying them, and drawing lessons about the need for international brotherhood. The schools emphasized the need for social cooperation in a common cause, and they promoted scrap drives to teach cooperation as well as to collect scrap. The curriculum placed new emphasis on physical education, vocational education, and adult education. The schools promoted the idealistic, John Dewey values of the teachers and principals who ran them much more than the conservative values of the establishment school boards.

School attendance rose, though unevenly, in both public schools and colleges. Everywhere blacks poured into the schools as never before, indicating that prosperity promoted education as well as the other way around. In the boom towns the schools overflowed, forcing the federal government to provide funds and, occasionally, schools and supervision when the counties failed. In nearly half the colleges, usually the stronger ones, the campuses overflowed with army-navy programs for future officers. Students supposedly received four years of higher education—often crammed into two years or less. Everywhere the teacher shortage was acute, for teachers drifted off to war or to higher-paying industrial jobs. Class sizes, therefore, rose faster than total attendance, and most people agreed that expanded school budgets should be a high postwar priority.[40]

Maryland in the 1940s, for whatever reason, had associated with it what was probably a larger proportion of the nation's prominent writers than it did at any other time in its history. H. L. Mencken was the dean, and despite his eclipse as a German sympathizer on the eve of the war, he remained almost a state symbol. Ogden Nash was a popular poet-humorist ("I never could have loved New York, loved I not Baltimore"). Emily Post was born in Maryland; Gertrude Stein and F. Scott Fitzgerald came and went; John Dos Passos and Upton Sinclair spent their later years in the state. Other writers included Hervey Allen (*Anthony Adverse*), Munro Leaf (*Ferdinand the Bull*), Fulton Oursler (*The Greatest Story Ever Told*), James M. Cain (*The Postman Always Rings Twice*), Dashiell Hammett (Sam Spade detective stories), Karl Shapiro (*V-Letter*), and historical novelists Philip Van Doren Stern, Van Wyck Mason, and William Seabrook. There was the philosopher Arthur O. Lovejoy, the classicist Edith Hamilton, the educator Stringfellow Barr, and journalists Hanson Baldwin, Gerald W. Johnson, Neil H. Swanson, and Hamilton Owens.

They were hardly regional writers, and no theme united them except the war and escape from it. The group was too large, however, to be dismissed entirely as a coincidental assemblage. Perhaps the best explanation was that Maryland lay near the center of the national consciousness and its expression.

Churches, like schools and culture, were healthy during the war, drawing from the fighting lessons of tolerance more than hatred. Roman Catholics, who were often of Irish or Italian background and

who were terrified of America's Russian ally, maintained a particularly
cool attitude toward the war, but both Catholic and Protestant
churches were centers of volunteer war effort. Attendance at the traditional churches rose sharply, and the multiplication of evangelical
sects temporarily abated.

The movie industry alternated between the absurd and the vicious
during war, but otherwise even the entertainment and sports industries
maintained a reasonable balance. Hollywood pandered to a glorification of war and unconscionable racist attacks on the enemy. Hollywood's local ally, the Maryland state board of movie censors,
maintained its tight sex code but relaxed its ban on "scenes showing
the cruelty and brutality of the enemy" on the grounds of the "necessity of conditioning a civilian population to war." Baseball and horse-
racing continued in Maryland, but they were curtailed somewhat by
restrictions on manpower and travel. Team owners were careful to
avoid the charge of frivolity by making extravagant contributions to
patriotic causes.[41]

People were tiring of the war when the end came: volunteer programs were lapsing, worker absenteeism growing, and strikes threatening; businessmen were beside themselves with complaints, and the
increased demand for consumer goods threatened the entire system of
rationing and price controls. These, however, were the frustrations of
rising expectations. It was a war of greater sacrifice and nobility than
people remembered, because the sense of sacrifice and nobility was
quickly lost. It was a war of greater benefits than people remembered,
because the benefits were soon exceeded. Only rather incidentally was
it a war of frustration and politics, but people remembered this very
well.

War and Politics

People in Maryland, like people in most states, never came to terms
politically with the depression and the New Deal, and they accepted
the controls and services the war brought only for purposes of winning
the war. From depression to war and on into the postwar world,
people were caught between the philosophical rejection of big government and the need for more of the things it provided.

The shadow over Maryland politics was Albert C. Ritchie, the four-
term Democratic governor (1920 to 1935), a symbol of best-govern-
ment-is-least conservatism. He considered Coolidge and Hoover to be
spendthrifts and he periodically surfaced as a possible Democratic
presidential candidate who might attack the Republicans from the
right. He was finally displaced in Maryland in 1935 by Harry W.
Nice, a pro–New Deal Republican who was so inept in dealing with
the Democratic legislature that his proposals for welfare and public
works programs were hardly noticed. Maryland voted by landslides
for Roosevelt and accepted the handouts Washington provided, but
through all of Roosevelt's administrations, Maryland's governors, its
United States senators, its Baltimore mayors, and the majority of its
legislators offered lip-service support at best, and in practice they were
usually uncooperative. Far from stimulating local government initia-

tives to end the depression, the New Deal preempted the task and curtailed local action.

Herbert R. O'Conor's administration (1939 to 1947) reflected the public schizophrenia. O'Conor's grandparents were Irish immigrants to Baltimore in the 1850s, and his father was manager of the city's fashionable Rennert Hotel. Born in 1896, O'Conor grew up in Boss "Sonny" Mahon's Irish Tenth Ward, which was located just south of Greenmount Cemetery, attended Catholic schools, received his law degree from the University of Maryland, and began his long-planned political career. Popular, glib, intuitively political, he sensed the public mood and played to it. As assistant state's attorney in Baltimore, he gained fame for kidnapping from the New York police a suspected murderer who was also wanted in Maryland, and in 1934, when Nice became the Republican governor, the flashy young O'Conor won election as the Democratic attorney general. Blithely he embraced both Ritchie and Roosevelt as his mentors.[42]

In 1938 the question was which of the state's Democrats would replace the hapless Nice. Prince George's Lansdale Sasscer came out as a champion of Roosevelt; Baltimore's Mayor Howard W. Jackson emerged as the urban establishment's anti–New Dealer; William S. Gordy from the Eastern Shore was the rural anti–New Dealer; and O'Conor mostly ignored anything touching on national politics or political philosophy. After the popular voting, which gave O'Conor a bare plurality, delegates to the Democratic caucus cast the deciding ballots. There Sasscer withdrew in favor of O'Conor, who won in the caucus and went on to defeat Nice with relative ease in the general election.[43]

In office, O'Conor's politically sensitive equivocation became clearer: modern management and rigid economy in the Ritchie tradition, rhetorical support for Roosevelt as a war leader, and an essential unwillingness to accept the expanded roles for state and federal governments which the increasingly complex and prosperous society demanded. Politically, in other words, O'Conor was rigorously middle class—for good management, economy, and skepticism of the New Deal were all middle-class views. Economically the poor gained most from the war, and their voice in government would eventually grow in proportion to their prosperity, but through the early 1940s the prosperous classes remained dominant in Maryland and all the more intense in their politics because of their relative economic decline.

Perhaps acceptance of modern management to replace patronage politics was all that could be expected from state government during the war years. Although efficient management was a progressive ideal that was raised to a high point by Ritchie in the 1920s, full acceptance of it by politicians who rose in the old patronage politics was slow. The evolution into modern bureaucracy lasted at least into the Mandel administration. Like all effective governors from Ritchie to Mandel, O'Conor perfected his technique of using these procedural reforms: the appointment of a high-level citizens' commission to publicize the need for action, old-fashioned patronage bargaining for legislative support, and then a popular call for legislation. O'Conor's successes as governor, besides mobilization, were his wartime steps toward legislative, executive, and, especially, judicial reforms. They were not substantive social reforms in the New Deal tradition, but procedural and management reforms in the Ritchie-Hoover mold.

The main commission report, undertaken between O'Conor's election and his inauguration, was by the Committee on the Structure of State Government, which was headed by Isaiah H. Bowman, president of the Johns Hopkins University, and included Dean Acheson, Glenn L. Martin, and Lansdale Sasscer. For the legislature, it recommended a legislative council of appointed members who would work year-round with a professional staff to prepare legislation, conduct preliminary hearings, and oversee the implementation of laws. For the executive branch it recommended creation of a budget bureau, which would receive all agency requests for money and prepare a budget within the bounds of professionally estimated revenues. The committee also recommended consolidation of numerous patronage regulatory agencies into stronger nonpolitical bureaus, especially a strong bureau of natural resources. For two years, while Roosevelt struggled to save capitalism and while the world went to war, the Natural Resource Administration provided the major political issue in Maryland, inspiring a dispute between conservationists, who wanted to save the Chesapeake oyster beds, and local oystermen, who resisted restrictions. O'Conor engineered a political compromise.[44]

Another administrative reform involved the courts and took three commissions and six years to be accomplished. First, a commission headed by lawyer Reuben Oppenheimer made recommendations that resulted in the elimination of scores of constables and part-time judges, especially in Baltimore, and their replacement by a smaller, nonpolitical professional court. Second, a commission headed by Judge Hammond Urner made recommendations that resulted in the elimination of 250 politically appointed county judges—often people lacking law degrees who depended for an income on the fines against those found guilty—and their replacement by 52 professional judges. Finally, a commission headed by Judge Carroll T. Bond transformed the state's highest court, the Court of Appeals, by replacing eight locally elected judges, many of them local political bosses, by a full-time, nonpolitical five-man court.[45]

Besides the procedural reforms, which continued during the war, O'Conor's other major program was rigorous government economy, and especially severe cutbacks in social welfare programs, even by the standards of Ritchie. Total expenditures for all state services dropped from $60.7 million in 1940 to a low of $48.6 million in 1943. O'Conor argued that the New Deal relieved the states of responsibility for social services, met complaints with calls for wartime sacrifices, and let department heads understand that their success was measured by how much of their agency's appropriations were turned back at the end of each year. The state asylum for retarded children reduced by more than half the number of inmates it accepted; state-supported county poorhouses received seventy cents per resident per day to cover all expenses; and the food allowance for state prisoners fell to fourteen cents per day.

Middle-class taxpayers appreciated the economies—as though the state was showing the federal government how it could operate. State

income taxes dropped during the war from a maximum of 2¹/₂ percent to 2 percent, maximum corporation taxes dropped from 6 percent to 5 percent, and state property taxes declined from 23¹/₂ cents
to 12 cents on each $100 of assessed value. Still, wartime prosperity
allowed revenues to flow into the state treasury, and toward the end of
the war O'Conor allowed expenditures to rise slightly, but even in
1945 total state expenditures remained about what they had been in
1938, despite a 10 percent increase in population and a 25 percent rise
in inflation. Maryland, complaining of federal power, used the war to
escape responsibility for its own social services (see table 2.7).[46]

The one state service that managed to expand during the war was
education, the state service that actively promoted middle-class values
and that had long been most acceptable to middle-class taxpayers.
Thomas G. Pullen, a powerful state superintendent of education,
played skillfully on the idea that education was not a peacetime luxury
that could be sacrificed, like welfare or health, but a tool of war. His
budgets grew almost without interruption, even slightly ahead of
statewide enrollments. In 1940 O'Conor and the General Assembly
appropriated money for adult education, especially for training
machine operators in the public schools. State support for teacher
salaries inched up, and in 1945 the General Assembly provided for a
35 percent increase in all public school operations, especially for
improved salaries, more teachers, better school libraries, and the addition to the high schools of a twelfth year of study. College appropriations also grew slightly during the war. Education, unlike other social
services, managed to avoid identification with either liberalism or
conservatism, and thus it developed apart from the passions over New
Deal politics.[47]

O'Conor's well-considered political center—of patriotism, good
management, and economy—would not hold in the increasingly prosperous and complex world that came with war. On O'Conor's left was
the growing political participation of the poor, especially blacks, who
demanded additional services. On his right was the growing intransigence of the comfortable, especially Republicans, who resented the
economic leveling of the war and the growing intrusion of government
into their lives. Even during the war both sides were gaining at the
expense of the center until the consensus of war dissolved into the
harsh frustrations of the late 1940s, when outspoken liberal execu-

Table 2.7. State Expenditures, 1938, 1940, 1943, and 1945
(in Millions of Dollars)

Expenditures	1938	1940	1943	1945
Administration (including war mobilization)	1.7	1.9	2.5	2.9
Capital investment, bonds	9.7	6.6	3.6	6.1
Education	9.0	10.5	12.1	15.1
Health, Welfare, Social Security	21.7	18.4	14.2	16.9
Highways	11.4	15.5	13.5	13.3
Police, Prisons	2.9	2.7	1.2	3.1
Supplement to counties and miscellaneous	2.9	5.1	1.5	2.8
Total	59.4	60.7	48.6	60.3

Source: Comptroller of the Treasury, *Annual Reports* (1938–1946).

tives like President Harry Truman and Governor William Preston Lane faced obdurate conservative legislatures and rebellious constituencies.

O'Conor and his complaisant legislatures faced pressures from the left in dealing, ever so tentatively, with problems of race, health, welfare, and libraries. In every case the state responded to rather than initiated action, but by responding, the state moved unwittingly toward the postwar world. First was the problem of race, as black prosperity impelled the courts and the legislature to action. When federal courts ordered the state to provide at least minimally equal college education for blacks or accept them into white colleges, O'Conor in 1935 obtained $250,000 to purchase Morgan College from the Methodist church. After seven Maryland counties lost suits that would have allowed them to maintain separate salary scales for white and black teachers, the state put up funds in 1941 for salary equalization. And when two thousand middle-class blacks from 125 churches and fraternal organizations marched on Annapolis in 1942 to protest unequal treatment, O'Conor appointed a commission to make recommendations and secured the first token appointment of blacks to the Baltimore school board and police department.[48]

In the field of health, the talk of a national system of socialized medicine, promoted especially by the unions, impelled local conservatives to offer alternative plans. In Maryland, physicians led the way, obtaining from the state a promise of a direct subsidy for their treatment of indigent patients. The program was not funded, so it hardly mattered except as a promise for the future, and after the war it was absorbed into a program for expanded state health clinics. In the field of welfare, the state, embarrassed by a series of newspaper exposés of barbaric county poorhouses, agreed in principle to assume control, although, again, funding and substantive action awaited the more thorough transformation that came after the war. Finally, the county libraries, which faced virtual extinction in the stringent budgets of depression and war, gained at least the promise of state aid as the war ended. Libraries, like schools, served especially the people who paid substantial taxes.[49]

The 1940 elections in Maryland reflected the peculiar conglomerate of O'Conor's bid for middle-class approval, the continuation of Democratic machine politics, and popular support for Roosevelt at the national level. O'Conor campaigned for Roosevelt but not for the New Deal, supporting the straight Democratic ticket with the disturbing argument that "Hitler would be delighted to see national defense bogged down by a change in administration." Democrats won all six Maryland congressional seats, although three of them were neutral or hostile to Roosevelt. Senator George L. Radcliffe, a lukewarm New Dealer, won reelection over the anti-New Dealers O'Conor supported in the primaries, and then, like Roosevelt, Radcliffe won the Maryland general election.

By 1942 a larger threat to O'Conor's centralism came from Maryland's growing Republican party. The only statewide election that year was O'Conor's own bid for reelection, which was supposed to produce an easy victory, but the then-unknown Theodore R. McKeldin came within a hair's-breadth of an upset. The core of McKeldin's

Franklin D. Roosevelt congratulates Glenn L. Martin during a 1945 tour of the giant Baltimore County aircraft plant. At center, Governor Herbert R. O'Conor beams. Courtesy of the *Baltimore Sun*.

support were middle-class Republican conservatives, but McKeldin himself was more liberal than O'Conor, and his supporters included workers and, especially, blacks, whom O'Conor ignored. In 1942 Republicans elected two congressmen from Maryland, and the following year McKeldin, with liberal support, became mayor of Baltimore. In 1944 Roosevelt carried Maryland by his smallest margin ever, and O'Conor tried to maintain his merger of conservatism and party loyalty by arguing that Roosevelt was more conservative than Thomas E. Dewey. In 1946 Maryland Democrats barely held onto their senate seats, and their margin in the General Assembly shrank to an unprecedented low. Democrats averaged a 62 percent margin in all statewide elections from 1936 to 1941, but from 1942 to 1946 their margin dropped to 54 percent.

The Republican rise in Maryland in the mid-1940s was part of a national trend, and it reflected the intense feelings of many anti–New Dealers, but it was not wholly what it seemed, for it marked hardly a pause in the growth of larger and more paternalistic government. For one thing, Republicans like McKeldin and Dewey obtained much of their support from people who wanted more services as well as those who wanted fewer services. More importantly, however, the poor showing of New Dealers was explained largely by the low turnout of working-class voters, who were satisfied with wartime prosperity. The dissatisfied are more likely to go to the polls than the satisfied. In 1936, 1937, and 1938 an average of 55 percent of Maryland's eligible voters went to the polls, but from 1944 to 1946 this figure dropped to 34 percent. Except for the era of good feelings in the 1810s and the prosperous second decade of the twentieth century, World War II marked the lowest political participation in Maryland history.

The people not voting in the mid-1940s were those who gained most from the war: blacks, blue-collar workers, newcomers, residents of the boom towns. The voters with high participation, on the other hand, were the affluent, who were not sharing proportionately in the rising wealth, the conservatives, who were disturbed by change, the old residents, who were overwhelmed by newcomers, and those who were left behind in the rural counties of declining population. Politics moved to the right during the war largely because conservatives were angry and liberals were content. When the situation was reversed after the war, Harry Truman and William Lane were prepared to take the next steps toward centralization and expanded social services. O'Conor stuck with his dwindling center of conservative Democrats. In 1946, after two terms as governor and with all the power of the Democratic organization behind him, he won election to the United States Senate by a bare 50.2 percent majority. He spent the rest of his career looking for American Communists; he blamed them for destroying his middle-class world.[50]

Most people in Maryland thought of the war as a temporary crisis that would be followed by normal times. O'Conor had three commissions planning for the postwar world, and none was very good because they all made the mistake of starting with 1940 instead of 1945. The war was not an interlude for America, but a transition. Politically it brought new alignments of interests, new bureaucracy, and still larger government controls and services. Economically it brought prosperity and population mobility that was just beginning, especially with the rise of the suburbs. Socially it stimulated democracy, especially in the rise of blacks. Emotionally it brought new frustrations and enemies, especially in the Cold War. World War II, like all our wars, speeded up history and offered a new beginning.

The population swirl of war, which people thought extraordinary, became the norm of American life. To be sure, movement was always characteristic of the nation, but its acceleration in the 1940s continued after the war and fundamentally transformed local institutions and ways of thought. Much of the increased movement was technologically based, as more automobiles and airplanes allowed easier movement to and fro. One author calculated that from 1940 to 1980 the average American increased his travel distance, not counting walking, from 2.2 to 6.4 miles daily.[1] Movement also meant change of residence. The old American ideal of a homestead that was passed along to children gave way to an ideal of families changing residence with each job promotion, so that by the 1960s the average American family moved every five years. Movement from farms and cities to the suburbs and from one part of the nation to another meant that provincialism faded, but so did community stability. The magnitude of the population changes in Maryland was somewhat greater than the national average.

The rise of the American suburbs involved the greatest population movement in history, larger and faster than the Mongols crossing Asia or Europeans crossing the Atlantic or Americans crossing the continent. For centuries rich merchants had retreated to summer country houses, and for decades the upper middle class had trickled out to spacious lots around the country clubs. After World War II, however, movement reached explosive proportions. In the five years from 1946 to 1951 Maryland's suburban population doubled; in the ten years from 1951 to 1961 the suburban population doubled again; and in the twenty years from 1961 to 1981 it doubled once more. Each wave brought a distinct culture of its own to the suburbs: first of cheap housing, then of cook-outs and shopping centers, and finally of industrial parks, high rises, and minority groups. America for so long had been a nation of farmers; then, by the late nineteenth century, it was a nation of cities; and by the late twentieth century it was a nation of suburbs (see figure 3.1).

The suburbs, as we have seen, dated from the trolley, the automobile, and the government's depression-era home loans to the prosperous, and until after the war suburban developments remained mostly affluent Republican enclaves, isolated from the counties around them. More than people realized, however, the war signaled change, for war industries boomed on the outskirts of Baltimore and military installations spread around Washington. Often war workers reversed the earlier flow by commuting daily from the city to outlying jobs, and government-constructed emergency housing in places like Middle River and Andrews Field gave a new dimension to suburbia. Also, as an omen of permanent change, the servants were no longer streaming out to the houses around the country clubs. Homemakers were embracing the new technology of dryers, dishwashers, freezers, and quick foods which became identified especially with suburban life.[2]

The Rise of the Suburbs

The age of swirl—the Jones Falls Expressway at 28th and 29th streets in Baltimore. Courtesy of M. E. Warren.

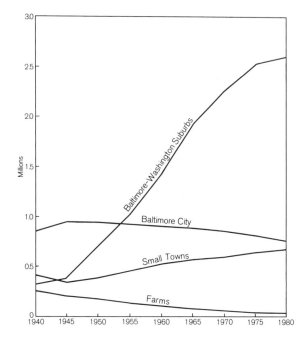

Figure 3.1.   Population: City, Suburbs, Towns, and
Farms, 1940–1980
Source: U.S. Bureau of the Census.
Note: Suburbs are defined by the census as "Standard
Metropolitan Area," with city and farm populations sub-
tracted. The suburban area includes Anne Arundel, Balti-
more, Montgomery, and Prince George's counties in 1940,
adding to them Howard and Harford counties in 1960, and
Carroll and Charles counties in 1980.

The years immediately after the war, 1945 and 1946, were less a
time of new movement than of returning home. Troop demobilization
took a full year; many Maryland war industries, like Martin Aircraft
and Bethlehem Steel, cut production sharply, and there was little new
construction. Women and blacks especially dropped out of the labor
force, either voluntarily or because of cutbacks, to return home, often
to the farm. Meanwhile veterans streamed back to crowd into homes
with relatives.

Housing became the nation's most pressing social problem. Dividing apartment houses and renting rooms became a patriotic act, and
housing codes, such as existed, were tacitly forgotten. Maryland Congressman J. Glenn Beall introduced, and Congress approved, a Vet-
eran's Emergency Housing Act to authorize the sale of government
barracks and government construction machinery to provide and
build civilian housing, with preference given to veterans. Baltimore
and Anne Arundel counties took title to 4,500 family units that had
been designed as temporary facilities for war workers or troops. The
counties sold the facilities to private firms, which maintained them,
often as slums, for decades. Montgomery County, in an act of public-
spirited patriotism, authorized purchase of 475 temporary units, plus
30 trailers, to be erected in public parkland, with the provision that
they be demolished in five years. Prince George's County acquired 33
barracks and gave them to the University of Maryland for student
housing. Entrepreneurs bought hundreds of additional units and
rented them at a rate the traffic would bear. The new residents did not
belong to the country clubs. Suburban development was taking a
sharp turn to the left.[3]

Again federal policy shaped the change, particularly through the
G.I. Bill, which offered veterans housing loans that were subsidized by
two or three percentage points. By aiding veterans instead of subsidizing urban housing for the poor or further supporting the well established, both of which were debated options for relieving the housing
shortage, Congress sent to the suburbs thousands of young people
who were usually just starting their families. What they wanted was
not luxury, but economy.

By 1947 the money was available, the construction business was on
its feet, and the boom was on. Huge firms that had been building
military bases launched developments of thousands of homes at a
time; old local firms began by building a few dozen units each; and
countless veterans entered the contracting business with little more
than a pickup truck. Early in 1947 the four suburban counties had
about 75,000 housing units; that year another 9,000 were completed;
the next year 14,000 were completed; then 18,000, 20,000, 26,000.
In the five years from 1947 to 1952 more new houses sprang up in the
four suburban counties than had been built there in all the preceding
centuries. During these five years the four counties accounted for more
than 80 percent of the state's total new construction.[4]

The two largest developments, which came to symbolize the rest,
were Viers Mill Village, located north of Washington, and Harundale,
to the south of Baltimore. Viers Mill contained 1,105 identical four-
room Cape Cod bungalows, each with a basement, each selling for
$8,700. Harundale contained 1,013 homes in two styles, with three
or four rooms, built on a concrete slab, selling for an average of
$6,900. The builders of the projects, one from New York, the other
from Washington, never thought of themselves as community developers; they were strictly construction firms. They provided their own
streets and temporarily provided for sewage disposal, since that was
faster than waiting for county action, but they gave no thought to
street maintenance, schools, or shopping facilities, access roads or
parks, fire or police protection. These were things for their buyers to
work out with their government. Least of all did the builders consider
things esthetic. Bulldozers leveled the land as they would have for any
army camp, construction crews set up Quonset huts to prefabricate
the walls, roofs, and windows, and truckers hauled in foundation
slabs. As the Viers Mill and Harundale houses reached completion in
1948, observers on nearby elevations could contemplate the entire
development of identical, fragile-looking boxes, their view unob-
structed by a single tree.[5]

Viers Mill and Harundale were typical of several projects that were
almost as large and scores that were smaller. In Prince George's
County were the Queenstown Apartments, with one thousand units,
and similar apartment, duplex, and single-family developments in
Chillum, Langley Park, District Heights, Hillcrest Heights, and Glass-
manor. In Montgomery County major projects appeared in Twin-
brook, Woodside, Parkwood, and Wheaton Woods. In Baltimore
County multiple- and single-family projects spread along Merritt Bou-
levard through Essex and Dundalk, and in Middle River, Towson,

Catonsville, and Liberty Road–Woodlawn. All of these projects were near the city line, their commuter residents depending not on the trolley but on the automobile. About 45 percent of the developments were composed of single-family units, about 30 percent were made up of apartments of mostly two and three stories, about 25 percent were composed of duplexes.[6]

The new occupants entered the suburban counties at the rate of one thousand each week, arriving about equally from the city, from surrounding small towns and farms, from out of state, and from their own extraordinarily high birth rate. Mostly they were commuters into the city, not executives, usually, but white-collar workers: clerks, bureaucrats, accountants, teachers, and salesmen. Employment opportunities followed, rather than led, the migration into the suburbs. Until well into the 1950s the suburbs received a growing proportion of their income from the city and spent a growing proportion of their money there. Almost all of the new immigrants were white, but otherwise they were ethnically diverse. Catholics scattered widely through the new housing, and Jews, who were generally excluded from the prewar county club developments, were welcomed everywhere and moved into the suburbs in slightly larger numbers than their proportion of the population.[7]

The chief mark of the influx seemed to be confusion, caused primarily by the absence of planning, zoning, or even building codes to control the explosion. County governments, incapable of standing between the public demand for housing and the developers' eagerness to supply it, became paralyzed with confusion and dissent. At Viers Mill, for example, homeowners were enraged at the county's failure to provide schools, street maintenance, police protection, and garbage disposal. Neighborhood property owners were angry at the flooding caused by the construction. The Viers Mill residents brought a class action suit against the developers for construction flaws, and they named the county government as a codefendant, claiming it failed to enforce the building codes. Helplessly county officials wrote to Maryland congressmen asking for a congressional investigation of the Viers Mill builders for "apparent cheap construction . . . and exorbitant profits." Hearings and suits dragged on but never amounted to much because the value of the Viers Mill houses rose by 70 percent within the next two years (property values in Harundale rose by 80 percent), so claims of profiteering and poor construction fell largely moot.[8]

Despite the confusion, the more important theme in this development was the general satisfaction of the new migrants. For most of them, the little boxes or garden apartments were infinitely better than the barracks or rooming houses in which they were huddled when the war ended, and infinitely superior to the rural shacks or urban tenements they remembered from a depression childhood. For one thing, the new homes were better inside than out. They had central heating and modern kitchens and bathrooms with tubs that were built-in instead of standing on iron legs. For another thing, the new suburbanites were young. In Harundale the median age of couples was 28 years, and they had 1.5 children, and in Viers Mill the median age of

all residents was 21 years. As long as the ambitions of the young
residents remained intact, the little houses provided an ideal place in
which to start a family.[9]

The new developments began immediately to bustle with community activities. Common grievances against the builders brought residents together, and obtaining their due from the counties demanded
political action. Nonaffluent and ambitious, the migrants were mostly
liberal, creating a new element in the old balances between rural
residents and country club suburbanites. More than in the cities or the
older suburbs, the newcomers joined in with local church groups, day-
care centers, bridge clubs, commuter pools, and neighborhood cook-
outs. Homogeneity produced camaraderie, home ownership inspired
pride.[10]

The best demonstration of satisfaction was that new residents kept
pouring in and real estate values kept rising. Not until the mid-1960s,
after the first wave of settlers had passed, did relative property values
decline in the inexpensive postwar developments. Then, in the mid-
1970s, many of these developments, including Viers Mill and Harundale, revived, this time as stable blue-collar enclaves with pride of
ownership, slow turnover, mature trees, and property values of up to
ten times the original purchase price.

While the new residents were satisfied, many Americans viewed the
postwar suburbs with disdain or even anger. People shook their heads
over the bulldozed landscapes, the cracker-box sameness, the prefabricated economies. The old country club suburbanites felt invaded.
Often their own property values were brought down by the developments, their schools overflowed, their taxes rose, their influence was
diminished, and their exclusive image was tarnished. The besieged
county political establishment and its mostly rural supporters alternated between attacks on the newcomers and bids to charm them.
Urban people, rich and poor, were almost unanimously hostile to the
new suburbs, for they were the ones left behind—and urban property
values lagged. Most of all the would-be intellectuals, symbolized by
the Baltimore *Sunpapers,* focused on the cheap suburban developments as representing a low-grade homogenization and anonymity of
American life. Novelists, playwrights, newspaper feature writers, and
academic sociologists denounced the postwar housing as "identical
boxes spreading like gangrene" and filled with "swarms of neuter
drones." The 1950s suburbs replaced "mass culture" as the scapegoat
for the fear and distaste felt by the upper middle class for the rest of
the population.[11]

Even while the critics were writing, however, they were falling behind
the times, for the character of suburbia by the 1950s was changing.
Inexpensive housing construction declined sharply after 1951, garden
apartment construction nearly ceased, and larger homes were becoming prevalent. Primarily the change resulted from economic forces. For
one thing, the real income of Marylanders rose by 70 percent during
the 1950s and by another 75 percent in the 1960s, and it rose most in
the middle levels, so that the money available for suburban-style hous-

ing soared. For another thing, many of the veterans in the first post-war wave were ready by the mid-1950s to move up to better housing, and many conservative urban dwellers, put off by the cheap construction of the first wave, were now ready to make their move. Moreover, federal financing policies changed to require substantial down payments, thus helping to shift construction toward more expensive homes.[12]

Competition, meanwhile, was growing among construction firms. Mammoth builders found it more profitable to invest in smaller, more expensive, developments; middle-sized firms appealed to people who wanted to design their own homes; and shoestring operations, which could only afford to build cheap homes, collapsed entirely. A simple six-room Georgian design, fitting with the Maryland tradition, was the most common style in the Washington and Baltimore suburbs, although the split-level and the picture-window ranch house, which became the 1950s cliché in the West and South, also spread through the Maryland suburbs. Construction was widely scattered, reaching out just beyond the areas occupied by the low-cost housing of the 1940s. The average price of new homes in the Washington suburbs rose from $6,300, in 1947, to $11,800, in 1957, to $34,000, in 1965.[13]

The rise of zoning in the 1950s brought a new focus for suburban politics, although zoning influenced elections more than it shaped patterns of suburban migration. Every county and almost every development was a different story of government agencies versus reformers, planners versus developers, and older residents versus newer ones. Each story involved special interests on both sides, alliances, bargains, betrayals, ideologies, and bitter elections. Almost every episode mattered terribly in the short run, for fortunes were won or lost, neighborhoods flourished or decayed, and the just and unjust were alternately victorious. In three of the four suburban counties historians have reviewed these zoning wars in detail, and journalists have filed hundreds of stories. The theme of the furor is that neither the planners nor the developers had much of an edge in being right; that the mistakes had a way of correcting themselves over time; and that by the end of the 1960s the furor and corruption were mostly gone as both planning and pragmatic exceptions came to be taken for granted. In the long run, however, the outcome of the zoning wars was determined less by idealists than by economic forces, which shaped all the suburbs more alike than not.

In Montgomery County, idealists dominated both sides of the issue: planners who wanted controls battled liberals who wanted cheap housing. In the 1940s the county's zoning authority lay with the Maryland-National Capital Park and Planning Commission, which persuaded the county council to meet national housing needs with cheap housing. This caused a revolt of the country club suburbanites, who in 1948 overthrew the county organization and in 1952 gained control of Park and Planning. For ten years afterwards the planners, the reformers, and the developers all fell in with the natural market forces by supporting single-family homes built on fairly large lots. In 1962 another group of reformers came to power along with the developers, arguing that the county needed apartments, jobs, and commercial and industrial development, that exclusive single-family restrictions were undemocratic, and that restrictive zoning was un-American. The planners agreed until 1968 and another major change came: a new county executive began to wind down the battles by supporting both single-family units and jobs and both planning and exceptions. Again, the planners adjusted their philosophy to political reality. Generally, in all the changes, Montgomery County kept taxes and services high in a way that pushed back small farmers, kept blacks out, and allowed government to remain relatively corruption free. This story, with different particulars, characterized the zoning histories of Harford and Howard counties as they became predominantly suburban.[14]

Baltimore, Anne Arundel, and Prince George's counties, meanwhile, arrived at the same point through a more painful route of political corruption. In these three counties the old-time political organizations entered the postwar world with the conviction that all development was good, that low taxes and minimum services promoted development, and that politicians and developers had much to gain from each other. Anne Arundel established a zoning commission in 1946 and Baltimore County in 1947, but zoning was primarily a means of benefiting the political organization by regularizing the charges for exceptions. Planners' designs often benefited developers more than established residents, notably by raising tax assessments to drive out farmers, but otherwise plans were made to be altered. In Prince George's County in the late 1950s, 31 percent of the building permits were issued as exceptions to Park and Planning zoning recommendations. Public disclosures showed that real estate developers contributed more to Baltimore County campaigns than all other contributors combined, and large real estate contributors were named to the zoning board itself.[15]

Slowly in Baltimore, Anne Arundel, and Prince George's counties, the middle class prevailed over the near-legalized corruption. In 1962 the prozoning reformers elected Spiro Agnew as county executive in Baltimore, and when he went on to be governor in 1966 they elected Dale Anderson. In 1962 Prince George's County elected Jesse Baggett as chairman of the county council, and in 1965 Anne Arundel County reformers elected Joseph W. Alton as county executive on a prozoning platform. In every case the entrenched corruption was stronger than the reformers: the pretense of honesty only transformed campaign contributions into secret bribes. Agnew, Anderson, Baggett, and Alton were convicted of collecting money in exchange for zoning favors, and all but Agnew went to jail. With the convictions, however, if not with the elections, the reformers were winning. Maryland's notorious corruption of the 1950s and 1960s was largely the adjustment of old political systems to modern needs for suburban planning. By the late 1960s suburban voters had generally prevailed over their politicians, and planning, zoning, open hearings, and reasoned exceptions to the plans were all an accepted part of suburban life. By 1970 the zoning battles faded from suburban politics.[16]

During the nearly two decades of zoning wars the growth rates in the erratically idealistic counties and the counties with near-legalized corruption remained almost identical, except that the counties with idealistic zoning were more effective in keeping out the poor and, especially, blacks. From 1948 to 1968 Montgomery County increased its median family income from 4 percent to 34 percent above that of neighboring Prince George's County. Howard and Harford counties increased their margin over Anne Arundel and Baltimore counties. Idealism, then, was an ironic ally of elitism, and corruption was an ally of egalitarianism.[17]

Along with better housing and zoning battles, supermarkets and shopping centers also came to the suburbs in the 1950s, further stimulating suburban growth and further transforming American lifestyles. Ancestors of the shopping centers were the large Washington and Baltimore Sears Roebuck stores of the 1920s, which were located outside the main shopping district and had their own parking lots. In 1946 the Hecht Company in Washington became the first area department store to open a suburban branch, in Silver Spring. The first full-scale shopping center in Maryland, however, was Edmondson Village, which opened in 1947 on the western edge of Baltimore. It had all the attributes of the new movement in American merchandising: a single developer, architectural unity, ample off-street parking, a branch of a major department store (Hochschild-Kohn), a supermarket, a theater, a restaurant, and more than twenty other stores. It was one of the first and finest centers in the country, merchants and public were equally delighted, and real estate developers noted a surge of development for miles around.[18]

Investors were cautious; it took surprisingly long for the shopping centers to multiply. Outside of Washington came Friendship Heights (1949), Langley Park (1954), Wheaton (1955), Congressional Plaza (1958), and Prince George's Plaza (1958); outside of Baltimore came Eastpoint (1956), Mondawmin (1956), Westview (1958), Harundale (1958), and Towson Plaza (1959). Their vitality in their original form was surprisingly short, only about fifteen years, and by the 1960s their regular multiplication, revitalization, expansion, and occasional closing was an accepted part of the suburban mosaic.[19]

The shopping centers of the 1950s were the breakthrough in transforming the suburbs from urban bedroom communities into self-contained living and working areas. Government agencies and industry, sales and services, doctors and lawyers, banks and churches, came to the suburbs. In the 1950s the Maryland suburban population increased by 87 percent, but retail sales increased 22 percent; in the 1960s population increased by only 5 percent, but sales increased by 165 percent. During the 1950s and 1960s public and private investment in commercial, industrial, and public facilities almost equaled investment in housing. The suburban counties made a virtue of the change, creating boards to attract new industries, to help finance industrial parks, and, less effectively, to supervise their choice of location.[20]

The major public expenditure was for roads. The new highways

Edmondson Village, outside of Baltimore, was one of the first shopping centers in America. Courtesy of the *Baltimore Sun*.

were not built only during the 1950s and 1960s, of course, and they were not built only in the suburbs, although they had their greatest impact there. Most of all they served people on the urban outskirts who were the greatest travelers, and in serving them they promoted suburbanization. Of the fifteen major highways in Maryland, each costing more than $100 million to construct, all but two were completed between 1952 and 1972, and all but two slashed through the suburbs:[21]

1939	Ritchie Highway, Baltimore-Annapolis
1952	First Bay Bridge
1954	Baltimore-Washington Parkway
1955	John Hanson Highway, Washington-Annapolis
1956	I-70, Baltimore-Frederick
1957	Baltimore Harbor Tunnel
1957	I-270, Washington-Frederick
1959	I-83, Baltimore-Harrisburg
1962	Jones Falls Expressway, Baltimore
1962	Baltimore Beltway
1963	I-95, John F. Kennedy Highway, Baltimore-Wilmington
1964	Washington Beltway

1970   I-70, National Freeway, Frederick-Ohio
1971   I-95, Baltimore-Washington
1982   Baltimore City Freeways

The highway programs stimulated the suburbs in many ways, often by simultaneously hurting the cities. Most obviously they improved job access for suburbanites, allowing the middle class to move to the outskirts without relinquishing their downtown livelihoods. The superhighways seldom harmed suburban neighborhoods, which were protected by green-swathed right-of-ways—in fact, residences near the the right-of-ways increased in value—but when highways slashed through urban neighborhoods, property values plunged. Planning was most effective in protecting suburban right-of-ways from housing developments long before the roads were built, so few families were uprooted when construction occurred. For construction of the entire Washington Beltway, only 185 Maryland families were forced to move. The urban freeways, meanwhile, displaced thousands of people, spreading slums and misery. Essentially the highways subsidized the middle-class, auto-owning, shopping-center culture. Most of all, the highways hastened the transition from railroads, which concentrated population at their urban terminals, to trucks, which pulled industry to the outskirts. Manufacturers discovered that their access to markets and to their white-collar workers was greater along the beltways than in the city.[22]

In the 1960s, then, the suburbs—with their generally middle-class housing, their generally self-contained economy, their glittering shopping centers and roads—lost their image of cheapness and instead seemed to become the vital center of American life. On one hand they had replaced the small town as the symbol of the good life, and on the other they had replaced the city as the apparent shaper of opinion and style. Television became central to all America (70,000 sets were owned in Maryland in 1950 and 1,000,000 in 1960), and the television image makers elevated suburbia into middle America. Americans, according to the television image, were a nation of split-level and ranch houses, of young wives in station wagons carrying children to baseball practice and young husbands keeping lawns free from crab grass. Intellectuals continued to complain about the homogenized suburban culture, but books like *The Man in the Grey Flannel Suit* and *The Lonely Crowd* reinforced the generally happy image more than they threatened it. The error in the image was in its supposition that the suburbs were all there was. They had triumphed too much.[23]

By the 1970s variety was becoming a new theme of suburban migration. Far out, northwest of Washington and Baltimore, the very rich built homes that rivaled the 1920s estates, and close in, southeast of the cities, the poor were taking up the modest housing of the 1940s that was growing older. Some of the new immigrants were too poor to afford the automobiles that built the suburbs, and they depended instead on public transportation to take them to the city or to suburban industrial parks.

High-rise office buildings and apartments began to appear, not primarily in the suburban centers like Silver Spring and Pikesville, and not as a means of economizing on land prices, as in the past, but scattered throughout the suburbs, isolated from everything but the interstates, and designed to recapture the urban tempo in a bucolic setting. Apartment living became a matter of taste rather than of economics. Typical of the high rises, and among the first, were the Grosvenor Park apartments, which opened in 1963 far out in Montgomery County. Three great seventeen-story towers, each with some five hundred luxury apartment units, offered residents urban throb amidst an endless horizon of highways and trees. Doctors, lawyers, architects, and brokers often commuted for miles along the beltway to other towers that served as offices. From 1955 to 1970 apartments increased from composing 15 percent to composing 33 percent of the Maryland suburban housing construction. Suburban planners began to visualize a series of urban clusters radiating out from the central cities, but there was no reason for such groupings besides system itself, and actual development, as usual, defied the planners.[24]

New patterns of living included condominium apartments and town houses. Condominiums, which had long composed at least half of European urban housing, came to Maryland in the mid-1960s as a means for apartment owners to escape rent-control regulations and obtain quick profits, and as a means for apartment dwellers to obtain tax-deductible interest on their mortgage payments. Typically an apartment building owner gave tenants six months to buy their apartment plus a share of the hallways and land. The condominium movement spread rapidly, so that by 1979 condominiums comprised 12 percent of Maryland's suburban housing. The counties made half-hearted attempts to appease renters by imposing restrictions on conversions to condominiums, but the restrictions never lasted long against market forces. The new town houses were also mostly condominiums, involving private ownership of the units and cooperative control of upkeep and a central square. Town houses were similar to the row houses that were so famous in Baltimore in the nineteenth century, but by the 1960s they were often suburban and usually grouped around courts rather than toe-to-toe along a street.[25]

The shopping centers, often nearing the end of their planned fifteen-year lifetime by the late 1960s, were undergoing changes, notably by evolving into covered malls. The first enclosed mall in Maryland, at Harundale outside Baltimore, was in 1958 a decade ahead of its time, the second in the country after one in Minneapolis. Harundale was built by James W. Rouse, a builder who was regularly ahead of his time. Its enclosed mall with year-round temperature control and ample seating invited people to visit as well as shop and became a meeting place for homemakers and teenagers, or the place for the family's evening outing. By the 1970s dozens of malls were competing in size and glitter, including Rouse's Columbia Mall (1972), which won architectural awards, and White Flint Mall, which opened outside of Washington in 1978 and featured several of the country's most expensive shops. As places to visit for pleasure, the malls appealed to impulse buying, and thus they marked a change in American merchandising, away from giant department stores and toward independent boutiques, art shops, and restaurants.[26]

The suburban migration took place amidst much concern and many wrong assumptions about race. During World War II the federal government enticed about fifteen thousand blacks into Baltimore County for war work, but elsewhere in the suburbs blacks remained as they had been since the Civil War, mostly living in isolated pockets that were widely scattered through the suburban area and making up 10 to 20 percent of each county's population. The suburban migration of the late 1940s and 1950s was so exclusively white that few developers imagined it could be otherwise. In Baltimore County developers bought up black housing and blacks left, but elsewhere developers generally kept their distance from the black enclaves. The communities were mostly ignored and were provided with a minimum of public services—usually they lacked street lights, paving, sewage connections, and garbage disposal. The enclaves increased only in proportion to their birth rate, as almost no new black migrants came in, so that the proportion of blacks in the suburbs sharply declined from 1940 to 1965, from 11 percent to 3 percent in Baltimore County, from 15 percent to 7 percent in all the suburban counties. White suburbanites liked to assume that the segregation was voluntary, but developers confirmed the assumptions by generally refusing to sell to blacks for fear of lowering property values.[27]

What developers failed to acknowledge was that the same forces that propelled whites to the suburbs affected blacks as well, and that economic forces actually pointed toward eventual integration of the suburbs. Federal policy paved the way, first with urban slum clearance, then with block grants to suburban counties for improvement of their mostly black enclaves, and finally with open housing legislation. Slum clearance followed from the federal housing and highways acts of the 1950s, which destroyed more housing than they created. By the 1960s, as these acts began to have their effect and as the suburbs recoiled at the prospect of black immigrants, the government changed the terminology from slum clearance to urban renewal and placed the emphasis on upgrading existing facilities.

Urban renewal replaced zoning as the major suburban political issue. On one hand suburban advocates pointed to the need for either improving or eliminating the miserable suburban enclaves of blacks and to the need to improve white areas like Catonsville, Towson, Dundalk, Silver Spring, and Hyattsville, which were blighted by bad planning and drained by neighboring shopping centers. On the other hand blacks feared removal and whites feared renewal meant a black influx, rising taxes, and change. The greatest battles came in Baltimore County. In 1961 officials created a Redevelopment and Rehabilitation Commission to obtain federal funds, but opposition proved overwhelming. Crowds appeared at public hearings to denounce what they assumed would amount to low-cost housing for blacks and required improvements for landlords. In 1964 County Executive Spiro Agnew sought $20 million in federal funds to rebuild Towson and $7 million for Catonsville, but again there was an outcry, and a public referendum rejected the application for funds. By 1975 federal agen-

cies were soliciting applications from the county, and County Executive Theodore Venetoulis was eager to respond, but this time the
county council and the legislative delegation vetoed the applications.
Altogether the county lost between $20 and $40 million. Urban
renewal grants offered similar opportunities and drew similar opposition in the other counties, inspiring dozens of angry public hearings
and swinging numerous local elections, although most county leaders
were generally more successful than those in Baltimore County in
finessing the opposition by obtaining small grants, one at a time.[28]

For all the excitement about urban renewal, the new laws against
housing segregation were eventually far more important in transforming the suburbs. The General Assembly passed an open housing law in
1967, but voters petitioned the law to a referendum and defeated it
with large majorities in all of the suburban counties except Montgomery. In 1968 Congress prohibited discrimination in the advertisement,
real estate brokerage, financing, rental, or sale of housing, and in
1971 Maryland passed its own law in order to take over the enforcement. Public reaction was mild because white suburbanites assumed
the law was unenforceable in controlling individual sales, and in this
they were correct. What did happen, however, was that mortgage
money was suddenly made available to blacks, and real estate agents
were happy to make new sales. Also, as soon as there were a number
of blacks who were willing to press their rights, major development
projects opened up, followed by entire neighborhoods.

The black migration to the suburbs did not begin until about 1965,
but then it became a rush. In 1965 local real estate dealers estimated
that only two hundred blacks moved from Washington and Baltimore
to the Maryland suburbs; in 1970 about two thousand moved to the
suburbs; and by 1980 approximately twenty thousand blacks were
moving out each year. Put differently, 88 percent of the suburban
growth during the decade of the 1970s was black (see figure 3.2).
They came, of course, like whites had come, for the better life of the
suburbs, and because of the continuing decline of the central cities.

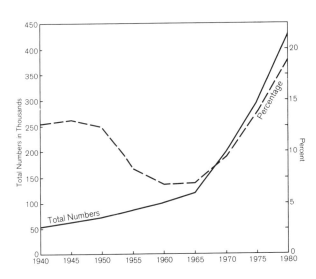

Figure 3.2. Blacks in the Suburbs, 1940–1980
Source: U.S. Bureau of the Census.
Note: Solid line and numbers on left are numbers of
blacks in Maryland suburbs. Broken line and numbers on
right are blacks as a percentage of the Maryland suburban
population.

Mostly they were poorer than whites, and mostly they moved into poorer housing. The tendency of whites to flee meant that a certain segregation continued, though in a less complete form than in the cities or in the earlier separation of the white suburbs and the city. Integration, however incomplete, was the ultimate triumph of variety in suburban life.[29]

By the 1970s the rapid growth of which the suburban counties were once so proud became a source of embarrassment. Partly the changed perspective was a conservative reaction to the black influx, but it was also a liberal concern with exhaustion of resources. The strongest antigrowth sentiment was often heard in outlying Carroll, Harford, Howard, and Charles counties, where strictures against suburban sprawl became the common political rhetoric. New civic groups appeared in Montgomery County, not only, in the exclusive tradition, to oppose public housing, drug rehabilitation centers, and juvenile halfway houses, but also in the new no-growth tradition, to oppose shopping centers, high rises, and highways. In the mid-1970s Anne Arundel, Baltimore, and Prince George's counties all allowed their sewerage disposal capacity to lag and then utilized this incapacity to declare a moratorium on new construction. The moratoriums did not last, but they marked a winding down of the suburban movement.[30]

Subways reached the Washington suburbs in 1978 and the Baltimore suburbs in 1983. They tended to lessen the distinction between urban and suburban, but otherwise they had less impact than either advocates or critics had predicted. They were not, after all, much different from the trolleys that had been abandoned four decades earlier. Although suburban neighborhoods fought bitterly over particular routes, the pressures for and against the subways were about balanced, so that subways never became an important element in suburban politics. Their cost was extraordinary, some $4 billion for Washington and $1 billion for Baltimore, mostly of federal money, but their construction only took up where the highway construction left off. Initial ridership was high but it did not grow as anticipated. Taxpayers bore not only construction costs but over half of the operating costs, as well. Subways tended to stabilize but not improve traffic problems. Prices of land near the subway stops rose sharply, and high-rise apartments were concentrated there. Subways thus contributed moderately to the suburban immigration of blacks and older people who did not own automobiles.[31]

As the suburbs increased in population concentration, in variety of living arrangements, and in ethnic mix, their difference from the central cities lessened. Growth slowed, the influx of poor and older populations grew, and the suburbs began to feel the economic pinch of the cities. Some scholars believed the chief theme of the entire postwar population swirl was "from downtown to no town."[32] It was one way of saying that the suburbs had triumphed.

The Model Communities

Dreamers since Plato have imagined designing a community so ideal as to lead the world out of its unplanned confusion. Occasionally investors—like proprietor George Calvert—shared this dream, if only in hopes that a planned community would turn them a profit. In the mid-twentieth century, as housing developments of a thousand units became commonplace, developers sometimes teamed up with social planners, and experiments in model communities multiplied. In Maryland, four of these experiments—Greenbelt, Bowie, Columbia, and Rossmoor—were among the most important anywhere. They were all very different from one another, and they symbolized divergent paths to the future. The world did not exactly fall into step behind them, but it generally acknowledged that each one was a little bit ahead of its time.

The first and most famous of the experiments was Greenbelt, the New Deal's chief model of community development and probably the most ambitious experiment in public housing in American history. Its enemies called it "the first communist town in America," a label proved all the more damaging when the experiment's friends occasionally agreed to the label's suitability. The inspiration for Greenbelt came from England, where the Fabians—Robert Owen, John Ruskin, and Ebenezer Howard—seeking alternatives to urban slums, developed the concept of small, planned, garden cities, surrounded by farmland, in which the residents jointly owned and managed the town's factories and farms. In the 1910s philanthropists and investors launched the first two experiments in England, Letchworth and Welwyn, and in the 1920s one was founded in Radburn, New Jersey.[33]

Meanwhile the New Deal faced the challenge of making work for the unemployed, moving people off submarginal farm lands, providing low-rent housing for residents of the urban slums, and generally searching for an economic system that worked better than the one at hand. Rexford Guy Tugwell, head of the Farm Resettlement Administration, became the chief enthusiast for the Greenbelt experiment, although Mrs. Roosevelt and the president also took a personal interest in it. Tugwell gave up on the idea of worker-owned factories and farms as being too radical, but he imagined a thousand new towns emerging with cooperatively owned housing and stores. In cooperation with the leading city planners of Europe and America, he drew up plans for twenty-five such towns, obtained money from Congress for eight, and completed three: Greenhills outside Cincinnati, Greendale outside Milwaukee, and Greenbelt—the largest town and the only one completed according to plan—outside Washington.

The government acquired nineteen square miles near Berwyn, Maryland, and through 1937 and 1938 employed some nine thousand workers for the largest make-work project in the Washington area. Bureaucrats discussed whether to use earth-moving equipment to move faster or wheelbarrows to employ more workers and Roosevelt facetiously suggested using teaspoons. The town was beautifully designed. It was composed of 884 housing units—a mixture of apartments, vaguely like garden apartments, and connected houses, vaguely like row houses—all facing inward on a series of parks which stretched along a wooded crescent-shaped plateau. In the center of the crescent were the community facilities: a model progressive school, in which religious services were held on Sundays, a theater, a town newspaper office, a swimming pool, a playground, a restaurant, and cooperative stores. Outside the crescent were a lake, garden plots that could be utilized at no cost by residents, and a health co-op. The government owned everything, but residents paid rents to amortize the costs, and residents governed all operations. Dwellings were unfurnished, but specially designed furniture was available at cost from the co-op.[34]

There were 12,000 applicants for 884 units, so it was possible to handpick residents. Those chosen were white, mostly high school graduates and white-collar workers, all with family incomes of between $1,200 and $2,200. During the war the government added another 1,000 housing units, much like the first, but the development was still short of its planned potential maximum. For most observers and residents Greenbelt was a triumph. The town attracted half a million tourists each year, foreign planners put aspects of the plan into effect around the world, and resident enthusiasm was extraordinary. The authors of at least three doctoral dissertations, five master's theses, and hundreds of journalistic accounts bombarded Greenbelt residents with questionnaires and consistently found one of the highest rates anywhere of community loyalty and participation.[35]

Still, fierce and often reasonable skeptics remained. Idealogues, of course, believed capitalism was at stake. Area real estate operators and businessmen, with some justice, saw unfair competition. Residents at first sometimes complained of communal intrusiveness in their lives, for the community passed ordinances about such things as how clothes were to be hung on the line. The most telling criticism was of construction costs—an average of $15,395 each for the first units, three times the price of comparable private housing. Costs were high because of the huge land buffer around the town, because of the construction emphasis on jobs for the unemployed, because artificially low rents added to capital costs, and because of experimentation and inefficiency; but the fact remained that taxes from a free economy subsidized the planned economy. City planners kept asking why the country did not follow the lead of happy Greenbelt, and the answer was that neither public nor private investors could justify a system that lost money.

In 1952 Congress forced the government to sell the experiment. Residents formed a co-op to buy the housing, the shopping center, and some of the surrounding land, although most of the land went to the nearby federal Agricultural Research Center, to a national park, and to private developers. During the next thirty years many of the cooperative features remained, including most of the cooperative housing and stores, and residents continued to display greater than average loyalty to the town. The biggest change, however, came from residents' greed, as they yielded to the temptation to keep taxes and rents low by selling off more and more of the common land. Conventional suburban developments encroached, and from 1950 to 1970 the town's population increased from 7,074 to 18,199. The original experiment merged off into the rest of suburbia, except that housing values and community loyalty diminished in proportion to distance from the old core. Greenbelt, in other words, was not a failure, and,

Bowie, one of the largest cities in Maryland, is a bedroom community outside of Washington, D.C., that was designed after many polls of potential buyers. Surveys since have found the residents, except for teenagers, to be generally happier than residents of cities and rural towns. Photograph copyright *Washington Post,* reprinted by permission of the D.C. Public Library.

apart from original costs, its weaknesses lay less in the planning than in the expectations for democracy.[36]

The town of Bowie, meanwhile, was in many ways the antithesis of Greenbelt, although, like most antitheses, the two acquired many resemblances. Bowie was born not in government paternalism but in corporate capitalism, and not in idealistic concern for community but in realistic calculation of the kinds of houses people wanted to buy. Bowie really was not a model town at all if *model* implies guidance toward an improved society. It was, rather, a prototype—an especially pure expression of the bedroom communities that characterized suburbia.

Bowie was a Levittown, built by the corporation that had already named three towns for itself, in New York, Pennsylvania, and New Jersey. To avoid the connotation of cheap which the name had acquired, the Levitts called their Maryland development Belair, after a nearby plantation, but residents called it Bowie, after a nearby railroad stop. It was located only six miles from Greenbelt. Instead of shrinking (19 square miles became 3 in Greenbelt), the Levitts' original 3.5 miles expanded to 11. Instead of nearly two thousand housing units, the Levitts built more than nine thousand, making Bowie one of the largest developments in the country—except for the other Levittowns, which were larger.

The Levitts never dealt much with town planners, even though planners adored the Levitts. The company was teacher, not pupil. When the county hired professional planners to advise it on containing Levitt, the planners became major spokesmen for noncontainment. The company was mostly run by a middle-level management who lived in houses not unlike those they designed and who were committed to making a profit by giving customers the best buy for their money. The best housing meant traditional design, lots of interior space, a nice-looking general area, and rigorous economy. Winding streets were worth the price but sidewalks weren't; grass and shrubbery were necessary, but not trees; air conditioning would sell, but not insulation.

The Levitts had few theories of community. Do the customers want racial segregation? All right, segregation. Do they object to uniform house design? Give 'em five to choose from. The company built small elementary schools and donated land for high schools and churches—which enhanced the value of the houses, promoted good will, and provided a tax write-off—but after that, the residents would have to tax themselves to pay for expanded elementary schools and for high school and church buildings. If people wanted parks or community centers, Levitt happened to have some vacant lots to sell them. Planning and financing of local institutions was mostly up to the residents. They could have any kind of schools, churches, parks, community facilities, fire and police protection, and government they wanted. These involved hidden costs that came several years after the first houses were sold, as residents learned they had to tax themselves. Leaving taxes and services to them was a deliberate company policy designed to direct disputes inward rather than against the builder.[37]

In 1960 the first five model homes opened, and throngs from Washington and Baltimore drove through the miles of winding streets where more than 1,000 homes were under construction. As sales poured in, Levitt expanded. By 1963, 3,000 units housed 11,000 residents; by 1968, 9,000 units housed 33,000 residents. Corporate changes took place when Levitt sold out in 1968 to International Telephone and Telegraph, and sales slowed. In 1977 Starrett Corporation bought the unsold land and cut corners to build inferior houses at inflated prices. Population peaked at 9,700 units and 43,000 people. Two years later, when the county revoked the company's building license, the Virginia Land Company acquired the property. As children of the peak years grew up and left home, population declined, stabilizing in 1980 at about 38,000.

Bowie was a bedroom development; it had no jobs and little cohesion as an economic or social unit. Its residents felt little sense of mutual dependence, little sense of serving as a model for living, little boosterism, little sense of pride in the home team. In the very center of the town the developers had left almost two square miles with hopes that the land might become an urban center of high rises and office buildings, and grandly they talked of a potential population of 300,000. The developers, however, were never ready to put up the investment to make Bowie a satellite city in fact. Even the major shopping centers that served the town appeared on the fringes and were built by rival developers. Bowie could never claim the sense of identity and community which the early residents of Greenbelt cherished and to which the residents of Columbia and Rossmoor so eagerly aspired. Like most of suburbia, Bowie was a place, not a community.[38]

The ultimate question about Bowie concerned the quality of life there. Was it enough to have the best house for the money? How important was community? If suburbia was the ultimate expression of what America had become, and if Bowie was an exaggerated expression of suburbia, then the quality of its life became a key to understanding the America of the late twentieth century. This logic did not escape the sociologists who came to study the various Levittown communities, to compare life there with life in the cities and small towns. Out of these studies came some convincing conclusions. Overwhelmingly the sociologists rejected the 1950s notion of suburbia as anonymous and unhappy. Overwhelmingly they found that by standards of other times and other places suburbia was well off, and the Levittowns were better off than most.

Most notably, with one exception, Bowie seemed to strengthen family life. Studies showed that, despite lengthy commutes to jobs, families spent more time at home than comparable families in cities and small towns; children received closer parental supervision; the divorce rate was measurably lower than it was in other environments. The home rather than the community became the center of family activities and leisure time. The exception, never fully explained, was for adolescents, who lacked meeting places in which to gather and alternative life styles to explore, such as those found in cities and towns, and whose dissatisfaction and deliquency rates were actually higher than in other environments.[39]

Critics attacked the loneliness and boredom of suburban life, but the questionnaires and interviews showed that there were more and deeper friendships among Levittown neighbors, more mutual visiting, more club memberships, more neighborly cooperation, and a more optimistic view of the future than in cities or towns. Critics spoke of rootlessness in such a new development, but the annual 15 percent turnover rate in Bowie was less than the 20 percent national average. With relatively little variation in incomes, the Bowie population was uniformly lower middle or middle class, and the class tensions of older places were lacking. Critics, then, denounced the homogeneity, but the absence of class tension was balanced by a greater degree of ethnic and religious integration than occurred elsewhere in America. Television viewing was less frequent in Bowie than in the cities, and about the same as in small towns; newspaper and magazine readership was higher than in cities or small towns.[40]

Political philosophers such as Ortega y Gasset theorized that people living in a uniform way as they did in Bowie would become dull, apathetic, disengaged from society, and subject to fascist hysterias, but evidence pointed to a contrary conclusion. Voter participation was greater than anywhere in the area except Greenbelt; Bowie politics was generally more liberal than elsewhere in the area; and Bowie officeholders, both Democratic and Republican, were resented by the rest of the county for dominating county offices disproportionately. Greenbelt with its socialist origins and concern for community, and

Columbia, Maryland, is a multitude of villages, each with a distinctive style. Designed by philosophers and architects, Columbia was intended to promote human and community values. Photograph copyright *Washington Post,* reprinted by permission of the D.C. Public Library.

Bowie with its free enterprise origins and concern for profits, both confused philosophers, for they both differed from their surroundings in ways that were primarily alike.[41]

Columbia, Maryland, was a marriage of the Bowie and Greenbelt ideals—a private enterprise development with the primary aim of making community a marketable commodity—but Columbia was also designed to provide the vibrance of a city. As a housing development it eclipsed Bowie to become the second largest city in Maryland after Baltimore, and its residents came not so much for housing as for a style of life. Columbia was private enterprise communalism, and it was urbanism in a country setting.

The central figure behind Columbia was the mighty James Wilson Rouse, one of the great figures of American planning. Born in Easton, Maryland, in 1914, a graduate of the University of Virginia and the University of Maryland Law School, he worked for various federal and urban planning agencies in the 1930s and 1940s, led the way in awakening Baltimore to urban renewal in the 1950s, built Harundale as the second enclosed mall in America in 1958, launched Columbia in the 1960s as one of the nation's most successful planned communities, and designed Harborplace in the 1970s as one of the country's most sparkling urban showpieces. Rouse was prophet, philosopher, and promoter—a man with a mission to make life better for people, a conviction that urban civilization was the way to do it, and an ability to translate ideals into reality and profit.

It is clear from his abundant writing and speeches that his ideals preceded his designs for specific projects. The plan of Columbia followed a decade of speeches made against the formlessness of 1950s suburbia and its homogenized neighborhoods. Levittown developments seemed to him "irrational," "anti-human," "out of scale with people, beyond their grasp and comprehension, too big for people to feel a part of, responsible for, important in. . . . The individual is immersed in the mass." The solution, he believed, lay partly in community, such as that in small towns and urban neighborhoods, but equally in variety, a mixture of incomes and races that would produce the excitement of a city.[42]

Through 1964 and 1965 Rouse consulted with panels made up of the country's most prominent sociologists: Herbert Gans, Christopher Jencks, Alan Voorhees, Henry Bain, Donald Michael, Wallace Hamilton. They began by developing goals—hundreds of pages about "enrichment of lives," "individual freedom," "education as a life-long process," and "government sensitive to the service needs of the people." Gradually the generalists gave way to panels of specialists to advise on architecture, recreation, schools, government, health, and religion. It was a great day for planners. Seldom had they been taken so seriously.

Inevitably, there were compromises. The main dilemma lay in the goal of basing the new city on citizen participation and the reality of its basic structure being in place before the first residents arrived. Rouse and his sociologists agonized at violating their most basic tenet before they began, although the result was probably to everyone's advantage. The practical dilemma was persuading the people of Howard County to approve an enterprise that would displace much of the county population and soon outnumber the rest. The resolution was costly to the developer and placed restrictions on Columbia residents for many years until, by the 1980s, they in fact controlled in the county government.[43]

The town, located between Baltimore and Washington, grew about as planned. One thousand people in 1968 increased to 57,000 in 1980, when economic conditions curtailed expansion toward the projected 100,000. There was an urban core with high rises and a major shopping center, nine satellite villages located around smaller commercial centers, and a large industrial complex on the eastern perimeter. There was a wide variety of housing styles, an abundance of recreational facilities, and highly progressive schools. Most remarkable was the adherence to the ideal of Columbia being a city complete with diversity and jobs. Rouse's belief in diversity fit exactly with the federal housing policy of breaking up the urban ghettos by bringing subsidized housing into suburbia, and Rouse collected federal subsidies for about 8 percent of his housing units. He directed housing advertisement toward middle-class blacks, so that Columbia's population remained consistently around 20 percent black. The median income of Columbia residents was about 30 percent above that of people in the surrounding area, but a significant 5 percent of the residents earned double the town's median income, and 5 percent remained at less than half of the median. There were 32,000 jobs in the town of 57,000 people.[44]

Columbia was a success, more successful than most of suburbia, more successful than Greenbelt or Bowie, both in its profits to its developers and in its satisfaction to residents. Questionnaires showed a remarkably happy population, low residential turnover, and property values accelerating faster than in the surrounding areas. The developer, in fact, turned control over to the residents, increasing resident satisfaction but also diminishing the attractiveness of continuing developer investment, thus slowing growth. The village organization did not much succeed in creating community, for people established their social and economic connections across village lines, and village government proved cumbersome, but citywide loyalty proved greater than anticipated. Class and, especially, race consciousness continued, of course, but instead of fragmenting society, its mixture gave Columbia its identity of pluralism, which was its chief source of distinction and pride. More, possibly, than any city in Maryland, Columbia believed in itself; it believed in America.[45]

While Columbia was dedicated to openness, there was another kind of model town, typified by Rossmoor Leisure World, which elevated exclusiveness into a utopian ideal. Rossmoor was designed for a particular group—the retired, the fearful, and the affluent—but the combination of community and exclusiveness was in varying degrees the appeal of most suburban developments. Initiated by a California developer, Ross W. Cortese, who had built similar towns on the West Coast, Rossmoor opened in suburban Washington in 1966 with about sixteen hundred residents and a plan for sixteen thousand more. Residents bought apartments, town houses, or single-family houses, but the corporation retained responsibility for upkeep and grounds. The company maintained a luxurious clubhouse area containing restaurants, recreational facilities, hobby shops, religious facilities, and medical care. Security was tight. Visitors were admitted through gatehouses and carried passes, and guards patrolled the fenced perimeter. The company newspaper provided a controlled fare of what its editors considered suitable for their charges. Close communalism was the product of a conservative company and conservative residents, who were secure from the socialism emanating from places like Columbia.

Rossmoor's success was modest, except in the number of communities which imitated it. The developer overestimated the number of affluent retirees and their eagerness to separate from the rest of the world. Sales declined as fears of urban violence abated and as interest rates rose. The corporation liquidated its holdings in other cities and sold off much of its Montgomery County land, although Rossmoor gradually increased to around four thousand residents. Similar retirement communities, slightly more modest, were Heritage Harbor in Annapolis and Crestwood in Frederick.[46]

Utopianism as an ideal, planning as a concept, development as an investment, even sprawl as a reality—all merged together indistinguishably. There was Coldspring in Baltimore, which was designed to bring the middle class back to the city. This area was planned to accommodate twelve thousand and was developed through an unusual combination of public and private funding; its residents were a deliberate mix of age and race, and its architecture was striking. There was Montgomery Village outside of Washington, which was planned for thirty-five thousand and was an upper-middle-class Bowie boasting especially fine public facilities. There were developments of estates valued at half a million dollars in Potomac, and there were condominiums in Annapolis featuring private yacht docks. Every housing project was a social experiment. Model communities by 1980 meant little more than communities that had used planners. Planning had become essential to life, and it did not necessarily mean the subordination of individuality.

The suburbs and the model communities were stories of extraordinary growth, but the mirror image was a corresponding decline of the city. In 1920 slightly more than one-half of the people of Maryland lived within the Baltimore City limits, and their standard of living was the highest in the state. By 1940 Baltimore's population had slipped to 47 percent of the state's population, and its standard of living had slipped as well. By 1960 the city's percentage of state population was down to 30 percent. By 1980 it had dropped to 19 percent, and the city had the state's highest rate of welfare, unemployment, and crime. Baltimore's decline and its efforts to save itself were typical of the story in most eastern industrial cities.

Decline of the City

Through the depression and the war, Baltimore never imagined that it was in trouble. Political bravado and business boosterism combined to boast of progress that was hardly there. During the administrations of Mayor Howard W. Jackson (1931–1943), a Democratic machine functionary, construction of federal courthouses, implementation of WPA street-paving programs, and development of about five thousand garden apartments as public housing projects allowed people to imagine that the city was improving. The housing program was called slum clearance, it displaced as many as it housed, and it may have actually lowered city revenues by replacing privately owned dwellings with non-tax-assessed public ones. Under the administrations of the optimistic Republican Theodore R. McKeldin (1943–1947), wartime bustle, a real but temporary influx of population, and federal construction of forty-eight hundred temporary housing units made the city seem to be bursting at the seams. In 1945 McKeldin appointed a Redevelopment Commission to continue the New Deal–inspired slum clearance, not for economic revitalization, but to serve the poor and to please the esthetic sensibilities of the rich.[47]

The optimistic mood hardly changed in the 1950s, as postwar construction, satisfying pent-up needs of the previous fifteen years, was less widespread than in the suburbs but widespread enough to nourish the illusion of progress. Under Mayor Thomas D'Alesandro, Jr. (1947–1959), a machine-allied Democrat, city planners regularly altered census estimates to reflect what they imagined the real figures should be. City taxes and debts rose sharply and services lagged, but against the memory of the depression the hardships were difficult to measure. The mayor allowed the city's congested waterfront airport to be moved to the suburbs, thus diminishing congestion. The mayor boasted more of building Memorial Stadium for athletic events, and he boasted of constructing twenty-five new schools. Slum clearance continued with the construction of about thirty-five hundred federally financed units, mostly in high-rise apartments that proved to be disastrous designs for low-cost housing.[48]

Other 1950s programs tacitly admitted that population and business were flowing from the city and offered the first lessons in what would not work to stem the flow. The Baltimore Plan for housing renewal, in which city health, fire, and building code inspectors swooped down on a targeted slum area and ordered landlords to meet all legal standards, began after the war and gained wide acclaim in the 1950s. Landlords either rebuilt their properties or sold out to someone who would. This worked well enough for upgrading a few blocks, and property values and tax assessments rose accordingly, but rents also rose, of course, so that ultimately the program only pushed the poor into other areas, and conditions and rents there fell in much the same proportion as they rose in the upgraded areas. Another major program offered low-cost city loans for private construction of ten large parking garages. The mayor touted the program as "The Road Back," as a means of keeping suburban shoppers in the downtown stores. In the short term, however, the program was a scandal, for Mayor D'Alesandro's friends, it seemed, got the loans, and in the long run the garages did little to alter the attractiveness of suburban shopping centers.[49]

Even into the 1960s Baltimore politicians failed to come to terms with urban failure. The administration of J. Harold Grady (1959–1962) was too inept and conservative to recognize the problems. Then Grady accepted an appointment as a federal judge, and his successor, Phillip H. Goodman (1962–1963), lacked the vision or authority to promote revival. Meanwhile, however, businessmen were reading the signs, and the census of 1960 could not be fudged (see table 3.1).

The migration from the city began in the mid-1940s, just as suburbia began to boom, and it accelerated slightly through the ensuing decades, especially after the 1968 urban riots. The decline was in fact more evenly continuous than it appeared, because the unusually high postwar birth rate camouflaged the net losses of the 1950s, and the

Table 3.1.   The Decline of Baltimore

	1940	1950	1960	1970	1980
Population	859,100	949,708	939,024	905,787	786,775
Average population change, per month	+450	+758	−92	−283	−983
Population as a percentage of the metropolitan area	79	71	52	44	36
Percentage of state black population	19	24	35	46	55
Percentage of votes cast in state elections	48	40	30	21	17
Difference between city median family income and state median (in dollars)	—	+9	−650	−2,243	−5,600

Source: U.S. Bureau of the Census, *County and City Data Book* (1947–1983); idem, *State and Metropolitan Area Data Book* (1979–1982).

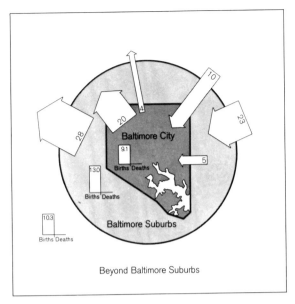

Figure 3.3. Baltimore City and Suburban Migrations, 1955–1970
Source: Adapted from Sherry Olson, *Baltimore* (Cambridge, Mass., 1976), p. 67.
Note: Figures with arrows are average annual migrations in thousands. Figures on bars are average annual excess of births over deaths per 1,000 population.

subsequent decline in births exaggerated the net losses of the 1970s (see figure 3.3).[50]

Patterns of living in the city changed as crowding diminished, as families were replaced by single people, and as houses were replaced by apartments. The city's population dropped, and the number of separate households there increased only slightly, from 275,000 in 1947 to 289,000 in 1977. This meant that the average household size declined from 3.4 to 2.7 people, and urban density declined accordingly. As families moved to the suburbs the city became a place for broken families, single people, and older couples. The percentage of people living in owner-occupied houses declined from 52 percent in 1950 to 43 percent in 1977, and the newer living units were mostly apartments and condominiums. The city made valiant attempts to reclaim abandoned dwellings, or to bulldoze them and auction the land, but continually after 1965 about fifteen thousand dwellings were legally vacant.[51]

The most obvious change in the population was, of course, from white to black. This change, like others, was not exactly as it appeared, for it was much less white flight from blacks than observers believed, and much more simply the flight of the affluent from the city. The exodus began well before school integration in 1954, and as soon as suburban racial barriers fell in the late 1960s there was a net exodus of blacks as well. Large numbers of unskilled and mostly black migrants from the south and the surrounding countryside entered the city during the 1940s and 1950s, and their large birth rates increased the number of blacks disproportionately through the 1960s. The exodus of the affluent continued remarkably evenly through the entire period.

Urban employment remained steady, at around 400,000 jobs, but sources of employment changed—from manufacturing, construction, and trade to government, health, and education. The number of retail stores in the city dropped by one-half, from 14,116 in 1940 to 7,006 in 1972. Partly this exodus was the departure of gasoline stations to the suburbs and the replacement of neighborhood groceries by super-markets.[52]

Sociologists analyzed many questionnaires to discover why people left Baltimore for the suburbs, but the answers were obvious. About two-thirds of the emigrants spoke of the greater attractions of the suburbs: its better housing, open spaces, better living conditions, and, increasingly, its greater convenience to jobs. About one-third noted a dislike of the city—its schools, lack of safety, neighborhood conditions (often meaning race), and poor street maintenance and services—as a reason for moving.[53]

The greatest change in the city was a replacement of wealth by poverty, power by powerlessness. As the rich and the middle class moved out, they left behind their old houses for the people who could afford no better. In 1950 the city had 40 percent of the state's richest population quartile, and in 1977 it had only 13 percent (the Baltimore suburbs increased from 25 percent to 34 percent their share of the richest quartile); conversely, Baltimore increased its proportion of the poorest quartile of the state's population from 27 percent to 34 per-cent (and the suburbs retained about 18 percent of the poorest). From 1950 to 1977 the median income of the city dropped from 98 percent to 68 percent of median suburban income. All of this meant a decline in urban leadership: 13 percent of the most successful people were in the city, 34 percent in the suburbs. Total library circulation in the city declined from a peak of 4.7 million volumes in 1964 to 2.1 in 1982. Certainly able people remained in Baltimore, but they composed a smaller proportion of the total there than anywhere else in the state.[54]

The exodus of money and talent, along with the influx of the poor, brought to the city the crunch of rising costs and plunging revenues. Costs surged, especially for welfare, housing, health care, and police protection, and this caused corresponding cutbacks in schools, street maintenance, and garbage disposal, which hastened the middle-class migration to the suburbs. To some extent the city found itself responsi-ble for providing services to the booming surrounding area, especially services such as roads, buses, hospitals, and libraries. Even as the city's population shrank to 19 percent of the state's, the city remained responsible for 56 percent of the state's public housing, 55 percent of the state's welfare payments, and 35 percent of the state's hospitals. This was the main justification for pouring state and federal funds, raised from suburban taxes, into urban revitalization.

The plunge in revenues was even sharper than the rise in costs. Federal and state revenue sharing was generally indexed to population and declined accordingly. City revenues from income taxes and sales taxes dropped faster than population as the rich left in disproportion-ate numbers. Worse than these was the decline in revenue from prop-erty taxes. In 1940, when the city had 47 percent of the state's population, it also had 54 percent of the total assessed wealth of the state, but by 1980 these figures had plunged to 19 percent and 12 percent (see figure 3.4). Property taxes rose from 65 percent above taxes in the suburbs to 145 percent above (see figure 3.5). This typi-

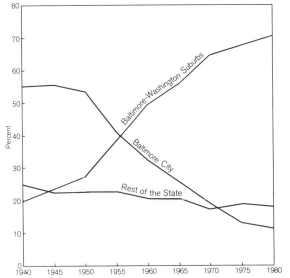

Figure 3.4. Assessed Wealth by Region, 1940–1980
Source: State Department of Assessments and Taxation,
Annual Report (1940–1980).
Note: Wealth in each region is shown as a percentage of
total state wealth.

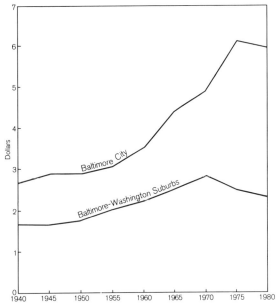

Figure 3.5. Property Taxes, City and Suburban, 1940–
1980 (Per $100 of Assessment)
Source: State Department of Assessments and Taxation,
Annual Report (1940–1980).

cally involved adding a 20 percent premium to urban housing costs, again serving to hasten the migration to the suburbs. Even the urban renewal projects, when they came, were mixed blessings, for the projects substituted mostly non-tax-paying public buildings for tax-paying private property. From 1940 to 1980 the proportion of non-tax-paying property in the city—such as state office buildings and public housing projects—rose from 13 percent to 27 percent of the total property in the city.[55]

To bridge the gap between rising costs and falling revenues, the cities depended increasingly on various kinds of grants from the state and federal governments. From 1940 to 1980 the percentage of Baltimore's budget composed of these grants increased from 18 to 61 percent. Since urban political power was eroding as quickly as revenues, this increasingly meant reliance on the generosity of others. As suburban costs also rose, and especially during the Reagan conservatism of the 1980s, the generosity proved limited.

Awareness of these dilemmas began to dawn in the mid-1950s, especially among businessmen. Banding together in their own self-interest, they awoke the politicians and the public to the reality of urban decay, and for the next fifteen years, until Mayor William Donald Schaefer assumed the leadership in 1971, business dominated the city's effort to stem the tide. At least three times before—when Baltimore was besieged by the British in the War of 1812, when it fell into Know-Nothing rioting in 1858, and after the great city fire of 1904—businessmen had coalesced to assume control of affairs. The decay of the 1950s, like the earlier occasions, was a crisis in which

politics was too important to be left to the politicians. The businessmen won many victories, and Baltimore's efforts at urban renewal
emerged along with Pittsburgh's and Milwaukee's as one of the country's most successful; but still the tide rolled on.

The individual who started the businessmen's effort was the
remarkable James Rouse. Impatient at what government was doing,
he established his own planning and development corporation. In
1954 he called city leaders and businessmen together to talk about
joint efforts they might make to obtain aid under the new federal
housing programs. Later that year he spoke to the chamber of commerce, calling on business to organize along the lines of the Pittsburgh
model, in which the top executives of the city incorporated themselves
to promote urban development. Early in 1955, 87 executives incorporated as the Greater Baltimore Committee.

The Greater Baltimore Committee began with about ninety-seven
thousand dollars in dues and contributions and within a few years
managed an annual budget of over one million dollars. It rejected use
of city planners because that seemed to tie plans to a particular city
administration, and it rejected the notion of hiring outside consultants
to design a plan that, it believed, would easily be forgotten. Instead,
the committee insured its autonomy and continuation by employing
its own planner, David A. Walker from Harvard University, who soon
had plenty of assistants. The committee then sold its designs to the
city, to its own members, and to outsiders. The committee established
six goals and boosted each of them with a promotional subcommittee:
improved port facilities, industrial parks, the Jones Falls Expressway,
a civic center, improved urban transportation, and comprehensive
urban renewal. The final goal was vague, but Rouse headed that
subcommittee and it eventually swallowed up most of the others.[56]

First came port improvement. The city piers were originally built by
the city, but by the late eighteenth century they had fallen under control of the shipping companies, by the late nineteenth century they
were owned and operated by the railroads, and by the 1950s they had
fallen into the decay that was assured through railroad management.
The Greater Baltimore Committee dispatched its spokesmen to
Annapolis in 1955 to oppose city takeover of the piers and the following year offered its own plan, modeled after those of New York and
New Orleans, creating the quasi-public Maryland Port Authority. The
legislature, in special session, gave the Port Authority full control over
harbor facilities and the revenue from a tax of one-half of 1 percent on
all corporate profits in the state with which to modernize them. Over
the next twenty years the Maryland Port Authority spent $198 million
for new piers and loading facilities at the old Locust Point and Canton
facilities and for an entirely new facility at Dundalk, where the old city
airport had been.

The Port Authority was a success at reviving the port but not at
reviving the city. Its peculiar mix of public and private management,
with competing public, leased, and subsidized private piers, was mas-
terfully efficient. Its control of the terminals gave it substantial control
over the railroad, truck, and air traffic in the state in a way that was
beneficial to both the industries and the public. It pioneered various

kinds of containerized shipping, by which railroad boxcars, truck trailers, and entire trucks were moved on and off ships without being reloaded. Baltimore retained but did not improve its position as one of the half-dozen leading ports of the nation. From 1956 to 1979 total trade declined from 52 million tons to 45 million tons. Midwestern grain exports moved to the St. Lawrence Seaway, and U.S. coal exports dropped, although exportation of these bulk items was replaced by importation of more expensive goods, mostly automobiles from Germany and Japan. Modernization and innovation, if rapid enough, allowed some enterprises to hold their own.[57]

Similar to the Maryland Port Authority was the Maryland Food Center Authority, an incorporated group of wholesale food distributors and public representatives who received about $80 million in state funds to buy up downtown food distribution centers and sell them for industrial sites and to build and lease new distribution sites in the suburbs. Their efforts concentrated jobs in the city, relieved urban traffic congestion by moving trucking out to the expressway arteries, and served incidentally to lower consumer food prices. In 1976 the wholesale markets moved to the suburbs, near Jessup.[58]

The port and food authorities, and urban renewal generally, represented a kind of postcapitalism that confounded the theories of Karl Marx. Government came to the aid of capital, not labor, and it sought to promote more than to regulate, but it promoted jobs as well as profits, and it benefited consumers as well as investors. As postindustrialism moved the economy from manufacturing to service employment, postcapitalism moved the economy from private to public investment. In politics, economic policy became the leading public question, and it was a difficult issue for democracy to handle.

In 1959 James Rouse, David Walker, and the Greater Baltimore Committee unveiled their plans for Charles Center, the first phase of their still grander design for urban renewal. Two volumes of designs won rave reviews in the architectural journals, and models delighted downtown businessmen. The project, managed, like the port and food authorities, by a conglomerate of the Greater Baltimore Committee and the city, acquired twelve blocks in the heart of the downtown district. Construction began in 1961 and was mostly complete within fifteen years, generally according to plan: eight major office buildings, an apartment complex, a hotel, a theater, underground parking, many shops, and two handsome public squares. About $35 million of the costs came from federal, state, and city funds, and about $145 million came from private investment, although federal agencies agreed in advance to rent much of the office space. It was pretty, and it bustled with office workers during the daytime, but it fell mostly silent at dusk, and there were no signs of its producing a domino effect in reviving the surrounding areas.[59]

As politicians gained inspiration from the Greater Baltimore Committee and the Charles Center showpiece, other bits of urban renewal appeared in the city. In 1958 the state began its own urban renewal initiative by bulldozing several thousand slum dwellings around Mount Royal Railroad Station to build three massive state office buildings. Mayor Theodore McKeldin initiated a publicized homesteading program, by which persons could buy an abandoned dwelling from the city for one dollar, provided they brought the dwelling up to housing code standards and moved in. Even with the additional boost of low-cost city loans, however, fewer than one hundred houses were remodeled each year. Slightly more successful was a Turnkey program, which involved about two hundred houses a year; through this program developers could obtain abandoned houses and loans and restore them for rental or for guaranteed sale back to the city for use as low-cost housing. This program was excellent from the standpoint of retaining the architectural integrity of the old city, and it provided good housing for the poor, but it worked only insofar as federal and city funds subsidized it. McKeldin also obtained federal and city loan subsidies for the invigoration of middle-class enclaves like Bolton Hill, Federal Hill, Fells Point, and Dickeyville. These areas were moderate success stories, attracting affluent and, often, single people who liked a sophisticated urban environment. McKeldin initiated plans for the Coldspring housing development located at the edge of the city and intended for moderate- and upper-income families, but after fifteen years only five hundred units had been completed.[60]

Baltimore's nadir coincided with the administration of one of its weakest mayors, Thomas D'Alesandro, III (1967-1971). Charles Center and other projects continued, but President Lyndon Johnson shifted the federal emphasis away from big construction and toward the War on Poverty, the Community Action Program, and the Model Cities Program. In the late 1960s these agencies provided up to $20 million a year for neighborhood revitalization, mostly in welfare, health care, day care, and job-training projects, but also for housing improvements, schools, and recreation centers designed to promote urban neighborhood morale. Rising expectations promoted discontent as well as improved morale, however, and the urban riots of 1968 balanced the millions of dollars' worth of improvements against millions of dollars' worth of ruin. These failures, compounded by Vietnam, made D'Alesandro's last years as miserable as those of Lyndon Johnson. The urban exodus reached its peak.[61]

The most controversial urban renewal efforts and the hardest to evaluate were those in urban transportation. One the one hand trolleys, buses, and subways guaranteed suburban commuters access to urban jobs; on the other hand they allowed all but the poorest to move out. From 1948 to 1979 ridership on city trolleys and buses declined from 236 million to 75 million. The privately owned Baltimore Transit Company collapsed in 1969. First it sold out to General Motors, which provided new diesel buses, and then, in 1971, General Motors sold both the company and the new buses to the city, which ran them at a deficit. By 1979 the average fare of thirty-two cents carried an additional twenty-nine cents in public subsidy. The long-anticipated Jones Falls Expressway was completed in 1962, and a web of interstate connectors, each costing over $200 million in mostly federal funds, traversed the city in the early 1980s. One author estimated that all the renewal efforts displaced twenty-five thousand housing units, mostly poor, a total greater than the number of public housing units. Spray paint on ghetto walls spelled out "Urban Renewal Go Home."[62]

Baltimore's urban renewal has centered around the harbor, which has become one of the most beautiful in the world. Courtesy of the Rouse Company.

Doubts about urban renewal were well founded, but the brightest episode in Baltimore's renewal was yet to come, as D'Alesandro was replaced as mayor in 1971 by Schaefer, as Model Cities gave way to block grants that could be used as a city wanted, and as Charles Center was eclipsed by the still greater Inner Harbor project. Schaefer, a bachelor who was married to the city, a true believer in urban renewal, maintained a close alliance with Rouse but otherwise overwhelmed and largely absorbed the Greater Baltimore Committee.

In area and cost the Inner Harbor project was roughly four times that of Charles Center. Its centerpiece was Harborplace, two glittering malls on the waterfront which were built and run by Rouse. Harborplace contained 134 shops, all of them small: restaurants, gift shops, boutiques, and art shops. Jugglers, jazz groups, and bagpipes performed in the plazas. The year it opened, 1981, 18 million people visited, more than the number at Disneyworld that year. The National Aquarium, the Maryland Science Center, a city convention center, a junior college, and a marina added to this area's drawing power. Nearby were a dozen new office buildings, a luxury hotel, and luxury apartments. Design was supervised by some of the world's leading architects: Joseph Hudnut, Holmes Perkins, Pietro Belluschi, and Louis Kahn. Here, finally, was a return of the downtown vibrance that the city had been losing for forty years. The cost of the Inner Harbor project was about $700 million, composed half and half of public and private funds. The federal government provided another $700 million for an eight-mile subway system to serve the downtown, considerably short of the thirty-two-mile system the city wanted.[63]

The greatest success of renewal was revived morale. The glittering waterfront, the mayor's extraordinary popularity, the involvement of

business leaders, the continuing construction, the winning athletic
teams, and the dynamic neighborhoods allowed Baltimore to think of
itself as a model for the nation. Mayor Schaefer played the theme hard
with city fairs, slogans, and promotions.

Political scientists expressed special interest in the mutual reinforce-
ment of morale and neighborhood vitality. While cities such as Philadelphia and Chicago had developed centralized bureaucracies in the
1950s, Baltimore had retained much of its ancient ward politics, with
each neighborhood claiming its own piece of the budget pie through
its representatives on the city council. Baltimore, too, had tried to
centralize, but when every bureaucracy—schools, housing, sanitation,
health, police, and the rest—lacked sufficient funds, everyone turned
against city hall. The shrewd Schaefer turned the tables. By actively
encouraging each neighborhood to establish its own priorities and by
providing the neighborhoods with funds to realize their goals, the
city's administration retained balance and direction.[64]

Mayor Schaefer was certain of his primary accomplishment in
office: "Neighborhoods," he said "have improved themselves. Neighborhoods have developed a sense of pride. Neighborhoods are working." The neighborhood improvement associations came together to
protest a proposed placement of a freeway, to establish a neighborhood crime watch, to claim federal rehabilitation funds, or to express
themselves on trash removal and zoning. Schaefer embraced the community groups as allies instead of enemies, concentrating housing
renewal in the wards that most wanted housing renewal and school
construction in the wards that most wanted schools.

Neighborhood associations, it turned out, flourished better with
contention than with homogeneity. Diverse ethnic groups, differing
levels of wealth, and the abundance of special interests actually
increased community participation, increased community power, and
usually promoted willingness to accept the outcome of community
deliberation. The disproportionate power of the rich and active,
moreover, proved a source of strength rather than weakness to the
neighborhood organizations, for the rich and active had the greatest
stake in the community and were drawn into its improvement. This
was a strikingly different political culture from the old ward politics
where power lay in patronage, and it was different from the poverty
programs of the 1960s which had placed power in the hands of the
poor. Community was a rediscovered arena for politics and for middle-class values as well.[65]

By the 1980s the ultimate result of urban renewal was far from
clear. Morale was a vague and volatile commodity that could turn
sour in any election—or even with the departure of a football team.
The cost of urban renewal, borne mostly by people outside the city,
was more than $1,000 per urban resident. Charles Center and the
Inner Harbor plus all the neighborhood improvement projects
involved less than 20 percent of the urban jobs and residents. Three
more major downtown department stores closed in the late 1970s,
leaving two, the number usually found in an ordinary shopping mall.

The number of jobs and the population continued to decline, and
the proportion of the population below the poverty line continued to

rise, but the new problem of the 1980s was the drop in outside aid. The suburban middle class who voted for Reagan was short on compassion for the city. Federal aid dropped from a 1972–1982 average of $425 million each year to a 1982–1984 average of $134 million a year. Combined state and federal aid in 1982 was $1,134 million, but in 1984 it was $562 million. *Esquire* magazine in 1984 featured Schaefer as "the best mayor in America," but a little noticed volume of statistics that year featured Baltimore as "the myth of the urban renaissance."[66]

Baltimore remained the hub of the metropolitan area and of the state, as cities everywhere remained the hub of civilization. Its renewal efforts excited everyone. The city remained the hub of decay as well as vitality, however, of failure as well as success.

In the population swirl between 1940 and 1980 the small towns appeared to offer the last refuge of stability. Each town had its own story: the decline of coal mining and railroading in Cumberland, Frostburg, Westernport, and Lonaconing; the decline of oystering in Crisfield; the growth of the chicken industry in Salisbury and Berlin; the growth of the resort industry in Thurmont and Easton; the Baltimore-Wilmington overflow into Elkton; the suburban Baltimore-Washington overflow into Frederick; the Frederick overflow into Walkersville; and the Salisbury overflow into Fruitland.[67] For all the particular stories, however, the towns hardly changed in size, ranking or number (see table 3.2).

Despite apparent stability, major internal changes, much like those taking place in the cities, were coming to the towns. Most notably the changes involved the growth of outlying areas, or suburbs, even outside the tiniest hamlets. New towns like Walkersville and Fruitland were suburbs of Frederick and Salisbury, and every town sprouted developments that were outgrowing the original core. Total town population increased by only about 15 percent, depending on the definition used for *town;* even though the farm population was declining, the total population in the counties grew by 24 percent. This meant that the rural population clustered around the towns and commuted in for jobs. As town and surrounding areas merged, town governments declined in importance. The small metropolitan areas looked to the counties for schools and services, so that after 1953 no new cluster sought municipal status.

Jobs increased around the town fringes, and commerce inside declined. Small industries appeared on the fringes of the old business districts, either inside or just outside the town boundaries, to take advantage of the labor fleeing the farms. Main Street languished as new shopping centers appeared on the outskirts. Housing in town became dilapidated, while new developments appeared on the outskirts and were strung out along the highways. Almost every small-town movie theater was gone by 1980, although there were new ones in the shopping centers. Hotels around the railroad station closed, and new motels opened along the highways. In seventeen of Maryland's twenty small towns, the black population grew faster than the white.

The Small Towns

Table 3.2. Nonsuburban Towns Having Populations Greater than Two Thousand

	1940	1980
Cumberland	39,483	25,933
Hagerstown	32,491	34,132
Frederick	15,802	27,557
Salisbury	13,313	16,429
Cambridge	10,102	11,703
Frostburg	7,659	7,715
Easton	4,528	7,536
Crisfield	3,908	2,924
Brunswick	3,856	4,572
Westernport	3,565	2,706
Elkton	3,518	6,468
Chestertown	2,760	3,300
Pocomoke	2,739	3,558
Lonaconing	2,429	1,330
Snow Hill	1,926	2,192
Berlin	1,439	2,162
Thurmont	1,303	2,934
Centreville	1,114	2,018
Walkersville	731	2,212
Fruitland	—	2,694

Source: U.S. Bureau of the Census.

Note: The census definition of *town* changes. There are about twenty additional towns with a population between one thousand and two thousand, and their stability in size, ranking, and number is similar to those of more than two thousand. It takes about two thousand people to support a doctor, a school, a grocery store, and a bank.

In the 1960s businessmen in the towns, as in the large cities, looked toward urban renewal for rescue. Usually business was the progressive force, overcoming politicians, old residents, and labor. The first step was usually a highway over or around the town, involving displacement of some people, a break-even for downtown business, a short-term boom in construction, and a considerable long-term boost to

Easton, Maryland, population 7,536. In size and social structure the small towns of America have not changed much for almost a century. Photograph by A. Aubrey Bodine, courtesy of the Peale Museum, Baltimore.

Taylorsville Farm, Carroll County. In 1980 the median Maryland farm income was $9,595; the median farm value was $381,200. Photograph by A. Aubrey Bodine, courtesy of the Peale Museum, Baltimore.

suburban business. The next step—especially for the larger towns of Cumberland, Hagerstown, Frederick, Salisbury, and Cambridge—was new government facilities, subsidized housing, and downtown plazas. They were financed, as in the cities, by a mixture of funds, in this case federal, state, town, and private, and their face lifts gave the towns a sense of keeping up with their suburbs.

Finally, whatever happened to the farm? For three centuries America *The Farm* had been a land of farms, and even in 1940, despite the depression, the farm seemed to embody the basic and natural way of life, to be the source of American values like self-reliance, and to be the place where hard work would always produce a just reward. On the one hand the farmer triumphed as production soared in the mid-twentieth century, for agriculture more than industry was the nation's economic miracle. On the other hand soaring production was the source of the farmer's failure, for prices plunged despite efforts of government to peg them, and most farmers were forced to abandon the rural life and work for someone else in the suburbs or city.

Throughout history urban growth has depended ultimately on an increase in farm productivity. In 1940 each Maryland farm provided food for approximately 43 people; in 1980 each one provided food for 240. The increase came from technology, which brought tractors and electricity to the farm, slowly after 1912 and rapidly after 1940; it came from a ten-fold increase in the use of fertilizer after 1940; and it came from the agricultural experiment stations of the late nineteenth century which in the 1940s finally began to bring major results with better animal breeding and chemically enriched feeds, with superior seed strains, with weed and insect control, and with new techniques of farming such as raised pens and twenty-four hour feeding of chickens. From 1939 to 1979 total crop yield in Maryland, measured in terms of 1979 dollars, increased by 190 percent; yield per acre increased by 375 percent; yield per farm man-hour increased by 655 percent. Wheat farming declined, and tobacco and vegetables remained stable; but livestock, corn, and fruit increased three times over, and poultry, dairy, and soybeans increased ten times (see table 3.3).

For the farmer, the rise in productivity was as much a loss as a gain, for rising productivity meant declining prices. The farmer spent enormously more for his fertilizer and machinery, but profits hardly changed. In 1960 the average Maryland farm family was actually making 18 percent less in real income (measured in constant dollars after deducting expenses) than it had made in 1920. From 1940 to 1980 the average real family income of all people in Maryland rose slightly more than 100 percent, but the farm owner's real family income went up only 28 percent. The highest goal of federal farm policy (which almost never was realized) was to maintain farm income at 90 percent of "parity," which meant 90 percent of the position the farmer held in the economy, relative to other groups, in the period from 1910 to 1914. Most farmers were left to settle for a position below that of their grandparents, or else find occupation elsewhere.[68]

The large farmers grew larger and the top 8 percent produced almost half of the total crop, but the majority of farmers remained poor. In 1940, 32.8 percent of the Maryland farm families had cash incomes of less than $250, 57 percent had no electricity, and 70 percent had no indoor running water. By 1980 real improvement was only moderate, for still 27 percent of the farm-owning families received an annual income of less than $2,500. These were the farm owners; altogether about 50 percent of the farm residents existed at this subpoverty level. Poorest of all were the migrant workers, holding steady at about four thousand people, mostly immigrants and blacks who came from Florida each summer to work in the vegetable fields and orchards. Farm owners provided barrackslike shacks without bathrooms, no one asked questions about minimum wages, and in 1966 the average workday lasted 11.8 hours.[69]

The apparent bright spot in farm decline was the rising value of rural acreage, but this too was a mixed blessing. The value of the average Maryland farm, its land and buildings and machinery, increased from $6,506 in 1940 to an astronomical $381,200 in 1980. This could only be realized, however, if the farmer abandoned his calling. In the meantime, the farmer's return on investment plunged to 2.5 percent, and if his labor was calculated in, his return on investment became a negative number (see table 3.4). Only expectation of

Table 3.3.   Farm Productivity, 1920–1979

	Total Crop Value (1979 $ millions)			
	1920	1939	1959	1979
Poultry	13	42	151	283
Dairy	17	71	164	189
Beef-hogs-sheep	27	29	86	87
Corn	37	52	33	99
Wheat and grains	73	29	13	18
Tobacco	20	24	42	30
Fruit	3	10	11	15
Soybeans	—	—	17	72
Vegetables and potatoes	30	29	46	30
Greenhouse and forest	3	5	24	30
Other	3	5	2	3
Total farm income	226	296	589	856

Source: U.S. Bureau of the Census.

Note: Crop value means costs plus profits; the increase in commodities is far greater. The 1920 figures are interpolated from total production less farm consumption. Dollars are adjusted, according to the Consumer Price Index, so that a 1979 dollar is equivalent to 45¢ in 1959, 21¢ in 1939, and 30¢ in 1920.

Table 3.4.   The Decline of the Farm

	1940	1960	1980
Total farm population	243,000	112,000	45,000
Number of farms	42,100	27,100	17,500
Percentage of Maryland population on farms	13.3	3.6	1.0
Percentage of Maryland land in farms	66	59	44
Average income, after costs, per farm (in 1980 $)	7,452	6,242	9,595
Average farm value (in 1980 $)	30,980	86,877	381,200
Average farm return on capital (not including family labor) (in percent)	24.0	7.1	2.5

Source: Maryland Department of Agriculture, *Maryland Agricultural Statistics* (1962–1980)

Note: A 1980 dollar, adjusted according to the Consumer Price Index, is equivalent to 45¢ in 1959 and 21¢ in 1940.

continued capital appreciation or unwanted loss of farm life or inertia kept farmers in business at all.

Federal and state governments tried, but never very effectively, to help agriculture. Agricultural agents kept offering improved farming techniques, as if that might help. The federal government poured in subsidies to establish price floors, to reduce production by paying farmers to put land in forest, or as direct handouts. State and local governments poured money into welfare, which was received by a disproportionate number of rural families, passed laws to insure health and educational benefits to migrant workers, biased tax assessments in favor of agricultural property, and offered subsidies to farmers who retained their land in farming instead of selling it to developers.[70]

What it all came to, however, was the continuing flow of population from the farm to the suburbs and city. The flow peaked in periods of war, when industrial wages were high, and slowed in times of urban unemployment, especially in the five years after 1978. Mostly the young left, so by 1980 the average age of the Maryland farmer was 56. Rich farmers left to obtain an easier and higher return on their capital, and the poor left for the higher wages of the town.

All of the population changes—the rise of suburbs and model towns, the decline of the city, the internal changes in small towns, and the near disappearance of the farm—had slowed by 1980. The years from

1940 to 1980 seemed to bracket an era of the greatest population swirl in history. The smaller the unit of measure—from nation, to state, to community, to individual—the greater the magnitude of upheaval seemed. For most of the people who moved, life was better, and this was why they had moved, but for almost everyone the life of stability, if it had ever existed, had become a life of swirl.

The war ended as it began, with cheers and foreboding. Cheers were justified, for the state was being propelled into the greatest binge of growth and prosperity in its history, even surpassing that of the war; but foreboding was also justified, for rapid change brought unease, and win-the-war consensus exploded into raucous contention. Conservatives wanted to repel the New Deal to regain a predepression normalcy, and liberals wanted to press ahead with a major expansion of the welfare state.

From 1945 to 1953 President Harry Truman expressed the will of a majority but not at all the consensus of the country in transforming the New Deal into the Fair Deal. Enemies reviled him. In Maryland from 1947 to 1951 Governor William P. Lane assumed a similar role and suffered a similar fate. Truman and Lane were both men of four-square common sense; they were courageous and unpretentious, and

4
The Postwar Discomfort of Harry Truman and William P. Lane

William P. Lane and Harry S Truman at dedication of Friendship Airport. Courtesy of the *Baltimore News American*.

they proceeded pragmatically to do what had to be done. Neither of them was able to soothe the deep frustrations people felt, and neither was popular, but in retrospect they were both among the most far-sighted leaders of the twentieth century. They dragged their constituencies, protesting, into the modern world.

The Postwar Mood

The paradoxes of V-E and V-J days foreshadowed the tenor of the coming years. Victory in Europe came in May 1945, but it was tempered by sadness over Roosevelt's recent death and dread of the battles still ahead. Victory over Japan came in August 1945, but it was almost overshadowed by awe at the atomic explosions that ended the war. In Baltimore and throughout Maryland and America, townspeople turned out to celebrate V-J day. The following day Glenn L. Martin, one of the state's largest employers, announced that its work force would be cut in half.[1]

The professional planners, including planning commissions and large investors, were especially pessimistic when the war ended. Two major planning commissions, one for the state and one for Baltimore, had been issuing reports since 1943, all predicting dire depression ahead. And yet, almost every assumption of the planners was proved wrong: that war plants would be useless for peacetime production, that women and blacks would retire from the labor force, that living standards would drop back to prewar levels, and that public works projects would be necessary to provide jobs for the returning veterans. The state had saved back $30 million, half a year's revenue, for the kind of public works the depression had required. Companies like Glenn L. Martin thought they were beating the competition by making cutbacks before the new depression came. As demand actually rose, those announcing cutbacks found they had outguessed themselves.[2]

Far from depression, the postwar years were characterized above all by soaring prosperity. Factory reconversion, fueled by the federal government's virtual write-off of wartime loans to industry, took weeks instead of years, and the reconversion created demand for extra labor in the process. Most wartime rationing ended with V-J day, and consumer demand—pent-up demand from depression as well as war—for nylons, appliances, autos, houses, and services, exploded. Greatest was the demand for housing, and suburban counties almost doubled their populations within five years. State and local governments fueled the boom with their new courthouses, waterworks, and schools. Veterans returned rapidly: 70 percent were demobilized within a year, finding plenty of jobs if they wanted to work, but often returning to school instead, upgrading their skills and value in the workplace accordingly. Enrollment in Maryland colleges doubled from the fall of 1945 to the fall of 1946, and enrollment in vocational schools quadrupled. With the G.I. Bill providing free tuition, conditions in the colleges were frantically crowded. At the University of Maryland at College Park students were packed six to a dorm room, stood for hours in the dining-hall lines, and rushed to classes in hopes of obtaining a seat.[3]

From 1945 to 1951 Maryland's per capita annual income increased by 39 percent, from $1,272 to $1,769. The increase in consumer expenditures was almost double the increase in income, although inflation of about 20 percent modified both figures somewhat. The expansive mood was stronger than the statistics allowed. The most popular movie of 1946 was *The Best Years of Our Lives,* about the good life returning veterans faced. From every outward appearance, these were happy times.[4]

The anxiety that underlay these years was also real, however, for prosperity was as disconcerting as depression would have been. Ever growing were the implications of Hiroshima and the apparent intransigence of the Soviet Union. More immediate were the problems of inflation, which stemmed from consumer demands, and everyone's suspicion that others were prospering more than he or she was. Class rivalry focused in unprecedented bitterness on the strikes that swept the state.

Within weeks of V-J day the War Labor Board lifted its compulsory arbitration regulations, and walkouts spread through the cargo docks of Baltimore and the textile and rubber plants of Cumberland. In 1946 there were serious strikes in the coal, steel, and railroad industries of Maryland, and in 1947 there were still worse disruptions among telephone and construction workers. Altogether Maryland lost about 200,000 man-days of labor due to strikes in late 1945, many times the loss for any year of the war. This surged to a loss of 1,400,000 man-days in 1946, and 1,620,000 days in 1947. Actually, in the peak period, this was only about 1 percent of the total labor in Maryland, but strikes were highly visible, and they had a domino effect on the lives of almost everyone. To non-strikers, the walkouts were outrageous. People looked to Washington, and Congress in 1947 passed the Taft-Hartley Act over Truman's veto. The act reinstituted certain kinds of labor arbitration and, combined shortly with increased minimum wages, worked well enough. By 1948 strikes in Maryland dropped sharply, to about 200,000 days lost each year, a figure generally maintained over the next three decades.[5]

The state's political caldrons, meanwhile, were bubbling. Local politicians could only lose by taking a stand on labor questions, and generally they left that strictly to Washington, but they could not avoid a growing public clamor for services, particularly for roads and schools, nor could they avoid the question of who would pay for them. Late in 1945 and early in 1946 Maryland had the air of a lame duck about it as it hung on to its wartime budget, waiting for a new election, new leadership, and a new 1947 biennial assembly. With the 1946 gubernatorial election, when Lane replaced O'Conor, passionate divisions over issues emerged, and voter participation in local affairs reached a new peak.

Lane was not a giant; he did not dominate his times. But by facing alternatives calmly and courageously he, like Truman, launched the state into the postwar era along a progressive course. He emerged out of two old traditions in Maryland politics: that of the patrician and that of the county boss. His father's people had migrated to Washing-

The Good Politician

ton County in western Maryland before the Revolution, and his mother's people had migrated there from ancient southern Maryland
tobacco plantations. Lane's father had served as a waterboy for the
Union Army at Antietam, had attended Princeton, and was later noted
for having participated in the famous first intercollegiate football
game of 1869, when Princeton defeated Rutgers, 6 to 4. The father
returned to Hagerstown as a banker, lawyer, newspaper publisher, and
militia colonel, a squire of the little town, an Episcopalian and a
Democrat.

The son, William Preston Lane, Jr., was born in 1892 and finished
first in his class at the University of Virginia, where he absorbed the
Virginian lore of honor, public service, and state's rights. He was a
National Guard captain in the United States border skirmish with
Mexico in 1916, and he was a major in France. In 1918 he won the
Silver Star for unusual valor, and newspaper reporters frequently
thereafter spoke of his valor in politics. He returned home to inherit
the bank, the newspaper, and the law practice, and to marry Dorothy
Byron, daughter of the town's second most prominent family. The
family fortune was secure. The young man set out for political adventure—all this in the Maryland patrician tradition of the Carrolls, War-
fields, Harringtons, and Ritchies.[6]

Lane's rise was also typical of the organization politics of the day,
which was marked by constant insurgencies. The Washington County
Democrats were controlled by a mossback boss, J. Hubert Wade. The
organization eagerly embraced the patrician war hero in 1919 and
elected him at once to the school board. The ambitious young Turk
was not satisfied, however, and a few months later, when the organization supported John Walter Smith, a former governor, for reelection, Lane and his friends, looking to pick a fight, announced their
support for the Democratic challenger, Albert C. Ritchie.

The 1919 split among Washington County Democrats assured
county support for the Republicans, but Ritchie won statewide, and
the Lane insurgents enjoyed control of the governor's local appointments. Four years later Lane carried the county for Ritchie, and the
Lane organization was secure. Such was the operation of local politics. In neighboring counties similar Ritchie bosses were emerging:
Judge William C. Walsh in Allegany and Garrett counties, David C.
Winebrenner in Frederick County, and E. Brooke Lee in Montgomery
County. Lane, Walsh, Winebrenner, and Lee were Ritchie's knights of
the west, closely allied, rising and falling together for three decades.
Organization, far more than issues, was the game. Politics was Lane's
profession now, but it was no coincidence that business was improving also. The Baltimore and Ohio Railroad and then the Pennsylvania
Railroad employed him on long-term retainers as their representative
in western Maryland.

In the 1930s Lane rose to statesmanship and political disaster from
which few imagined he would ever recover. Ritchie, running in 1930
for a third term as governor, needed a county man to balance his own
city support, and Lane was nominated for attorney general. Lane
easily rode Ritchie's coattails to victory, and many considered him
Ritchie's heir apparent. Unfortunately for Ritchie, the young man

found a cause he believed in and devoted his term of office to waging a war on lynching.[7]

The first episode occurred in October 1931, when a mob in Wicomico County attempted to lynch an accused black rapist, and then beat to insensibility the lawyer, Bernard Ades, who defended the accused man. H. L. Mencken thundered for the *Sunpapers,* and Lane investigated. Two months later another mob, urged to "heroic action" by the *Worcester County Democrat,* pulled an accused black murderer, Matt Williams, from a hospital and burned him to death. This time there was national concern, and Lane worked in vain for convictions, infuriating the local populace. Then, two years later, a Somerset County mob of five thousand seized from jail a feeble-minded black, George Armwood, who was accused of tearing the dress of a white woman, and cheered while he was beaten, hanged, mutilated, and burned.

Local officials again refused to take action even against those who acknowledged their role in the lynching, and Lane called out state police and the National Guard to make arrests. The accused were held in the Salisbury jail while mobs fought a pitched battle with the militia and violence spread through the county between police and citizens, blacks and whites. Eventually local judges freed all of the boastful lynch leaders, but Lane had one more play. He accepted an invitation to testify before a congressional investigation of lynching. There, before a national audience, he excoriated the racism of Eastern Shore mobs, called for a national antilynching law, and, to dramatize his message, read into the record the names and evidence against the Somerset County leaders he believed had escaped conviction.[8]

Lane was a national hero, and his action marked a turning point in public outrage against lynching in America, but he had become an embarrassment to Ritchie. The Democratic organization dumped Lane in 1934, electing Herbert R. O'Conor, a man who courted mobs, as attorney general. Lane, and the Lane-Walsh-Winebrenner-Lee organization, laid low for the next four years, but by 1938 they had reemerged in their counties, making peace with Governor-elect O'Conor. From 1938 to 1946 the Lane organization worked smoothly in Washington County, supporting O'Conor dutifully and Roosevelt enthusiastically. Memories of the lynchings faded.

Lane was primarily a practical politician, not a philosopher—his actions stemmed from facts surrounding a particular case, not from abstract principles—and yet Lane was sufficiently profound to be able to relate pragmatic politics to basic principles of government. In so doing he provided a significant philosophy for state government in the twentieth century. The pragmatic politician analyzed the three basic political problems of his times: majority rule, liberalism, and federalism. In each case New Deal reality and traditional state's rights found peace with each other.

Lane's fear of the majority must have been inspired at the University of Virginia, where it was as basic as the alphabet, but it was sharpened by the events in Somerset County, which were the keenest experiences of his life. "The doctrine of the divine right of the majority," he wrote, "is as wicked, as brutal, and as dangerous to human liberty, as the now repudiated doctrine of the divine right of kings. . . . There has not been a dictator who has not claimed that he holds a mandate from the majority." Lane cited the mobs of the French Revolution, the mobs who attacked the abolitionists, and the mobs who supported Hitler. What he was really thinking of, but seldom quite mentioned, were the lynch mobs of the Eastern Shore, and the mob spirit during his own administration which demanded new services and rejected new taxes, which lashed out sometimes hysterically to find scapegoats in the labor movement or in foreign conspiracies. Lane's solution lay in constitutionalism, the bulwark of free speech and thus of reason. Here was a blending of liberalism and conservatism: freedom as the limit of democracy and thus the bulwark of democracy.[9]

Lane's acceptance of welfare-state social services was almost entirely pragmatic; it was only coincidentally associated with the idealism of New Deal planners, although it came to about the same thing. Probably Lane followed the same path that led Truman to the Fair Deal. Both had learned, perhaps reluctantly, that their constituencies demanded roads, schools, hospitals, and charity that only government could provide, and that the prosperous constituency of the 1940s demanded far more than constituencies had been willing to settle for in Ritchie's day. As between services and taxes, most people chose services, even though those same people refused to acknowledge the either-or nature of the choice—either taxes and services, or minimum taxes and minimum services—on a subsequent election day. It was especially hard for Lane politically that he insisted on paying for services as they were provided. All for practical reasons, he was a big spender, a budget balancer, and, eventually, a scapegoat for public frustrations over the taxes it cost.[10]

By any measure of historical judgment, Lane was right on the problem of majority rule and public services, but he was probably more wrong than right in his third major conviction—that the states rather than the federal government must assume the burden of public services. "Unless the states have the wisdom and courage to carry upon their own shoulders the responsibility of giving to their peoples those things which they are now demanding of the federal government," he warned, there would be a disastrous "trend toward nationalization, compounding the American people into a common mass." For all of Lane's own effort to persuade Maryland to accept that burden, much of the expansion of services did have to come at the national level. Certainly there were costs involved, but they probably amounted to less than the disaster Lane foresaw.[11]

Lane's political sense, supported by his philosophy, allowed him to win the gubernatorial election of 1946, and he enacted a huge program into law. He was so bold and successful that he was elected chairman of the Southern Governors Conference in his second year, and chairman of the national Governors Conference in his third year. He was so bold and successful that he was turned out of office altogether in his fourth year.

Party politics, which pretended to be subordinate to common purpose during the war, burst forth grandly in the election of 1946, flaunting the hoopla of bosses struggling for control, powerful lobbies, big spending, and sharp issues. The state's leading Democrat, Governor O'Conor, ran for the Senate, defeating incumbent Democrat George L. Radcliffe in the primary and a retired brigadier general, D. John Markey, in the general election. In each case O'Conor won narrowly by promising to oppose the Russians more vigorously than his opponents. The larger battle was for the governorship and control of the Democratic party of the state.

Late in 1945 Lane announced first for the Democratic primary as a Fair Deal candidate from the west, calling for expanded public services, and making a strong appeal to Baltimore by calling for state reapportionment, which would benefit the city. He was eager to ally any precinct bosses of the city who were willing to challenge the city's superboss, William Curran. Next in the race was Congressman H. Streett Baldwin, boss of Baltimore County, fiercely anti-black, anti–New Deal, and anti-Communist. Third was State Comptroller Millard Tawes, reluctant candidate from the Eastern Shore, the front man for Curran. Baldwin attacked Lane's supporters as "Communists, agitators and left-wing radicals" who were out to "subvert the ranks of the Democratic party." Lane attacked Tawes as a small-time hack, a front for Curran. Tawes said very little.[12]

Lane won the primary easily because postwar voters demanded the social services he promised, and because antibossism was strong and anti-Communism had not yet crested. That was the lesson of 1946 politics. The general election was lackluster, based on party loyalty and personality, as Lane won handily over the liberal Republican mayor of Baltimore, mellifluous Theodore McKeldin. Lane, like Truman, was an honest man who could use organization politics but not be dominated by it. He could play tough politics, and he had somewhere to go.

Maryland's Fair Deal

In all matters regarding public services, Maryland ended the war as a deeply conservative state, more like the South than the North. By the end of Lane's administration it was a liberal state. In 1945 per capita expenditures for state services were $36.68, 14 percent below the national average. By 1950 expenditures were $61.27, 2 percent above the national average.[13]

The new administration dismissed out of hand the reports of the professional planners and depended instead on a special citizens' commission headed by Judge Joseph Sherbow. The formation of such commissions was a standard procedure for launching major state programs; for support by the members assured important commitments to the report from the outset. The Sherbow Report was especially significant. It was written largely by a remarkable staff member, V. O. Key, a young professor at Johns Hopkins who eventually became the nation's leading political scientist. A thoroughgoing study of the sources of revenue at all levels of local government, it was liberal in that it led to greatly expanded services, but it was conservative in calling for expenditures at the most local level and in viewing expenditures not as largesse but as investments that would pay off in increased income for individuals and the state. In the short run Maryland adopted this view and benefited; in the long run, as Lane feared, in Maryland and elsewhere centralized state bureaucracies continued to grow at the expense of the states.

Specifically, the Sherbow Report showed that town and county governments were failing because their revenues depended on property taxes, which had reached a practical limit. New services, which modern society demanded, had to come from income, corporation, and sales taxes, which could only be levied at the state and national level. The solution, according to Sherbow and V. O. Key? Let the states levy the taxes and pass revenues along to the localities to spend.[14]

Lane understood, and he forced the program through the 1947 General Assembly, the most effective session in Maryland's twentieth-century history. Mostly the program was a matter of establishing new state taxes, and this required all the persuasion the governor could muster. He appealed to moderates with the logic of the Sherbow Report, and to liberals with idealism. He appealed, one at a time, to all those who would benefit from taxes: the destitute local governments, parents and teachers of schoolchildren, the police, the road-builders, the staffs and the families of inmates in hospitals, prisons, and welfare institutions. He utilized his appointment powers to the utmost, rewarding loyal legislators and punishing recalcitrants. Most of all, he forced the question of taxes into the either-or framework.

The General Assembly gave Lane what he wanted, perhaps realizing better than he who would have to pay the political price. First came a new sales tax of 2 percent on all items costing more than nine cents, a not-so-novel idea: Maryland was the twenty-second state to adopt such a tax. Then came corporation taxes, up from 1 1/2 percent to 4 percent, gasoline taxes from four to five cents per gallon, income taxes from 2 percent to 2 1/2 percent, and taxes on investment income from 2 percent to 5 percent. Lane's political enemies were entirely correct: taxes rose more in Maryland during his four-year administration than they rose in any other state. It did not do Lane much good at reelection time to reply that people were enjoying the benefits, or that one of the most prosperous states still paid taxes only barely above the national average. A more serious charge was that several of the taxes were regressive, paid mostly by those who were least able to pay.[15]

From 1945 to 1951 the state budget increased more than 25 percent each year, from $60 million to $219 million (see table 4.1).[16] The most important increases from the standpoint of government procedures were the grants to counties and towns, up from $1.6 million to $14.6 million in direct appropriations, plus at least that much more that was appropriated for schools and hospitals and was given to the localities to spend. Most of the money came with strings attached—that it be matched in specified ways and spent for specified purposes. To receive anything at all the counties and towns had to submit to state audits and follow streamlined procedures as outlined in the Sherbow Report. Legislation granting money to the localities was highly complex, changing from year to year as state priorities changed and as political deals in the governor's office and the legislature required. Control of revenue collection centralized power at least as much as local spending decentralized it. The state sought particularly to equal-

Table 4.1.   State Expenditures, 1945 and 1951
(in Dollars)

Expenditure	1945	1951	Percentage Increase
Administration	2,888,000	8,123,000	181
Capital investment, bonds	6,124,000	27,810,000	451
Education	15,145,000	47,048,000	210
Health	5,888,000	19,057,000	236
Highways	13,287,000	67,609,000	409
Police and prisons	3,065,000	7,201,000	135
Supplement to counties	1,584,000	14,597,000	821
Welfare, Social Security	11,037,000	22,852,000	107
Miscellaneous	1,259,000	5,033,000	236
Total	60,277,000	219,330,000	264

Source: Comptroller of the Treasury, Annual Reports (1945, 1951).

ize educational, health, and welfare facilities, transferring a disproportionate share of the revenues from rich suburban counties to the poorer rural ones.

The state service that improved most in the postwar years, in response to the greatest demand for improvement, was education. Probably more than ever before in American history, education seemed to be the golden door to individual and social improvement. During Lane's administration teacher salaries increased 53 percent, from an annual average of $2,317 to $3,543. State incentives to the counties financed the construction of 208 new schools or major additions, and average class size declined from forty to thirty-three pupils. Operating budgets tripled for the state's colleges and universities. Parents and teachers remained Lane's most loyal constituents.[17]

State road building came in response to a different constituency: businessmen, farmers, and road builders. The program cost even more than the schools, and was paid for mostly by the gasoline tax (whose revenues were spent in the counties where the tax was collected so that road use partially dictated expenditures) and by bonds for which the bill came due in the future. The state built over eleven hundred miles of new roads in four years, including ninety-three miles of new dual highways, notably the Baltimore-Washington Parkway and the Annapolis-Washington Parkway. The administration claimed that one of the poorest road systems in the country rose to an above average rating. The state joined with Baltimore and federal agencies to move Baltimore's congested air terminal from the downtown area to the Friendship Methodist Church community on the city's outskirts. Areas that benefited most from roads and public projects showed, if anything, a negative correlation in their support of Lane between the 1946 and 1950 elections. Neighborhoods are offended more often than they are pleased by improvements in their midst.[18]

The most spectacular road project, which eventually became a symbol for Governor Lane and was named for him, was the Chesapeake Bay Bridge. It cost $45 million in the late 1940s and is one of the nation's most significant engineering feats. Discussed since the turn of the century, the bridge had symbolic importance, in tying together the

The William Preston Lane Memorial Bridge reoriented Eastern Shore economy from Philadelphia to Baltimore and Washington. Courtesy of M. E. Warren.

diverse halves of the state, and economic importance, in weaning the Eastern Shore from its railroad dependence on Philadelphia and Wilmington. A major private financing plan for the bridge failed in the Great Depression, and a public financing plan was interrupted by World War II. Then, under Lane's guidance, the whirlwind 1947 General Assembly gave approval to bond financing, to be repaid by tolls. After delays to restudy tunnel or bridge alternatives, construction began early in 1949, and the first traffic crossed in 1952. As a travelers' convenience it was a huge success, and it probably served to integrate the state and modernize the Eastern Shore. Decades later, however, there was still doubt over whether it had brought prosperity to the shore or had encouraged the ambitious to move out; and Eastern Shore reactionaries still wondered whether modernization and integration with the rest of the state was a mixed blessing.[19]

The third Lane program, along with education and roads, was expanded public health facilities, especially new hospital facilities for tubercular patients and the mentally ill. The movie *Snakepit* was making the rounds, and the *Sunpapers* ran a dramatic series showing mentally ill local children in dungeons, ankle deep in filth, and adults chained together, forty to a room. The General Assembly approved new facilities at Rosewood, Mt. Wilson, and Spring Grove, plus an important psychiatric institute for research at the University of Maryland. Expenditures for Maryland mental patients rose, and the state quickly rose from nineteen to sixth in such expenditures among all the states.[20]

During the remainder of Lane's term, following the session of 1947, the state expanded its Fair Deal program as revenue allowed. A special legislative session in 1948 increased state employees' salaries; the 1949 session added more appropriations for schools, roads, and hospitals; and the 1950 session followed the recommendation of the Sherbow Report in implementing annual legislative sessions and annual budgets.

There were also things left undone. Lane put off the promised reapportionment of the state because Baltimore politicians who publicly embraced expanded city representation really preferred not to upset their local balances. Perennial efforts to rescue the declining oyster industry failed because oystermen preferred immediate small profits to the larger ones that conservation would bring in the future. Plans for an organized and expanded system of higher education lay moldering on the shelves.

For all of Lane's successes his, like Truman's, was a harassed administration. People were uneasy in the modern world. Politicians were embroiled in ferocious disputes over legalizing or outlawing gambling in some county, in expanding or curtailing the season for some race track, or in firing or appointing roads and police commissioners. All this was the daily chaff of politics, but it was carried on with greater harshness than usual. For the public, much more than for politicians, anger focused on the new taxes, especially the sales tax. Merchants apologized for the tax by sneering that it was "Pennies for Lane," and the slogan became better known than the governor himself. People tossed pennies when he appeared in public until he was forced to cancel public appearances. On one occasion, when Lane's wife presented roses to the winner at a racetrack, people tossed pennies and booed until she was reduced to tears. Lane called a special session of the legislature to increase the amount exempted from tax from nine to fourteen cents, and he promised that if he were reelected he would call another special session to increase the exemption to fifty cents.[21]

More serious was public demand for anti-communist legislation, with its implication that local radicals were responsible for Russia's growing power abroad, and maybe for liberal programs in Maryland as well. Lane, like most of the legislature, knew better, but in 1948 he dutifully appointed the antisubversive study commission that the legislature demanded, and the following year he sadly, and without comment, signed its recommendations into law.

When Lane announced for reelection in 1950 he had the support of almost every leader of the Democratic party, almost every newspaper, and almost every responsible voter, but that was not enough. In the Democratic primary, where he was expecting no opposition, George P. Mahoney, a Baltimore contractor, entered at the last moment, calling for expanded state services and an end to the sales tax, not worrying about how the budget might be balanced. Lane won, but, to everyone's surprise, by the narrowest margin. In the general election the liberal Republican Theodore McKeldin, former mayor of Baltimore, won easily, calling, like Mahoney, for more services and fewer taxes. For all their frustrations about taxes, every politician recognized the demand for expanded services as well.[22] Actually, McKeldin raised taxes during his first year in office, and in fact he may have pushed along Lane's progressive program faster than Lane could have done. The Fair Deal was secure and was consolidated by an amiable Eisenhower, who pretended he was against it. There was no other way to go.

What the Maryland political experience of 1945 to 1951 seemed to say about America was, first of all, that there was an irresistible demand for public services. The postwar era was not the death of New Deal liberalism, as national historians sometimes say, but its transfer to local initiative and its triumph. At the community, county, and state levels, where the local establishments had long resisted big spending, there was now surging demand for better schools to provide an avenue of opportunity, for new roads to accommodate a torrent of cars, and for systematized public care to replace private charity for the afflicted, diseased, and poor. The movement for public services gained strength from the swelling numbers of southerners who migrated to the factory areas, from rural black immigrants to the cities, and from civil service workers who moved to the suburbs, and they faced little opposition. Locally, almost all politicians were calling for big spending for new services.

Second, Maryland reflected the national trend toward power concentration even while voters called for decentralization. The nation was increasingly collecting the taxes and assuming the powers that had once belonged to the states, the states were taking over from the counties, and the counties from the communities. Lane justified the efficiency of centralized revenue collection and standardized services by reverting revenue and delegating administration to the localities, although the trend still veered toward centralization. Lane and most of his generation were mistaken, however, in assuming that centralization was necessarily so dire. There was probably more fairness and honesty in centralized bureaucracy than in community politics.

Finally, Maryland demonstrated the dilemma of an able leadership that had no reasonable alternative to the direction it was taking. For all the unanimity of demand for public services, people harbored immense resentment at having to pay for them. Lane reasonably faced the alternative of more services and more taxes, or fewer services and fewer taxes, and the choice was plain; but voters could angrily demand more services and fewer taxes without bothering about the contradiction.

The matter-of-fact, nonidealistic, dogged liberalism of Truman and Lane provided a certain stability to government but did not still the seething public frustration. Voters turned on both of them and then began looking under beds for even more diabolical villains. The triumph of liberalism did not bring peace of mind.

Communism and the cold war were mostly matters of philosophy and foreign relations, but occasionally American communities were caught up in the complex issues of liberty and equality, democracy and totalitarianism, appeasement and coexistence, war and peace. This chapter is a look at communism and the cold war from the grass roots up, especially during the years from 1944 to 1952, when the attention of Marylanders was most intensely focused on these issues.

Marxism and the Communist party were in fact quite real in Maryland before 1950, and, by coincidence, the two most prominent Americans accused of subversion, Alger Hiss and Owen Lattimore, were both Marylanders. The Maryland anti-communist movement was more zealous than anti-communist movements elsewhere. Well before McCarthyism became a national phenomenon, the state passed the strongest loyalty oath in the country, compiled lists of its undesirable citizens, and pressed the federal government for stronger action against communism and the Soviet Union. Then, early in the 1950s, the state backed off and tried to separate itself from these frightening matters.

The first important Maryland discussion of Marxism took place in 1866 at the Baltimore convention of the National Labor Union. The convention provided one of the significant bridges by which the European idea traveled to the New World. Marxism found its first applicable expression in Maryland during the bitter strike against the Baltimore and Ohio Railroad in 1877, when strike leaders spoke of a war on capitalism, and after the strike was crushed, when almost half the voters in Baltimore and western Maryland cast ballots for the socialist candidates of the Workingman's party. Thereafter, Marxism and its various expressions waned and reemerged periodically into the 1920s but never received more than 5 percent of the state's votes.

In 1919, following the Russian Revolution, the American Communist party broke away from the socialists and determined to follow the example of the Soviet Union. This provoked furious reaction in America, and during the following year the federal government arrested 2,700 presumed Communists, including at least 62 in Baltimore. Most of those arrested in Baltimore—and eventually released—were Russian immigrants who were presumed to be loyal to the revolution in the old country. For a short time in the early 1920s the party almost disappeared, but as persecution ended and the depression arrived, a reconstituted Communist party emerged.

There is not much mystery left about the party that developed in Maryland during the depression. Despite the cult of secrecy, party members were too much inclined to apostasy and confession, and investigatory enemies were too powerful to leave them much cover. Many literate people have provided accounts of their experiences in the party, and freedom of information laws have forced police agencies to release most of their records. Probably no other political group in Maryland history has such an accessible record.

During the early 1930s about seventy-five communists in Baltimore were loosely organized as a subdistrict of the party's Philadelphia

Communism in Maryland

branch. The first major organizing effort came in 1934, when New York headquarters dispatched Earl C. Reno and Harry Fields, both native Americans of working-class background, to organize Maryland and the District of Columbia as District Four, with headquarters in Baltimore. By 1938 District Four had about one hundred and eighty members in Baltimore, about one hundred and fifty in Washington and its suburbs, about fifty in Cumberland, and about fifty more scattered through the state. These members paid their dues of between 50 cents and $1.25 a week, depending on their income, and they were available at any time to man picket lines or distribute leaflets. If those who occasionally paid dues or attended were included, the number of visible communist sympathizers in the state doubled. In addition, as enemies claimed, for every member there were four or five fellow travelers who were not afraid of the communist label, read the *Daily Worker,* and were ready to sign petitions or consider the party's advice in elections. Altogether, this means some five hundred party members in Maryland, and maybe two thousand active sympathizers.[1]

To appear on the ballot in Maryland a party had to have received 1 percent of the vote in the preceding election or present a petition signed by at least two thousand voters. Always in the 1930s the party was forced to petition, and a major portion of its effort was directed to appearing on the ballot. Between 1920 and 1940 the party managed to offer one of its members for most statewide elections, usually gaining about one thousand votes of some four hundred thousand cast. Generally the votes were widely scattered in every county and every ward of Baltimore, indicating a protest against major candidates rather than a positive vote of a closely knit group. People noted, of course, that the total communist vote was always smaller than the number of petitioners, and investigations revealed that many of the names on petitions were fraudulently obtained.[2]

During the 1930s the party sought publicity. Although records of membership were secret because of fear of reprisals, meetings were generally open. There were ten or twenty cells in Baltimore—the number varied considerably from year to year—and each was attended by twenty or thirty members and visitors. Cells were organized primarily by industry, although members could float from one cell to another. Meetings were generally held every two weeks and were devoted to discussions of theoretical Marxism, world and national politics, and, especially, strategy for promoting party goals within a particular industry or plant. Every few months a city or district meeting was held, and frequently a party speaker, such as Earl Browder, William Z. Foster, or Elizabeth Gurley Flynn from New York headquarters, attended. Meetings were generally reported in the press, and sometimes they attracted more than a thousand people. One of the most successful communist enterprises was the organization in 1936 of a demonstration in which several thousand people protested the Baltimore docking of the Nazi cruiser *Emden.*

Communist speakers often excited opposition, and violence was always nearby. A party-sponsored mixed-race dance in 1933 produced the expected melee. In 1937 a clash between the fascist group calling itself the Baltimore Blackshirts and the communists produced a miniature riot. The following year a communist-led strike for peace at the Johns Hopkins University resulted in scuffling. Strikes, at which communist soapbox orators were almost certain to be present, often resulted in fights, and newspapers regularly commented on the degree to which communist parades were orderly. Party rallies centered around celebrations of Lenin's birthday, May Day, and the anniversary of the Russian Revolution.[3]

World War II served to strengthen the party, particularly in terms of its acceptability, primarily because of communist determination to subordinate all criticism of capitalism to an allied victory. The party ceased offering candidates for office after the 1940 election, partly as a result of scrutiny of its election petitions, but also because of its strategy to support the war effort. Instead of supporting strikes it opposed them. Its chief propaganda effort favored an early second front against Hitler. In 1944 its national convention actually dissolved the American Communist party, changing the group's name to the Communist Political Association and its nature to that of a study club. In an effort to demonstrate acceptance of the American system, the association endorsed Roosevelt for a fourth term, and this reinforced the Republican charge of Democratic party–Communist party complicity.[4]

The end of the war brought a major upheaval in American communism as the hard-liners reasserted themselves and re-created the party in its most pro-Soviet form. Delegates from District Four at the 1945 national convention joined in denouncing the party's wartime leader, Earl Browder, who had argued that the party could operate within the boundaries of the United States Constitution. The radicals, led by William Z. Foster, maintained that communism must develop primarily through the expansion of the Soviet Union and that the aim of local units was to promote that end. Moscow, through public announcements, supported the revolt against Browder, but American Communists viewed the party's swing as a movement of local units against conservative national leadership. In October 1945 the District Four convention in Baltimore expressed unanimous support for the radical triumph.[5]

The pro-Moscow stance doomed the American Communist party, for it permanently severed the tenuous alliance of communism with American liberalism and American labor, and it directed public wrath against the party. The party of the left, as Europeans liked to say, had become the party of the east.[6] In the short term the party grew; membership in Maryland peaked from 1945 to 1948 at 450 members in Maryland and 280 in Washington. No longer were off-and-on members allowed. It was still a pitifully small number, a fraction of what the party's enemies imagined.

The postwar party growth spurt was based not so much on rejection of capitalism as on personal frustration. Many of the new members were veterans who were dissatisfied with available peacetime jobs, many were blacks who were angry about discrimination, many were workers who were radicalized by bitter postwar strikes. A large majority of the postwar members were laborers—steelworkers, longshoremen, textile workers, coal miners, and others—as they had been in the 1930s. At least one-third of the postwar membership was black.

The party cultivated a proletarian base, discouraging the membership of students, librarians, and clerks. Weekly dues rose to almost 10 percent of members' income, and there were frequent drives for contributions. Most of the money covered local expenses, although some went to New York headquarters. Money flowed up; probably there was never a net balance of outside support flowing into the state.[7]

The chairman of District Four was appointed by New York headquarters, and, after discussion above and below, he appointed about seven others who served with him as an executive board. This board included a secretary for organization, a secretary for labor, the chairman of the Baltimore cells, the chairman of the Washington cells, an attorney, a secretary, and a treasurer. Board members worked together almost daily and met formally each Friday evening. The board worked with a central committee, which included about twenty-five elected delegates and met monthly in the mid-1940s, but by 1948, as government surveillance increased, the committee seldom met more often than semiannually. Theoretically the committee made policy for the district, but in actuality it relayed decisions from above back to the rank and file.

The members of the executive board were hard-line and hard-core, about equally middle class and proletarian in background, mostly natives of Maryland, frequently Jewish. Most of them were full-time paid party workers, living in the 1940s on wages of twenty-five to seventy-five dollars weekly, depending on family size. New York headquarters paid them from local dues, but money was always tight, and sometimes the party defaulted on salaries. The leaders were cool headed and able, suitable for managing a corporation or serving on a governor's council. Their lives were difficult and dangerous, but communism provided them with a tightly knit intellectual system, persecution provided community and excitement, and leading a movement that they believed represented the future provided a personal fulfillment. They never thought of themselves as acting on orders from Moscow, but they accepted the dogma that the triumph of the Soviet Union was desirable, and their stands on peace or strikes or race were, if not directed to that end, at least not contradictory to it.[8]

The chairman of District Four from 1938 to 1941 was a native of Baltimore, Albert E. Blumberg, a graduate of Johns Hopkins who held a doctorate in philosophy from the University of Vienna and was a philosophy instructor at Hopkins from 1933 to 1937. Remembering anti-Semitism in Vienna and angry about the depression, he joined the Communist party in 1933, rose rapidly to local leadership, and went on to serve national headquarters as legislative advisor and Washington lobbyist. Al Lannon, district chairman from 1941 to 1946, was a Brooklyn-born seaman who had jumped ship in the 1930s to study in the Soviet Union and who returned to this country as a party organizer. He was nonintellectual, warm, and engaging, a Communist of the heart. The toughest executive of the group was the classic old Bolshevik Philip Frankfeld, who was chairman from 1946 to 1951; Frankfeld was born in New York in 1907, once held a job as a postal worker, and became a full-time party organizer in 1922. He studied in Moscow in 1931, was a union activist with a record of more than twenty arrests for radical activity during the 1930s, and was a corporal in the Second World War. He was erudite and hard-driving, a tough disciplinarian. George E. Meyers, District Four chairman from 1951 to 1952, was a labor organizer who moved leftward into the party. He was the son of an immigrant Cumberland coal picker who, Meyers claimed, nearly starved during the depression. Herbert Kransdorf, chairman from 1952 to 1954, was a New York seaman who had long been a labor organizer for the party. In addition to serving as chairmen, Blumberg, Lannon, Frankfeld, Meyers, and Kransdorf also occupied various positions on the executive board.

Other leaders included Maurice Braverman, a taxi driver studying at night to join the bar. Ostracized by the legal community for taking on radical clients, he joined the party in 1942 and served as its local attorney, although he never received a party salary. Dorothy Rose Oppenheim Blumberg, wife of Albert Blumberg, was the beautiful daughter of a wealthy Baltimore industrialist and a graduate of Goucher College. Regina Frankfeld, wife of Philip Frankfeld, was a Jewish refugee from Hitler and a Baltimore public school teacher. William C. Taylor was a black steelworker. Leroy H. Wood was a steelworker and professional union organizer. One of the best-known Maryland party leaders was Mary Stalcup Markward, a Washington beautician who was especially respected for her brilliance and loyalty—and who, for the entire period of her membership (from 1943 to 1950), was an undercover informer for the Federal Bureau of Investigation. All of these people held positions on the board in the 1930s, 1940s, and 1950s.[9]

The party's leadership was always on the lookout for people to recruit into its ranks from below, but there was a big gap in dedication and ability between leaders and followers. The various federal and state government investigations identified at least two hundred members of the Maryland party, and about forty were called before hearings to testify. Most party members had been born before 1915, approximately one-fifth of them in eastern Europe, especially Finland. The great majority were workers, frequently in steel, and they usually had not completed high school. A few were small shopkeepers, but only a handful were clearly of the middle class—an occasional physician, minister, lawyer, or concert pianist. Almost all members of the rank and file declined to testify against themselves, but it is clear that their radicalism was largely emotional rather than theoretical, and their value to the party was limited.[10]

For all the ruthlessness of revolutionary theory, Maryland Communists thought of themselves as standing for brotherhood and humanity. Certainly in their own eyes, and probably in fact, they tended as a group to be warm and humane people who were sentimental more than cynical, and concerned for the downtrodden. To be sure, novelists and psychologists often note the close relationship between idealism and ruthlessness. But generally Maryland Communists were less concerned by their failure to promote ultimate revolution than with what they regarded as their successes in awakening the United States to the danger of fascism and in promoting better working conditions for labor and civil rights for blacks. In this regard they saw themselves as their conservative enemies did, as the militant advance guard of liberalism.

Despite the solidarity and authoritarianism of the party, tensions were inevitable in such a self-conscious and theoretical group, tensions as old as Bolshevists and Menshevists, Stalin and Trotsky. There were the leaders and the rank and file, there were the foreign-born working-class old timers and the native middle-class recruits, there were practical reformers and those more interested in ultimate ends, there were those concerned with strikes and demonstrations and those concerned with party discipline and security. In a general way, the tensions between these groups explained the split between Browder and Foster. Immense variation characterized this dialectic in Maryland, but, despite ceaseless internal disputation, the local party's development can be understood less in terms of ideology than in terms of personality of its leaders and the evolution of the national party line.[11]

Increasingly after 1945 Maryland Communists went underground, a move that alarmed enemies almost as much as did the party's pro-Moscow line. Public parades and rallies became rare, and usually only Frankfeld's and Blumberg's names were used publicly. The party maintained a cluttered three-room suite in the Baltimore slums, variously on Eutaw, Franklin, and Liberty streets, replete with hammer-and-sickle flag on the door; this provided an official address, which by law was required to be placed on all publications. District and city-wide meetings ended, and admission to cell meetings was limited to members. To insure security, the number of cells was greatly increased, to more than sixty in Baltimore, while membership in each one was held to fewer than a dozen, and by 1952 to only three or four. Floating between cells ended. Policy came to the cell through meetings of the central committee, by word of mouth, through couriers from the executive board, and through publications like the *Clarion* from Baltimore and the *Daily Worker* from New York.[12]

The party's chief effort was in promoting liberal causes, claiming credit for liberal legislation, and seeking reliable new members. The weekly literature and cell discussions focused more on domestic than on foreign affairs: the need for continuation of price and rent controls, for public housing, for legislation to outlaw racial discrimination; support for prolabor candidates such as President Truman and Maryland Governor William Preston Lane; and opposition to antilabor politicians such as Maryland Senators Millard E. Tydings and Herbert R. O'Conor. Even its foreign policy stands, although always supportive of Soviet stands, were usually much like those of many noncommunist Americans. A major party effort went into publication of the tabloid periodical the *Clarion,* which appeared during 1946 and 1947 and proclaimed the party's liberal views.

To promote its cause more directly, the local party made valiant efforts, which were never successful, to gain control of unions, particularly in industries such as steel in Baltimore and some of the building trades in Washington. Short of gaining control of labor, the party supported strikes of any kind and rushed to join and claim credit for those that occurred without its instigation. The party was far too small to think of revolution within the foreseeable future, and investigators and apostates never suggested that there was evidence of sabotage or espionage.[13]

The Maryland Communists devoted themselves in 1948 to the presidential campaign of the Progressive party candidate, Henry Wallace, but communist support by then was a kiss of death. Although Wallace won ten thousand votes in Maryland—2 percent of the total cast and enough to shift Maryland's electoral vote from Truman to Dewey—the Wallace vote almost certainly would have been larger without communist support. Wallace was among the last in his party to discover and denounce his communist allies, and he left the Progressive party himself in 1949. The Maryland Communists were able in 1950 to use the Progressive party hulk to field their own candidates, who each received about five hundred votes.[14]

Party efforts after 1949 were dedicated primarily to staying alive. Frankfeld ostentatiously supported Maryland's first loyalty law of 1947 (which required candidates for office to swear loyalty), claiming that Communists were in fact loyal; but in 1949 the second loyalty law effectively outlawed the party, and it desperately fought the law. All members from the Washington cells were ordered into Maryland to campaign, and lack of zeal brought fines and even expulsion from the party.[15] Communist opposition only eased the passage of the bill, however, first through the legislature in 1949, and then in a statewide referendum in 1950. Just over a year later, Philip Frankfeld, Meyers, Braverman, Wood, Regina Frankfeld, and Dorothy Rose Blumberg were sentenced to jail. Kransdorf was left, and he pretended the party was still alive, but membership had dwindled to a few score, several of whom supported themselves by selling information to the state and federal governments.[16]

The jailing of the party leaders in 1952 nearly spelled the end for Maryland communism, although the final paroxysm was internal. Unexpected continuing postwar prosperity hurt the cause, and during the Korean War (1950 to 1953), many of the rank and file would not oppose the United States as doctrine required. Intellectuals reeled under the Soviet Union's suppression of the Hungarian revolt in 1956. The final straw was Khrushchev's 1957 denunciation of Stalin's brutalities, for the faithful learned that they had been deluded in denying those brutalities. The party disappeared as an organized structure; the *Daily Worker* ended publication.[17]

The Communist party was a faith and a way of life for people, and it made a partial comeback as persecution ended and as the New Left appeared on American campuses in the 1960s. The party attracted about one hundred members during the 1960s and 1970s, members who once again were card carrying and moderately public in their activities. Membership consisted largely of older people from the earlier days, but a few young members were attracted to the historical name and the old radical leadership. The literature was stridently antimilitarist and prolabor, but half a dozen other left-wing groups considered the party hopelessly rightist because of its support for the most liberal of major party candidates.[18] Of the old Maryland leadership, only George E. Meyers remained in the party, as national secretary for labor. The Blumbergs, Braverman, Kransdorf, Taylor, and

Wood all left the party and became moderately successful in other occupations. All retained pride in what they regarded as party accomplishments and sympathy for party aims. Reno and Markward denounced it and turned to the right. Frankfeld and Lannon were dead.

Historians in recent years have gained considerable understanding of the American communist movement, and the Maryland story supports their findings. The movement was real enough, it had deep American roots, and a certain type of people found a congenial home in its conspiratorial atmosphere. The party was not engaged in subversion because it was too weak, but it did reject the constitutional system and embrace the theory of revolution. It was not exactly in the service of a foreign state, but it idealized the Soviet Union, somewhat like Zionists idealized Israel, and it saw Soviet goals and its own as identical. The movement failed in America because conspiracy was hardly necessary to further most of its views, because the movement was tiny and easily destroyed, and because its diehards finally became disillusioned by Soviet actions. The party was hardly a threat to America. Its main significance, at least after 1944, was its usefulness to its enemies.

Origins of the Anti-Communist Movement

Communists believed, theoretically, in revolution, but opponents of communism constituted a revolution—or at least a revolt—against the New Deal, centralization, bureaucracy, and the philosophical ambivalence of the age. In Maryland, the anti-communist movement had little to do with foreign policy, or with the geopolitical logic of Winston Churchill and George F. Kennan, and it preceded the national emergence of Senator Joseph McCarthy. It grew out of local political rhetoric and out of the concerns of specific groups—notably, conservative politicians, Catholics, military groups, and businessmen. Each for different reasons coalesced around the hunt for Communists. The cold war events of Yalta, NATO, the Berlin Blockade, and Korea certainly fed the local anti-communist movement, but there could be little doubt that local excitement also fed the cold war.

Anti-communism, like communism, had a long Maryland heritage, dating back at least to the red scare of the 1920s and to the rhetoric of the 1930s which charged the New Deal with taking deliberate steps toward Marxist goals. A high point in the rhetoric came in the otherwise muted presidential campaign of 1944, after the Communists had endorsed Roosevelt, when the Democratic and the Republican side each wrapped itself in the flag to imply that the other side signified treason. Roosevelt was partially responsible, claiming that Republicans were "making a deliberate effort to place political advantage over devotion to duty." Local Democrats intensified the message. "Hitler and Hirohito want you to discard your Commander-in-Chief!" said a Maryland billboard. On the day before the election the Maryland Democratic party sponsored a newspaper advertisement that read, in part, "To a soldier's Mother. . . . Why do you suppose the Jap and Nazi radios are urging the election of Dewey? . . . Don't Gamble With the Life of Your Son! Vote to Keep Franklin D. Roosevelt as the Head of Our Government!"[19]

The Republicans' Thomas E. Dewey responded similarly: "In Rus-

sia a Communist is a man who supports his government," he said. "In
America a Communist is a man who supports the fourth term so that
our form of government may be more easily changed." Dewey frequently quoted communist Earl Browder's endorsement of Roosevelt,
and publicly he wondered if Roosevelt had made "deals" to accommodate Stalin after the war. In Maryland the *Sunpapers'* best-known
columnist, Frank Kent, devoted at least nine columns to the Demo-
cratic-Communist alliance, and the Maryland Republican party made
it their central campaign theme. "What Are You Doing to Offset the
Communist Menace?" cried one advertisement. Another spoke of
"The New-Deal-Fourth-Deal-Communist Forces," and another
screamed of "Hordes of Communists, fellow travelers and collectivist
well-wishers working incessantly to capture key positions."[20]

Roosevelt won, but by a smaller margin than before, and the direction of opposition was fixed. Frustration gripped conservatives, for
Roosevelt appeared invincible and big government continued to grow
bigger. For conservatives the drift to communism, or even the conspiratorial drive to communism, was a self-satisfying explanation of all
they disliked in the modern world, and their attack on communism
was a way to argue that the country was losing its old freedoms.

In the Maryland elections of 1946 not all conservatives used the
anti-communist rhetoric, but some in each party extended it beyond
the earlier excesses. In the Democratic gubernatorial primary, H.
Streett Baldwin attacked his liberal opponent, William Preston Lane,
saying, "Communism is the only issue in this campaign." He charged
that Lane was "surrounded by fellow travelers, parlor pinks and out-
right Communists, headed by such men as Harold Ickes, James
Roosevelt and Henry Wallace." In the general election for governor,
the Republican candidate, Theodore R. McKeldin, steered clear of
such language, but the party headed its advertisements with "Ameri-
canism or Communism?"[21] Still more portentous was the victorious
senatorial campaign of former Governor Herbert R. O'Conor, who
was never one to miss a trend and who outdid his Republican challenger in identifying liberalism and subversion. The search for treason
became the theme of O'Conor's senatorial career, and he became
chairman of the American Bar Association's Committee on Subversion. On the national scene he was later surpassed in ability, if not in
shrillness, by Senators Patrick A. McCarran, Joseph R. McCarthy,
and Richard M. Nixon.[22]

Maryland politicians in 1948 temporarily backed off the communist
issue. For one thing, President Truman grasped the political message
of the 1946 elections and partially defused the issue by his own loyalty
drive of 1947 which forced the resignation of 6,414 federal employees
for whom there was insufficient positive evidence of patriotism. Also,
Henry Wallace's 1948 communist-supported presidential candidacy
served to lift the burden of radicalism from other candidates. But by
the 1950 elections the campaign technique of charging opponents with
radicalism surged stronger than ever, and by then other major forces
promoted the rhetoric.

The strongest organization to join the anti-communist crusade in
Maryland was the Roman Catholic church, guided especially by

Father John Francis Cronin. From 1933 to 1967 Father Cronin was a professor of labor economics at St. Mary's Seminary in Baltimore. A dedicated liberal, he wrote a dozen volumes on the rights of labor and the dangers of communist atheism. Father Cronin worked directly with the Baltimore union movements during the 1930s, came to know the local Communists thoroughly, and regularly offered "Cronin" candidates in union elections when he suspected the party was gaining control. Party officials considered him their most effective opponent. Meanwhile the Maryland Catholic weekly, the *Catholic Review,* crusaded against communist atheism in Spain and the Soviet Union. During the war the journal kept up the attack, publishing at least as many articles and editorials against Stalin as against Hitler.[23]

The Catholic church's alarm increased as the war ended and communism began its suppression of religion in eastern Europe, and Father Cronin took his anti-communist crusade to the national level. In 1945 Father Cronin presented the bishops of the Church with a 148-page document entitled "The Problem of American Communism" which was based on his privileged though unofficial perusal of the files of the Federal Bureau of Investigation and the House Un-American Activities Committee. Although the bishops did not act officially on the Cronin report, Cronin was appointed liaison on the subject of communism between the church hierarchy in the United States, the government of the United States, and the United States Chamber of Commerce. It was a powerful nexus.[24]

Ethnic groups in Maryland, meanwhile, shared letters from relatives about hardships of Soviet occupation in the old country, and churches with large eastern European congregations held masses for their oppressed brethren. In March 1946, almost a year prior to the Marshall Plan or the theory of containment, the Maryland Knights of Columbus began a letter-writing campaign to persuade Congress to take a stronger stand against the Soviet Union. A few months later the Knights of Columbus launched a series of six local radio broadcasts designed "to expose the evils of Communism."[25] By the end of the year the Maryland chapters of the Hibernians, the Catholic War Veterans, the Maryland Action Guild, the Catholic Daughters of America, and the Federation of Catholic Alumnae all passed resolutions urging stronger American opposition to communism. Politicians placed their strongest anti-communist advertisements in Catholic journals.[26] The Maryland Board of Motion Picture Censors, whose interests in the past had been mostly limited to sex, outlawed the showing of a documentary film, "Our Polish Land," on the grounds that it "showed priests and nuns freely entering their churches when, according to all reports, their persecutions and denial of freedom by the Russian-Communist dominated Polish government was actually taking place."[27]

The Maryland Masons, who also had strong European connections, shared the Catholic concern about communist atheism. In 1947 the Maryland Grand Lodge departed from its traditional nonpolitical stance to denounce communist imperialism and launch a campaign to awaken the public to its danger.[28] Protestant churches generally came late and hesitantly into the anti-communist movement, although fundamentalist groups particularly warmed to the concept of good versus evil.

Other major groups that came early and ardently to the anti-communist movement were military officers, veterans' organizations, and the police. Often they knew firsthand, better than the war-weary public, the nature of the Soviet Union's occupation policy, but, also, they lived on violence and enhanced themselves by projecting a worthy enemy. Brigadier generals and colonels were favorite speakers at service clubs immediately after the war, and well before American policy had hardened, their message frequently was of the Soviet Union's intransigence. J. Edgar Hoover launched a major publicity campaign in 1946 to alert the nation to the hard-line dogma of the American Communist party, and his agents became regularly available on the speaker's circuit. Within the year, Maryland associations of the American Legion, Veterans of Foreign Wars, Catholic Veterans, Jewish Veterans, and the Twenty-Ninth Division were mobilized. Local police chiefs, themselves often active in veterans' organizations, were frequently leaders of the anti-communist movement. They provided the inside information that often served as inspiration for others.[29]

Maryland business leaders came later to the anti-communist crusade, but they were ultimately the most important group. Chafing under wartime economic controls that continued after the war, they were responsive to the extreme rhetoric of the politicians. More specifically, businessmen were disturbed by labor unrest—involving the most crippling strikes in American history—which began late in 1945, peaked in 1947, and continued intermittently into the 1950s. Maryland was far from the worst-hit state, but it had more than the average amount of strike activity.[30]

Although every major union in Maryland prohibited communist membership by 1946 and denounced communist support, the Communists claimed credit for the strikes, and many businessmen were ready to accept their claim. Roosevelt himself had encouraged the idea that wartime strikes approached treason, and it was easy for those hurt by labor unrest to think of the postwar strikes as nothing less than sabotage by the Soviet Union. Father Cronin formulated the argument for the United States Chamber of Commerce, and the National Association of Manufacturers took up the cry. Local business journals like *Baltimore* and the *Manufacturer's Record* repeated the refrain: strikes were the manifestation of communist subversion.[31]

During 1946 and 1947 a long list of Baltimore civic clubs and trade associations appointed committees to alert the nation to the communist menace: the Bar Association, chamber of commerce, junior chamber of commerce, Civitans, Farm Bureau, Kiwanis, Lions, Medical Society, Optimists, Rotary, along with groups representing canned foods, furniture, laundries, lumber, petroleum, grocers, and truckers. The Crusade For Freedom emerged to broadcast radio messages into eastern Europe. The National Education Fund provided anti-communist speakers to public groups. Other groups were the Association for the Preservation of American Ideals, the International Brotherhood of Christians, the Minute Women of the United States, and the Baltimore All-American Conference to Combat Communism.[32]

The Baltimore Kiwanis Club proposed an "organization of organizations" to fight communism, and in September 1948 ninety delegates from fifty organizations attended a meeting to form the Maryland Committee against Un-American Activities. Wilmer C. Carter, a local insurance executive and state senator from Baltimore, was elected chairman, and a few weeks later William C. Crane became the salaried executive director. Crane named chairmen for each county of Maryland and soon claimed that the number of participating organizations had doubled.[33]

For Maryland, at least, the crusade against communism was fully launched by late 1948. This was hardly a "red scare" in the sense that people were frightened, as many had been in 1919, but the crusade provided a banner under which different groups could march for different ends: conservative politicians to gain election over liberals, Catholics to lash out at atheism in eastern Europe, paramilitary groups to enhance themselves through a worthy enemy, and businessmen to vent their outrage over strikes for which Communists claimed credit. This was a wave of public opinion, swelling from the grass roots, ready to reshape democracy in order to save it. National and international events paralleled the movement, obviously serving as an impetus to the surging local opinion, but also being affected immeasurably, as well (see table 5:1).

For Maryland, the catalyst for this shift from organizing to taking direct action was the trial of Alger Hiss. Its impact everywhere was great, but especially so in Maryland. The Hiss family had been part of the Baltimore social establishment since the eighteenth century, and a Baltimore suburban avenue was named for the family. Alger Hiss was an honor graduate of the Johns Hopkins University, and, in recognition of his distinguished career in the Department of State, Johns Hopkins honored him at its June 1948 commencement. Two months later Whittaker Chambers, a former *Time* magazine editor, accused Hiss of being a communist spy and led reporters to Hiss's Carroll

Table 5.1.   The United States and the Cold War

Year	Foreign	Domestic
1945	Soviet occupation of Eastern Europe	
1946		Major labor unrest; Communists claim credit
1947	Marshall Plan to rebuild Western Europe	Truman orders loyalty tests for U.S. employees
1948	Soviet Union blockades Berlin	Trial of Alger Hiss
1949	NATO created Communists win China	
1950		Senator McCarthy makes charges McCarran Act requires registration of Communists and sympathizers
1950–1953	Korean War	
1954		Censure of McCarthy

County farm, where treasonous documents were hidden in a pumpkin patch. The first trial, in November, ended with a hung jury, and the second trial, in 1949, ended with Hiss convicted, not of espionage, but of perjury for claiming to be innocent. Many people were upset by the indirection of the case against him and were still more upset by the implication that New Dealers generally were tinged with disloyalty. For others, however, the trial cemented the link between liberalism and treason.[34]

The anti-communist movement came earlier to Maryland than to the rest of the nation, and almost certainly it was more intense there than in most states, but it also faded rapidly and actually did less damage to liberty and liberalism than might have been expected. It was an alarming surge of public opinion that momentarily threatened democratic institutions, but it was checked in time, and largely by the inexorable operation of those institutions.

Protecting Democracy

The movement found its most irresponsible expression in the General Assembly, where public opinion brought assembly concurrence with actions that often passed because delegates trusted the executive branch and the courts to redress their excesses. This yielding to constituent passion appeared notably in the foreign policy resolutions that swept the General Assembly from 1947 to 1953. Resolutions of this sort were irrelevant to the legislature's work, and they were unheard-of in the assembly before or after, but they passed, usually without opposition, as a means of pleasing constitutents and as a courtesy to the occasional delegate who cared about them.

Foreign affairs first surfaced in the 1947 Maryland legislature, when the delegates, after long but wholly favorable discussion, informed President Truman and the Congress that worldwide communism was "a derogation of the basic principles of democracy and a menace to international unity." In the next meeting of the assembly in 1949, foreign relations resolutions became a regular agenda item under the heading "Communist Bills." The assembly condemned the trial of Cardinal Mindszensky, the suppression of Lithuania, the occupation of Czechoslovakia, and the government of Bulgaria, and it called for the expulsion of the Soviet Union from the United Nations. It called for an independent Israel as a bulwark to freedom, and it wrangled inconclusively about advising the United States to withdraw from the United Nations. Foreign policy resolutions continued to be made until 1953; they often concerned small details of international relations, and they were always formally dispatched to members of Congress and the Department of State. The resolutions reflected opinion, uncontained by international realities, which was too strong at least for local legislators to resist.[35]

The General Assembly moved from foreign to defense policy in 1949 by holding hearings on the readiness of the state to prevent sabotage and repel invasion. The state adjutant general, Major General Milton A. Reckord, testified that the federal government was unprepared, and he urged the state to develop plans for its own defense. The legislature responded by creating the Maryland Civil

Defense Agency, whose work would be carried out by a paid staff of
twelve, plus volunteers, who would work with the federal government, the state National Guard, and with state and local police to
protect citizens against foreign attack, subversion, and natural disasters. Two years later the assembly approved a $2.5 million bond issue
for defense equipment, including an underground headquarters bun-
ker in Pikesville. The Assembly authorized the agency's director to
enter into "Mutual Aid Pacts" with other states to insure exchange of
men and equipment in times of crisis.

For a short time, from late 1949 to early 1951, the Civil Defense
Agency took itself seriously. Its director, Colonel David G. McIntosh,
named deputy directors for every county and called for 160,000 volunteers—young men who would study first aid and maintain around-
the-clock air raid watches. Colonel McIntosh published an
educational pamphlet, *America's Defense against Communism,* and
he launched a journal, *The Old Line Alert,* to maintain morale among
the volunteers. Other states developed similar organizations, and in
1951, when Maryland interest was beginning to wane, Congress
agreed to provide the state defense forces with specified matching
funds. Still, the anticipated volunteers were slow in coming, and few
lasted more than a couple of weeks, and anticipated county support
never materialized. By 1954 the Maryland organization had ended its
annual war games, had ceased expressing itself on international
affairs, and was concentrating almost entirely on providing emergency
aid for communities hit by fires, floods, and storms.[36]

The volunteer defense force was relatively harmless; more alarming
was the General Assembly's mobilization against subversion. In 1947
Prince George's County Delegate William H. McGrath, a retired colonel in the military police, offered an amendment to the state constitution which barred from state or county employment anyone who
advocated overthrow of the government. Although the amendment
did not define *advocate* or *overthrow,* and the Communist party conspicuously testified in favor of the amendment on the ground that it
did not include them, it passed the General Assembly unanimously,
and the following year it won ratification by a vote of 203,000 to
84,000.[37]

The amendment lacked teeth, and the 1948 assembly requested that
Governor Lane appoint a commission to design a more comprehensive
legislative program "for the exposure and expurgation of subversive
activities." Lane hesitated, but the request had passed unanimously,
and in July he appointed a commission of eleven members. The chairman and ablest member was Frank B. Ober, a graduate of the Harvard
Law School and a leading Baltimore attorney. A month before the
legislature's action Ober had made a much-heralded speech to the
annual convention of the Maryland Bar Association in which he
argued that an impending struggle with the Soviet Union required the
most stringent measures. He condemned "free speech fanatics . . . who
are unwilling to sacrifice an ounce of free speech dogma for a pound of
democratic survival." He outlined the type of antisubversive law which
he believed the state should have, the tactics for its adoption, and the
means of making it acceptable to the courts. The Bar Association

responded to Ober with shouts of approval. Other members of the governor's commission included six lawyers, six veterans, and five members of the General Assembly.[38]

The commission worked through the fall of 1948 and presented its 115-page report late in the year. The commission boasted that the report was based in part on secret information supplied by the FBI, and the report's tone was "we know more than we can tell," "it's later than you think." The report claimed there were 100,000 Communists in the United States and 2,700 in Maryland, and it warned ominously, "There were but 50,000 Communists in Russia at the time of the 1918 Revolution." It offered the complete text for a comprehensive law, copied in part from the Smith Act, which was a 1940 congressional law against subversion, and in part from Truman's loyalty order, but it went much further than either.

The proposed law was in fact overwhelming. It required (1) a lengthy and detailed loyalty oath of all public employees; (2) the attorney general actively to seek out subversives in public or private life and bring indictments; (3) educational institutions to file annual reports demonstrating what positive steps they were taking to eliminate radical influences; (4) and, most of all, the attorney general to maintain records on anyone reported to be disloyal, including reports from anonymous informers, and to make this information available to prospective employers.[39]

The anti-communist movement mobilized to support the bill, legislators were deluged with positive mail, and testimony before a legislative hearing was overwhelmingly favorable. Governor Lane was conspicuously silent, and the attorney general protested that the law thrust his office into police work and that its enforcement should at least be the responsibility of another agency. Scattered opposition came from Quakers who did not approve of oaths, from liberals who spoke timidly against the concept of anonymous informers, and from labor unions who saw themselves coming under attack. The bill passed, however, virtually without change, by a vote of 31 to 0 in the Senate and 115 to 1 in the House. The lone dissenter was a former school teacher, John N. Newcomer, from Washington County. His vote was unexpected and caused momentary consternation, but then the House of Delegates broke into applause for their colleague's courage. He never stood for election again.[40]

Governor Lane signed the bill without comment on April 22, 1949, and since the legislature had voted it an "emergency measure," it went into effect immediately, amidst considerable national publicity. Favorable editorials appeared throughout the country. Senator Karl Mundt of South Dakota praised it as the best anti-communist law in America. Mississippi and New Hampshire copied it almost verbatim. A Maryland state senator exulted that "as long as our flag flies, as long as Francis Scott Key is remembered, we shall remember Frank Ober."[41]

The Maryland Civil Liberties Union, the CIO and miscellaneous liberal groups obtained enough signatures to force the law to referendum in the 1950 election, but they were no match for the establishment. The law's supporters included almost every newspaper in the state; Catholic and veterans' groups were fully mobilized; and business and service organizations were at the peak of their anti-communist enthusiasm. The law won public approval 259,000 to 79,000—some 77 percent of the electorate accepted the need even for anonymous informers. The favorable vote was largest in rural areas, but the vote was sufficiently overwhelming to defy further analysis. Democracy can be fierce, it can consume itself.[42]

And yet, for all the sweeping language of the law, surprisingly little ever came of it. Two Communists resigned from the Baltimore school system because of their inability to take the oath, exactly four Quakers were fired from state employment because of their refusal to take it, and some years later the eminent Johns Hopkins scientist Bentley Glass gleefully declined to serve on the governor's Science Advisory Council because of the oath. At the University of Maryland, which was the largest single state employer, everyone signed, although during the next twenty years about twenty prospective faculty, including some very prominent figures, broke off negotiations with the university on learning of the oath. There were not many other would-be state employees who refused to sign.[43]

The state attorney general's staff remained unfriendly to the law that had been thrust upon them, for they doubted its constitutionality and disliked its political overtones. Dutifully the attorney general appointed a Subversive Activities Unit, which went to work looking for someone to prosecute, but, despite the eager cooperation of local police, the unit never obtained enough information to bring a single indictment. The unit prepared a "counterespionage" training program for local police, who compiled biweekly summaries of radical activities which they gleaned from surveillance, from paid informers, and from newspaper clippings.[44]

To insure vigilance in the schools, the Subversive Activities Unit contacted about ninety colleges and private schools. One-third of them reported that they were adopting a form of the oath required of public school teachers, another third, including the Johns Hopkins University, reported they were doing nothing beyond what they had always done, and the rest never bothered to respond. College presidents and principals were more inclined to be defensive of their institutions than to seek possible public favor with purges. A bureaucracy first of all protects itself. None of the schools was contacted again. Recognizing that it had no sanctions, the attorney general's bureaucracy discontinued its attempted enforcement of the law.[45]

Collecting information on residents was the most ticklish task of all, a task clearly uncongenial to the state's lawyers. Still, reports came in, mostly from police, volunteer patriots, and students reporting on their teachers, until the attorney had files on about three thousand people. The office released information only when employers asked about specific individuals, and then only when the lawyers were persuaded that the information would stand up in court as justification for non-employment.[46]

When the Ober Law gained public approval in the 1949 General Assembly and then in the 1950 referendum, local groups looked for ways to take action on their own. While the Ober Law was still under consideration, the Baltimore Board of Education ordered principals to root out "any person whose loyalty to our American ideals is not clear."[47] The Cumberland City Council in 1950 ordered police to "register" local Communists, and nearby Hagerstown and Martinsburg copied the ordinance. Cumberland veterans' groups conducted a "Loyalty Day" on which they asked citizens to sign a pledge saying they would search for subversion. The Cumberland police commissioner explained that he "was spending most of [his] time investigating Red activities," that he had assigned night watchmen to the task, and that he had captured two elderly textile workers who had once been Communists and had failed to register.[48]

In Baltimore, two longshoremen were mobbed and fined for disturbing the peace when onlookers concluded that their strike literature was communist inspired.[49] The Baltimore American Legion in 1951 compiled a list of twenty-one Hollywood actors whose movies they planned to picket, but they ceased picketing because it seemed to provide favorable advertising for the films.[50] The Maryland Boy Scouts ordered an investigation of subversion among its members.[51] Methodist laymen created an organization called the Circuit Riders "to rid the Methodist Church of subversive forces."[52] Vincent Godfrey Burns, designated by the General Assembly as the state's poet laureate, composed a book-length rhyming epic on the dangers of communism:

Now the Reds are masters of the political arts
They've got peace on their lips and murder in their hearts,
They'll talk about friendship and coexistence
But what they really want is to lower our resistance,
They have only one purpose from day to day,
To conquer the world and the U.S.A.[53]

The Alger Hiss case, the Ober Law, and many local initiatives preceded the national anti-communist movement, but when the voice of Senator Joseph R. McCarthy of Wisconsin was finally raised, his charges seemed to focus especially on Maryland, for his first-named target was Professor Owen Lattimore of the Johns Hopkins University, and his most famous victim was Senator Millard E. Tydings of Maryland. In February 1950 McCarthy moved to the forefront of anti-communism with a speech that claimed that the United States Department of State "knowingly" employed Communists. Pressed for names, he cited only one: Owen Lattimore. The Hopkins professor had been director of Hopkins's famous School of International Relations since 1939, and he also served periodically as advisor to Chiang Kai-shek and the United States Department of State during the period of Mao Tse-tung's relentless triumph. Congress ordered the Senate Armed Services Committee, which was chaired by Tydings, to investigate the charge. After three months of publicized hearings, the Tydings committee concluded that McCarthy's charges were "a fraud and a hoax," "perhaps the most nefarious campaign of half-truths and untruths in the history of this republic."[54]

Far from settling the matter, Tydings's strong language invited challenge. Two members of the committee dissented, saying the hearings had been hasty and had passed over the more general charges of communist influence in government. This was true, for Tydings was eager to get the hearings over before the elections, including his own, that were coming up in November, and he deliberately dealt, like a judge, with specific charges instead of with McCarthy's generalities. McCarthy lusted for revenge, and Lattimore made matters worse by rushing into print with an intemperate book, *Ordeal by Slander,* that contained inaccuracies.

The Maryland election of 1950, therefore, was not only a referendum on the Ober Law, for which the anti-communist movement was mobilized, but also a referendum on the five-term conservative senator who was now accused of protecting Communists in government. Tydings's opponents rallied around a political unknown, John Marshall Butler, who remained as quiet as possible. Senator McCarthy contacted his supporters to aid Butler. Clint Murchison of Texas came up with ten thousand dollars, and others contributed smaller amounts, and together Butler's supporters contacted the Chicago public relations genius Jon M. Jonkel. Jonkel was personally liberal, but he was a professional, and he later boasted that the campaign added a new dimension to political advertising. Jonkel played on the theme of "whitewash." Articles and advertisements linked the names of Tydings, Hiss, and Lattimore, making the most of any occasion when they had been seen together. "Do you feel you know for sure," asked Jonkel, "that there are no Communists or Communist influence in our Government?" The Maryland Committee against Un-American Activities linked the Tydings campaign to the Ober Law referendum, establishing a theme for many editorial writers: "Are you for or against the Communists?" Tydings's defense was to claim that he, too, was a militant: "Tydings has introduced and fought for more defense legislation than any other man in the Senate," his campaign boasted.

Four days before the election, on November 3, came Jonkel's masterpiece, a four-page tabloid, *For the Record,* distributed by hand at shopping centers across the state. Its headline proclaimed, "Senator Tydings Says: There Is Not a Single Pro-Communist in the State Department," and underneath were the pictures of Dean Acheson, Alger Hiss, Owen Lattimore, and former Communist party Secretary Earl Browder. A different picture, showing Browder whispering to Tydings, carried a caption noting, in small print, the picture was a "composite"—for people who knew what *composite* meant. Jonkel was subsequently fined five thousand dollars for corrupt political practices for circulating the picture, but Butler won the election with 326,000 votes to Tydings's 283,000. Senator McCarthy promptly renewed his attack on Lattimore, who was called back to testify and then indicted for perjury on the basis of errors, not in his testimony, but in his self-defense book. The trials dragged on for three years before charges were dropped. Lattimore moved to England.[55]

The 1950 election was the high point but also the turning point for the communist issue in Maryland politics. The issue produced not only the victories of the Ober law referendum and Senator Butler, but also probably the margin of victory for Republican Governor Theodore McKeldin—even though he denounced the extremists both in the election and in office—and for three Republicans of Maryland's six congressmen. With Republicans in power, however, it was no longer convenient to imply that government was communist dominated. Butler went as far as expediency allowed in disavowing and even apologizing for the campaign that led to his victory, and in the 1952 state elections, candidates largely avoided the issue of communism altogether.[56]

At the national level, where Truman was still president, anti-communism continued to flourish. Late in 1950 the McCarran Internal Security Act passed over Truman's veto. This act resembled the Ober Law in that it prohibited employment of, and required registration of, radicals, and it also prohibited people with mistaken political views from immigrating into the United States. Senator Herbert R. O'Conor of Maryland boasted that the state provided inspiration for the bill, and he served as the Democratic whip for its passage. Anti-communist enthusiasm contributed in 1952 to the election of Dwight Eisenhower and the control by Republicans of both houses of Congress. Like McKeldin, however, Eisenhower held himself aloof from the popular passion and slowly emerged as the turning point for its decline on the national scene. The Senate censure of McCarthy came in 1953.

The Communists themselves were almost forgotten as the political rhetoric reached its peak, and arrests of Communists were anticlimactic. Federal prosecutors moved first against the party leaders in New York, and then, in March 1952, arraigned the avowed leaders in California and Maryland. The prosecutors ignored the Ober Law and the McCarran Act because of their questionable constitutionality, and brought charges instead under the old antisubversive Smith Act of 1940, which had been directed against the Nazis. Seven members of the Maryland party appeared before the court to explain that they were really members of the FBI, and they identified the "real" state communist leaders: Philip Frankfeld, Regina Frankfeld, George E. Meyers, Leroy H. Wood, Maurice Braverman, and Dorothy Rose Blumberg. The leaders admitted they were Communists, and the issue became whether communism was subversive. Prosecutors offered short quotations from Karl Marx's Communist Manifesto and rested their case. The defense read less inflammatory passages and rested. This was a battle of quotations. The jurors found the passages sufficiently incendiary, and the judge handed down sentences of between two and four years. Appeals courts upheld the convictions, although in the late 1950s, after the defendants had served their terms, federal courts determined that membership in the party was not necessarily subversive.[57]

The 1952 arrests, even more than the election of McKeldin, marked the decline of anti-communism in Maryland. They virtually destroyed the party, revealing a minuscule movement of leaders who were forlorn rather than threatening, and they defined subversion as membership in the Communist party, not as advocacy of liberal programs. Congressionally inspired investigators returned to Maryland in 1954 and again in 1957 to publicize the names not only of leaders but also of members of the former party. This time, however, public opinion was distinctly unfriendly to the investigators, most newspapers refused to list the names that investigators sought to publicize, and the

Sunpapers subsequently boasted that no more than half a dozen of the people mentioned had lost their jobs.[58]

The Ober Law fell slowly into oblivion. By 1953 the attorney general's Subversive Activities Unit spent most of its time parrying demands of extremists for some kind of action. One official, lacking anything else to do, copied the license plate numbers of visitors to a World Federalist rally, and when this became the object of newspaper ridicule, the official resigned, saying the only way to enforce the law was to repeal the Constitution. The courts, meanwhile, nibbled away at the law and finally, in 1968, ruled that the heart of it was unconstitutional. The attorney general petitioned the General Assembly to allow him to shred the records of the Subversive Activities Unit. The assembly declined to act, and the records have remained, well guarded, for historians.[59]

The anti-communist movement, then, succeeded in crushing the little Communist party in Maryland and contributed significantly to the Republican election victories in 1950 and 1952. In Maryland exactly six Communists plus Alger Hiss went to jail, about a dozen, including Owen Lattimore, lost their jobs, and probably several dozen more failed to obtain employment in the state. Intangible costs were greater, as forums were closed to controversial speakers, as teachers hedged their lectures, and as liberals and mavericks faced intimidation in public and social gatherings, PTA meetings, and private clubs. Within a decade student radicals would be intimidating conservatives in a similar manner.

The anti-communist movement died in Maryland—not so quickly elsewhere in the country—as the Communists in Maryland were routed and as people awakened to the excesses that the Ober Law and the Lattimore and Tydings episodes represented. It died in Maryland as bureaucrats, who were objects of the movement's wrath, became responsible for executing the new laws but sought instead to protect the traditional laws and institutions. It died when Republicans—with leaders like McKeldin and Eisenhower—came to power, and when they discovered that it was necessary to accept and expand the controls and services the conservatives hated. Finally, the movement died as the Korean War required local politicians to turn international matters back to the professionals. Ultimately anti-communism served as exorcism of nostalgia for a predepression era that was no longer suited to the modern world.

Korea and Vietnam

The disappearance of international matters from state history after 1952 may be more remarkable than its earlier prominence therein. The Korean War was different from previous American wars—but set the stage for subsequent ones—in being a war of national decision makers rather than of popular enthusiasm. Even if, in some way, anti-communism contributed to the war, its outbreak in an obscure corner of the world met with no cheers. The extreme anti-communist crusaders were not enhanced by it and were not conspicuous as volunteers to help wage it. People responded to the war dutifully, with a mix of determination and skepticism, but it was not Maryland's war.

There were no parades, no Maryland units, no monuments to its heroes, and little community support beyond what was paid for by the national government.

The military services declined to classify Korean War enlistments or casualties by states. Probably, based on Maryland as a proportion of the national total, about 88,500 Maryland troops served, including about 24,000 draftees plus 64,500 volunteers, who were attracted mostly by jobs and adventure. Local newspapers, which tried to count state casualties, calculated some 460 battlefield deaths, somewhat below the proportion of deaths nationally.[60] An unforeseen local result of the war was the migration of more than fifteen thousand Koreans to Maryland who immediately became one of the state's largest foreign-born groups.[61]

The economics of the war served to turn local attention away from international events rather than toward them. Federal military expenditures from 1950 to 1954 rose from 30 percent to 70 percent of the federal budget, and this brought special benefits to a state that had a disproportionate share of military supply facilities. Wages and profits grew, full employment brought labor peace, and, even without new taxes, the state government revenue increased more than 10 percent a year, and the increase was used for schools, roads, health facilities, and other public services. As the war ended, Governor McKeldin reversed the local rhetoric of the late 1940s, assailing the federal government for its preoccupation with war and calling for the states to show the way toward improvement in the quality of life at home.[62] Prosperity turned the frustrations of the late 1940s into the euphoria of the 1950s.

The cold war roared on after Korea, costing about 40 percent of the national budget, and people worried, but the cold war became a subject for experts, for Washington. The state legislature fell silent on international matters, local defense budgets dwindled away, and local candidates, even for Congress, tended to keep away from frightening cold war issues. International politics did not figure in a single gubernatorial election after 1952, or a state referendum, and senatorial and congressional elections were overwhelmingly concerned with domestic issues. Foreign affairs, like religion, could be discussed among individuals, but such issues seldom divided communities and were best kept out of state and local affairs. People in Maryland had largely excluded the slave question in a similar way before the Civil War. The confrontation between the United States and the Soviet Union continued through containment (1953–1964), Vietnam (1963–1973), detente (1963–1979), and then rearmament (1979–).

The Vietnam War was even larger and longer than Korea, and public opinion was bitterly divided, but the division lay largely outside a local context. At first newspaper opinion in Maryland and polls taken nationally supported American involvement, but by mid-1967, as draft calls and costs mounted, national and state polls showed a majority believed intervention to be a mistake. The most important debates on the war took place within the foreign policy establishment, where military experts slowly concluded that American policy was doomed.[63]

Protest also surged from the grass roots, especially from the college campuses, and student protests contributed to ending the war. Student antiwar opinion mixed with fear of the draft, with the civil rights movement, with demands for reforms in education, and especially with a generational revolt against authority. The movement was intense in Maryland, reaching a peak in 1969 and 1970 with huge antiwar parades in Baltimore and Washington, hundreds of student arrests, and riot-torn campuses patrolled by the National Guard. Although the student revolts never seized the levers of local power, the movements of the late 1960s resembled the anti-communist movement of the late 1940s in its mass support and shrillness.[64]

The American troops were the ones caught in the middle. About 170,000 troops served from Maryland, including 33,000 draftees and 136,000 volunteers, not quite double the number serving in the Korean War. The 908 Maryland residents who died in battle provided slightly more than Maryland's proportion of the total troops who died in service. The number of Maryland troops who received less than honorable discharges was 11,000; the number of Maryland draftees who refused to serve was 3,740. As happened after most wars, refugees poured into this country; more than four thousand Vietnamese settled in the state.[65]

American foreign policy continued to swing after Vietnam, first in the 1970s toward detente, with the SALT talks, friendship with China, and the Camp David accords, then in the 1980s toward rearmament again, brought on by the Iranian hostage crisis, the Soviet invasion of Afghanistan, and the Soviet downing of a Korean airliner, and public opinion shifted accordingly. After 1952, however, with the partial exception of Vietnam, opinion seemed to follow Washington rather than lead it. Foreign affairs opinion was hardly a state or community bailiwick, and it seldom emerged through local institutions and seldom consciously mixed with other concerns of society. Communism and anti-communism, war and peace, fell back into the hands of philosophers, diplomats, and soldiers—with whatever consequences for democracy.

In sum, then, communism was a small but real force in Maryland until about 1944, when it withered as an idea, or until 1952, when it was finally crushed as an organization. Anti-communism, meanwhile, was a mass movement that was born in postwar frustration and served as an equally serious threat to democracy, but it too died quickly around 1952 without doing significant damage. Possibly anti-communism helped awaken America to the cold war, for better or worse, but there were far larger forces in the awakening. After about 1952 foreign affairs rose to the national arena or descended to individual deliberation. Except briefly again during the Vietnam War, local organizations, local political rhetoric, and local and state governments shunned world matters as irrelevant and divisive. Both state and nation were better off for the disengagement. Local communities were never very astute in foreign affairs.

Theodore Roosevelt McKeldin took office as the Republican governor of Maryland in January 1951. In this, as in many other ways, the state slightly anticipated the nation. The following year, McKeldin nominated Dwight D. Eisenhower at the Republican National Convention, and Eisenhower became president in 1953.

McKeldin and Eisenhower were warm and sensible men, appropriate symbols for a happy decade. Both men were elected in reaction to long Democratic rule that had initiated and sustained a trend toward ever-bigger government and welfare services, but neither of them much slowed the trend; instead they broadened the base from which it grew. Both men emerged out of anti-communist hysteria, but they tempered that emotion and helped remove it from partisan politics. Their administrations coincided with the greatest advances in civil rights since Civil War reconstruction. When the Supreme Court in 1954 ordered the beginning of school integration, McKeldin took steps to promote compliance in Maryland, and Eisenhower moved, somewhat more hesitantly, in Little Rock. Prosperity and real growth characterized the decade, less frenetically than in the decades before and after, but supported by an assumption that good times stretched endlessly ahead. The 1950s were closer to "normalcy" than any decade since the 1880s. They established a new base line for nostalgia.

6
The 1950s Euphoria of Eisenhower and McKeldin

Dwight D. Eisenhower and Theodore R. McKeldin, seated, campaign in Baltimore. The two Republicans were close friends. McKeldin had nominated Eisenhower for president in 1950 and they campaigned together often. Courtesy of the *Baltimore Sun*.

The Happy Governor   McKeldin was the tenth of eleven children born to an illiterate Scotch-Irish Methodist father and a devout Catholic mother in a poor section of south Baltimore. Throughout his life he repeated the stories of his youth, and mostly they were true. He got his name, he explained, when in 1900 his stonecutter-turned-policeman father was assigned to guard Theodore Roosevelt, who was campaigning in Baltimore. As Roosevelt left the stage of the Lyric Theater he slapped the elder McKeldin on the back exuberantly, saying, "How're ya, Red?" and two weeks later the delighted father named his newborn son after the candidate. He got his party affiliation, he liked to explain, "because my grandfather came from Scotland and saw people enslaved because they had faces that were not his color. He enlisted in the Union Army and was killed in the Battle of Monocacy in Frederick County. . . . That made my father a Republican, and I'm his son and it made me a Republican." He was a teetotaler, he said, because he remembered the tears in his mother's eyes when his father came home drunk, and he remembered watching, at the age of ten, as his father walked up the aisle of the Bennett Memorial Church to swear off liquor forever.[1]

McKeldin was such an extrovert, and he had a smile so big and a rhetoric so grandiloquent, that people wondered if he was genuine, but mostly he was what he claimed to be. The facade never wavered. "I am a hand-shaker. I like people," he said.[2] His ebullience masked neither hidden motives nor profound philosophy.

He was deeply religious, not in a denominational sense, but in his conviction that religion meant love of humankind. He seldom spoke without making religious allusions, and when people trooped into his office to ask favors he often began the encounters by offering them a rosary, a testament, or a yarmulke. Whether McKeldin was running for office or not, he frequently visited two or three churches, preferably black, each Sunday to preach; he was equally at home, though, in white Protestant, Catholic, or Jewish pulpits. "My honest ambition was to be a preacher," he said. "It's still in my heart. I would have been a preacher if I had had a high school education." He withstood criticism to commute fifteen death sentences when he was governor, but at the end of his life he wept about his greatest failure: "I am ashamed to say I hanged four men. The public clamor was such that I yielded to it. May God forgive me." He always liked to embrace people, especially during the civil rights upheavals, with the salutation, "My brother, my brother!"[3]

Besides religion, McKeldin believed in education—his own youth was a struggle for schooling—and in oratory. People liked to say of whatever position he obtained that he had talked his way into it. After seven years of attending public school he got a full-time job in a bank at age 14, and the same day he enrolled for a high school equivalency in the night classes of Baltimore City College. On weekends he worked as a gravedigger. One summer he spent twenty dollars for twenty-five Dale Carnegie speech classes at the YMCA, and the next year he taught the course. Graduating from the University of Maryland Evening Law School in 1925, at age 25, famous as the school's best orator, he was hired by the Fidelity and Deposit Company to give pep talks on company loyalty to its agents throughout the country. On a business trip to New York State he met Honolulu Manzer, whom he married. Two years later he volunteered his services to William F. Broening, the Republican Baltimore mayoral candidate. Broening won an upset victory in the Democratic city and appointed the boy orator, who was almost as well known as he, to serve four years as his executive secretary and stand-in speechmaker. Broening and McKeldin were much alike. McKeldin in retirement called Broening "the greatest politician I've ever known . . . because he came out of poverty and never forgot it."[4]

During the 1930s McKeldin practiced law, founded the Baltimore Junior Chamber of Commerce and served as its president, founded Santa Claus Anonymous (which became a major Baltimore depression charity for poor children), and talked city politics. In 1939 McKeldin was a lightly regarded and easily defeated Republican candidate for mayor of the city, and in 1943, when the Democrats divided between incumbent Mayor Howard W. Jackson and boss William Curran, McKeldin was the lightly regarded upset winner. A Republican could only win in Baltimore or statewide when Democrats divided, and McKeldin sensed when the divisions were coming and exploited them.

As mayor from 1943 to 1947 he established the political style that guided his career. Instead of attempting to dominate the unanimously Democratic city council as his Democratic predecessors had done, he stood back from the council, offering his patronage indiscriminately to one faction or another in exchange for major items, and relishing and even encouraging council stalemate on everything else. His fellow Republicans were the ones left out, and they were outraged, for they received almost no patronage, while their titular head enjoyed credit for a moderately successful administration. The appointments McKeldin made outside the Democratic factions went to blacks, Jews, women, or independent liberals, and in this way he established a small but passionate personal constituency. He was always unpopular within his own party in Maryland, but he left the party with the choice of winning very little with him or nothing without him. "I should have been a Democrat," he once confided. "The Democrats are closer to the common people." He and his voice were a one-man party.[5]

The mayor initiated, or encouraged the council to initiate, progressive reforms in the city Charter which primarily involved transferring positions from patronage to civil service. As a Republican who had not shared in the long alliance between the Democratic organization and the Baltimore Transit Company, McKeldin pressed successfully in the courts for $2.6 million in back taxes from the city buses.[6] With these funds, plus released revenue savings from the war years, McKeldin and the council joined the state's program for building Friendship Airport on the edge of town, rebuilt the famous Lexington Market, expanded the city water supply, rebuilt schools, and launched a slum clearance program. The spending was carefully balanced in the traditional way, with a certain amount for each council district. The spending made everyone look good.

In 1946 McKeldin, who still had one more year to serve as mayor, reluctantly allowed Republicans to nominate him for governor, to succeed O'Conor and run against Lane. The postwar reaction against

incumbent parties gave him a surprising margin in twelve of the
twenty-three counties, but it similarly worked against him in Baltimore, where he lost to Democrats who were reunited under Curran,
and thus he lost the election. He finished out his term of mayor
successfully, but wisely chose not to seek a second term in 1947,
retiring with honor, leaving the office to Curran's new man, Thomas
D'Alesandro, Jr.

In 1950 Maryland Republicans accepted McKeldin without enthusiasm but without opposition to run against Lane for a second time.
For McKeldin it was a campaign that always afterward embarrassed
him, because he rode the public frustration, which he did not share,
over communist subversives, and also the public frustration over the
sales tax, for which he had no alternative. Still, his was the biggest
Republican victory in Maryland history—victory in twenty of the
twenty-three counties plus a comfortable margin in Baltimore—
amounting to 58 percent of the vote. "I was not elected, Mr. Lane was
defeated," he acknowledged ruefully. "Actually, Mr. Lane was not
defeated, the sales tax was defeated." As for the tax, within a year
McKeldin was saying, "I made a mistake."[7]

McKeldin's inaugural speech exuded humanity but was otherwise
indecisive, wavering between his liberal instincts and his campaign
rhetoric. He spoke of the Korean War and, vaguely, of civil defense.
He spoke of enforcing antisubversive legislation, but his emphasis was
on enforcement "that is not repugnant to the letter or spirit of our Bill
of Rights." He spoke in general terms of efficiency in government, free
enterprise, and the hope for lower taxes, but he never mentioned the
sales tax, and he waxed poetic in speaking of the need for better
hospitals and schools. "Not a thing he said nor a pledge he made," said
a Baltimore *Sun* editorial, "could not have come as well from a Democrat."[8]

Three major advisors followed him to Annapolis and represented
the range of contacts for a successful Maryland politician. First was
his secretary and alter ego from his law practice, Mildred K. Mom-
berger, "Mrs. Mom" to almost everyone. She was a worshipful but
practical woman who worked sixteen and more hours a day, arranging his schedule, drafting his letters, even consulting on policy. Hers
was the instinct of the typical middle-class voter.[9]

Second was the hard-nosed back-room wheeler-dealer, M. William
Adelson, McKeldin's former law partner, who was considered one of
the toughest lawyers in Maryland. Adelson was officially a Democrat,
but he masterminded all of McKeldin's elections. He knew every Democratic and Republican club in the state and delighted in making
bargains with them that the man in the front office could not afford to
know about. Adelson wangled McKeldin's bills through the Democratic Baltimore City Council and the Democratic General Assembly
in Annapolis, mostly by controlling patronage. "See Bill," said the
governor freely to favor seekers, "He's my patronage man. . . . my
closest political advisor." Occasionally Adelson held minor political
offices himself, such as director of Lexington Market and director of
Friendship Airport, and after McKeldin left office he was a registered
Annapolis lobbyist for insurance and savings and loan companies. He

was known by most legislators as "the Candy Man," ostensibly for his habit of calling everyone "Sweetie Pie," but also for his late-night, high-stakes poker games in which key legislators always seemed to win. This was mostly politics for the love of it; Adelson died in modest circumstances.[10]

The third key advisor of the McKeldin years, as idealistic as Adelson was shrewd, was Simon E. Sobeloff, one of the ablest and most honorable men ever to serve the state. The son of immigrants who settled in East Baltimore, he entered the Maryland bar with one of the highest scores ever recorded, subsequently became city solicitor and then United States attorney for Maryland, and was selected by McKeldin as the chief judge of the Maryland Court of Appeals, the first Jew ever to serve on that bench. Sobeloff was appointed by Eisenhower as solicitor general of the United States, where he presented the government's case in the 1954 Brown decision, and finally served as chief judge of the United States Court of Appeals. Always he was the champion of the underdog, dedicated to civil liberties and the Bill of Rights. In private law practice and in public service Sobeloff and McKeldin were closest allies, promoting each other's causes and careers. The five-hundred-page Sobeloff Commission Report on state administrative reorganization, issued in twelve parts in 1951, 1952, and 1953, completed the overhaul of state government that had been begun by Sherbow and Lane.[11]

Along with his acceptance of Sobeloff reforms, McKeldin brought to the governorship a traditional commitment to business, much like Eisenhower's. It was the commitment of his party and his times. McKeldin was out of state an average of one day a week, speaking to business groups, Kiwanis clubs, chambers of commerce, insurance and plumbers' conventions. "I think I have been a good salesman for the state," he said. At his urging, state agencies compiled statistics and published pamphlets to attract industry. For all his rhetorical concern for the common man, his tax and labor policies did not frighten businessmen. Environmental programs lagged, and welfare expenditures declined. State manufacturing value increased by about 60 percent during his administration. Business employment rose about 20 percent. Profits rose faster than wages.[12]

The major program for business, begun in 1956, was the Maryland Port Authority. Stimulated to take action by Eisenhower's St. Lawrence Seaway Project, which threatened to preempt Baltimore's midwestern trade, the state committed an initial $15 million to a consortium of state, city, railroad, and shipping leaders for terminal and harbor improvements. The program was barely launched when McKeldin left office, but it established an imaginative alliance of government and business that was to have a bright future.

McKeldin viewed his role as governor not to be the initiator of programs, nor primarily the manager of an executive bureaucracy—in these jobs he was far less effective than Lane—but to be an inspiration to the people, an orator. The governorship was a bully pulpit for business, for civil rights, but mostly for virtue itself. He averaged one hundred forty major addresses a year—three a week—plus countless more impromptu homilies for office visitors, discourses for street-corner gatherings, and Sunday sermons. Eisenhower performed the role of inspirational leader as a military hero and an avuncular model citizen; McKeldin provided the inspiration more actively. It was as though the 1950s needed a spiritual leader, or a symbol of leadership, more than it needed leadership itself.

McKeldin employed several speechwriters—Sobeloff and journalists Albert Quinn and Gerald W. Johnson—but the speeches were mostly his, begun with jottings on scraps of paper, embellished with apt quotations and lines of poetry from sources near at hand, dictated to his secretary and polished. While governor he published a textbook for speech students called *The Art of Eloquence.* Occasionally he repeated the best speeches or best stories, but the variety was enormous. They are catalogued among his papers both chronologically and by topic: "Alcoholism, Automobile Safety, Aviation, Bill of Rights, Boy Scouts, Business," runs the list. "Cancer, Capital Punishment, Catholic Groups, Charity, Christmas. . . ." The thickest file is on religion. His most quoted sentence came from an Eisenhower rally, where he made an uncharacteristically partisan attack on the Democrats: "The plundering potentates of the Potomac and the pusillanimous parasites of the palace guard are having their last ride on the merry-go-round of privilege and pelf."[13]

Religion and politics came together in McKeldin's concern for Jews, blacks, and women. This was good politics, for this was McKeldin's personal constituency. "The minority groups—they elected me," he said. But his concern was sincere and had consequence. Much of what he did was rhetorical and symbolic; he made racial tolerance and women's rights the subject of speeches, for example, and he made conspicuous appointments of Jews, blacks, and women to offices where they had never served before. While governor he remained president of the American-Israel Society, toured the country to sell Israeli bonds, and twice visited Israel. He worked publicly and behind the scenes to promote integration of Baltimore theaters, stores, and lunch counters in 1952 and 1953; ordered the integration of state ferries and beaches in 1954; and promoted school and hotel integration in 1955 and 1956. The governor was working in a positive rather than a negative way, and this pointed the state forward instead of backward.[14]

The General Assembly   The growth of executive power at the expense of the legislature was one of the most striking features of American government in the twentieth century, and it was more evident at the state than at the national level. In Maryland it began with Governor Albert Ritchie (1920–1935), who used the media and patronage to create a personal constituency far broader than that of any legislator, and then used his power to obtain constitutional changes that gave the governor almost exclusive control over the budget. The Ritchie amendments required the governor to offer the assembly a balanced budget and gave the assembly authority to make cuts only by adding to the state surplus, which was a thankless task, and to make additions only by adding new taxes, which was a virtual impossibility. The amendments went even beyond the power given to the federal Bureau of the Budget by Harding, Roosevelt, and Johnson. The budget authority and the bureaucracy that went with it, coupled with the ability of men like Lane and McKeldin, which was vastly superior to the ability of most of the part-time members of the assembly, created a government far different from that of the nineteenth century, when the legislature ruled. The governor, once merely the administrator of laws passed by the assembly, was now the chief spokesman for the people and the primary initiator of governmental change. He was a far better reflection of the popular will than the faction-stalemated, interest-dominated General Assembly. For its part, the assembly exercised its supervision over county affairs, put off executive proposals until enough public pressure built up, let off steam in moderately harmless resolutions about communist subversion, and served as ombudsmen for individual citizens.[15]

The Sobeloff Commission, including among its members some of the finest business and academic leaders of the state, recognized these changes and attempted to modernize government accordingly. It provided a recent history of all state agencies, compared their operation to those of agencies of other states, and outlined costs and benefits of modernization. Gradually, as the governor paid the political price for them over the next six years, the recommendations gained approval: centralized state purchasing, accounting, payroll, and licensing agencies; a standardized merit system and salary scale; better planning for public works; improved administration of health, welfare, highways, and prisons; and a new parole system became realities. All of this was normal, periodically necessary government reorganization, ably promoted by Sobeloff and McKeldin, grudgingly approved by the legislature.[16]

The most important Sobeloff recommendation was for county home rule, which would take from the legislature its greatest and most abused power: its almost absolute control over the internal government of the counties. The 1867 Maryland Constitution, in an effort to prevent black or Republican counties from infringing on white Democratic power, required assembly approval of almost every expenditure or ordinance within each county. In practice this placed county power squarely in the county's delegation to Annapolis. Legislative courtesy required unanimous approval of all recommendations made by a county delegation. Up to half the bills in the legislature, and half its time, was spent approving everything from a clerk's salary raise in Garrett County to zoning easements in Somerset.

Sobeloff's home rule recommendation, then, was an effort to strengthen the legislature by getting its mind on state business, and incidentally to promote efficient county government and break up county machines. For four years the legislature fought valiantly for its privilege, but McKeldin, with broad support from good government leagues and from almost all county newspapers and county citizens, eventually prevailed. In 1956 home rule passed as a constitutional amendment for those counties that wanted it, although in the next six years only Baltimore City and the five suburban counties of Baltimore and Washington succeeded in throwing off the delegation yoke to adopt home rule.

Two other governor's commissions further addressed legislative failure, one mostly in vain, the other successfully. Richard W. Case, a prominent Baltimore lawyer, headed the Tax Survey Commission, which showed how additional revenue could be raised and tax collection procedures modernized, but failed to persuade the assembly to come to grips with inequitable tax assessments and overlapping state and county tax levies. More successful was the State Roads Commission Report of 1953, conducted by the state's own bureaucracy, which established a twelve-year road improvement priority program that began to preempt annual legislative logrolling for a wider road in one county in exchange for a bridge in another.[17]

The General Assembly of the 1950s was remarkably close to the ideal of democratic theory, in which truly average citizens serve, and far from the eighteenth- and nineteenth-century practice, in which the legislature served as a governing elite. The distaste that literate journalists and suburban liberals expressed for legislative mediocrity was only recognition of the legislature's ordinariness. Only one-fourth of the members of the General Assembly had a college diploma, although one-third were lawyers and over one-half had some form of education beyond high school. Almost one-half of the legislators were new to Annapolis with each election. They were considerably older than the median age of the voting population. There were few women and fewer blacks. There was little difference between the composition of the Senate and House, and little change in either during the decade (see table 6.1).[18]

A few of the legislators, mostly lawyers, made almost a full-time job of politics, but most legislators held assembly work to a few days a week when the Assembly met: three months in odd years and one month in even years. Leadership went to the few, of course—old-time local leaders like George W. Della of Baltimore, Harry T. Phoebus of Somerset, or Perry Wilkinson of Prince George's; or else to young men building a career, like Blair Lee from Princeton, Charles Mathias from Yale, Louis Goldstein of Calvert County, or Marvin Mandel of Jack Pollack's sidewalk school. Pay was six hundred dollars annually, and except for a handful of homemakers and retired people, everyone had regular occupations (see table 6.2).[19]

Legislative style and concerns reflected the legislature's antiquated function. In 1950 legislators still had roll-top desks, and, counting guards and secretaries, there was one staff member for each four members. The assembly of these years would be the despair of political scientists looking for significant ideological divisions; it would totally frustrate Marxists looking for significant class divisions; even the special interest influence of lobbyists was probably exaggerated by the newspapers. The reality of legislative politics was mostly of smaller stuff: factional intrigue to promote regional advantage and personal ambition. "I think of myself first as the Senator for Somerset County," said Senator Phoebus, "and second as a Senator for Maryland."[20]

McKeldin and the assembly conducted their ballet in four major acts—the sessions of 1951, 1953, 1955, and 1957—each act interspersed with the political campaigns that were in considerable part

Table 6.1.   The General Assembly, 1951 and 1959

	1951	1959
Legislators with college diplomas	25%	26%
Republicans	30%	7%
Women	3.2%	3.2%
Blacks	0	1.3%
Newly elected	49%	43%
In office 2–10 years	34%	45%
In office 10+ years	16%	12%
Average age	46	47.5

Source: Maryland Manual (1951–1959).

Table 6.2.   Occupational Profile, 1950s General Assembly

Occupation	Percentage
Law	35
Business (salesmen, merchants, grocers, restaurant owners, manufacturers, etc.)	16
Blue-collar labor (steelworkers, policemen, bus drivers, barbers, tailors, oystermen, etc.)	13
White-collar labor (accountants, teachers, bankers, secretaries, etc.)	9
Farming	9
Real estate and insurance	8
Auto sales and repair	6
Contracting	3
Miscellaneous	1

Source: Maryland Manual (1951–1959).

their object. These provide four chronological lessons in the operation of state politics.

The governor was especially weak in the 1951 session, for he was new to Annapolis and he was still caught between his campaign rhetoric and his better instincts. The direction of the session emerged, as was often the case, in the first week of legislative organization, when Jack Pollack's city delegation, in alliance with Baltimore County, was crushed by a rival alliance of Curran's city delegation and the Eastern Shore. The victors were led by two Eastern Shoremen who were not members of the assembly; State Comptroller Millard Tawes and University of Maryland president H. C. "Curley" Byrd, who controlled the farm extension agents of the state. The victors claimed their prizes: defeat of reapportionment for the suburbs, defeat of Richard Case's tax reform, defeat of state efforts to control the Chesapeake oyster beds, defeat of court reform, defeat of bonds for Baltimore harbor improvement, and autonomy for the University of Maryland. Autonomy was highly desirable, as it freed university appointments and operations from political interference, although with Curley Byrd as president people wondered if the act got the university out of or only further into politics. One other highly desirable assembly action came as Tawes, the Democratic comptroller responsible for the budget, joined with McKeldin in blocking what would have been a popular cut in taxes.[21]

The election of 1952 became bright for McKeldin when he was called on in his capacity as orator to nominate Eisenhower. McKeldin's action won the lasting enmity of conservative Republicans, notably Joseph France, president of Midcontinental Oil Company and the leading Republican financier in Maryland, who was supporting Robert Taft; but Eisenhower's victory over Adlai Stevenson strengthened the governor. McKeldin came closer to statesmanship during the campaign than anyone else in Maryland, downplaying the antisubversive rhetoric that most candidates were using. The demagogic George P. Mahoney used the communist issue to defeat the organization-supported Lansdale Sasscer for the Democratic nomination to the United States Senate, and in turn Republican J. Glenn Beall defeated Mahoney. Republicans picked up an additional congressional seat. State Democrats, though still making up 70 percent of the General Assembly, were in organizational shambles.[22]

The Democratic chaos made McKeldin's second legislative session, of 1953, worse than the first. Newspaper reporters called it "the worst session in Maryland history." For almost two weeks the legislature could not meet at all while Democrats wrangled over the election of house and senate officers. Finally the Republicans tipped the balance, in favor of ineptitude. Indecorum prevailed. Home rule, judicial reform, conservation of the oyster beds, automobile inspection, all failed. Special interest groups succeeded in reducing taxes on liquor, farm equipment, and savings banks. Time spent on local legislation increased to 60 percent. At the end of the session ten bills were declared void for internal contradiction, indecipherability, and unrecorded votes. Boasting that it had embarrassed McKeldin, the Democratic majority only embarrassed itself, for in fact the executive offices were working well enough without legislation. A record budget went through unscathed.[23]

Election year 1954 provided sweet payoff for the governor and a curious vindication of the democratic process. George P. Mahoney and Curley Byrd tore at each other in the Democratic primary in order to challenge McKeldin's reelection. In the midst of the primary the Supreme Court announced its school integration decision, and the two Democrats outdid each other in appealing to segregationist sentiment. Byrd won by the narrowest margin, withstanding Mahoney's demand for recounts and litigation. Then McKeldin, to the dismay of conservatives, actually embraced the Court's exraordinary decision. "Come, come, Dr. Byrd," he taunted. "Come out of the bog of bigotry, out of the puddle of prejudice." McKeldin accused Byrd of mismanaging the university, of putting football ahead of academic standards. When Byrd charged McKeldin with legislative mismanagement, he was deluged with words. "I have no anger tonight," said the governor, "about the foolish charges that have been leveled against me in these dark descending hours of the opposition's star." McKeldin lost the Eastern Shore and southern Maryland, but he won the election easily, the first Republican governor in the state's history to gain reelection. Otherwise, the Republicans lost a congressman, and their representation in the assembly declined from 30 percent to 21 percent.[24]

McKeldin, who was bolder than Eisenhower, relished his image as the state's progressive and devoted his second inaugural address to tolerance, the Bill of Rights, and the ending of ideological and racial bigotry; but the address went over the heads of the assembly. Again in 1955 there was an intense struggle to organize, which, told briefly, resulted in the Pollack wing of the Baltimore city delegation (which was supporting Thomas D'Alesandro's reelection as mayor) allying itself with western and southern Maryland to control the senate; the anti-Pollack, anti-D'Alesandro wing of the city delegation allied with Tawes and the Eastern Shore to control the house. Such stuff, with endless embellishment, was the heart of local politics in the 1950s.

McKeldin's liberal budget with new taxes and services passed, but significant programs for conservation, insurance regulation, automobile safety, reform of the court system, and reform of the election laws all failed. Probably the failure of reform was a reflection of a happy, prosperous period.[25]

The legislature sometimes worked better in its short, even-year sessions, which were supposed to deal only with emergencies and budgets. The 1956 emergency was a Baltimore bus strike, which the legislators investigated to see if Communists were responsible. To halt the strike the assembly gave the governor authority to seize the buses, which he did. A second crisis came with the death of H. L. Mencken, Maryland's renowned cynic, and assembly debate on a resolution "expressing its sorrow." After referral to five committees the resolution passed, with delegates from six Eastern Shore counties angrily opposed. McKeldin gained approval of a Maryland Port Authority by which the state would supervise and expand harbor facilities for transportation and trade. City advocates boasted that they had obtained the $15 million facility cheaply: $1.5 million in pork-barrel acts for Anne Arundel County, $500,000 for Baltimore County, and $10,000 for Somerset County. McKeldin persuaded the assembly to bring state employees under social security, and—the ultimate expression of an affluent and happy society—to assume some responsibility for the Baltimore Symphony Orchestra.[26]

The 1956 political swirl reflected satisfaction. Eisenhower again won big over Stevenson, carrying on his Maryland coattails the conservative John Marshall Butler back to the Senate over the ubiquitous George P. Mahoney, who stood for whatever he thought people wanted but could never figure out what it was.

McKeldin's 1957 legislature, combined with the short session of 1958, provides the fourth lesson in 1950s legislative behavior. Mostly it was routine. Legislators were still opposed to procedural change, especially if it was labeled reform, but they felt prosperous and expansive. Taxes and services again rose, especially for education. Russia's Sputnik launch of 1957 added patriotic urgency. Even McKeldin hesitated at legislative largesse, for he was eager for counties to assume a larger share of the tax burden for schools, but the county-oriented legislators, like congressmen who cried abstractly for local rights, really preferred that a centralized agency, less identifiable by the voters than themselves, be responsible for levying taxes. McKeldin, who had won his office by promising to abolish the sales tax altogether, now joined with Tawes to increase it from 2 percent to 3 percent.[27] The placid, quietly petty 1950s were about to give way to Tawes and the fervid 1960s.

State Services

Neither the governor nor the assembly was the main branch of government in the 1950s—the bureaucracy had emerged as the decisive branch. The various state agencies continued to grow, although less than before and after McKeldin (see table 6.3).[28] Actually, like so much of the apparent affluence and expansion of the 1950s, these budget increases were partly illusory. When the 105 percent increase is

Table 6.3.   State Expenditures, 1951 and 1959
(in Millions of Dollars)

Expenditure	1951	1959	Percentage Change
Administration	8.1	11.4	+ 41
Capital investment, bonds	27.8	51.7	+ 87
Education	47.0	121.2	+158
Health	19.1	37.7	+ 97
Highways	67.6	123.8	+ 83
Prisons and police	7.2	17.4	+141
Supplement to counties	14.6	35.5	+143
Welfare, Social Security	22.9	46.7	+104
Natural Resources and miscellaneous	5.0	4.7	− 6
Total	219.3	450.1	+105

Source: Comptroller of the Treasury, *Annual Reports* (1951, 1959).

adjusted for a 30 percent increase in population, a 29 percent increase in personal income, and inflation of 17 percent, then the real rate of increase in state taxes and services during McKeldin's administration was down to about 30 percent. This was still a significant expansion—people accepted extension of the welfare state from Eisenhower and McKeldin when they rejected it from Truman and Lane—but it was also a slower growth in government than occurred in the Democratic administrations before and after.

The greatest expansion came, at the demand of the young and increasingly middle-class population, in education. The surging state population brought in workers of child-bearing age, the end of the baby boom was not in sight, and middle-class prosperity meant that more people were going to school and staying there longer. The state's public school population increased 58 percent from 1951 to 1959, and budgets increased even faster. Schools were everyone's favorite expenditure, including McKeldin's. The hard-driving superintendent of schools, Thomas G. Pullen, made the most of it. The chief need was teachers, and to attract them, teacher salaries rose 45 percent, from an average of $3,543 to $5,117. This significant change in status for teachers—from the economic level of unskilled to skilled workers—was a status they would maintain and improve. School construction costs rose at an even greater pace, from $31 million a year in 1951 to $63 million annually at the end of the decade. The movement from rural and neighborhood schools to consolidated schools continued, along with a more varied curriculum and greater emphasis on social adjustment.[29]

State-sponsored higher education meant almost entirely the University of Maryland, which increased its full-time enrollment from about 11,000 to 15,000 and its part-time enrollment from 17,000 to 30,000. The state teachers' colleges and black colleges together enrolled only about 3,000 students and received a pittance from the state, and the new junior colleges, with a total of 3,000 students, still depended entirely on county support. The University of Maryland's budget grew substantially in the 1950s. The increase in state funds of approximately 80 percent was a result not so much of public enthusiasm for higher education as of, first, the political ambitions of Curley Byrd, and, after 1954, the persuasive case for quality made by the university's scholarly new president, Wilson H. Elkins.

State road building was another state function that grew significantly. The automobile (800,000 state registrations in 1951; 1,300,000 in 1959) was basic to the decade's prosperity. Here was one case where bureaucrats generally were ahead of legislators, and legislators, strangely enough, were ahead of the road building lobbyists who emerged so powerfully in later years. In 1951 the State Roads Commission presented the legislature with an extensive study of highway safety, calling for hundreds of improvements from straightening curves to widening bridges. This led in turn to a much larger study, adopted by the assembly in 1953, which established a twelve-year plan of road construction priorities. The planners utilized airplane surveys and computers for calculating present and future road use, and garnered national awards for their vision.

During the decade new expressways opened from Baltimore to Washington, from Baltimore to Harrisburg, from Washington to Frederick, and across the Eastern Shore. The most spectacular project of the period was a $130-million tunnel under the Baltimore harbor which diverted north- and southbound traffic around the city. Most of the roads were paid for by tolls and bonds. McKeldin embraced the road building program and demanded frills—picnic tables, anti-billboard regulations, and safety programs—which the legislature resisted but finally approved. An increase in the number of state police officers from 250 to 470 resulted in a decline of the highway death toll from 7.6 per million miles in 1951, which was one of the highest in the nation, to 5.4 in 1957, which was one of the lowest.[30]

Smaller in terms of dollars than the growth in education or roads, but larger in terms of life expectancy, were the changes taking place in health care. The biggest change in the lives of the American people in the 1950s stemmed from the greatest medical research breakthroughs in world history. Penicillin and sulfa drugs, developed during the war, came into common use, and antibiotics, the Salk vaccine, tranquilizers, cortisone, and fluoridation gained immediate acceptance. The state public health bureaucracies grasped the significance of these breakthroughs and saw to it that they were in common use by the end of the decade. Mostly the changes brought relief from pain and longer, happier lives. There were also some less-anticipated, less-welcome side effects.

As new drug therapies eased the ancient scourges of tuberculosis, venereal disease, and insanity, the fine new sanitariums that Lane and McKeldin had rushed to completion became monuments to a dark age past, and then were adapted to new purposes. Salk vaccine for polio, given by state nurses to all school children, virtually ended the disease that most terrified parents. Penicillin for venereal disease, along with new contraceptive devices, prompted a sexual revolution that was to have undreamed-of consequences in the decade ahead. Fluoride, added to 65 percent of the state's water supply by 1958, allowed dentists to redirect the focus of their work from relief of pain to more profitable cosmetology. Longer lives created a new nursing-home industry. Once-modest physicians became members of one of the highest-ranking status groups in American society.[31]

Other state services fell behind the state's growth rate. Maryland continued to operate like a southern state in its maintenance of a large prison population under harsh conditions. It retained about 174 prisoners per 100,000 population, the highest rate in the country except for Georgia. Following Sobeloff's recommendations, the state created a professional parole board to replace wardens' advice to the governor, slowly expanded its work program for prisoners, and opened a modern facility for mentally retarded prisoners in which doctors engaged in a new enthusiasm, psychiatric research.[32]

The state service that lagged most significantly was welfare, partly because the affluent middle class could not see that poverty remained and partly because the federal government assumed much of the burden through social security. The apparent increase during the period in welfare expenditures was only a result of the inclusion of teachers and other state employees into the social security system. State and county expenditures for the deaf, the blind, orphans, the aged, and the poor averaged $9.36 per capita, compared to a national average of $19.99. The governor, the assembly, and the state bureaucracy were not particularly concerned about the lag.

Expenditures for parks and for conservation of the oyster and crabbing grounds of the Chesapeake actually declined, despite McKeldin's pleas, and chiefly in response to the watermen themselves, who preferred laissez faire to state regulations.[33]

Looking back over his administration—his own role, that of the assembly, and that of the bureaucracy—McKeldin was generally pleased with the results. As he said of Eisenhower's, it was a good administration, not a great one.[34] Probably, like Eisenhower, he could have been elected for a third term if that had been constitutional and if he had wanted it, although neither he nor Eisenhower successfully transferred his office to a Republican successor, for theirs was a triumph of personality, not of party. Neither Eisenhower nor McKeldin created the self-satisfied period that they symbolized, but they both promoted its social harmony, its prosperity, and its slightly pallid good intentions.

McKeldin's greatest personal hour lay ahead. From 1963 to 1967 he again served as mayor of Baltimore, an office for which he was probably better suited than he was for the governorship, and in this later period, which called for heroes, he almost became one by promoting racial justice and walking the streets when racial revolution threatened. Ultimately, however, the 1950s style of middle-class generosity to blacks was doomed, and after McKeldin left office the explosion came.

Postwar prosperity required massive adjustments in social relations which sometimes assumed extreme or even revolutionary proportions. The anti-communist movement of the late 1940s constituted one such adjustment, and the student revolts of the late 1960s produced another. The greatest upheaval, however, was the black revolt against segregation and poverty. In some ways the black movement was a revolution, including, as it did, the classic stages of slowly building pressure, exploding idealism, radicalism and violence, and, finally, institutionalization. In a larger sense, however, it was evolution, for its roots extended back to emancipation, it never went backward, as revolutions usually do, and it was far from over, even by the 1980s. The racial adjustment that took place between 1940 and 1980 was only the revolutionary phase of a much greater evolution.

Maryland encapsulated the movement because it contained both its southern and northern halves. In Maryland, as in the South, change began slowly, through court action, and then blossomed into the fervor of sit-ins. Then, as in the North, the movement burst into urban violence. Finally it was absorbed into the system. In retrospect the movement appears inevitable, the product of prosperity, and in retrospect it looks even larger than it did to participants.

For Maryland blacks the decade of the 1920s was the low point, at least since slavery. Blacks composed about 17 percent of the state's population, and they were segregated by law into separate parts of town, separate railroad cars and buses, separate parks and sporting events, separate restaurants, water fountains, and toilets, separate hospitals and jails, and, usually, separate stores and separate menial jobs. Baltimore was the only major city in the nation which had legally separated blocks for black and white residents. No Baltimore blacks were employed in the police or fire department, and blacks were generally forbidden admission to public libraries, museums, art galleries, and banks. The state's public schools in 1920 spent an average of $36.03 per year for each white child and $13.20 for each black child. Maryland in the 1920s had one of the largest state memberships in the Ku Klux Klan; there had been sixteen lynchings in the state since 1884; and even respectable politicians made "niggers" the scapegoats for the ills of society. Black adult and infant mortality rates were almost double those for whites. To be sure that these conditions did not impinge on whites, the state in 1927 created the Interracial Commission, dominated by whites and dedicated "to encourage thrift, industry, education, sobriety, and all the virtues." For five years the commission issued reports that congratulated the state on harmonious race relations, but then it stopped reporting. All this was the background against which to measure change.[1]

What blacks did have was the relative prosperity of the 1920s, the social welfare legislation of the 1930s, and the soaring prosperity that came after 1940. In the 1920s in Maryland blacks had some special advantages: a secure right to vote, an urban concentration that allowed them to act in concert, and leaders who had been toughened

The Bases of Hope, 1920–1955

rather than demoralized by degradation. They had the *Afro-American,* probably the strongest black newspaper in the United States, which was published by the remarkable Carl Murphy. They had strong churches under politically minded ministers, and they had some aggressive female leaders like Lillie May Jackson and her daughters. These things, especially the rise of prosperity, formed the bases of hope that eventually prevailed over custom and law.

The modern civil rights movement in Maryland began in the mid-1930s with the revival of the Baltimore chapter of the National Association for the Advancement of Colored People. The Baltimore NAACP had been organized in 1913 but had languished until 1935, when notorious Eastern Shore lynchings focused attention on Maryland and the national organization, on the inspired recommendation of the *Afro-American,* selected Lillie May Jackson to revive the Baltimore chapter. Born Lillie May Carroll, she claimed that one of her forebears was an African chieftain and that another was Maryland's Revolutionary aristocrat Charles Carroll of Carrollton. She was deeply religious, a fundamentalist who was opposed to alcohol, tobacco, and dancing. She built a real estate empire with her preacher husband, Kieffer Jackson, and she pressed her black tenants for maximum rents, which she used for good causes, in the same aggressive way that she demanded greater efforts from her followers and greater concessions from her enemies. Governor McKeldin remarked that he would rather have the devil after him than Mrs. Jackson.[2]

Baltimore's and New York's NAACP chapters alternated in these years as the two largest in the country, and Baltimore's strength lay in the plain people who made up the core of Jackson's support. She combined militance with nonviolence. In the early years she clashed with intellectuals, black and white, who feared she moved too fast and thus alienated too many, and she replaced many of the polite preacher-teacher intellectuals on her board with labor leaders and longshoremen. Then, in later years, she clashed with the mostly black intellectuals who argued that violence promoted racial pride. Reform movements in America have always failed in the hands of intellectuals, while they usually have flourished under pragmatists. Jackson knew where she stood; she was a good executive and a superb publicist; and she always carefully allied herself with the black churches and the *Afro-American.* Jackson's NAACP, the black ministry, and the newspaper were the triple generals in the crusade—the three avenues of protest—for the Maryland civil rights movement.[3]

There were hard-won early victories for the movement in the 1930s, small but sustaining victories for the newly militant organization. Jackson organized a buy-where-you-can-work campaign, a militant picketing of local stores that were dependent on black patronage but refused to hire black workers. The campaign won some concessions, especially from the A&P grocery stores—maybe the first concessions in Maryland that had ever been won through black power. Political mobilization and deals with white candidates forced the Baltimore Police Department to hire a number of blacks, but then the department determined to hire only black college graduates, and they were not issued uniforms or given power to make arrests.[4]

Theodore McKeldin, Justice Thurgood Marshall, and Lillie May Jackson at the Sharp
Street Methodist Church, Baltimore. Mrs. Jackson, beautiful as a girl, disliked pictures
of herself because her face was distorted as a result of a bungled operation in a doctor's
office after she had been denied admission to a white hospital. Courtesy of the Lillie
May Carroll Jackson Museum.

A breakthrough came on the legal front, in the NAACP tradition,
when Donald G. Murray, a black graduate of Amherst, won his suit
for admission to the University of Maryland Law School. The
NAACP selected the case carefully: it included a well-qualified appli-
cant, the postgraduate level of education, an institution in a border
state, and a brilliant local lawyer, Thurgood Marshall, who himself
had been denied admission to the University of Maryland Law School.
Baltimore friends had helped Marshall pay for his education at
Howard University, but he remembered the rejection bitterly. "The
first thing I did when I got out [of Howard] was to get even," he said.
Marshall won his case in 1934, the first big victory in his own career,
the first major attack on segregated education—which culminated in
Marshall's arguments in *Brown* v. *Board of Education*. Following the
Murray case, the Maryland legislature, to avoid "indiscriminate mix-
ing," appropriated a fund of $30,000 a year to finance out-of-state
education for blacks.[5]

Marshall and the NAACP also launched legal attacks on the system
in which Maryland teachers were paid about half the salary of whites.
The black Defense League, a coalition of ministers and lawyers, had
won salary equalization in education in Baltimore in 1926, but the
counties lagged. Marshall proceeded county by county, winning
equalization in Montgomery County in 1937, and then in six other
counties, until the legislature accepted the inevitable and in 1941
enacted salary equalization for teachers throughout the state.[6]

World War II more than the court decisions generated change in
black conditions. Wars are usually forces for social equalization, as

manpower becomes scarce and wages rise. From 1940 to 1942 some thirty-three thousand blacks poured into Baltimore—some three hundred per week—increasing the black population of the city by 20 percent. About half of them came from the Maryland countryside, especially from southern Maryland and the Eastern Shore, and half came from the South. Mostly they came for low wages, for even in 1942 about 94 percent of the black jobs in the city were menial or unskilled. Still, their arrival marked the end of tenant farm share-cropping in Maryland, the independence of money wages, and the concentration of blacks under Baltimore's strong black leadership.[7]

The surge to the city brought terrible crowding, for the war allowed little housing construction, and there was intense white opposition to enlargement of the segregated ghetto areas. A 1942 survey calculated that 20 percent of the city's population—the black percentage—was crowded into 2 percent of the city's shelter space. Rents skyrocketed, and eight people in a room became commonplace. Again, however, the frustration served to strengthen black leadership.[8]

Jackson, the ministers, and the *Afro-American* editors calculated their strategy and kept in close touch with leaders in other cities where conditions were similar. In Washington in 1941 the black labor leader A. Philip Randolph emerged with the concept of a nationwide black disruption of the war effort through a massive march on Washington. President Roosevelt was duly alarmed and made a trade: cancellation of the march in exchange for an order requiring equal pay in government and defense industries and a Fair Employment Practices Commission for enforcement. Black wages did begin to rise, and some blacks realized they had won with threats. In Baltimore, particularly, the NAACP kept the pressure on, cooperating with the local FEPC for full implementation of orders, publicizing inequities, and even threatening strikes. There were tension and racial incidents and continuing violation of the FEPC regulations, but there was also unprecedented economic progress, if only because of the wartime labor shortage. Most war plants and unions actually boasted of compliance.[9]

Other groups, both more and less radical than Jackson's, emerged during the war. The Urban League, mostly run by whites, promoted black economic opportunities and harmonious race relations. Fearful that public pressure did more harm than good, it worked with employers behind the scenes to promote job-training programs. It especially encouraged congressional passage, and then the state's adoption, of the War Training Program, which provided federal money to the public schools to train unskilled adults for skilled jobs. By 1943 more than eight thousand adults were enrolled in Maryland, the majority of them black. Notable wartime gains in Baltimore included the rights of blacks to drive taxis and to own taverns.[10]

Individual black entrepreneurs emerged, notably Baltimore's black millionaire Willie Adams, who made his money in liquor and gambling and wanted the recognition that accompanied wealth. Adams mobilized protesters and employed lawyers to gain the right of blacks to use the city's golf course. The city first set aside one afternoon a week for blacks to use the course, then built a separate golf course, and finally, in 1946, agreed to integration, creating probably the first legally integrated public recreational facility in Maryland. Jackson was contemptuous of what she regarded as a frivolous cause, but Adams was on his way to a new career of political power.[11]

Wartime prosperity and progress for blacks brought tension that found outlet in street violence and a corresponding escalation of black demands. In February 1942 a black was shot in the back and killed by a white policeman for resisting arrest after he had attempted to ride in an unlicensed taxi. A grand jury charged the policeman with homicide one day, and met with the police chief and pardoned him the next. The *Afro-American* noted that ten blacks had been killed by the police in four years and had had no action taken against them. Mayor Howard Jackson had no comment, and the NAACP began organizing for a march on Annapolis.

On April 23, 1942, thousands of blacks, representing 125 religious, civic, and fraternal organizations, rallied at the Sharp Street Methodist Church in Baltimore. Some two thousand delegates then headed for Annapolis by chartered buses and trains. They filled both houses of the General Assembly, and Lillie May Jackson, Carl Murphy, and others made a two-hour plea to Governor O'Conor. The protestors were calm but resolute, calling for an end to police brutality and for black representation on the city school board.[12] Again, as in the threatened march on Washington, the show of strength and the argument were successful, and O'Conor replaced the ineffectual Interracial Commission of 1927 with a new Commission to Study the Problems Affecting the Colored Population. This commission was only educational, but it deliberately tied black progress to patriotism, and it thus increased both the willingness of employers to accept black workers and the willingness of the city to accept federal housing projects to accommodate the black influx from the farm. By the end of the war, black employment had risen from 7 percent to 17 percent of the state's industrial labor force, Baltimore and its suburbs had over six thousand new federal housing units for blacks, and Lillie May Jackson's NAACP had over twenty thousand members. Black progress had become like a ratchet—each step forward provided a base for the next one.[13]

By the end of the war, blacks were beginning to realize that their greatest power was in the ballot box and that their best allies could be elected officials. Roosevelt was the first black ally, even though he sometimes pretended he wasn't, and in 1936 black voters in Maryland, who had been Republicans since the time of Lincoln, generally voted Democratic. Jackson and the *Afro-American* led the way. Even more significant, however, was the switch back, when in 1943 Baltimore blacks cast the deciding votes in favor of Republican Mayor Theodore McKeldin. The three black wards that had been 54 percent for Roosevelt in 1936 were 74 percent for McKeldin in 1943. Both conviction and politics pushed him to be worthy of their support. McKeldin appointed blacks to almost all city boards: education, health, recreation, planning, and the rest. He ordered city employment of blacks, notably as police officers, librarians, and nurses. He worked with the federal government to obtain additional black housing, with the Urban League to find private employers for blacks, with

the unions to promote acceptance of black workers, and with the
NAACP to persuade the local press, notably the *Sunpapers,* to soften
their emphasis on racial crime and to expand their coverage of black
achievements. Mostly McKeldin's efforts from 1943 to 1947 were
rhetorical and symbolic, not quite for integration but, rather, for
expanded opportunities. In most cities racial tension mounted after
the war as jobs became scarce, but postwar Baltimore maintained and
continued progress amidst considerable good will.[14]

The NAACP was keenly aware of the power of politics. Black voter
registration became a major concern of the late 1940s, so that from
1940 to 1952 the number of black voters approximately doubled. In
1946 Willie Adams's wife, Victorine, organized the Colored Democratic Women, which became a core of black voting power which was
nongeographic and separate from the Democratic clubs—and more
powerful than most of them.[15] In 1948 it was almost as though Harry
Truman had learned from McKeldin. Truman championed federal
legislation to insure black fair employment, and he mostly lost the
South's support, but he won election as president in 1948 by the
margin of black votes in the middle and northern cities (56 percent of
Baltimore's black voters in the fifth, fourteenth, and seventeenth
wards voted for Truman). He also provided rhetoric that boosted
black hopes and sometimes won white sympathizers.

The Maryland governor's race of 1950 showed how well politicians
had learned about black voting power. The Democratic candidate was
William P. Lane, a liberal supporter of Truman's civil rights program,
and the Republican candidate was the black voter's friend from Baltimore, Theodore McKeldin. The state seemed to have progressed far
from the racist campaigns of the 1930s, but actually 1950 was only an
interlude when politicians could seek black support without threatening whites. The Republican McKeldin won for governor as he had
won for mayor, with black votes, and two years later 68 percent of
black voters in the three black-dominated wards of Baltimore supported the Democratic presidential nominee, Adlai Stevenson. Black
voting solidarity was extraordinary: voters in these three wards
switched parties five times in eighteen years (see table 7.1)[16]

From McKeldin's election as governor in 1950 until the beginning
of school integration in 1954, black gains continued, though they
were still mostly symbolic and still mostly at the instigation of the
governor, who was conscious of the necessity of pleasing a constituency without unduly rousing an opposition. Most people, whether

Table 7.1.   Baltimore Black Voters, 1934–1952
(in 5th, 14th, and 17th Wards)

Year	Majority Party	Candidate Supported	Percentage of Votes
1934	Republican	Nice over Ritchie	66
1936	Democratic	Roosevelt over Landon	54
1943	Republican	McKeldin over Jackson	74
1948	Democratic	Truman over Dewey	56
1950	Republican	McKeldin over Lane	79
1952	Democratic	Stevenson over Eisenhower	68

they were for the changes or against them, viewed the gains as rights for a few successful blacks, not the elevation of many. The gains involved rights more than integration; they did not much threaten anyone; opposition was cantankerous rather than angry. Each gain was a story unto itself, usually involving careful planning and pressure by the black leadership, behind-the-scenes support by the governor or other powerful white politicians who wanted black support, and, finally, reluctant action by the agency involved. A list illustrates how many gains were made in these years, but does not tell of the great battles required to make them:

1951   McKeldin appoints blacks to most state commissions
        McKeldin replaces Commission to Study the Problems Affect-
            ing the Colored Population with Commission on Interracial
            Problems and Relations
1952   Baltimore's Ford Theater integrates
        Most Baltimore department stores agree to wait on blacks
        Baltimore opens two baseball diamonds for blacks
1953   Dorchester County hires first black police officer
        Cambridge and Salisbury open hospitals to black doctors
        Baltimore's Lyric Theater books Marian Anderson, first black
            performer (although no hotel will give her a room)
        Baltimore fire department hires first blacks
        McKeldin opens state parks to blacks
1954   Baltimore dime-store lunch counters begin to open to blacks
        Baltimore Public Housing allows integration
        Baltimore elects Harry Cole as first black to General Assembly
        Baltimore public schools first in United States to accept
            Supreme Court's integration order[17]

The high point for all America of this first period of legal action and gradually rising hope came in education with the *Brown* v. *Board of Education* court decision and the response, notably in Baltimore, to its implementation. There were reasons Maryland became the first legally segregated state to accept the decision, one year ahead of the court's deadline: it was the northernmost segregated state, its blacks were relatively prosperous, its black leadership was strong, its political leaders were either enlightened or sensitive to black voting power, and its progress toward other types of integration had been fairly smooth. Besides Governor McKeldin and Mayor D'Alesandro, there was Baltimore's school superintendent, John H. Fischer, who promoted integration as an expression of progressive educational theory. In 1952 Fischer persuaded the school board to admit fifteen advanced black high school students to the city's only technological school, Baltimore Polytechnic. The action was well publicized, for it violated local law, but there was no trouble, and the city fathers were soon boasting of their enlightenment.[18]

The decision in *Brown* v. *Board of Education*, which ordered all schools to begin after one year to integrate with deliberate speed, came on May 17, 1954. That evening Jackson and her friends celebrated with lemonade and cookies, proud that one of their own, Thurgood Marshall, had been the landmark case's chief attorney. The next day Governor McKeldin and Mayor D'Alesandro issued statements hailing the decision and promising to uphold the law. A week later Superintendent Fischer called the school board into session and gave them a carefully prepared plan for compliance, not for 1955, as required, but for the fall of 1954. The board consulted with the state attorney general to make sure the Supreme Court outranked the city ordinances, and on June 3 the board voted unanimously to proceed. The following day the Catholic archbishop announced that the state's Catholic schools would voluntarily comply, and two weeks after that the University of Maryland announced it would accept undergraduate blacks to its classes and dormitories. It seemed as though the Supreme Court had encouraged state leadership to do what it had wanted to do anyway.[19]

That fall integration in Baltimore proceeded fairly easily, as about two hundred blacks entered white schools widely scattered through the city. Hundreds of photographers and reporters flocked to the first city in the nation to comply with the Court's order; the news magazines published profiles of the city, and CBS made a special documentary. After a month pickets appeared around several schools in the blue-collar area of south Baltimore, white high school gangs urged a student strike, and crowds around the schools became unruly. The pride of civic leaders was stronger than the protest, however. Churches and media denounced the mobs. The police arrested strike leaders, the courts issued injunctions against picketing, and the protest collapsed. The abortive protest had come either too late or too early, but it seemed to have cleared the air. The middle-class liberals had triumphed. Opposition had been crushed, and integration in Baltimore proceeded with little incident, slowly increasing momentum. The following year, 1955, about 7 percent of the city's black pupils attended school with whites; in 1956, 14 percent; and in 1957, 26 percent.[20]

With the Brown decision, and with Baltimore leading the way in implementation, the period of litigation and behind-the-scenes leadership was ready to give way to something larger. The quiet hope of an oppressed people was about to burst forth into a crusade.

The Movement, 1955–1968

The civil rights movement—The Movement, as participants like to say—was a wave of almost religious sentiment shared by blacks and whites together in favor of justice for all people. It lasted for about thirteen years, from 1955 to 1968, beginning with the black bus boycott in Alabama, gaining impetus from the Gandhi-like sit-ins that spread to Maryland in the early 1960s, culminating in the march of a million people to Washington in the summer of 1963 to hear Martin Luther King proclaim his dream and in the enactment of the federal and state civil rights laws of 1964 and 1965. Blacks led the movement, demanding justice, but it was equally a white movement, especially of the educated middle class, inspiring idealism and brotherhood. "We

Shall Overcome" was the movement's hymn. It was the triumph of hope; it was the birth of bitterness and despair.

The movement had its beginning in Montgomery, Alabama, on December 5, 1955, when Rosa Parks, who was black, sat down in the wrong bus seat and stubbornly decided not to move. The next Sunday her hitherto unknown preacher, Martin Luther King, urged blacks in the city to boycott the buses, and for almost a year blacks walked or made up carpools to get to work, until the bus company neared bankruptcy and decided that blacks could sit anywhere. The boycott was an old weapon, one Lillie May Jackson had used, but the serene dignity of Rosa Parks and the inspiring benevolence of Dr. King's sermons were new weapons, and they were aimed at the nation's conscience.

In Maryland the transition to popular crusade came slowly. It began to appear in community pride over the first school integration, in newspaper and television coverage of the Alabama boycott, and in public support for accelerating local change. The determinedly upper-middle-class *Sunpapers* reflected the mood. In the 1920s they were outspokenly hostile to blacks as a source of crime, a threat to middle-class values. By the 1930s the anti-black stance faded, but the papers still pandered to prejudice by conspicuously identifying miscreants by race and by conspicuously ignoring black achievements. By the 1940s this attitude in turn had evolved to patronizing sympathy, and by the mid 1950s to full support. The major dailies in Washington and Wilmington followed a similar course, as did the national news magazines and networks, with the small-town Maryland newspapers lagging by about a decade. In 1955 the *Sunpapers* launched a major front-page series entitled "The City We Live In," which was an exposé of injustice to blacks.[21] The papers gave sympathetic coverage to the Alabama bus boycott. Society pages began to cover black weddings, and sports-page editors launched a small crusade for the integration of athletic teams and facilities.

Encouraged by Governor McKeldin and Mayor D'Alesandro, other politicians began to discover that liberal racial stands were popular not only with black voters but with a growing number of whites, as well, and the bureaucracy began to take up the cause of black civil rights. In 1955 the Baltimore City Council authorized publication of a 249-page book, *A City in Transition,* boasting of the city's progress in civil rights and openly promoting the need for more. The leadership was leading. The following year, after long debate, the council passed a far-reaching equal employment ordinance, patterned after a similar one in Philadelphia, which outlawed racial discrimination for employment by city or private firms within Baltimore. There was no means of enforcement, but the ordinance created a small city bureaucracy to publicize violations and to lobby for still stronger legislation. In 1956 Governor McKeldin ended the separate listing of black and white applicants for state jobs. In 1959 there were at least thirty antisegregation bills and resolutions offered in the General Assembly, most of them introduced by delegates from Baltimore, the Washington suburbs, and the western counties.[22]

The newspapers and the state civil rights bureaucracies kept a running box score of their victories. The great efforts here involved not so much the behind-the-scenes manipulation that was evident in the early 1950s, but more the development of public opinion.

1955   Baltimore department stores allow blacks to try on clothes
        McKeldin ends segregation in the National Guard
1956   Baltimore Equal Employment Ordinance
        McKeldin eliminates separate lists for state job applicants
1957   Most Montgomery County restaurants agree to serve blacks
        Most state professional organizations (except dentists) agree
            to accept black members
1958   Most Baltimore movies open to blacks
        Most Baltimore first-class hotels accommodate blacks
1959   Prince George's and western Maryland restaurants begin to
            integrate[23]

Blacks remained the center of the movement in Maryland, but whites also poured in, organizations multiplied, and leadership diffused. Mostly white organizations dedicated to ending segregation included the Council of Churches, Clergymen's Interfaith Organization, Commission on Human Relations, Americans for Democratic Action, AFL-CIO, the League of Women Voters, Panel of American Women, and the American Civil Liberties Union. Lillie May Jackson's NAACP swelled with white members. Mostly black organizations, like the Southern Christian Leadership Conference, Congress of Racial Equality (CORE), and the Student Non-Violent Coodinating Committee (SNCC), also appeared. The black organizations particularly emphasized political action, and the first statewide black political leaders emerged. In 1954 Harry Cole from Baltimore became the first black delegate to the General Assembly, and in 1958 Verda Welcome and Irma Dixon were elected. There were major black voting registration drives in 1957 and 1960, adding at least 50,000 black voters to the rolls, and by 1968 ten blacks were delegates in the General Assembly.[24]

The movement's grandeur grew in proportion to the bigotry of its opponents. In 1957 the nation watched federal paratroopers in battle gear escort frightened black children to school through the howling mobs of Little Rock. In February 1960 people watched while black college students in coat and tie waited to be served at the Woolworth lunch counter in Greensboro, North Carolina, while white hoodlums poked at them and jeered. Here was precisely the Gandhi-King technique: civil disobedience to unjust laws, dramatizing the gulf between justice and injustice, gaining attention to promote reasonable negotiation. Within weeks college students everywhere had discovered the most effective way yet to promote the cause of racial justice.

In Maryland, just one month after Greensboro, black students from Morgan State College, joined by whites from Johns Hopkins and Goucher, staged a sit-in that won desegregation of the lunch counters in the Northwood Shopping Center near the Morgan campus in Baltimore. Warmed by their easy victory, they moved downtown to picket the major department stores to employ black clerks. Black students from Maryland State College began integrating Salisbury lunch counters that fall, and restaurants and movie theaters the following spring. White students in College Park launched a boycott of the Little Tavern, which was the last town eating establishment to refuse black customers, and then they began an intermittent three-year picketing campaign to get black clerks in the local stores and banks. In Baltimore and the Washington suburbs, students were thrilled to discover and pounce on a recalcitrant merchant.[25]

The most publicized sit-in was organized by mostly white clergy to protest black exclusion from the Gwynn Oak Amusement Park in Baltimore County. Baltimore rabbis seem to have made the first contacts; the Presbyterian president of the World Council of Chuches, Eugene Carson Blake, arrived from New York to participate; and Baltimore's Roman Catholic Cardinal Lawrence Shehan provided a pastoral letter saying, "We [Catholics] have a special obligation to place ourselves in the forefront to remove the injustices and discriminations which remain." On July 4, 1963, the clergy led protestors to the park, where 275 were arrested, including 36 clergy. Three days later the protestors reappeared for another 100 arrests, this time including 7 clergy. Newspapers and television featured the story, sermons rang out all over the world, and a month later, after publicized negotiations, the amusement park welcomed blacks.[26]

From 1960 to 1963 the desegregation movement spread slowly to other parts of the state, notably the fifty-mile stretch of roadhouses along Route 40 between Baltimore and the Delaware line. For years African diplomats traveling between Washington and New York had been discomfited by the segregation, and had lodged protests and received soothing apologies. In March 1961, however, President John F. Kennedy, newly inaugurated, determined to make an issue of this segregation through an elaborate public apology to the chargé d'affaires from Sierra Leone. This invited other Africans to make similar complaints, and, willingly enough, the African delegations banded together for a joint protest. Kennedy negotiated with Governor Tawes, who issued a profuse apology and urged the restaurants, at least, to serve black diplomats. Reporters from the *Afro-American* dressed in lion-skin togas to dramatize the absurdity: foreign blacks could usually get service but local blacks could not. Baltimore and Philadelphia students organized freedom rides, by which well-dressed blacks sought arrest and publicity for trespassing in segregated facilities. Dozens were arrested through the summer of 1961, but the climax came in September when three Philadelphia blacks refused to pay their fifty-dollar fine, refused to post bail, and went on a seventeen-day hunger strike to protest their jailing. For weeks the affair made headlines, until the judge relented and released the prisoners.

All this merely fueled the issue. The Kennedy government, still pretending foreign relations were at stake, sent State Department agents into the towns along Route 40 to promote integration. The Congress of Racial Equality called for a freedom ride on November 11 during which two thousand students, black and white, would be willing to accept arrest for trespassing. The restaurateurs, hemmed in by local intransigence and ordinances, begged Governor Tawes to intervene, and after a week of frantic negotiations between Tawes's office, local governments, restaurateurs, the State Department, and CORE, a compromise settlement emerged: thirty-five of about forty-seven restaurants would accept black customers, CORE would call off its march, and Governor Tawes would introduce legislation at the next General Assembly session which would bar discrimination in public accommodations forever.[27]

Many students were disappointed to be denied arrest for a noble cause, and a group from Hopkins, Goucher, and Morgan rallied to lament their easy triumph and to look for new frontiers. Here was the essence of a revolution: the movement was outrunning its participants, victories were coming faster than the proponents could handle them. The students agreed to contact their colleagues in the Eastern Shore colleges and to launch a spring sit-in offensive in Easton, Chestertown, and Cambridge.[28]

The time had come by 1962 for political action that would legally eliminate segregation once and for all. Tawes promised it for the 1962 General Assembly, and public opinion seemed to be calling for it. Polls showed the majority of voters still marginally opposed, but opinion was shifting rapidly, and newspapers and volunteer organizations were clamoring for action. The opposition knew theirs was a rearguard cause. They lacked ideology and organization and largely acknowledged their biases as uncharitable. The opposition was strongest, of course, in the eastern and southern counties, where blacks were most numerous and where racial segregation was not easily replaced by economic segregation.

Tawes, true to his promise, in January 1962, offered his open accommodations bill outlawing segregation in restaurants, hotels, theaters, stores, beaches, and recreational facilities. Legislative leaders, fearful that the issue would deadlock the assembly, agreed to table the bill for a special session of the assembly in March, immediately following regular business. By then the bill was toned down, in Maryland's peculiar way, to apply only to Baltimore and eight counties (Baltimore, Charles, Montgomery, Prince George's, Frederick, Washington, Allegany, and Garrett), omitting the remaining fifteen. Still, probably never since reconstruction had a session been so dramatic, as legislative banter and horseplay gave way to evangelical passion and tears. The bill failed, sixty in favor, forty-three opposed, and nineteen abstaining, lacking two votes to obtain a majority of the votes cast. Proponents of brotherhood wept, but of course they would be back. The Baltimore City Council and the Montgomery County Council, feeling that their people had been rebuffed by the state's reactionaries, passed their own open accommodations ordinances.[29]

The 1962 setback was temporary, for late that same year came a court-mandated legislative reapportionment that sharply reduced rural power, and early in the 1963 legislative session Tawes's open accommodations bill passed by a vote of ninety-three to twenty-eight. It applied to Baltimore and twelve counties, with Howard, Harford, Cecil, and Anne Arundel added to the list of the previous year. The assembly gave the state Commission on Interracial Problems and Relations power to enforce the act through subpoenas and cease and desist

orders. In the summer of 1963 came the great march on Washington
and Martin Luther King's speech, and in the fall came President Kennedy's assassination. In March 1964 the Maryland General Assembly
voted eighty-three to fifty to apply open accommodations to the entire
state. Finally, three months later, President Lyndon Johnson persuaded Congress to pass a similar law, the Civil Rights Act of 1964,
hardly different from the Maryland law. From 1963 to 1968, even
while civil rights idealism gave way to violence, state and federal
legislation proceeded almost in tandem, with Maryland generally a
little bit ahead (see table 7.2).

Maryland's 1965 Fair Employment Act passed without fanfare and
took effect before the federal statute outlawing job discrimination
both in hiring and promoting by both public and private employers.
Two years later the state passed an Open Housing Act, more than a
year ahead of corresponding federal legislation, which outlawed discrimination in the sale of new houses and apartments. Voters petitioned the act to referendum and defeated it, 343,447 to 275,781, but
the referendum made no difference, for by then the federal law was in
effect. More important than the state or federal housing law was the
Maryland law, hardly noticed, which forbade lenders from discriminating against house buyers, even of older houses. For Maryland and
the nation, legislation marked the high point of civil rights sentiment,
even though the legislation came after that sentiment was sharply on
the wane. Legislation lagged behind opinion, and opinion lagged
behind events.[30]

From the beginning the movement had been led by blacks, and the
reasons were simply that blacks demanded a better place for themselves, that affluence in World War II provided an economic base for
take-off, that black ballots were effective, that legal breakthroughs
like the *Brown* decision made progress feasible, and that each success
in the movement fueled the next one. It was also, however, a white
movement. White court decisions and executive action allowed blacks
to secure better jobs, to ride the buses, and integrate the schools.
Within twenty years after World War II, whites accepted economic,

Table 7.2. Civil Rights Legislation

Date	Maryland	United States
1963	Open Accommodations for twelve counties	
1964	Open Accommodations for entire state	Civil Rights Law: Open Accom-modations and Fair Employ-ment after one year
1965	Fair Employment effective immediately	Voting Rights (did not apply to Maryland)
1967	Open Housing (passed by assembly but defeated by voter referendum)	
1968	Open Housing for home financing (lenders cannot refuse blacks in white areas)	Open Housing

educational, and social integration in a way that had been inconceivable twenty years before. The reasons for the change in white opinion are harder to explain.

Partly the answer lay in the Western world's embarrassment over Hitler's racism and in the changed conclusions of social scientists who once supported but now denounced notions of racial inferiority. Maybe part of the answer lay in the vague concept of cyclical idealism, which had reoccurred in the abolitionist movement of the 1850s, in the populism of the 1890s, and in the New Deal of the 1930s. This concept gained support from the civil rights movement's close association with the fervid antiwar, antipoverty, and environmental concerns of the 1960s. One of the most interesting explanations of the civil rights movement was essentially Marxist—the idea that the middle class was so secure by the 1950s that it no longer needed a subservient class, that machinery had reduced the number of unacceptable jobs so that subjugation was no longer necessary (that dishwashers and frozen foods, in other words, had eliminated the need for black servants), that the middle class, as a result of its security and comfort, was willing for those on the bottom rung to rise as high as they could. Whatever the reasons, America was experiencing a change of revolutionary proportions.

The Violent Phase, 1963–1968

Revolutions, however, usually turn violent and devour their own, and this, too, happened in Maryland. In June 1963, in the little Eastern Shore town of Cambridge (population 11,000), the hitherto peaceful sit-ins erupted into the movement's first urban rioting. The significance of Cambridge was that it signaled the transition of blacks from victims to part-instigators of violence. The scene of action was shifting from the South, where peaceful demonstrations promoted legislation that ended segregation, to the North, where blacks protested because they were poor and where protests did little to alleviate poverty. Beginning in Cambridge, the black goal of integration mixed with the new black goal of separation. "We Shall Overcome" evolved into "Burn, Baby, Burn."

Salisbury and Cambridge, the two largest towns on the Eastern Shore, had been progressing toward integration almost as admirably as Baltimore and the Washington suburbs. Although the Eastern Shore towns were generally of southern traditions, and both were one-third black, they were proud of recent progress. In Salisbury, sit-ins of black students from nearby Maryland State College brought lunch counter integration in 1960 and general restaurant integration in 1961. Cambridge, if anything, had a better record. A token black had served on the city council since 1900, attending all meetings except the annual banquet, from which he was excluded. His colleagues sent his dinner on a paper plate to his home. Similarly, one or two establishment blacks served on the school board, hospital board, housing authority, and zoning commission, and three served on the police force. The town establishment considered itself realistic, even progressive. Unemployment was moderately high, for the seafood packing industry was in a depression, but nine small manufacturers had arrived between 1958 and 1963, and all accepted black workers. A town-sponsored Equal Opportunity Commission actively promoted jobs for blacks. In 1962 three of the town's four major restaurants accepted blacks, although the movie theater, bowling alley, and about eighteen quick-food lunch counters were still negotiating or were firmly segregated. In January 1963 about twenty students, black and white, arrived from Swarthmore College in Pennsylvania and other colleges in New York and Baltimore to stage a sit-in and lead demonstrations. The outside element was a little different, stimulating local opposition, but still not alarming.[31]

What was different in Cambridge was the emergence of Gloria Richardson, a strong woman, like Lillie May Jackson in many ways, but of a younger and angrier generation. Richardson was scion of the town's black establishment, granddaughter of Maynaidier St. Clair, who had been the black city councilman for fifty years. She was the daughter of Charles St. Clair, who was a funeral director and probably the town's richest black. She was one of the few blacks from the town to have gone away to college—to Howard University, where she was a brilliant student—and one of the few college graduates to have returned. But things went badly. She wanted to teach, but for reasons of discrimination or depression there were no jobs. Her marriage failed. For a while she was on unemployment, and then she obtained a job in a factory and was fired for lack of manual dexterity. She was one of the ablest persons in the county, but she was a failure, and she was angry.

During the winter and spring of 1963 the protestors grew increasingly strident. The local black establishment recoiled from them, denouncing the protests as counterproductive, as worsening race relations rather than improving them. To the activists, however, harmony was not a goal, and the protests were obviously gaining more support from heretofore nonpolitical street blacks than they were losing from moderates. Intellectually, the movement was evolving from acceptance of a few to rights for all—to militance and black pride. Lillie May Jackson's Baltimore NAACP withdrew from Cambridge and was replaced by leaders from the more militant Philadelphia NAACP and by leaders from CORE and SNCC who came from Baltimore, New York, and Atlanta. The forms of protest included sit-ins, picketing, parades, and boycotts—unmixed with negotiations, as in the past, centering not on the moderate establishments that might yield but, defiantly, on the most intransigent. The purpose of the demonstrations changed; they no longer were meant to impress others with the justice of a cause, they were to vent generations of anger. Integration was less important than the discovery of pride in standing up to whitey. It was in this atmosphere that Richardson emerged, not as the instigator, originally, but as the toughest, smartest, most militant, most admired among the other protestors, the person who knew the area best, the natural leader. People around her called themselves the Non-Violent Action Committee. Delegates from the Philadelphia NAACP, CORE, and SNCC waited for Richardson's orders.[32]

Black militance bred opposition, but not primarily in the city council. Opposition was represented by the police chief, Brice A. Kinna-

Gloria Richardson, proud and angry, gained control of black protesters in Cambridge in 1963 by passionate rhetoric and disdain for the bayonets. Courtesy of the *Baltimore News American*.

mon, and by aggressive whites, who were also often unemployed, often from the rural countryside and attracted into the little town, like blacks, for the excitement that mass emotion provided. Tempers flared, fights broke out, arrests mounted—all this caused the black movement to grow in size and intensity. As the black movement outgrew its instigators, its most outspoken participants emerged as leaders.

The reasons for the transformation from idealism to anger, then, lay mostly in the process by which it occurred. It lay in the frustration of blacks in the middle and northern states for whom integration was not enough. It lay in the anger of unemployed blacks and the shift in participation from students to the unemployed. It lay in the evolution of leadership from people with attainable goals to the crowd itself. Idealism died when the protest grew larger than the aim it was meant to achieve.

From March to June the transformation from prayerful sit-ins to riots was evident almost from day to day. The city government accepted sit-ins as long as they were not disruptive, and pickets as long as they did not impede access, but many whites were resentful and taunting, and the protestors grew increasingly aggressive, and police made arrests. By mid-May about seventy blacks and five whites had been arrested. On May 15 a swelling crowd of blacks surrounded the city jail, and the police, claiming to feel threatened, arrested sixty-two more. Mayor Calvin Mawbray called for the state Commission on Interracial Problems to investigate and make recommendations, and he called on Richardson to curtail demonstrations in exchange for a moratorium on arrests, but Richardson angrily refused, and the demonstrations and arrests continued. On a balmy June 10, loudspeaker trucks toured the mostly black second ward calling for a massive turnout, and that night there were twenty-five arrests. The enraged or excited prisoners destroyed the plumbing and mattresses in their cells.[33]

The following night black youths began stoning white cars and smashing white-owned store windows, and the first shooting began. During the next two days, five whites were wounded by gunfire, five stores and the home of the moderate black on the school board were firebombed, and many blacks and whites were hurt by rocks and fighting. The city petitioned Governor Tawes to declare martial law, and 475 troops arrived with fixed bayonets.[34]

The unprecedented rioting was both exciting and frightening. News and television coverage was mostly sympathetic to the blacks, as civil rights reporting from the South had usually been, thus emboldening Richardson's followers and further disorienting the town's whites. Everyone, especially the town government, talked of negotiations, as if the situation amounted to war. Tawes first invited both sides to Annapolis, and when Richardson refused to attend, he sent delegates to Cambridge with an offer to obtain an open accommodations ordinance through the Cambridge City Council in exchange for a promise to end demonstrations. Richardson would have none of it. Meanwhile United States Attorney General Robert Kennedy was in touch with Mayor Mawbray, and on Sunday morning, June 16, he met in Washington with the Cambridge black leaders: Richardson, her friend Barbara Jew, Philip Savage of the Philadelphia NAACP, and Reginald Robinson of SNCC. Kennedy explained that in exchange for a one-year moratorium on demonstrations, he was able to promise that Cambridge would provide immediate equal service to blacks in its twenty-four eating places, would accept an open accommodations ordinance that would outlaw all types of discrimination, and would integrate its schools for every grade in the fall term; that a biracial commission would be created to seek jobs for blacks in the town; and that the federal government would guarantee a new public housing program. Savage and Robinson were delighted, and Kennedy thought all had agreed. Three days later, at a rally in Cambridge, Richardson announced the gains, boasted of what militance had accomplished, and pointedly denied that she had made any assurances that demonstrations would cease. Kennedy believed Richardson had betrayed him. That evening Tawes dispatched another 500 troops.[35]

The troops remained for twenty-four months, until May 1965, and racial tension remained great in the little town, but the first Cambridge crisis was over. Integration was general, but grudging. The open accommodations ordinance, proposed as an amendment to the city charter, actually failed. Mayor Mawbray had calculated that he and the white establishment could carry half the white votes, and blacks, who constituted 30 percent of the total vote, would put it over. In fact, almost two-thirds of the whites voted against the ordinance, and with Richardson urging blacks to stay away from the polls, only half of them cast ballots. By that time, however, the matter was moot, for state and federal laws applied.[36]

What happened in Cambridge could have happened elsewhere, for the climax of idealism everywhere evolved toward anger and resistance. In February 1963 more than four hundred students from Morgan State University were arrested for pressing into suburban theaters, and the following February, Maryland State College protests in Princess Anne, not far from Cambridge, evoked a vicious reaction by white hoodlums and police that sent sixty students to hospitals. At Glen Echo outside Washington, and at Gwynn Oak and Patterson Park in Baltimore, there were demonstrations, rock-throwing, broken windows, fights, and arrests that involved aggression on both sides.[37]

Even more threatening was the changing rhetoric on both sides that played on fear and hatred. In the spring of 1964 George Wallace, the southern symbol of segregation, entered the presidential primary against Lyndon Johnson and concentrated much of his campaign in Maryland. He pointedly began his Maryland campaign in Cambridge, and for the next two days there was rock-throwing, and the National Guard felt barely in control. Wallace came to the University of Maryland where eight thousand students turned out for the largest political rally the campus had ever staged. Mostly the students jeered, but a few weeks later Wallace received 42 percent of the state's Democratic vote.[38]

Tension mounted through the summer of 1964, still one year before any significant rioting took place outside of Cambridge, as rumors of violence spread. Governor Tawes and Mayor McKeldin issued a joint statement, heralded by newspaper headlines, that "outside agitators" were descending on Baltimore, that there was danger of "looting, destruction and bloodshed," that police were to remain on alert and judges were to extend maximum penalties for incitement of riot, and that contingency plans were being made for a ban on liquor sales and a curfew.[39]

Central to the growing sensitivity and to continued progress in black rights was the role of national, state, and local human rights bueaucracies. The state Commission on Interracial Problems had a paid staff of eight by 1965, plus scores of volunteers, and most county and town governments had equivalent organizations. Officially designed to promote good race relations and to enforce the new civil rights legislation, they usually interpreted their role, reasonably enough, to be the promotion of black rights, and the best way to do this, obviously, was by promoting an awareness among blacks of the injustices they were still suffering. The organizations had the budgets and official standings of professionals, and they had the fervor of amateurs. Through the 1960s the tone of the agencies' reports changed—from pleasure at what had been accomplished to anger at what had not been. The Baltimore Community Relations Committee boasted in 1965 of distributing 149,000 copies of its bitter pamphlet, "Are You Being Discriminated Against?" Other pamphlets spoke of the "seething frustration" of the oppressed and disadvantaged. The posture of the bureaucracy was changing; rather than reacting against injustice, the agencies were actively promoting black progress. Government was almost urging revolution against itself.[40]

Elsewhere in the country black power slogans spread and rioting erupted. Harlem rioted in the summer of 1964, Watts in 1965 left thirty-four dead, Chicago was the major disruption in 1966, and in 1967 tanks rolled through the streets of Newark and Detroit firing machine guns into apartments, killing about one hundred. CORE and SNCC both adopted the black power slogans in 1966, and the Black Panthers emerged with their strange fusion of sensitivity and savagery. CORE held its 1966 convention in Baltimore and announced that this would be its target city for the coming year. Mayor McKeldin bravely addressed the convention, embracing black power for its efforts to improve black living conditions, and promising to cooperate fully. For the rest of the year, for as long as McKeldin was in office, Baltimore maintained its uneasy peace.[41]

Again, however, little Cambridge provided the trigger. The National Guard had left in 1965, and extremists on both sides looked to the town as a symbol. In July 1967 the National State Rights party held a racist rally in Cambridge. Richardson, who had been on the sidelines, replied in an angry radio talk, and on July 24 the famous H. Rap Brown, head of SNCC, arrived to deliver what rhetoricians have called one of the great speeches of American history. Standing on the hood of a car in front of a burned-out building, he held the black crowd at fever pitch for almost an hour. Reporters on the edge of the crowd recorded the speech and the cheers. The speech was in the language of the ghetto, vulgar and funny, admiring violence if not actually advocating it, full of hatred and overstatement. Almost immediately after Brown finished there was shooting. Brown left town, but fires began to break out in the black ward. The police chief ordered the fire trucks to watch from a nearby shopping center. Blacks pleaded in vain for help while the black school and two blocks of the district burned to the ground.[42]

In Cambridge, the blacks were finally crushed. The National Guard returned briefly, but there was no more trouble. Richardson and other militants left town. Brown maneuvered through indictments and trials, jumped bail and went underground, and four years later was killed by police in New York after an apparent robbery. Cambridge had heralded the start of violence, and it also heralded its inevitable conclusion, even though a larger episode was yet to come with Agnew and the burning of Baltimore.

Spiro Agnew was elected governor in November 1966, elected, ironically, as a civil rights liberal over George P. Mahoney, who had captured the Democratic nomination by playing on conservative white

Burn, Baby, Burn! In 1967, H. Rap Brown visited Cambridge and that night the black district went up in smoke while the white fire department watched from a nearby shopping center. Courtesy of the *Baltimore News American*.

racial fears. Actually, Agnew was neutral rather than liberal on racial matters, and he was a conservative on everything else, and he was from the most racially conservative county in the state. Now, in much the same way that Eisenhower and Nixon were freed by their elections to be as liberal as they wanted on communism, Agnew was freed to be as conservative as he wanted on race. His biographers agree that his turning point from neutralism came in late 1967, when he received the recording of the Rap Brown speech. He played it over and over, invited others in to listen, and judged them by their reaction. Moderate black legislators like Verda Welcome and Parren Mitchell and whites like McKeldin were accustomed to the ghetto language of overstatement and were amused, but Agnew's more sheltered friends were shocked, as he was. To Agnew, the world was divided between most blacks and liberals, who half-admired the Rap Brown oration, and conservatives, who saw civilization at stake, and Agnew waited for the chance to strike for civilization.[43]

The chance came quickly, on April 4, 1968, when about 450 black students from Bowie State College marched on the State House to see

Baltimore, like most industrial cities, erupted in flames after the assassination of Martin Luther King, Jr. In Baltimore, 1,049 businesses were destroyed before 12,000 United States troops established order. Courtesy of the *Baltimore Sun*.

the governor, demanding improved dormitories and classrooms. There was no violence, but Agnew refused to see them and called for the state police to mobilize. The police ordered the students to leave the State House, and then surrounded them and arrested 227. To underline his resolve, Agnew ordered the troops to proceed immediately to Bowie, where they arrived at seven in the evening to close the institution, giving the remaining students five minutes to vacate their dormitories and leave the campus.[44]

Momentarily in Baltimore black moderates and militants came together in dismay and outrage, and tension mounted. That evening Martin Luther King was assassinated in Memphis. Most black communities erupted in one way or another, but now, for the first time, Baltimore was as ready for eruption as any other. It would have happened with or without Bowie, with Agnew or anyone else as governor, for it was mostly senseless black aggression, but now there was particular provocation as well.

The looting began on Gay Street in mid-afternoon, Saturday, April 6, about when it started in other cities, two days after King's death. Teenagers were in the forefront, attacking clothing and grocery stores; adults followed, attacking liquor and appliance stores. Drunkenness and hilarity mixed with anger; looting mixed with stoning cars and firebombing. All Saturday night the rioting increased, spreading over the entire city, and Agnew called out the National Guard. All day Sunday it continued to grow in intensity, and Agnew called it an insurrection and asked for federal troops. On Monday and Tuesday armored vehicles patrolled the streets, and the rioting grew sporadic and then died. The troops in Baltimore refused to use gunfire, and the death toll was light. Altogether there were 11,900 guardsmen and troops, 5,512 arrests, 1,208 major fires, 1,049 businesses destroyed, and 6 deaths. Washington's statistics were similar: 13,600 troops, 5,310 arrests, 919 fires, 10 deaths. There were few disturbances in the suburbs or in the smaller towns of the state.[45]

Agnew insisted on the last word, to add insult to injury. On Wednesday he called in one hundred leaders of the moderate black community of Baltimore: Lillie May Jackson and the ministers, people who were exhausted from walking the streets for days trying to restore order. Instead of thanking them, as they had expected, Agnew berated them as cowards who were secretly allied with the criminals and who shared responsibility for what had occurred. About eighty people in the audience walked out, and Agnew refused to allow those who remained to explain themselves. Black leaders felt as shattered as their communities, all the more that the insult made Agnew famous as the man who had spoken back, the man Richard Nixon and the backlash could embrace for vice-president.[46]

The 1968 riots were the end, so suddenly, of the hope that had blossomed into fervor and then anger. The revolution was over, exhausted in extremism. There could be no more sit-ins or demonstrations for civil rights. Whites, already pushed out of the movement by black separatism, turned their anger against the war in Vietnam and their idealism to environmentalism and the rights of women, the aged, homosexuals, and Indians. Blacks felt crushed by the riots, they still faced problems of lagging education and poverty, and they were forced to swallow their anger. Still, not much had been lost. Legal rights were secure, schools and jobs were becoming available, and the civil rights bureaucracy was just gearing up.

Affirmative Action, 1965 and After

By the summer of 1968 the impetus to forward motion was gone, but the movement did not go backward. The federal and state civil rights laws that marked the movement's culmination created the bureaucracies that guaranteed it immortality. The federal law created eight major agencies to promote fairness in voting, employment, housing, education, and federal contracts.[47] Mostly the federal agencies encouraged state and local agencies to undertake the day-to-day enforcement of the laws, but they provided the direction and much of the financial support. The federal agencies took the lead in promoting legislation for other minority groups—women, the aged, and the handicapped— and the federal government provided funds especially for job training programs. Most of all, however, the federal bureaucracy developed the concept of positive initiatives to promote the status of minorities.

The phrase "affirmative action" came from Lyndon Johnson's 1965 Executive Order 11246, in which he instructed government agencies to issue contracts and grants only to those firms that offered a plan, complete with goals and timetables, in which they demonstrated their positive efforts to enhance the status of minority groups. By 1970 firms were aware that their affirmative actions were an important factor in receiving contracts, and local governments were aware that their plans were an important factor in receiving grants. Suddenly big corporations and local governments were scurrying to find new ways of pleasing the federal bureaucracy. The affirmative actions of the firms doing business with the government became a yardstick of rights against which grievances were brought against smaller businesses. Companies and local agencies which had taken a progressive step by eliminating racial information on employment forms in the mid-1960s reversed themselves in the early 1970s in order to monitor and encourage the employment of blacks.[48]

State agencies were more important than national ones, both for enforcing the civil rights laws and for promoting affirmative action. The central agency was the old Commission on Interracial Problems, which was reorganized in 1968 as the Maryland Commission on Human Relations. Primarily it heard grievances—about two thousand each year—mostly from people with employment complaints, but also in housing and public accommodation matters. The agency lobbied and obtained new state legislation, especially to extend its coverage from race to sex, age, the handicapped, homosexuals, and even the obese. It conducted workshops and issued pamphlets to make people aware of their rights, and it worked with state and local government offices, with unions and professional associations, and especially with private companies, either behind the scenes or through court action, to promote not only nondiscriminatory but also affirmative action programs. It worked with agencies such as police departments that had problems with minorities, and with entire communities that felt abused by a lack of public services, by construction projects, or by unusual ethnic tensions. From 1968 to 1978 its professional staff increased from thirteen to sixty-nine. By 1978 at least half of its attention went to the problems of white minorities. The divergence of the bureaucracy from its original purpose was a loss to blacks, whose condition remained such an overwhelming problem of American life.[49]

Far more important than the federal or state agencies were the affirmative action divisions in almost every personnel office in Maryland—in every department of state government, every county and town, every school system, and almost every major corporation. Operated at department or company expense, the divisions were necessary for demonstrating initiatives in employing and promoting minorities and for allowing employees to file grievances according to their rights under the civil rights laws. Such operations were the price an agency paid for receiving federal contracts and grants. Usually staffed by minorities, the operations were eager and effective. Larger state departments, counties, and institutions like Bethlehem Steel employed from six to thirty affirmative action officers; throughout the state there was one for every thousand or so employees. Few jobs were left unmonitored.[50]

White acceptance of the new programs was surprisingly complai-

sant. On one hand, riots and bureaucracy marked the final collapse of
the civil rights movement's vaguely paternal middle-class idealism; but
on the other hand, riots and bueaucracy also marked the collapse of
virulent racism, which evolved—if only for reasons of compulsion and
fear—into a grudging accommodation. Soon the once-beautiful senti-
ments of McKeldin and Lyndon Johnson seemed dated and fatuous,
and the overt racism of Agnew, Mahoney, and George Wallace seemed
vulgar and dangerous. After 1968 there was not a single statewide
political campaign in Maryland with significant racial overtones, and
the white mobs that had sprung up in Cambridge and elsewhere in the
1960s melted away as completely as the rival black organizations.
Racial issues were not only boring, they were positively distasteful. It
was a matter for government to handle, not for public debate.

For blacks, the riots and bureaucracy brought equally swift realization of what did not work and what did. At first, in 1968, many black
leaders were seized with despondency as they viewed the near-universal condemnation of the riots and the physical destruction of ghetto
neighborhoods. Soon, however, despondency gave way to recognition
that only violence had failed, that black pride and even black progress
remained intact. Within a year after the riots the militant organizations in Maryland either expired, like SNCC and the Cambridge Non-
Violent Action Committee, or else they reorganized as moderate
organizations, like CORE, which transformed itself into a job-training program.[51]

For most blacks, both individually and organizationally, the challenge was no longer legal rights, but economic gain. A certain sense of
black pride remained or was enhanced, but for many, solidarity was
no longer quite so necessary, for each individual had to make his or
her own way according to his or her own talents. Old moderate
organizations like the NAACP and the churches tended to regain their
stature, adding black pride to their ancient litany of hard work and
education. The strongest new leaders were political. From 1968 to
1978 the number of black representatives in the General Assembly
increased from ten to nineteen, and in some counties and towns the
proportion of elected blacks approached the proportion of black voters. As a caucus, the black representatives failed, for there was little
common ground for legislative action. As role models for success, as
nudges to the bureaucracy for affirmative action, as power brokers
and spoilsmen for their communities, they were often splendidly successful. Lillie May Jackson, who did so much to launch the movement, was dead; Gloria Richardson, who represented the violent
phase, had left the state; the new political leaders were people like Aris
Allen of Anne Arundel, Tommie Broadwater of Prince George's, and
Clarence Mitchell III, Verda Welcome, Clarence Blount, and Troy
Brailey of Baltimore.

The important result, of course, was the change in the conditions for
black people as a result of hope, idealism, violence, and bureaucracy.
While the relative costs and benefits of each are too entwined to
measure, it is clear that the condition of blacks in Maryland changed
remarkably from 1940 to 1980, and mostly for the better. Black prog-

ress since 1940 was most evident in improved health and housing, which came especially in the general prosperity of the 1940s and 1950s. Black progress relative to whites was most evident in education and employment, which came with the new laws of the 1960s and 1970s.

From a numerical standpoint, the growth of the black population in Maryland was probably a sign of well-being, both absolutely and relative to other parts of the country. From 1770 to 1920 the black proportion of the state's population declined from 47 percent to 17 percent; from 1920 to 1960 the proportion remained steady, despite the largest influx of whites in the state's history; and from 1960 to 1980 the black population grew to make up about 23 percent of the state's total. The black increase came mostly from a high birth rate, consistently about 40 percent above the white birth rate, plus a small influx of blacks, mostly from the South. The surge after 1960 was primarily migration from Washington into Prince George's County. Movement within the state was, like that of whites, chiefly from farms to the towns, from towns to the city, and from city to the suburbs. About 62 percent of Maryland blacks lived in urban areas in 1940 and about 89 percent in 1980—in both cases slightly ahead of the rate of white urbanization.

Much of the black growth and well-being came from medical progress and expanded health programs for the poor, for black life expectancy increased much faster than white. Improved infant care from 1940 to 1980 meant that an additional thirty white children lived for every one thousand born, and an additional fifty-six black children lived. The total white death rate declined by 41 percent, meanwhile, and the black death rate declined by 48 percent. Blacks still lagged behind whites, but the gap was narrowing.

The rise in the basic level of subsistence from 1940 to 1980 benefited all Americans, but especially those at the bottom who aspired to enter the middle-class mainstream. The rise from deprivation to adequacy is greater than that from adequacy to luxury. In 1940 the majority of black households were without central heat, one-third were without electricity or full plumbing, and one-fourth were crowded more than one person to a room. By 1980 these numbers were down to a negligible level, and most blacks could at least aspire to a middle-class education and middle-class way of life (see table 7.3). The number of Marylanders below the Census Bureau's poverty level fell from 17.4 percent in 1969, when the calculations began, to 11.2 percent in 1979. Blacks remained a steady 40 percent of the total beneath the line, to be sure, but at least the total number of blacks below the line was diminishing.[52]

One of the greatest indicators of black progress, and the place where blacks made the most remarkable progress in narrowing the lag behind whites, was in education, the traditional avenue of social mobility. From 1940 to 1980 the median number of school years completed by Maryland whites rose by 45 percent (from 8.4 to 12.2 years), but the median years completed by blacks jumped by 75 percent (from 5.8 to 10.1 years). The number of whites in the population who had completed high school increased by 129 percent (from 13.1

Table 7.3.   Blacks and Whites in Maryland, 1940, 1960, and 1980

	1940	1960	1980
Percentage of state population			
White	84.3	83.6	77.3
Black	16.6	16.7	22.7
Percentage of urban dwellers			
White	58.8	75.8	77.9
Black	62.0	75.2	89.4
Birth rate per 1,000			
White	16.6	23.2	12.1
Black	22.7	32.8	17.2
Infant mortality, per 1,000 births, after one year			
White	41.7	22.3	11.5
Black	76.6	44.9	20.9
Death rate, per 100,000			
White	11.4	8.6	6.7
Black	16.2	10.5	8.4
Percentage of households without full plumbing			
White	29.3	3.7	1.3
Black	35.7	9.8	3.9
Percentage of households with more than one per room			
White	11.9	9.5	1.5
Black	26.0	13.7	7.7
Median school years completed			
White	8.4	11.0	12.2
Black	5.8	8.1	10.1
Percentage who are high school graduates			
White	13.1	24.6	30.0
Black	3.4	12.5	20.7

to 30 percent of the total white population), but the number of blacks who had completed high school increased by 509 percent (from 3.4 to 20.7 percent of the total).[53]

Median income increased similarly; it was still behind that for whites, but the gap was narrowing. In 1959, when the calculations were first made, Maryland black family incomes were 50.7 percent of those of white families; in 1960 the black percentage had risen to 58.6; in 1970, 67.0 percent; and in 1980 it fell back to 62.2 percent (see table 7.4). In Maryland blacks were about ten percentage points closer to whites than they were in the rest of the nation.[54]

The most spectacular progress of all, as revealed in the gross census figures, came in the entry of blacks into prestigious jobs. The proportion of blacks in managerial and professional positions still lagged behind that of whites, but by 1980 most positions seemed to be open to talent, and statistically the number of blacks in almost every type of job had risen from token to significant. Blacks in sales and craft jobs approximately equaled the black proportion of the population. Their proportion in labor and janitorial positions, on the other hand, though still large, was definitely declining (see table 7.5).[55]

Federal census calculations of average health, education, and income conditions did not tell the whole story, and more refined analyses were seldom available at the state level. Other studies of smaller

Table 7.4.   Family Income, 1950–1980

	1950	1960	1970	1980
Median (in $)				
White	3,128	6,703	11,635	25,886
Black	1,614	3,926	7,798	16,104
Black percent-				
age of median	50.7	58.6	67.0	62.2

Source: U.S. Bureau of the Census, *Characteristics of the Population* (1950–1980).

Table 7.5.   Blacks in the Workplace, 1940–1979 (in percentages)

	1940	1960	1967	1979
Officers and managers	2.9	2.9	2.0	7.4
Professional-technical	4.6	6.3	4.8	9.5
Sales and clerical	2.4	5.8	5.8	16.2
Craft and operatives	6.9	14.2	16.2	23.5
Labor and service workers	44.3	45.1	46.7	41.0

Source: U.S. Bureau of the Census, *Characteristics of the Population* (1940–1980).

communities, however, demonstrated that most of the progress came to those blacks located in the top quarter or top half of the income scales, where the gap between blacks and the corresponding white quartile was narrowing even more than the averages indicated; but the gap between blacks and whites in the lower quartiles was as great or greater than ever. The success of many blacks made still more bitter the failure of others. The other side of the statistics of progress was that unemployment, crime rates, and family disintegration for poor blacks were much more significant than they were for the white population. The magnitude of these problems for poor blacks generally exceeded what it had been forty years before, and probably exceeded the magnitude of the problems for correspondingly impoverished whites. These figures required major reservations to claims of success for the black revolution, and they pointed toward the continuing significance of poverty and failure in the late twentieth century.[56]

Still, however much qualified, the final word must be of success. In the mid-nineteenth century, America underwent its greatest internal revolution to end slavery, and in the mid-twentieth century, it underwent another upheaval to end segregation. In a long-term perspective, each revolution attained more than its instigators dared hope.

The 1960s: Camelot and J. Millard Tawes

Out of the 1950s euphoria burst the moral idealism of the 1960s; out of sustained prosperity came dreams of utopias; out of consensus that government could be beneficial to all came demands that it do everything; out of social improvement came unreal expectations and revolt against the society that has done so well. Locally and nationally the years from about 1959 to about 1967 were vastly good, with exponential growth rates and visions of Camelot, even if the growth rates were not permanent or the visions real.

The administrations of Governor J. Millard Tawes from 1959 to 1967 fit better the era of rising expectations than either of the corresponding presidential terms. President John F. Kennedy's administration from 1961 to 1963 terminated artificially, stimulating mythology in his martyrdom. President Lyndon B. Johnson's administration from 1963 to 1969 outlasted its time and exploded in the raucous din of urban riots and Vietnam. After the moral idealists came the deluge.

The Unlikely King Arthur

There was nothing romantic in the origins or talents of J. Millard Tawes. The middle name came from Millard Fillmore, the American president his parents somehow most admired. The name is aptly reminiscent of J. Alfred Prufrock, T. S. Eliot's symbol of mediocrity. Tawes was cut out to be an accountant with green eye-shades sitting on a high stool in a small-town firm, and he was—but he was also an able governor, maybe, because of the times, a great governor, of a progressive state. The times made the man: an accountant became the symbol of rapid change, an old machine pol became the agent of reform, Prufrock became King Arthur.

John F. Kennedy points Millard Tawes toward Camelot. Courtesy of the *Baltimore Sun*.

The established Tawes family of Somerset County on the Eastern Shore was another distinct shade in the mosaic of Marylanders—distinct, but typical of a significant group, like the patrician Lane family of Washington County or the ethnic-immigrant O'Conor and McKeldin families of Baltimore. On the father's side was the Tawes clan and on the mother's side was the Byrd clan, both of which had lived in Somerset County since the seventeenth century. For more than 250 years the same Eastern Shore families had been farmers and watermen, hardly changing in total numbers, gently fluctuating through time in rank and condition. James B. Tawes, the governor's father, was on the rise, a blacksmith who grew prosperous from inventing and manufacturing a new kind of oyster tongs until they were made illegal because they destroyed the crab eggs on the floor of the bay. The father then established a lumber business, a seafood box-manufacturing company, an ice and electric company, and a bakery that popularized Tawes bread through the entire county. In the town of Crisfield, population 2,500, James Tawes was easily one of the two or three leading citizens.

The streets of the town were paved with oyster shells, and steamboats loaded seafood, potatoes, and watermelon at the wharves. Economically the area was tied by the railroad to Delaware and Philadelphia, but politically it was Maryland, and politics was one of the few ways in which an Eastern Shoreman could join the outside world without emigrating. The father was content at home, but his middle son expanded the family's mobility further.

James Millard Tawes was born in 1894, one of three sons. He attended the public schools uneventfully, worked summers in the family enterprises, and talked of being a lawyer, but went instead to a junior college in Wilmington for two years, and then a business school in Baltimore for two more years, where in 1914 he earned a certificate in accounting. The next year, at age 21, he married Helen Avalynne Gibson, who came from a local family that was probably related to his own from centuries before, and next to his parents' house he built his own modest brick house, where he and his wife lived for the rest of their lives, except while they lived in the Governor's Mansion. Millard Tawes became manager of the lumber business, kept the books for the other family businesses, and taught the men's Bible class at the Methodist church. The accountant was the most relaxed and popular member of the family. He played the trumpet in the firemen's band, joined the Elks and the Moose, became a state officer in the Knights of Pythias, and founded the local Rotary Club. By the time he was in his mid-thirties Millard had gained a respectability apart from his father's and a congeniality unexcelled in the little town.

Politics on the Eastern Shore was seldom a lifetime career, as it was in the city; usually it was a duty assumed by people already recognized as part of the county establishment—men like Millard Tawes who ran lumber companies, taught Sunday School, played the trumpet, and enjoyed public affairs. He was known as a Democrat, his name would strengthen the ticket, his election would not hurt the family enterprises. In 1926 a group asked him to run for the General Assembly but he declined. Then, in 1930, the chairman of the Somerset County

Democratic party, Wallace M. Quinn, implored him to join the county slate, for almost any office. This time he agreed; he would run for clerk of the court, an administrative job that amounted to hiring bailiffs and issuing court orders and would take only one day a week.

Tawes was elected, and he loved the job. All the politics of the county swirled around the courthouse, and after a day spent with the account books, he delighted in attending the political and lodge meetings of the evenings. People looked to him as the expert on county finances, and officials in neighboring Wicomico and Worcester counties invited him over to consult on budget matters. He was reelected in 1934, and by 1938 he was permanently hooked on the excitement of politics. His most prominent connection was William S. Gordy, president of the Salisbury Bank and the state comptroller. Gordy was announcing as a Democratic candidate for governor, and he would support Tawes for the statewide election to his former position.[1]

Gordy had occupied that office for seventeen years, from 1921 to 1938, not only as comptroller, but also as Eastern Shore leader of Governor Ritchie's long-invincible Democratic oganization, and even when Ritchie lost to Republican Harry Nice in 1934, Gordy remained in office. The position seemed to belong to him, and to the Eastern Shore, to be passed along to his chosen protégé. Gordy, like Ritchie and Tawes, represented conservative accounting procedures, like those followed in a small-town bank. Basic policies might be highly political, but daily operations were scrupulously honest. Tawes, aged 44 now, fully appreciated his insider support and played to it, sending 250 telegrams to state party leaders seeking their approval of his candidacy. Gordy himself went down to defeat in 1938: Herbert R. O'Conor was elected governor. But the competent, congenial Millard Tawes won easily the mostly unnoticed election for state comptroller. Four years later O'Conor barely won reelection, but Tawes won again, unopposed in both the primary and the general election.[2]

The job of comptroller, like that of attorney general and state treasurer, is designed for the party insider. All three should be appointed rather than elected positions. Tawes, who headed up five hundred employees, was in charge of tax collection, revenue disbursement, daily accounting, and revenue projections. The treasurer, with a dozen employees, was responsible for investing state surpluses. Placement of an incompetent in any of these positions does no particular harm, for the governor is responsible for policy, and the bureaucracy carries on. For a man who is both accountant and politician, however, the comptroller's position is a dream. He can become the acknowledged master of technical budget detail, of which items the state can and cannot fund. Almost unnoticed by the public, he can on the one hand shape the governor's fiscal policies, and on the other hand greatly influence the administration's support in the General Assembly. Tawes was perfect for the job, relishing equally the balance sheet and the brokerage among political factions.

Tawes worked well enough with O'Conor during their eight years from 1938 to 1946, and even better with the party pros who met regularly for lunch at the Emerson Hotel in Baltimore, or in Annapolis hotel rooms when the legislature was in session. Everyone liked him and respected what he said about the budget. He was a pristine politician in that he was bound to no convictions that might interfere with his clear reading of public opinion.

The qualities that made him popular with insiders occasionally gained unfavorable public notice. There was a report that salary checks for the Tidewater Fisheries Commission were lost for a week when a friend of Tawes's failed to obtain a fishing license, and the newspapers reported that government officials underwent special audits of their expense accounts when they refused to find jobs for Tawes's friends.[3] In 1943 Tawes received the greatest newspaper publicity of his term as comptroller when Rives Matthews, a newcomer to Somerset County, purchased the county's weekly and revealed that Tawes had used a state limousine to circumvent wartime gasoline rationing and attend his son's wedding in Georgia. The Somerset rationing board, in a twelve-minute hearing, accepted Tawes's flimsy explanation that he was observing state financing in Georgia, even though he could not remember the capital of the state. The Somerset County prosecutor arrested Matthews and jailed him for libel. "He has been riding everybody every week," said the prosecutor. "It causes dissension down here." When the state rationing board overruled the county, censured Tawes, and withdrew his gasoline coupons for a year, the comptroller transferred ownership of the automobile to his wife and renewed his gasoline allotment. The case against Matthews dragged on for a year, until he left the state. At the least, Tawes had been indiscreet in use of the automobile, and his friends had been outrageously zealous in harassing a fine journalist. More importantly, the incident revealed the vicious small-town background Tawes still had to overcome.[4]

Tawes had intended to run again for comptroller in 1946, but instead he allowed himself to be used by Baltimore's boss William Curran, who was looking for a candidate for governor. Curran, a whipping boy for the rising William P. Lane, hoped to reestablish his grip on the Democratic party by reinvigorating the old alliance of the city, party insiders, and the Eastern Shore. Curran, however, was fading, and the congenial Tawes, only half-comprehending, marched to his slaughter. Weeks before the election his own campaign manager resigned in disgust: "You have submitted yourself to the complete control and domination of Curran and submit meekly to his dictates." Lane won the election with 104,000 votes; Tawes received 86,000 votes, chiefly from the Eastern Shore, and H. Streett Baldwin of Baltimore County received 46,000. The Curran organization never came up with the campaign funds it promised, and Tawes found himself ten thousand dollars in debt and a wiser man.[5]

Tawes, now 50, was still due twelve more years of apprenticeship, although he hardly thought of himself as waiting for something larger to come along. A few months after the election, Lane made peace by appointing him to the largely honorary position of state banking commissioner, in charge of banking regulations, and in 1950, when the state comptroller died, Lane reappointed Tawes to his old office to fill the last months of the term and to prepare for election to the position. Although McKeldin was elected the Republican governor in 1950,

J. Millard Tawes as the old pol.
Courtesy of the *Baltimore Sun*.

Tawes was elected Democratic comptroller, winning easily against token opposition. Still largely unnoticed by the press and public, he was more than ever his party's inside man. McKeldin courted his support, which he offered cheerfully in exchange for favors to his Democratic friends.

Genuine modesty confirmed his position as the man everyone else could trust, a mediator for the factions in the Democratic party who had no apparent ambition to be their manager. His Annapolis office swirled with visitors offering confidences and hoping he could obtain something for them from McKeldin. His status rose still further with the election of 1954, as he stood aside while George P. Mahoney and H. C. Byrd tore at each other to run against McKeldin. Maybe Tawes sensed that the nomination was not worth much, for McKeldin, along with Tawes, returned to his office. Even more than before he was the acknowledged dean of his party, the budget expert, everyone's friend. At the end of his term in 1958 he had served as comptroller for seventeen years; he was in his sixties, generally had no obligations to anyone, was serenely pleased with what had already come in his good life, and was willing to accept whatever else might come. In politics the job at hand was the next election.[6]

The common—and quite correct—wisdom among Democrats was that Maryland Republicans won only when the Democrats were divided, and the Democratic insiders in 1958 were determined on harmony. Seldom have the insiders been so unified, thanks to Tawes's congenial mediation, and seldom in recent times has a party ticket been so thoroughly bargained out behind closed doors before being presented for public acceptance. Everything came together on January 8, 1958, in a grand party caucus at Carvel Hall, an old Annapolis hotel. Tawes would be the party's nominee for governor, Thomas D'Alesandro of Baltimore would run for the United States Senate, C. Ferdinand Sybert of Howard County would run for attorney general, and Louis L. Goldstein of Calvert County would run for comptroller. Party delegates called this the "Harmony Ticket."[7] Of course, outsiders could challenge anyone, and the several mavericks led by George P. Mahoney weakened D'Alesandro in the primary; but otherwise the Tawes-D'Alesandro-Sybert-Goldstein ticket won nomination without much contest. In state and local elections the day of the caucus was not yet over, and in fact the caucus often put up better candidates than pure democracy could produce. The party pros, no matter how self-seeking—or because they were self-seeking—required a basic competence along with loyalty; they could not tolerate a demagogue like George P. Mahoney who offered the people only what they wanted and who principally won the support of people who did not fully understand him.

The Democratic victory in the general election of 1958 was, throughout the country, the party's greatest since 1940. It was a proclamation of optimism, of readiness for another takeoff like that of the Lane-Truman years. Most of the 1950s had been a McKeldin-Eisenhower interlude that had transformed conservative business and professional people from critics of to participants in the welfare state. The Republicans had dismantled none of the Democratic apparatus;

they had only broadened the base of its support. The 1958 vote for the Democrats was not a repudiation of the incumbent Republicans so much as a declaration of readiness for the next step forward.

In Maryland, as generally elsewhere, it was a pleasant election, without recrimination. For governor the Republicans nominated the candid and soft-spoken James P. S. Devereux, a retired marine general and hero of Wake Island. He stood for liberal things: expanded higher education, expanded public health programs, prison reform, industrial development. Tawes stood for the same things, only adding to the list care for the aged, utility regulation, and legislative reapportionment. Tawes won, 485,000 to 278,000. Although D'Alesandro lost his race for the Senate to J. Glenn Beall, who looked younger and fresher, Maryland Democrats occupied every seat in the House for the first time since 1940. In Massachusetts John F. Kennedy won reelection to the Senate by a margin even larger than Tawes's, and he was poised to become president two years later. He *looked* more like King Arthur, but he was no more successful in his program than the Maryland accountant was in his.

The Soaring Sixties

The period from 1959 to 1967 was probably the best since the American Revolution for a politician to be successful. Provided the politician got out in time, before the riots and Vietnam, failure was almost impossible. Growth throughout the country was real, and growth was exaggerated in Maryland. From 1960 to 1970 the state's population increased by 26.5 percent, creating a boomtime atmosphere. Median family income in the state increased from $6,309 in 1959 to $11,057 in 1969; even when it was adjusted for inflation, it amounted to a real increase of 22.3 percent, the greatest in American history except for the brief period of World War II.[8] The most important figure was the stock market, which is not an index of anyone's wealth but of everyone's optimism. More than any set of figures, it offers real growth and perceptions of the future compounded together, a graph of American zeitgeist. The Dow Jones averages rose slowly in the O'Conor and Lane administrations, steadily under McKeldin, feverishly under Tawes, and then they fluctuated violently under Agnew, Mandel, Lee, and Hughes (see figure 8.1).

Nothing in Tawes's inauguration inspired particular optimism, except that he was safe; certainly he didn't frighten anyone. His speeches usually avoided politics and issues, relying instead on platitudes.[9] Behind the scenes he consulted with anyone who wanted to have a say, promising little, but rigorously true to his word, giving everyone a sense of being dealt with fairly.

His chief advisor was George M. Hocker, which somewhat shocked middle-class sensibilities because for twenty-five years Hocker had been a professional beer lobbyist in Annapolis, but politicians regarded him as forthright and honorable. Tawes explained that his friend was "a college man. . . . I need the advice of people like that."[10] During his first year in office Tawes seemed to be particularly under the influence of Baltimore boss Jack Pollack. Tawes's first political appointments were so completely Pollack's, including members of Pol-

Figure 8.1. Gubernatorial
Administrations and the Dow
Jones Averages, 1939–1982
Source: John J. Esposito, ed.,
*Moody's Handbook of Common
Stocks* (New York, 1984), p. 25.

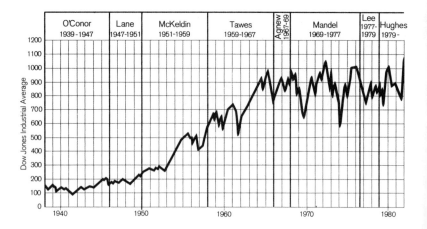

lack's own family, that the assumption that the governor was paying
off old debts was unavoidable, but after that, to Tawes's credit, the
two drifted apart and eventually boasted of mutual enmity.[11] Also
advising Tawes were Thomas B. Finan and Louis Goldstein, who were
ubiquitous party stalwarts, Odell Smith and Edmund Mester, who
were young hangers-on, and Lloyd "Hot Dog" Simpkins, who was an
old attorney friend from down home in Somerset County.

The Tawes program for the next eight years developed, not from
any personal philosophy, but pragmatically, from the balance between
available money and popular new services. Tawes was a bureaucrat
who believed in bureaucracy, and the one program that increased most
spectacularly was government administration itself—by 460 percent.
The administration's central agency was a new State Planning Department, created in 1959, which soon had a staff of over one hundred. It
was a built-in initiative for new programs, telling people what they
wanted before they knew they wanted it, always ready with draft
legislation to expand every other agency of government. Tawes pulled
the department's programs off the shelf as money became available,
and in these flush times it was plentiful. If he had thought of it in
advance he could have called his program the five modernizations:
education, roads, regional industrial development, health, and environment. Except that Tawes budgeted more for administration and
environment and less for roads, the same priorities and about the same
rate of increase prevailed as under McKeldin. Tawes's first and last
budgets illustrate the priorities of the boom times (see table 8.1).[12]

Education was the most important program for Tawes, as it had
been for McKeldin, exceeding highways for the first time as the leading state expenditure. "When the history of this Administration is
written," said Tawes, "the achievement we have made in education
[will be] set down as our greatest achievement." [13] The combination of
baby boom, immigration into the state, and affluence meant that
thirty thousand additional students were entering the public schools
each year, the equivalent of twenty large new schools. The state took
from the counties the initiative for responding to the demand and also
for insuring a general equalization of standards in the rich and poor

Table 8.1.   State Expenditures, 1959 and 1967 (in Millions of Dollars)

Expenditure	1959	1967	Percentage Change
Administration	11.4	63.9	+460
Capital investment, bonds	51.7	112.1	+117
Education	121.2	276.0	+128
Health	37.7	83.7	+122
Highways	123.8	169.8	+ 37
Natural Resources	4.7	12.0	+155
Prisons and police	17.4	35.0	+101
Supplement to counties	35.5	71.3	+101
Welfare, Social Security	46.7	92.0	+ 97
Total	450.1	915.8	+103

Source: Comptroller of the Treasury, *Annual Reports* (1959, 1967).

counties, becoming the tenth state in the nation to provide state support for local schools. The pro-education zeal of the rich counties balanced the willingness of the poor ones to accept a subsidy. In 1963 a conservative commission to study the tax burden, headed by Harry Hughes of Caroline County, drifted afield to call primarily for additional school aid at the expense of new taxes. From 1955 to 1965 teacher salaries rose 62 percent. The state approved a special bond issue for vocational-technical schools in each county, and it paid homage to technology by appropriating nearly a million dollars for a state educational television system that was supposed to beam lessons into the classrooms.[14]

Even more, this was the golden age of higher education. President Kennedy was racing the Russians to the moon, and additional knowledge, especially scientific knowledge, seemed to promise that progress would continue forever. The Gallup poll showed that 77 percent of the people believed that cancer would be cured within a decade.[15] "It's not water, or real estate, or labor, or power, or cheap taxes which bring industry," said a General Assembly report, "it's brainpower."[16] This was the only time in American history when the college professors seemed to hold the key to the future. The governor, who was awed by colleges, brought Wilson H. Elkins, president of the University of Maryland, and Milton Eisenhower, president of the Johns Hopkins University, into his closest counsels.

To guarantee progress, and to meet the projected baby boom influx from the high schools, Tawes appointed a commission headed by General Edwin Warfield, a Maryland aristocrat, which recommended that the University of Maryland take over three small teachers colleges—Towson, Frostburg, and Salisbury—and make them into huge branch campuses of the university. When this recommendation proved politically unpopular, Tawes appointed a second commission, under John N. Curlett, a Baltimore businessman, which called for a tripartite system of higher education: the University of Maryland would be at the top, six state teachers colleges would be elevated into liberal arts institutions to occupy the middle, and an indefinite number of community colleges would reign below—all to be coordinated by an advisory Commission for Higher Education. Tawes and the assembly agreed in 1963, and this became the structure that would guide higher education into the future.[17]

Fueled by unprecedented state support, the University of Maryland grew from 13,850 students in 1955 to 36,980 in 1966, from the twentieth largest to the tenth largest university in the country. At Tawes's urging, it created a new campus, which opened in Baltimore County in 1966. Enrollment at the state colleges grew from 5,067 students in 1955 to 16,651 in 1967. The community colleges grew, too, from four institutions with 1,452 students to eleven institutions with 20,580 students. They were constructed mostly with state funds, and the state matched local funds for their operation. Tawes and the assembly gave about one million dollars to the private institutions each year to keep them satisfied and prosperous.[18]

Tawes's second modernization was in road building, although the extraordinary spending came primarily from the federal government, which was proceeding with the vast interstate highways system as part of the optimism of the 1960s, which, incidentally, tided the national economy over from the early 1950s expenditures for the Korean War to the late 1960s expenditures for Vietnam. The federal government bore 90 percent of the cost, and construction provided a large part of the prosperity of the period—the Baltimore and Washington beltways, and the Baltimore-Wilmington, Baltimore-Hancock, and Washington-Frederick interstates (see chapter 3). Other, less spectacular, projects appeared over the state, paid for by a huge increase in revenues from gasoline and automobile taxes. There was money enough for some highway beautification, and for safety inspections, which reduced automobile fatalities.[19]

The third program was economic development, which had been promoted by McKeldin and was institutionalized by Tawes. Gone were the days of benevolent laissez faire, for industries depended as much as labor on active government aid. Tawes created a Department of Economic Development to entice corporations to relocate into Maryland, an Industrial Development Corporation to insure private loans to new industry, and a Development Credit Corporation to provide state loans if private money was unavailable. Other agencies promoted convention business and tourism. The agencies claimed responsibility for attracting at least six industrial plants and at least two thousand jobs each year.[20]

The state undertook responsibility for entire regions that fell below average in prosperity. The idea of regional development dated back to the Tennessee Valley Authority of the 1930s and was revived with the Canadian-American St. Lawrence Seaway project of the 1950s. In 1960 the Department of Economic Development persuaded Tawes to convene in Annapolis the governors of the eleven Appalachian states to discuss that region's laggard economy. President Kennedy was delighted, and the following year he creatd a presidential Appalachian Commission to study the area; in 1964 President Johnson, acknowledging Tawes's leadership, established a federal Appalachian Regional

Development Program to build roads and schools and to create jobs by reviving mining and promoting industrial development.

Tawes, something of a hero in Appalachian development, created a Delmarva Council by which Delaware, Maryland, and Virginia joined together to employ a public relations firm to promote industry in the Chesapeake area. Everyone wanted a development commission. In 1963 five counties around Baltimore formed a Regional Planning Council, and in 1965, when the General Assembly closed down the gambling industry in southern Maryland, Tawes created a Tri-County Council to trumpet the virtues of that region. Except for Appalachia's success in getting federal aid, the commissions mostly competed against each other, and a large portion of the jobs they created were for their own employees.[21]

The fourth modernization was in health, for an optimistic society wanted to believe that suffering was conquerable and that an affluent America was generous. If professors were prophets, physicians were gods. In 1959 the state agreed to pay hospitals on a cost basis instead of per patient basis for charity cases: services improved, and costs doubled. The state appropriated unprecedented sums for medical research. It established public nursing homes for the aged. The number of patients in mental hospitals declined from 8,916 in 1959 to 8,102 in 1966, due mostly to new drug therapies, but the state built seven new mental hospital buildings and increased operating costs from $20 million annually to $37 million. Probably this reflected improved services to patients; certainly it reflected improved status for physicians.[22]

Finally, one of the most successful of the routine modernizations was expanded care for the environment. Led by the bureaucracy's and by Tawes's own enthusiasm for the Chesapeake Bay, the Maryland legislature generally preceded rather than followed the public fad for environmentalism that came late in the decade. In retrospect, environmental legislation may have been Tawes's most progressive achievement.

In 1962 Maryland became one of the first states effectively to control water pollution from industrial plants, sewerage overflow, and toxic detergents. The Department of State Planning created a new state Department of Water Resources, which in turn initiated cooperation with neighboring states to design master plans for control of runoff, erosion, reservoirs, and pollution in the Susquehanna and Potomac River basins. Success there led to development of one of the first air pollution programs and a state Air Pollution Control Council.[23]

The governor was particularly aware of the disastrous decline in the Chesapeake Bay seafood industry, most notably in oystering, which had declined from over 15 million bushels annually in the 1880s to 1 million bushels in the early 1960s. The reason for the decline lay primarily with the adamantly independent watermen of Maryland and Virginia, who, cutting off their noses to spite their faces, refused to respect seasonal controls or reseeding programs. The watermen prevented local politicians from interfering with their harmful laissez

faire, and local politicians in turn defeated the efforts of every governor since Ritchie to rescue them. Tawes accepted the challenge, and
after waging an epic battle full of intrigue, he finally destroyed the old
waterman-controlled Tidewater Fisheries Commission and created a
modern Department of Chesapeake Bay Affairs, which had nonpolitical management, full facilities for scientific research, and appropriate
police authority. Seafood production rose at a spectacular rate. Watermen cursed and enjoyed their newfound profits. Tawes also established a boat tax, which financed shore conservation and boat safety
measures for the bay.[24]

As the affluent 1960s population sought recreation, the number of
state parks doubled during Tawes's administration, from seventeen to
thirty-four, from 17,000 acres to 38,000. Even more spectacular was
the development of Assateague, a twenty-one-mile-long island off the
coast of Maryland, and Chincoteague, a nine-mile extension of the
island into Virginia, into a national park. A storm in 1962 focused
attention on the isolated area as one of the most beautiful seashores in
the world, extraordinarily rich in wildlife, but a seashore that was
threatened by both natural and commercial destruction. The bureaucracies in Annapolis and Washington studied the area, and in 1965
Maryland (followed later by Virginia) donated its part of the island to
the federal government for costly and sensitive development as a
national park.[25]

Prosperity, an effective bureaucracy, and competent political management made Tawes into a progressive governor; popular enthusi-
asms were to make him into a symbol of morality as well.

The Liberation Crusades

The product of prosperous optimism is idealism, fervor, and rebellion.
The reform spirit that began under McKeldin as a happy flute tune
swelled under Tawes to dominate the decade and exploded under
Agnew and Mandel in a discordant crescendo of urban and campus
riots. The moral fervor lasted about fifteen years, from a year or two
before Tawes until five or six years after, and marked a period in
America much like the years before the Civil War, the Progressive era
before World War I, and the New Deal era of Franklin D. Roosevelt
and Harry Truman. In the 1960s the ironic symbols of idealism were
the pragmatic politicians, John F. Kennedy, Lyndon B. Johnson, and J.
Millard Tawes.

The three great crusades of the 1960s—of blacks, women, and
youth—occurred, like those before them, in the name of liberty. Each
movement emerged slowly from suburban prosperity, and each gradually rejected the middle-class consensus and revolted against suburbia.
None of the movements was unique to Maryland, and none was
directly related to Tawes, but they, more than he, defined the decade,
and he was astute enough to accept rather than oppose them.

The greatest of the crusades was the civil rights movement (see
chapter 7), and it served as impulse to the others. McKeldin actively
promoted the black movement, and Tawes probably secretly opposed
it, but Tawes sensed the direction of events and guided the General
Assembly to its partial acceptance of integration in 1963 and its com-

prehensive acceptance the following year. Maryland hailed Tawes as a civil rights leader, although he never boasted of it. Not one of his four hundred public addresses during eight years of office dealt primarily with minority rights, and the official sixty-four-page history of his administration does not mention the subject.

The second crusade of the 1960s was that for the equality of women, an offspring of the ideal of racial equality which followed a similar path of aspiration, self-consciousness, and anger and which culminated, as revolutionary movements do, in improved conditions but disappointed expectations.

The Maryland women's movement of the 1960s had roots in the early suffragist struggles. In 1894 a group of Quakers in Sandy Spring, Maryland, launched a state movement for the right of women to vote, and by 1900 Baltimore had become a hub of state and national rallies. By the 1910s there were right-to-vote chapters in every county, suffragists in every local patriotic parade, bobbed-haired orators on soapboxes at street corners and courthouse squares, and armfuls of petitions at every session of the General Assembly. The assembly narrowly but regularly rejected the petitions on the grounds that women in politics would weaken the family, and in 1920 the assembly narrowly rejected the United States constitutional amendment that passed without Maryland and finally gave women the right to vote. For the newly enfranchised, the fight had been a gallant one.[26]

For the next forty years, from 1920 to 1960, women voted about like men, expressing little concern for their other rights, accepting as a matter of course the continuing discrimination in jobs, wages, education, and manners. The main organizational heritage of the suffragists was the League of Women Voters, which was dedicated not to women's issues, but to nonpartisan good government and to keeping voters informed on issues and candidates. From 1920 to 1960 the proportion of women in the Maryland work force grew moderately, from 23 percent to 34 percent of the total. Women were usually found in lower-paying jobs, and their wages, when they held the same jobs as men, averaged about 65 percent of the wages paid to men.[27]

The turning point, and the immediate origin of the 1960s movement, was not discrimination as much as suburban boredom. The clarion call was Betty Friedan's 1963 book *The Feminine Mystique,* which informed suburban women that they were trapped in "a comfortable concentration camp," that they were slaves to husbands and children, and that they were being suffocated by family togetherness, neighborhood cookouts, and banal garden clubs. Blacks were gaining liberation; it was time for women to find personal fulfillment, to discover identity and pride, to demand lives of their own. Women were excited by the concept, and men were mostly sympathetic.

President Kennedy established a commission to study the matter, Congress added women to the Civil Rights Act of 1964, and Governor Tawes, spotting a new constituency, appointed a Maryland Commission on the Status of Women. For three years the commission deliberated, preparing an enormous set of demands for new legislation in the broad categories of education, employment, family protection, and legal rights. Meanwhile at least scores, and probably hundreds, of women's groups were forming in Maryland. Most important was the National Organization for Women (NOW), which established a Maryland chapter in 1968 and dedicated itself primarily to economic and educational equality. It was sufficiently prosperous to establish a professionally staffed legislative office in Annapolis.[28]

The more women thought about their condition, the more angry many of them became. Women, like blacks after the Civil Rights Acts, faced the frustration of discovering that legal equality was not enough. New groups, often more radical than NOW and eager for direct action, established job placement centers for women, day care centers, homes for battered women, legal aid programs, abortion centers, and consciousness-raising seminars. An outstanding Marxist journal, *Women: A Journal of Liberation,* originated in Baltimore. Kate Millet became a spokesman for the new mood with her 1970 book *Sexual Politics,* which argued that women were subordinated, subjugated, and figuratively raped by all the customs of American life. She promoted the word *sexism* and the title "Ms."

Still, even into the 1970s, when the Tawes administration gave way to Spiro Agnew and Marvin Mandel, most people were more concerned with promoting equality than they were possessed by anger. In 1970 the Johns Hopkins University first admitted women to its regular undergraduate program, and most colleges added courses or even departments in women's studies, much as a few years earlier courses had been added in Afro-American studies. The Maryland Commission on the Status of Women, renamed the Commission for Women, became institutionalized with a state-supported staff. It published newsletters, arranged seminars, worked to promote changes in state and local laws, and conducted hearings and brought suits against discriminating employers. In 1971 the agency was absorbed into the Department of Human Resources.[29]

In 1972, when Congress was first considering an Equal Rights amendment to the Constitution, the Maryland General Assembly voted 120 to 1 in the house and 39 to 0 in the senate to adopt an identical amendment to the state's constitution. Later in the year, almost without debate and almost unanimously, the assembly ratified the federal amendment. The people of Maryland approved the state amendment by a vote of 697,000 to 236,000. The suburban counties provided the largest approval, by a margin of more than six to one; only rural and Republican Garrett County was opposed.

Maryland's unusually quick approval of ERA brought unusually quick realization of the problems it posed. Sympathetic legislators introduced more than eighty bills in the 1973 assembly to bring existing statutes into accord with the amendment, only to discover that women's groups opposed more of the bills than they supported, notably in the areas of labor law, alimony, welfare payments, athletics, privacy, military service, and prison sentences. People were not so much opposed to equality, but equality was complex. The assembly tossed the problem to the bureaucracy—the commission Tawes had created—and during the next decade about two hundred of its recommendations became law.

One stumbling block came over the question of state aid for abortions. Catholics and fundamentalist Protestants were violenly opposed to abortion, and the issue subtly polarized the women's movement between careerism and traditional values. Moderate women turned bitterly on the radical feminists, who began to withdraw from public view. By 1980, when ERA was failing elsewhere in the country, the Maryland assembly was receiving many petitions, mainly from women's groups, for repeal of its earlier approval of the amendment.[30]

The revolutionary force of the women's movement was gone, but the movement's gains were secure. Women made up 34 percent of Maryland's work force in 1960; in 1982 that figure had risen to 46 percent. While women remained concentrated in lower-paying jobs, especially clerical and sales positions, and their careers were interrupted by childbearing, the courts were pushing toward equal pay for equal work. The number of women in Maryland medical, law, business, and engineering schools increased from about 5 percent in 1960 to 34 percent in 1983. Public schools eliminated sexist references in textbooks, and women's clubs received state support to hold fairs and seminars which advertised the social, economic, and legal rights of women. One of the most conspicuous gains was in politics, where, in 1982, women occupied about one-fifth of the state's elected offices, a greater proportion than that held by women in any other state east of the Rocky Mountains (see table 8.2).[31]

Finally, there was the youth revolt, which, like the others, peaked and turned angry in the 1960s, and then faded, leaving an altered society in its wake. In the nineteenth century, as distinct middle-class values evolved, Americans first recognized adolescence as a stage of life, and by the 1920s "sophomoric" had become a standard condescending label for youthful rebellion. During World War II parents who were more guilty about their neglect of family than they were insightful about their children created the concept of juvenile delinquency. After the war, as the middle-class suburban way of life came to prevail, the consciousness and self-consciousness of young people

Table 8.2.   Women in Government, 1938–1982

Year	Number in General Assembly	Number in Congress
1938	4	0
1942	4	0
1946	2	0
1950	5	0
1954	5	0
1958	6	0
1962	10	0
1966	15	0
1970	11	0
1974	19	2
1978	28	4
1982	37	3

Source: Maryland Manual (1938–1982).

burgeoned. The baby boom that began in the 1940s increased the proportion of young people in society; prosperity and educational opportunities extended their dependence on parents; better nutrition resulted in earlier maturity; and automobiles fostered independence. While most Americans cultivated conformity in the 1950s, young people identified with James Dean in the movie *Rebel without a Cause* and made a hero of Elvis Presley.[32]

Rebellion centered, as it had in the women's movement, in prosperous suburban areas, and Maryland was at the forefront of rebellion. In the 1960s conformity became a term of disdain for students, and polls showed "success" giving way to "self-realization" as a goal of adolescent life.[33] College and high school students, encouraged by faculty, rebelled against dress codes, dormitory regulations, and course requirements. Long hair, free speech, "hippie" clothing styles, and rock music spread. The Beatles, Bob Dylan, Janis Joplin, and Timothy Leary became gurus. New and easy contraceptive devices relaxed sexual mores, and use of marijuana and other drugs became fashionable. The Maryland Drug Administration estimated that by the mid-1970s one-half of high school seniors were smoking marijuana at least once a month. Young people called themselves flower children, cultivated Eastern religions, ate "natural" foods, celebrated the brotherhood of all peoples, and sometimes retreated to counterculture communes. To be sure, pacifism lived in tension with violence, and the flower children could become very angry. Every year from 1966 to 1971 some rock concerts at the Civic Center in Baltimore ended in fights, with 12 to 140 arrests each year, until finally no more concerts were held.[34]

The youth movement also took on a political dimension in the 1960s, and hence a seriousness, as students protested against segregation, war and capitalism. From 1963 to 1968, primarily at Princess Anne, Morgan, and Bowie state colleges, at least three hundred mostly black students were arrested at sit-ins. From 1968 to 1972 at least two hundred mostly white students were arrested for staging antiestablishment and antiwar protests, most of them at College Park. Almost all college and high school publications, if they were free of censorship, carried Marxist and Maoist columns. Student associations like the Students for a Democratic Society flourished on most campuses and deluged Baltimore and Washington with underground publications and graffiti.

The outcome of the youth movement was farther reaching than elders liked to admit. Schools and colleges rewrote their rules and requirements, and the General Assembly, in a series of votes from 1968 to 1973, lowered from 21 to 18 the age for drinking beer, for voting, and for legal maturity. In politics the young people may have had their greatest impact, for partly through their efforts, or at least through the opinions they expressed most passionately, segregation ended, the United States left Vietnam, and Lyndon Johnson and Richard Nixon were driven from office.

Reaction came in the mid-1970s, of course, as political conservatism descended and unemployment caused self-realization to give way again to careerism. Hair became shorter, dress neater, schools stricter;

drug abuse declined; and the 1982 General Assembly raised the drinking age back to 21. Still, reaction did not cancel the achievements of youth, for many of the changes in manners, education, language, sexual attitudes, and deference were permanent. The young, like blacks and women, had in fact gained a degree of liberation.

The idealism of the 1960s did not find only passionate expression, it also found expression in more ordinary reforms: abolishment of slot machines in Maryland, control of the corrupt building and loan industry, modernization of the courts, legislative reapportionment. Reform also entered the operation of politics itself.

The Politics of Morality

One of the best indexes to American moral sentiment is the attitude toward gambling. During cynical times, like the 1920s, 1950s, and 1980s, gambling flourishes, and during times of idealism, like the 1900s, 1930s, and 1960s, moralists seek to ban it. Maryland, as one of the most ethnically diverse and tolerant states, was usually one of the most enthusiastic in embracing gambling and one of the last to curtail it. State-sponsored lotteries began in 1791, helped launch the University of Maryland in 1807, and financed any number of public monuments and firehouses, semipublic canals and railroads, and private inns and churches. After the Civil War, to curtail the inevitable public corruption in the system, the state discontinued lotteries, and then in 1920, to curtail the inevitable private corruption in horse racing, the state provided for socialized gambling by taking over supervision of the tracks for a percentage of the take. Much of the state's reputation for moral laxity, including the jailing of Governor Marvin Mandel, stemmed ultimately from that.

The Great Society of President and Mrs. Lyndon Johnson and Governor and Mrs. Millard Tawes. Courtesy of the *Baltimore Sun*.

During the 1940s a new kind of gambling, one-armed bandits and pinball machines, appeared around the army camps. To play the one-armed bandits, customers put a coin in a slot and pulled a lever that spun a set of wheels; if a certain combination of pictures appeared— lemons or cherries—the machine returned several coins. The pinball machines offered free games as payoff which could be exchanged by the proprietor for cash. Anne Arundel County legalized the machines for a percentage of the profits in 1943, and in the late 1940s, following public referendums, three southern Maryland counties, St. Mary's, Calvert, and Charles, did likewise. Charles County prospered most, tapping the Virginia trade with piers from Virginia out into the Maryland Potomac.

Since most states and the other counties of Maryland outlawed the machines, a huge industry of casinos, bars, and motels emerged in the 1950s in the southern Maryland counties. In 1951 United States Senator Estes Kefauver, investigating organized crime in America, noted its involvement with slot machines, and estimated that Maryland had more of these machines than any other state, including Nevada. Congress, more sensitive to reform sentiment than Maryland, forbade the transportation of machines across state lines, but this only brought to Maryland the manufacture of the machines as well. Subsequent investigations revealed that Baltimore and Anne Arundel counties provided most of the machines that were transported illegally to the rest of the country.[35]

At the peak of slot machine prosperity in 1963 there were 4,927 machines in the four counties, with annual receipts of about $62 million in coins. The machines returned about 65 percent to the customers and paid about 15 percent to the casino proprietor, about 5 percent to the county in taxes, and about 15 percent to the anonymous owners. For local businesses, the 15 percent take was only the beginning, for profits on liquor and motels brought in an additional $10 million. For county residents, taxes on the slot machines almost eliminated property taxes and provided for some of the most generous public services in the state. Finally, the owners always appeared benevolent by giving frequently to churches and charities, most notably funds for a modern hospital for Charles County. It was hard for Annapolis politicians to become indignant, for they could guess the source of anonymous campaign contributions. One reporter, carefully studying the campaign contributions from Anne Arundel County, estimated that more than $50,000 from gambling interests went toward the 1958 election of Governor Tawes. Surely, if there was ever a savvy politician they could count on, he was it.[36]

Still, the mounting forces on the other side were stronger. The suburban liberals who voted for Adlai Stevenson and Estes Kefauver in the 1950s were more powerful when they voted for the Kennedys and Tawes in the 1960s. Newspaper exposés of the influence of gambling and organized crime increased. Good government leagues began suggesting that the gambling-influenced politicians were the same ones who opposed civil rights, reapportionment, and consumer legislation. The suburban communities looked down on the tawdry casinos and the prostitution and shootings that seemed to go with them, and horse-racing communities like Baltimore felt left out. Tawes understood politics better than his old crony contributors.

The reform initiative came, as usual in the twentieth century, from volunteer citizen groups. In 1958 a group of Baltimore lawyers, physicians, and businessmen incorporated themselves as the Maryland Crime Investigating Committee. They compiled statistics on organized crime and gambling, made speeches before service clubs, collected contributions, and demanded state action. The following year Anne Arundel political reformers, chiefly homemakers, issued a daring pamphlet listing the names of convicted racketeers, chiefly from Chicago, who were now living in the county and accusing them of dominating county politics. Grand juries demanded action. Finally in 1962 Tawes appointed his own blue ribbon commission, which demanded the end to the slots and paying pinball machines. Tawes and the General Assembly yielded first to the demands from Virginia to close the piers that led from the Virginia shore to the Maryland casinos, and in 1963 the assembly, under Tawes's leadership, agreed to outlaw all Maryland gambling machines. To soften the blow to the local economies the machines were phased out over a five-year period, finally disappearing in 1968. Property taxes in the gambling counties did rise, as predicted, but the growth in suburban population more than offset the decline in gambling revenues.[37]

Outlawing the slots did not change much, for one kind of gambling replaced another, a pattern established since the earliest settlement. As slots died, legal horse racing and bingo games surged, and the illegal numbers rackets surged even more. Numbers dated from the 1920s and reached a peak in the early 1970s. Bettors chose a number from 1 to 999, then checked it at the end of the day against a randomly selected number, usually the last three digits of the day's stock market sales. Winners won about six dollars for each ten dollars invested, and the 40 percent profit went to the brokers and the sponsor. Law enforcement officers considered this the high point in Maryland's history of organized crime, popularly considered to consist of the Mafia. To counter this, in 1973 (another year of conservatism) the numbers racket was socialized into a state lottery that quickly became the largest in the country, in both total sales and per capita sales. State profits, overhead, and corruption cost state lottery customers about 51 percent of their wagers, at least 10 percent above the take of organized crime.

Waves of concern about gambling come and go, and one such wave coincided with the Tawes years, but gambling itself continues, only partly modified by reformers' laws. By the mid-1970s fairly reliable estimates placed state gambling at about $350 million annually for horses, $200 million for the lottery, $50 million for bingo, and perhaps $500 million for illegal numbers and miscellaneous private wagers. This accounted for about 6 percent of the state's per capita income, probably about the percentage it has always been. Moralists still object, chiefly now to the corruption that frequently accompanies the industry and to the fact that the overhead and profits of 30 percent to 50 percent are paid chiefly by the poor. Betting per capita in zip code areas of lowest income is more than ten times that in areas of highest income.[38]

Another basic reform, and another attack on the apparent alliance of racketeers and establishment politicians, came with the imposition of controls over the Maryland building and loan associations, sometimes called savings and loan associations. These associations were the largest in the nation in the 1950s, for Maryland was the state where they operated with the fewest regulations. There were more than four hundred such associations, controlling over one billion dollars, constituting a rival to the state banking system, and providing a huge unregulated supplement to the local money supply. The associations had a romantic and admirable history, dating back to the 1850s, when residents of ethnic communities began incorporating to pool and protect each other's savings and to offer home building loans to members. Often they were run through weekly neighborhood meetings and had no professional managers. Their record through the Great Depression was outstanding, far better than that of the audited banks.

Trouble came in the 1950s as scoundrels began to realize the associations' potential for corruption. Scores of new associations appeared, especially in Prince George's and Montgomery counties, often with allegedly "hot" money, especially from Morocco and Panama. They paid their officers vast salaries and enlisted local politicians as figurehead officers in order to gain respectability and guarantee continued nonregulation. The tainted associations offered depositors high interest, speculated on real estate around the world, and periodically filed for bankruptcy and disappeared with depositors' holdings. In 1960, 174 new associations opened, and at least eight members of the General Assembly were officers in them. Within a year, even at the peak of the real estate boom, 5 of the companies had filed for bankruptcy.

Tawes the banker, like McKeldin before him, sought regulation as a means of curtailing swindling. He appointed a commission, which enlisted the support of the reputable old associations, and when the General Assembly, under the leadership of two floor managers who were officers in the new associations, succeeded in gutting the proposed legislation, Tawes won the ardent support of the press and suburban liberals who were even more outraged by conflict of interest politics than they were by swindling. Eventually Tawes prevailed over the assembly and over a referendum that Baltimore boss Jack Pollack required be held on the measure. A new state bureaucracy emerged to dismantle the disreputable associations and police the others. Tawes the insider had again prevailed as few outsiders could have in transforming a system that had created him.[39]

Yet another object of middle-class moral indignation focused on the Baltimore police courts, or magistrate courts, which represented the worst of the old-time political patronage. The twenty-seven part-time judges in these courts were appointed to four-year terms by the governor at the behest of the Baltimore delegation to the assembly. Some were not lawyers at all, but political hacks who turned out the vote for their districts, and often they were subject to favoritism and deals. Lane and McKeldin met with violent reaction from the Baltimore politicians when they tried to reform the system, and as protests from the press, civic organizations, and bar associations grew, it was again the insider who dismantled the system.

Tawes obtained a citizens commission report, joined with the suburban counties, and challenged the Baltimore delegation head-on. His reform bill created highly paid, nonpolitical, professional judgeships and gave them new facilities for psychiatric counseling and new authority over probationary sentencing. Again Jack Pollack petitioned the reform to referendum, again in vain.[40] In 1966, when the politically ridden Baltimore police force won notoriety as one of the country's most mismanaged systems, Tawes again took from the Baltimore politicians the initiative for reforms. Tawes's program led to the force receiving an award, three years later, as one of the nation's best-managed police forces. Tawes pressed for court reforms in some of the counties, and he modernized the state appeals courts. He was such a good politician that he could attack the political system.[41]

One of the most consequential reform crusades, along with those for civil rights and women's rights, was the long battle over legislative reapportionment. The struggle was as old as colonial and state governments and consisted of expanding areas against stable ones, reformers against entrenched political establishments, liberals against conservatives. Maryland's history could be told through its major reapportionments: of 1689, 1776, 1831, 1851, 1864–1867, 1901, and 1918. With the growth of suburban counties in the 1940s and 1950s the struggle began again.

Reform organizations appeared in all the metropolitan areas, notably in the Maryland Committee for Fair Representation and the League of Women Voters. The statistics they wielded were impressive: in voting for the 1960 General Assembly, one voter in Kent or Calvert County had the power of four voters in Baltimore City, ten voters in Prince George's, or thirteen voters in Baltimore County. Although Baltimore and the four suburban counties had 74 percent of the population, they formed a minority in the General Assembly, for twenty rural counties with 26 percent of the population had 51 percent of the delegates. A University of Virginia study ranked Maryland fourth among the most malapportioned of 48 states. The principle of fair representation was usually much more important to the reformers than the substantive issues that divided urban and rural counties.

What sharpened the cause was the tendency of the political machines in the metropolitan areas to oppose reapportionment, for machine power depended on small numbers of representatives, tight organization, and the ability to strike deals and trade votes with the rural counties. The reformers, therefore, not only were struggling for additional representation in the assembly, they also were fighting the organizations of William Curran and Jack Pollack in Baltimore, of Christian Kahn in Baltimore County, Louis Phillips in Anne Arundel, Brooke Lee in Montgomery, and Lansdale Sasscer in Prince George's.

The federal movement for reapportionment was ahead of the local movement. The bombshell was dropped in 1962, when the Supreme Court under Chief Justice Earl Warren announced in *Baker* v. *Carr* that representation within states must reflect population changes.

This, along with television, was the greatest blow the American party system had undergone, the beginning of government by Gallup poll. The results remain uncertain.

When the courts specifically ordered Maryland to take action, Tawes called the General Assembly into special session in May 1962, and under the governor's arm-twisting leadership the assembly approved a plan drafted by William C. Walsh of Cumberland to add to its membership nineteen delegate seats from the metropolitan areas. In 1964 the Supreme Court went further, declaring unconstitutional equal county representation in state senates, which followed the federal constitutionally established representation for states in the United States Senate. Tawes responded with another special session in October 1965, this time to pass two bills, one by Harry Hughes of Caroline County which essentially defied the courts, and the other by William S. James of Harford County which was accepted by the courts in time for the 1966 elections.[42]

Establishment politicians were in such disarray, the suburban anti-party momentum seemed so irresistible, the anticipated liberal changes appeared so great, that the next logical step seemed to be to rewrite the state constitution. It was a century old, and much amended, and rewriting constitutions is a reformer's dream. Reform groups and the League of Women Voters petitioned, and Tawes had no objections. The 1966 legislature agreed to let the matter go to referendum, and with the suburban counties leading the way, the state voted overwhelmingly to proceed. Tawes, in retirement, would be named the constitutional convention's chairman.[43]

J. Millard Tawes in retirement walks past his boyhood home in Crisfield. Courtesy of the *Baltimore Sun*.

Elections in the 1960s, like pressure groups and legislation, reflected the prevailing optimism, the growing suburban distaste for organization politics, and the growing concern with moral issues. Especially as the decade wore on, disagreements sharpened over civil rights and politics took on the harsh edge that foreshadowed Agnew, Mandel, violence, and disgrace.

The only statewide election in 1960 was for president. John F. Kennedy easily defeated Wayne Morse in the Maryland Democratic primary and then defeated Richard Nixon in the state in the general election, chiefly with black votes in Baltimore and liberal votes in the Washington suburbs. Incumbents or liberals won all state congressional seats.

Suburban liberal and anti-organization sentiment was especially strong in 1962. Tawes, despite his fine record, barely withstood charges of being the organization's man. In the primary Tawes edged by an unknown suburban liberal, David Hume, who attacked him on the left, and the perennial outsider, George P. Mahoney, who attacked him on the right; in the general election Tawes barely edged by a liberal Prince George's County Republican, Frank Small. In the United States Senate election, Daniel Brewster, a liberal congressman from Baltimore County, replaced the mossback Republican John Marshall Butler. Carlton R. Sickles, a liberal anti-organization Democrat from Prince George's county, won a statewide race for the extra at-large congressional seat that the state had obtained from the latest census report. The following year Republican Theodore McKeldin defeated the Democratic organization to become the mayor of Baltimore again.

In 1964 the Tawes Democratic organization took its licks from both the right and the left. First, the organization made comon cause with liberals to oppose George Wallace. The organization won by the narrowest margin, carrying Baltimore and seven western and suburban counties, but losing sixteen mostly rural counties. The organization also won in the general election, where Lyndon Johnson defeated Barry Goldwater, but the margin in Maryland was much smaller than that nationwide. George Wallace and the Johnson-Goldwater campaign brought new stridency in the political rhetoric. Then, in the Senate primary, when the Tawes organization made common cause with the rural counties to support the stalwart Louis Goldstein, the organization was overwhelmed by the liberal outsider Joseph Tydings, who went on to easy victory in the general election. The days of organization were nearly over, although *Baker* v. *Carr* had still not come to the General Assembly, and Marvin Mandel in 1964 was elected Speaker.[44]

In 1966 there was only one statewide election, but it must rank as one of the most disastrous in the state's history. With Tawes out, with reapportionment in effect, and with the Democratic organization in shambles, the victor in the wide open Democratic gubernatorial primary was George P. Mahoney, this time making his appeal as an outspoken racist. The Republicans nominated Spiro T. Agnew, who was making a good living now, after a lifetime of failure, as a politician accepting payoffs, twenty-dollar bills delivered to his office in brown paper bags, from government contractors.

The liberal movement of the 1960s made strange heroes, strange in Tawes and stranger still in Agnew. The sheer growth in population and wealth and the routine expansion of state services during the period was remarkable enough, but the moral overtones associated with growth gave the decade the marks of a classic liberal movement. Even routine legislation—for new schools, beltways, health programs, Appalachian regional development, oyster conservation, and air and water pollution control—passed with a certain moral enthusiasm. Still closer to morality were the issues of civil rights, women's rights, the youth revolution, gambling control, building and loan regulation, court reform, and reapportionment.

In 1967, after eight years in office, Tawes, the able political Prufrock, retired gracefully, perhaps somewhat bewildered at being hailed as the state's greatest reform governor—at least until Agnew.

If an astute nineteenth-century traveler like Alexis de Tocqueville visited mid-twentieth-century America he would probably be struck most by our prosperity, but then he would note the extraordinary degradation of a significant minority. He would note that one-third of blacks were desperately poor, and one-third of the poor were black. He would note that the poor were hardly neglected, for they were the object of varying policies and soaring benefits; but he would also note that their overall condition hardly seemed to be improving. From 1940 to 1980 the public costs of welfare, including social security and medicare, edged ahead of the costs of transportation, education, and even war. One-fifth of the nation's population apparently could not accommodate to the rigors of a competitive society and was doomed to drag miserably behind.

Government care of the poor was older than is sometimes realized, for it was buried in the annals of local government. After about 1935, however, welfare programs centralized, and social services changed in concept and scope. People began to think less in terms of benevolence toward the poor and more in terms of society prospering or languishing as a unit. The new way of thinking justified larger government and new benefits for all people, especially for the poor. In an absolute

9

Poverty and the Welfare State

Hard times in Garrett County—for some people the Great Depession never ended. Courtesy of the University of Maryland, Baltimore County.

sense poverty declined: few went hungry after 1940; but for those at the bottom, social instability increased. Rates of family disintegration, crime, drug addiction, alcoholism, and suicide grew fastest among those who benefited most from the new social programs.

Origins of Welfare   For three centuries welfare laws in Maryland served to assuage the conscience of the prosperous and keep the wretched out of sight. In 1660 the Maryland General Assembly required the counties to take care of their poor, lest they be deliberately driven to the next county; and in 1768 the assembly required each county to maintain an alms-house to care for the diseased, blind, crippled, insane, and destitute. Counties contracted with the rural family that agreed to maintain the almshouse at the lowest cost. A theory of asylum developed during the nineteenth century decreed that deviants of all kinds—the insane, paupers, criminals—should be isolated and subjected to stern discipline, and that hard work and virtuous living would restore them to health. Theorists argued that "outdoor aid," subsidies given to people living in their own homes, would only confirm slothful habits; "indoor aid" provided in well-supervised institutions, the theorists declared, would instill habits of work and ambition. This basic philosophy prevailed until the Great Depression. By 1900, in addition to county jails and almshouses, the state maintained two prisons and three asylums and made contributions to more than one hundred private asylums, hospitals, orphanages, and nursing homes, which were usually run by churches or ethnic societies.[1]

From 1900 to 1930 social consciousness grew, along with a certain optimism that poverty could be permanently eliminated from society. Charles H. Grasty of the *Baltimore News* ran exposés of the desperate lives of the poor; Cardinal James Gibbons of Baltimore preached a social gospel; labor leaders like David J. Lewis of Allegany County promoted workmen's compensation; academic leaders like Dr. William Welch of the Johns Hopkins Medical School obtained stronger public health laws; and social leaders like Charles J. Bonaparte of the Baltimore Municipal Art Society made it fashionable for the ladies of high society to spend an afternoon each week as "friendly visitors" providing counsel to the poor. In 1900 the state created a Board of State Aid and Charities to oversee institutional requests for aid, and gradually this group shifted the emphasis away from institutional grants and toward fairer per capita grants to the counties.

Maryland's early-twentieth-century programs for workmen's compensation, health care, and prison control were remarkably progressive. The state's Workmen's Compensation Act of 1902, which insured workers and their families against injury on the job, was the first in American history, although more than a decade passed before it won final court approval. The state health program, guided by Johns Hopkins Hospital physicians in the 1920s, transformed the role of state asylums from caretaking to therapeutic, created four new state tuberculosis sanitariums, and established health offices in each county with statutory authority to collect vital statistics, supervise treatment of communicable diseases, and inspect water supplies. The state prison control board instituted a parole system, gained authority to inspect county prisons, and established separate state facilities for juveniles. These new institutions benefited all classes, but they mostly benefited the poor and were adopted in a sense of charity.[2]

During the Great Depression, as unemployment in Maryland approached 40 percent, poverty was no longer the plight of the forgettable but a threat to everyone. For over a century cities like Baltimore had provided soup kitchens in time of extraordinary unemployment, and in 1930, well before the federal government acted, the city made appropriations for free food. The Citizens Emergency Relief Committee coordinated city aid with an outpouring of philanthropy from churches and ethnic groups. In 1932 President Herbert Hoover provided emergency relief that citizens' committees in the counties and towns administered. Then, like a whirlwind, came the New Deal, with programs for farmers, manufacturers, merchants, bankers, students, and the unemployed. It came less from demands of the poor or concern for them than from the assumption that all of society fell and rose together.

The New Deal provided the boldest welfare program until that of the 1960s, and probably the most successful ever. For two years Franklin D. Roosevelt continued Hoover's Federal Emergency Relief Administration grants to localities for direct distribution to the needy. Maryland received about $9 million but then refused the federal request for matching this sum with local funds. By 1935, however, Roosevelt planners had concluded that charity was degrading and contributed nothing to the larger dilemmas of unemployment and low productivity. Roosevelt turned instead to the Works Progress Administration (WPA) to give people the dignity of working and to give the public the benefit, however marginal, of their labors. Other programs—the Public Works Administration, Civilian Conservation Corps, and National Youth Administration—accomplished a similar purpose on a smaller scale.

From 1935 to 1939 the WPA spent at least $38 million in Maryland, paid wages to at least 10 percent of the state's workers, and incidentally left Maryland with 509 new buildings, 167 miles of new roads, 101 parks and playgrounds, and 72 miles of water mains. People complained that WPA wages were too high or too low, that its workers were lazy, that it was badly administered, and that it unfairly competed with private industry. It did not, moreover, solve the problem of the depression. What it did do was come closer than anything short of war to solving the problems of welfare and unemployment. All the indexes of social well-being rose (unlike in the 1960s), and social well-being increased most conspicuously among the poor. The program died during World War II, and afterward programs of medical care, housing, and income supplements were more politically appealing.[3]

A more lasting New Deal program, and one with even greater long-run implications, was social security, by which the federal government provided insurance against unemployment, injury, and old age. The establishment of social security was probably the longest step ever taken toward the welfare state and probably the most universally approved. The implications of social security were larger than the funds it distributed because, for one thing, the program began to transform the problem of poverty into the problem of economic stability, blurring the distinction between the workers and the poor. For another thing, it began to transform concern for the poor from charity, with its implied condescension, into a matter of human rights: employment and a subsistence income came with citizenship. Most of all, social security raised the problem of economic well-being from the local to the national level. Private philanthropy and local governments were generous during the depression, but of course the problem was too great for their resources. Most states, on the other hand, certainly including Maryland, hardly seemed to make an effort to deal with the problem, and thereby they weakened federalism forever.

The Maryland state government's primary answer to the depression, apart from rigid parsimony, which caused its once-fine state hospitals and prisons to decline drastically, came in 1939 in the form of transforming the Board of State Aid and Charities into the State Board of Welfare. This changed the agency from a citizens' commission to a professional bureaucracy, its concern from charity to economic rights, and its activity from distributing local funds to distributing mostly federal money.[4]

New Deal concern for economic recovery also brought a new initiative in public housing. Towns had built public markets, wharves, and workhouses from the colonial period; building codes to regulate private construction dated from the eighteenth century; and park planning boards and zoning commissions dated mostly from the 1920s. But government construction of housing, with government rents based on family income, represented a new dimension of social management. In 1937 the United States Housing Authority provided funds for ten low-cost housing projects to accommodate 2,556 families in Baltimore, Annapolis, and Frederick. Federal housing programs increased during the war, not to improve the quality of life, but to attract workers into the war industries. By the end of the war about eight thousand publicly owned units had been built by the federal government but mostly transferred to state ownership and control.[5]

During and immediately after the war the most rapidly developing public service was public health. Medical science, flourishing in government hospitals, was producing the greatest medical miracles of all time: the sulfa drugs, penicillin, antibiotics, antihistamines, steroids, tranquilizers, and cortisones. Life expectancy in the United States increased from 62.9 years in 1940 to 68.7 years in 1950, the greatest leap in American history. Life expectancy continued to rise, reaching 74.1 in 1981. Social security in the 1940s took responsibility for children with heart defects, orthopedic problems, a harelip, and burns. Millions of soldiers came to think of full medical service as a right of citizenship, and President Truman, twenty years ahead of his time, made national health care a touchstone of postwar liberalism.

In Maryland physicians shared the wartime concern for public welfare and, fearing socialized medicine, led the way toward improved services for the needy. In 1943 the Maryland Medical Society persuaded the state to replace its almost random annual donations to various hospials with a per diem specified for welfare patients. Two years later the Medical Society lobbied the legislature and convinced it to accept a system by which the state paid private physicians their regular fees when they treated anyone certified as needy. This was, to be sure, a conservative means of opposing more extensive health insurance, and the state often failed to fund the program adequately, but the program generally took care of the neediest cases.[6]

Physicians also took the initiative, after careful consultation among themselves, for calling in the *Sunpapers* to do a remarkable exposé of the scandalous wartime neglect of the state insane asylums. The doctors took advantage of the publicity to push the state toward creation of three specialized state hospitals for the aged, a psychiatric facility at Patuxent for the criminally insane, and a psychiatric institute at the University of Maryland for research. The Medical Society promoted the transformation of the advisory Board of Mental Hygiene into a full-time Department of Mental Hygiene staffed by professionals who had executive authority over the state mental institutions.[7]

The Maryland Department of Health, meanwhile, was expanding its authority. It undertook programs for supervising private hospitals, promoting factory safety inspections, improving nurses' training, creating state nursing homes, and providing free dental inspections for all schoolchildren. In 1949 the Department of Health, far stronger than the Department of Welfare, took over supervision of the poor who were in need of medical care. During the 1950s the General Assembly, accustomed to transforming medical will into law, required the counties to support their local health boards exactly to the extent that the state's Department of Health deemed necessary. The public was alternately appreciative and awed by medical authority. In Maryland and elsewhere the welfare state was growing fastest from the self-interest of physicians, who constituted one of the most conservative interest groups in society. The poor had scarcely asked for the new benefis they so enjoyed.[8]

During the 1950s, when most people remembered the depression and felt prosperous, the public almost forgot about poor people and worried instead about slum removal. The poor became, as they had been before the New Deal, objects of charity rather than claimants of rights. Philanthropy in the form of Community Chest drives reached new peaks, but government welfare barely held its own. Dilapidated housing, however, was a different problem, an offense to middle-class esthetic sensibilities, a drain on the tax base, and a challenge to the construction industry. If poor people were driven out, maybe so much the better.[9]

Slum removal began modestly in Baltimore with the emergence of a Citizens' Planning and Housing Association, which was dedicated to enforcing the health and housing codes in behalf of indoor plumbing and at least one room for each adult. In 1945 the city's health, housing, plumbing, and fire inspectors descended on a targeted area of

The 1950s Slum Removal

Sharp Street to cite violations and require landlord improvements. Since rents were generally high in the 1940s, most landlords made the necessary improvements and simply expelled tenants who had surplus family members or ones who could not afford the rent increases necessary to finance the improvements. Within two years Sharp Street was again rapidly deteriorating, providing the clear lesson that one block of renewal made little difference in terms of either misery or economics. Also in the late 1940s Baltimore business leaders obtained public funds to move the downtown airport to the suburbs and to disperse warehousing away from the congested port. Both were esthetic boons to the city, and few made the connection between the resulting decline in urban jobs and the rise in unemployment.[10]

In 1951 the housing inspectors, again under middle-class pressure to clean up the slums, targeted a twenty-seven-block area of East Baltimore for strict housing code enforcement. This time the procedure for selectively enforcing the housing codes gained favorable national publicity as the "Baltimore Plan" for slum clearance. This time, however, there was political turmoil as owners protested what they called harassment, turned out hundreds of long-term tenants, and sold out altogether rather than make the necessary repairs. Rents skyrocketed and both owners and tenants felt abused. Five years later a careful study estimated that the human costs of enforcing the housing codes exceeded the benefits.[11]

Meanwhile the federal government was reentering the scene with the federal Housing Acts of 1949 and 1954, which were designed to stimulate the lagging building industry and incidentally to appeal to middle-class sensitivities with the promise to reduce both rural and urban blight. Another housing act, of 1959, provided loans for slum clearance and government construction of apartments for the aged. From the early 1950s to the early 1970s, when direct rent subsidies largely replaced public housing, federal purchases of slums and construction of low-cost housing affected about one thousand Baltimore City families each year and about five hundred other families scattered through the state. The total number of publicly owned units increased from the eight thousand that had been created during the depression and the war to about thirty thousand by 1975. A writer describes these projects as "the plain rows of the 1940s brightened by their wash lines, the cagelike towers of the mid-1950s with yellow and turquoise balconies, midrise housing for the elderly of the 1960s, and the townhouse groupings of the 1970s."[12]

Federal housing projects, however, did not keep pace with federal demolition of existing units. The federal Highways Act of 1956, which marked the beginning of the interstates, spent over $500 million in Maryland, ten times the federal expenditure for housing. Planners made the most of the potential for slum clearance. During the next twenty years highways and other government building projects destroyed about two thousand family units each year, mostly of the cheaper sort. Displaced residents scrambled for what they could find, pushing blighted areas deeper into marginally prosperous neighborhoods.[13]

The cities were just discovering by the mid-1950s that drastic measures were necessary for survival, and Baltimore moved slowly toward economic renewal. The year 1956 launched the Port Authority Project, involving some $200 million during the next twenty years for publicly managed docks, warehouses, and rail and truck terminals. Simultaneously the city created an Urban Renewal and Housing Agency to promote actively federal funding for low-cost housing and city funding for construction that would attract people rather than displace them. The agency selected a twenty-seven-block area around Harlem Park and another fifteen blocks around Gay Street for renewal. It obtained federal and city funds to eliminate shacks in the inner alleys, built miniparks with concrete turtles in the center of blocks, and provided cheap loans to enable owners to add new roofs and aluminum siding. Again, however, it was hard to find long-term gains: the rents rose, the total population of the area declined as the poorest were pushed out, and within five years the effects of the effort were almost invisible. The mostly black residents were hardly consulted by planners, and the landlords even less so. Especially for the residents, urban renewal was a program of the bureaucrats which still meant black removal.[14]

Efforts by the smaller towns and the state government lagged behind the initiatives of Baltimore and the federal government. Cumberland, Hagerstown, Frederick, Towson, and Salisbury all accepted with some eagerness the federal funds for road projects that displaced poor tenants, and all accepted with some qualms the federal grants for housing projects that partially rehoused them. The state created its Department of Economic Development in 1959, but this agency was active in courting new industry, and another decade passed before it added a housing arm to promote living quarters for workers.[15]

Labor organizations, like urban developers, also prospered during the 1950s, and prosperity led them also toward a from-the-top-down concern for the poor. The unions enjoyed their most prosperous period ever, their membership up nationally during the decade from 22 percent to 26 percent of the labor force. Labor contracts improved, adding generous security packages of medical and retirement benefits and wages that escalated with inflation. For the well employed, social security rose steadily, rising most for old-age benefits. Even while the gap between workers and the unemployed grew, the gains of labor highlighted the needs of the poor, and by 1960 labor leaders, like urban developers, were ready to support new welfare initiatives.[16]

The prosperity of the 1950s evolved into the still greater prosperity of the 1960s, and the public attitude toward the poor blossomed briefly into generosity. About the time of Tawes's election in 1958 and Kennedy's in 1960, people began to think more optimistically than ever before in terms of all classes prospering together. Perhaps the mood was a reaction to the blandness of the Eisenhower-McKeldin years; certainly it was related to the rising moral fervor over civil rights. Intellectually the concern with poverty gained momentum from such

The 1960s War on Poverty

books as John Kenneth Galbraith's *The Affluent Society* (1960), which celebrated American prosperity, Michael Harrington's *The Other America* (1963), which spoke of those left behind, and Daniel P. Moynihan's *The Negro Family* (1965), which saw elimination of poverty as the only permanent assurance of racial justice and family stability. Politically the movement had one origin in Kennedy's 1960 presidential primary trip to West Virginia, when he and the national press were genuinely jolted by the poverty there, and later, when his strategists saw the issue of poverty as a key to winning the black vote. In any case, with simultaneous enthusiasm, Maryland and America undertook their war on poverty. The enthusiasm waned about 1968, when urban riots spread and Richard Nixon and Spiro Agnew were elected, but many of the poverty programs went on, sustained by their momentum. Total government health and welfare expenditures rose from about 5 percent of the gross national product in 1960 to about 20 percent in 1982—the most dramatic increase in government activity of the twentieth century.[17]

The first nationally significant poverty program of the 1960s actually began in Maryland six months before Kennedy's election, when Governor Tawes invited twelve Appalachian area governors to Annapolis to seek federal funds for areawide redevelopment. Presidents Kennedy and Johnson embraced the Appalachian Regional Development Program, one of several area programs by which the federal government experimented, much as it had with the Tennessee Valley in the 1930s, in transforming one of the poorest areas of the country. The billion-dollar program provided roads, schools, subsidized housing, and subsidized industrial development. It continued during the next twenty years, an apparently permanent part of Appalachian life. Such programs seldom fade away. Only three of Maryland's counties were affected, and they benefited—each received about $1 million a year —but the program did not alter their status as three of the poorest counties of the state.[18]

Other programs came from Washington. Kennedy launched the food stamp program in 1961, by which the poor could buy food at a discount according to their need, and by the 1980s about 10 percent of the Maryland population used the subsidy. Also in 1961 Kennedy expanded the program of Aid to Families with Dependent Children, which actually was a part of social security, to provide a direct dollar subsidy to families with children. Designed to keep families together, the subsidy was a kind of minimum income guarantee for families whose adults earned less than required to keep them at the subsistence level. Payment doubled in the first five years, then doubled again, and by 1975 about 3 percent of Maryland families received this support.[19]

Unrecognized as part of the war on poverty was the burgeoning of the profession of social workers. Nationwide the number of professionals rose from a plateau of twenty thousand between 1936 and 1959 to fifty thousand in 1969, and to eighty thousand in 1979. The University of Maryland in 1961 began the state's first School of Social Work and Community Planning, which was soon one of the largest anywhere, awarding two hundred degrees each year. The new professional creed was not charity, but reform. The University of Maryland

After the riots of 1968, which burned out many of the stores, people turned to the Community Action Centers for aid. Courtesy of the *Baltimore Sun*.

"dedicated itself toward helping the system function better rather than treating the individuals who are victims of the system." Its graduates, mostly employed by the state, were dedicated to transforming the state.[20]

The heart of the war on poverty was Lyndon Johnson's creation in 1964 of the Office of Economic Opportunity. Designed by sociologists, including Daniel P. Moynihan and Adam Yarmolinski, OEO put into practice the 1960s theory of reform. Partly this meant reforming the poor themselves by giving them education, job training, and the work ethic ("get poverty out of the poor"), and partly it meant awakening the poor to political consciousness so they could demand reform of the system in ways that would eliminate poverty ("get the poor out of poverty"). OEO included a Head Start Program, which tutored young children for school; a Job Corps, which trained dropouts for jobs; Upward Bound, to help promising poor youths get into college; and VISTA, which encouraged middle-class people to enter the slums as missionary counselors. The agency's keystone, however, was the

Community Action Program, CAP, which provided money directly to neighborhood groups to use for their own benefit.

Baltimore was one of the first cities in the country to qualify for CAP funds because, propelled by the same forces that impelled Congress, it was already moving in the direction Congress favored. The city's initiative came from civil rights organizations, especially from the interfaith clergy, which had already provided a 207-page "Plan for Action on the Problems of Baltimore's Disadvantaged People." A few months later, in February 1965, OEO agreed that the Baltimore plan fit their CAP goals exactly and provided an initial grant of $4 million, and the city was to provide nominal 10 percent matching funds. The money came, not to the state or city and not to existing welfare agencies, but to a board of eleven members, four of whom were to be chosen from among recipients of the poverty funds. The board, appointed by the mayor but largely independent of him, was in political trouble from the start, for state and city officials were skeptical, existing welfare agencies and civil rights organizations believed they had been bypassed, and the board's inexperience was assured. The Baltimore board had five directors in its first three years. One of them, Parren Mitchell, used his visibility in the position to gain election to Congress. Another went to jail for larceny.[21]

The Baltimore CAP board approved distribution of funds to about forty-five neighborhood councils located in the poorest sections of the city. County boards distributed funds to about thirty-five councils elsewhere in the state. Each neighborhood council included at least one prominent neighborhood political or business person, at least one social worker, and at least four "poverty representatives." The neighborhood council, then, employed workers and distributed funds for the local programs: day-care centers, job training and placement, legal services, small business loans, consumer protection services, education in homemaking and nutrition, counseling in deliquency and drugs, and, especially, neighborhood "organization." Each council supervised about thirty salaried workers and thousands of dollars. Internal council politics were fierce and opportunities for corruption considerable. The total spending in Baltimore rose from $4 million in 1965 to a peak of $15 million in 1969, and ended with $11 million in 1974. This was more than half the expenditures for the entire state. All together it amounted to about $300 a year for each of the families at the bottom 10 percent of the economic scale.[22]

Other programs, born in the expansive spirit of aid to the poor but increasingly providing services for everyone, came in the late 1960s. In 1966 medicare, which supplied mostly free medical care for people over age 65, and medicaid, which supplied mostly free medical care for the needy, were established. These two programs soon overshadowed all other forms of welfare in terms of cost, providing an average of about $300 a year for every family in Maryland. Also in 1966 Congress created a new Department of Housing and Urban Development, which launched a Model Cities Program of direct grants to cities, mostly for subsidized construction loans for public housing. Two years later Congress provided for rent subsidies so that low-income families could mix with the rest of society. Initiative came from the federal government, which had the money for it, but local legislation in Maryland kept abreast. The state provided reasonably generous matching funds for federal welfare (1961), juvenile services (1966), consumer protection (1967 and 1969), new centers for alcoholics (1968), and liberalized abortion (1970).[23]

Programs like medicare and consumer protection benefited everyone, and by the late 1960s public enthusiasm for the poor had about run its brief course. President Johnson's attention and congressional largesse shifted to Vietnam, prosperity soured into recession, and the 1967 and 1968 urban riots outraged middle-class taxpayers. Public hostility turned especially on the Community Action Program. Critics argued, accurately enough, that the government was employing two thousand community organizers in Maryland to persuade the poor that they were the victims of injustice, and the riots occurred exactly in the neighborhoods where CAP was active. The organizers' message—that the poor had to speak for themselves—was easily misunderstood even by its purveyors as authorization for aggression and revenge.

Local officials in Baltimore and elsewhere joined the attack on OEO and CAP, if only to justify transfer of funds from its nearly independent boards into the growing Model Cities Program, which left localities free to administer funds through existing local agencies. When Nixon assumed office in 1969 the shift was assured. Congress dismantled OEO and abolished CAP. "War against poverty" took on the sardonic ring of "War to make the world safe for democracy."

The war on poverty, even apart from its impact on poverty, was not all failure, for it probably, as intended, broadened political participation, developed economic opportunities, revitalized neighborhoods, and transformed attitudes. It also left its mark politically; from Baltimore alone, one CAP employee won election to Congress, three went to the General Assembly, one became city council president, and one became mayor. Almost all local and state advisory commissions—such as those for health, education, transportation, and housing—accepted and retained consumer or poverty representatives. Government agencies and private corporations retained many of their training programs, internships, and paraprofessional appointments, if only for reasons of public relations. Neighborhood organizations, generally stronger in poor neighborhoods than in rich ones, continued to be the basis of the vaunted neighborhood vitality of subsequent urban renewal. Finally, in the matter of attitude, the odium of accepting charity disappeared, for better or worse, and the new concept of "entitlement" was secure. Even lost wars have large consequences.[24]

Failure Carries On

More remarkable than the decline of public interest in poverty was the actual expansion of most social services. During the Nixon, Ford, and Carter administrations—during those of Mandel, Lee, and Hughes—when the mood of the electorate and the rhetoric of politicians turned cool toward welfare, the expenditures for social services increased faster than before. Much of the expansion was built-in. Political reality meant that programs like social security, medicare and medicaid, food stamps, and rent subsidies could hardly be curtailed, even when costs rose far beyond anything anticipated for them. Declining economic growth, rising unemployment, and the aging of the population made the services more essential than ever. The social service bureaucracy was secure, and its logic in favor of expanding particular programs was often compelling.

The welfare programs lacked philosophical or organizational cohesion. Maryland social workers shuffled the poor among a bewildering array of agencies: social security, food stamps, rent subsidy, general public assistance, Aid to Families with Dependent Children, foster care, medicaid, state unemployment insurance, and job training and counselling. A state inventory in 1977 counted ninety-four different medically related programs, sixty-eight welfare programs, and fifteen for the aged. Presidents Nixon and Carter each tried to bring order to the system and to nationalize it with a guaranteed minimum income or a reverse income tax. Congress rejected both plans but added two more: the Supplemental Security Income of 1973, which guaranteed minimum income for the aged and infirm, and the Comprehensive Educational Training Act of 1973, which offered funds to public agencies and private companies for establishing training programs. The states were left to administer the various funds, but their responsibility for the local poor diminished.[25]

Maryland moved with the times by changing regularly the name of its supervisory agency, and each new name was more euphemistic: the Department of State Aid and Charities, begun in 1900, became Welfare in 1939, Social Services in 1970, and Human Resources in 1975. During the 1970s this agency transferred its responsibility for juvenile detention to the Health Department, but it added new programs for youth organization, job training, homemaker counselling, released prisoner counselling, and insuring minority rights.[26]

Total welfare expenditures in Maryland were confused by the constant juggling of programs, but from about $285 million in 1969, expenditures reached $663 million in 1979, including housing subsidies and medicaid, but not medicare or regular social security payments. This amounted to about $5,782 a year for each of the families in the bottom tenth of the population—a miserable subsistence, of course, for a family with no other means of support. The federal portion of the total rose from about 55 percent to 75 percent. Maryland's welfare effort, in terms of contributions relative to personal income, number of people covered by welfare, and adequacy of coverage, was near the national average—Maryland ranked about twentieth among the states. Overhead costs were incalculable, but the State Department of Human Resources, which administered most of the nonmedical programs, reported 3,520 employees in 1979—one employee for each thirty-two families in the poorest tenth, or one for every $68,000 in nonmedical funds expended.[27]

Housing and construction policies in the 1970s had a sharper focus. Public housing construction ended in 1973 in favor of direct rent subsidies, which in Maryland rose to $44 million by 1979. The major new federal policy, however, was to award grants of money directly to the cities and counties which made the best case for the use of federal money in upgrading their communities. President Nixon called the policy a "new federalism" by which localities would assume responsibility for experimentation, and successful programs would be copied by others.[28]

The awards began as "model cities" grants that were designed to produce a few showcases. During the first four years, from 1969 to 1973, Baltimore collected $41.5 million for downtown renewal, and Prince George's County collected $6.7 million for projects just outside Washington and for rebuilding the little town of Upper Marlboro. In 1974 the program was broadened to "block grants," and Maryland received about $25 million a year, which was used by sixteen communities for urban planning, urban renewal, "open space" parks, water and sewer lines to low- and medium-cost housing projects, and community recreational facilities. In 1977 the government responded to the inevitable protests of those left out by expanding Maryland's grants to $50 million a year and awarding them to communities on almost a per capita basis. Although guidelines for grant awards required that some emphasis be placed on urban renewal, the elderly, and moderate-income housing, the localities were no longer primarily interested in the poor. Baltimore City, which continued to obtain a disproportionate share of the federal money awarded to the state, obtained funds for deluxe facilities to spark downtown renewal and for subsidizing Coldspring, which was projected to be the city's largest housing project and was designed to attract the affluent back into the city.[29]

All together from 1940 to 1980 the costs of welfare programs rose from about 4 percent of the GNP to 20 percent, and the recipients of welfare increased from about 2.5 percent of the population to 14.5 percent.[30] What was the impact of this apparent largesse on the poor themselves? The answers were clear even if they were contradictory. First, absolute poverty declined significantly; second, the place of the poor relative to the rest of the population remained almost exactly the same; and third, demoralization of the poor increased.

The number of desperately poor people in Maryland declined almost exactly as the economy rose—that is, the number of poor people declined rapidly from 1940 to 1968, when the economy expanded rapidly, and it declined slowly thereafter, as the economy cooled. In 1940 about 26 percent of American families lived on $650 a year or less, and in 1982 about 6 percent of families lived on $4,200, which was equivalent in 1982 dollars (see table 9.1). These figures are

Table 9.1.   Poor Families in America, 1940–1980
(in Percentages)

Year	Below $650 Annually in 1940 Dollars	Below "Poverty Level"	Less than Half U.S. Median Income	U.S. Income Received by Poorest 20%
1940	25.9	—	22.4*	4.1
1950	17.4	—	20.4	4.5
1960	11.5	22.2	20.2	4.8
1970	6.1	12.6	19.1	5.4
1982	5.9*	15.0	19.8*	4.7

Source: U.S. Bureau of the Census.

* estimate.

not broken down by states, but calculations for other years indicate that the proportion of poor people in Maryland remained slightly below the national average. The decline in absolute poverty from 26 percent to 6 percent was significant. In 1959 the federal government established a more sophisticated "poverty level," which was calculated by area income and area costs for subsistence. The proportion of people living in Maryland who were below this level declined from about 18 percent of the population in 1959 to 12 percent in 1982. Again, the decline was significant.[31]

Still, the decline in poverty was partly illusory because many luxuries of 1940 had become virtual necessities by 1980—things like indoor toilets, central heat, medical care, and television. To the hopeless and depressed, a certain amount of recreation, transportation, tobacco, and alcohol may be as important as food and shelter. Poverty had declined if the poor did without everything but food and shelter, but of course they did not. Relative poverty, in other words, had hardly changed from 1940 to 1980; the gap between the majority who were comfortable and the minority who were poor was as great as ever. About 20 percent of families still received less than half the country's median income; the poorest 20 percent of the population still received about 5 percent of the total national income; and about 20 percent of the population still were irregularly employed, accepted one kind of welfare or another, and felt themselves to be essentially out of the mainstream.[32]

The dilemma of poverty was entwined with unemployment, and steadily after World War II the picture darkened. The rise in unemployment was more apparent in averages by decade than in annual fluctuations: from 4 percent in the 1940s, national unemployment rose to 4.5 percent in the 1950s, 4.8 in the 1960s, and 6.2 in the 1970s. Unemployment was a major cause of poverty, and it grew even as poverty seemed to decline. For each person unemployed there was usually a family on welfare. In 1975 there were 128,000 Maryland workers unemployed, and 313,000 individuals struggling to survive below the poverty level. The poor, who were least subject to self-discipline and the work ethic, struggled in a declining market for the least attractive jobs.[33]

According to almost any measure, social demoralization increased, especially after about 1960. Probably it was growing among all classes, but it was growing more discernibly among the bottom 20 percent of the population, and its growth was greatest among the poorest 5 percent. It appeared most starkly in the weakening of family ties. Among the most prosperous 90 percent of the population the number of families headed by women increased from 1960 to 1980 from 9.3 percent to 14.2 percent, but among the bottom 10 percent of the population the families headed by women increased from 26 percent to 50.3 percent.[34] Other figures were hard to break down by income level, but they were usually related to poverty: the number of divorces in Maryland averaged about 5,100 annually in the 1950s and 1960s, then rose to 9,252 in 1970, and to 17,150 in 1980; the caseload in Maryland juvenile delinquency courts increased 150 percent in the 1970s; the caseload in Baltimore's domestic relations court increased 165 percent. Suicides, steady since World War II, rose in the 1970s by 24 percent. One of the starkest figures was the birthrate, a biologist's measure of well-being, which declined in Maryland from 24.8 live births per one thousand people in 1960 to 14.2 in 1980.[35]

The most dramatic illustration of social demoralization appeared in crime statistics. Although crime was by no means limited to the poor, those living below the poverty level were twice as likely to be arrested and more than twice as likely to be victims of crime. Maps of reported crimes coincided almost exactly with maps of poverty concentration. The number of crimes hardly changed, relative to total population, from 1934, when uniform compilations began, until 1960—when suddenly the numbers began to rise. Crime rates increased more than 300 percent in the decade of the 1960s, and more than 200 percent in the 1970s. Since 1934 Maryland, for most types of crime, remained consistently above the national crime rate (see table 9.2).[36]

Drug abuse and alcoholism also increased among all classes, of course, although police and hospital records showed remarkable correlations with poverty. Drug-related arrests in Baltimore remained constant to 1960, but then increased 230 percent in the next fifteen years. The numbers of people treated for alcoholism from 1940 to 1980 can hardly be compared, for the huge increase was less a measure of alcoholism than of more available care. Alcohol consumption may be a sign of social well-being rather than of demoralization, but in either case it increased slowly to 1960, and then rapidly (see table 9.3).[37]

Social demoralization was probably related to television, to Vietnam and Watergate, and to the declining economic growth rates of the 1970s, but the most obvious explanation, especially among the poor, who so conspicuously led the way in all of these statistics, lay with the unrealized expectations of the civil rights movement and the war on poverty. A rise in living conditions came about without a rise in status, and television showed the deprived how different they were. Job training accompanied by a rise in joblessness demonstrated the futility of the effort.

Table 9.2. Crime, 1934–1982 (Incidents per 1,000 Population)

Year	Violent Crime (Murder, Rape, Aggravated Assault)		Property Crime (Burglary, Larceny, Auto Theft, Etc.)	
	Maryland	United States	Maryland	United States
1934	.88	.68	10.2	14.7
1940	1.36	.65	10.3	15.0
1950	1.61	.73	10.9	11.1
1960	1.41	1.60	7.9	9.6
1970	6.25	3.61	27.2	23.8
1980	8.52	5.80	57.8	53.2
1982	5.06	5.55	44.4	49.9

Source: Federal Bureau of Investigation, *Uniform Crime Reports* (1935–1982).

Table 9.3. Alcohol Consumption in Maryland, 1940–1980 (per Capita Gallons per Year)

Year	Liquor	Beer and Wine
1940	1.39	19.77
1950	1.31	—
1960	1.42	20.49
1970	2.21	22.50
1980	2.67	26.01

Source: Comptroller of the Treasury, *Alcoholic Beverage Division Reports* (1940–1980).

A portrait of the poor showed some changes from 1940 to 1980, but more striking was the changelessness. The proportion of the poorest 5 percent who were urban grew from 45 percent to 75 percent, and the number of families headed by women grew from 20 percent to 50 percent. Otherwise the portrait was distressingly static. Geographically, except for the move toward the cities, the distribution of poverty remained the same; it was concentrated in the Appalachian counties of Garrett and Allegany, in the counties radiating out from Somerset on the lower Eastern Shore, and in the cities in proportion to their size. Every study showed the proportion of blacks among the poor to be about the same, somewhere between 29 and 35 percent of the total. About 75 percent of the poorest 5 percent lived in families, and 25 percent lived alone; about 60 percent were under age 18 or over age 65; about 55 percent of the adults worked at least part time. At least one-third of the poor remained in poverty for generations, others moved in and out. Most distressing was the psychological portrait, similar in 1940 and 1980, similar in Maryland and around the world: helpless, cynical, and fatalistic people lacking ties to institutions or ideology; irresponsible people concerned with immediate gratification, concerned not at all for the future; angry people, inflictors and victims of physical abuse. These traits were inherent not in people but in poverty; and they disappeared when conditions improved—but meanwhile poverty contorted the poor.[38]

Alexis de Tocqueville, then, would be left with the ironies he loved. The nation of democracy, more than European nations, was the nation of inequality, and its age of greatest prosperity was also an age of poverty. A historically local problem had become more nationalized than any government activity except foreign affairs, and one of the most centralized activities was one of the most disorganized. While Americans reached out to blacks and other minorities, they were little interested in poverty, but even though no one was much interested in the poor, a huge structure had evolved to serve them. The improvement of living conditions of the poor could be weighed against the decline in most measures of their social well-being. Alexis de Tocqueville might conclude that the more Americans did about poverty, the more it remained about the same.

Prosperity more than anything else was the force from 1940 to 1980 that transformed Maryland and America, and that transformation was overwhelmingly good. For most people the American creed of progress still existed. For the poor the creed, as always, remained a myth.

Spiro Theodore Agnew's two-year administration as governor, in 1967 and 1968, paralleled the final years of Lyndon Johnson's administration, when huge liberal programs reached their peak, the war in Vietnam flared out of control, and the American cities erupted in riots. The Agnew gubernatorial administration portentously foreshadowed the appalling national combination of Richard Nixon, Agnew, and Watergate. These were difficult times for America, when the 1960s idealism showed its underside.

Except for corruption, there was a good deal that was pleasant about Agnew's life and administration. He was the ultimate suburbanite, the candidate of Kiwanis Clubs and the PTA, the triumph of modernity over the old guard and the old style of politics. Along with his election came statewide reapportionment, much progressive legislation, and a well-meaning attempt to rewrite the state's old constitution. The newcomers were naive, and the overheated atmosphere consumed them. Except for an unusual naïveté that exposed human nature too clearly, Agnew actually represented modernity and cleanliness in politics.

Spiro Agnew was born in November 1918 above a flower shop in downtown Baltimore, but a few months later his family moved out to what was then the suburb of Forest Park, and after that he and his parents, and then he and his wife and children, moved every few years from one suburb to another, as suburbanites do when the family fortunes shift slightly up or down. Strangely for a politician, Agnew always seemed more conscious of status measured by wealth than of status measured by power.

His father was Theofrastos Anagnostopopoulos, a migrant from Greece who arrived in Baltimore in 1910 at age 32, shortened his name, and opened a restaurant. The father was successful and became a leader of the Baltimore Greek community. In 1917 he married Margaret Akers Pollard, widow of a Virginia veterinarian and mother of a ten-year-old son. After Spiro, usually called Ted, was born and the family moved to Forest Park, both parents continued to work long days in the restaurant, and an aunt ran the home for the two boys. Forest Park was a pleasant neighborhood of shingled bungalows with big front porches and overhanging sycamores. Their mostly happy home was dominated by a stern father. The boys were embarrassed by their father's accent and would have little to do with his Greek associations. In the depression the family moved to a slightly smaller house, then to a slightly larger one.

In elementary and high school the young Agnew was academically average and socially nearly invisible. He played the piano, banging out the "Star Spangled Banner" for the weekly high school assemblies, but except for that teachers and classmates hardly remember him. He was 1 of 4 in a class of 163 students who had no achievements noted under their pictures in the 1937 high school yearbook. Certainly he was unusually shy. One biographer, Theo Lippman, believes that he was sensitive about his family being a shade less prosperous than some of

10
Spiro T. Agnew's Crusade for Good Government

The Ultimate Suburbanite

Spiro T. Agnew, with Richard Nixon in the background, campaigns for good government. Courtesy of the *Baltimore Sun*.

the neighbors. Still, he entered the Johns Hopkins University in the fall of 1938, declared chemistry as his major, joined a fraternity, and spent a lot of time playing ping-pong—but he failed several subjects and withdrew after one semester.

He went to work for an insurance company and became an assistant underwriter in the sprinkler leakage department at a salary of $18.00 a week. There he met a file clerk, Elinor (Judy) Judefind, who made $17.00, and they became engaged. He was drafted in September 1941, went to officer candidate school in Kentucky, got married, and was assigned as a second lieutenant to an infantry supply company. He was sent to France and acquitted himself well under fire. He apparently overcame his youthful shyness, for his men remembered him as a good leader. He won a Bronze Star but did not obtain a promotion.

After the war his life typified that of the white-collar population with its suburban migrations. At first he and Judy crowded in with Judy's parents in the in-town suburb of his childhood, while he found a job as a law clerk. He used the G.I. Bill to study law at the University of Baltimore and to buy a tiny house out in Baltimore county, north of Towson. The law school was unaccredited, but he obtained his degree quickly. His firm refused to give him a raise, however, and so he tried practice on his own, and then went to work as an adjuster for an insurance company. In 1950, as the Korean War began, he was drafted again, but it was a mistake, for he had three children, and he was released after three months.

He became an assistant personnel manager in the Schreiber Food Stores of Baltimore, mostly to mediate with the butchers' union and to shake down shoplifters without getting the store sued for false arrest. His salary rose to $5,000, and the family moved to another suburb near Towson. These may have been the happiest years of his life. A group of neighbors, calling themselves "the Group," became especially close and spent Saturday nights bowling or at each other's houses, talking sports and singing, with Agnew playing the piano. They never talked politics. Besides the Agnews, there were a real estate manager, two salesmen, a retired marine major, a manager for an oil burner equipment company, and their wives. This was where Agnew belonged. Even after Spiro became vice-president of the United States, he and Judy returned at least once a month to the suburbs to talk football and sing with the Group.

In 1953 Spiro left Schreiber's to try law practice again on his own. His chief client was the butchers' union, which he represented against his old bosses, but he was forced to supplement his income by serving as a legal researcher for the court of appeals. Agnew was approaching 40, and none of his law-related jobs had been very profitable. He spoke to his law associates about opportunities in politics and on their advice switched his registration from the Democratic party, which dominated the county and was crowded with lawyers, to the tiny Republican party, where opportunities seemed greater. He became president of the PTA at the school where his son was in junior high school, and then, after seven years with a perfect attendance record, president of the Loch Raven Kiwanis.

Agnew discovered he was a good public speaker, and he spoke out in support of the favorite local cause of the white-collar suburbanites—the cause of home rule. Ostensibly the cause was nonpartisan, but actually it was an attack on the entrenched Democratic machine, which was an alliance of rural voters in the northern part of the county and factory workers in the southeast corner. The Democrats were dedicated to rapid growth, but to minimum schools and services, especially in the new developments. Home rule would presumably free the county from the iron grip of the Democratic legislative delegation, which had to approve all county ordinances. Home rule would presumably bring broadly representative government with freely elected commissions to control taxes, services, and zoning. Agnew's voice in the Kiwanis Club was not instrumental, but in 1956 home rule passed. That fall Agnew appeared at the little Republican party office and asked if he could campaign in favor of Republican candidates to the new county council, and for the next month he worked indefatigably in the most humble job in American politics, ringing doorbells and handing out flyers for the local party candidates. The Democrats elected the old boss, Michael J. Birmingham, as the new county executive, but the Republicans, in an upset, captured four of the seven seats in the new county council. The faithful Republican workers lined up to collect their reward.[1]

What Agnew wanted and got was a seat on the county's new zoning board, a one-year appointment at a salary of $3,600, far better than court research to supplement his legal practice, and ideal for obtaining visibility. Baltimore County almost doubled its population in the 1950s; fortunes in real estate depended on zoning decisions; opportunities for collecting legal fees were limitless. The county had a professional staff that established zoning regulations, and the zoning board met about once a week to listen to appeals. Temptation in the suburban boom was as ubiquitous as crabgrass. "If I were interested," Agnew liked to say to his friends, "there is not a case that comes before me that I could not make a minimum of $10,000 on, under the table."[2]

But Agnew was superb in the job: firm and fair, without a hint then or later of impropriety. From time to time others were tainted, but not Agnew. At the end of the first year he was reappointed to a three-year term, and his fellow board members elected him chairman. Occasionally he was criticized, and he was thin-skinned, as shy people are likely to be, and never forgot an insult. But mostly his decisions received praise for being made on the basis of the total long-range welfare of the county. Many people believed that the zoning board alone justified home rule, and the gutsy chairman of the zoning board was partially responsible for its success. In his dedication to the public interest, Agnew never surpassed the years from 1957 through 1961; they were the peak of his career.

He was good because he had time for the job and because he wanted to earn a reputation for fairness that could win him a judgeship in a local court. In 1960 he made the mistake of running against sitting judges, which was almost never done, and he lost badly, but the election did not diminish his effectiveness on the zoning board. When

Democrats on the county council denied him reappointment to the
zoning board for 1962, good government leagues were outraged.
When he announced that he would run for county executive, the
citizens' groups were delighted.[3]

Agnew became the first Republican in sixty years to serve as chief
executive of Baltimore County. He won the election because the
ancient Democratic organization was badly split between its rival
bosses, Michael J. Birmingham and Christian H. Kahl. He won as the
candidate of the rising white-collar suburbs, the opponent of crony
rule, because of his reputation as Mr. Clean. And he won because the
sharks who did business with the county thought they spied a mark
who was softer than the bosses, and they supported and befriended
him. His new friends in the election included J. Walter Jones, I. H.
Hammerman, Jerome B. Wolff, Lester Matz, John C. Childs, and
Samuel A. Green—a lot of new friends all at once, and rich, impressive people. They all eventually confessed to schemes of extortion.

Agnew's career as county executive from 1962 to 1966 has been
scrutinized by biographers, reporters, grand juries, and prosecutors as
closely as any county administration has been in modern times. It is a
case study in the new suburbanization—a case study of what happens
when the new white-collar suburbanites triumph over the old-style
politics of the courthouse gang. It is a story of moderately efficient
day-to-day administration and small immediate accomplishment, of
mostly good intention and tragic naiveté. Agnew's administration was
less corrupt than administrations before and after, but it was more
blatant and stupid about the corruption it was involved in.

Everyone agreed, then and later, that the new administration
brought at least marginally better management than existed before,
including experts instead of cronies in most jobs, more businesslike
procedures, better bookkeeping. Agnew fought valiantly but in vain
for good PTA things like urban renewal for Towson and Catonsville,
outlawing pinball machines, getting firemen and police out of political
campaigns, modern garbage incinerators to replace landfills, handgun
registration, and a pooling of resources and services with Baltimore
City. The biggest issue was civil rights, and Agnew was ahead of rural
and blue-collar voters in opposing George Wallace, who campaigned
in Maryland, in advocating a limited open accommodation ordinance,
and in obtaining a county Human Rights Commission. But Agnew
was a 1930s liberal who believed in racial harmony, not a 1960s one
who believed in black advances. When the Human Rights Commission supported sit-ins at Gwynn Oak, he denounced the agency and
forced the resignation of its chairman.

As for corruption, Agnew curtailed and refined it. Instead of traditional big shakedowns from the engineers, contractors, and insurance
people who did business with the county—shakedowns for campaign
contributions and jobs for scores of party workers—he expected only
modest payments for personal use. He was not much interested in
building a party organization, just in living a little better. He moved
into a richer development.

Personally as well as politically Agnew represented a suburban politics, not of personal attachments, but of impersonality and clean

image. He was dignified and righteous, distant from fellow workers in government, at his best when making a speech. Reporters repeated the word *impeccable* to describe both his dress and his manner; he was the kind of man who never had a hair out of place. This new style was still too cool for Baltimore County in the early 1960s; the victory of the newcomers was not secure. Agnew knew he could not be reelected in 1966, and he was looking for a job. The old machine returned to win with an easy victory, and it ruled for two more terms before it finally collapsed.[4]

The governors of Maryland seem so much to be the product of their times, as though no one else could have served just when they did, and yet the results of each election seem accidental. Agnew won as county executive against a three-to-one Democratic voter registration because the Democrats were splintered; he won as governor against a two-to-one Democratic majority for the same reason; and in 1968 Richard Nixon and he were elected as president and vice-president with 43 percent of the vote, while Hubert Humphrey and George Wallace and their running mates between them obtained 56 percent of voter support.

Governor, Vice-President, and Felon

Agnew's Baltimore County friends, especially Hammerman, Jones, and Wolff, were eager for Agnew to run for governor, and early in 1966 he somewhat reluctantly made the rounds of his fellow Republicans in the state. He contacted Republican Congressmen Charles McC. Mathias and Rogers C. Morton and Republican county leaders Joseph W. Alton of Anne Arundel, J. Glenn Beall, Jr., of Allegany, and David Scull of Montgomery. None saw a chance of winning against Millard Tawes's Democratic organization, and all were pleased to allow Agnew to run for governor in exchange for making a few speeches in their behalf locally. Agnew may not have cared about his chances of winning, despite the excitement of his friends. Name recognition as a result of being a gubernatorial candidate would help him as a lawyer, maybe even boost his chances for that judgeship he really wanted.

For the same reason that Republicans were reluctant, Democrats were eager to run. The Tawes organization supported an able but conservative party stalwart, Thomas B. Finan, which prompted Congressman Carlton R. Sickles, a fast-rising young liberal, to enter the race. Five more Democrats, including several of some stature, plunged in, and then came the perennial candidate, George P. Mahoney, with money and energy and a willingness to play the racial demagogue. At his KKK-attended rallies, Mahoney attacked the state's new Open Accommodations Law and the pending open housing legislation with his slogan "Your Home Is Your Castle—Protect it." Mahoney obtained only 30 percent of the Democratic votes, but that was slightly more than any one of his opponents, and there was no runoff.

So Agnew had the support in the general election of everyone in Maryland who was on this side of the Dark Ages. Backed by plenty of money, he ran a good campaign. An ad agency developed a nice jingle, "My kind of man—Ted Agnew is," and a bouncy model sang it on television commercials. Agnew spoke well and made the most of Mahoney's resemblance to Lester Maddox, who was swinging ax handles at blacks while he ran for governor of Georgia. "The electorate must choose," said Agnew, "between the bright, pure, courageous flame of righteousness [and] the evil of a fiery cross." At the last minute an able independent candidate, Hyman Pressman of Baltimore, appeared in the race, but he drew about an equal number of votes from both candidates and did not affect the outcome. Agnew won with slightly less than a majority of the votes, mostly from the suburbs, except that Baltimore County was against him. Analysts calculated that over 80 percent of the black vote went to Agnew.[5]

Except for in the most intimate circle, the staff and appointments of Agnew's administration were mostly good. On the inside were Jones, Hammerman, and Wolff, who were responsible for the deals and payoffs. Beyond that, however, were ambitious young people dedicated to modern management: E. Scott Moore, Arthur Sohmer, John G. Lauber, Cynthia Rosenwald, C. Stanley Blair, Vladimir Wahbe, and Robert J. Lally. Outside of that circle was the sound and experienced Democratic legislative leadership: the ultimate insider, Marvin Mandel, who was Speaker of the house, the statesmanlike William S. James, who was president of the senate, and bright young Harry Hughes, who was senate majority leader. Agnew knew that he had no hope of launching a legislative program of his own, even if he had been interested in doing so. His hope for success lay in joining in the programs of the Democratic leadership, and that suited him well enough.

Agnew kept his distance, as he had in the county, from both the bureaucracy and the legislature. Administrative technique, natural shyness, and disinterest in details coincided. He worked from 10 to 5, took two afternoons for golf, and kept the weekends free. His desk was usually bare. Except in the inner circle and the Group which he regularly visited back in the Towson suburbs, he avoided small talk and called people only by their last name.[6]

The 1966 election was one of the most notable in Maryland history, not only because of Agnew and Mahoney, but also because it marked the culmination of a twenty-year struggle over legislative reapportionment. In 1960 the 75 percent of the voters who were in the suburbs controlled 50 percent of the votes in the General Assembly and only 30 percent of the votes in the state senate. Righting the balance was one of the major causes of good government leagues in the suburbs, and slowly state and federal courts came to their aid. In 1962 the United States Supreme Court in *Baker* v. *Carr* moved toward the principle of one man, one vote, and later that year the Maryland Committee for Fair Representation won a state decision that required the Maryland General Assembly to increase the membership of the house from 123 to 145 to accommodate growth in the expanding counties. Still this was not enough, and bad feelings between the suburban counties and the Tawes administration made the last years of that administration difficult. Finally, in 1965, the courts ordered that even the state senate must be reapportioned. The reluctant Tawes persuaded the still more reluctant legislature to increase the number of senators from 29 to 43, so that the large suburban counties had up to 8 senators and several rural counties had to share a senator. All this took effect in the same election that made Agnew governor. Not only was the governor the ultimate suburbanite, but for the first time the suburbs dominated both houses of the General Assembly. The newcomers were inexperienced, but they were bursting with eagerness to remake the old order.[7]

In Agnew's first year, then, 1967, it was as though a dam had burst, and in one of the best legislative sessions ever progressive programs burst forth that had been bottled up for years. Most important was a revised tax code, generally called the Cooper-Hughes Bill, after a scholar-bureaucrat, Paul Cooper, and Senator Harry Hughes. The bill had failed in Tawes's last year, but the suburbanites pushed it through even though it transferred money from the rich suburban counties to the poor rural ones. Mostly it was a progressive income tax ranging from 2 percent to 5 percent, replacing the old flat-rate tax, and a large share of the huge new revenues was to be apportioned to the counties on the basis of their needs, thus helping them to relieve their regressive property taxes.

The newcomers had just begun: there was money left for air and water pollution control, alcohol rehabilitation centers, mental health clinics, strip-mining controls, reforestation, driver education courses in the schools, a public television station, and a consumer protection agency. All these things came primarily from legislative initiative, but the new legislators were the kind of people who had elected Agnew, and he supported them.[8]

The grandest scheme, typical of the naive times and the good intent, was rewriting the entire state constitution. Seldom in Maryland history has so much effort gone into so little. It was just as well that Agnew had little to do with it. The existing constitution dated from 1867 and was already much amended. Before he left office Tawes appointed a commission to advise on revision, the legislature approved, and the people elected a 143-member commission that hired a professional staff of 105 and deliberated for six months. A wise constitutional lawyer, H. Vernon Eney, was chairman of the constitutional convention, former governors Lane and Tawes were members, and political scientists flocked in from around the country to offer advice.

The result was a splendid document, resembling something a graduate school seminar might have written. It expanded civil liberties, lowered the voting age, liberalized voter residence requirements, provided regular automatic reapportionment, created a lieutenant governor, reorganized the executive branch into twelve cabinet positions with powerful secretaries, reorganized the court system, provided for standardized statewide property assessments, expanded the power of local governments, encouraged the creation of regional, city, and suburban government, and called for new programs in education, natural resource control, and consumer protection. It was a model document, and almost everyone assumed it would pass.

People were suspicious of such sweeping reform, however, and too many entrenched interests were opposed, and when the new constitution was presented in 1968 for voter approval it did not even come close to passing. During the next ten years most of the provisions passed, one at a time, as they should have in the first place, either as constitutional amendments or as legislation. Meanwhile, the convention allowed new state leaders to mingle with the old timers and receive a nice workout in constitutional government. In more ways than one, the Agnew years were educational. The suburbanites were coming of age.[9]

State government reform was in the air, partly because of the activist suburbanites, and maybe also because Lyndon Johnson's administration was growing so fast that the states felt compelled to keep up. A Tawes-appointed commission headed by a Baltimore businessman, John N. Curlett, made a report called *Modernizing the Executive Branch of the Maryland Government,* and Agnew sent aides to New York to learn the executive techniques of Governor Nelson A. Rockefeller, whom he particularly admired. Out of it all came the beginning of a much-expanded and reorganized executive bureaucracy, most of which developed in subsequent administrations. Meanwhile the Citizens' Commission on the General Assembly, and then a state-funded Eagleton Foundation Report criticized the operations of the General Assembly. These reports recommended higher legislative salaries, year-round committees, and greatly expanded legislative staff support, all of which emerged full blown in the following decade. The state courts underwent the largest expansion of all. Agnew stood personally apart from most of these things, but they were launched by the times and by the constituencies he represented.[10]

More than he was caught up in governmental changes, however, Agnew was caught up in these fervid years of 1967 and 1968 in the explosion of the civil rights movement into violence. He was elected governor as a friend of civil rights and left it as an enemy, but in fact he never changed. He supported fair treatment for blacks as long as they acted like white people; he opposed special schemes to help them get ahead; and he was outraged by demonstrations designed to change the laws. This was as close as he came to philosophical conviction and consistency on anything in public life. As a politician, he sometimes spoke at one end of his own spectrum without developing the other, but he never altered his principles. For the times in which he served, what he stood for was not enough.

Agnew accepted the legislature's Open Housing Act of 1967 (using his influence to restrict its application to apartments and large developments), and he accepted the legislature's repeal of an ancient law against interracial marriage. The larger race-related events of Agnew's administration have been discussed in connection with the black revolution. There was Rap Brown's inflammatory Cambridge speech, which Agnew played over and over to visitors. There were the student strike at Bowie State College, the student sit-ins and arrests at the State House, and Agnew's closing of Bowie on five minutes' notice. Most of all there were the Baltimore riots, which were an insurrection no one could have handled, but which rocketed Agnew to national fame. When he called in the black moderates to blame them for "allowing" the riots, he was in effect condemning all blacks equally and thus the entire civil rights movement. This finally allowed white conservatives to feel superior, and Richard Nixon found a running mate.[11]

The last year of Agnew's governorship, although only the second, was less happy than the first. The legislature passed minor laws easing abortions and allowing certain compensation for crime victims, but otherwise found no direction. Agnew quarreled with the elected Democratic comptroller, Louis Goldstein, without whom he could scarcely hope to comprehend the state's finances. Agnew curtailed meetings with his own budget director and with legislative leaders. Jones and Hammerman raised their payoff rates for contractors doing business with the state, and business people and politicians began to gossip about the payoffs.[12] Agnew turned his attention to supporting Rockefeller's bid for the Republican presidential nomination, and when that collapsed (amidst some embarrassment for him, for he had no prior notice of Rockefeller's withdrawal), he spent his time speaking out for Nixon.

The 1968 Republican National Convention took place in Miami, and Agnew headed the Maryland delegation. After a long process of elimination Nixon impulsively selected Agnew as a running mate because he was a clean-looking type who was apparently halfway between the liberals and conservatives in the party and was willing to promise absolute loyalty. People outside the Maryland area were astonished and mildly pleased by the look of the well-groomed suburbanite; local people who were aware of the gossip were outraged. The *Washington Post* called it "the most eccentric political appointment since the Roman emperor Caligula named his horse a consul."[13]

Nixon assigned Agnew the campaign job of counteracting the George Wallace appeal, and Agnew warmed to the job. He resurrected 1950s rhetoric by calling Democratic candidate Hubert Humphrey "squishy soft on Communism," and he called his ubiquitous hecklers "the delegation from Hanoi." He declined to visit an area in Detroit with the observation, "When you've seen one city slum, you've seen them all." He called Polish voters "Polacks" and referred to a reporter as "the fat Jap." He made jokes calling liberals fags, ridiculed Senator Fulbright and Dr. Benjamin Spock, and appeared to call for vigilante action against student hippies. Above all, he attacked the press in a way that cast doubt on anything reporters said of him. Journalists and intellectuals were "effete impudent snobs," "hopeless hysterical hypochondriacs," and "nattering nabobs of negativism."[14]

Meanwhile the journalists picked up the talk among contractors and politicians in Baltimore and Annapolis, and the *New York Times*, especially, ran stories about Agnew's unexplained increase in net worth, his purchase of land at the end of the second Chesapeake Bay Bridge just before its construction, and his about-faces to veto or support highly lobbied bills.[15] Amidst the screaming campaign rhetoric of race relations and Vietnam, however, no one paid much attention to these stories. Probably on balance Agnew was a net boost to the Nixon-Agnew ticket, especially in his appeal to the working people of middle America. As Baltimore County had voted against him when he ran for governor, now Maryland voted against the Republican ticket for president.

As vice-president, Agnew discovered, like his predecessors, that he had little to do, but he enjoyed the perquisites of office, especially his fine suite in the Sheraton Park Hotel. New friends appeared, even richer than those in Baltimore, people like Nixon's associate Charles G. "Bebe" Rebozo and singer Frank Sinatra. When asked what he liked about public life, Agnew replied on one occasion with the simple statement, "the trappings of wealth." Agnew continued to make speeches for Nixon, especially defending the war, but they were more moderate than his speeches in the campaign, and he made useful trips abroad as a dignified American spokesman.[16]

Nixon hesitated in 1972, then accepted Agnew as running mate for a second time, this time against George McGovern and another Maryland resident, an in-law of the Kennedy family, R. Sargent Shriver. Nixon and Agnew were quieter than before, for the cracks of Watergate were appearing. The Republicans wrapped themselves in the flag and let the Democrats slaughter themselves. With the election, however, began the events that led both Agnew and Nixon to resign— a critical time for America, an especially sad time for Maryland (see table 10.1).

It began with a small-time investigation of kickbacks in Baltimore County. The investigators, mostly Republicans, were not looking for big game; the statute of limitations had run out on Agnew's time there. The prosecutors subpoenaed records of engineers who did business with the county, discovered their payoffs easily enough, and offered them immunity if they would testify against the politicians who awarded the contracts. This was exactly the kind of good government activity that Agnew's elections and administrations had promoted. When witnesses were asked for the "whole" truth, however, they pointed not only to Democratic County Executive Dale Anderson and his cohorts, but also to Agnew as the preceding county executive, and then, astonishingly, to Agnew as governor and vice-president. The payments to Agnew for his influence in obtaining state and federal contracts, said the witnesses, were still going on.

The prosecutors went to their superior, United States Attorney General Elliot L. Richardson, for advice. A man of utmost honor, Richardson was aware of Nixon's troubles and feared that two simultaneous trials or impeachments could actually imperil American democracy. He instructed the prosecutors to proceed and informed Nixon. The president, suspicious of the prosecutors' motives, ordered that an independent review of the evidence be made by Henry E. Petersen, who was suggested by Agnew. Petersen, unfamiliar with the Baltimore County background, was more horrified than the prosecutors. Nixon asked congressmen of both parties to review the case, and they were convinced. Richardson, with the aggressive support of Nixon's aide, General Alexander Haig, wanted desperately to avoid a public trial that might coincide with Nixon's, and they offered a deal: Agnew could resign, let the prosecutors' evidence be made public, and accept a minor penalty for income tax evasion, or else he could stand trial for conspiracy, extortion, and bribery and face the probability of jail. On October 11, 1973, two weeks before Nixon's impeachment hearing began, Agnew submitted his resignation and stood before the

Table 10.1.   The Nixon-Agnew Resignation Chronology

Year	Agnew	Nixon
1968	October. *New York Times* charges kickbacks	
	November. Election	November. Election
1972		June. Watergate break-in
		September. Woodward-Bernstein articles begin
	November. Reelection	November. Reelection
1973	January. Baltimore County investigation against Dale Anderson begins; witnesses implicate Agnew	April. Haldeman, Ehrlichman, and Dean resign or are fired
	August. Case against Agnew complete, becomes public	May–November. Senator Ervin holds hearings on Watergate
	September. Independent Nixon investigation confirms Agnew guilt	
	October. Agnew resigns to avoid trial	October. Congress begins impeachment hearings
1974		August. Nixon resigns to avoid impeachment
1981	April. Agnew convicted of receiving kickbacks, 1962–1973; repayment ordered.	

federal court in Baltimore to receive a fine. Frank Sinatra gave Agnew $200,000 to pay the fine and back taxes, with a little left over, and Agnew moved to California. A scholar who compiled 2,685 pages of incriminating documents noted that "few criminal investigations have ever uncovered such detailed evidence of wrongdoing." Congress named Gerald R. Ford to be vice-president.[17]

Agnew wrote a book maintaining his innocence in which he claimed the prosecutors were politically motivated, the witnesses lied to save themselves, and General Haig was conspiring to be Nixon's successor.[18] This version ignored the evidence the prosecutors provided and stimulated a group of George Washington University law students to sue, in the name of Maryland taxpayers, for recovery of the kickbacks. The case dragged on for two years, witnesses paraded in, and, as in Watergate, the world obtained a view of sordid government.

The case concentrated on the years when Agnew was governor. Jones and Hammerman were the bagmen who asked for "political contributions" from those who did business with the state, especially architects, engineers, and contractors. The suggested amount was 5 percent of the contract, to be paid in cash in installments as the work was completed. The state roads commissioner, James B. Wolff, awarded the contracts, which were then approved by the governor. Wolff had kept meticulous records of the transactions: the bagmen received 25 percent of the take, Wolff received 25 percent, and 50 percent went to Agnew. Some contractors described how they had declined to pay and, despite low bids, had suffered accordingly. Three contractors testified that they made payments directly to the governor and then the vice-president, avoiding the middlemen; two of them told of making trips to the White House itself. Whisked through security, they met the vice-president with some awe. Each made small talk and delivered his envelope containing about $2,000 in bills, which Agnew placed in his coat pocket. Agnew always came at a low price.

Ironically, Jones, Hammerman, and Wolff were all wealthy businessmen and well-known philanthropists; they had been caught up in the glamor of power and promoting a friend. Most of the contractors were honorable men and were distressed at what they were forced to do to stay in business. Good intention did not serve them; many went to jail. One contractor who refused to pay, Wilson T. Ballard, was an ardent Republican who repeatedly visited Agnew to tell him that the payoffs were ruining the party, and Ballard testified that Agnew put him off with promises of reform. Agnew's own lawyer, George W. White, in a peculiar maneuver, was forced to testify against him, admitting that Agnew's only real defense was "it's been going on for a thousand years." The court ordered Agnew to pay back $147,500 in bribes, plus interest, and two appeals courts unanimously upheld the judgment.[19]

Agnew's fall evokes sadness more than anger. He was an ordinary man, an immigrant's son who was on his way to becoming a good lawyer, a fine spokesman for the new suburbs and good government, and an outstanding zoning commissioner. Then he was sucked up into government over his head, befriended by con men, and hoisted on his own petard of good government. He saw others on the take, and he took his share, which was actually less than they were taking, but he was too inexperienced to weigh the difference between party contributions and personal gain. It was a story that Mark Twain or William Dean Howells might have told—of American innocence, of coming of age too fast.

Maryland corruption, of which more revelations were to come, was the old order of politics making way for the new. The newcomers found it hard to resist temptation for personal gain, and the old-timers found it hard to understand the newcomers' rules against political favors. The newcomers in the suburbs provided a new boost to American democracy, but it took them a while to learn, and they took backward steps along the way.

The larger significance of Agnew and Nixon was not corruption but the gradual disintegration of 1960s idealism and an old political culture. Historian Arthur M. Schlesinger, Jr., has viewed the Agnew phenomenon as a watershed between an old politics of economic interests and a new suburban politics of status and image. Politics before 1966 meant preoccupation of voters with lower taxes, expanded services, bureaucratic benefits, labor and industrial policies. The new politics meant the concern of voters with a candidate representing his or her personal values, ethnic group, or social aspiration.

Within this new politics, Agnew and Nixon represented suburban values and fears: values of family, patriotism, law and order—belonging to the Kiwanis Club, listening to the music of Lawrence Welk, and cheering the Baltimore Colts—and fears of Communists, college intellectuals, hippies, blacks, liberals, the press, and big-city sophistication.[20] The new politics was eclipsed again under Marvin Mandel, and subsequent candidates would create new images, but Agnew's suburbia would prevail.

11
The Culture of Bureaucracy

The population move into suburbia paralleled an occupational move into bureaucracy; these were the most rapid population and occupational changes in American history. What representative democracy was to the eighteenth century, what industrialization was to the nineteenth, suburbanization and bureaucracy were to the twentieth. Each century's change brought disruption and costs, but the changes may have added proportionately to the health and welfare of the human race.

Primarily bureaucracy meant experts sitting in offices and managing society, but bureaucracy was a culture larger than this. It developed almost as rapidly in business as in government, and today one-third of all American workers sit in offices, managing the rest. Mostly, however, bureaucracy became synonymous with government, and its growth became a measure of the growth of government itself. From 1940 to 1980 the proportion of all Maryland workers employed by state, local, and federal agencies increased from 5.9 percent to 24.5 percent. In 1940 there was one government employee in Maryland for every thirty-nine Marylanders; in 1980 there was one for every ten.[1] Voters, of course, commanded this army of 407,000 bureaucrats, although voters sometimes wondered who was in command of whom.

The State Bureaus

Centralized, specialized modern management developed in nineteenth-century organizations like the Catholic Church, the armed services, and the great business corporations, but it came slowly to government, where people feared centralization and where jobs went mainly to the party faithful. By the 1910s, however, reformers were urging government to imitate the successful business corporations, and the middle class was seeking for itself the jobs that went to party hacks.

The new management techniques were instituted first in the executive branch. Maryland in 1916 under Governor Emerson Harrington became the first state in the country to adopt a modern executive budget. It was designed by Frank Goodnow, president of the Johns Hopkins University and the governor's chairman of the Committee on Efficiency and Economy in the State Government. In Maryland before the Goodnow reforms, and in other states, state bureaus for schools, roads, or prisons had their own bank accounts, which were often supported by their own taxes, and bureaus and legislators bargained with each other with little concern for statewide priorities. The executive budget of 1916 brought all state agencies under the governor, making him and his budget experts responsible for total revenue estimates and a single balanced budget, and the legislature was limited to making budget reductions. The executive budget was a modern and efficient concept, and it was subsequently adopted by the federal government and by most states and localities.[2]

The next step came in 1920 when Governor Albert C. Ritchie, exemplifying the business spirit of the decade, created the state's civil service system. Ritchie employed professional management consultants, the Griffinhagen firm of Chicago, to draft a plan for Maryland government according to business principles, and then he obtained support for its major provisions by inviting comments from a 108-member citizens' study commission. The result, after appropriate constitutional amendments and legislation, was civil service and the State Employment Commission. Within the first year the commission administered sixty different kinds of tests and assumed appointment authority over 1,516 of the state's 2,693 jobs. Ritchie also reduced the number of elections in the state, especially for state and county commissioners. He created a centralized state purchasing agency, which was responsible for buying supplies for all state hospitals, prisons, and other agencies.[3]

Centralization, the merit system, and the governor's budget leadership continued to grow during the depression and World War II. Periodic government study commissions prompted the process, but the major boosts to executive power were the burgeoning federal programs for roads, hospitals, welfare, and education. Most of the federal programs were channeled through state agencies, which grew, through federal funding, without the state having much say in the matter. From 1930 to 1950 state expenditures grew more than 500 percent, from $39 million to $205 million; but federal expenditures through state executive agencies grew more than 800 percent, from $2.2 million to $19 million. Federal programs were reasonably well supervised and audited, generally enhancing the reputation of the executive bureaus.[4]

Executive and bureaucratic budget control developed further in the 1950s, as the state budget bureau undertook supervision and auditing of county and municipal finances, acquired computers to provide daily analyses of revenues and expenditures, and largely replaced line-item budgeting with program budgeting. The line-item budget produced an illusion of precision by listing each state employee's salary, but it obscured in massive detail the totals for programs like education. The program budget produced an illusion of simplicity by offering legislators totals for major programs, but it obscured specific expenditures and ultimately further cowed the legislature and the governor himself. The governor's budget staff grew from twenty in 1950 to more than one hundred by 1975.[5]

Even more intimidating to the General Assembly was the growth of the governor's planning staff. In the 1940s the governor occasionally employed engineers at nearby universities to advise him on the statewide development of roads and parks or to draft model zoning ordinances. By 1950 the governor had a staff of nine planners, including a sociologist. In 1960 twenty-seven planners were concerned with all aspects of population and economic change and were largely responsible for establishing priorities of other state agencies for new facilities. The 1970 staff of forty-nine was dedicated to "promoting the general welfare," controlled all federal development grants, and was responsible for coordinating future plans for all state agencies and for county and municipal agencies as well. By 1980 the staff had grown to more than two hundred. It advised other agencies, prioritized their future needs, and issued reports on critical state concerns which advised voters and elected officials. In most matters following the advice of the staff was not mandatory, but its data and logic usually prevailed.[6]

Governor Marvin Mandel in 1970 created an Office of Legislation with a staff of about forty to draft the planners' plans into law and then to seek legislative approval at the appropriate time. A legislator soon learned that for matters of consequence it was usually necessary to persuade this office to introduce his or her measure as an "administration bill." Officials in the Office of Legislation might bargain with a legislator, modify his or her bill, and then accept it, perhaps in return for the legislator's support on something else.[7]

Finally, as part of the growth of bureaucracy and executive authority, from 1968 to 1972 came administrative reorganization—the structuring of a cabinet system by which the governor sought control over the 250 bureaus and departments he headed. The movement for executive grouping of government agencies according to the function they performed and their centralization under department chiefs began at the federal level with the Hoover Commission report of 1948, and was subsequently copied by most of the states. Agnew, who was a weak governor, began the reorganization by forming commissions and task forces as a means of comprehending the system he headed, and Mandel, who was a strong governor, consummated it as a means of exerting control over an often independent bureaucracy. The cabinet system marked the effective end of the citizens' commissions setting policy for agencies like education or health and the end of bureaus circumventing the governor by doing favors for legislators in exchange for favors.[8]

For Agnew and Mandel, as for most governors, the process of centralization was immensely costly, both politically and financially, for the bureaucracy had a life of its own. Bureaus resisted change, enlisting constituents and interest groups to their cause, especially if change involved becoming subordinate to other bureaus. Mandel eventually won the epic reorganization battle, after suffering minor losses to groups like agriculture and education, but he won chiefly by upgrading almost everyone in rank and salary. Far from cutting expenses, as promised, reorganization created order at the price of a new management level. Jurisdictional disputes dragged on for years, and in Mandel's time may have even outbalanced the orderliness he created, although eventually order did emerge and the new structure became as solidified as the old.

By the mid 1970s the executive branch was reasonably well ordered into twelve departments, each under a cabinet officer reporting to the governor. The Budget Department and the Planning Department were the supervisory agencies. General Services (care of government buildings), Personnel, and Licensing provided routine government housekeeping. The public service agencies were Agriculture (which was very small), Economic and Community Development (encouraging business, zoning, culture), Health, Human Resources (welfare), Natural Resources (parks), Public Safety (police and prisons), and Transportation. Education remained outside the structure, not directly administered, but fully coordinated, by the governor's financial authority. The comptroller, who supervised tax collections, and the attorney general, who supervised legal affairs, were separately elected officials but operated as cabinet officers.[9]

The executive branch changed greatly from the mid 1910s to the mid 1970s, and it would reshuffle but probably not change greatly in the near future. Even its growth has slowed. The ancient American fear of executive authority faded because the bureaucracy was stronger than the executives it served. It largely insulated weak governors from their mistakes, and it ignored or exposed bad ones.

The surge of executive authority eclipsed the General Assembly until belatedly, in the 1960s, the assembly evolved its own professionalism and bureaucracy. Legislatures in America reached a peak in the American Revolution, when they served as the forum for the new ideas being developed by a public-spirited gentry. They adjusted adequately to nineteenth-century politics, in which professional politicians bargained to obtain public largesse for their constituents. In the twentieth century, however, as government increasingly became administration, legislatures were left almost without function—except doing favors for the people back home and vetoing governors' unwarranted initiatives. Until 1943 Maryland legislators were paid only five dollars a day when the legislature was in session, and until 1950 the legislature met only once every two years. Newspapers delighted the public with stories of delegates spreading Limburger cheese over each other's desks, tying together the shoes of members who were sleeping, and engaging in revelries and brawls.

Gradually the assembly reawakened, out of pride and out of concern for the growth of executive authority. In 1939 the assembly created a Legislative Council, which served as a standing committee between sessions to prepare important legislation and to keep delegates informed of affairs of government. During the 1940s the council employed its first full-time staff member to help it keep track of business, and the assembly employed its first auditor to examine the governor's budget. In the 1950s, when Republican McKeldin became governor, the Democratic assembly moved into annual sessions, revised its rules to encourage rather than discourage the passage of legislation, and flaunted its authority by rejecting much of McKeldin's program, even the good parts. The large suburban counties began supplying their delegations with secretaries and budget experts. Governor Tawes in the 1960s astutely pandered to the assembly, feeding it bills for the very purpose of encouraging their defeat and thus stoking the assembly's pride. Tawes saw to it in 1962 that William S. James of Harford County became president of the senate and in 1964 that Marvin Mandel became Speaker of the house. They were the strongest leaders the assembly had had for half a century.[10]

Legislative reapportionment, long talked of but finally ordered by the Supreme Court in 1966, brought still greater legislative transformation. In the short term it was a setback for the assembly, for naive suburbanites replaced experienced delegates, but in the long run the new delegates engineered a legislative renaissance, for the presence of women and blacks added decorum and purposefulness, and the newcomers acknowledged their inexperience and demanded a bureaucracy to help them. The assembly employed a group of political scientists from Rutgers University to provide a study, which was entitled

Strengthening the Maryland Legislature, and within the next few years the assembly enacted most of the professors' ninety recommendations into law.[11]

Mostly this meant adding many bureaucrats: the General Assembly's full-time staff increased from 12 in 1966 to 119 in 1969; its operating budget rose from $675,000 in 1960 to $3.9 million in 1970, and to $14.5 million in 1980. The most important new legislative bureau was the Department of Fiscal Services, the legislature's answer to the governor's Budget Department. The development of such legislative bureaus in most states during the 1960s was a significant transformation of American government. No longer did the governor deal directly with the General Assembly, but one professional bureaucracy proposed a budget to another professional bureaucracy. The governor's economists could never say to their boss, the governor, that they had created a budget that proved politically unacceptable; and the legislature's economists could never say to their employers, the assembly, that they had studied the governor's budget for a year and had nothing to criticize. Now one group of economists and their computers negotiated with another, each largely concerned that their elected employers receive plaudits for statesmanship.

To create professionalism among legislative delegates, to free themselves from the expectations of favors from lobbyists, and to provide themselves with just rewards for their labors, members of the General Assembly worked valiantly to raise their own salaries. Twice, in 1966 and 1968, voters rejected constitutional amendments to raise salaries from $2,400 to about $7,000. Finally, in 1970, the assembly obtained voter approval of an impartial board that would establish an undetermined "appropriate" remuneration, and the next year salaries rose over 350 percent, to $11,000. It was a remarkable one-year jump, and of course salaries continued to rise, but the turnover in delegates dropped in half at the next election, and the quality and independence of delegates increased significantly.

The General Assembly during the 1970s instructed its major committees to meet year-round and gave each of them a professional staff. It took from the counties the responsibility for providing delegations with receptionists, secretaries, and other staff, thus giving the small delegations the advantage of larger ones. It established an ethics committee, a financial disclosure law for delegates, and restrictions on lobbyists, all designed to raise the standards and reputation of the branch of government generally held in lowest esteem by the public. The American legislature would probably never regain its eighteenth-century eminence, but its new professionalism and bureaucracy made it a moderately effective check on the larger armies of the executive.[12]

The branch of government that grew the most—from a budget of about $1/2 million in 1940 to $1 million in 1950, $3 million in 1960, $15 million in 1970, and $45 million in 1980—was the judiciary. The multiplication of judges, investigators, prosecutors, defenders, and clerks seemed to reflect the increasingly litigious temper of an impersonal society, just as larger government encouraged concern with personal and civil rights. Bureaucracy, in other words, was both a cause and a result of change. For all the costs, however, there was greater justice for a greater proportion of people toward the end of the century than there had been toward the beginning.

Until 1940 most cases in Maryland, civil and criminal, came before local trial magistrates whose salaries depended primarily on the fines they collected or on a percentage of the settlement they ordered. Most were appointed, or reappointed, by the governor every two years, depending partly on their political loyalty. Many were not lawyers at all, and most of them had other jobs. Business firms, especially loan operators and real estate companies, liked to have one of their officers serving as a magistrate in order to give respectability if not judicial advantage to the firm. Above the magistrates, for serious cases and to hear appeals, were twenty-six salaried judges organized into eight circuit courts. The chief judges of the circuit courts came together occasionally to hear appeals from the circuit courts.[13]

The first steps taken were toward professionalism. In 1940 the state curtailed the fee system by pooling all fines, and magistrates collected fixed salaries from the pool. In 1943 the state increased the number of salaried judges and created a full-time Court of Appeals. In 1961, after a decade of commission recommendations and political maneuver, the state made the Baltimore City judges professionals, placing them on a full-time basis and largely removing them from politics. Although this did not apply outside Baltimore, it provided an example that greatly improved the quality of county appointments. In 1966 the state consolidated the authority of the Court of Appeals over lower courts, created the Commission on Judicial Disabilities to review judges' competence, and created a new Court of Special Appeals to ease the growing workload by dealing with specified types of cases.[14]

The biggest changes came in the early 1970s, as the crime rate rose and as civil rights litigation reached a peak. In 1971, after appropriate constitutional amendments, the state took over completely the old magistrate courts, transforming them into state district courts with professional judges. Each judge had a staff of experts to obtain background information on the accused, to prepare the case for trial, and, if necessary, to supervise parole. Maryland's well-staffed four-tiered court system—district, circuit, special, and appeals courts—had 180 judges and more than 1,500 other employees. Quasi-judicial agencies were consolidated as part of the judiciary: the attorney general's office, including state attorneys; the Public Services Commission, which fixed utility rates; the Workmen's Compensation Commission, which adjudicated accident claims; and other boards that adjudicated tax and zoning judgments. Maryland's was generally considered one of the best systems in the country.[15]

There were still other frontiers, however, for the judiciary. In 1972, following the Supreme Court's *Miranda* decision, Maryland created an Office of the Public Defender, which employed hundreds of attorneys to defend indigents accused of crimes. Finally, in 1974, Maryland created an open-ended Division of Consumer Protection, which was established as part of the attorney general's office to seek out business fraud. Justice increased, and so did the number of lawyers.[16]

All together the executive, legislative, and judicial branches of state government by 1980 depended far more on their eighty thousand bureaucrats than on their two hundred elected officials. Honest and corrupt governors could come and go, liberal and conservative legislatures could succeed each other, but the stability and direction of government services was established. And the size and power of the bureaucratic army were greater at the county and local level than they were at the state level.

The Local Bureaus

State and local governments were inextricably entwined in their bureaucracies, sources of revenue, and provisions for public services. The nineteenth-century tension over whether governor or county legislative delegation provided the patronage jobs was generally replaced by tension over whether state or local bureaus controlled the revenues and provided the services.

Maryland has 24 counties (counting Baltimore City, which operates like a county), and about 150 towns, the same number as it had a century ago. The counties and towns were created by the state, not by the people who lived in them. They had no constitutional rights, but operated entirely under the approval of the governor and the General Assembly. This meant that counties had no laws or ordinances that were not approved by the General Assembly, and the county delegation to the assembly had almost complete control over the county. Legislative courtesy dictated almost automatic approval of any local bill proposed by a local delegation, but even in the 1980s almost half the time of the General Assembly was spent approving matters like a restaurant license fee for one county or a dog leash ordinance for another.

Baltimore City pointed the way toward change for some counties. Since the nineteenth century, when Baltimore had contained more than 50 percent of the state's population, it had maintained a kind of "home rule" by which the mayor and the city council had the final say in most matters. In 1948 Montgomery County obtained home rule by constitutional amendment, and in the next two decades seven other counties, mostly the largest ones—Prince George's, Baltimore, Anne Arundel, Harford, Howard, Talbot, and Wicomico—adopted home rule. The remaining fifteen preferred to remain largely under their county delegations.[17]

The system was peculiar to Maryland and it created two quite different kinds of county government, but the counties that created a large elective structure to make their laws and those that chose to remain with their relatively autocratic delegation rule had about equal advantages. The home rule counties had an elected county executive (or mayor, in Baltimore City) and an elected council. The heads of the service agencies—police, education, welfare, and the rest—were appointed by the executive and the council and were usually professional and reasonably nonpolitical. The counties that remained under the rule of their delegations, on the other hand, had no executive and had a council that only made recommendations to the county delegation. In these counties the heads of service agencies were mostly appointed by the governor, the agencies' policies were generally shaped by appointed citizens' commissions, and the agencies were usually more conservative than agencies in the home rule counties. In both home and delegation rule counties, however, bureaucracy emerged beneath or around the governing authority, integrated itself with its counterpart on the state level, and carried out the daily services.

Town government, except for large cities like Baltimore, did not lend itself to the growth of bureaucracy, and consequently after about 1940 town government grew increasingly anachronistic. Incorporated towns had emerged when communities, isolated in a rural countryside, wanted services such as police protection and garbage disposal which the counties did not provide. Eventually, however, the counties began to provide these services, especially for suburban areas, and the towns ceased to have much purpose. The intimacy and personal politics of towns interfered with the development of an impersonal bureaucracy of experts, so that town services were generally less efficient than those of the more impersonal counties. No new town sought incorporation after 1953. Except for Baltimore, the seven largest communities in the state—Silver Spring, Bethesda, Wheaton, Towson, Dundalk, Catonsville, and Columbia—remain unincorporated.[18]

While town governments waned, regional associations grew. Mutual interests of Washington area political bosses (notably, E. Brooke Lee of Montgomery County and Lansdale Sasscer of Prince George's County) resulted in one of the earliest such associations in America, the Washington Suburban Sanitary Commission of 1918, which provided water supply and sewerage disposal for two of the largest counties in the nation. The same bosses created the Maryland National-Capital Park and Planning Commission in 1927 to supervise, if not control, park development and zoning. Obviously, even in 1918 and 1927, bureaucracy had begun to create incomprehensible and euphemistic names for its bureaus. In 1965 the same counties formed a Washington Suburban Transit Commission to develop buses and subways. The Baltimore area began more tentatively about 1957 with a Regional Planning Council to consolidate water, garbage, police, and transportation services. Cooperation also came to rural areas. Federal grants required common administration of many road, school, conservation, and zoning functions through the Appalachian Regional Commission. Southern Maryland and the Eastern Shore created commissions whose functions did not go far beyond advertising to attract tourists.[19]

What caused local government to swell even beyond the perimeters of federal and state government was the central governments' delegation to the localities of the administration of public services. The federal and state governments insisted that the counties retain responsibility for education, health, and welfare, for example, even though federal and state agencies dictated what the programs should be and supplied most of the money for them. As a result, the number of federal employees in Maryland grew sixfold from 1940 to 1982 (from 23,121 to 135,000), and the number of state employees grew ninefold (from 9,176 to 86,800), but the number of local employees grew twelvefold (from 14,748 to 185,200).[20] The local responsibility for administration, if not for policy, tended to perpetuate the federalism that was a distinct part of the American heritage, and administration was probably the better for it. The overlap, however, resulted in tension over control of tax sources and confused funding for public services.

Local and state taxes became so entwined during the period from 1940 to 1980 that it was meaningless to speak of one without the other. Comparison of state-level taxes or of state-level expenditures for public services with those of other states creates a false impression; state taxes and services must be combined with local taxes and services to obtain a true comparison. For example, in Maryland the counties collected certain taxes for reversion to the state, and the state reverted up to one-third of its collections to the counties. State reversions differed, moreover, depending on local needs and local willingness to match them.

Bureaucrats cared more than the public about who levied particular taxes and performed particular services, and there were endless squabbles and adjustments between the levels of government.[21] The trend was for collecting to concentrate at the higher levels, which passed revenue back down the line, although federal and state governments kept the pressure on localities by making grants provisional or matching funds. Each level of government looked constantly for new sources of revenues, and the revenues from each source increased enormously (see table 11.1).

Income and sales taxes grew most. An income tax first existed in Maryland from 1777 to 1779 and again from 1840 to 1850, but the modern tax began in 1937 at .5 of 1 percent and then rose by about 1 percent each decade. By 1967, when the levy was 5 percent, the state allowed the counties to establish a piggyback tax, which added an additional 2.5 percent in most counties. The income tax was probably the fairest and most acceptable tax. A sales tax of 2 percent came in 1947 amidst vast public outcries. It provided a sharp boost to state

Table 11.1.   State and Local Revenues, 1942–1977

	1942*	1957	1967	1977
Total state-local revenues (in $ millions)	145	601	1,622	5,867
From U.S. government	8	51	207	1,208
Property tax	72	196	483	1,077
Sales tax (including liquor)	7	137	338	928
Income tax	10	71	217	922
Auto tax	14	69	127	271
Licenses, business, gambling, etc.	33	77	250	1,400
Percentage from U.S. government	6	8	13	21
Percentage from state taxes	38	47	46	45
Percentage from local taxes	56	44	41	34
Per capita state-local revenues	$59	$209	$ 440	$1,418
Revenues per $1,000 personal income	$53	$ 94	$ 129	$ 187

* Figures for 1942 are partly estimated.

and local income in the 1950s, but it leveled off as a source of revenue despite its gradual rise to 5 percent.[22]

Property taxes, which in the nineteenth century brought in up to 90 percent of state and local revenues, declined relatively as a source of funds. Originally, after the American Revolution, they were highly progressive and were levied on the chief source of wealth. Property taxes grew increasingly unpopular, however, as land ceased to be an important source of wealth, as special interest groups like farmers and apartment developers used their influence to imbalance property taxes, and as inflation made property taxes burdensome to fixed-income and long-time homeowners. Automobile taxes also declined relative to other taxes, much as roads declined as a proportion of state expenditures.[23]

Types of taxes and magnitude of tax burdens were remarkably similar throughout the country, for there was no magic way of paying for the services people wanted. The states and counties watched each other carefully, and the rich ones led the way. Maryland was about average among the states in adopting the new income and sales taxes, in assuming the tax burdens of the counties, and in curtailing property taxes, but its total tax burden lagged considerably behind its wealth. In 1982, when Maryland ranked ninth among the states in per capita wealth, it was tenth in per capita state and local taxes and twenty-second in per capita taxes relative to income.[24]

The Culture

By 1980 the people of Maryland paid over one-fourth of their income to federal, state, and local government, and over one-fourth of the state's population received their livelihood from government jobs. By a considerable margin, government workers were the largest single occupational group in society. There were 160,000 local, 135,000 federal, and 85,000 state employees, compared with 20,000 at Bethlehem Steel, which was the state's second largest employer. Insofar as there was a typical American, that person was no longer a farmer or an industrial worker, he or she was a bureaucrat: middle class, suburban, educated, and prosperous.

The number of government workers in Maryland was only slightly larger, and their prosperity only slightly greater, than elsewhere, for despite proximity to Washington, Maryland ranked tenth among the states in per capita federal employees. During the 1940s most government salaries lagged behind salaries in the private sector, but salaries rose as government grew, and by the 1970s, with federal employees leading the way, government salaries were generally ahead of others. Government work, moreover, was notably secure, job turnover was lower and retirement benefits were better than in business, and job satisfaction was above average.[25]

Like the farm in the eighteenth century and the factory in the nineteenth, bureaucracy projected its values to all society. The country's work ideal was no longer persevering toil or fearless entrepreneurship, but cautious management and technical expertise. The successful politician was no longer noted for aristocratic heritage or for granting

The United States Social Security headquarters in the Baltimore suburbs employed 20,000 clerks. It symbolized the emergence of suburban bureaucratic service industries. Courtesy of the *Baltimore Sun*.

personal favors, but for management efficiency and image. Taxes were based no longer primarily per capita, where all paid equal taxes regardless of their wealth, or on property, but mostly on income and consumption. The political ideal was no longer majority rule or equal opportunity, but a certain degree of equality, at least for the meritorious.

The word *bureaucracy* was vaguely pejorative, but there was no alternative to its operation. The use of experts and hierarchy was as ubiquitous in private enterprise as in government, for bureaucracy was as necessary for providing a complex society with efficient organization as machines were necessary for providing wealth. There were problems with machines and with bureaucracy, but no one could reasonably be against either one. The problems of bureaucracy were the problems of an advanced society.

First there was impersonality, which was a bane of modern society and was inherent in bureaucracy. The public railed against indifferent office workers and mail that was misanswered by computers. In fact, office workers tended to confer their loyalty on the bureau or the company rather than on those they served. They often valued relations with colleagues more than relations with clients. Abstract policies prevented agencies from fulfilling a greater justice, which exceptions might allow. Parents felt helpless to influence schools, and patrons to influence the transit system. Office workers learned to speak a non-English language that sidestepped responsibility: "It is thought necessary . . ." or "This office regrets. . . ."

Second, the reliance on experts tended to compartmentalize government, if not life itself. Bureaucratic data overwhelmed governors, legislators, and voters. Insofar as everyone was an expert, no one could comprehend the whole. Probably the rise of experts was related to the drastic decline in liberal arts education during the 1950s and 1960s and the rise of vocationalism. Probably it was related to the steady decline in voter participation, from 58.9 percent of the eligible voters in Maryland in 1940 to 50.4 percent of the eligible voters in 1980. Popular cartoons like *Peanuts* and *Doonesbury* and humorists like Woody Allen established the theme of individual impotence in a mass society.

Third, there was the tendency of bureaucracy toward self-aggrandizement, especially the self-aggrandizement of administration. Every bureau wanted more for its program and tended to measure its success by growth. Usually the relative cost of administration increased rather than decreased with the amount of service performed. Bureaus tended to take care of administrative needs first. Workers created an etiquette of rank as levels of administration multiplied, and they wrote memos to each other, making and dispatching appropriate copies, on planning plans and coordinating coordination.

Fourth, although all the frustrations were interrelated, was the problem of diffused authority. Worker dependence on collegial rather than client approval bred timidity. Circular checks and balances of authority buried alike the incompetent worker and the brilliant one. Caution and consensus worked to homogenize bureaus at low common denominators, and critics complained that they homogenized society. The aggressiveness of an aristocratic and capitalistic society seemed to be replaced by the security of a bureaucratic one.

Finally, there was the problem of accountability. One of the strengths of bureaucracy was its ability to ride out the blunders of corrupt elected officials, of which Maryland had its share, and to ignore popular hysterias and bad laws such as those which arrived in the 1950s with anti-communism. The other side was the tendency of school officials or military experts or transportation bureaus or professional social workers to brush past public doubts about their policies. Elected officials and public alike sometimes felt helpless against a branch of government which seemed to have an independent life of its own.

In the last analysis, however, the balance sheet was positive. The public that railed against impersonality, compartmentalization, self-aggrandizement, diffused authority, and accountability demanded still more public services. Neither conservatives nor liberals offered alternative ways of obtaining them. The frustrations of a middle-class society were no greater, of course, than those of an aristocractic or wholly competitive one. Along with the problems came the relative social stability of society, the economic security of a majority, and the breadth, however shallow, of American culture. Bureaucracy was not the immediate cause of what was bad or good; it was merely the reflection of its times: this was an age of bureaucracy.

Americans have always led the world in concern for education. Within a few years of its settlement, backwoods North America was the most literate society the world had known, and today education is the only social service for which Americans outspend every other major nation. "I find education everywhere, and in America it is everywhere, it is thought about everywhere, but only in America is it done as much as it is thought about," said Gertrude Stein, who went to school in Maryland. "They do it so much in America that they do it even more than it is thought about."

For the first three centuries after settlement the struggle for education was more of a personal than a social goal, the struggle of individuals for self-improvement, occasionally with aid from churches, philanthropists, and the government. During the early decades of the twentieth century, however, when so much of America was being institutionalized, philosophers like John Dewey began working to transform education into a social goal, the means by which society assured itself of progress and harmony. The schools flourished under Dewey's philosophy of progressive education, and some of their finest triumphs were in Maryland.

The movement for progressive education reached a peak in Maryland from about 1940 to 1955. It was a golden age for the schools, when they were confident, the public accepted them matter-of-factly as the center of every community, and their main problem was expanding fast enough to accommodate the growing number of students. The years from 1955 to about 1970 seemed to mark a second period, a period less of confidence than of fervor. Integration came, which was a triumph of progressive thinking but also a challenge to it; Sputnik soared, which stimulated American education but implied that education was at least as good in totalitarian countries; and then the schools and colleges became the site and even the object of attack for the greatest student insurrection in American history. Finally, the years from about 1970 into the 1980s seemed to mark a third period and a new educational outlook. People demanded a sharper focus for the schools and greater results, less transformation of society and more of the aid to personal advancement that had marked the country's first three centuries.

Dewey's contacts with Maryland were direct, beginning with his own education at Johns Hopkins and proceeding through the criticisms of the state's educational system which he inspired in 1913 and 1915 and on through the reforms that two of his finest students, Albert S. Cook and Thomas G. Pullen, put into effect in their successive terms from 1922 to 1964 as state superintendents of education. In a physical way Dewey, Cook, and Pullen provided more schools to more people; in a philosophical way they moved the schools away from rote learning and corporal punishment and toward education based on eagerness to learn. They were less concerned with individual achievement than with social adjustment. They were less concerned with instilling a body of knowledge than with helping students face the problems of

Triumph of Progressivism, 1940–1955

life. They emphasized the contextual nature of truth and called on the schools to rebuild society by applying reason to social problems.[1]

Their first job was to establish a school system sufficiently powerful to undertake such a vast transformation of society, and their progress began, ironically, when a famous 1913 study of the American school system showed how far Maryland was behind. According to this survey, Maryland schools ranked thirty-sixth in "general efficiency," forty-sixth in average school attendance, and forty-seventh out of the forty-eight states in tax money spent per pupil. The outcry, led by the Baltimore *Sunpapers,* was predictable, and Governor Phillips Lee Goldsborough proclaimed public education to be his first priority. As if by plan, two of Dewey's associates at Columbia University, Abraham Flexner and John Bachman, agreed to make Maryland a model of what could be done with public education at minimum cost. Flexner, who was also educated at Johns Hopkins, was already famous for his scholarly exposés of the nation's medical schools. In Maryland alone at least three profit-oriented medical colleges and two dental colleges closed as a result of his crusade. Flexner and Bachman had also designed the model school system of Gary, Indiana, which had gained much publicity. Their study of a state system, *Public Education in Maryland,* published in 1915, was the most comprehensive state survey ever made, a high-water mark of the progressive movement. Flexner and Bachman limited their attention to the public schools, visiting almost every one in Maryland, interviewing 10 percent of Maryland teachers, and in the process dissecting the structure of Maryland politics. Politics, they found, was the heart of the problem, with school boards, superintendents, and even teachers appointed as part of the patronage system. They laid bare the system's corruption, which extended from diverted school funds to student absenteeism. Educational progressivism began, then, with professionalism and efficiency.[2]

The Maryland General Assembly was impressed, and the Flexner-Bachman report resulted in passage of the 1915 school laws, the basic public school code that became a national model and has lasted in Maryland for seventy years. The laws began to take the county school boards out of politics with staggered terms; established compulsory attendance and attendance officers; required teacher certification and minimum salaries; established teacher tenure and a retirement system; and provided that the state appropriations that dribbled into private academies be diverted into a state equalization fund to aid public schools in the poorer counties.[3]

The man who actually constructed the Maryland school system was Dewey's student, Albert S. Cook, who was superintendent of schools in Baltimore County from 1900 to 1922, state superintendent from 1922 to 1942, and one of the ablest superintendents anywhere, at least until he was replaced by his successor. His twenty-year administration was an almost endless record of victories: upgraded teachers' salaries, an extended school term, free school books, professional control and modernization of the county curriculum, equalization of the state schools, consolidation of the one-room rural schools, vocational education (1917), special training for the handicapped (1929), adult education (1939), high school equivalency exams (1941), and equalization of salaries for white and black teachers (1941). From 1915 to 1940 the percentage of 5- to 15-year-olds attending school rose from 73 percent to 97 percent, and the percentage of teachers with postsecondary training increased from 10 percent to 95 percent. The greatest change, however, was the transformation of teaching procedures. Through teacher training requirements and summer and in-service teacher workshops, often taught by missionaries from Columbia University, Cook transformed education from memorization to excitement, from drill in fundamentals to discussion of social issues, from punishment to cooperative projects. The history of the Cook administration was the history of the success of American education.[4]

By the early 1940s the structure of progressive education was essentially in place, where it basked almost unchallenged in another long administration, that of Thomas G. Pullen. Cook represented the development of progressivism; Pullen represented its triumph. To mark the cordial transition of administrations of one of Dewey's students to the next, the two men commissioned their mentors from Columbia University to evaluate their past progress and future challenges. The resultant 420-page report demonstrated that Maryland's schools were among the nation's most advanced. The report utilized all the fashionable clichés: "teaching children, not subjects," "the whole child," "intrinsic motivation," "creative self-expression." For the future the report deemed that "the chief need is intensive and continued development . . . which will help every pupil in Maryland to realize as fully as possible the blessings of American democracy and will prepare him in the best possible way to meet the immediate emergencies." In trying to be specific about school goals, the report hardly mentioned reading, writing, or arithmetic:

1. To develop through successful living in a cooperative group . . . an appreciation of the American way of life and the interdependence of all peoples.
2. To develop . . . a gradual realization that man's conception of truth changes.
3. To know and observe the essential rules for healthful living [such as] team work and a willingness to participate in games.
4. To develop . . . appreciation of the fine and useful arts . . . thereby enabling the individual to live an increasing rich and worthy life.
5. To acquire such skills and information in the so-called fundamentals as the foregoing objectives would require.[5]

World War II slowed school growth but greatly enhanced the role of the schools in promoting social values. From 1940 to 1945 school population rose 2 percent—up slightly in the elementary schools (due to population increase), down in the high schools (due to available jobs), and up sharply among blacks (who often for the first time could afford clothes to wear to school). Educational budgets in the state rose 45 percent, reflecting public faith in education. Education was the only major public service to grow during the war years. Even school construction continued, often financed by the federal government to accommodate the growing population around the war plants. Average class size increased from thirty-three to thirty-six as teachers were drafted or went into higher-paid war work. Enrollment in physical education, vocational courses, and adult education increased especially.[6]

For most people, however, the schools more than any American institution became the bulwark during the war of the country's values, the chief national agency for promoting individual sacrifice in a common cause. Kindergarten children lisping the "Pledge of Allegiance," elementary children selling war stamps, high school students discussing the "Problems of Democracy"—these were the assurances that the American cause would triumph. The school building itself, flag flying, was the center of community defense activity, the rallying point for blackout alerts, rationing registration, and scrap drives. Dewey's concept of education's social responsibility was more apparent in the wartime mission of the schools than in the language of the 1941 report.

The schools' wartime values were more likely to be Deweyite liberal than xenophobic conservative. Unlike during World War I, during this war no effort was made to eliminate German language or German music from the schools, and there was little glorification of military action. Instead the war was an opportunity to teach the need for cooperation in a common cause, the value of democracy, the importance of social justice, and the necessity for international brotherhood. At a statewide meeting, county superintendents debated wartime changes in the curriculum, specifically denounced "racial and national animosities," and reaffirmed the definition of American values as democracy, first of all, and after that tolerance, social justice, and world peace. There was hardly a word in their report that could be viewed as unfriendly to German or Japanese culture, but there was bitter denunciation of American prewar isolationism and express enthusiasm for the American-Soviet alliance. All of this reflected a fine wartime consensus for the country, but it also laid the basis for the first telling attacks on progressive education, when conservatives after the war challenged these liberal assumptions.[7]

In the last years of Governor O'Conor's administration (1945–1946), under Governor Lane (1947–1950), and during most of Governor McKeldin's administration (1951–1958), public school development was the highest single priority of state and local government. Public schools seemed to be the institution that would insure the well-being of society and perhaps the improvement of human nature. Public enthusiasm for schools was probably ahead of public school leadership, although Pullen and the county superintendents were ready enough to point the way toward more and better schools.

The postwar school boom reflected general confidence in education, but more simply it reflected the baby boom, which began in 1945, reached a peak in 1957, and then took another twenty years to pass through the schools. In addition to the birth rate, which kept moving beyond expectations, was the continued increase, beyond anything Dewey had imagined, in the number of people demanding additional education. The first surge after the war came in the high schools and colleges, as returning troops and war workers sought to upgrade their skills; by the early 1950s the elementary schools were bulging; and at every point along the way the drop-out rate declined. Total enrollment in Maryland schools and colleges increased from 376,000 in 1945, to 602,000 in 1955, and on to its all-time peak of 1,147,000 in 1972. After the surge began it seemed so inevitable and permanent that statisticians blithely calculated the point near the end of the century when projected school budgets would exceed the projected income of everyone in the state. The adjustment to stability would be even more difficult than the adjustment to growth (see figures 12.1 and 12.2).

The first problem in meeting the surge was obtaining teachers. In 1945, when other salaries were still frozen, the legislature provided a bonus and then a raise, and the teachers' colleges and later the University of Maryland offered free tuition to aspiring teachers. In 1947 the state partially funded another major salary increase and required the counties to supplement it, and in 1949 it established a moderately generous retirement program. From 1945 to 1955 the number of teachers doubled, and average salaries rose 115 percent, from $2,063 to $4,404, during the greatest decade of progress the teaching profession ever enjoyed.

Pullen kept construction and operating costs well ahead of teachers' salaries. The two thousand schools of 1930 were consolidated by 1955 into approximately one thousand, and well over half the stu-

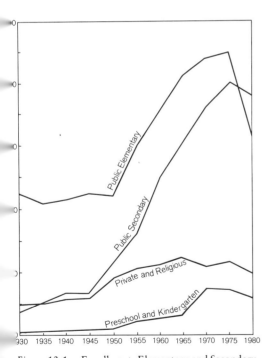

Figure 12.1. Enrollment, Elementary and Secondary Schools, 1930–1980
Source: Department of Education, *Annual Report* (1930–1980).

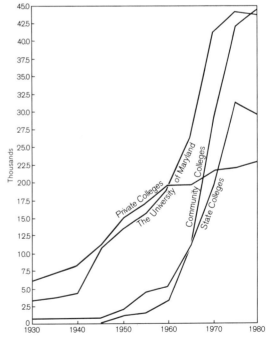

Figure 12.2. Enrollment, Colleges and Universities, 1930–1980
Source: State Board of Education, *Record* 6 (Feb. 1981): 3; Council of State Governments, *Book of the States* (1941–1981).

dents rode buses. The once romantic one-room rural schools, which to progressive educators symbolized the old order, gave way to modern plants with guidance counselors and vice-principals. Guidance counselors were especially important as the schools undertook the responsibility of matching individual capacities to social needs. In 1945 the General Assembly approved the addition of a twelfth grade, and over the next six years Pullen organized the elementary and high schools into a three-tiered system of elementary, junior high, and high school. The federal government began a free, or mostly free, hot lunch program to make the schools an attraction rather than a barrier to the very poor. There were new federal and state programs for vocational training, for vocational rehabilitation of adults who had lost their jobs, and for adult educational enrichment. The state made the schools responsible for county library programs, and directed that they especially encourage the use of bookmobiles, which made books available in remote areas. By the 1950s "special education" was the new frontier as more than one thousand teachers went to homes, hospitals, and even prisons to provide services for the deaf, blind, ill, or retarded.[8]

These years of triumphant progressivism were rich in educational philosophy. Simply put, the theory was one of loving little children, believing in goodness and equality and potential of students, favoring cooperation over competition. People who went into teaching were either naturally sympathetic to this creed or else they were persuaded by exposure, so that school personnel were in remarkable accord. "Teachers have gradually changed their emphasis from subject matter as an end in itself to the child as the center of the program," said Pullen. State officials expressed delight with the new Child Study Institute at the University of Maryland, where aspiring teachers studied child behavior. Instead of emphasizing subject matter, the good teacher helps "the child to develop as a member of the group." Instead of assigning lessons, the good teacher "plans experiences." Instead of the teacher giving tests, the "teacher and the pupil look together for evidences of growth."[9] School officials took great pride in the fact that teachers had almost ceased to fail students for unsatisfactory work, especially in the elementary grades (see figure 12.3).

The public generally was only dimly aware of the extent of the changes that had taken place. Occasionally parents in PTA meetings objected to the language of *educationese* that came from school officials. Still more occasionally conservatives railed that the emphasis on cooperation and justice was subversive to their world of competition, but such charges were usually linked to foolish implications of communist conspiracy, and these were easy for the schools to refute. It would have been more telling for conservatives to charge the schools with promoting conformity, but that would have been difficult for conservatives wearing grey flannel suits.[10]

Colleges also grew rapidly from 1940 to 1955, from about 13,000 to 35,000 students, and they also reflected the strong progressive tide. Six different types of higher education served the state, if not as well as the public schools, at least well enough. First, of course, was the venerable Johns Hopkins University, in the company of nearby Prince-

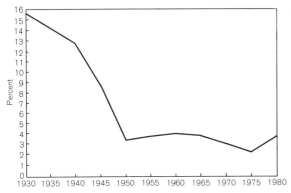

Figure 12.3.   Public School Students Not Promoted, 1930–1980 (Failures As a Percentage of Total Enrollment)
Source: Department of Education, *Annual Report* (1930–1980).

ton and the University of Virginia, all three of them dedicated to research and to helping the prosperous assume positions of social leadership. Taxpayers were especially pleased with Hopkins because it offered prestige and cost the state nothing, although the legislature often gratefully provided it with gifts. Second were the private colleges—Goucher, St. John's, Washington, Western Maryland, and a dozen more—which served as an extension of the middle-class family, instilling the values of character and hard work. Third was the University of Maryland, which did almost everything—a little research, a bit of character building—but especially it had responsibility for providing professional training in medicine, law, dentistry, pharmacy, nursing, engineering, agriculture, athletics, education, business, science, journalism, the humanities, and the arts. It was the largest and by far the fastest growing, partly because of its flamboyant political president, H. C. "Curley" Byrd, who served from 1935 until he ran for governor in 1954, and partly because of the growing demand for its practical training. Fourth were the three little white teachers colleges whose curriculum Pullen limited to teacher training. Fifth were four weak institutions, partially supported by the state, for blacks who happened to want an education. Finally, portentously, there were three new two-year junior colleges, a kind of thirteenth and fourteenth grade, which were established in 1946 and 1947 mostly by the counties but with Pullen's encouragement, offering classes mostly in the high schools at night for students who were not quite ready to make a full commitment to higher education.

For the colleges these years of triumphant progressivism brought an emphasis not so much on social adjustment as on practicality. Especially rapidly growing were the University of Maryland and the junior colleges, which provided the utilitarian training that helped their graduates get better jobs. Almost every discipline moved toward practical application. Medical schools, for example, shifted their emphasis from diagnosis to treatment and created new departments of cardiology and psychiatry; law schools moved from theory to case study and legal clinics; new schools of business, journalism, architecture, and library science appeared. The proportion of students and faculty in the humanities declined sharply after 1940, and the proportion in science, social science, and engineering correspondingly increased.[11]

If progressive educators had been able to evaluate their years of triumph, they would have boasted particularly of the harmony that hung over the college campuses, and for that matter over the country. The pranks of the 1920s and the hardships of the 1930s were mostly forgotten. The war years were marked by a common purposefulness, the postwar years by the seriousness of returning veterans, and the 1950s by cheerful conformity. Students affected a neat "Ivy League" look, shouted "Rah! Rah!" at football games, and read William Allen White's *The Organization Man*. The progressive educators could justly claim that their promotion of social adjustment had worked. They should have enjoyed their triumph; it was not permanent.

Integration

Both the creed and the criticism of progressivism paled beside the problems of integration. Genuinely equal education was an extension of the creed, and most educators promoted it for that reason, but quickly integration overshadowed progressivism, for it was the greatest adjustment the schools ever faced. As it was so often, Maryland in the process of integration was the nation in microcosm. The western part of the state, having few blacks, adjusted with moderate ease; the big urban center grew increasingly black; and the southern and Shore counties resisted fiercely and then made the most successful adjustment of all. On balance the results were probably about halfway between the hopes of the advocates and the fears of opponents.

Following the Supreme Court's *Brown* decision in May 1954, Baltimore that fall led the nation in adjusting to integration because two years before the decision its progressive school superintendent, John H. Fischer, had deliberately prepared the way with an unusual freedom-of-choice school assignment policy (see Chapter 7). A freedom-of-choice policy meant that, rather than having to attend school in his or her own neighborhood, a student could attend any school assigned to his or her race on a first-come, space-available basis. After the Supreme Court spoke, Fischer merely erased the racial qualification. Integration, then, only meant in practice that any black student could, if he or she particularly wanted to, attend a white school. "We believed it wrong to manipulate people to create a segregated situation," said Fischer. "We believe it equally wrong to manipulate people to create an integrated situation." For the first decade after the *Brown* decision, this is what most people thought the Court had said, and it was what most people accepted.[12]

From 1954 to 1964 freedom of choice emerged as the state's policy. Montgomery County, led by its churches, its PTA, and its League of Women voters, in 1955 abandoned assigned schools and adopted the new policy. Statewide the Department of Education worked with the State Commission on Interracial Problems to implement the policy. Each one made annual reports on its progress. In 1960 they both announced that school integration was "complete" in Baltimore and in the five western counties, where the freedom-of-choice policy was official, and that integration had begun in nine other counties where local judges had admitted black students to white schools without county school board action. Counties of the Eastern Shore, like the

Deep South, resisted even token integration as a matter of principle, but the courts were closing in. By 1964 there were only four counties with no integration, and they had all promised the courts they were making "progress" toward freedom of choice.[13]

By 1964 most Maryland blacks had attained the right to attend white schools if they bore the cost of transportation and sometimes the burden of abuse, but this had not eliminated segregation. Despite the anxiety of adjusting to a new concept, the schools themselves, and the great majority of students, were hardly affected. Even in Baltimore, which boasted of "totally" integrated schools—since almost every school had a handful of students of a different race—there were more black children in an essentially segregated situation than there had been when segregation was compulsory: in 1954, all black children (52,000) were in all-black Baltimore schools, and in 1964, 95 percent of black children (but a number that had risen to 80,000) were in schools that were more than 95 percent black. Elsewhere in the state, segregation remained even more complete: 82 percent of the black children living outside the city were in all-black schools.[14]

The second change in direction came from outside the state, as the *Brown* decision had, when Congress responded to the Civil Rights movement and the assassination of President Kennedy with the Civil Rights Act of 1964, which gave the Department of Health, Education, and Welfare authority to take positive action to eliminate school segregation wherever it existed. The HEW officials looked, and they found it abundantly in Maryland, as elsewhere.

From 1965 into the 1970s federal officials replaced freedom of choice with a new policy of school districting which was specifically designed to promote racial mixing. The concept was blacks and whites together in neighborhood schools. Under freedom of choice the state had prodded itself, and Baltimore had led the way. Under school districting, HEW took the initiative, and it decided that the recalcitrant counties of the Eastern Shore should provide the lead. The state Department of Education called a meeting of county superintendents to urge compliance, but otherwise it washed its hands of the problem. HEW announced guidelines and required the counties to show how they were in compliance—or face cutoff of all federal school support as well as HEW suits for court-ordered compliance.

Each county's was a separate story of HEW negotiations, court suits, divided school boards, angry communities, and buffeted school officials. Superintendents resigned, school boards held special elections, and at one point Somerset County, the poorest in the state, suffered a cutoff of federal funds. The design of school districts, the assignment of teachers, the regulation of school activities, even the content of courses, was subject to negotiation.

More remarkable than the struggle, however, was the adjustment that within five years was generally secure and fairly uniform in all the counties. Usually neighborhoods were defined to include both races, and neighborhood elementary schools served both. Although neighborhoods tended to be predominantly black or white, most schools were partially integrated. Usually the high schools served much larger areas, and they were much more racially mixed; often the formerly black high school served the ninth and tenth grades and the formerly white school served the eleventh and twelfth grades. There were proportionately fewer black teachers than black students, but almost all schools had teachers of both races. A few whites withdrew to attend private schools, and there was intermittent minor violence, but otherwise teachers, students, and eventually parents accepted the new way of life as inevitable. In Baltimore in 1970 only 9 percent of black students were in schools with 40 percent or more white students; in Prince George's 49 percent of blacks were in schools with more than 40 percent whites; but in the rest of the state 94 percent of blacks were in schools with more than 40 percent whites. In terms of real integration, the southern and Shore counties of Maryland, like the southern states, were ahead of the suburbs and cities. Perhaps the fairly homogenous way of life and the personal contacts within small-town environments eased the way.[15]

By 1970 it dawned on HEW that the suburbs and cities were lagging, and it therefore prepared for the third phase of school integration: neighborhoods were to be broken up and students were to be bused about until each school reflected accurately the racial makeup of the country. Here was the most radical thrust of school integration. HEW tested it in several school systems, notably in nearby Prince George's County, which was the tenth largest school district in the country, and in the city of Baltimore. In neither case was the result encouraging.

Prince George's County, with a school population larger than six of the states, had a 20 percent black population that was rapidly growing and highly concentrated along the county's boundaries with Washington. From 1965 to 1970 the number of blacks in schools that were mostly black increased, so that for most blacks segregation was increasing. HEW issued its own order to begin busing, on penalty of losing federal funds, and it simultaneously brought court action to support its order with orders from the federal court. The court's action was most decisive. Following the Supreme Court in *Swann* v. *Mecklenburg,* a North Carolina case, the court ordered Prince George's busing to begin on January 29, 1973, in the middle of the school year.

It was a tense day, like the start of freedom of choice in 1954 in Baltimore and the start in 1966 of districting on the Eastern Shore. This time 30 percent of the county's children, mostly black, were bused out of their own neighborhoods and into a distant one. Again there were many reporters, a few demonstrators, valiant efforts of teachers and principals to maintain order, and then grumbling acceptance by all concerned. This time, however, the objections were more sustained. Blacks were as skeptical of busing as whites. The costs of transportation were large, the program weakened rather than strengthened neighborhoods, and the long-term impact was to promote white exodus. From 1970 to 1983 the proportion of white children in Prince George's public schools dropped from 80 percent to 45 percent.

Two years after the Prince George's experiment began, HEW

ordered busing in Baltimore City, and the proportion of whites in public schools there declined to 20 percent. The Maryland General Assembly asked Congress to intervene to halt busing, but Congress took no action.[16]

Busing remained in Prince George's and Baltimore, but it did not expand to other counties, and its importance declined. Even in Prince George's County it began to break down because the Prince George's integration quotas were based on a minimum number of blacks in each school, and as the number of blacks in the county rose, the quotas became almost meaningless and the proportion of students being bused steadily declined. It was as though HEW acknowledged it had made a mistake, especially after Reagan's election in 1980, and HEW seemed content for demographic change to wash the mistake away. The courts also slowed the pace. If counties or cities were becoming predominantly black, then logic dictated busing from one county to another, but the Supreme Court in a 1975 Detroit case rejected that possibility.[17]

Integration proceeded in much the same way in the colleges, first too slowly, then with bureaucratic precipitance. Maryland institutions generally welcomed blacks who asked for admission after 1954, and when few blacks came to previously white schools, professors and students became among the most active advocates of additional civil rights initiatives. About 1968, however, HEW entered the picture, pushing hard for affirmative action by which the colleges were actively to recruit black faculty and students. At first this recruitment proceeded successfully and the number of blacks attending white colleges rose significantly, but again there were unanticipated results. Once-black colleges were threatened with extinction, to the distress of blacks, and once-white colleges attracted unqualified blacks who became bitter about their failure.[18]

The important questions concerned the impact of integration on the schools, the students, and on society itself, and their answers were not definitive. Certainly the public school system remained intact. For all their problems, of which integration was only one, the public schools continued to grow, even ahead of the private schools. Private and religious schools gained a few students with each step toward integration, but their overall enrollment actually dropped from a peak of 20 percent of the total school population in 1950, to 14 percent in 1970, then back to 16 percent in 1982. Private school enrollment in Maryland was a product of prosperity more than a product of integration.

Teachers complained that the main cost of integration was an increase in disciplinary problems and absenteeism. School rowdiness paralleled the general rise in violent crime in America, but the correlation with integration was too close to ignore. Prince George's County experienced an increase in reported daily "assaults" from 1.8 in the year before busing to 5.2 in the year following it.[19] Statewide daily school absences increased from a 1930–1965 average of 7.7 percent to a 1970s average of 11.5 percent (see figure 12.4).

School integration did not appear to be related to declining test scores. Although blacks scored lower than whites, and the black school population was rising, the county with the greatest decline in

Figure 12.4.   Daily Absences in Public Schools, 1930–
1980 (As a Percentage of Total Enrollment)
Source: Department of Education, *Annual Report* (1930-
1980).

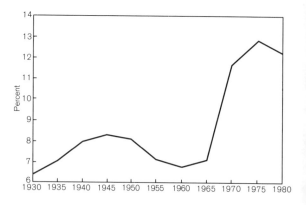

scores was Garrett, which had actually two blacks in its entire system. In Prince George's, which had far the greatest influx of blacks, the decline was much less than the average decline in the state. Test scores exist for only a brief period, in the 1970s (see table 12.1).

School integration probably contributed to residential segregation, and especially to the white migration from Baltimore City. When HEW used busing to overcome neighborhood segregation, this appeared to promote white flight from Prince George's to surrounding counties and thus promoted a much larger racial segregation by county.[20] Integration probably increased black opportunities. An increasing proportion of blacks went on to college and professional schools. Almost all polls showed students to be much more open-minded than their parents on racial matters. Integration probably promoted an amalgamation of teenage culture, notably in music, possibly in language and religion.

The most important concern was the children themselves. They had withstood the experiments of progressive educators without being seriously damaged, and they withstood the experiments of social engineers as well.

Radicalism, 1955–1972

Although integration was the chief blow to progressivism, surging enrollment, concern with quality, attacks on the left, and then the student rebellion also buffeted education. Each of these forces, like progressivism and integration, appeared temporarily to herald the transformation of all American society, and the wonder was that the schools remained so much the same.

By the mid-1950s the baby boom was cresting, and parents' concern for their children's education was the single most important business of state and local government. Each week Maryland added thirty new classrooms, each year it employed three thousand new teachers. Fervor for education overwhelmed regard for any particular pedagogy or creed. The old Pullen progressives imagined themselves still fully in control, they felt augmented rather than diminished by the surging demand for their services, and they hardly noticed that their services were changing in the process. In fact, "teaching children" was very difficult; it was much easier for harried and inexperienced teachers to "teach subjects."

Table 12.1.   Effect of School Integration on Test Scores, 1973–1977

County	Percentage Blacks in Schools, 1980	Change in Black Enrollment, 1970–1980	Grade Level Score of 9th Grade, 1977	Change in Score, 1973–1977
Allegany	1.7	− .3	8.73	−.24
Anne Arundel	14.1	+ 1.2	8.63	+.13
Baltimore City	77.8	+10.8	7.13	+.30
Baltimore	11.7	+ 7.9	8.87	+.07
Calvert	30.8	−22.2	7.53	+.27
Caroline	21.8	− 4.2	7.83	−.33
Carroll	2.6	− 1.3	8.77	−.29
Cecil	5.0	− 1.6	8.57	+.10
Charles	25.9	−14.0	7.93	+.03
Dorchester	42.7	+ .7	7.87	+.14
Frederick	6.5	− 2.5	8.70	+.40
Garrett	0		8.43	−.34
Harford	9.4	0	8.97	−.03
Howard	14.6	+ 6.0	9.33	+.13
Kent	30.4	− 1.1	8.43	−.17
Montgomery	12.0	+ 6.9	9.53	−.07
Prince George's	49.9	+30.0	8.33	−.10
Queen Anne's	20.4	− 7.9	8.13	−.10
St. Mary's	22.8	− 3.8	8.17	+.17
Somerset	46.7	− 2.0	7.90	+.13
Talbot	29.8	+ 3.9	8.57	0
Washington	3.1	+ .6	8.27	−.10
Wicomico	29.4	+ .4	8.67	−.10
Worcester	37.4	− 7.4	8.16	+.43
Total	30.4	+ 6.3	8.46	−.20

Source: Department of Education, *Facts about Maryland Public Education* (1970–1984); idem, *Accountability Reports* (1974–1983).

Parental concern was not only for schools but also for quality education. This meant ever higher standards, and parental demand for standards included an element of attack on the educational establishment, but educators tried to embrace the movement. Following the publication of several popular books and the issuance of some PTA resolutions which attacked educational gobbledegook, Governor McKeldin called a 1955 summer workshop conference at Towson for the critics to make their case and for Pullen and the county superintendents to respond. The result, however, was a lovefeast, in which everyone called for more money for the schools, better teachers, and higher standards.[21]

After the Soviet Union launched Sputnik in 1957, concern for quality education sometimes bordered on hysteria. National magazines like *Life* and *U.S. News and World Report* devoted full issues to "The Crisis in the Schools," and teachers caught the enthusiasm for upgrading standards and curriculum. The legislature authorized another commission to make a comprehensive study, like those of 1915 and 1941. The 1958 study was in two parts. One, from a committee headed by J. Freeman Butts of Columbia University, offered unstinted praise to progress and progressivism; the other from a committee headed by Baltimore lawyer Enos S. Stockbridge, called for higher standards. Then the commission joined together to lavish praise with a hesitant qualification: "If there is any error over the last decade or two, it has been in veering too much toward methods of developing the child's personality and in failing to place sufficient emphasis on content requirements and achievement." The commission called for tougher standards, merit raises for teachers, special programs for gifted students, and greatly increased school budgets.[22]

The federal government, meanwhile, responded to Sputnik with the National Defense Education Act of 1958, the biggest federal venture into education since the land grant acts. The NDEA offered funds, to be matched by the state, for facilities and equipment to improve mathematics, science, and language teaching from kindergarten through graduate school; interest-free loans to students who wished to become teachers; and fellowships to outstanding graduate students in approved fields. Within the next ten years Maryland received more than $50 million, sometimes more than it could well spend, and federal contributions became a permanent part of every school budget.

The emphasis on quality in the public schools was not especially successful. Prodded by integration as well as by demands for quality, many school systems established special classes for the gifted, or track systems, which placed students in classes according to ability, but educators generally disliked the implied elitism and these innovations did not go far. For a while technology seemed to be the answer to growth and quality. Maryland established an educational television network, most school rooms acquired television sets, and the University of Maryland tried broadcasting its basic courses into dormitories, but the system never worked well and was soon forgotten. The quality fad caused foreign language enrollments to rise temporarily, but mathematics and science remained steady (see figure 12.5).

The emphasis on quality had its greatest impact on higher education, and especially on the University of Maryland. In 1954 the university's new president, Wilson H. Elkins, a Rhodes Scholar, took over an institution that had the country's best football team but was about to lose its academic accreditation. Elkins set about building a strong faculty government, libraries and laboratories, and rigorous admissions and retention policies. Contrary to legislators' expectations, raising standards increased the university's appeal. Each hike in admissions requirements caused a surge in enrollment, from 15,000 on the university's Maryland campuses in 1954 to 45,000 in 1970. The faculty turned increasingly to research, federal research grants increased to compose one-fifth of the institution's budget, and "publish or perish" became a faculty cliché. The university was admitted into membership with the top fifty institutions in the country, and Elkins became president of the accrediting association. Enrollments at the state community colleges were also surging, and many of the students attending these institutions aspired to enter the University of Maryland.

People in Maryland were more worried than pleased by the state's diversity of higher education. On the one hand it had become common

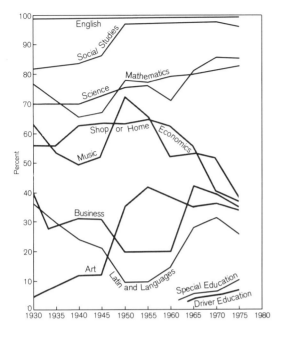

Figure 12.5 Public High School Students Enrolled in Selected Subjects, 1930–1978 (As a Percentage of Total Enrollment).
Source: Department of Education, *Annual Report* (1930–1977). Unfortunately, the Department of Education ceased compiling these statistics in 1975.

wisdom that higher education was the basis for prosperity and national strength, and on the other hand was the lingering suspicion that the intellectual was obtuse, arrogant, and liberal. The state's elite were accustomed to relying on Johns Hopkins, even though the proportion of students it served declined steadily, and the state's politicians were often hesitant to support the University of Maryland, partly because of its location in the alien Washington suburbs and partly because of its very success and intimidating size. State appropriations per student in all Maryland institutions of higher education remained among the lowest in the nation, more students left the state for higher education than were coming in, and the legislature ordered one restudy of the problem after another.

The plans for higher education moved the state's institutions steadily toward consolidation. First was the 1947 report of a commission headed by Baltimore attorney William L. Marbury which warned of the extraordinary growth that was to come and called for building up the University of Maryland and the new community colleges. Then came the report of the 1960 commission headed by Edwin Warfield, the grandson of a former governor, which also warned of frightening growth and called for Pullen's somnolent teachers' colleges to be upgraded into general liberal arts colleges and made into branches of the university. Pullen blocked the recommendation because he feared it would denigrate teacher training, but meanwhile Governor Tawes urged the university to establish its own undergraduate branch in Baltimore County. In 1962 came the best of the reports, by businessman John N. Curlett, which was the start of a unified tripartite system of junior colleges, state colleges, and the University of Maryland (see chapter 8). The legislature accepted the plan, which included an Advisory Council that was to maintain order among the three parts. This plan was the beginning of a unified structure, but the Advisory Council was the beginning of a bureaucracy that was more often the common enemy than the supporter of the particular institutions.[23]

Along with the rapid school expansion, the fervor for quality, and the particular emphasis on higher education, there was emerging among educators and students a groundswell of leftist sentiment which proved the swan song of progressivism and resulted in the greatest student rebellion of American history. The 1960s movement on the left was inspired by civil rights and reached a peak of idealism in the great society rhetoric of Lyndon Johnson's administration. The Vietnam War and the draft quickly transformed idealism into radicalism, and radicalism ended in the early 1970s shambles of Vietnam and Watergate. As usual, the schools reflected the rapidly changing mood to an exaggerated degree.

The leftist idea flourished among education theorists and then fed on students' sense of being crowded, anonymous, and restrained. Conservative critics had attacked the schools in the 1950s for promoting communalism rather than competitiveness, but the leftist critics of the 1960s accused them of being establishment enterprises that promoted docile workers.[24] The two attacks on Dewey's ideal of social adjustment were curiously similar, though aimed from different sides. In Maryland the high point of the new educational radicalism came at Towson in 1958 at the annual meeting of county superintendents and school board members. Melvin Tuman of Princeton told the cheering audience that "marks humiliate the kids," that "it is we who pass or fail—not the children." By accepting a society of rich and poor, "the schools are responsible for violence and the decay of the cities." He called on teachers to "take over the schools" and to "revolutionize society." This was heady stuff for school teachers and it became headier still as it seeped down to students. That spring high school teachers of Montgomery County voted a one-day moratorium on regular studies so that students could discuss "the animosities" in contemporary society.[25]

The greatest rebellion came in the colleges, and from 1968 to 1972 they seemed to be almost guiding the national mood. Clearly the rebellion was related to public questions, especially the civil rights movement. From 1963 on students at Johns Hopkins, Goucher, St. John's, Frostburg, and the University of Maryland at College Park joined together in sit-ins, risking arrest to demand that blacks be served in the local restaurants. Some of the earliest student demonstrations and some of the most violent occurred in the black colleges. More than four hundred students were arrested in 1963 at Morgan; at Princess Anne black students were arrested annually after 1964 and more than 170 of them in 1970; and in 1968 more than two hundred were arrested at Bowie.[26] After 1968 the rebellion was closely related to protests against the Vietnam War. It weighed heavily on many students that they were exempt from the draft but were subject to it if they failed or graduated. Others, including many faculty, saw injustice in the American intervention in a distant land, in the use of modern weapons against a primitive people, and in the bombing and invasion of countries near Vietnam. By the late 1960s almost every college had teach-ins, like sit-ins, where volunteer faculty talked about civil rights, the Vietnam War, and, occasionally, about the new drug culture.

Clearly, also, the student rebellion was against local educational conditions. Students were angry about the antiquated collegiate practice of in loco parentis by which the colleges usually required that female students wear skirts to class, that all students return to their dorms before midnight, and that beer not be consumed on campus. Administrators censored student publications and professors called the roll daily, as in high school, to see that everyone was in place. Students were angry about rigid academic requirements that stressed languages and mathematics and seemed to contain insufficient relevant material on contemporary social problems. More vaguely, students were angry about the impersonality and anonymity of huge educational plants, especially at College Park, which was the fifth largest campus in the nation with over thirty-five thousand students. Sometimes students were registered by number instead of name and their schedules were mutilated if their cards were. Professors frequently lectured to more than three hundred students, and graduate assistants graded final examinations. Often the faculty were more interested in their research and their professional status than in their students. In short, there was in fact a good deal to rebel against.

The first major student rebellion was at Berkeley, California, in 1964, the second at Columbia University in 1968; one of the next major outbreaks was at College Park. In the spring of 1970 several hundred students occupied a building to protest the denial of tenure to two popular philosophy professors, and the administration imprudently called police, who made eighty-seven arrests. Two weeks later, when United States troops invaded Cambodia, four thousand University of Maryland students went on a rampage, smashing hundreds of windows, setting fires in the administration building, and blocking nearby highways. That night the outbreak was the lead on network television news, and Governor Mandel called out the National Guard, placing the campus under martial law.[27] Twice more, in 1971 and 1972, there were rebellions, each smaller but angrier than the last, and twice more, troops occupied the campus. Most other campuses in Maryland and many high schools experienced similar, although less extreme, outbreaks. Some people briefly wondered if colleges would survive.

The period of rebellions passed rapidly, but its impact on education was lasting. In the public schools the leftward impulse promoted decentralization, with county systems distancing themselves from state supervision and individual schools from county superintendents. Communities, on the other hand, demanded a stronger voice in school control, not merely through polite PTAs but also through militant community action groups that advised principals on disciplinary codes, teacher assignments, and curriculum. Teachers also grew militant, obtaining state legalization of unions in 1968; though teacher strikes remained illegal, in 1969 and 1970 teachers in sections of Baltimore and Anne Arundel counties went out on strike.[28]

The schools reached out to new groups. The federal Head Start program funded preschool as well as summer school for disadvantaged children. The state provided new funds for vocational training for jobless adults and for programs to reach the handicapped, the children of migrant workers, and pregnant school-age girls. In 1968 the state required that driver education be taught in the schools, and the state Department of Education began actively to promote sex education. The leftward impulse even influenced school architecture. Designers created "open space" classrooms so that walls would not inhibit students' free expression, and they eliminated windows so that the "real world" outside would not interfere with the shaping of children's characters. Almost all schools relaxed their disciplinary codes, most high schools established smoking areas, and teachers tried not to notice what their students smoked. The leftward movement was a vague reassertion of progressivism, but it was also different; Dewey would not have claimed it as his own.[29]

The rebellions centered in the colleges and had their greatest impact there. In loco parentis died almost overnight. Campus pubs appeared, dorm curfews ended, and many colleges offered no objections if unmarried male and female students shared dorm rooms. The colleges made very strong efforts to serve students better, through improved advising programs, renewed emphasis on teaching, and elaborate grievance systems. Instead of as parents, the colleges liked to imagine themselves as intellectual supermarkets where students selected at will. The University of Maryland developed a preregistration system, which insured that the institution taught what students wanted to learn instead of what faculty wanted to teach. Fixed requirements almost ended, although usually field distribution requirements remained. Democracy developed to a fault, so that campus committees deliberated about almost everything. Students obtained a substantial voice in all committees, including those responsible for the appointment and promotion of faculty.[30]

For students, especially college students, 1968 to 1972 was a time of revolutionary liberty and revolutionary turmoil. For them it was the best of times and the worst of times, exhilarating and dangerous. Students changed the world more than they ever had before, they helped to end the presidency of Lyndon Johnson and the war in Vietnam and transformed forever the lifestyles of America. The drinking age, for example, was lowered by the General Assembly from 21 to 18, so that most college students could legally consume alcohol. The long hair and communes and anger faded with time, but casual informality would remain. There were terrible casualties in the revolt, for drugs and violence destroyed many lives, but the war between the generations resulted in a draw.

Parents and taxpayers found it hard to understand the youth revolt. Adults were generally worried when the most pampered generation in history challenged social values, and they were generally outraged when the best-schooled generation maliciously destroyed school property. Sometimes worry found outlet in anger. Once again it was time for fundamental changes in the educational system.

Along with the conservative backlash against student insurrection came the realization that school enrollment was declining. In 1972, for the first time since the depression, fewer people were attending school in Maryland than had the year before. The decline, moreover, was just beginning. From 1972 to 1981 school and college enrollment dropped by 17 percent; in the elementary schools it was down 32 percent. The birth rate was down 45 percent. An aging population was shifting its interest from education to health, environmentalism, defense, and tax relief. From the depression to the 1960s politicians could hardly promise enough for the schools, but by the 1970s they were outdoing each other in calling for educational accountability.

Accountability first became a fad in business, especially as managers of the new conglomerates of the 1960s tried to measure cost-effective productivity in each of their units. By the 1970s people were applying the concept to bureaucracy, and with student revolts and enrollment decline, it became especially apt as a measure of the school systems. The 1972 Maryland General Assembly was rife with anti-education sentiment. One bill called for ending teacher tenure, another called for educational vouchers by which parents could claim their share of state support to pay private school tuition; the bill that passed was the Maryland Accountability Act. Like similar acts in a dozen other states, it called on the Department of Education to administer annual reading and mathematics tests to all schoolchildren and to evaluate annually the effectiveness of each teacher in each school.[31]

Educators were adept at bending to public pressure, but they did not hide their hostility to accountability. Teachers especially felt threatened, partly because they resented the scrutiny, but mostly because they philosophically rejected the notion that academic achievement was the primary purpose of the schools. To teachers, pupils with academic talent were not necessarily better or more promising children than those with good values or strong motivation or fine social adjustment. For teachers, rewarding only the academically talented students and branding the rest inferior not only was demoralizing to a class, but it was also decidedly harmful to individuals and to society.

Hesitantly, accompanied by verbiage about the fallibility of tests, the schools in 1973 offered the first statewide standardized tests to third, fifth, seventh, ninth, and eleventh graders. More than one year later the Department of Education published the results as obscurely as it could—in three huge volumes—and in subsequent years it made the results as incomparable as possible. In 1975 it eliminated tests for eleventh graders, whose grades were worst; in 1978 it eliminated ninth graders; and in 1980 it switched to another test altogether. One explanation of the shift was that teachers were giving their students answers in advance and principals were tampering with test results.[32]

The schools had good reason to be embarrassed. Maryland, the eighth highest among the states in per capita support for education, was generally below the national average in academic results. The tests showed first that student achievement declined as students were exposed to the schools, for third grade students were at or above the national averages on accountability tests, but ninth grade students were a full year behind the national averages (see table 12.2). The tests showed further that the schools were declining over time. Scholastic Aptitude Tests are given to graduating high school seniors. From 1972 to 1982 the mean Maryland score on these tests dropped from 942 to 889—from 8 points below the national average to 4 points below.[33]

There were many explanations for the decline, none entirely satisfactory. For one thing, a larger proportion of young people were in school than previously, and a larger proportion were attending college, so more marginal students were taking the tests. Maryland may have had a greater success in keeping students in school than other states. Integration, on the other hand, did not seem to be a factor, for the decline was at least as great in private schools and in counties with small or declining black enrollment as it was in counties with large and growing black enrollment. Other explanations were vague: the increase in television viewing, changing family patterns, the possible change in social values from self-discipline to indulgence, and increasing school rowdiness. Although the correlation may have been false, a surplus of teachers produced a rise in the employed proportion with graduate-level teacher training, from 24 percent to 35 percent, in precisely those years in which test scores were falling. Perhaps teacher training in education was a negative factor in teacher quality. Certainly the expanded opportunities for women in other careers drained teaching talent from the schools. In any case, most parents felt the quality of teachers was declining.[34]

As rapidly as possible the schools shifted public attention from accountability to basic competency. The two programs sounded similar, and the competency program adopted "Back to Basics" as its slogan, but while accountability tested all students and honored the high achiever, competency sought only to insure that the weakest students attained a minimum proficiency. The studies and statewide meetings about competency began early in 1973, and by the fall most county boards had adopted an emphasis on basic competence as pol-

Table 12.2. Reading Comprehension Grade Level in Public Schools, 1974, 1977, and 1981

	3rd Grade	5th Grade	7th Grade	8th Grade	9th Grade
1974					
National average	3.7	5.7	7.7	—	9.4
Maryland average	3.6	5.3	6.9	—	8.4
1977					
National average	3.7	5.7	7.5	—	9.3
Maryland average	3.8	5.4	6.9	—	8.4
1981					
National average	3.3	5.5	—	8.4	—
Maryland average	3.0	5.5	—	8.6	—

Source: Department of Education, *Accountability Reports* (1974–1983).

Note: The 1981 test is not comparable to earlier years because of a change from the Iowa Basic to the California Achievement Test.

icy. Mostly it meant a renewed stress on first grade reading. The Department of Education held special reading clinics for elementary teachers, encouraged parent or high school student volunteers to serve as reading tutors, and provided supervisory reading teachers or visiting reading teacher experts to visit the schools having unusual difficulties.[35]

In 1977 a new state superintendent, David W. Hornbeck, announced that measurable minimum competencies would be the keystone of his administration. The aim, he explained, was to insure survival skills: the ability to read cookbooks, phonebooks, sales receipts, and newspaper advertisements. He persuaded the General Assembly to make passing the the competency test a legal requirement of graduation, and he appointed an official with a remarkable title: deputy superintendent for competency. The percentage of eleventh graders who passed increased from 87 percent in 1977 to 89 percent in 1979, but then the test was changed so that annual comparisons were impossible. Critics claimed the tests proved that a large proportion of high school seniors were illiterate, but the Department of Education maintained that they demonstrated improvement. The Department of Education increased from eighteen to twenty its minimum number of credits for graduation.[36]

In a different sense accountability meant budget constraints. Enrollment was declining, economic growth was slowing, and taxpayers were losing their enthusiasm for education—but meanwhile school costs continued to soar, especially for fuel. The schools eliminated marginal programs, especially curtailing courses in languages and driver education. From 1970 to 1980 Maryland teacher salaries fell from their historic peak of $565 above the median United States family income to $3,407 below it. The number of teachers declined slightly, although the number of administrators greatly increased, presumably to supervise the reductions. The greatest turmoil came over closing schools. Communities fought to save schools, but school boards had little choice. From 1975 to 1982 the number of elementary schools in the state declined from 936 to 776.[37]

The public was more concerned with accountability for its colleges than for its public schools, not to insure quality, but to impose order and control costs. People were concerned about the behemoth at College Park, where students had destroyed state property. The institution claimed that academic freedom required autonomy from state controls; its branches spread to Baltimore County and the Eastern Shore. People were concerned about the costs of duplication, as the six teachers colleges became general colleges and aspired to become universities. There were twenty-two junior colleges, now called community colleges and providing new kinds of professional training, all clamoring for aid. Private colleges wanted the state to provide support or even take them over entirely. Meanwhile, higher education was the fastest growing state expense: from 1940 to 1970 it rose from 15 percent to 44 percent of the state's education budget, from 2 percent to 15 percent of the state's total budget.

The General Assembly looked to the Advisory Council on Higher Education, created in 1963, to bring order, but mostly it contributed to disorder. It instituted program control in the colleges and blocked new areas of study, required faculty to sign time sheets, and generally pitted institutions against one another. In 1973 the General Assembly called for a massive study of the problem, and the resulting Rosenberg Commission recommended a new bureaucracy that would administer both the public schools and higher education. The public schools persuaded the legislature to leave them alone, but in 1976 the heavy bureaucratic blanket fell over the colleges. Actually it did little except require the colleges to employ new administrators to correspond with the state administrators. Control came, not from the new administrators, but from enrollments, which topped out in 1972, and especially from the General Assembly's determination to curtail spending. From 1970 to 1983 the budget for higher education declined from 44 percent to 29 percent of the state's budget for education, from 15 percent to 10 percent of the state's total budget.[38]

The colleges and universities felt keenly the change in mood from expansion to consolidation. In the late 1960s students drove conservative presidents and deans from office, but in the mid-1970s the regents encouraged the early retirement of liberal ones. Voices lowered and so did expectations. Faculty reasserted its right to judge academic quality, and in about 1975 grade inflation abruptly reversed. Students withdrew voluntarily from faculty committees. The University of Maryland, after an extensive curriculum study, sharply increased its basic course requirements in English, mathematics, and history, and this caused the community colleges to adjust their requirements accordingly. Scholarships for the able increased; programs for the disadvantaged declined. The greatest college change, besides that of mood, came in enrollment shifts out of theoretical courses in humanities and social sciences and into vocational fields like computer science, engineering, and business management. Once lowly business courses became the most prestigious on campus. Idealism and passion were out of date. Students were not very interested in understanding the world, much less changing it. They worried, as students in the 1930s had, about getting jobs.[39]

From the depression to the 1930s few institutions in American society changed so much as education, and few remained so much the same. The school system shuddered but endured securely enough under the seemingly quickening pace of change. Progressivism, integration, rebellion, and accountability reflected the swirling passions of society, but teacher and student faced each other, one mind trying to reach another, much as they always had.

The protection of resources such as oysters and soil, open spaces and wildlife, pure water and air, is a story about the continuation of life on the planet, and a story of still uncertain ending. In the twentieth century for the first time large sections of America—sections like Maryland—filled with population to levels previously known only in Europe and Asia and learned, as the Old World had, that growth was not the only law of life. Stagnation was not inevitable, either, but continued well-being depended on the development of new attitudes and restraints. Surprisingly, perhaps, Maryland became a leader in the movement for environmental management.

During the 1930s and 1940s economic concerns forced Maryland's attention on the conservation of resources—with mixed results. In the 1950s and 1960s suburban affluence brought highly successful programs for public recreational facilities and open spaces. Then, during the 1970s, the critical problem of pollution emerged, and, after belatedly awakening to nearly disastrous water and air conditions, the state launched a vast and costly cleanup. It may have been the best effort anywhere, and in some ways the Maryland environment was better in 1980 than it had been since the American Revolution. The long-term costs and benefits of environmental management remained in uncertain balance, however, especially as problems of pollution clashed with problems of energy and economy.

13
Environment and Environmentalism

Maryland, like most places, had a long history of resource depletion, sometimes impoverishing society for generations, but then sometimes reviving with environmental management. The shortage of land and timber near navigable streams contributed in 1688 to the colony's first major insurrection. In the 1760s the iron veins began to give out, and Maryland's first industrial capitalism failed. The greatest calamity was the collapse of tobacco soon after the Revolution. Although there were many causes, including the curtailment of foreign markets, Marylanders blamed the collapse on worn-out land that had been drained of its primordial nutrients. The tobacco counties stagnated for more than a century. In the 1840s wheat began its decline, as the new fields of the Midwest proved richer, and in the twentieth century oystering and coal mining nearly disappeared. Almost every major resource that had built the state ran out. Eventually most of these industries revived partially through state management, but they never reapproached their zenith.

The most important of the recent depletions was the oyster, for oysters grew in publicly owned waters and had to be managed within a political context. State controls should have worked and should have provided the lessons for control of other resources, as they did in Virginia, but in this case Maryland provided a lesson in failure. Local economic interests prevailed over conservation controls, and so the greedy destroyed their own livelihood and much of their folk culture. The oyster story is a lesson in needless resource depletion that should frighten a world facing more portentous losses of food and fuel.

Natural Resources

Oystering on the Chesapeake has followed a tradition of more than a century, but the 1980 industry was a fraction of the size it had been earlier. Photograph by A. Aubrey Bodine, courtesy of the Peale Museum.

Oysters are an ancient food; they were much more important throughout most of history than they are now, were cherished by the Greeks and Romans for their supposed aphrodisiac quality, and were a major objective of the Vikings in their conquest of Europe. Archeologists look for mounds of shells as guides to ancient settlements in Europe and to Indian and white settlements in America. Plentiful oysters and other seafood encouraged settlement around the Chesapeake. Although too perishable to be a trading staple, oysters were sought after by almost everyone. People "tonged" with ten-foot scissorlike forks for a few bushels at a time. The food taken for the population around the bay probably stimulated oyster growth rather than lessened the supply. A handful of the landless who lived almost solely on the shellfish came to be known as watermen. During the 1830s New England traders, in their winter off seasons, first brought large ships into the bay, dragged huge iron dredges along the bottom, and then raced back to sell their catches in Philadelphia and New York. Local people resented the intrusion, Maryland passed laws against dredging by strangers, and local sheriffs encouraged people to shoot at the outsiders. Local dredgers—"drudgers" in local parlance—only occasionally took a haul to the cities.

In the 1870s and 1880s the Chesapeake oystering boom came on like a frontier gold rush as a new steam canning process proved suitable for oysters and as the railroad reached the lower bay. At the peak year of 1886 Maryland was producing for the world over 15 million bushels of oysters. More than six hundred vessels worked out of the little railroad terminus at Crisfield, saloons and burlesque houses lined the town's streets, and each day (Sundays excepted) twenty to thirty railroad cars laden with oysters headed north.

Big money brought tumult: brawling drunks on the crowded streets, shanghaiing of immigrants from Baltimore to work the winches on the boats, dynamiting of boats owned by rival packinghouses, and fighting between those who claimed exclusive control over riverbank oyster beds and those who claimed that all the water was common property. The state attempted to enforce order by restricting the dredgers who destroyed the seed oysters and the hibernating crabs and by reserving the shallows for tongers. The state in 1868 authorized an oyster navy of tongers to enforce the law, but the dredgers defied regulation. In the notorious Battle of the Little Choptank River in 1888 three official boats with cannon attacked fourteen well-armed dredgers. For three days the battle raged, neighbors against neighbors. Finally the deputized tongers rammed and sank two dredging vessels, eleven men drowned, and the deputies brought back twenty prisoners in manacles. The oyster navy grew to more than one hundred officers, the largest bloc of patronage appointments in the bay counties, but peace between tongers and dredgers—much less effective conservation regulation—was almost impossible. The oyster catch fell from 15 million bushels a year in the 1880s to 6 million in the 1900s, and then to around 2 to 4 million bushels each year from 1930 to 1984.[1]

Conservationists understood the situation well enough: the solution was simply a matter of leasing the public oyster bars to private developers to farm on a systematic basis. Other states did so. Scientists claimed that the bay would produce 100 million bushels. While the Maryland harvest dropped from 15 to 3 million bushels, in Virginia, where the saline water was less suited to oysters, the harvest increased from 2 to 9 million bushels. In other states, however, the oystermen had relatively little political power, and the state could force them to accept a program that was in their own interests. In Maryland, on the other hand, independent watermen were politically powerful; they refused to accept restrictions on the public waters, and so they almost destroyed themselves.[2]

Every twentieth-century Maryland governor sought legislation that would stem the collapse. In 1907, after twenty-five years of alarms and surveys, the General Assembly approved the Haman Oyster Act, copied from a similar Connecticut statute, which allowed local people to lease nonproductive submerged areas for seeding at the rate of one dollar per acre per year. At first watermen were enthusiastic and tied up the courts in establishing claims, but enthusiasm was short-lived. Small leasers who seeded their bars could not stop raiders, and packing companies that employed their own guards invoked local wrath against supposed monopoly. In 1912 the General Assembly established a tax on oyster packers to finance the state purchase of shells, which were used to reseed the public oyster bars. Uncontrollable dredgers usually destroyed the newly seeded beds long before the three or four years required for the oysters to reach maturity. Through the 1920s Governor Ritchie tinkered vainly with the leasing and seeding laws, calling the oyster problem "the most serious consideration of this administration." In 1935 the state created the Chesapeake Biological Laboratory at Solomons, the first such organization in the country; the laboratory employed a number of scientists to search for ways to increase the oyster catch without disturbing the watermen.[3]

In 1941 the oyster problem led to creation of a state Bureau of Natural Resources. Governor O'Conor took advantage of a thorough oyster study and enlisted the state's conservation enthusiasm to promote the progressive measure. O'Conor had a more political motive—to bring under control the appointees of the oyster navy and the oyster inspectors. Theoretically they were already under the governor's control, but in fact it was the other way around. The appointees and the watermen were one, and they generally controlled their county delegations and thus their own appointments. The governor was left to do their bidding or lose county support. As for the Bureau of Natural Resources, the watermen would have none of it. O'Conor was caught between the progressive conservationists he had loosed and the angry watermen he had provoked. He compromised, obtaining the bureau after a statewide referendum, but creating a separate Tidewater Fisheries Commission that had only nominal ties to the bureau, so in fact leaving the watermen to their own devices. The oyster problem created one of the first and strongest environmental bureaus anywhere, even though the oyster industry went uncontrolled. The bureau eventually became one of the thirteen departments of state government and the umbrella for all environmental concerns.[4]

During the late 1940s and into the 1950s and 1960s, oyster policy, more attuned to politics than to conservation, veered radically. For Governor Lane, the liberal, the policy meant appointing strong Tidewater Fisheries directors who promoted leasing and an oyster tax to pay for policing and seeding. The result, besides the demolition of able directors, was violence in the bay, as dredgers, often from Virginia, raided the leased bars. Lane's police boats mounted machine guns, and every year saw fatalities. Then Maryland and Virginia drew up a "treaty" of mutual law enforcement that went to Congress, where it was ratified. Governor McKeldin, the amiable politician, allowed the leasing to lapse and poured state tax funds into the futile seeding program that added only marginally, if at all, to production.[5]

Finally Governor Tawes, a waterman himself, established the lasting modus vivendi through a policy concerned less with oyster production than with effective government. First, he gained control over Tidewater Fisheries by greatly enlarging its scope, giving it responsibility for recreational fishing and bay boating (an industry larger than oystering) and staffing it with a mostly nonpolitical bureaucracy. Second, he greatly increased the oyster seeding program so that by 1979, when oystermen harvested 2.1 bushels, the state was purchasing and planting 6.1 million bushels of old shells and seed oysters. Third, he increased the state's Chesapeake research program and made it part of the University of Maryland. Finally, when Tawes retired from the governorship, he agreed to serve under Governor Agnew as head of

the newly created Department of Natural Resources, a fully centralized agency under a professional staff. All of the programs that Tawes
had established as governor were thereby institutionalized. The new
agency was stronger than the watermen but was careful not to antago-
nize them. It continued to subsidize their little industry and otherwise
left them alone.[6]

Total seafood production hardly changed from 1930 to 1984—
oysters declining slightly and crabs increasing slightly. Seafood was a
negligible portion of the state's economy for all the ruckus it caused. In
terms of rescuing a resource, the state failed, and needlessly. The
watermen, although subsidized by major seeding and research programs, remained virtually free of state restrictions. A 1977 study calculated that there was a two-dollar per bushel state subsidy for each
seven-dollar bushel sold.[7] In the process of buying off the watermen,
however, the state created a significant agency for other purposes,
especially for the promotion of recreational lands and for pollution
control.

Land depletion was the other major resource problem that occupied
the state, with somewhat better results. Early colonial laws required
that a certain amount of corn be planted and restricted tobacco in
order to extend productivity, and from 1800 to 1820, when tobacco
collapsed, the Chesapeake area led the country in the creation of
agricultural societies, agricultural fairs, and agricultural journals
which were dedicated to reform. In 1833 the state appointed a state
geologist to look for deposits of marl that could be used for fertilizer,
and in 1848 it appointed a state chemist who advised farmers on
fertilizers. In 1859 Maryland opened the third agricultural college in
the country, and in 1862 Charles Benedict Calvert of Riversdale was
the chief founder of the United States Department of Agriculture.
Although agriculture continued to lag behind industrialization after
the Civil War, federal experiment stations, extension agents, and,
finally, New Deal price supports maintained considerable farm prosperity.

The New Deal addressed the specific issue of soil as a natural
resource in the Soil Conservation Act of 1936, and the following year
Maryland agreed to match the federal funding for the act's operation.
For each county, funds supported one or two professional soil advisors
who worked with local farm councils to control erosion, construct
farm ponds, establish pastures, improve wood lots, and control silta-
tion and flooding. Farmers who agreed to curtail soil-depleting crops
such as tobacco, cotton, and wheat in favor of soil-enriching crops
such as soybeans and timber received cash allotments for investment
in erosion control. At any given time from 1940 to 1980 about 20
percent of the farmers were receiving such payments. Thus farm prosperity grew in Maryland and in America even while the number of
farms declined, and farm productivity per acre soared even more.
Farm soil conservation was a resounding success of federal policy and
local administration.[8]

Another land conservation program centered on shore erosion.
Action began with a geologist's report in 1949 which showed that
Maryland had lost exactly 24,712 acres over the previous ninety-six

years—over one square mile every three years. Bay county legislators expressed alarm, Tawes appointed a commission to investigate, and in 1964 the legislature approved a measure by which the state would assume up to half the cost—along with property owners, counties, and the federal government—for building jetties, seawalls, and bulkheads, and for planting cover crops over sand dunes. The program grew rapidly, and a Coastal Zone Administration emerged to administer it. Eventually the state assumed complete licensing authority over the use of tidal and seafront property. In this program, Maryland was ahead of most states, and strict controls appeared socially desirable.[9]

Finally, although Maryland neglected its declining coal-mining industry, the state became involved when strip mining scarred the land. After heavy pre–Civil War investment in the Chesapeake and Ohio Canal, which was designed to ship coal but was replaced by the railroad, Maryland restricted its mining concern to passing safety inspection laws, beginning in 1874, and providing injury insurance, beginning in 1912. Coal production reached a peak of 5.5 million tons in 1907, worth even more than oysters at their peak, but when coal began its decline (less than half a million tons were mined in 1948), people assumed more or less correctly that there was little the state could do about it. The western counties lacked the political cohesion and power of the Eastern Shore.

Into this laissez faire industry, strip mining entered in 1943, without state encouragement, which would have increased profits, and without state opposition, which would have saved the land. Strip mining tore away vegetation, leaving huge unsightly, acid-filled pools and gravelly heaps of overburden. The land was almost permanently unusable and its acid runoff poisoned farmland and streams for miles around. A citizens' committee concerned equally with economic and esthetic devastation and petitioning for state aid appeared in Cumberland in 1950. Then, in 1955, the state passed its first strip-mine law, licensing strip miners and requiring them to post bond for land restoration. During the next twenty years strip mining almost completely replaced deep mining, production rose modestly to about 3.5 million tons, and the standards for reclaimed land increased. A state Land Reclamation Bureau approved environmental impact studies before strip-mine permits were issued, allowed local residents to approve the restoration before bonds were returned, and used permit fees to restore lands destroyed before the law was in effect.[10]

In short, while special interests made seafood protection the great failure of resource conservation, public interests made land protection the great success. Half a century of government effort left seafood production exactly where it had been, and at great public cost. The government, on the other hand, had added immeasurable fertility and hundreds of square miles of usable land to the economy. Other notable successes came with timber, wildlife, water, and air, but the concern for these resources was less economically than socially motivated.

In Search of Nature

The more America urbanized the more it yearned for the redemptive air of the countryside. A twentieth-century nation of suburbia—sani-

State forest land in Garrett County. Almost half the land surface in Maryland is forest, more in 1980 than any time since the American Revolution. Courtesy of the Maryland Department of Economic and Community Development.

tized, prefabricated, machine-tooled, and affluent—gave rural names to its housing developments and demanded state support for wildlife, parks, and open spaces. Once fulfilling such esthetic and recreational needs was recognized as a legitimate function of government, politicians could gain by declaring their loyalty to nature, and spending was limited chiefly by the relative priority of other social needs. This meant that such spending was often a conservative impulse, coming from and for the benefit of the affluent.

Only the earliest wildlife laws were motivated by economic more than spiritual needs. A 1694 law established seasonal limits for certain types of fishing, and a 1730 law established a deer-hunting season from August to December and subjected violators to a fine of 400 pounds of tobacco. A 1768 law, still in effect, restricted the placement of fish barriers in major rivers, and an 1831 law, expressing concern for the shortage of terrapin, prohibited masters from serving it to slaves more than twice a year. Probably the first legal concern for nature as an esthetic resource was a law of 1870 which forbade killing songbirds: mockingbirds, bluebirds, swallows, robins, wrens, and doves. It passed by a close vote in the General Assembly, after the inclusion of an amendment that exempted the counties of the Eastern Shore.[11]

The origin of the state forestry and state park system was philanthropy, an unusual stimulus to public action. John and Robert Garrett gave three square miles of land in Garrett County to the state in 1906 with the provision that the legislature establish a forestry bureau. The brothers, grandsons of the builder of the B&O Railroad for whom the county was named, claimed to have been inspired by Theodore Roosevelt's advocacy of conservation and the outdoor life. The General Assembly agreed to the Garretts' condition and accepted land from other philanthropists in succeeding years, and in 1916 the state began to buy land on its own. By 1930 the state owned thirty-one square miles. The New Deal's Resettlement Administration gave the state some sixty more miles of forest land which it bought up as nonproductive farms in order to move people to the cities, and the New Deal's Civilian Conservation Corps provided the labor to turn some of the state's forests into parks (see table 13.1).[12]

During the 1930s and 1940s state management was more concerned with preservation of timber resources than with recreation, although the two aims were always mixed. By 1950 the state owned about 5 percent of the forest land in Maryland and, in an interesting experiment in state capitalism, received slightly more than 5 percent of the total income from forest products. What made this program work was that there was no hint of competition with private owners, for prices depended not on a neighbor's productivity but on the efficiency of Maryland forests relative to those of Georgia and Oregon. The Maryland Department of Forestry, moreover, lavished its profits, and additional tax subsidies, as well, on the promotion of private preserves. The state assumed responsibility for fire prevention, forest disease control, tree marking, licensing and supervising sawmills, and, most notably, for reseeding. Forest rangers advised private owners on the types of trees to plant and then provided them with up to seven million seedlings each year. From 1930 to 1980 the amount of forested land in Maryland increased from 35 percent to 47 percent of the total land surface, and forest productivity increased 150 percent. Forestry was an especially popular state agency, and it cultivated its popularity. Its lands were available to hikers, it supervised the beautification of roadsides, and as the suburbs grew, it helped developers establish the proper shade trees.[13]

By the 1950s the recreational uses of state land were more important than the economic uses. A postwar recreation boom jammed the meager facilities. The files of Governors Lane and McKeldin swelled with demands for more. McKeldin, who would have preferred racially integrated parks, used legislators' segregationist sentiment to justify a near doubling of appropriations. During the prosperous 1950s the

Table 13.1. State Forests and Parks, 1930–1980

Year	State Forests		State Parks		
	Forests	Square Miles	Parks	Square Miles	Visitors
1930	7	31	0	0	—
1940	9	163	6	6	536,000
1950	10	187	9	7	777,000
1960	11	189	19	26	5,300,000
1970	12	192	39	70	7,500,000
1980	10	188	35	125	5,064,000

Source: Department of Forestry, *Annual Reports,* (1930–1980); Board of Natural Resources, *Annual Reports* (1930–1980).

Note: In the 1970s certain areas were transferred from forests to parks and called Natural Environment Areas.

state increased its number of parks from nine to nineteen, and attendance increased sevenfold. The park service shifted its focus from maintenance of remote scenic spots to creation of recreational facilities near centers of population. In 1962 it added a Division of Recreation and Leisure Services, with counselors who offered nature walks, and concession stands that sold refreshments and souvenirs. The state established a tax on recreational boats and used the proceeds to develop water safety programs and marina services.[14]

City, county, and federal parks had old origins, but by about 1950 they too were expanding rapidly. Baltimore parks dated from philanthropies of the 1820s, and a City Parks Commission began to buy park land in the 1850s. In the Washington suburbs, the Maryland-National Capital Park and Planning Commission of the 1920s acquired most of the stream banks for parks. Montgomery County instituted a parks recreational program in 1942 and by the 1950s claimed to have among the best such facilities in the country. Within the decade, however, the parks budgets nearly doubled, and other counties—Baltimore, Frederick, Prince George's, Harford, Anne Arundel—authorized bond issues for parks and created recreational departments. Towns and counties established tennis courts, golf courses, swimming pools, and skating rinks and employed recreational directors to organize basketball and softball leagues.[15]

Federal lands were located mostly in the western states, but in 1964 Congress authorized that profits from government oil land leases be distributed equally among all the states and counties for parks. Maryland's share began at $5 million a year and rose steadily. Governor Tawes, meanwhile, assumed leadership in the local political battles that were necessary to give Assateague Island to the federal government in 1965; Assateague was the only federal park in the state.[16]

The most fervent outdoors advocates were the hunting, fishing, and wildlife enthusiasts who supported state forests and parks but also sought a great deal more. They established the position of state game warden in 1896, and they obtained a major source of independent funding for state gamekeeping with state hunting licenses in 1918 and fishing licenses in 1929. These funds made the hunting, fishing, and wildlife agencies among the most prosperous of the state agencies, jealously eyed by the others and by governors in tight-budget years. Funds went into the study of wildlife habits; the purchase of wildlife refuges, which provided animal shelters and feed, and fish hatcheries, which distributed trout and bass into the streams of the state; and the propagation of turkeys, pheasants, quail, raccoon, deer, and other animals. In 1937 the hunters and preservationists obtained an even greater windfall with a federal tax on hunting equipment, and later on fishing gear, which was distributed to the states for the purchase of wildlife preservation refuges. Hunting and fishing increased, like the use of state parks, in approximate proportion to the rise of middle-class prosperity (see table 13.2).[17]

By any measure the increase in wildlife was spectacular. From 1930 to 1980 the January waterfowl population grew from 500,000 to 900,000. Deer, which in 1930 were nearing extinction in Maryland, became a traffic hazard despite a lengthened season; raccoons, which

Table 13.2.   Hunting, Fishing, and Wildlife, 1930–1980

Year	Hunting Licenses	Fishing Licenses	Deer Killed	Wildlife Preserves (in square miles)
1930	74,000	14,000	31	0
1940	77,000	24,000	300	10
1950	120,000	73,000	1,300	17
1960	159,000	100,000	4,600	55
1970	182,000	122,000	7,000	92
1980	172,000	138,000	13,300	157

Source: Game Warden, *Annual Reports,* (1938–1949); Board of Natural Resources, *Annual Reports* (1950–1984); *Maryland Conservationist* (1924–1984).

also had become nearly extinct, adapted themselves to suburban living to become a common pest; wild turkeys, which some believed to have disappeared altogether, became a common hunters' quarry; eagles, falcons, and beaver returned to the state. The Federal Endangered Species Act of 1973 sent enthusiasts into a scramble for species to save and resulted in the identification of 46 kinds of reptiles, 51 mammals, and 280 birds which qualified for especially delicate promotion.[18]

More or less related to the search for nature was the search for the purity of earlier days. The simple past seemed to offer balance to the clangor of modern life, and if the state could promote wilderness, it seemed appropriate for it also to promote the balm of history. In 1961 the General Assembly created a Historical Trust to obtain historic sites and encourage private restorations. Soon federal funds became available to supplement state appropriations and some of the grandest structures of colonial America came under state supervision. The park service also developed historical sites, maintained battlefields and dressed park employees in Civil War uniforms, and restored manor houses and staffed them with guides wearing colonial dress and demonstrating crafts such as candle making. In 1965 the General Assembly launched a major program to excavate the original settlement at St. Mary's City and to publish its findings and establish a museum. The impetus to the program was crass, for St. Mary's City imagined itself a new Williamsburg, but the scholarly results were more significant than tourism. In 1968 a state office of archaeology appeared, again encouraged by federal funds. The office, empowered to halt highway or private construction projects, identified thirty-three hundred prehistoric or historic sites and predicted the discovery of twenty thousand more.[19]

The search for nature emerged most notably in the 1950s and peaked in the late 1960s as conservatives like Governor Tawes and the hunters made common cause with hippies on their communes and with the radical chic of downtown condominiums. Fads for indoor plants, organic farming, and natural foods swelled. One of the bestsellers of 1958 was Charles Reich's *The Greening of America,* concerning the need for rejecting corporate America by returning to nature.

The bureaucracy did not lag; quickly it brought the public will to fruition and beyond. As secretary of the newly reorganized Department of Natural Resources, Millard Tawes possessed the political skill to unify and subordinate the mass of overlapping conservation, forestry, parks, and wildlife agencies, and he brought an able staff to offer new initiatives. He obtained for the department the most lavish government building in the state, a building surrounded by a garden of state flora. The garden was subsequently named for his wife. Tawes launched an Environmental Trust Program that offered tax advantages to land owners who agreed to place permanent restrictions on their land's development, and a Scenic Rivers Program that sought to zone or purchase scenic river frontage for "a setting of natural solitude."[20]

Most importantly, however, Tawes and his successor, James B. Coulter, launched what came to be known as the Open Spaces Program. Capitalizing on the forestry and wildlife tradition of independent funding, the program called for a special tax of $1/2$ of 1 percent on all real estate transactions, which was to be devoted to the purchase of lands for state and local wildlife refuges and parks. The real estate lobby protested in vain, and natural areas came into public ownership at a rate never attained before. Environmental scientists rather than recreational directors guided the Open Spaces purchases, and they placed emphasis on the rich wetlands of the Chesapeake and, always, on a carefully balanced ecology. Theoretically the state would eventually be returned to the pristine condition it was in before it was disturbed by Indians. Newspaper editors hailed the act as a model for other states to follow.[21]

Although state programs continued to grow, the public search for nature after about 1970 clearly leveled off or even waned. Park attendance dropped sharply, and applications for hunting and fishing licenses declined, probably mostly because of shrinking middle-class prosperity during the 1970s, and possibly because of a rising crime rate in the parks. The growing emphasis on wildlife preservation may have cut into the interest in hunting. The disappearance of farm communes and the decline of plant and natural food stores marked the passing of a fad. Still, as society grew ever more congested, it was comforting for people to know that nature remained at least within visiting distance.

Pollution and Productivity

Delight in growth was so prevalent among Americans that until the 1970s few people thought of its dangers. Gubernatorial addresses, newspaper editorials, everyday conversational rhetoric, boasted of population increases and new technologies as guarantees rather than as threats to a brighter future. The first general doubts began to arise as people realized that the environment, notably the water and air, was becoming dangerously contaminated. The country was strangling in its numbers, in its nondegradable plastics and synthetics, in its sewerage and garbage, its pesticides, detergents, aerosol fluorocarbons, oil spills, auto emissions, industrial effluents, nuclear radiation, heat diffusion, and noise. Antimodern conservatives and antitechnological radicals coalesced in alarm. Their immediate and practical concern was cleaning up the water and air. The centuries-old crusade for growth was muted in the 1970s by a crusade against pollution.

Bethlehem Steel in Baltimore County was one of the world's largest steel plants, and still in 1980 one of the state's largest employers. Courtesy of the *Baltimore Sun*.

Government supervision of sewerage disposal, to be sure, preceded the general alarm over pollution. Beginning in 1874 the state Health Department maintained an Office of Sanitary Engineering that had the authority to order towns to establish sewerage disposal systems, and occasionally the Health Department, prodded by imminent threats to human life, sought injunctions against industrial dumping into streams or excessive coal smoke emanating from urban chimneys. In 1918 the Washington suburbs created the unusual intergovernment-controlled Washington Suburban Sanitary Commission, which had authority over water supplies, sewerage disposal, and flood control. By 1954, however, most Maryland towns still piped their sewerage, untreated, into the nearest river.[22]

A much clearer beginning to public concern with pollution came with Governor O'Conor's appointment in 1945 of a Water Pollution Commission to inform the state of conditions and recommend action. Naturally the commission recommended permanence for itself and began to devise ways of improving the water supply, not only for health, but for recreation and aquatic life as well. It publicized regulations against dumping garbage into waterways and against ships dumping oil into the bay. It fought with the overlapping bureaucracy of the Health Department, each stimulating the other with publicity about its own effectiveness and with requests for additional legislative authority. The main reason Maryland became one of the national leaders of the antipollution crusade was that the state already had in place a bureaucracy—two, in fact—that plotted ways of exciting interest in the cause.[23]

On through the 1950s and into the 1960s the rival agencies expanded, gaining the scientific knowledge, establishing the bureaucratic machinery, and learning the political skills on which their mission depended. The water commission developed twenty volumes of maps showing the relative purity of the state's water supply and assumed control of dam building, reservoir and farm pond construction, and even well digging. The agency changed its name from Water Pollution Commission to Department of Water Resources, implying an evolution from inspecting violations to managing them. It required all industrial plants to filter their wastes through a $1/32$-inch screen and to meet toxic standards. It required new plants to obtain dumping licenses in advance, and plants around Baltimore were required to pipe their runoff from the shores of the harbor to the central channel. The Health Department's Office of Sanitary Engineering changed its name to Environmental Health and expanded its horizons from sewerage to toxic effluents and radiation and air. By the mid-1960s each of the state's two agencies had a budget of over $1 million annually and a staff of more than fifty.[24]

One or two of the state's programs, especially the soapsuds flurry, brought widespread attention to the pollution problem. The soap companies developed a new nondegradable detergent in the late 1950s that was clogging the country's sewers and rivers with foam. Newspaper pictures showed forty-foot banks of suds along the Mississippi River. When a Johns Hopkins group identified the offending compound, the state's water agency persuaded Governor Tawes to appoint a commission of scientists and politicians to negotiate with the soap companies and armed it with the threat of banning their products within the state. The companies developed an acceptable substitute and in 1965 withdrew the last of the offending soaps. Two years later the state health agency won attention by persuading the General Assembly to pass one of the nation's most far-reaching air quality laws, giving the agency power to set air quality standards and, if necessary, to close factories and halt traffic.[25]

Federal antipollution agencies, meanwhile, were growing in the same way, almost unnoticed at first and impelled only by the logic of their cause, but increasingly enlisting the public in their enthusiasm. Federal support for towns' sewerage treatment plants began in 1948 and grew to cover 50 percent of the costs in 1966. The government in 1961 established an agency for research in and publicity on water purity and two years later offered grants to states for research in and publicity on air quality. The shift by federal and state bureaus from regulation to publicity was crucial, for it was not scientists but public opinion that had to set effective standards. The bureaucracy did its best work in publicizing its research and allowing the public to decide what must be done.[26]

The first alarm in the antipollution movement which gained much public attention was rung by a Maryland woman, Rachel Carson, once a part-time professor at the University of Maryland and a wildlife journal editor whose book *The Silent Spring,* published in 1963, was an account of the disastrous consequences of new chemicals, especially pesticides. The same year President John F. Kennedy's secretary of interior, Stuart Udall, wrote about the environment in *The Quiet Crisis,* which some of its readers believed should propel him into the presidency. In 1968 the biologist Paul Ehrlich published *The Population Bomb* on the terrible implications of unlimited growth, and in 1972 environmentalist Barry Commoner's book *The Closing Circle* publicized the image of "spaceship earth" squandering its resources and choking on its refuse. The books were only peaks in a mountain of popular magazine articles and newspaper editorials. College students rioting against the Vietnam War carried environmentalist banners and stuck wildflowers in soldiers' gun barrels. Old conservation groups grew in Maryland and new ones emerged: the Wildlife Federation, Sierra Club, Isaak Walton League, Friends of the Earth Society, Chesapeake Bay Foundation, Clean Air Coalition, Maryland Conservation Council, Nature Conservancy, and Ecology Action Group. The Baltimore telephone directory included two environment-ecology- or pollution-related entries in 1960, nine in 1970, and fifty-one in 1980.[27]

Environmentalism became a national crisis with good reason, for the new antipollution laws were not keeping up with worsening conditions. The main contribution the Maryland bureaus had made by 1965 was demonstrating clearly that the bay, the rivers and streams, the ground water from wells, and both urban and rural air were measurably dirtier than they had been a decade or half a century before. Partly the crisis was one of population, which more than doubled in Maryland from 1940 to 1965. There was simply less space in which the water and air could purify itself. Partly the crisis was one of technology and affluence, of more automobiles, new pesticides and chemicals, new plastic and synthetic throwaways. Garbage in Maryland was increasing from 1950 to 1970 at the rate of 3 percent per person per year. Partly the crisis was one of increased life expectancy; many diseases were largely conquered, but cancer, presumably stimulated by pollutants, surged enormously. In fact, prosperity could not continue if environmental conditions worsened.[28]

The public alarms in the late 1960s came at the right time politically, when tax revenues were still plentiful and when the nation needed diversion from its failures in Vietnam. Radical students and Rotary Club businessmen could agree on the need for a clean environment, and even the great corporations, which were often the targets of the legislation, could only disagree on particulars. Maryland's threat to the soap companies and California's threat to ban certain makes of automobiles made the corporations generally more sympathetic to national than to state standards of regulation. In 1970 the vast federal Environmental Protection Agency came into existence. That same year President Richard Nixon made environmentalism the keynote of his State of the Union address, and in the spring he declared Earth Day, when ministers prayed, suburbanites hauled in station wagons filled with old newspapers, Boy Scouts dredged ponds for old tires, and schoolchildren picked up litter in the parks.

The Environmental Protection Agency, independent of all other departments of government, brought together all the random environmental laws of the past and quickly obtained a multitude more. It established minimum national standards for water and air quality, established automobile emission regulations, banned aerosol cans, banned DDT as a pesticide, restricted cigarette advertising, required cities to publish their daily air pollution index, and required all federal and local agencies to obtain "environmental impact" approval before undertaking any new activity. Major federal funds went to the state for cleanup and policing.[29]

Maryland, already a leader in these matters, welcomed the new federal programs. Most of the new funds went to the state's Department of Natural Resources, which under James Coulter raced to be among the first to meet the federal regulations and to claim the federal bounty. From 1970 to 1976 a multitude of additional state laws consummated the subtle transformation from policing to management of water and air conditions. Taxes on tankers supported the state's oil spill cleanup, taxes on industry supported cleanup of forgotten chemical dumps, and taxes on coal supported cleanup of abandoned mines. In 1974 the state passed a noise pollution law, adopted from a Baltimore City ordinance, and passed over the objections of the building industry to give the state authority to halt construction projects and arm police with decibel meters to monitor trucks and automobiles.[30] State pollution control expenditures were small by the standards of health, welfare, or education costs, but no part of the state's budget was rising faster (see table 13.3).[31]

Coulter's most innovative program, along with Open Spaces, was the Maryland Environmental Service, a semipublic corporation that contracted with towns or private corporations to treat sewerage or to dispose of garbage or wastes according to the stringent new standards. Anyone could contract voluntarily with the agency, but if a town or corporation was found to be in violation of federal or state regulations, Coulter could order his agency to take over and bill the offender. Counties and towns fought the agency as an infringement on their autonomy, although increasingly they came to accept it. The great corporations liked the program from the start and stood in line to be accepted into it. The agency experimented with recycling waste products. It purchased used oil from filling stations and industry for repurification, and it purchased old tires, which it tied together to make huge offshore fishing reefs. It launched a major research pro-

Table 13.3. Pollution Control, 1951–1980

Year	Water Pollution Control Expenditures ($)	Per Capita Expenditure Rank among States	Air Pollution Control Expenditures ($)	Per Capita Expenditure Rank among States
1951	57,000	—	—	—
1961	160,000	8	38,000	6
1969	2,855,000	4	242,000	6
1971	13,137,000	3	973,000	4
1980	35,678,000	7	2,529,000	16

Source: U.S. Bureau of the Census, *State and Local Government Special Studies, Environmental Quality Control, 1971, 1980* (1972, 1982).

gram at Beltsville to experiment with the agricultural use of sewerage sludge and a pioneering program in Baltimore for the pyrolysis of garbage to transform it into electrical energy. Economically the programs mostly failed, as did many of the 1970s environmental enterprises, but the failures also taught useful lessons.[32]

As public anxiety over pollution evolved into near panic over energy shortages, Coulter was again in front, eager to assume responsibility for the state's energy needs. Oil prices began rising sharply in 1971, the first heating oil crisis came in the harsh winter of 1973, gasoline lines reached their peak in 1978, and in 1979 came the near catastrophe at Pennsylvania's Three Mile Island nuclear plant, which sold energy to Baltimore. Coulter, in 1971, obtained a state law requiring electric utility companies to demonstrate their ability to meet needs at least ten years into the future, and two years later he obtained an environmental surcharge tax on all electrical use to help them plan their future. The tax, in the way of Coulter's bureau, was free from annual legislative review. Soon he had a nine-million-dollar-a-year power plant design program staffed by a small army of environmentalists and engineers who were responsible for the land purchases and design of all new facilities. When the Baltimore Gas and Electric Company set about building the state's first nuclear plant in Calvert County, Coulter was ready with a state nuclear policy. The Calvert Cliffs project soared in cost from an anticipated $300 million to an actual $852 million, but economists calculated that it saved consumers at least $250 million each year after it began operation in 1975. Federal agencies smiled on the Maryland programs, recommending them as models to other states.[33]

The tide of environmental management was irresistible in the 1970s, but it was not without strains. Nationally the auto and oil industries set public pollution anxiety against public energy panic to frustrate or delay enforcement. Locally the towns and corporations faced costs that were in fact very high. The towns, compelled to establish secondary and tertiary treatment of sewerage and waste, complained most, even with the federal government bearing up to 75 percent of the costs. From 1972 to 1980 Maryland municipalities spent a total of $1,015,000,000 on new treatment facilities, or $232 per person.[34] "Almost without exception," wrote one state official, "every sewerage project in Maryland has been undertaken at [our] suggestion, urging, insistence, formal order, and when administrative processes were exhausted, by court order."[35] Big government was intrusive, and necessary. Bethlehem Steel, the state's largest corporation, was generally cooperative, spending over $125 million from 1972 to 1980 for purification devices, but still it paid fines of $16 thousand in 1972 and an extraordinary $500 thousand in 1977 for falling behind deadlines. Such costs contributed, of course, to the decade's terrible inflation.[36]

The bottom line, as people in the 1970s said, was environmental improvement, which was only partly measurable during the decade. Scientists changed their minds about which pollutants mattered, measuring technology changed, and weather and population varied, but generally some three hundred locations indicated moderate improvement from 1970 to 1980 in both air and water quality. Fish reappeared in rivers where they had been unknown for a century. Most people claimed that windowsills were cleaner, water tasted better.[37] Attitudes changed, so that stealing a Christmas tree from a park or tossing beer cans along the road carried a new opprobrium. Cigarette smoking, formerly sophisticated, became an embarrassment. Most of all, Americans were coming to terms with a lower standard of prosperity and a slower rate of growth.

By the late 1970s environmentalism was waning as a public enthusiasm, even though its bureaucracy was in place and occasionally able to reawaken interest in specific causes. Ronald Reagan in 1980 pitted environmental controls against economic growth in order to campaign for growth, and his secretary of interior, James Watt, cut drastically the federal funds for environmental programs. The Maryland General Assembly in 1979 and 1980 modified its wildlife and pollution controls as a means of courting industrial development. Occasionally the bureaucracy pushed forward. In 1983 the federal Environmental Protection Agency, encouraged by Maryland Senator Charles Mathias, called Chesapeake area governors into a "Summit Conference" to consider the bay's continued or growing pollution. Governor Hughes was especially excited. He explained to the 1984 General Assembly that bay cleanup had become his highest priority, and actually it was his first significant legislative initiative in six years of office. The startled legislature provided certain zoning controls around the shoreline and appropriated a modest $40 million to encourage towns and industries to refine further their waste and sewerage discharge.[38]

The environmental movement was a product of prosperity, much like the popular movements for civil rights, care of the poor, women's liberation, consumer protection, ethics in government, and the rest. Like them, it was institutionalized and mostly successful. Resources were better protected, parks and wildlife more plentiful, and water and air purer. To be sure, the costs were harder to pay as the economy contracted, and the crusaders were tiring.

14
The 1970s Aftermath of Idealism: Richard Nixon and Marvin Mandel

Two old pols, Marvin Mandel and Richard M. Nixon, assumed office on the same day, one as governor, the other as president. Both were successful in their first years beyond the hopes of their most ardent supporters and both won reelection by unprecedented majorities. Both, however, were secretive men who came under the unrelenting hostility of the press. Nixon was driven from office in August 1974, and his successor, Gerald Ford, served slightly over two years and was defeated in his bid for popular election. Mandel was driven from office in June 1977, and his successor, Blair Lee, served slightly less than two years and was defeated in his bid for election.

There were probably circumstances in the 1970s that called forth similar men and drove them along similar paths, but we must not make too much of the similarities, for the careers of Nixon and Mandel also demonstrate the role of unique events in shaping the course of history. For Mandel, the particular event was a middle-aged love affair of epic proportions, an affair reminiscent of the one forty years before, when Edward VIII gave up the English throne to marry Wallis Warfield Simpson, another Maryland divorcée.

The Outsider as Insider

Jewish, poor, excluded from the gentlemen's clubs of Baltimore, Mandel felt himself the outsider. As operator, confidant, bargainer, deal maker, he was the ultimate insider. The political organization was the road from the ghetto, was the cocoon of self-protection and harmony. From his childhood to his bitter prison term, Mandel responded to the forces around him from this dialectic of insider-outsider far more than from personal values or ideology. A shy but cunning man, always pragmatic, he sounded Maryland's last hurrah of machine politics.

Mandel's political successes constituted a high point of Maryland's ethnic history. A handful of Jews arrived in Baltimore after the American Revolution, mostly from England and Holland, and in 1826 first obtained the right to vote. In the 1850s many more arrived, escaping the political turmoil in Germany. Mostly they were middle-class people, as the first Jewish migrants had been, moving with reasonable ease into merchandising, skilled trades, and even the professions of urban life. By 1880 there were approximately ten thousand Jews in Baltimore, comprising 1.5 percent of the city's population, usually residing in Fells Point and the eastern half of the city.

The largest growth came around the turn of the century as a result of the pogroms in Russia, the Baltic, and Poland. Some 24,000 East European Jews landed in Baltimore in the 1880s; 18,000 in the 1890s; 40,000 in the 1900s; and 25,000 in the 1910s. A few moved on to other cities, but most were desperately poor and huddled where they landed. They entered the garment business in great numbers, crowding into hundreds of sweatshops to produce clothes for pennies less than their competition. Mandel's grandparents were part of this migration, arriving in the early 1890s. They died young, and by the next generation the family was uncomfortable talking about them.

The newcomers worked mostly for the German Jews, who were more acclimated and who owned the sweatshops and then the huge downtown garment factories. By the 1890s the German Jews were living mostly along Eutaw Place in the northwest. Soon the Orthodox Russian Jews from the eastern part of the city crowded in around them, and the richer Reform synagogues moved out to Forest Park and Pimlico. In the 1920s the process repeated itself, and the richer Jews moved still farther out of the wedge, toward Fallstaff and Pikesville. Once again the process repeated itself in the 1950s, as blacks moved into Forest Park and Pimlico and the Jews dispersed still farther, to Stevenson and Randallstown in Baltimore County.

Baltimore Jews had sharp internal divisions in the 1920s—German and Russian, Zionist and Socialist, Reform and Orthodox, rich and poor—but they were also gaining an unusual unity that was to last for forty years, until one of their own became the state's first Jewish governor. Unity started to emerge through the *Jewish Times,* which began publication in 1919, the Baltimore Hebrew College, which opened the same year, and the Associated Jewish Charities, which was formed in 1921. Philanthropy was an especially important bridge between rich employers and poor workers. Most of all, however, unity evolved through a developing political consciousness that was probably stronger in Baltimore than in any other American city. In New York, Philadelphia, and elsewhere Jewish voters were too scattered or too few to have a major political impact, but in Baltimore a concentrated and disciplined vote gave them a power comparable to that of the Boston Irish. Politics, like education and money, became a major avenue to upward mobility.

Jews had occasionally served in elected offices since before the Civil War, but in 1903 the first two Jews were elected to the city council, primarily as representatives of an ethnic constituency. The numbers grew with subsequent elections, and in 1924, by mutual consent of Jews and non-Jews, Baltimore redistricted itself, giving Jews virtual control of the Fourth District but essentially excluding them from the other five. Skilled Fourth District managers traded the Jewish vote to one faction or another in the city and state, even one party or another, in proportion to the favors and patronage they received in return. For decades the power of the Jewish organization in the Fourth District was nearly absolute, especially under boss Jack Pollack in the 1940s and 1950s, and the Jewish organization's leverage in city and state elections gave it an extraordinarily disproportionate share of power and appointments. Mandel became governor with the backing of this power, displacing Pollack in the process, and not forgetting his friends. To be sure, during Mandel's terms as governor, conditions were changing. Blacks took over the Fourth District, and Jews took over the Fifth, and then, as still greater affluence dispersed Jews farther into the suburbs, the political organization began to crumble. The triumph of ethnic assimilation was that by the time Mandel left office, Jewish voters had largely lost their sense of ethnic identity with him.[1]

Marvin Mandel was born in 1920 in a tiny row house in one of the poor sections of Pimlico. His father, Harry Mandel, worked as a garment cutter in a factory downtown and sometimes as a union organizer and when a heart attack forced him to retire from the factory, he opened a small neighborhood liquor store. His mother, Rebecca Cohen Mandel, was the strong one in the family. She insisted that the homework be done, and she sometimes gave Marvin a nickel to squander—when the family could afford it. Once he cried when he lost his nickel, but the family did not have another one.[2] For many years when he was growing up he sold newspapers at the Pimlico Racetrack, and he dreamed of being a professional baseball player or boxer. He was small, about five feet six inches, but he was macho athletic.

His mother insisted that he attend City College, the public high school for bright students, and he did well enough, participating in almost all sports and becoming extremely popular. He was quiet, but he liked people and was the kind of person friends confided in. Girls especially liked him, and he reciprocated. His favorite was Barbara Oberfeld of Reform German-Jewish heritage, whose parents lived a few blocks farther out and owned a trucking firm. They were in love from at least the age of 15. She was as bouncy and voluble as he was taciturn. He called her Bootsie. People saw them everywhere, hand-in-hand, at the ice cream parlor, the skating rink, ball games, the senior prom.

When Marvin graduated from high school he received an offer to play baseball for an Eastern Shore professional team, but his mother insisted on college. She was probably the first person in the family's history to have dreamed of such a thing. The parents took a mortgage on the house to pay for Marvin's education, and in the fall of 1937 he arrived at the University of Maryland in College Park. Within a few weeks he hurt his arm pitching, and that ended his athletic career; he was only mildly interested in classes, so the best part of college became fraternity life: he was active in the best Jewish fraternity, Tau Epsilon Phi, and he acquired a tuxedo for the dances. But two years were either enough for Marvin or all his father could afford, and in 1940 he returned to Baltimore, took a twelve-dollar-a-week job as a shipping clerk, and enrolled at the University of Maryland Law School. He was not an honor student, but he graduated in May 1942 and passed the bar exam. The following week he and Bootsie were married, and a few weeks later he answered his draft call. He served through the war as a noncommissioned officer, teaching riflery in Aberdeen, Maryland, and then in Texas. Long afterward, Bootsie remembered the year in Texas with special nostalgia. The couple had lived above a garage, and the months went by like a long honeymoon.

After the war Marvin and Bootsie rented a Pimlico row house, and Marvin went into practice with a law school friend, Stan Franklin. Theirs was a squalid practice of defending pimps and whores from Baltimore's notorious Block and occasionally one of the big-time racketeers who was caught violating the liquor laws or selling pornography. Mandel was always sensitive about the fact that lawyers in the big firms were often busy when he telephoned and often failed to return his calls. Still, however unfashionable, the job paid the rent. He took to smoking a pipe and started repeating the explanation that lasted through his political career: "It helps keep your mouth closed."[3]

Two children, Gary and Ellen, came along. The Mandels bought a lot out in Fallstaff, in an area that was mostly woods. For six years they saved, visiting the lot on weekends. Their dream house was finally completed in 1954, and they lived there until 1969, when they moved to the Governor's Mansion. The Fallstaff house was a simple two-story, 8-room brick house, vaguely colonial. There was no shrubbery, and the white shades were always drawn, making it appear bare. The main room was the den, where the television was usually on. A wall of shelves held bowling trophies, pipe racks, cocktail glasses, and about fifty books, including a worn encyclopedia, a medical dictionary, and a set of *The Bedside Esquire*. Mandel almost never worked at home, except for a great deal of talking on the telephone. He and Bootsie went to the movies about once a week and to baseball and football games.[4]

The center of Mandel's life, more than his law practice or even his family, was politics. Pollack's organization needed him more than he needed it, but the association was congenial, to say the least. Mandel disliked canvassing, and he was no public speaker, but people in the neighborhood liked him, and he found himself inevitably on the inside of the deals and gossip. In 1950 Pollack's man, Sam Friedel, a city councilman and later a congressman, offered Mandel the organization's support to run for election as one of the three representatives from the Fifth District to the State Central Committee of the Democratic party. The committee was an association of insiders, a way for the party clubs and workers to keep in touch. Bootsie loved the idea of a campaign. There was almost no competition, but she led the way as she and Marvin rang doorbells together, and they won overwhelmingly. To Jack Pollack, the campaign energy and the margin of victory was as impressive as the man himself was likable and loyal.

Within a year came a larger opportunity, when one of the Pollack representatives to the General Assembly resigned and Pollack and the Central Committee deadlocked over naming a replacement. There were negotiations and trades and deals, until both sides agreed that the congenial young Mandel was an acceptable compromise. In 1952 he joined the General Assembly in Annapolis, an appointed rather than an elected delegate. Bootsie came along, delighted, and watched from the balcony as Marvin was sworn in.

He was the ideal delegate, hard working, cooperative, unassertive for himself; he had no ideology to accommodate, and he was eager to smooth over controversy. He was everyone's friend, aware of special interests, always available to broker one person's cause with another's. He hated confrontation. A standing joke was that he always excused himself to go to the men's room when people raised their voices, but he was the one who later visited each antagonist separately and worked out the compromise. He never seemed to be for or against anything except making the system work.

Just one year later, when the chairman of Baltimore's delegation died, Pollack and Mayor Thomas D'Alesandro struck a deal by which the 32-year-old Mandel would become chairman of the city's delegation to Annapolis. Few would have called him the city's strongest delegate, but he was the one who could bring others together. That same year he was appointed chairman of the House of Delegates Ways and Means Committee. He did his homework to understand the budget (better, people said, than anyone else in the State House), and he understood better still the stake that the governor and the various delegates had in each part of it.[5]

Mandel kept winning elections back home—he won nine and lost none in his lifetime—not so much because of personal popularity with his constituents, although his supporters never failed to get their share of jobs and favors, but because of the unswerving support of the organization, the contributors, and the insiders. Keeping one's balance was sometimes hard in the shifting political sands. In 1962 Pollack and Governor Millard Tawes became enemies as Pollack demanded too much in the way of patronage and Tawes became embarrassed by his alliance with the tough city machine. Mandel hesitated, then joined with Tawes to lead the Fifth District against its long-unchallenged boss. Mandel won by a small margin.

The newspapers cheered his heroism, calling him the giant killer, the anti-organization progressive. The next year Mandel collected his reward, utilizing the support of Governor Tawes and the *Sunpapers* to win election as Speaker of the House of Delegates, replacing A. Gordon Boone, who went to jail for defrauding investors in a savings and loan scheme. As delegate, as chairman of the Baltimore delegation, as Speaker, and later as governor, Mandel came in to replace someone who left office prematurely; in the last two cases his predecessors were felons. Pollack, who also had questionable associations, was wounded by Mandel's rise but not destroyed. Most of Pollack's party workers remained in place, and Fifth District contributors like Irvin Kovens remained equally close to the old boss and to the new one they were supporting in Annapolis.[6]

Mandel was at his best from 1963 to 1969 as Speaker of the house. This position enhanced his natural role, the one he had always played and would continue to play as governor: the presiding officer, the facilitator. New levers of power—the power to make house committee assignments, the power to call up or ignore any legislator's bill, the power to influence the governor's appointments—were at his command. First Tawes and the old guard, then Agnew and the suburban liberals, courted him, and both had reason to be confident they were receiving maximum return through his brokerage. If politics was the art of consensus and the possible, then Mandel's style was politics at its best.

From 1963 through the 1966 session of the General Assembly, Tawes and Mandel, the ultimate county and city insiders, were closest allies. Theirs was the old-style politics, astute enough to give free reign to the idealistic reform fervor of the 1960s. With Agnew and the reapportioned legislatures of 1967 and 1968, Mandel was even more central. Both the Republican governor and the suburban liberals could trust him to balance realization of the popular will with the maximum harmony possible. Mandel's leadership in the house and William S. James's dignified leadership in the senate helped Agnew, like Tawes, accumulate a mostly admirable legislative record.

Mandel worked nearly full time at politics during his years as Speaker, taking maybe one day a week for his legal practice. There was not much money. Bootsie said he owned one green suit and a maroon jacket. He spent a minimum amount of time with constituents back home, and a maximum amount listening to fellow legislators, especially in late-night drinking and gossip parties. The less he said, the more people told him. He sipped bourbon, very moderately. Intoxication came from the things he knew and from appreciation of the favors he imparted. Most week nights he shared a room with Dale Hess, a delegate from Harford County, at the Maryland Inn in Annapolis, where most legislators stayed. This was an odd friendship, for the talkative Hess was a wealthy real estate operator whom nobody much trusted, but, then, nobody thought much about the association. Sometimes Bootsie came to Annapolis at the beginning of the week or the end, to give Marvin a ride, to sit in the State House observers' balcony, and to enjoy the parties and gossip herself.[7]

One night early in 1964, one night when Bootsie was not there, Mandel met Jeanne Dorsey at a dinner party in the Maryland Inn. She was beautiful and young, intensely aggressive and political, the wife of Senator Walter B. Dorsey of St. Mary's County. Marvin and Jeanne Dorsey later claimed there was electricity in the air from the moment they met. From that evening on, Mandel was sometimes out of touch with either Baltimore or Annapolis for a whole day or night at a time.[8]

When Agnew resigned after serving two years as governor to become vice-president, he seemed unbothered that he was leaving his office to the opposition party. The only person Agnew consulted besides his cronies was Mandel, the leader of the Democrats, and Mandel advised him that the vice-presidency was a great opportunity. Late in 1968, when Agnew was campaigning, Maryland really had no governor, and then in January 1969, when Agnew's resignation took effect, it fell to the joint senate and house to choose his successor. The senate supported William S. James, their president and a man of impeccable honor; the house supported Mandel; Mandel won, 126 votes to 54 votes for James and scattered votes for a few others.[9]

As usual, Mandel had risen to the top, not by popular election, but through the admiration of the insiders who thought they knew him. The public reaction was mild. Blacks, most Democrats, and many Republicans were glad to see Agnew gone. Liberals expressed mild concern about Mandel's Pollack-Tawes-machine associations, but legislators and reporters offered a chorus of assurances that the quiet little man would bring progress and harmony. Agnew, the outsider, had failed; give the insiders a chance.

Marvelous Marvin

Mandel's administration fell into three phases: the first two years as appointed governor, which were marked by spectacular legislative triumphs; the first elected four-year term, which was marked by adequate management of the bureaucracy and growing press hostility; and the second elected term of follies, which ended in resignation and disgrace. The stages, like those of Nixon's presidency, illustrated the varied dimensions of executive leadership. As a manager of politics and legislation, Mandel was a great governor; as a day-to-day manager of bureaucracy, he was good; as a moral leader for the people, he was a failure. Finally, however, even the disasters of Mandel and

Nixon provided the irony of a democratic process that corrected its errors.

Mandel had enough notice of his elevation to the governorship to pick his staff carefully—a blend of cronies and statesmen. The inner core, as with Agnew, was made up of cronies: Irvin Kovens, the millionaire furniture store owner and Teamster consort, and Dale Hess, who was majority whip in the house. They were unpaid advisors, not appointees; Mandel was never stupid, like Agnew. For his most conspicuous appointment, the governor surprised everyone by naming as his secretary of state his apparent opposite, Blair Lee III, who was from the liberal Montgomery County suburbs instead of the old city machine, and who was WASP and patrician rather than ethnic.

Mandel's personal staff—Maurice Wyatt, Frank H. Harris, Michael S. Silver, Ronald L. Schreiber, Edmond R. Rovner, Joseph G. Anastasi, and Frank A. DeFilippo—were of a type: glib and tough, if they were not from the Fifth District, they were at least able to play its hardball politics. Mostly they were legislative or press contacts, for legislative and public relations seemed to come first and count most. As for other appointments, Mandel took his time, waiting until he had the best possible deal for making friends and conciliating opponents.

Mandel's speech accepting the governorship was as weak as his staff was strong. "Make no mistake," he said in reference to his legislatively appointed status, "I shall govern." But he did not suggest then or later to what end. Reporters delving into his past votes, analyzing his speeches, or interviewing him could find very little that resembled vision or direction. He was equally for maximum services and minimum taxes, for county and state power, for city and suburbs, environment and productivity, consumers and producers, management and labor. After two statewide elections and nine years as governor, Mandel remained an enigma: people still had no sense of what he stood for besides a method of operation. All of this was more reassuring than alarming, at least in the beginning. Good local and state government may lie in management rather than in causes. Ideological and moral guidance may best be offered at the national level. Even there, the people preferred Nixon in 1968 and 1972 to Hubert Humphrey and George McGovern. Perhaps civil rights, Vietnam, and campus riots had exhausted ideology.[10]

With the 1969 and 1970 legislative sessions, Mandel's team was off and running, off to the best two years in Maryland legislative history, better than under Tawes, better than the first year under Agnew and reapportionment. To be sure, the Mandel start was related to both Tawes's and Agnew's successes, for the 1969 and 1970 sessions were the high points of the government activism that had been building throughout the 1960s. It did not much matter whether the liberal Kennedy or the conservative Nixon or the neutral Tawes, Agnew, and Mandel was its leader—government had major new roles to assume, and the executive was a good facilitator or a poor one. Reasons for the 1960s government activism, we have noted, were simply that the postwar baby boom was peaking at its offsprings' productive years and prosperity was unparalleled. There were minor fluctuations in the prosperity during the decade—Agnew's second year saw an especially sharp decline in public optimism as measured by the stock market—but the peak was reached between 1969 and 1973. The Nixon and the Mandel programs were nearly identical: not attacks on discrimination and poverty, for those crusades were on the wane, but concerns for government reorganization, environmentalism, consumer protection, and government ethics. Nixon and Mandel contributed to the last concern in ways they had not intended.

Mandel's legislative liaison team quickly got to know all the delegates, their spouses and friends, the special interests they represented, the issues on which they could and could not compromise. The team tried to get each delegate what he or she wanted—whether in legislation or in jobs and flattery—and to get his or her vote for Mandel's projects in return. "Never let a person leave your office without him thinking you have done him a favor," Mandel told his aides. Just before crucial assembly votes, Mandel and his aides used to bet on the result. The aides usually came within three or four votes of being correct, but Mandel usually won the bets, calling the results exactly. The administration boasted that during the first two sessions, ninety-three of the ninety-five administration bills passed the General Assembly, and these were almost the only bills that passed. Delegates either persuaded Mandel to sponsor their bills or they considered them dead.[11]

The first year started nicely, when it turned out there was plenty of money for almost any program delegates wanted, provided the governor approved, and at the end of the year, to pave the way for 1970, Mandel called a special session to distribute an extra surplus. Agnew, not understanding the budget and having to depend on the unfriendly advice of his Democratic comptroller, Louis Goldstein, had allowed no growth in the 1968 legislature's budget for 1969, and he so feared a deficit for 1970 that he left after paving the way for an increase in the sales tax from 3 to 4 percent. Mandel quickly learned from Goldstein that the coffers were bulging, but without saying much he let the "Agnew sales tax" pass so the coffers might bulge still more (see table 14.1).[12]

What Mandel wanted first from the 1969 and 1970 legislatures was a comprehensive reorganization of the executive branch of government, which had been called for by the rejected 1967 constitution and then by a specially appointed study commission. Reorganization meant combining 248 executive agencies into twelve major departments headed by cabinet-level secretaries; thus, Maryland would have one of the first complete cabinet systems in the country. Reorganization turned out to be a bigger battle than Mandel expected, for bureaucrats and public interest groups fought the combination and subordination that was required, and they fought change itself as the basic missions of all the executive departments were evaluated and redefined. With political skill and plenty of money, however, Mandel won the fight—a fight that few executives in modern times have ever won more than piecemeal—and the state was better for it.[13]

Reorganization gave the governor twelve powerful secretaryships to distribute. Governor Tawes and the brilliant James B. Coulter at the

Table 14.1.　　Annual Budgets, 1967–1984

Governor	Year	Total ($ thousands)	Percentage Increase over Previous Year
Tawes	1967	885	15.5
Agnew	1968	1,107	25.0
	1969	1,157	4.5
Mandel	1970	1,387	19.8
	1971	1,536	10.7
	1972	1,799	17.1
	1973	2,117	17.7
	1974	2,497	17.9
	1975	2,815	12.7
	1976	3,169	12.6
	1977	3,551	12.1
	1978	3,889	9.5
Lee	1979	4,339	11.6
Hughes	1980	4,778	10.1
	1981	5,231	9.5
	1982	5,646	7.9
	1983	6,162	9.1
	1984	6,481	5.2

Source: Comptroller of the Treasury, *Annual Reports* (1967–1984).

Department of Natural Resources were outstanding appointments. Able or moderately able people headed the departments of personnel, general services, agriculture, police and corrections, planning, and transportation. The appointments to health, economic development, licensing, budget, and welfare were mostly political and weak. The record was barely adequate, unequal to the opportunity reorganization had offered. Observers usually evaluated Mandel's appointments to other offices, including the courts, in a similar way: sometimes they were good, often they were purely political.[14]

Closely related to reorganization as a means of modernizing government was guiding through the legislature and then through referendum a set of constitutional amendments which accomplished most of what the failed 1967 constitution had sought to obtain. These included amendments to create a lieutenant governor, permit longer legislative sessions, provide automatic legislative reapportionment, allow a nonpolitical body to fix legislative salaries, and allow home rule for counties that wished to break away from dependence on their legislative delegations in the enactment of local ordinances. All were unspectacular reforms, but they showed the governor, whose background was in the old machine politics, responding to the new suburban demands for modernity. Everything whisked through as proposed.

The court system came in for notable reform. A constitutional amendment created district courts to replace the magistrates, who often were no more than political hacks. The legislature created a public defender system to provide lawyers to indigent litigants, and Mandel appointed Senator William S. James to head a commission that undertook a twenty-year project of reviewing, codifying and modernizing Maryland laws.[15]

Government reorganization and reform were just the beginning of Mandel's first two whirlwind years. Environmental protection was a popular enthusiasm, stimulated by Ralph Nader and the student activists, but reasonable enough for legislators to accept and possibly a way of appeasing the students. Mandel had never been an environmentalist before, but he, like Nixon, sensed the movement and embraced it, through an ambitious Open Spaces program, by which the state bought up land for recreational use; control of waterfront development; preservation of wetlands; air and water pollution controls; strip-mining controls; state inspection of town and county water and sewerage disposal systems; and state disposal of junk cars and the fencing off of junk yards from public view.

Consumer protection was closely related and was marked by another flood of laws. These allowed the state to issue cease and desist orders whenever merchandizing fraud appeared, established state control of health insurance programs, required full disclosure in the sale of homes and automobiles, controlled drug sales, restricted giveaway programs with purchases, and halted distribution of unsolicited credit cards. There is little evidence that Mandel viewed the legislation as comprehensive environmental and consumer protection programs, or even that he took much pride in it except as one-by-one legislative triumphs, but all together the legislation added up to remarkably progressive programs.

Finally, in these first two Mandel years, there were miscellaneous laws (each of which would have been called a program in earlier administrations), which capped off the government activism that reached into 1969 and 1970. The state created a Mass Transit Agency, which assumed responsibility for developing subway systems for Baltimore and the Maryland suburbs of Washington. The state made a major contribution to low-cost housing and created drug addiction treatment centers. On the liberal side, the legislature, after emotional debate, passed one of the country's most liberal abortion laws. On the conservative side, in response to student disruptions, it placed restrictions on the growth of the University of Maryland and required that the Pledge of Allegiance be recited daily in the public schools.[16]

The successful governor loved his job, and people loved him. He was at his office by eight o'clock in the morning, munched a hamburger at his desk or with legislators for lunch, remained in his office until nine or ten o'clock in the evenings, spent an hour or two having a nightcap in the office with the staff or in town with the boys. Observers noted his outsider-insider awareness when he instructed state officials to be sure that state bank deposits, bond sales, and insurance contracts were distributed beyond the inner circle of establishment firms that had traditionally handled them, and when he allowed the presidents of the most venerable banks and brokerage houses to wait a little before they were ushered into his office. Staff, legislators, bureaucrats, citizens, were in and out of the office; "Marvin wants" was the government's password.[17] More than ever before or since, people seemed to look to government to provide the kind of society they wanted, and they looked to Mandel more than people had looked to any governor in Maryland history to bring it about. "Marvelous

Marvin," the phrase went, among people unable to quite fathom the wizardry.

Bootsie presided in the Governor's Mansion, redecorating and being interviewed, but Bootsie and Marvin were no longer together much. Once or twice a week Marvin was out of town, attending a political caucus or a dedication, and every week or two, his blank calendar belied the fact that he took off in an unmarked car to Leonardtown in St. Mary's County to visit Jeanne. The neighbors in Leonardtown knew, of course, and then the staff and the gossipy legislators, and then Bootsie. She was embarrassed and hurt, and sometimes she telephoned Leonardtown to find her husband and berate Jeanne. Otherwise people chuckled; hardly anyone was scandalized.[18]

For a political animal like Mandel, the first two years as governor were only preparatory to the 1970 gubernatorial election. He had become chairman of the state's Democratic Central Committee, so in every way he was master of the party machinery, and he had the legislature in the palm of his hand, but no one was certain how the state would respond to a Jewish candidate who in public was far from charismatic. The key to the election was to shut out all other possible candidates, first by getting them positions elsewhere as judge, congressional candidate, or running mate, and second by co-opting all possible sources of campaign funding. This was where Irvin Kovens, Mandel's old friend from the Fourth District, came in.

Kovens operated one of the largest purchase-by-installment furniture operations in the east, but his interests went far beyond that, to banking in Pennsylvania, gambling in Nevada, and real estate in Florida. At various times federal investigators had probed his half-million-dollar gifts to the daughter of Teamster President James R. Hoffa, his acceptance of kickbacks for arranging Teamster loans, his gambling casinos in Las Vegas, his alleged defraudation of union pension funds in Florida, and his political contributions in several states. People said the Mafia was weak in Baltimore because Kovens had the town sewed up and was too tough for the outsiders. His hobby, especially in later years, was politics: financier to the Pollack organization, contributor to Agnew, godfather to Mandel. Mostly he was in it for ego reward, to be close to power. He seemed in his greatest glory hosting Mandel at a racetrack box, standing guard at the door, admitting or not the powerful and fashionable people who hovered about.[19]

Kovens's job in the 1970 election was to line up every possible contributor a full year in advance, before any rival could stake a claim and while Mandel still had favors to dispense. Kovens contacted architects, contractors, engineers, bankers, and businessmen who did business with the state; major state employees; and aspiring politicians, and he carefully registered their names and the amounts they chose to contribute. A single fund-raiser in October 1969 attracted seven thousand "friends" to the Baltimore Civic Center and netted $640,000—more than anyone had spent before in an entire statewide election.

The election itself was almost anticlimactic. The ticket was overwhelming, headed by Mandel, with Blair Lee for lieutenant governor, Louis Goldstein for comptroller, and Francis B. Burch for attorney general. Mandel ads were everywhere. There was no significant opposition in the Democratic primary, and in the general election the Mandel ticket buried the Republican candidate, Agnew's secretary of state, C. Stanley Blair, by more then two to one, the largest mandate of any governor in Maryland's modern history.[20]

The pace from 1971 to 1974 was less frantic than that of the first two years, but the governor's control, at least over the legislature, remained secure. Always the legislature attracted a disproportionate share of his attention. Here was the marketplace of ideas where he could broker without commitment, and if the pace was less frantic in the early 1970s, that was because government activism was slowly waning. Consumer protection was the major program that went forward: the state required licensing of auto and appliance repair shops, itemizing ingredients in ground meats, and itemizing bills for funerals; new state agencies were established to supervise rent increases, to control health costs, and to provide insurance for people rejected by private automobile insurance firms. Conservation, too, went forward at its slightly slowed pace as the state created a soil conservation program for the Potomac basin and a program for state intervention in local zoning decisions. Educational programs, especially compensatory education for disadvantaged children, aid to community colleges, and full assumption of school construction costs, grew. Mandel was especially proud of school construction as a boon to education, although future legislatures became frightened by the growing costs. In 1973, two years after the United States Congress lowered the voting age in federal elections, Maryland reduced its legal age of maturity from 21 to 18. The legislature also went through its statutes to eliminate anything relating to sex discrimination.[21]

State expenditures for all services increased through the 1960s and 1970s, but there was surprisingly little change in emphasis during the administrations of Tawes, Agnew, Mandel, Lee, and Hughes. Transportation commitments went up somewhat with the Baltimore and Washington area subways of the mid-1970s, and the costs of state employee retirement mounted, but otherwise state services grew similarly under these five governors (see table 14.2).[22]

One issue, however, was emerging preeminent—the issue that eventually overwhelmed the Mandel and Nixon administrations—and that was the issue of public ethics. Mandel's first brush with the ethics problem came only weeks after he assumed office, when, with some fanfare, he proclaimed a sweeping executive order about public ethics, and then seemed to back away from it. The order, which he was later forced to read at his trial, and which he read with great embarrassment, applied to appointed (but not elected) officials. It required them to make full disclosure of their financial interests, forbade them to accept significant gifts, prohibited their use of inside information for private gain, and established a Board of Ethics for enforcement of the order. The press became miffed rather than pleased, however, because appointments to the board looked political, and because Mandel declined to offer an understandable public disclosure for himself. The irony was that his reluctance may have stemmed from embarrassment over his impecuniosity.[23]

Late in 1972, as Nixon's presidential campaign reminded people of

Table 14.2.   State Services, 1959–1983 (Average Annual Percentage Change)

	Under Tawes (1959–1967)	Under Agnew (1968–1969)	Under Mandel (1970–1978)	Under Lee (1979)	Under Hughes (1980–1983)
Education	11.5	22.0	12.4	11.0	8.3
Transportation	9.0	6.5	19.7	5.0	7.3
Health	11.3	20.5	16.7	10.0	11.8
Welfare	17.0	12.5	12.3	5.0	11.3
Insurance and retirement	10.1	15.0	26.3	16.0	14.8
To counties	8.0	4.5	3.7	10.0	7.3
Police and prisons	13.4	19.0	12.5	18.0	13.0
Natural resources	9.3	18.5	13.8	11.0	11.0
Other	11.8	− 7.0	16.2	38.0	8.0
Total budget	10.7	14.7	14.4	11.6	9.2

Source: Comptroller of the Treasury, *Annual Report* (1959–1983).

Note: All percentages show an *increase* except "Other" under Agnew.

Mandel's 1970 expenditures and as Watergate first emerged, the press discovered that Mandel along with House Speaker Thomas Hunter Lowe and others had acquired a small plot of land in Talbot County, a gift of Dale Hess. At the next legislative session delegates introduced a host of reform bills to require financial disclosure by elected officials and to regulate campaign costs, and in the frantic last day of the session, the most far-reaching law accidentally passed. It was the strictest law in the country, requiring officials to list their wealth every six months and firms doing business with the state to list their campaign contributions. A special session late in 1973 weakened the law, and the 1974 session weakened it still further, but it served at least to sensitize people to the issue. Mandel lay low, letting the General Assembly have its way on the matter. Where he erred was in failing to realize that public ethics was replacing civil rights and environmentalism as the reform issue of the 1970s.[24]

By 1973 Mandel's relations with the press were fast declining. He had come to office sensing the importance of the press, full of promises for regular press conferences and easy access. The promises, however, violated his basic nature, which was to listen rather than talk, and his political technique of distributing favors did not work among reporters. More than legislators or the public, reporters were disturbed by the absence of intellectual content in the administration, the cynicism of the governor's personal staff, and the governor's social association with Kovens and Hess. Partly it was a matter of taste: well-bred reporters from the patrician *Sunpapers* and the pretentious *Washington Post* did not like the tough language of the Fourth District. Mandel especially came to consider the press attacks as representing establishment attacks on democracy. Editors responded that they ultimately supported him in campaigns—but that was because he had eliminated credible opposition. News stories brimmed with hostility. The press had got Agnew in 1973, and, with good reason, it was now after Nixon and Mandel.[25]

Meanwhile the grand passion grew. When Mandel was enjoying growing acclaim from 1968 to 1972, and when he was suffering growing attack after 1973, the sparsely furnished little house in Leonardtown became an increasingly important haven. He and Jeanne had met in 1964, when he was still Speaker of the house; a year later she had a son, Paul, of whom Mandel was very fond; in 1968 she obtained a divorce from her husband. She lived with her four children and won election to the Leonardtown town council from 1968 to 1972, when she decided not to run again and face gossip about her paramour. Colleagues on the town council often disagreed with her liberalism, but they admired her ability and toughness.

Theirs was a touching love story, except for the pain it caused his family, and except for the financial costs, which he couldn't afford. Each one had everything the other needed. She was young, 27 when they met, and enormously vibrant; he was 44, worried about the short life span of males in his family, worried about middle age. She was Jeanne Blackistone Dorsey of the aristocratic Blackistones who had produced a governor of Maryland in the seventeenth century, long before the pretentious gentlemen's clubs and brokerage houses. The Blackistones had come on hard times; Jeanne's father was a waterman; and the way back, through her marriage into the ancient Dorsey clan, had ended in failure. Mandel, on the other hand, was ashamed to mention his grandfather's name, but he was governor. She was verbal and dominating; he was taciturn and eager to be dominated. She was stylish and sophisticated; he was old-shoe dowdy. Both were politically cunning, but she was ideological and he was pragmatic; she was aggressive and he was accommodating. Most of all, they were in love.[26]

In December 1970, just after the huge popular gubernatorial mandate, the lid almost blew off the affair. Returning from Leonardtown just after midnight, the governor's unmarked car, driven by a patrolman, crashed into a car careening out of a nightclub. The driver entering the highway was killed, Mandel was hurt and in pain for weeks, both cars were demolished, and newspapers pressed for explanations. Mandel lied that he had been attending a political caucus, and the newspapers exposed the lie and left readers to surmise about the scandal. Worse than the newspapers was explaining to Bootsie. Two weeks later he gave her a forty-five-hundred-dollar diamond bracelet that he could not afford. Kovens obtained it for him from friends in New York.[27]

Mostly incidental to the love affair, but maybe as a result of a simultaneous boredom and arrogance that came with his election victory, Mandel turned his attention to national politics. Late in 1971 his staff succeeded in getting him elected as chairman of the National Caucus of Democratic Governors—elected as a compromise among better-known executives, and elected despite the opposition of Georgia Governor Jimmy Carter, whom Mandel never forgave. The following year the governors met in San Francisco. Bootsie remained at home, but Jeanne attended, and for the first time he introduced her to his staff and to reporters.[28]

Finally, in the summer of 1973, they made their decision. Mandel read to reporters a statement that echoed the statement issued by Edward VIII. "I am in love with another woman," he said, "and I intend to marry her." He hoped people would accept the situation but he was unsure of their reaction and was ready to accept the consequences. To marry Jeanne was one of the few nonpolitical decisions he ever made.[29]

The story made headlines throughout the country, and the headlines grew as the story developed. Bootsie pretended complete surprise, and the actual announcement, read to her by an aide one hour before Mandel read it to reporters, probably was a surprise. She knew of Jeanne through third parties and had spoken about the affair, but friends guessed that Mandel's inability to face confrontation meant that he and Bootsie had never discussed it. Bootsie struck back. "I don't know what in the world he is talking about," she said. "My husband climbed out of my bed this morning. He has never slept anyplace but with me. . . . I think the strain of the job has gotten to him. . . . He should see a psychiatrist." Reporters had a field day. "I intend to go on living at the mansion," said Bootsie. "I intend to remain Mrs. Mandel." That night her husband moved across town to the Hilton Hotel, where he remained for five months, running up another bill he could not afford, and then he moved into an apartment. A patrolman took his clothes to the mansion each week to be cleaned by the laundress there. Most people were amused rather than upset, arguing about which of the threesome deserved sympathy. Eventually Bootsie gave in and left the mansion, and on August 13, 1974, thirteen months after their separation, she and Marvin were divorced. One hour later Marvin and Jeanne were married in a Jewish synagogue. "I wish them the happiness they deserve," said Bootsie. The newlyweds exuded happiness, waved to the crowds, and went off in a camper to barnstorm for reelection, just three months away.[30]

The celebrity status of the couple attracted crowds during the campaign, and people warmed to their obvious infatuation, so that the remarriage became an asset rather than a liability. Otherwise Mandel's second election for governor was like his first. He co-opted or squeezed out his Democratic opponents, and Kovens conducted his fund-raisers even earlier than before, sixteen months before the election, this time raising over $1 million. Token Democratic opponents complained of the governor's cronyism and bullying control over the legislature, and Republican candidate Louise Gore attacked Mandel for being a Democrat who supported consumer and environmentalist legislation, but the margins of victory in both the primary election and the general election were almost as large as before. Newspaper reporters were miffed most by the lack of credible opposition. Their distaste for Mandel's style, along with their suspicion concerning his apparently ballooning affluence, grew. Worst of all, he was so concerned with his wife that he was ignoring them. Press conferences became rare and more hostile than ever.[31]

The first Mrs. Mandel, Barbara, retained the mansion for almost a year after the Governor moved to a nearby hotel. Barbara left her portrait to hang with those of the other first ladies. The divorce settlement specified that it alone would represent the Mandel administration. Courtesy of the *Baltimore News American.*

The follies of Mandel's final two and half years were, first, that he lost his consuming interest in governing, and, second, in the words of a *Washington Post* reporter, that he was loving beyond his means. He was arriving at the office at nine or even ten o'clock, and frequently taking two-hour lunches in the little town's French restaurant. Before his second marriage he had always dined with a bottle of catsup on the table, and now he inquired about wine vintages. Usually Jeanne was

The winners, reelection 1974: Marvin Mandel and his second wife, Jeanne, in the foreground; behind, Lieutenant Governor Blair Lee, Attorney General Francis Burch, and Comptroller Louis Goldstein. Courtesy of the *Baltimore News American*.

there at lunch, along with lobbyists and people of fashion instead of only politicians. Legislators and even staff waited days for an appointment, and evening caucuses virtually ceased.[32]

Worst of all—because of the image they established, the lies they evoked, and the costs they entailed—were the vacations. Immediately after the 1974 election, Marvin and Jeanne took a publicized honeymoon trip to Israel and then on to England, where they explored the Blackistone genealogy. Twice in December they were off to Florida, and in January 1975, in the midst of the legislative session, they were in Jamaica. First Mandel explained lamely that he had won the Jamaican trip as a door prize, then that he and Jeanne had paid their own way, and finally it developed that they were guests of Steuart Petroleum, which was seeking legislative approval to build a refinery in St. Mary's County. Aides tried to shield the governor from the press, but reporters discovered still other trips: to Alaska, Wyoming, South Carolina, and, frequently, Florida. Exposés mounted, and it finally turned out that the governor, usually with his wife, had been a nonpaying guest on nine out-of-state trips and on many Maryland weekends in between. Hosts included contractors, developers, utilities companies, oil refiners, and old friends Kovens and Hess.[33]

While Mandel learned to enjoy his wife's style of good living, she delighted in the game of government. He was inaugurated the first time in a business suit, but Jeanne directed his second inauguration like a movie production, dressing all the principals in tails, white ties, and top hats. She attended conferences and offered advice, praised or scolded aides, and once publicly scolded Lieutenant Governor Blair Lee for what she regarded as a blunder by his staff. She particularly liked to attend press conferences to watch Mandel perform and to guide his remarks by way of little gestures that told him when he was doing well, when he should elaborate, and when he should stop talking. Staff and reporters came to feel they were communicating through an intermediary.[34]

The governor's experience and power were still strong enough that supervision of details by him was not essential. His legislative successes of 1975, 1976, and 1977, though increasingly mixed with occasional defeats, were still substantial. Consumer and environmental protection remained the major essentially "liberal" programs. Legislation passed controlling prescription prices and permitting dispension of generic drugs, prohibiting smoking in designated public places, prohibiting ocean dumping, providing state supervision of nursing homes, and guaranteeing the privacy of school records and bank accounts. The administration established a new bureaucracy to promote the interests of the aging, and it won a major battle to expand the subway systems in the Baltimore and Washington areas. Lost battles included mandatory automobile inspections, prisoner rights, and removal of college scholarships from political control. Legislative leaders—Steny H. Hoyer and Roy N. Staten in the senate; John Hanson Briscoe and Benjamin Cardin in the house—remained closely allied to Mandel. These legislators were not as dependent on the governor as their predecessors had been, but their alliance with Mandel assured good order.[35]

Administrative equanimity began to break up as scandals larger than vacations emerged. Reporters learned that state funds often lay in non-interest-paying banks and that State Treasurer John A. Luetkemeyer and Natural Resources officer Louis N. Phipps had significant holdings in the banks in which they made state deposits. Attorney General Francis B. Burch acquired beach property under circumstances never fully explained. Two personal aides of the governor, Maurice Wyatt and Michael Silver, were called before grand juries investigating corruption in Baltimore County. Alford R. Carey, a personal friend of the governor and head of the school construction program, went to jail for forgery and embezzlement. Another friend, Gerald R. Siegel, just freed from a securities fraud scandal, was appointed to supervise state bond sales. Most disturbing of all, the ubiquitous Tidewater Insurance, Inc., which was owned by Mandel's closest associates, and which, it turned out, had promised Mandel a

Marvin Mandel and his wife,
Jeanne, face the camera after his
conviction for accepting money
from friends and influencing legislation in return. Courtesy of the
Baltimore News American.

job after he left office, seemed to profit directly from Mandel's administration. Tidewater had been founded by George Hocker, Tawes's
patronage advisor, to serve as a bridge between politics and business.
Its ownership had fallen principally to Dale Hess and Harry W.
Rodgers. From 1968 to 1973 Tidewater increased from 5 percent to
25 percent its share of the insurance coverage bought by construction
firms doing business with the state. One Tidewater subsidiary was an
engineering company that boosted by $2 million its share of state
contracts when Mandel assumed office.[36]

The denouement began in November 1975, when a federal grand
jury indicted Mandel for accepting bribes from five of his closest
friends, all of them involved with Tidewater: Irvin Kovens, Dale Hess,
Ernest N. Cory, Harry Rodgers, and William A. Rodgers. Everyone
admitted the friends had provided gifts, and they were embarrassing.
What Mandel did for his friends in return was the question before the
jury. Mandel and Jeanne sat through the trial in agony as prosecutors
dragged out the details of the gifts: the diamond bracelet Marvin had
given Bootsie after the 1970 accident; an engagement ring worth
$2,600 for his son Gary's fiancée; $800 for new clothes he needed as
president of the National Caucus of Democratic Governors; payment
of the hotel bill when he had to leave the Governor's Mansion; at least
$155,000 for settlement fees to persuade Bootsie to grant the divorce,
then the lawyers' fee for the divorce, then the honeymoon trip, then
more when alimony payments fell behind. Prosecutors estimated the
total to be $415,000, including a share in Security Investment, Inc., a
subsidiary of Tidewater whose value soared when it leased the land on
which the United States built its huge Social Security complex.[37]

The fact was that the governor's salary was $25,000 annually and he had two expensive wives to maintain. He was in over his head, and there was at best a narrow line between accepting money for campaign expenses and accepting a little in between elections.

There was abundant circumstantial evidence to indicate that something was expected in exchange for these gifts, but prosecutors found the connection difficult to prove. It all hinged on legislation for the seedy Marlboro Racetrack in Prince George's County. The track was small and limited by law to a short racing season, but the 1971 legislature approved expansion of the track and lengthening of the season. Mandel vetoed the legislative action as harmful to other tracks. The value of Marlboro plummeted, and Kovens and his friends bought it for about $1 million. Early the following year, without fanfare, the legislature overrode Mandel's veto and the track doubled in value. The prosecution argued that Mandel must have known who owned the track and must have encouraged the override, and that therefore the gifts to him were bribes for allowing the legislature to act contrary to his will. Later in the 1972 session Mandel supported a further extension of the Marlboro racing season, which he once had wanted to curtail. The extension would have doubled again Kovens's investment, but this time the legislature was suspicious and refused to act.[38]

The trial embarrassed the judicial system as much as it embarrassed Marvin and Jeanne. In June 1975 the first judge in the case was removed, after appeal, for conflict of interest. Then, in December 1976, after ninety witnesses and ten thousand pages of testimony, the second judge was forced to declare a mistrial when it developed that two separate attempts had been made to bribe the jurors. Two men were convicted and went to jail. No one knew who put them up to the bribery, but reporters imagined they saw connections to Kovens. The third attempt at trial suffered delay when Mandel was hospitalized for two months with a stroke. When the trial began again in June, Mandel, still seriously ill, relinquished his office—temporarily, he thought—to Lieutenant Governor Blair Lee. Finally, when the jury went out it remained deadlocked for thirteen days until the judge virtually ordered it to reach a decision and it trailed out to report "guilty" for Mandel and the five codefendants. Within days, at least two of the jurors reported in the newspapers that they believed Mandel was innocent.[39]

Still the comedy—or tragedy—went on. The Mandel lawyers appealed, of course, on many grounds, but mainly on the ground that the conviction was based on "mail fraud," which was a catch-all law that allowed federal prosecutors to bring charges against state officials who failed to provide the honest government that they used the mails to proclaim. In Mandel's case the mail fraud charge extended to use of the mails to transfer payments from the Kovens-Hess group to the governor. Three judges of the United States Circuit Court, ranked just below the Supreme Court, voted two to one to overturn the guilty verdict, not on the facts of the case, but because of the unusual use of the mail fraud charge. Then, instead of allowing this judgment to stand, as was customary, the entire court, bitterly divided over the

federal law, considered the case again and voted three to three, thus
allowing the guilty verdict to stand. By coincidence, two more judges
were appointed to the court and wanted to review the law, and again
the court deadlocked, four to four. Yet another judge was appointed
by a process unrelated to the case, and he wanted to break the tie, but
the sitting justices hastily closed the case before he arrived.[40]

No one associated with the case was satisfied, but the end had
come. The Supreme Court declined to act. Mandel and each of the
codefendants faced one to three years in jail. Circumstantial evidence
of the governor's wrongdoing was overwhelming: huge gifts, huge
conflict of interest, huge benefits to the givers of gifts, were all facts.
Perhaps the exact nature of the quid pro quo, the peculiar charges,
and the court's bungling hardly mattered. A costlier result for society,
in the Mandel case as in Watergate, was the growing distaste for
government itself.

During the appeals Mandel and Jeanne moved to a small house in
Annapolis, where further tribulations awaited. Bootsie sued for lapse
in alimony payments, and the state, inventorying the Governor's Mansion, sued for recovery of $23,800 worth of furniture that had disap-
peared since Mandel assumed office. During Mandel's final days in
office, said the state, Jeanne had charged to the Governor's Mansion
$1,544 in grocery bills for tuna fish, cake mix, Kosher salami, tooth-
paste, and dog food, all of which had been delivered to their little
house. The Mandels returned some of the furniture and paid back
$9,250. In July 1980 police arrived to take Mandel away in handcuffs
to a prison in Florida.[41]

Jeanne visited as often as she could, and she waited. After fifteen
months President Ronald Reagan pardoned the former governor, and
he returned to Maryland, not repentant, but subdued. He and Jeanne
set themselves up as "consultants" in a small office that they occupied
together each day. Friends believed they were happy. They occupied a
fine house now, and lived very comfortably. By mid-1980s Mandel
and the trial, like Nixon and Watergate and most of the previous
decade, were much out of fashion.

The Problem of Corruption

Corruption was the political theme of the mid-1970s, whether because
of increased crime in the wake of rapid government expansion or
because of Watergate and investigative reporting or, most reasonably,
because of a new standard of political morality that came with the rise
of the white-collar suburbs. The country was mired in Vietnam and
Watergate, both of which were political scandals of a sort, and stories
of Mafia influence abounded, but Maryland more than any state was
the symbol of corruption.

By the standards of its own past and by those of other states,
Maryland was reasonably well governed and progressive, and its
1970s record resulted not only from rampant political crime but also
from vigorous prosecution. The time and place coincided, however, to
establish for Maryland the most remarkable record of proven scandal
for any state in any period of American history. Two successive governors, a United States Senator, two congressmen, a Speaker of the

House of Delegates, eight other members of the General Assembly, and fourteen major state and county officials were indicted (see table 14.3).[42]

Pattern and lack of pattern emerged from the list. First, the crimes were highly disparate, hardly related to one another like the political crimes of Louisiana during Reconstruction or of New York in the time of the Tweed Ring. Each Maryland politician was operating mostly on his own, accepting favors and providing them in the way many assumed politics was supposed to work. Second, the personal nature of the crimes transcended political boundaries of Democrats and Republicans, liberals and conservatives, machine tickets and reformers. Baltimore and its suburbs provided a slightly dispropor-tionate share of the grafters, but other areas were well enough repre-sented. Third, the sums involved were small considering the amounts politicians were handling. Mandel accepted at least $415,000 in gifts or bribes, which was by far the largest amount, but no one became rich in office, and state auditors never suggested that a significant portion of public funds were diverted or even that the state failed to obtain approximately its money's worth on its contracts.

Holding office in Maryland or American government has always been a way to further self-interest, and charges of corruption have come mostly as attitudes toward government have changed. For the Calvert proprietors and their colonial supporters, the very purpose of government was to make money for the people in power. Great fami-lies like the Dulaneys and Carrolls gained power in proportion to their wealth and wealth in proportion to their power. One historian esti-mated that before the Revolution at least 10 percent of the colony's gross annual product went as profit to those who governed.[43] In the 1810s the state sold privateering charters to allow select adventurers to prey on foreign commerce. From the 1810s through the 1850s the state bought great quantities of stock in banks, canals, and railroads, which used the public money for investment and then regularly found ways of pushing the state investors out. In the 1850s, as political machines developed, Baltimore police and firemen fought pitched bat-tles for control of the polls and the ensuing patronage.

Machine politics of patronage and favors reached a peak from the 1870s to 1940s. Patronage held the party workers together; large favors to the rich brought campaign contributions and small personal favors to the poor brought votes. In a personal society, where every-one counted on favors, patronage seemed to work. The machine sometimes appeared larger than government itself. In 1890 state Trea-surer Stevenson Archer was convicted of embezzling $130,000, but the money was never found, for it probably went to the Democratic party, whose governor promptly pardoned Archer. Writers Frank Kent and Bradford Jacobs have shown how Governor Edwin Warfield in 1904 defeated legislation to restrict the bank he owned, how Isador Rayner in 1906 bought his seat in the United States Senate, how Governors Austin L. Crothers and Albert C. Ritchie finagled the bal-lot boxes. Ritchie was a patrician of personal probity who paraded as a reformer, but he controlled the state organization with an iron hand. He saw that the twenty-million-dollar contract for the Conowingo

Table 14.3.   Political Corruption, 1962–1979

Office	Name	Indicted	Allegation*	Result*
Governor	Spiro T. Agnew	1973	Bribery	Resigned; fined $10,000; returned $147,000 in bribes
	Marvin Mandel	1975	Accepted $415,000 in gifts, failed to control assembly	3 years
U.S. Senator	Daniel B. Brewster	1971 1975	Bribery, $14,500 Bribery, $4,500	6 years, overturned Fined $10,000
U.S. Congressman	Thomas F. Johnson	1962	Bribery, $25,000	6 months and $5,000
	William O. Mills	1971	Accepted $25,000 gift	Suicide before trial
Senator, Md. Senate	Harry T. Phoebus	1966	Tax fraud	3 months
	Frank J. McCourt	1971	Tax fraud	1 year
	John W. Steffey	1975	Soliciting gifts	4 months
	Joseph W. Staszak	1979	Owned tavern while on liquor board	Died before trial
Speaker, Md. House	A. Gordon Boone	1963	Bribery	3 years and $1,000
Delegate, Md. House	Leonard S. Blondes	1971	Bribery, $5,000	Fined $2,500
	W. Dale Hess	1975	Bribery	3 years and $40,000
	James A. Scott	1973	Heroin traffic	Murdered before trial
	George J. Santoni	1976	Bribery, $14,600	5 years
Commissioner, State Roads	Jerome B. Wolff		Confessed to taking $50,000 in bribes	Granted immunity for testimony
Head of Construction, state schools	Alford B. Carey, Jr.	1975	Embezzlement, $22,000	3 years
County Executive, Anne Arundel	Joseph W. Alton, Jr.	1974	Bribery	18 months
County Executive, Baltimore	Dale Anderson	1973	Bribery, $38,000	5 years
County Commissioner, Prince George's	Jesse Baggett	1971	Bribery, $3,500	15 months
County Administrator, Baltimore	William E. Fornoff	1973	Bribery	2 years and $5,000
County Treasurer, Kent	Elizabeth Cowding	1975	Embezzlement, $8,000	10 years
Councilman, Baltimore	Dominic M. Leone	1975	Bribery, $5,000	Murdered before trial
	John A. Schaefer	1975	Conflict of interest	30 days
Public Works Administrator, Baltimore	Ottavio F. Grande	1977	Bribery, $55,000	4 years and $10,000
Sheriff, Frederick	R. O. Baumgartner	1973	Embezzlement	4 years
Sheriff, Howard	Frank J. Pelz	1974	Bribery	2 years and $2,000
State's Attorney, Baltimore	Samuel A. Green, Jr.	1973	Bribery	3 years
Court Clerk, Baltimore	Paul L. Chester	1974	Coercing campaign contributions	2 years and $3,000
Police officer, Baltimore	Twenty-two officers	1973	Bribery, gambling	Various

Note: These allegations and sentences, taken from newspaper stories and court records, are condensed from legal language and may have been altered by plea bargaining or in other ways.

Dam went to his friends, and in 1932 he saw that his supporters obtained advance notice and withdrew their deposits before he closed the banks. The issue-oriented politics of the 1930s and 1940s damaged the political machine, but it held on for a decade or more, especially in Baltimore City and in Anne Arundel, Prince George's, and Baltimore counties.[44]

As the middle class grew, especially in the white-collar suburbs of the 1950s, and as bureaucracy grew, so hostility to the machine grew also. Suburbanites lacked the party loyalty of urban and rural areas, and they had little to gain from the personal favors the party machine offered the poor or the contracts it offered the rich. The bureaucracy, for its part, was at constant war with patronage appointments, and it was outgrowing them. Suburbanites and bureaucrats wanted government not of favors but of impersonal rules that applied alike to all. Governors O'Conor, Tawes, and Mandel represented the old politics of patronage and favors. They were strongest in the city and in rural areas. Governors Lane, McKeldin, Agnew, Lee, and Hughes represented the new antiparty order, and they were strongest in the suburbs. The old politics was based on favors. The new politics was based on the assumption that favors were corrupt.

The actual exposure and attack on the old politics came from the bureaucracy, specifically the bureaucracy of the federal judiciary. From 1960 to 1977 the number of federal prosecutors, mostly young lawyers eager to make a name for themselves by attacking the most conspicuous crime they could find, increased from 589 to 1,621. There was little question of their authority, at least since the 1868 adoption of the Fourteenth Amendment to the Constitution, although for almost a century presidents held prosecutors back from political cases for fear of losing votes. After about 1960, however, attacks on political manipulation were more likely to be popular than unpopular, even locally, and Attorneys General Robert Kennedy and Ramsay Clark encouraged them, beginning in New Jersey and Illinois. Nixon's attorney general, John N. Mitchell, called off the attacks from 1969 to 1972, but then Richard G. Kleindienst and Elliot L. Richardson pressed ahead again. Late in 1972 a group of Maryland's United States attorneys led by George Beall and Barnet Skolnik, one a Republican, the other a Democrat, visited New Jersey to learn procedures for obtaining indictments of political figures. They returned to launch investigations in Anne Arundel and Baltimore counties, and the trail got hot.[45]

Maryland was the ideal spot for uncovering wrongdoing. It had rapid population growth and a pell-mell rush for services, as well as pockets of the old patronage politics in an otherwise reform-oriented climate and major newspapers ready to join in the exposés. Beall and Skolnik began by issuing blanket subpoenas for financial records of engineers and contractors doing business with the counties or the state in order to discover contributions or payoffs to public officials. Other avenues for investigation led through developers who wanted zoning changes and through racetracks, slot-machine interests, liquor dealers, and savings and loan companies that wanted favorable laws or regulatory rulings. Once prosecutors were known to be investigating an official, bureaucrats often passed along information about a superior. Prosecutors and newspaper reporters met in downtown bars to find out what one another knew.

The Maryland convictions were suitably spectacular, and many of the worst miscreants went to jail. From 1977 to 1979 the General Assembly expanded its ethics laws, providing for lobbyist registration, sunshine laws (which opened most political meetings to public view), fuller disclosure of assets by candidates and elected officials, and fuller disclosure of contributions by agencies doing business with the state. It also created a bureaucracy with subpoena power to enforce the laws. After 1977 the indictments dropped off sharply; prosecutors backed away, moving on to other states and to other types of crime such as drug smuggling.

The political culture of the Mandel years faded less because of the prosecution and the laws, however, than because of population changes that dictated the ultimate triumph of the suburban vote and the suburban ethic. By the late 1970s—by the time Jimmy Carter and Harry Hughes were elected—clean looks and demonstrable civic virtue were major qualifications for holding public office. The legacy of Mandel, besides a love story, was effective government; the ironic legacy was a new standard of ethics as well.

The Institutionalization of Culture

Corruption and political disenchantment were not the only themes of the 1970s, and in perspective they will probably not be the largest themes. The decade was also a time of cultural development and humanistic expression which may someday appear as a golden age. Mandel was certainly no more responsible for the cultural expression than McKeldin was responsible for the suburbanization and consensus of the 1950s, or than Tawes was responsible for the idealistic ferment of the 1960s. The suburbanization, the idealism, and the cultural expression, moreover, were not at all limited to a single decade. For enemies of Mandel and Nixon, it sticks in the craw that theirs was an age of culture. Still, these were the conspicuous features of these decades, and the leadership embraced them. The 1970s especially saw an unprecedented flowering of scientific investigation, scholarship, historic restoration, art, music, dance, theater, and athletics. Culture was the ultimate expression of the prosperity that had been soaring, at least for the affluent two-thirds of the population, for more than three decades.

The major theme in the cultural boom of the 1970s was its institutionalization, as committees, corporations, and, especially, governments assumed responsibility for cultural endeavor. The once lonely artist became, if not a bureaucrat, at least a grantsman. Government support was not entirely new, and government's growing responsibility for culture was seldom the intent of its generosity. Government had long supported universities and cared for historical records, and in 1916 Baltimore became the first city in the country to support a symphony orchestra. Each of the new initiatives of the 1970s came for compelling reasons and for specific constituencies that had never imagined themselves becoming bureaucratized. The new institutional patrons of the arts were seldom restrictive, and the new patronage vastly increased the quantity, though probably not the quality, of cultural expression:

1947   Commercial television begins

1949   Cone art collection given to Baltimore Museum

1950   Baltimore Opera begins under Rosa Ponselle

1952   Historic Annapolis, Inc., begins restorations
       Johns Hopkins begins first intensive care unit in United States

1958   Atomic Energy Commission moves to Montgomery County
       Academy of the Arts established in Easton
       Baltimore Colts win world football championship

1959   Goddard Space Flight Center opens in Prince George's County
       Baltimore Colts win world football championship

1961   Maryland Historical Trust provides grants of about $1 million a
          year plus tax advantages for restoration of historic sites
       Baltimore Ballet organized
       Bureau of Standards, science research center, moves to Mont-
          gomery County

1963   Center Stage Theater established in Baltimore

1964   Wye Institute promotes culture of Eastern Shore, Queen Anne's
          County

1966   Arts Council provides over $1 million a year to art institutions
          and to arts councils in each county
       Maryland Public Broadcasting for educational and cultural
          radio and television programs begins
       St. Mary's City Commission begins research and restoration of
          seventeenth-century city
       Baltimore Orioles win world baseball championship

1967   Maryland Institute College of Art acquires Mt. Royal Railroad
          Station, Baltimore
       Morris Mechanic Theater opens in Baltimore
       Merriweather Post Pavilion opens in Columbia
       Maryland Historical Society in Baltimore acquires new building

1968   Bicentennial Commission begins 1976 celebration
       Chesapeake Maritime Museum opens at St. Michaels, Eastern
          Shore

1970   National Institutes of Health, established in Montgomery
          County in 1938, soars as world center of medical-scientific
          research
       Baltimore City Fair, celebration of neighborhoods and ethnic
          groups, begins
       Baltimore Orioles win world baseball championship

1971   Baltimore Colts win world football championship

1973 Johns Hopkins physicians develop first heart pacemaker

1974 Committee for the Humanities awards about $500,000 a year
      to promote lectures, exhibits, conferences, on the humanities
      Mayor's Advisory Committee on Arts and Culture established
      in Baltimore
      Commission on Afro-American History and Culture estab-
      lished
      Walters Art Gallery opens new building, Baltimore

1976 Maryland Science Center Museum opens in Baltimore

1977 Peabody Institute merges with the Johns Hopkins University
      Commission on Ethnic Affairs promotes ethnic culture

1979 Daniel Nathans and Hamilton Smith at Johns Hopkins win
      Nobel Prizes for medical research

1980 Charles Center and Harbor Place in Baltimore increasingly
      acclaimed as showcases of modern architecture

1981 National Aquarium opens in Baltimore

1982 Maryland Heritage Committee promotes celebration of state's
      founding
      Meyerhoff Concert Hall opens in Baltimore

1983 Baltimore Orioles win world baseball championship

1984 Hall of Records acquires new building in Annapolis[46]

The largest cultural institutions were federally funded and they promoted scientific research. After World War II, government research
proceeded in atomic energy, weapons, and medicine, but after the
Russian launch of Sputnik in 1957, the programs expanded vastly.
The National Science Foundation was established to provide funds to
universities and other agencies, and the space program began. All of
this had a double impact on Maryland: the burgeoning research at the
Johns Hopkins University and the University of Maryland, and also
the clustering in the Maryland suburbs of such federal research agencies as the Atomic Energy Commission, Goddard Space Flight Center,
the Bureau of Standards, and the National Institutes of Health. These
in turn attracted high-technology private industries and consultants
who bid on government research contracts. By the 1980s Maryland
had one of the highest concentrations of scientists in the world.

A different kind of cultural expression developed locally in the
1950s and 1960s as people recognized the twin ravages of urban decay
and suburban sprawl and turned to the government for aid in historical preservation. At first preservationists sought only zoning protection, and then chambers of commerce discovered the marketability of
preservation. State and local agencies emerged to make surveys, to
provide grants, and to insure tax writeoffs for restoring historical
landmarks. Annapolis led the way in Maryland, and Baltimore and St.
Mary's City followed, and by 1980 there were over three hundred
protected sites scattered widely over the state.[47]

The Governor's Mansion, called Government House. Although a nineteenth-century structure, it combines the best features of many nearby Georgian homes, and it reflects the state's preoccupation with the aristocratic elegance of its eighteenth-century past. Photograph by A. Aubrey Bodine, courtesy of the Peale Museum.

Meanwhile, with historic preservation as a precedent, cultural groups were increasingly successful in obtaining city or state funds, usually on a matching basis, for art galleries and concert halls. From 1968 to 1983 the state contributed some $43 million for such facilities. Baltimore, seeking its renewal, obtained a large share of the total for such projects as the Maryland Science Center, the Baltimore Museum of Art, Center Stage, the Morris Mechanic Theater, and the Meyerhoff Concert Hall.[48]

In the 1960s and 1970s cultural enthusiasts were seeking government institutions that would directly subsidize artists and humanists and would thereby improve public taste and character. Government was subsidizing everything else, the argument ran, so there should be something for culture as well. The General Assembly created a Public Broadcasting System, partly to provide educational television for the schools, but when the schools lost interest, the station became a major producer of cultural programs for the state. An arts council became a funnel for continuing state support for museums and musical groups, and a humanities council distributed public funds for lectures, exhibits, and conferences. Ethnic groups, emerging from the civil rights movement, claimed their share of the public funds for cultural museums and ethnic fairs. By the 1980s about $25 million a year in state funds, plus a like amount from federal, local, and private sources, went into these activities.[49]

The ultimate question concerned the impact of institutionalization on culture. For science, support was largest and the result clearest. Scientists after 1960 obtained almost all the support they wanted, support came almost without restriction or corruption, and almost everyone acclaimed the result as beneficial to society. In other fields the results were harder to evaluate.

Numerical measures showed that production and consumption of books and art increased enormously. The number of books borrowed from all public libraries in Maryland increased from two per capita per year in 1940 to seven in 1980. The number of museums increased from five to thirty, although attendance at the largest museums did not keep up with population increase. The number of art dealers listed in Maryland telephone books increased from about twelve to about one hundred sixty. The number of reported musical performances in the Baltimore area increased from about sixty a year to about six hundred. Exposure to high culture increased even more than the figures indicate if the new technologies—paperback books, high-fidelity recordings, inexpensive art reproductions, and television—were counted in.[50] The census showed that the number of people devoted professionally to cultural expression increased from 3,970 in 1940 to 21,908 in 1980—from one performer for every 458 people in the state to one for every 192 (see table 14.4).

The writers and scholars working in the decades after 1950 were probably less widely recognized than those working immediately before 1950, although the decline in recognizable names was an American phenomenon, not a local one. Maybe apparent decline was related to an overwhelming number of writers or to our inability to recognize contemporaries.[51] The most prominent Maryland writer was John Barth, a sophisticated wordsmith vaguely like H. L. Mencken, and for whom Maryland was often both subject and residence. Other writers associated with the state included Katherine

Table 14.4.   Professional Artists, 1940–1980

Profession	1940	1950	1960	1970	1980
Actors	71	79	36	286	992
Artists	689	1,141	1,566	2,396	3,463
Athletes	130	197	437	1,303	1,068
Authors	139	214	759	1,302	815
Dancers	118	272	178	151	276
Designers	301	471	895	1,968	5,541
Editors, reporters	791	1,650	2,258	4,603	6,155
Entertainers	153	360	541	1,613	1,153
Musicians	1,578	1,924	1,408	1,766	2,445
Total	3,970	6,308	8,078	15,388	21,908
	458	371	383	254	192

Source: U.S. Bureau of the Census, "Occupations of Employed Persons," in *Characteristics of the Population, Maryland* (1940–1980).

Anne Porter, Leon Uris, Anne Tyler, and Josephine Jacobson. Scholars doing major work after 1950 included George Boas in philosophy, Rachel Carson in environmental studies, and C. Vann Woodward and Bruce Catton in history. An unusual galaxy of journalists included Russell Baker, William Manchester, George F. Will, Garry Wills, and Jonathan Yardley.[52]

Changes in literary styles were difficult to identify within a state context, but changes in art and architecture after 1950 provided a conspicuous transformation of the landscape. For half a century before, Maryland, like most America, had been traditional and backward in accepting the new styles. The Baltimore Museum of Art had opened in 1923, the Washington Art Gallery in 1931, and the Walters Art Gallery had opened to the public in 1935, but they were displays of old wealth more than outposts of a living culture. A few artists in the 1930s came and went—Leon Kroll, Lee Gatch, and Grace Turnbull, a talented society matron whose flirtation with social activism and modern art gained her a reputation for eccentricity. Still more peculiar to the few who knew them was the taste of two wealthy sisters, Claribel and Etta Cone, who were quietly, almost secretly, gathering one of America's finest collections of modern European art. From the 1910s to 1950 they ferreted away their masterpieces in a tiny apartment on Eutaw Place in Baltimore, far from public sneers.

The transformation after 1950 was dramatic and rapid. The Cone collection became public and international acclaim made it a source of civic pride. Talented Eugene Leake arrived to invigorate the Maryland Institute College of Art, and major studio programs developed in the colleges, notably around Herman Maril and Mitchell Jamison at the University of Maryland. Artists like Clyfford Still and Grace Hartigan came to Maryland to teach and paint; students like Joyce Scott and Tom Green blossomed. By the 1970s modern styles were issuing from the palettes of every schoolchild, were for sale in discount drugstores, and were ubiquitous in office buildings and courthouse squares.

A similar lag and renaissance came in architecture. The first significant revolt from derivative and theatrical nineteenth-century styles came in the 1930s with art-deco influence on movie theaters and the town of Greenbelt, and with the influence of Hugo Gropius's form-follows-function industrial buildings of the 1930s and 1940s. By the 1970s modern architecture was the basic style of almost every architect, standard for everything except private homes. Its greatest monuments were entire "environments"—Columbia, Charles Center, Cold Spring, and Harborplace. Eventually the most advanced designers found modernism so traditional that they began calling themselves post-modernists and toying with a free-style classicism.[53]

Culture, public interest in it, and the twentieth-century styles reached a peak in the 1970s, but in this culture there was no obvious reflection of Maryland as a particular place. Elsewhere in America—in the South or in New York or California—remnants of regionalism persisted, but the significance of Maryland's culture was its Americanness. Maryland's modern culture was its modern history, its prosperity, suburbanization, anxiety, and change—its love stories and its corruption—its O'Conors, Lanes, McKeldins, Taweses, Agnews, and Mandels. Culture reflected and prevailed over them all.

15

The Respite of Ford and Carter, Lee and Hughes

By the late 1970s four decades of prosperity and expansion were winding down. From 1940 to 1978 the real per capita income in Maryland increased by 4.5 percent a year, a total increase of 154 percent; but from 1978 to 1982 real per capita income actually declined, by $110. The national growth rate dropped from an average of 3.8 percent annually to .1 percent annually. Meanwhile, the state's unemployment rate rose from an average of 4.5 percent to 6.7 percent.[1] The 1970s recession was the worst since that of the 1930s, and its implications were far reaching, for Americans imagined the country running down, resources giving out.

The nation's discouragement centered in economics, but it was related to the military failure in Vietnam, to Watergate, and to public weariness with the crusades for the rights of blacks, the poor, women, and the young. Discouragement was also related to the energy crisis, which dealt crippling blows to basic industries, and to the accident at Three Mile Island, which diminished hopes for a nuclear solution to the energy crisis. Americans in the late 1970s faced well-established trends they had long ignored: the continued weakening of the family and the schools, the decline of the cities, the growth of crime and drug use, the growth of fundamentalist religions, the culture of narcissism.

On one point almost everyone agreed: government was not the solution, but part of the problem. States and counties imposed ceilings on new taxes, and voters looked for antigovernment candidates for public office. A similar antigovernment mood after the Civil War and Reconstruction brought six presidents between Ulysses Grant and Theodore Roosevelt whom few could remember and a group of Maryland governors who were more anonymous still. Now came the caretaker Gerald Ford in 1974, the outsider Jimmy Carter in 1977, and the genial Ronald Reagan in 1981. Their Maryland counterparts were Blair Lee in 1977 and Harry Hughes in 1979. The transition to the 1980s was hardly a reactionary time, for existing programs seldom came under attack. People simply wanted a moratorium on new programs. The post-Watergate, post-Mandel leaders were successful in proportion to their fresh looks, their ordinariness, their willingness to stay out of the way.

The Uncomfortable Blair Lee III

Francis Preston Blair Lee III fit the needs of the time in terms of his relaxed manner but not in terms of his family heritage or his ties to the Mandel past. Heritage matters for governors, not so much as an explanation of their action in office, but as a reflection of the state itself, for leaders partially personify the people who elect them. Maryland was the immigrant ethnic heritage of O'Conor, McKeldin, Agnew, and Mandel; it was the aristocratic heritage of Lane and Lee; it was the old but unpretentious heritage of Tawes and Hughes.

Blair Lee was the direct heir of one of the most aristocratic families in America, rivaled only by the Randolph and the Adams families. Marylanders were neither much impressed by that fact, as Virginians would have been, nor put off by it, as people in the western states would have been. About twenty Blairs and Lees in the family, along with maternal Ludwells and Fitzgeralds from the Virginia side and

Carrolls, Diggses, Clagetts, Sasscers, and Bowies from the Maryland side, had become the subjects of biographies. The most simplified line was overwhelming (see figure 15.1).[2]

The mantle of family lay heavy on Blair Lee. "The family has been run by ghosts," said one of his sons. "My earliest feeling was, how do you join the list on the wall?"[3] The tension in Blair Lee's life was between wanting and not wanting to be governor. He believed he owed it to his father, and he dutifully put in sixteen-hour work days as acting governor; but he lacked ambition and ruthlessness, he was too secure to take the job seriously, and there was nowhere he wanted to lead people. Except to add to the family's credentials, Lee had little reason to be governor. He was not sufficiently ordinary for a time of blandness, and he and the electorate both came to accept the fact.

Born in 1916 at the family estate in Silver Spring, Blair Lee III grew up amidst ancestral portraits, hunting dogs, the swirl of a huge family, and the constant echo of political debate over the issues of the day. His senator grandfather was a populist liberal, his father a curmudgeonly conservative. He followed the family tradition and attended Princeton, joined the clubs his ancestors had founded or joined, and majored in history. He attended Georgetown Law School and traveled as an aide to McGeorge Bundy, who served as President Roosevelt's trade negotiator with Mexico. In 1941, at age 25, Lee enlisted in the navy and became a lieutenant commander on a destroyer escorting merchant ships to Murmansk. He returned to Maryland to marry Mathilde Boal of Bryn Mawr, daughter of an ambassador. Lee cut the wedding cake with the admiral's sword that had belonged to his great-grandfather.

There was little connection for Lee between livelihood and occupation; inheritance took care of the first, and beyond that he cast about for something worthwhile to do, for an avenue into the public life that the family took for granted he would lead. He took over his father's county newspaper, the *Maryland News,* which mostly had until then been an organ for his father's political organization, but Lee estab-

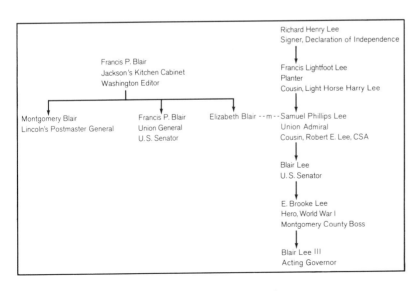

Figure 15.1. The Blair-Lee Families

Francis Preston Blair Lee III and family. Lee is at the right, Mandel at the left, and Colonel E. Brooke Lee broods in the rear. Courtesy of the *Baltimore Sun*.

lished its independence and it won a press award as the best weekly in the state. He served on the Maryland-National Capital Park and Planning Commission and the county zoning commission, which did not hurt the family's livelihood and gained him a reputation as a reformer as well. In 1954 and 1958 he won election to the state senate, mostly as a pro-zoning candidate of the suburban reformers, but also with untrumpeted support from the remnants of his father's more development-minded organization. With ties to both sides in county affairs, and with more time and money for the job than most delegates to Annapolis had, he emerged in his first term as chairman of the county delegation. In Annapolis he continued as a moderate and mediator, gained some distinction for working with the prickly state teachers' union, became noted for the eloquence of his language, and was named by reporters in 1958 "legislator of the year."[4]

Although they both had been schooled in organization politics, Lee and Governor Tawes—the suburbanite and the rural manipulator—were never friendly, and when the Tawes organization put together its state ticket for 1962 there was no place on it for Lee. Brashly Lee announced for the United States Senate, challenging the party stalwart Daniel Brewster, who was ready to move up from a congressional seat. Both were able, but Lee found himself teamed up with a motley crowd of anti-Tawes mavericks headed by the disreputable George P. Mahoney, who wanted Tawes's job as governor. Lee carried his home county but lost almost everywhere else. He relearned his father's lesson that leaders don't stray from the pack. "I deserved to lose," he said. For the next four years he paid the price of exile, working with the county planning board, and then in 1966 he won back his seat in the state senate. His career was still on schedule, drifting toward something the family would find acceptable.[5]

In 1969, when Marvin Mandel was about to succeed Agnew, Lee's sense of style was offended as it had been offended by Tawes, and Lee led the futile effort to name Senator William S. James instead. Again, Lee smelled exile. The evening after the vote, however, when legislators gathered in a bar to congratulate Mandel, the new governor asked Lee to be his secretary of state, the new governor's first and most conspicuous appointment. It was a typically brilliant move for Mandel, for Lee would give Mandel the touch of class and generosity he needed. Lee called his father, who was ecstatic and told him to accept. The appointment was only a test; Lee proved loyal to his boss; and a few months later Mandel asked Lee to be his running mate in the position just created by constitutional amendment, lieutenant governor. The election victory with Mandel was easy, and for the next seven years, from 1970 to 1977, the two were a perfect team: the pol and the patrician.

By heritage Lee was a number one man, but by nature he was a number two: loyal, hard-working, unaggressive, pleased enough to have something useful to do, relishing the role of insider but not saddled with responsibilities that would curb his natural insouciance. Men with strong fathers are often content to be number two. Mandel relied on Lee increasingly, first as a tie to the gentry of the legislature and the state, second as the office expert on budget matters, and finally as the czar of everything relating to education. Lee was largely responsible for the continuing growth of support for college and public school appropriations, even after the campus riots and the public disenchantment with education. When Mandel was riding high Lee boasted that he was the governor's alter ego, that the two were so close that each one spoke for the other. To his credit, Lee was not as close as he thought. He never quite understood the levers of power or that he was himself only one of the many levers.[6]

Occasionally Lee stumbled. Mandel sent a fat cat, Joseph Klein, a Washington area developer, to manage Lee's 1970 campaign. Lee allowed Klein to put up half of the $75,000 needed for the campaign, while, unaware of the connection, Lee supported legislation in the General Assembly which favored developers. Three years later Lee promoted state construction projects in Prince George's County, unaware that the builders were major contributors to Mandel. When Mandel's wife expelled him from the Governor's Mansion just prior to the 1974 reelection, Lee generously picked up part of the governor's hotel tab without realizing it looked as if he was buying himself a place on the ticket. None of these were serious stumbles, although each one made Lee's father furious. The stumbles were part of the carefree manner that was the lieutenant governor's charm and value.[7]

Blair Lee became acting governor on June 4, 1977, following Mandel's stroke just as the final corruption trial got underway. Mandel and Lee both believed the assignment was temporary, that Mandel was innocent and would resume his duties. Mandel was constitutionally limited to two terms, however, and everyone took for granted that Lee was the heir apparent. Mandel's conviction provided Lee with a seven-teen-month trial run and a great deal of publicity.

Lee's easy manner made him likable, but he was out of scale for people who yearned for the ordinary. Tall, silver-maned, he looked like a man in a liquor ad. He was the first governor in the state's history who scaled down his living arrangements when he moved from private life into the Governor's Mansion. His wife was an expert canoeist, a swimming instructor, and a leader of Girl Scout backpacking expeditions, and she was not about to curtail her life to host tea parties for ill-bred senators. The Lees' eight children, growing up in the 1970s, reflected too poignantly the turmoil people wanted to escape. Most of the children eventually settled down to college and corporate life, but meanwhile they experimented with rebellion. One was arrested for possessing marijuana, another lived in a West Virginia commune, and one was a San Francisco suicide.[8]

Lee served at the pleasure of Mandel, who could withdraw the delegation of power at any moment, and so loyalty to the old order and use of the old staff was the basis of Lee's power, but election in his own right depended on a show of independence. Lee's position as acting governor became more secure after Mandel's conviction in August 1977, but it was still subject to revocation if an appeal succeeded. In January 1978, after one successful appeal, Mandel actually did take over again for two days simply to demonstrate his presence as governor in the new year. Lee was unwilling to fire the Mandel cronies, but he quietly shifted a few—Frank H. Harris, Michael S. Silver, Alan M. Wilner, Neil Solomon—away from the governor's office. The new appointments he made were good, notably Harry A. Cole and Rita C. Davidson, the first black and the first woman, to the Court of Appeals.[9]

The mood in Annapolis changed from conspiracy to openness, from pomp and limousines to informality, from love of power to hope for popularity, but also from tight control to off-handedness. The change from Mandel to Lee was like that from Nixon to Ford. The new leadership was transition to, and unwitting foil for, the new mood of antigovernment. Lee loved the press conferences that Mandel hated, for example, and he bantered cleverly with reporters, but he also willingly mused aloud about issues he had not fully considered. He showed his hand too soon, changed his mind too often, did not take time to line up supporters or let others share credit; he seemed more eager for approval than for result. Lee opened the 1978 legislature with a call for stronger ethics laws and tax reform, but little developed in either area. Steny Hoyer, the president of the senate who also wanted to be governor, obtained a milder and better-drafted antibribery law, and legislators scuttled tax reform in favor of more popular tax cuts. The legislature permitted Lee to have his way mainly on a new prison site, and when he chose a Baltimore location he guaranteed himself the loss of the neighboring wards.[10]

These minor political bobbles hounded him, but the press was generous and so he appeared popular in the state, and few imagined he would be deposed in the 1978 election for governor. He was heir to the Mandel organization, yet he was situated above its scandals. He reflected the change from the activism of the early 1970s to the relaxed style of the late 1970s. Still, as between the insider and outsider, or between experience and freshness, many preferred the latter.

The Laid-Back Harry Hughes

Harry Roe Hughes was a smaller man whose origins lay in the small-town Norman Rockwell America for which people of the late 1970s had grown nostalgic. An all-American actor like Ronald Reagan could have played the role of Harry Hughes, or vice versa. Born in 1926, Hughes grew up in the quiet little Eastern Shore town of Denton in a Victorian house with a big front porch. There were no gentry in his heritage, but rather generations of ordinarily successful farmers, schoolteachers, merchants, and canners. A great-grandfather Roe and a grandfather Roe had each served briefly in the state senate, not primarily as politicians, but as public servants in the manner of the small-town establishment. Hughes's father was a stockroom manager for an electric company, his mother a schoolteacher.

His career flowed out of the setting: happy school days (four years of elementary school spent in his mother's class), playing the trumpet in the high school band, pitching for the high school team, and in 1943, at age 17, enlisting in the navy air corps. He attended the University of Maryland after the war, joined a fraternity, played baseball one summer for a semi-pro team, graduated with a major in business administration, and married a childhood sweetheart. In 1952 he graduated from George Washington Law School and returned to Denton to join the local law firm and the Rotary Club. In later life he recounted no intellectual influences other than his mother and the distant model of Adlai Stevenson. Just two years out of law school he won election to the General Assembly, and in 1958, still fresh and diligent and without guile, he moved up to the state senate. In 1964 he ran for Congress and was defeated, but he remained in the state senate.[11]

Law practice in the little town was slow, so Hughes had plenty of time to be a good delegate and senator. He did his homework, followed the party leadership, and came to be an insider, first as chairman of the finance committee, then as senate majority leader. His specialties were taxation and finance, and his main concern was distributing state revenues to the localities. The high point of this effort was the Cooper-Hughes bill of 1966, which Hughes drafted. The bill increased and graduated the state's income tax, allowed counties to add a surcharge to income taxes collected in their area, and provided that the revenue increase be passed along to the counties and towns. All this was a highly progressive transfer of the tax burden from property to income. The bill failed by a single vote, but most of its substance passed the following year, after Hughes had left the senate. Hughes, like his mother, was a bit more liberal than his constituents on civil rights and money for the schools, but otherwise he did not stray far from the pack.[12]

Twelve years in the General Assembly was enough, and in 1966 he declined to run again. Ahead were possibilities of appointment to an administrative post, appointment to the bench, or a partnership in a

Harry Hughes was an ardent supporter of Jimmy Carter, although the Hughes administration also bore some resemblance to that of Ronald Reagan. Courtesy of the *Baltimore Sun*.

law firm. Hughes negotiated with Governor Mandel, and Mandel offered him the position of secretary of the new Department of Transportation. For Mandel it was paying off past political debts, obtaining new fealty from a respected Eastern Shoreman, and co-opting a possible rival. For Hughes it was a major career advancement. He and his family moved to Baltimore.

From 1971 to 1977 Hughes administered one of the state's largest bureaucracies, consisting of six thousand employees and an annual budget of $500 million. He was hardly a transportation planner—he was always uncomfortable with policy making—and he was only adequate as a day-to-day manager, but he was successful as a negotiator who engineered the merger of diverse air, rail, highway, port, and mass transit agencies, and he dealt skillfully with legislators, federal agencies, and local political jurisdictions. The Hughes department was due considerable credit for rebuilding Friendship Airport into Baltimore-Washington International and for supervising the planning for the subway systems in the Washington suburbs and in Baltimore.[13]

Ambitious people in government began scurrying when Mandel faced trial, and on May 27, 1977, just one week after Lee took over as acting governor, Hughes astonished the Mandel-Lee staff by announcing his resignation. He left with a flourish guaranteed to make headlines, charging that Mandel and his associates had overruled his recommendation to award a twenty-five-million-dollar contract to a California firm to supervise construction of the Baltimore subways. Mandel and the Board of Public Works had scrutinized the bids, had considered the bidders' past performances, had considered the bidders' estimates of possible future costs, and had chosen a Baltimore firm headed by Victor Frenkil, who had been a major contributor to the Mandel campaigns. On the surface it looked like skulduggery, exactly what Mandel was on trial for. Almost no one noticed that the Frenkil bid was $7.5 million below the California bid, or that the California firm eventually agreed to lower its bid by $3.5 million and finally received the contract. Hughes, meanwhile, with unaccustomed opportunism, had found an issue that not only cleansed him of the Mandel past but allowed him to run against it. Six weeks later, amidst fanfare about clean government, he announced his candidacy for governor.[14]

The 1978 campaign, conducted in the shadow of Mandel's trial and appeals, generated little interest, for people were not so much outraged by scandal as they were disgusted with government generally. If the Mandel administration looked bad, then the court process that brought him down looked worse. Voter participation, as in the 1976 and 1980 presidential elections, was way down. The chief contest was in the Democratic gubernatorial primary. Harry Hughes, all-American and boyish looking, with many socially prominent Baltimoreans in his campaign staff and with the support of the *Sunpapers,* won 37 percent of the vote. Acting Governor Lee, of unquestioned honor but intimately part of the old administration and a lackadaisical campaigner, won 34 percent. Theodore Venetoulis, a former chief executive of Baltimore County, fresh and antigovernment like Hughes, won 24 percent of the vote. Walter S. Orlinsky, a liberal Baltimore City councilman, won 4 percent. The general election was even quieter, as

Hughes won a routine Democratic victory over the Republican, former Congressman J. Glenn Beall, Jr.[15]

Hughes began slowly, cautiously—and the beginning proved to be the essence. If caution reflected a lack of philosophical commitment, that was what people wanted him to lack; if it reflected insecurity, most people were glad for him to feel a bit insecure; and this was the means of his success. Appointments came slowly, mostly of respectable but inexperienced people whose appointment gained little attention. The personal staff was made up mostly of outsiders, people from the campaign or from the Department of Transportation. Cabinet appointments were not cronies, not stars, and not a team, but a mélange of holdovers, both liberals and conservatives. Ejner J. Johnson in licensing got rid of some deadwood; Charles R. Buck in health attracted a good staff; Kalman R. Hettleman in human resources proved responsive to the needs of the poor; Lowell K. Bridwell in transportation persuaded the General Assembly to provide the gasoline tax increase he wanted; but none of Hughes's appointments developed notable programs, and turnover in the cabinet was frequent.

Other Hughes appointments over the years to the courts and to state boards were good, better than those of Tawes and Mandel. Largely unencumbered by political debts, since he had almost no legislative program to promote, Hughes was free to examine candidates largely on their merit. He claimed to spend more time on appointments than on any other administrative activity, agonizing over résumés and interviewing hundreds of candidates each year. He was more comfortable responding to nominations than recruiting.

Harry Hughes, like Jimmy Carter, was naturally sympathetic to the underdog, willing enough for government to serve humanitarian causes, and in an earlier day he might have put his heart into liberal programs more eagerly than Tawes or Mandel. For Hughes and Carter, however, the days of liberal programs were gone, at least for the duration of their terms of office. Neither they nor anyone else were much interested in income equalization or restrictions on business practices or new initiatives in civil rights, health care, or welfare. Few people were very enthusiastic about more consumer legislation or environmental controls, or thought that additional money would help the schools.

This faltering of liberalism after its forty-year surge was a major phenomenon of the late 1970s. In part liberalism collapsed from its own successes in expanding the middle class; from the rise of near-universal education, health care, civil rights, and women's rights; from the liberation of youth from parental and collegiate authority; from the collapse of formalism. In part liberalism faltered from its failings in the war on poverty, in taking democracy to Vietnam, in the equalization of the races and sexes. The left collapsed as labor became a conservative interest group and as young people abandoned idealism for careers in the corporate-bureaucratic culture.

Hughes's inaugural address and his state messages thereafter contained little of agenda or promises, but rather warnings that growth was slowing, that government had to be curtailed, that optimism was unjustified. This was a political message unheard for decades, and for many realism sounded better than promises. Hughes acknowledged that the state budget presented by his predecessor looked fine to him, but he would respect changes the legislature wanted to make.

Hughes's neutralism was an almost nineteenth-century view of government. "The governor," he said, "is not the policy-making body in the state; policy is for the General Assembly to establish."[16] The governor merely executed the laws. Unlike his predecessors, he took no part in the General Assembly's search for its own leadership. Press conferences were few and dull, not because Hughes was holding back like Mandel, but because he did not have much to say. Reporters disliked the lack of news and criticized the administration for being bland, dull, invisible, and weak, but the public was not antagonized, and few were enumerating particular goals toward which stronger leadership should be moving.[17]

The main program of the late 1970s, then, was a negative one, the curtailment of taxes and bureaucracy. It began in 1978, prior to the economic downturn in Maryland, and it came, strangely, from middle-class property owners in the suburbs who had long been the source of liberal programs. Now, however, suburbanites were frightened by property taxes that were rising out of proportion to their incomes. Suburbanites were chiefly responsible for California's Proposition 13, and in 1978 Prince George's County adopted a TRIM amendment to its charter, establishing a permanent ceiling on revenues collected from property taxes. The 1978 General Assembly under Lee rolled back state property taxes by 10 percent and ordered a freeze on property taxes for the elderly. State legislative candidates in the 1978 election found themselves caught in the frenzy for tax relief, and the 1979 legislature set to work returning revenues already collected. Hughes, wiser than the legislature, preferred to use the funds to prepay the state's capital investments or to give them to the counties for health and welfare, but he went along with the legislative insistence on more conspicuous and more middle-class-oriented rebates: elimination of the sales tax on utility bills and farm equipment, and allocations to the counties for further relief of property taxes. The 1980s legislature continued, returning surpluses for the local support of education and mass transit. By 1981 surplus tax funds were gone, but the next three sessions maintained a tight rein on new expenditures and cut back sharply on state employee pension benefits.

Curtailment of taxes was not only for the economic savings provided but also a means of attacking bureaucracy. In this, however, Hughes and the Maryland legislature, like Carter and Reagan and their congresses, were less successful in responding to the public mood. Bureaucracy was bad mostly in the abstract; each office performed desirable services. Budgets for most agencies tightened from 1978 into the 1980s, and their growth rates slowed, but there was no turning back. The public cry for curtailment only balanced the cry for expanding particular services.

Concern for moral rededication—not the extension of human rights which preoccupied the 1960s, but a reaffirmation of ethics and family values—was another theme of the late 1970s and 1980s. Church attendance rose slightly after 1975, especially among conservative and ethics-oriented denominations. In the legislature, ethics bills proliferated in the wake of the Mandel trial, notably abolishing Baltimore's venerable institution of election-day walking around money. For three years the General Assembly debated state aid for abortions, finally concluding, against Hughes's wishes, that its curtailment would somehow strengthen families. The assembly reversed its earlier nod to permissiveness for the young and raised the drinking age from 18 back to 21. It rebuffed Hughes's wish for a liberalized prison parole system in order to mandate minimum sentences for offenders. A governor's task force dedicated itself to opposing "extremism and violence" and drafted a multitude of laws to that vague end. Minor legislation extended blue laws, restricted divorce, and curtailed public access to information from state agencies.[18]

Budget priorities into the 1980s reflected the conservative temper. A major appropriation for rebuilding Baltimore's Memorial Stadium, and increases for roads, prisons, and attracting business into the state, were approved. The only significant initiative that a 1960s liberal would have recognized, and a particular enthusiasm of Hughes, was tightening of water pollution standards and restriction of construction along the shores of the Chesapeake Bay.

Hughes yielded to the 1980s more skillfully than Jimmy Carter, though without the overt enthusiasm of Ronald Reagan. His 1982 reelection was the quietest in half a century. With few ardent supporters and no ardent opponents, he won easily, and the 1980s proceeded without interruption.

Fifty years after the great depression, forty years after World War II, thirty years after happy McKeldin, twenty years after Tawes's vision of Camelot, ten years after Mandel's triumphs and failure, the administrations of Lee and Hughes marked a respite, a lull, a taking stock. In 1984 Maryland celebrated its 350th anniversary, somewhat quietly. Blair Lee and Harry Hughes, both middle-aged men in the 1980s, could remember the administrations of O'Conor and Lane and they could think of themselves as successors easily enough. A straight line of continuity could be drawn between the 1940s and the 1980s: the same form of government and party structure, similar relations with the nation and outside world, a similar economic system, similar relations between the rich and poor, similar ideology, similar institutions of education, culture, and religion. There was something approaching discontinuity in race relations and styles of living, but even here the milestones of the earlier period remained in sight.

For all the continuity, however, these forty years also encompassed monumental change. In the largest perspective it was a transition from an industrial to a postindustrial age, from smokestack productivity to technicians and bureaucrats producing services, from urban to suburban, from status based on wealth to status based on expertise, from a work ethic that glorified competition to a consumption ethic that glorified self-realization and self-indulgence. Human nature was the

Continuity and Change

same, of course; happiness was neither greater nor less. But most people lived more comfortably for the changes.

The most obvious manifestation of change was growth, the fastest in the state's history. From 1940 to 1980 population rose 132 percent, real per capita income rose 154 percent, life expectancy rose 10.5 years. Growth brought swirling movement, and it was directed especially toward the suburbs. The suburban population grew from 23 percent to 63 percent of the state's total population, the city dropped from 47 percent to 19 percent, the farm population dropped from 13 percent to 1 percent, and the small towns and the counties without suburbs about held their own in numbers but lost many of their most upwardly mobile people. State sectionalism survived the swirl, but the balance of power shifted overwhelmingly to the suburbs. The old political culture, wherein the city organization negotiated with rural courthouse elites, was engulfed by suburban amateurs with an anti-party ethic.

Suburban occupations and middle-class values increasingly prevailed. As people moved from manufacturing and farming into white-collar services, the middle-income levels grew most. The wealth of the wealthiest 1 percent declined from about 30 percent to 20 percent of the state's total wealth, and the number of people beneath the poverty level decreased from about 25 percent to 6 percent of the state's total.[19] This democratization expressed itself in the rise of blacks and women, the enhanced pride of ethnic groups, the enhanced status of the handicapped, the greater independence of the young. Democracy expressed itself in the disappearance of servants and the decline of deference and formality. It attained notable successes in the expansion of schools and colleges, in the rescue and improvement of the environment, in a growing demand for high culture.

In government, where the electorate recharters course every two years, the transition of these years was most easily measured. The source of change was the surging middle class asserting itself over city and countryside; the instrument of change was bureaucracy; and the direction, at least until the late 1970s, was relentlessly toward greater controls and services.

World War II, far more than the depression, brought the mobilization and centralization of society which established the new direction. Then, in the late 1940s, under President Truman and Governor Lane, the new welfare state services prevailed over the bitter challenge of conservatives. In the 1950s, under Eisenhower and McKeldin, opposition Republicans accepted the welfare state. In the prosperity and optimism of the 1960s, under Kennedy and Johnson and Tawes, the middle class demanded for itself better schools, a better environment, and more consumer services, and they offered little objection when blacks, women, students, and the poor demanded equality for themselves. Momentum carried this idealism into the 1970s, under Nixon and Mandel, until the costs began to mount and disillusionment came. By the late 1970s, under Ford and Carter and Reagan, and under Lee and Hughes, the economy turned sharply down, taxes seemed too high, and the triumphant middle class sought respite from forty years of government activism.

Finally, along with the continuity and change from 1940 to 1980, generalizations emerged that gave these years a certain unity. The largest generalization, but one people had difficulty accepting, was the grandeur of this time and place. In all of human history, no people had a better chance or a better life or more obvious improvement in their physical condition than most Americans in these middle years of the twentieth century. The notion was embarrassing because it violated awareness of failures, but the well-being was there, if only relative to any other time and place. Concede the injustices and the dashed hopes: it was the best time any people ever had to be alive. Concede the diversity and ugliness that certainly existed: still, Maryland, precisely at the center of these times, was as ideal and beautiful a place to live as any on the globe.

A second conclusion crowds on the first. The years from 1940 to 1980 were not years of confidence, but of anxiety, revolt, and failure. There were external reasons enough for anxiety: the mushroom cloud, the loss of a major war, the uncertain economy, the sense of resources running out. There were still larger internal reasons for anxiety, mainly in the rapidity of change itself. Change brought the decline of the old as well as the new, it destabilized values in ways that destroyed individuals and weakened civic virtue, it caused the resentment of those left behind and promoted unrealistic expectations of those forging ahead. Resentment of change contributed to the conservative revolt of the 1950s, ostensibly against communism, but more generally against modernity. Expectation for change contributed to the liberation crusades of the 1960s, which culminated, after great pains, in riots and disillusionment.

A third conclusion, and this book's main theme, is the parallel between the local and national temper. The zeitgeist grew from specific events and from general technological and demographic change; it was larger than the leadership and the laws—it created them rather than the other way around. The parallel among communities and between state and nation offers a certain insight into the process of history itself. Whether other states reflect this parallel so fully, or better, or whether Maryland has special microcosmic significance is the subject of another inquiry.

State and local history underscore the importance of particulars and place in explaining the course of events. State history is an amalgam of particulars from which it is possible to make generalizations, but generalizations are not necessarily the average of the parts. Look up, and Maryland history is about all of America. Look down, and Maryland history is about the moment and one's self.

The most important part of this book may be the footnotes, for they will provide the basis for adding to the story. The notes are not meant as proof of what is in the text, and occasionally the sources listed take the argument opposite my own, but the notes detail the major sources that I found useful and that others should consider.

The starting place for gathering together a skeleton of facts about the recent past is public documents, an enormous and forbidding mass of irregularly printed materials, and sometimes typescripts, from almost every department of federal, state, county, and town government. Files of these documents exist in the Hall of Records in Annapolis, the State Department of Legislative Reference, the State Library, the Enoch Pratt Library, the University of Maryland, or, most reliably, in the offices from which they are issued. Some documents, such as the *Laws of the State of Maryland* or the *Proceedings of the General Assembly,* are overwhelmingly large, so that they can hardly be perused from year to year but must be used as references to answer specific questions. Other files, such as the annual reports of many government departments, must in fact be explored systematically, and I have cited only a fraction of those I actually used. Some of the most valuable documents are the reports of state ad hoc commissions or task forces, which usually are appointed by the governor. Among the best continuing reports are those of the departments of Natural Resources, State Planning, and Education, although an alarming trend is the decline in quality of reports in recent years. The more public relations experts take over, the more promotional and less informative reports become; the more records are computerized, the less administrators have to say about policies and the effectiveness of their operations. The *Maryland Manual* (Hall of Records, more or less annual since 1896), the *Maryland Statistical Abstract* (Department of Economic and Community Development, irregular since 1967), and the *Statistical Abstract of the United States* (U. S. Bureau of the Census, since 1878), must be kept continually at hand.

Similar to public documents are the reports and flyers from institutions, businesses, unions, service clubs, women's groups, and public interest organizations. These are mostly irregular and hard to find, but they are important in making observations about public concerns. Vertical files and catalogues exist in the Enoch Pratt Library, the Maryland Historical Society, and in county libraries and historical societies.

The second major group of materials, equally overwhelming to use, are the newspapers. Every day through these forty years scores of reporters and editorial analysts have searched for the facts and meaning of local events. Simply to read through newspaper files, however, leads the historian to everything and nothing, so that usually, as with legislative proceedings, it is necessary to begin with specific questions and then depend largely on newspaper clippings files, which are available by special permission in the major newspaper offices. Clippings have been collected most fully by the Enoch Pratt Library and maintained sporadically by the Maryland Historical Society, the University of Maryland, and some of the county libraries. These files, unfortunately, are subject to vandalism. Newspaper indexes are sometimes useful, and for critical events a day-to-day search is essential. Magazines such as *Baltimore* and *Maryland Magazine* contain useful stories. Events such as the Cambridge race riots, the Agnew and Mandel scandals, and Baltimore's renewal have been covered by reporters for national newspapers and magazines. These stories can usually be found through the periodical indexes.

Two collections in the Maryland Historical Society require special note. The War Records Collection of materials relating to Maryland's participation in World War II is one of the finest such collections made for any state and is the basis for chapter 2. The Oral History Collection, mostly converted to typescript, and particularly the McKeldin-Jackson materials on race relations, provides the basis for chapter 7. The existence of these two collections was one of the major inspirations leading me to write this book.

Manuscript collections and interviews are an important source, and if this had been a twelve-year project instead of a six-year one, I would have used them much more than I did. The official papers of the governors, deposited in the Hall of Records, are an enormous lode that I have only sampled. Documents and testimony presented before legislative hearings and governors' commissions are voluminous. Diaries and correspondence of prominent people and occasionally of ordinary ones exist at the Maryland Historical Society, the Johns Hopkins University, and the University of Maryland, and many remain in private hands.

Finally, secondary sources are numerous, but few are comprehensive. Amazingly, I could not find a single study of another state during this recent period that offered much guidance. Studies of national presidential administrations, and studies of such topics as wartime mobilization, anticommunism, civil rights, bureaucracy, poverty, environment, education, and culture, are abundant. Harry Bard, *Maryland, State and Government: Its New Dynamic* (New York, 1974), is good on the structure of government. Franklin L. Burdette, "Modern Maryland Politics and Social Change," in *Maryland: A History, 1632–1974,* ed. Richard Walsh and William Lloyd Fox (Baltimore, 1974) is good on elections. Theo Lippman, Jr., *Spiro Agnew's America: the Vice President and the Politics of Suburbia* (New York, 1972), is excellent on Agnew's early life, and Richard M. Cohen and Jules Witcover, *A Heartbeat Away: Of Vice President Spiro T. Agnew* (New York, 1974), is excellent on his fall. Bradford Jacobs, *Thimbleriggers: The Law v. Governor Marvin Mandel* (Baltimore, 1984), is an outstanding presentation of the case against Mandel.

Three good county histories deal with the recent period: Neal A. Brooks and Eric G. Rockel, *A History of Baltimore County* (Towson, Md., 1979); Ray Eldon Hiebert and Richard K. MacMaster, *A Grateful Remembrance: the Story of Montgomery County, Maryland* (Rockville, Md., 1976); and Harry Stegmaier, Jr., David Dean, Gordon Kershaw, and John Weisman, *Allegany County: A History* (Parsons, W.Va., 1976). Sherry Olson, Suzanne Ellery Greene, Lenora Heilig Nast, and others have compiled fairly comprehensive material on Baltimore, and there are other town histories. Special studies, mostly dissertations, exist on such subjects as reapportionment, the

constitutional convention, poverty, housing, desegregation, and education—except that dissertations on education should be avoided.

Several abbreviations run through the footnotes. The *Baltimore Sun*
and the *Baltimore Evening Sun* are cited as *Sun* and *Evening Sun,* and
the *Baltimore News American* is cited as *News American.* The *Journal
of Proceedings of the House of Delegates of Maryland* and the *Journal
of Proceedings of the Senate of Maryland* are cited as *Journal of the
House* and *Journal of the Senate.* Annual reports of state agencies are
usually listed as *Annual Report,* even though exact titles of the reports
often vary from agency to agency and from year to year; the titles of
the agencies also change over time. The Vertical File of the Maryland
Room of the Enoch Pratt Library in Baltimore is cited as VF-Pratt.
The War Records Division of the Maryland Historical Society and the
Oral History Transcripts of the Maryland Historical Society are cited
as WRD-MHS and OH, along with the appropriate box or transcript
number.

1. Sherry Olson, *Baltimore* (Cambridge, Mass., 1976), 17–29.

2. Department of Economic and Community Development, *Maryland Statistical Abstracts* (1967–1984); State Department of Assessments and Taxation, *Annual Reports* (1940–1984).

3. The best first-hand account of Isaac Freeman Rasin and his successor is John J. Mahon, "Sonny Mahon's Own Story," *Sun,* Oct. 1, 8, 15, and 22, 1922; also, Frank R. Kent, *The Story of Maryland Politics* (Baltimore, 1911); idem, *The Great Game of Politics* (New York, 1923); John R. Lambert, Jr., *Arthur Pue Gorman* (Baton Rouge, La., 1953).

4. Edwin Rothman, "Factional Machine Politics: William Curran and the Baltimore City Democratic Organization, 1929–1946" (Ph.D. diss., Johns Hopkins University, 1949); Joseph L. Arnold, "The Last of the Good Old Days: Politics in Baltimore, 1920–1950," *Maryland Historical Magazine* 71 (Fall 1976): 443–48; *Evening Sun,* Oct. 4–8, 1951, Jan. 27, 1965; *Sun,* Oct. 5, 1951.

5. *News American,* Mar. 14, 1977; *Sun,* Mar. 16 and 19, 1977.

6. *Sun,* July 8, 1977; *Washington Post,* June 6, 1978.

7. "The Crescent Club of Baltimore," *Frank Leslie's Illustrated Weekly* 63 (Dec. 11, 1886); 261–263.

8. *Sun,* Dec. 17, 1956.

9. See clubs by name, VF-Pratt; *Sun,* Feb. 14, 1938; Dec. 20, 1947; Dec. 12, 1956; *Evening Sun,* Feb. 28, 1940; Vincent Santavenere, "The United Democratic Club of the 26th Ward," VF-Pratt.

10. *Evening Sun,* Oct. 18, 1974; *News American,* Oct. 17, 1976.

11. Harold A. Williams in *Sun,* Apr. 20, 1947; Edwin Maryin in *News American,* Nov. 28, 1971.

12. Karen Chatmon, "William L. (Little Willie) Adams: Everybody's Advocate," (Baltimore) *Metropolitan* 4 (Nov. 1978): 6–10; Thomas B. Edsall in *Evening Sun,* Mar. 11, 1971; *Sun,* Mar. 19, 1979.

13. Evelyn L. Wentworth, *Election Statistics in Maryland, 1934–1958* (College Park, Md., 1959); *Maryland Manual* (1958–1984); Neal Friedman, "City Hall," *Baltimore* 67 (Oct. 1974); 38–39; *Evening Sun,* Apr. 20, 1964; Sept. 15, 1971; *News American,* June 8, 1977.

14. Articles on city politics by Dorothy Pula Strohecker, Morgan H. Pritchett, Lawrence N. Krause, and Joseph Arnold in Lenora Heilig Nast et al., eds., *Baltimore: A Living Renaissance* (Baltimore, 1982), pp. 229–50, "Cities Are Fun" (cover story), *Time,* 118 (Aug. 24, 1981): 42–48.

15. James Branch Clark, *The Eastern Shore of Maryland and Virginia,* 3 vols. (New York, 1950); Department of Economic and Community Development, *Community Economic Inventories* (1962–1977); EBS Management Consultants, *A Profile Study of the Eastern Shore of Maryland* (Centreville, Md., 1964); Department of State Planning, *The Counties of Maryland* (1968); U.S. Commission on Civil Rights, *A Crisis in Housing on the Upper Eastern Shore* (1971). For a similar political culture, see "Virginia: Out of the Byrd Cage," in *Transformation of Southern Politics... since 1945,* ed. Jack Bass and Walter DeVries (New York, 1976), pp. 339–68.

16. Frank Goodwin, *A Study of Personal and Social Organization: An Explorative Survey of the Eastern Shore of Maryland* (Philadelphia, 1944).

17. Harry Stegmaier, Jr., et al., *Allegany County: A History* (Parsons, W.Va., 1976); Neal A. Brooks and Eric G. Rockel, *A History of Baltimore County* (Towson, Md., 1979); Nancy M. Warner, *Carroll County, Maryland: A History, 1837–1976* (Camden, N.J. 1976); Department of Economic and Community Development, *Community Economic Inventories* (1962–1977); Thomas H. Hattery, ed., *Western Maryland: A Profile* (Mt. Airy, Md., 1980).

18. Harry M. Caudill, *Night Comes to the Cumberlands: A Biography of a Depressed Area* (Boston, 1963).

19. For a vaguely similar political culture, see "Tennessee: Genuine Two-Party Politics," in *Transformation of Southern Politics,* ed. Bass and DeVries, pp. 284–304.

20. Howard P. Chudacoff, *Evolution of an American Urban Society* (Englewood Cliffs, N.J., 1975), pp. 237–47; Sherry H. Olson, *Baltimore: The Building of an American City* (Baltimore, 1980), pp. 212–19; Ray Eldon Hiebert and Richard K. MacMaster, *A Grateful Remembrance: the Story of Montgomery County, Maryland* (Rockville, Md., 1976), pp. 220–22; Brooks and Rockel, *Baltimore County,* pp. 177–79.

21. Lata Chatterjee et al., *FHA Policies and the Baltimore City Housing Market* (Baltimore, 1974).

22. Olson, *Building of an American City,* p. 303; Blue Book, Inc., *Baltimore Society Visiting List, 1941* (Baltimore, 1940).

23. Brooks and Rockel, *Baltimore County,* pp. 349–68; *Sun,* Oct. 20, 1952; Oct. 11, 1971; Aug. 25–27, 1974; *Evening Sun,* Dec. 3, 1962; *Washington Post,* Aug. 20, 1970.

24. James C. Bradford, ed., *Anne Arundel County, Maryland: A Bicentennial History* (Annapolis, 1977), pp. 211–18; *Evening Sun,* Dec. 9, 1970.

25. Hiebert and MacMaster, *Grateful Remembrance,* pp. 262–326.

26. Lawrence Stern in *Washington Post,* Oct. 16, 1957; *Washington Post,* Oct. 6, Dec. 15, 1965; *Washington Star,* July 29, 1960, Nov. 6, 1964.

27. Wentworth, *Election Statistics; Maryland Manual.*

28. Hiebert and MacMaster, *Grateful Remembrance,* pp. 255–308; Constance McLaughlin Green, *Washington Capital City, 1878–1959* (Princeton, N.J., 1963), pp. 283–85; Washington Suburban Sanitary Commission, *Annual Reports* (1918–1984); Maryland-National Capital Park and Planning Commission, *You and the Maryland-National Capital Park and Planning Commission, 1927–1952* (1952).

29. Brooks and Rockel, *Baltimore County,* pp. 395–468; Hiebert and MacMaster, *Grateful Remembrance,* pp. 313–47; Bradford, *Anne Arundel,* pp. 214–18. Also, vertical files on county executives in county libraries of Annapolis, Towson, Rockville, and Hyattsville, and in VF-Pratt.

Chapter 2. Maryland's World War II

1. In 1945 the Maryland General Assembly established a War Records Division of the Maryland Historical Society as a memorial to Marylanders who served in World War II. The division's staff worked for almost ten years compiling what in some ways is the most complete record of the war years for any state. Some of the material was published in catalogue form in three volumes as *Maryland in World War II* (Baltimore, vol. 1: 1950; vol. 2: 1951; vol. 3: 1958); much additional material exists in 224 manuscript boxes preserved by the society. These materials (cited hereafter as WRD-MHS, *World War II,* and WRD-MHS, MS Boxes) provided the basis for this chapter.

2. (Baltimore) *Jewish Times,* 1933–1942; on Mencken, *Sun,* Sunday mornings, 1938–1941, and especially July 14, 1940.

3. *Baltimore* (Journal of the Baltimore Association of Commerce) (Oct. 1939), pp. 9–11 (Nov. 1939), pp. 5–7 (Jan. 1940), p. 12 (Apr. 1940), p. 9 (May 1940), p. 13; on Alex. Brown and Sons, "War and Business," *Baltimore* (Sept. 1939); *Report of the Maryland Agricultural Society* 24 (1939): 79; Baltimore Federation of Labor, Minutes (1933–1940), AFL Headquarters, Baltimore.

4. Glenn L. Martin, *Annual Reports* (1935–1945); WRD-MHS, MS Boxes 101–2.

5. Richard Polenberg, *War and Society: The United States, 1941–1945* (Philadelphia, 1972), p. 7; WRD-MHS, *World War II,* 3:175; *Sun,* July 12,

1940; Council of Defense, *Report of the Maryland Council of Defense, August 1, 1940, to September 1, 1942* (1942).

6. *Sun*, Nov. 27, 1940; Baltimore Federation of Labor, Minutes, Dec. 10, 1941.

7. *Report of the Maryland Council of Defense*; "Council of Defense," WRD-MHS, MS Boxes 70–76; WRD-MHS, *World War II*, 3:175–88.

8. *Laws of Maryland, 1941*, chap. 567.

9. *Laws of Maryland, 1941*, chap. 388; *Laws of Maryland, 1943*, chaps. 380, 153, 602.

10. *Sun*, Oct. 30, 1940, Jan. 6, Apr. 28, 1941; *Laws of Maryland, 1941*, chap. 33; *Sun*, June 18, Aug. 28, 1941; *Evening Sun*, Dec. 17 and 20, 1941; *Baltimore News-Post*, Dec. 17, 1941; *Evening Sun*, Feb. 24, 1942.

11. WRD-MHS, *World War II*, 3:175–252; Harry W. Kirwin, *The Inevitable Success: Herbert R. O'Conor* (Westminster, Md., 1962), pp. 296–98; *Sun*, Mar. 16, 1942; *Evening Sun*, Mar. 14, 1942; C. B. Lister, Secretary, National Rifle Association, "To All Members," Mar. 19, 1942, in VF-Pratt; *Baltimore News-Post*, Mar. 27, 1942; *Sun*, Sept. 18, 1944, July 31, 1945, Nov. 16, 1975.

12. WRD-MHS, *World War II*, 1:258–63.

13. Ibid. According to WRD-MHS figures, Maryland fatalities were approximately 303 per 100,000 state population, compared to 229 nationally (precise figures are not available because of crossing over between states).

14. WRD-MHS, MS Boxes 44–57; enlistments by county are detailed in WRD-MHS, *World War II*, 3:189–208.

15. WRD-MHS, *World War II*, 3:19–54.

16. Ibid., 3:55–138.

17. Ibid., 3:1–18.

18. Ibid., 2:429–33; U.S. Department of Labor, *Impact of the War on the Elkton Area, Cecil County, Maryland* (1944); Mary Heaton Vorse, "The Girls of Elkton," *Harper's* (Mar. 1943), pp. 347–54; S. G. Arthur, "How the War Ran over Elkton," *Nation's Business* (Oct. 1945), pp. 28–30, 131–32; "Triumph's Tribulations," *Fortune* (Mar. 1944), pp. 20, 30, 44.

19. Records of the Elkton USO in WRD-MHS, MS Box 191, especially interviews with Ruth W. Robbins, (USO director) by S. G. Grether, Apr. 20, 1948, and with Daniel L. McMenamin, Chairman, USO Board, by S. G. Grether, Apr. 12, 1948.

20. U.S. Department of Labor, *A Statistical Summary of Harford County, Maryland* (1943); interview with William S. James, attorney in Harford County, subsequently state senator, by E. K. Monke, May 8–9, 1947, WRD-MHS, MS Box 143; WRD-MHS, MS Box 105; WRD-MHS, *World War II*, 1:78–91, 99–107, and 2:72–74.

21. WRD-MHS, *World War II*, 2:389–97, 3:63–66; "Glenn L. Martin," VF-Pratt.

22. *Sun*, Aug. 27, 1942, Apr. 14, May 27, 1943; *Evening Sun*, Mar. 5, 1942, Apr. 14, 1943, Mar. 23, 1944, Feb. 2, 1951, *Baltimore News-Post*, Feb. 2, 1955; Federal Public Housing Authority, *Middle River* (Baltimore, 1944); Housing Authority of Baltimore, *The Story of Public Housing* (1945); interview with C. W. Burrier, Housing Director of Middle River area, by S. G. Grether, Nov. 26, 1946, WRD-MHS, MS Box 107.

23. The WRD-MHS compiled a history of almost every industrial company in Maryland for the years 1940 to 1945, detailed in *World War II*, 2:18–519.

24. U.S. Department of the Navy, Naval History Division, "Naval Air Test Center, Patuxent River, Maryland," a 430-page history compiled in 1945, Naval Library, Washington, D.C.; WRD-MHS, *World War II*, 1:206–13; interview with Alvin Pasarew by E. K. Monke, Aug. 2, 1946, WRD-MHS,

MS Box 179; *Evening Sun,* March 28, 1945; *Baltimore News-Post,* May 1, 1946; Regina Combs Hammett, *History of St. Mary's County, Maryland* (Ridge, Md., 1977), pp. 413–24.

25. Geoffrey T. Hellman, "That Was the War," *New Yorker* (Nov. 15, 1947), pp. 65–71; James H. Bready in *Sun,* Dec. 16, 1945; WRD-MHS, *World War II,* 1:134–37, WRD-MHS, MS Box 16.

26. U.S. Bureau of Foreign and Domestic Commerce, *Survey of Current Business* 31 (Aug. 1951): 18; U.S. Department of Commerce, *Area Development Report: Maryland* (Jan. 1948); U.S. Council of Economic Advisors, *Economic Report of the President* (Jan. 1948). Maryland fell from 15 percent above the national income average to 6 percent above because the fastest growth in the war was in agricultural income, which comprised more than 7 percent of the nation's income but only 3 percent of Maryland's.

27. (Baltimore) *Afro-American,* Mar. 7, 1942; Commission to Study the Problems Affecting the Colored Population, *Report* (1943).

28. Baltimore Department of Public Works, *Annual Reports* (1940), p. 270 (1943), p. 313.

29. Commission to Study the Problems Affecting the Colored Population, *Report* (1943), Housing Authority of Baltimore, *Story of Public Housing* (1945); U.S. War Manpower Commission, *Annual Reports* (1942, 1943); William O. Weyforth, U.S. War Manpower Commission, "Manpower Problems in the Baltimore Labor Market in World War II" (1946), in WRD-MHS, MS Box 91; WRD-MHS, MS Box 142.

30. U.S. Department of Labor, *Baltimore Women War Workers* (1948); Weyforth, "Manpower Problems"; U.S. Department of Labor, *Labor Information Bulletin: Women* (May 1947); U.S. Department of Commerce, *Current Population Reports: Population Characteristics of the Baltimore Area* (1947); U.S. Department of Labor, *Impact of the War on the Elkton Area.* Karen Anderson, *Wartime Women: Sex Roles, Family Relations, and the Status of Women During World War II* (Westport, Conn., 1981), concentrates on Baltimore.

31. *Baltimore Federationist* (AFL monthly, 1943–1980); interview with Frank J. Bender, Regional Director, CIO, by S. G. Grether, June 9, 1947, WRD-MHS, MS Box 69; Baltimore Federation of Labor, Minutes, 1940–1947.

32. War Production Board, *Summary of War Supply and Facility Contracts by State* (1945).

33. WRD-MHS, *World War II,* 2:1–17, 550–61; A. B. Hamilton, *Comparative Census of Maryland Agriculture* (College Park, Md., 1946); Maryland Agricultural Society, *Reports* (1939–1947).

34. *Sun,* May 19, 1935, Sept. 20, Dec. 6, Aug. 19, 1936; *Evening Sun,* Mar. 6, 1938, Apr. 14, 1945; Kevin Wood, "American Feelings toward the Germans during Both World Wars," in "Germans," VF-Pratt; interview with Morgan Pritchett, President of the Society of the History of the Germans, by George H. Callcott, Oct. 16, 1976; "Names Changes in Maryland," WRD-MHS, MS Box 211; "Report of the Baltimore Peace Center," WRD-MHS, MS Box 35; J. Edgar Hoover, "Accomplishments of the FBI in Baltimore during World War II," WRD-MHS, MS Box 90; files, American Civil Liberties Union of Maryland, Baltimore.

35. Hoover, "Accomplishments of the FBI"; interview with Captain Marshall Hanks, Chief, POW, Maryland area, by Harold Manakee, Mar. 28, 1946, WRD-MHS, MS Box 164; *Sun,* Aug. 6, 1943; WRD-MHS, MS Boxes 77–79.

36. State Department of Corrections, *Annual Reports* (1935, 1947); Baltimore Board of Police Commissioners, *Report for the Year* (1930–1950); inter-

view with Harold Donnell, Superintendent of prisons, by E. K. Monke, July 19, 1946, WRD-MHS, MS Box 32; Better Business Bureau of Baltimore, *Report* (May 1946).

37. James M. Hepbron, Chairman, Maryland Commission on Juvenile Delinquency, *Report* (1943); Baltimore Board of Police Commissioners, *Report for the Year* (1943), p. 17; *Laws of Maryland, 1943,* chap. 797; *Sun,* Apr. 28, 1943.

38. Jack Lait and Lee Mortimer, *Washington Confidential* (New York, 1951), pp. 63–68; 258–75.

39. State Board of Health, *Annual Reports* (1938–1950); Maryland Department of Health, *Public Health in Maryland,* (1942–1980); Baltimore Department of Health, *One Hundred and Thirty-Third Annual Report* (1947).

40. Maryland Department of Education, *Maryland School Bulletin* (1937–1947); "Redirecting the School Program in Wartime" is vol. 24 of the *Bulletin* (December 1942); State Board of Education, *Annual Reports;* Board of Education, Anne Arundel County, "Activities Emphasized in the Schools during World War II," WRD-MHS, MS Box 83; George H. Callcott, *A History of the University of Maryland* (Baltimore, 1966), pp. 335–37.

41. Maryland Board of Motion Picture Censors, *Annual Report* (1942–1943), p. 5; WRD-MHS, MS Boxes 31, 130.

42. Kirwin, *O'Conor,* pp. 1–152.

43. Franklin L. Burdette, "Modern Maryland Politics and Social Change," in *Maryland: A History, 1632–1974,* ed. Richard Walsh and William Lloyd Fox (Baltimore, 1974), pp. 773–904: Kirwin, *O'Conor,* pp. 189–233.

44. Isaiah Bowman, Chairman, Committee on the Structure of the State Government, *Report* (1939); *Sun,* Jan. 6 and 7, 1939; Kirwin, *O'Conor,* pp. 235–243.

45. Rubin Oppenheimer, Chairman, Commission on the People's Court of Baltimore City, *Report* (1938); Hammond Urner, "Bill and Constitutional Amendment of the Governor's Commission on the Inferior Courts," O'Conor Papers, Hall of Records, Annapolis; Carroll T. Bond, "Report of the Commission on the Judiciary," (Baltimore) *Daily Record,* Oct. 22, 1942; Morris A. Soper, "Reorganization of the Court of Appeals," *Maryland Law Review* 8 (Feb. 1944): 91–119; Kirwin, *O'Conor,* pp. 310–12, 369–88.

46. Comptroller of the Treasury, *Annual Reports* (1938–1946); *Evening Sun,* Mar. 10, 1941; Kirwin, *O'Conor,* pp. 394–96.

47. Maryland School Survey Commission, *The 1941 Survey of the Maryland Public Schools and Teacher Colleges* (1941); State Board of Education, *Annual Reports.*

48. Kirwin, *O'Conor,* pp. 257–67, 298–304, 383–84; Joseph P. Healy, Chairman, Commission to Study Problems Affecting the Colored Population, *Report* (1942); newspaper clippings in WRD-HMS, MS Box 142; (Baltimore) *Afro-American,* Feb. 7, Apr. 4, 11, and 25, May 16, 1942; *Sun,* Feb. 2, Apr. 25, 1942.

49. State Planning Commission, *Medical Care in the Counties of Maryland* (1944); Anna D. Ward, "Baltimore's Health and Welfare Expenditure in Wartime," *Councillor* 9 (Mar. 1944): 22–35; *Hospital Management* 59 (Feb. 1945); 104–6; Walter N. Kirkman, Chairman, Maryland Almshouse Commission, *Report* (1940); State Planning Commission, *The Free Public Library in Maryland* (1944).

50. Burdette, "Modern Maryland Politics," pp. 773–904; Evelyn L. Wentworth, *Election Statistics in Maryland, 1934–1958* (College Park, Md., 1959).

Chapter 3.
The Population Swirl

1. Calculated from figures in Alvin Toffler, *Future Shock* (New York, 1970, pp. 75–76.

2. See chapter 1 herein. Also, Morton Hoffman, "The Role of Government in Influencing Changes in Housing in Baltimore, 1940–1950," *Journal of Land Economics* 30 (May 1954); 125–40; Neal A. Brooks and Eric G. Rockel, *A History of Baltimore County* (Towson, Md., 1979), pp. 369–70; State Planning Commission, *Residential Development in Baltimore City and County* (1953).

3. *Sun,* Aug. 16, Sept. 11, 1950; Ray Eldon Hiebert and Richard K. MacMaster, *A Grateful Remembrance: The Story of Montgomery County, Maryland* (Rockville, Md., 1976), pp. 329–34; Brooks and Rockel, *Baltimore County,* pp. 369–72.

4. Homer Hoyt Associates, *Economic Survey of Montgomery and Prince George's Counties, Maryland* (Washington, D.C., 1955), pp. 10–18; Maryland-National Capital Park and Planning Commission (hereafter MNCP&P), *Inventory of Land Use* (1955); Washington Suburban Sanitary Commission, *Annual Reports* (1956–1984); *Sun,* Apr. 16, 1950.

5. Hiebert and MacMaster, *Grateful Remembrance,* pp. 330–34; *Montgomery County Sentinel,* Sept. 29, 1955; *Washington Post,* Nov. 6, 1947; *Sun,* June 5, 1949; *Evening Sun,* Mar. 24, 1952; *News American* Aug. 24, 1958.

6. MNCP&P, *Annual Reports* (1953, 1954, 1955, 1961); idem, *Residential Neighborhoods* (1956); idem, *Population Patterns* (1954); idem, *You and the Maryland-National Capital Park and Planning Commission, 1927–1952* (1952); Homer Hoyt Associates, *Economic Survey,* pp. 10–18, 27; State Planning Commission, *Maryland Population, 1930–1960, by Election Districts, Cities, and Towns* (1961); *Sun,* Sept. 11, 1949, Sept. 10, 1950, Sept. 14, 1952.

7. Homer Hoyt Associates, *Economic Survey,* pp. 42–66; MNCP&P, *Inventory of Land Use;* State Planning Commission, *Maryland County Economic Data Book* (1962): Derek Thompson et al., *Atlas of Maryland* (College Park, Md., 1977), pp. 77–85.

8. House Committee on Expenditures in the Executive Department, *Investigation of Viers Mill Village Housing Project,* 80th Cong., 2d sess., 1956, *News American,* Aug. 24, 1958.

9. MNCP&P, *Residential Neighborhoods; Evening Sun,* Mar. 24, 1952.

10. *Sun,* June 5, 1949, Dec. 17, 1951; State Planning Commission, *Residential Development; Montgomery County Sentinel,* Sept. 18, 1975.

11. John Keats, *The Crack in the Picture Window* (Boston, 1957); Robert G. Wood, *Suburbia: Its People and Their Politics* (Boston, 1959); Herbert J. Gans, *The Levittowners: Ways of Life and Politics in a New Suburbia Community* (New York, 1967), p. 180; *Sun,* Sept. 11, 1949, Sept. 10, 1950, Sept. 17, 1965.

12. Homer Hoyt Associates, *Economic Survey,* pp. 92–100; MNCP&P, *An Inventory of Community Resources for Montgomery and Prince George's Counties* (1955); idem, *Community Resources in Montgomery and Prince George's Counties* (1959).

13. MNCP&P, *Annual Report* (1967); idem, *Looking Ahead: A General Plan, 1958–1980* (1957); Homer Hoyt Associates, *Economic Survey,* p. 94.

14. Hiebert and MacMaster, *Grateful Remembrance,* pp. 330–61; MNCP&P, *An Economic Analysis of Land Use and Zoning in Silver Spring* (1954); idem, *Annual Report* (1962); M. Henry Eppes, *Home Rule in the Maryland Counties* (College Park, Md., 1975).

15. MNCP&P, *Annual Reports* (1961, 1962); Baltimore Regional Planning Council, *History of Regional Planning in the Baltimore Area, 1955–*

1964 (1964); *Sun,* Sept. 10, 1950; I. Alvin Pasarew, *Survey of Local Planning in Maryland* (Baltimore, 1948).

16. Brooks and Rockel, *Baltimore County,* pp. 372–85, 395–423; *Washington Star,* Oct. 9, 1977.

17. Income calculated from figures in U.S. Bureau of the Census, City and County Data Book (1952, 1962, 1972).

18. "New Shopping Centers Opened in Baltimore Area," *Baltimore* 51 (Oct. 1958); W. S. Hamill, "A Shopping Center Review," *Baltimore* 53 (Mar. 1960): 15, 48–49; *Sun,* Feb. 24, 1946; see shopping centers by name in VF-Pratt.

19. Homer Hoyt Associates, *Economic Survey,* pp. 116–36; MNCP&P, *Annual Report* (1957).

20. Homer Hoyt Associates, *Economic Survey,* pp. 126–56; MNCP&P, *Employment Patterns in Montgomery and Prince George's Counties* (1959); Prince George's County, *Annual Reports* (1962–1980); Baltimore Regional Planning Council, *Economic Report on the Baltimore Region* (1964); idem, *Patterns of Change in the Manufacturing Industry, 1955–1965* (1968).

21. State Roads Commission, *Annual Reports* (1940–1980); idem, *A History of Road Building in Maryland* (1958); idem, *A Review of the Twelve-Year Construction and Reconstruction Program . . . of Maryland* (1952); MNCP&P, *Master Plan of Highways* (1953); see highways by name in VF-Pratt.

22. State Roads Commission, *Maryland Capital Beltway Impact Study,* 7 vols. (1966–1967); Douglas H. Haeuber, *The Baltimore Expressway Controversy: A Study of the Political Decision-Making Process* (1974).

23. Sloan Wilson, *The Man in the Grey Flannel Suit* (New York, 1955); David Riesman, *The Lonely Crowd* (New Haven, Conn., 1950); Scott Donaldson, *The Suburban Myth* (New York, 1969); Wood, *Suburbia.*

24. MNCP&P, *Apartments and Their Impact on the Public Schools* (1959); idem, *Looking Ahead: A General Plan, 1958–1980* (1957); idem, *The Growth of Housing Units, 1960–1968* (1969); Prince George's County, *Annual Reports* (1960, 1962, 1964); Prince George's County Community Renewal Program, *An Economic Profile: Measures of Change* (1971); *Sun,* Mar. 1, 1959, Oct. 27, 1963.

25. Baltimore Department of Housing and Community Development, *Condominiums* (1980); "An Overview of Condominiums," *Real Estate News* 67 (Apr. 1979): 12–14; *Washington Post,* June 4, 1975; *Washington Star,* Nov. 9, 1979, May 19, 1981.

26. See Louis P. Bucklin, *Competition and Evolution in the Distributive Trades* (Englewood Clifs, N.J., 1972); see malls by name in VF-Pratt.

27. Brooks and Rockel, *Baltimore County,* pp. 389–94; Hiebert and MacMaster, *Grateful Remembrance,* pp. 304–6; 337–38.

28. Brooks and Rockel, *Baltimore County,* pp. 379–82; Prince George's County, *Annual Report* (1976); Baltimore Regional Planning Council, *General Development Plan* (1972); *Sun,* Feb. 15, 1959; Prince George's County Community Renewal Program, *Economic Profile.*

29. Maryland Commission on Interracial Relations, *Annual Reports* (1952–1968); Maryland Commission on Human Relations, *Annual Reports* (1949-1975); Montgomery County Suburban Fair Housing Committee, *Annual Reports* (1963–1968); *Washington Star,* Oct. 26, 1969.

30. Brooks and Rockel, *Baltimore County,* pp. 383–85; Hiebert and MacMaster, *Grateful Remembrance,* pp. 371–77.

31. Baltimore Mass Transit Administration, *The Baltimore Metro* (1984); Eric Garland, "Metro," *Baltimore Magazine* 74 (Aug. 1981); 57–60, 112–13; *Sun,* July 4, 1977, Jan. 6, 1978, Feb. 20, Dec. 22, 1983.

32. David R. Goldfield and Blaine A. Browell, *Urban America: From Downtown to No Town* (Boston, 1979).

33. Paul K. Conkin, *Tomorrow a New World: The New Deal Community Program* (Ithaca, N.Y., 1959), pp. 61–65; Joseph L. Arnold, *The New Deal in the Suburbs: A History of the Greenbelt Town Program, 1935–1954* (Columbus, Ohio, 1971), pp. 3–36.

34. Conkin, *Tomorrow a New World,* pp. 305–21; Arnold, *New Deal in the Suburbs,* pp. 45–46, 88–103.

35. Arnold, *New Deal in the Suburbs,* pp. 136–45, 162–84; George A. Warner, *Greenbelt, The Cooperative Community: An Experience in Democratic Living* (New York, 1954); Sally Scott Rogers, "Community Planning and Residential Satisfaction: A Case Analysis of Greenbelt, Maryland" (Ph.D. diss., University of Maryland, 1975), pp. 107–15; dissertations include those by Arnold, Rogers, and William Form; theses by Gerlad Boisvert, Sally Borchert, Cedrick Larson, Kaye Noe, and Stephen Polaschik.

36. Arnold, *New Deal in the Suburbs,* pp. 229–38; Rogers, "Community Planning," pp. 80–87, 107–15; Ken Schlossberg, "Greenbelt Has Been Deflowered," *Washingtonian Magazine* 3 (July 1968); 49–51, 75–76.

37. Gans, *Levittowners,* pp. 3–144; Kenneth Geremia, "Levitt's Belair in 1980," *Washington Post,* June 21 and 28, 1980.

38. Geremia, "Levitt's Belair"; City of Bowie, *Annual Reports,* (1968–1980); *Sun,* July 17, 1960; *Washington Post,* Aug. 29, 1964, July 24, 1965, Apr. 24, 1969; *Washington Star,* Dec. 15, 1976; *Bowie News,* Dec. 1, 1976.

39. Gans, *Levittowners,* pp. 206–89.

40. Ibid., pp. 154–79.

41. Ibid., pp. 189, 289–378.

42. The Rouse Company, Columbia, maintains files of Rouse's speeches, writings, and press coverage. Also see cover story, *Time* 118 (Aug. 24, 1981); 42–53; James Rouse, "It Can Happen Here," speech of Sept. 16, 1963, and "How to Build a Whole City from Scratch," speech of May 17, 1966, cited in Richard Oliver Brooks, *New Towns and Communal Values: A Case Study of Columbia, Maryland* (New York, 1974), pp. 12–20.

43. Brooks, *New Towns,* pp. 20–76.

44. Ibid., pp. 4–10, 93–121; Lynne C. Burkhart, *Old Values in a New Town: The Politics of Race and Class in Columbia, Maryland* (New York, 1981), pp. 2–22; *Washington Post,* Feb. 27, 1982; Rouse Company, *Annual Reports of the Columbia Association, 1965–1980.*

45. Brooks, *New Towns,* pp. 167–93; Burkhart, *Old Values,* passim.

46. *Rossmoor News,* 1966–1973; *RLW Today,* 1973–1980; *Washington Post,* Sept. 28, 1965, Apr. 24, 1966, Oct. 10, 1974, Sept. 7, 1978, Feb. 24, 1979; *Washington Star,* Nov. 21, 1967; *Montgomery Sentinel,* Sept. 30, 1976.

47. Baltimore Housing Authority, *Fifteen Years of Public Housing* (1952); idem, *Quarterly Review* (1947–1957); Commission on the City Plan, *Redevelopment of Blighted Residential Areas in Baltimore* (1945); Theodore R. McKeldin, *Fourth Annual Report on Municipal Activities, 1943–1947:* (1947); *Sun,* May 28, 1943, Mar. 4, 1947.

48. Thomas D'Alesandro, Jr., *Progress in Baltimore, 1947–1957* (Baltimore, 1957); idem, *Third Annual Report, 1949–1950* (Baltimore, 1950); *Sun,* Jan. 2, 1951, May 20, 1953, May 2, 1957; Martin Millspaugh and Gurney Breckenfeld, *The Human Side of Urban Renewal* (Baltimore, 1960).

49. James W. Rouse, *Report to the Mayor on the Operations of the Baltimore Plan* (Baltimore, 1952); D'Alesandro, *Progress in Baltimore;* State Department of Planning, *Capital Improvement Program for Baltimore* (1951); *Evening Sun,* May 20, 1957.

50. Maryland Department of Health, Division of Vital Statistics, Annual Reports (1940–1980).

51. Abel Wolman, Chairman, Task Force on Population Migration, *The Impact of Population Decline on Baltimore* (Baltimore, 1978), pp. 1–14.

52. Ibid., pp. 67–73.

53. Ibid., pp. 33–36.

54. Ibid., pp. 38–52.

55. State Department of Assessments and Taxation, *Annual Reports* (1940–1980). Assessments in both the city and the suburbs remained at about 60 percent of sale prices.

56. Clarence Miles, *Opening Days: Memoirs of Clarence Miles* (Baltimore, 1978); cover story, *Time* 118 (Aug. 24 1981); 42–53; Greater Baltimore Committee, *Annual Reports* (1955–1978); idem, *Charles Center* (1959); idem, *The Central Business District* (1959); Suzanne Ellery Greene, *Baltimore; An Illustrated History* (Woodland Hills, Calif., 1980), p. 267; Martin Millspaugh, "New Look for Old Baltimore," July 14, 1957; *Sun*, Jan. 7, Nov. 23, 1955; Lenora Heilig Nast et al., eds., *Baltimore: A Living Renaissance* (Baltimore, 1982), pp. 3–50, 279–92.

57. Maryland Port Authority, *Decade for Port Progress, 1967–1977* (1966); idem, *Annual Reports* (1956–1962); Maryland Department of Transportation, *Annual Reports* (1956–1962); Stanley J. Hille et al., *The Economic Impact of the Port of Baltimore* (College Park, Md., 1975).

58. Greater Baltimore Consolidated Wholesale Food Market Authority subsequently Maryland Food Center Authority), *Annual Reports* (1969–1980).

59. Greater Baltimore Committee, *Charles Center;* idem, *Annual Reports* (1955-1978); Jane Jacobs, "New Heart for Baltimore," *Architectural Forum* 108 (June 1958); 88–92; Baltimore Economic Development Corporation, *Baltimore Economic Profile* (1979); Greene, *Baltimore,* 206–12; Sherry Olson, *Baltimore* (Cambridge, Mass., 1976), pp. 48–54.

60. Baltimore Chamber of Commerce, *Metropolitan Baltimore: Growth Patterns, 1963–1967* (1968); Theodore R. McKeldin, *Baltimore Report: The Growing Years, 1963–1967* (1967); *Evening Sun,* Nov. 24, 1966; James W. Hughes and Kenneth D. Bleakley, Jr., *Urban Homesteading* (New Brunswick, N.J., 1975); Morton Hoffman and Co., *Housing Market Analysis: Baltimore City, 1964–1980* (Baltimore, 1965); Thomas N. Marndas, *Baltimore City's Vacant Housing Program* (Baltimore, 1975).

61. Thomas D'Alesandro III, *The Emerging City: A Report from the Mayor* (1971); *News American,* Nov. 30, 1969, Sept. 7, 1970; *Sun,* Dec. 6, 1970; *Evening Sun,* July 12, 1971; Louis S. Roseberg, The Low-Income Housing Effort in the City of Baltimore (Philadelphia, 1969); Michael A. Stegman, *Housing in the Inner City: The Dynamics of Decline, A Study of Baltimore, Maryland, 1968–1970* (Cambridge, Mass., 1972).

62. *Evening Sun,* June 16, 1956, Jan. 7–10, 1957; *Sun,* May 26 and 27, 1969, Feb. 9, 1971, Dec. 17, 1976, Jan. 20, 1978, June 16, 1979; State Roads Commission, *Annual Reports* (1940–1970); Maryland Department of Transportation, *Annual Reports* (1940–1981); Haeubner, *Baltimore Expressway Controversy,* Sherry H. Olson, *Baltimore: The Building of an American City* (Baltimore, 1980), pp. 360–77; idem, *Baltimore,* pp. 53–54.

63. Baltimore Economic Development Corporation, *Baltimore Economic Profile* (1979); Jeff Valentine in *Evening Sun,* June 18–22, 1979; *New York Times,* Aug. 27, 1980; *Time* 118 (Aug. 24, 1981); 42–53.

64. Matthew A. Crenson, *Neighborhood Politics* (1983).

65. Ibid.

66. Baltimore Department of Planning, *Retail Trade* (1957); *Evening Sun,*

July 29, 1977; *Sun,* Jan. 3, 1979; *News American,* Jan. 3, 1979; Donald P. Baker, "Is Baltimore Truly Back?" *Washington Post,* Nov. 24, 1984; Michael C. MacDonald, *American Cities, A Report on Myths of Urban Renaissance* (New York, 1984).

67. On the particular towns, see Department of Economic and Community Development, *Community Economic Inventory,* 72 vols. (1961–1976); published county and town histories; and VF-Pratt. On small towns, see Berton Roneche, *Special Places: In Search of Small-Town America* (Boston, 1982).

68. Ross M. Robertson, *History of the American Economy* (New York, 1973), pp. 293–320, 514–58; Gilbert C. Fite and Jim E. Reese, *An Economic History of the United States* (Boston, 1973), pp. 579–83; Gilbert C. Fite, *American Farmers: The New Minority* (Bloomington, Ill., 1981).

69. Maryland Department of Employment Security, *Maryland Farm Labor Report, 1948–1967;* Governor's Commission on Migratory Labor, *Progress in Meeting Problems of Migratory Labor in Maryland, 1963–1966* (1967); U.S. Bureau of the Census.

70. *Maryland Farm News,* 1934–1974; *Maryland State Grange Proceedings* (1940–1984); Maryland Department of Agriculture, *Agriculture Statistics* (1962–1984).

<table>
<tr><td>

Chapter 4.
The Postwar Discomfort
of Harry Truman
and William P. Lane

</td><td>

1. *Sun,* May 8 and 9, Aug. 14–16, 1945.

2. Maryland Commission on Post-War Reconstruction and Development, *Program and Activities . . . 1943–1945* (1945); Baltimore Committee for Post-War Planning, *Baltimore Plan for Post-War Activity* (1943).

</td></tr>
</table>

3. See University of Maryland and other college newspapers of the period; also, William L. Marbury, Chairman, Commission on Higher Education, *Higher Education in Maryland* (1947).

4. U.S. Bureau of the Census, *Historical Statistics of the United States,* 2 vols. (1975), 1:224, 297; Joseph C. Goulden, *The Best Years, 1945–1950* (New York, 1976), pp. 3–13.

5. U.S. Bureau of Labor Statistics, *Monthly Labor Review* (annual May issue calculates man-days lost by industry and by state); *Evening Sun,* Nov. 26, Dec. 3, 1945, Jan. 19 and 21, Nov. 23, 1946, May 10, 1947; *Sun,* Aug. 11, 1945, Mar. 5, Nov. 22, Dec. 5, 1956, May 26, 1947.

6. Lane Family Scrapbooks, William Preston Lane Papers, McKeldin Library, University of Maryland, College Park, Maryland; *Sun,* June 2, 1946.

7. Lane Political Scrapbooks, Lane Papers, College Park. Lane's secretaries maintained excellent scrapbooks of clippings from daily and weekly newspapers regarding Maryland politics.

8. Major coverage in *Sun,* Dec. 27–30, 1931, Oct. 21–Nov. 30, Mar. 14, 1933, Feb. 15, 22, and 25, 1934; *Evening Sun,* Dec. 12, 1931, Dec. 14, 1932, Feb. 2, Oct. 30, Dec. 4, and 12, 1933; *New York Times,* Jan. 24, 1932, Nov. 29, 1934; (Snow Hill) *Worcester Democrat,* Dec. 12, 1931.

9. Lane, "Shall Democracy Be Saved?" to Naval Academy, Dec. 10, 1948, Speeches File, Lane Papers, College Park; also, reported in *Sun,* Dec. 13, 1948. This speech was repeated many times in many forms. A later version was Lane, *Founder's Day Address, University of Virginia, April 13, 1954* (Charlottesville, 1954).

10. See especially "Inaugural Address, January 8, 1947," *Sun,* Jan. 9, 1947; and "Address to the General Assembly," Jan. 5, 1949, *Journal of the House* (1949), pp. 28–102.

11. Especially, "Welcome to the General Assembly," Jan. 3, 1951, *Journal of the House* (1951), pp. 13–20; "Bureaucracy," May 9, 1949, to National

Commission on Intergovernmental Relations, Speeches File, Lane Papers, College Park.

12. Lane Political Scrapbooks, Lane Papers, College Park; especially *Hagerstown Daily Mail,* Dec. 20, 1945; (Baltimore) *Afro-American,* Jan. 26, 1946; (Baltimore) *Home News,* June 13, 1946; *Sun,* Jan. 19, Apr. 17, July 7, 1946.

13. Calculated by Council of State Governments, *Book of the States* (1945), p. 186; idem, *Book of the States,* (1950), p. 224.

14. Joseph Sherbow, Chairman, Maryland Commission on the Distribution of Tax Revenues, *Report* (1946).

15. *Journal of the House* (1947); *Journal of the Senate* (1947); *Sun,* Jan. 16, Mar. 25 and 31, 1947, Oct. 22, 1950; *Evening Sun,* Apr. 17, 1947; *Baltimore News-Post,* Feb. 19, Mar. 29, 1947; "Legislation, 1947," Group 9927, Boxes 1–7, William P. Lane Papers, Hall of Records, Annapolis. Boxes 4 and 5 contain about eleven thousand cards and letters regarding the sales tax.

16. Comptroller of the Treasury, *Annual Reports* (1945, 1951).

17. Maryland Department of Education, *Annual Reports* (1945, 1951), especially (1951), pp. 10–11, 86, 129, 130.

18. State Roads Commission, *Annual Reports* (1945–1952); Vera Filby, "The History of Friendship," MS, VF-Pratt; Evelyn L. Wentworth, *Election Statistics in Maryland, 1934–1958* (College Park, Md., 1959).

19. W. S. Hamill, "The Story of the Bay Bridge," *Baltimore* 43 (July 1952); 18–19, 45–64.

20. Maryland Department of Health, *Reports of the Director* (1945–1951); *Evening Sun,* Jan. 9–16, 1949.

21. Especially political articles, *Sun,* Sept. 5 and 21, Nov. 11, 1947, May 25, 1948, Jan. 3, Mar. 3, 1949, Sept. 18, 1950; *Evening Sun,* Apr. 27, 1949; "Legislation," Groups 9927, 10630, 10631, Lane Papers, Annapolis.

22. For campaign of 1950, "Campaign, 1950," and Lane Political Scrapbooks, 1950, Lane Papers, College Park.

Chapter 5. Communism and the Cold War

1. House Un-American Activities Committee (hereafter HUAC), *Investigation of Communism in Baltimore* (1954), especially testimony of Earl C. Reno, pp. 4079–177; idem, *Hearings Relating to Communist Activities in the Defense Area of Baltimore* (1951), testimony of Mary Stalcup Markward, pp. 740–46; *Sun,* Mar. 30, 1940; *Evening Sun,* Feb. 19, 1951.

2. For votes, see "Election Returns," *Maryland Manual* (1898–1984); also, *Evening Sun,* Dec. 11, 1934; *Sun,* Aug. 31–Sept. 30, Nov. 5 and 29, Dec. 6 and 7, 1940.

3. *Sun,* Jan. 29, May 1, 1932, Nov. 11, 1933; *Evening Sun,* Mar. 4, 1933; *Sun,* May 1 and 2, 1934; *Evening Sun,* Apr. 19, 1934; *Sun,* May 3, Feb. 18, June 10, Nov. 11, 1935, Jan. 27, July 19, Oct. 19, Nov. 23, 1936, Jan. 25, 1937, Apr. 28, Sept. 1, Nov. 19 and 21, 1938, Jan. 8, Feb. 28, Apr. 25, Sept. 11, Dec. 9, 1939, and Jan. 8, 1940.

4. *Sun,* Feb. 2 and 3, 1941, Apr. 29, Nov. 13 and 25, 1942; Dec. 4, 1943, Jan. 11, Feb. 2, May 24, June 4, 1944; *Evening Sun,* Apr. 21, May 8, June 2, Oct. 7, 1944; HUAC, *Hearings* (1951), pp. 744–50.

5. HUAC, *Hearings* (1951), pp. 747–48; *Sun,* July 28, 1945; *Evening Sun,* Oct. 17, 1945; Interview, Maurice Braverman, by George H. Callcott, July 20, 1977.

6. David A. Shannon, *The Decline of American Communism* (New York, 1959), pp. 354–70.

7. HUAC, *Communism in the District of Columbia–Maryland Area* (1951), pp. 4482–89; idem, *Hearings* (1951), pp. 761, 786, 791; idem, *Investigation* (1954), pp. 4097–101; idem, *Investigation of Communist Activity in the Baltimore Area* (1957), p. 900; *Evening Sun,* Mar. 28, 1947; *Sun,* Jan. 19, 1948.

8. HUAC, *Communism* (1951), pp. 4502–3; idem, *Hearings* (1951), pp. 779–83; idem, *Investigation* (1957), pp. 894–925.

9. Information about individuals and their positions is scattered throughout hearings, newspaper stories, and trial records. In addition to citations in note 8, above, see *Sun,* Mar. 29, Aug. 29, 1940: *Evening Sun,* Feb. 19, 1951, Mar. 11, 18, 19, 1952; also interview, Albert E. Blumberg and Dorothy Rose Blumberg, by George H. Callcott, July 27, 1977.

10. HUAC, *Hearings* (1951), pp. 789–1119; idem, *Investigation* (1954), pp. 4121–64; idem, *Investigation* (1957), pp. 891–1086.

11. Interview, Albert E. Blumberg and Dorothy Rose Blumberg; interview, Maurice Braverman.

12. HUAC, *Hearings* (1951), pp. 764–67; idem, *Investigation* (1954), pp. 4098–99; idem, *Investigation* (1957), pp. 907, 1024–30; *Evening Sun,* Feb. 18, 1946; *Sun,* Apr. 27, May 26, 1946, Jan. 15 and 16, Nov. 8, 1947, Mar. 18, June 18, July 19, 1948, Aug. 26, 1949, Jan. 22, Feb. 28, July 3 and 25, 1950.

13. See the *Clarion,* which appeared in June, July, Aug., Oct., Nov., and Dec. of 1946, and Feb. of 1947. See also leaflets in "Communist Party," VF-Pratt; HUAC, *Hearings* (1951), p. 750.

14. *Sun,* Jan. 1, 1949, Aug. 9 and 10, Nov. 20, 1950.

15. HUAC, *Hearings* (1951), pp. 757–58.

16. HUAC, *Investigation* (1957), pp. 891–1086; Subversive Activities File, Attorney General's Office, Baltimore (hereafter Attorney General's Office).

17. HUAC, *Investigation* (1957), pp. 914–17; Shannon, *Decline,* pp. 354–70.

18. Subversive Activities File, Attorney General's Office; Roger E. Williams, "What's Happened to the Communist Party, U.S.A.?" *Saturday Review World* 1 (Feb. 23, 1974): 10–14; see, beginning in 1968, the *Daily World,* which replaced the *Daily Worker* after a ten-year lapse.

19. *Sun,* Oct. 28, Nov. 3–5, 1944; *Frederick News,* Oct. 25 and 28, Nov. 1 and 6, 1944; *Salisbury Times,* Nov. 4, 1944.

20. *Sun,* May 24, June 11, Aug. 23, Sept. 20, Oct. 1, 7, 8, 30, Nov. 1–5, 1944; *Frederick News,* Oct. 25, Nov. 3, 1944; *Salisbury Times,* Oct. 25 and 30, Nov. 1, 2, 4, 1944.

21. *Sun,* June 23, Sept. 23, Nov. 1 and 3, 1946; *Evening Sun,* Nov. 4, 1946; *Salisbury Times,* Nov. 1, 2, 4, 1946.

22. *Sun,* June 10, Nov. 1 and 2, 1946; *Cumberland Evening Times,* Nov. 1 and 4, 1946; Harry W. Kirwin, *The Inevitable Success: Herbert R. O'Conor* (Westminster, Md., 1962), pp. 417–547.

23. *Catholic Review,* passim; John Francis Cronin, *Rugged Individualism* (New York, 1937); idem, *Communism: A World Menace* (Washington, D.C., 1947); idem, *The Church and the Workingman* (New York, 1965); interview, Maurice Braverman.

24. Peter H. Irons, "American Business and the Origins of McCarthyism," in *The Specter: Original Essays on the Cold War and the Origins of McCarthyism,* ed. Robert Griffith and Athan Theoharis (Philadelphia, 1974), pp. 80–83.

25. *Catholic Review,* Mar. 15, 1946; John P. Bauernschub, *Columbianism in Maryland, 1897–1965* (Baltimore, 1965), p. 104.

26. *Sun,* Sept. 12, Oct. 5, 1945, Mar. 12, July 18, Aug. 18, Sept. 22, Oct. 1, 21, 27, 1946, Apr. 26, July 22, 1957; *Catholic Review,* Apr. 13, July 13, 1945, Jan. 25, Oct. 11, 1946.

27. Maryland Board of Motion Picture Censors, *Annual Report* (1948–1949) p. 4.

28. Carl N. Everstein, *History of the Grand Lodge of Ancient, Free, and Accepted Masons of Maryland, 1888–1950,* 2 vols. (Baltimore, 1951), 2:861–65.

29. *Sun,* Aug. 10, 1945, Nov. 1, 1948, June 3, Sept. 6, 9, 11, Oct. 13, 18, 1946, May 28, June 15, Sept. 9, 11, 1947.

30. For annual strike statistics, see U.S. Bureau of Labor Statistics, *Monthly Labor Review,* May issue.

31. Irons, "American Business," pp. 80–81. The following issues of *Baltimore:* 40 (Oct. 1947): 52–55; 41 (Feb. 1948): 10–26; 41 (Apr. 1948); 11; 41 (Aug. 1948); 55; 42 (Feb. 1949); 8, 25; 42 (Mar. 1949); 11. The following issues of the *Manufacturer's Record:* 115 (Jan. 1946): 68; (Mar. 1946): 29; (May 1946): 33; (June 1946): 33–35; (Nov. 1946): 37; 116 (Oct. 1947); 37.

32. See these organizations by name in VF-Pratt; *Sun,* Nov. 13, 1947, Nov. 1, 1948, June 3, 1949, Feb. 6, Nov. 6, 1950, Oct. 2, Nov. 3, 1951; *Evening Sun,* Oct. 5, 1950, Dec. 8, 1950.

33. Maryland Committee against Un-American Activities, Operation Anti-Communism (1950), pp. 1–3; *Evening Sun,* Oct. 29, 1948; *Sun,* Nov. 23, 1948, Aug. 6, 1950.

34. For the Hiss trial, see Maryland newspapers, Aug. 2, 1948, to Mar. 22, 1950; also, John Cabot Smith, *Alger Hiss: The True Story* (New York, 1976); Athan G. Theoharis, ed., *Beyond the Hiss Case: The FBI, Congress, and the Cold War* (Philadelphia, 1982).

35. *Journal of the House* (1982); *Journal of the House* (1949), pp. 374–75, 496–97, 674, 971, 972, 554, 459–60, 2000; *Journal of the House* (1950), pp. 173, 365–66; *Journal of the House* (1951), pp. 138, 486–87, 546, 774; *Journal of the House* (1952), pp. 497–99; *Journal of the House* (1953), pp. 68–69, 1563.

36. *Journal of the House* (1949), pp. 671, 1298–99, 1466, 1727; *Journal of the House* (1951), pp. 1174–81; 1824–1928; Civil Defense Agency, *Annual Reports* (1950–1969); David G. McIntosh, *America's Defense against Communism* (Baltimore, 1952); *The Old Line Alert,* June 1953–Feb. 1954; "Civil Defense," VF-Pratt; *Sun,* Nov. 3 and 7, 1963.

37. *Journal of the House* (1947), pp. 955, 1364, 1526, 2269–70; *Sun,* Oct. 28 and 29, 1948; *Maryland Manual* (1949), p. 135.

38. *Journal of the House* (1948), pp. 136–37, 151–53; *Journal of the Senate* (1948), pp. 22, 38, 70, 139–40; Frank B. Ober, "Communism vs. the Constitution," *American Bar Association Journal* 34 (Aug. 1948); 645–50; *Sun,* June 27, 1948.

39. Frank B. Ober et al., *Report of a Commission on Subversive Activities to Governor Lane and the General Assembly* (1949).

40. *Journal of the House* (1949), pp. 155, 558, 920, 1031, 1186, 1262, 1930; *Laws of Maryland, 1949,* pp. 96–105; William B. Prendergast, "Maryland: The Ober Anti-Communism Law," in *The States and Subversion,* ed. Walter Gellhorn (1952), pp. 140–83.

41. *Sun,* Apr. 23, 1949; *Washington Post,* Mar. 6, 1949; Prendergast, "Maryland," pp. 140–41.

42. See "Ober Law" in VF-Pratt for several score clippings and leaflets; Maryland Committee against Un-American Activities, *Operation Anti-Communism;* Prendergast, "Maryland"; *Maryland Manual* (1952), p. 272.

43. *Sun,* June 19, 1948; *Washington Post,* Mar. 4, 1949; Frank J. Donner,

"The Smith Act: Baltimore Version," *Nation* 175 (Nov. 8, 1952): 668; *Sun,* Apr. 2, 1949; Jan. 5, 1964; "Ober Law," "Communism," "Loyalty Oaths," etc., Files of Maryland Branch, American Civil Liberties Union, Baltimore; "Ober Law," "Loyalty Oath," Files of the Vice Chancellor for Academic Affairs, University of Maryland, College Park.

44. "Memorandum to Police," dated Feb. 22, 1953, in Correspondence File, Attorney General's Office.

45. State Aid Institutions File, Attorney General's Office; Thomas G. Pullen, *Report on Subversive Practices in the Montgomery County Public Schools* (1948); *Sun,* June 13, 1949.

46. Correspondence File, Attorney General's Office. Also interviews, Fred Oken, Director, 1963–1965, and Clarence W. Sharp, Director, 1973–1978, by George H. Callcott, May 24, 1977. Brief annual reports of the office appeared from 1952 to 1958 in *Report and Official Opinions of the Attorney General.*

47. *Sun,* June 19, Sept. 3, 1948; Baltimore Board of School Commissioners, *Annual Reports* (1946–1948), pp. 38–39; idem, *Annual Reports* (1948–1950), pp. 37–38.

48. Harry Stegmaier, Jr., et al., *Allegany County: A History* (Parsons, W.Va., 1976), pp. 428–29; *Sun,* Sept. 30, Dec. 8, 1950.

49. *Sun,* Jan. 27, 1950.

50. Ibid., Apr. 17, May 20, 1952.

51. Ibid., Aug. 4, 1952.

52. Ibid., Nov. 3, 1951.

53. Vincent Godfrey Burns, *Red Fuse on a World Bomb* (Washington, D.C., 1969), pp. 61–62.

54. Owen Lattimore, *Ordeal by Slander* (Boston, 1950); Fred J. Cook, *The Nightmare Decade: The Life and Times of Senator McCarthy* (New York, 1971), pp. 177–274.

55. Stanley Kelley, Jr., *Professional Public Relations and Public Power* (Baltimore, 1956), pp. 107–43; Senate Subcomittee on Privileges and Elections, *Hearings on the Maryland Senatorial Election of 1950,* 81st Cong., 2d sess., 1951; box 3 (1950), series 3 (elections), and boxes 1–7, series 2 (un-American activities), Tydings Papers, McKeldin Library, University of Maryland, College Park, Maryland; *Sun,* Nov. 5 and 6, 1950; (Annapolis) *Evening Capitol,* Nov. 6, 1950; *Hagerstown Herald,* Oct. 24, Nov. 3, 1950; *Salisbury Times,* Oct. 28, 1950; *Washington Post,* June 5, 1951.

56. *Sun,* Sept. 13, 1951; Oct. 30, 1952; May 12, 1957.

57. *Sun* and *Evening Sun,* Mar. 10–Apr. 4, 1952; Donner, "Smith Act," pp. 426–28.

58. *Sun,* Mar. 26 and 27, 1954; May 8, 10, 28, 1957; *Baltimore Daily Mail,* May 11, 1957.

59. Correspondence File, Attorney General's Office; *Sun,* May 11, 1953; *Washington Star,* May 17, 1953; *Evening Sun,* Jan. 27, 1971. The long court history of the Ober Law is reviewed in 389 U.S. 54 (1967) and 287 Federal Supplement 61 (District Court, Maryland, 1968).

60. In June 1953 the U.S. Department of Defense announced 24,965 U.S. battle deaths and 338 from Maryland; a subsequent figure was 34,200 U.S. deaths. This projects to about 460 from Maryland. *Evening Sun,* July 27, 1953; U.S. Bureau of the Census, *Statistical Abstract* (1980), p. 377.

61. U.S. Bureau of the Census, *Characteristics of the Population, Maryland, 1980* (1983), p. 22.

62. *Journal of the House* (1955), pp. 84–88.

63. George C. Herring, *America's Longest War: The United States and Vietnam, 1950–1975* (New York, 1979), pp. 252–72.

64. *Sun,* Oct. 16, 1969; May 9–20, 1970, May 4, 1971.

65. U.S. Bureau of the Census, *Statistical Abstract* (1980), p. 377; *Sun,* Jan. 25, 1973; *Washington Post,* Nov. 10, 1982; U.S. Bureau of the Census, *Characteristics of the Population, Maryland, 1980,* p. 22.

1. Theodore R. McKeldin, Jr., interviews by Charles L. Wagandt, Apr. 6 and June 10, 1971, Oral History Project, Maryland Historical Society; Baltimore, transcripts 8033; Theodore R. McKeldin, Jr., interview by Barry Lanman, Oct. 4, 1976, OH 8181; *Sun,* Jan. 14, 1951; Aug. 11, 1974.

2. McKeldin interview by Wagandt, May 9, 1973, OH 8033.

3. *Sun,* Apr. 25, 1943, Aug. 11 and 14, 1974; *Evening Sun,* Aug. 28, 1974; *News American,* Aug. 13, 1974.

4. McKeldin interviews by Wagandt, Apr. 6, 1971, May 9, 1973; *Evening Sun,* Apr. 25, 1943, Nov. 20, 1970; *Sun,* June 13, 1927, Aug. 11, 1974.

5. *Sun,* Oct. 22, 1950.

6. Ibid.

7. McKeldin interview by Wagandt, May 9, 1973; *Sun,* Nov. 25, 1967, Aug. 11, 1974.

8. McKeldin, "Inauguration, January 10, 1951," Speeches File, McKeldin Papers, McKeldin Library, University of Maryland, College Park, Maryland; *Sun,* Jan. 11, 1951.

9. *Sun,* Aug. 11, 1974; *Evening Sun,* Apr. 13, 1975.

10. *Sun,* Mar. 11, 1955; Nov. 26, 1967; Apr. 16, 1974; Jan. 1, 1975.

11. Abel J. Merrill, "Simon E. Sobeloff," *Maryland Law Review* 34 (1974); 491–97; Simon Sobeloff, *Commission on Administrative Reorganization of the State,* 12 pts. (1951–1953); Carl T. Richards, "Maryland's Administrative Reorganization: A Study of Decision-Making," (Ph.D. diss., University of Maryland, 1972).

12. *Baltimore News-Post,* May 15, 1958; *Sun,* Sept. 1, 1958; U.S. Bureau of the Census, *Census of Manufactures, 1963,* 3 vols., 3: 19–24.

13. Theodore McKeldin and John C. Krantz, *The Art of Eloquence* (Baltimore, 1952); Speeches File, McKeldin Papers, College Park; *Sun,* Feb. 12, 1952.

14. McKeldin interview by Wagandt, Mar. 29, 1973; Speeches File and American-Israel Society File, McKeldin Papers, College Park; Commission on Interracial Problems and Relations, *Annual Reports* (1951–1959); *Evening Sun,* Aug. 14, 1974.

15. Edward J. Miller, "Executive-Legislation Relations in Maryland: The Governor as Chief Legislator" (Ph.D. diss., University of Pittsburgh, 1973).

16. Sobeloff, *Commission on Administrative Reorganization.*

17. Richard W. Case, *Report of the Maryland Tax Survey Commission of 1949,* 4 pts. (1949–1951); State Roads Commission, *Proposed Twelve-Year Program for Road Construction, 1954–1965* (1952).

18. Compiled from biographical sketches in *Maryland Manual* (1951–1959).

19. Ibid.

20. *Evening Sun,* Apr. 17, 1953.

21. *Journal of the House* (1951); *Journal of the Senate* (1951); *Sun,* Nov. 2, 1950, Jan. 4, 1951, Apr. 3, 1951; Mar. 7, 1952; *Evening Sun,* Apr. 3, 1951.

22. McKeldin interview by Wagandt, June 30, 1971. For a chronological review of elections, see Franklin L. Burdette, "Modern Maryland Politics and Social Change," in *Maryland: A History, 1632–1974,* ed. Richard Walsh and

*Chapter 6.
The 1950s Euphoria
of Eisenhower and
McKeldin*

William Lloyd Fox (Baltimore, 1974), pp. 773–904; Elections File and Newspaper Clippings Files, McKeldin Papers, College Park.

23. *Sun,* Jan. 15, Feb. 16, Apr. 8 and 19, 1953; *Evening Sun,* Apr. 17 and
21, 1953.

24. McKeldin, Radio Transcript, Oct. 31, 1954, Speeches File, McKeldin
Papers, College Park; *Sun,* Aug. 11, 1974.

25. *Sun,* Jan. 6, 1955, Apr. 5, 1955; *Evening Sun,* Mar. 21 and 31, 1955;
May 5, 1955.

26. *Journal of the House* (1956), p. 614; *Journal of the Senate* (1956), p.
401; *Sun,* Feb. 2, 1956.

27. *Sun,* Mar. 11, June 10, 1958.

28. Comptroller of the Treasury, *Annual Reports* (1951, 1959).

29. For a summary of action by state agencies, see Theodore R. McKeldin,
The Governor Reports, 1951–1958 (Annapolis, 1958); for schools, see Maryland Department of Education, *Annual Reports* (1951–1959).

30. State Roads Commission, *Proposed Twelve-Year Program;* idem,
Annual Reports (1951–1959).

31. McKeldin, *The Governor Reports,* pp. 25–34.

32. Council of State Governments, *Book of the States* (1958), p. 401; State
Department of Corrections, *Annual Reports* (1951–1959).

33. Council of State Governments, *Book of the States* (1957), p. 198.

34. *Evening Sun,* Nov. 20, 1970.

Chapter 7.
The Black Revolution

1. Series by Thomas O'Neill, *Evening Sun,* May 18–23, 1942; Carter G.
Woodson, "The Negro in Maryland," *Negro History Bulletin* 12 (June 1949):
207–14; A. B. Hamilton and C. K. McGee, *Economic and Social Status of
Rural Negro Families in Maryland* (College Park, Md., 1948); Ira DeA. Reid,
The Negro Community of Baltimore (Baltimore, 1935); Herbert Lee West,
"Urban Life and Spatial Distribution of Blacks in Baltimore (Ph.D. diss.,
University of Minnesota, 1974), pp. 1–12; Maryland Interracial Commis-
sion, *Annual Report* (1928), pp. 9 and passim; Joseph R. Healy, Chairman,
Governor's Commission, Governor's Commission on Problems Affecting the
Negro Population, *Report* (1943).

2. Much of this chapter is based on the eighty typescript volumes of tran-
scripts of interviews conducted by the Lillie May Jackson–Theodore R.
McKeldin Oral History Project of the Maryland Historical Society, Baltimore.
I cite here the most useful transcripts by the name of the person interviewed
and transcript number. On Lillie May Jackson: her daughter Juanita Jackson
Mitchell, OH 8094, 8095, 8135; her daughter Virginia Jackson Kiah, OH
8097, 8126; her son-in-law Clarence Mitchell, OH 8154, 8198, 8209;
Vernon Dobson, OH 8131; Samuel Hopkins, OH 8121; David Glenn, OH
8112. Also, Blaine Taylor, "The Jackson-Mitchell Clan," *Baltimore* 66 (April
1973); West, "Urban Life," pp. 100–116.

3. Juanita Jackson Mitchell, OH 8095, 8097, 8135; Troy Brailey, OH
8147; Elizabeth M. Moss, OH 8140; Luther H. Stuckey, OH 8160; Enolia
McMillan, OH 8110.

4. Evelyn T. Burrell, OH 8138; Vernon Dobson, OH 8131; Juanita Jackson Mitchell, OH 8094.

5. Randall W. Bland, *Private Pressures on Public Laws: The Legal Career
of Justice Thurgood Marshall* (Port Washington, N.Y., 1973), pp. 5–11; John
Dorsey, "Thurgood Marshall," *Sun,* Feb. 20, 1966; Donald Murray, OH
8139; Juanita Jackson Mitchell, OH 8095; Elizabeth M. Moss, OH 8140.

6. Kenneth Gregory, "The Education of Blacks in Maryland: An Historical

Survey" (Ph.D. diss., Columbia University, 1976), pp. 349–51; Juanita Jackson Mitchell, OH 8095; David Zimmerman, OH 8173.

7. Governor's Commission on Problems Affecting the Negro Population, *Report* (1953); Hamilton and McGee, *Economic and Social Status*.

8. Governor's Commission on Problems Affecting the Negro Population, *Report* (1953), p. 123; West, "Urban Life," pp. 4, 21; Baltimore Urban League, *A Community Audit* (1950); *Sun,* Oct. 2, 1942, Mar. 23, 1943, Feb. 19, June 27, 1944, Feb. 12, 1950; Juanita Jackson Mitchell, OH 8138; John E. T. Camper, OH 8134.

9. Juanita Jackson Mitchell, OH 8183; Troy Brailey, OH 8147.

10. Governor's Commission on Problems Affecting the Negro Population, *Report* (1953), pp. 53–76; J. Harbey Kearns in *Sun,* Feb. 12, 1944; Troy Brailey, OH 8147; Evelyn T. Burrell, OH 8138; Willie Adams, OH 8210.

11. Willie Adams, OH 8210; Juanita Jackson Mitchell, OH 8095, 8097.

12. Governor's Commission on Problems Affecting the Negro Population, *Report* (1953), pp. ii–v; *Afro-American,* Mar. 7, Feb. 21, Apr. 4, 11, 25, May 16, 1942; *Sun,* Feb. 2, May 4 and 25, Sept. 25, 1942; Juanita Jackson Mitchell, OH 8183; John E. T. Camper, OH 8134; Elizabeth M. Ross, OH 8140.

13. West, "Urban Life," pp. 11–15, 25–28; Troy Brailey, OH 8147; John E. T. Camper, OH 8134.

14. McKeldin, OH 8033; Theodore R. McKeldin, *Fourth Annual Report on Municipal Activities, 1943–1947* (1947).

15. West, "Urban Life," pp. 88–91; "Baltimore: What Went Wrong?" *Black Enterprise Magazine* 2 (Nov. 1971); 40–48; John E. T. Camper, OH 8134; Robert Wells, OH 8102.

16. Census figures showed each of these wards to be 50 percent or more black throughout the period, and political managers regularly cited these wards to calculate the "black vote," but the actual number of black voters cannot be determined. For election figures, see *Sun* on day following elections. See West, "Urban Life," pp. 88–91.

17. Commission on Interracial Problems and Relations, *Annual Reports* (1951–1954).

18. John H. Fischer, "The New Task of Desegregation," *Nation's Schools* 56 (Sept. 1955); 43–48; Otto F. Kraushaar, Chairman, Commission on Interracial Problems and Relations, *Desegregation in the Baltimore City Schools* (1955); Elinor Pancoast, *Report of a Study on Desegregation in the Baltimore City Schools* (Baltimore, 1956).

19. Juanita Jackson Mitchell, OH 8095; Enolia P. MacMillan, OH 8110; *Sun,* May 18 and 19, 1954; Pancoast, *Report of a Study on Desegregation*.

20. Samuel Lee Banks, "Descriptive Study of the Baltimore City Board of School Commissioners as an Agent in School Desegregation" (Ph.D. diss., George Washington University, 1976); Reed Sarratt, *The Ordeal of Desegregation: The First Decade* (New York, 1966); Gertrude Samuels, "School Desegregation; A Case History," *New York Times,* May 8, 1955; Gregory, "Education of Blacks in Maryland," pp. 359–64; Thomas G. Pullen, OH 8026; Elizabeth M. Moss, OH 8140; Silas Craft, OH 8137; Robert B. Watts, OH 8120; David W. Zimmerman, OH 8073.

21. Weldon Wallace, "The City We Live In," *Sun,* Mar. 14–18, 1955; also, James R. Conant series, *News American,* May 20–31, 1962.

22. Maryland Commission on Interracial Problems, *A City in Transition* (1955); Baltimore Commission on Human Relations, *Annual Reports* (1956–1968).

23. Commission on Interracial Problems and Relations, *Annual Reports* (1955–1960).

24. See files on each organization in VF-Pratt; also, West, "Urban Life," pp. 88–99.

25. *Morgan College Spokesman,* May 4, 1960; Jan. 13, Apr. 27, 1962; *University of Maryland Diamondback,* Apr. 21, May 6 and 19, 1960; Commission on Interracial Problems and Relations, *Annual Reports* (1960–1963); David L. Glenn, OH 8112; Vernon N. Dobson, OH 8131; Lane Berk, OH 8146; Chester L. Wickwire, OH 8118.

26. Lenora Heilig Nast, "The Clergy and the Interfaith Movement, 1945–1980," in *Baltimore: A Living Renaissance,* ed. Lenora Heilig Nast et al. (Baltimore, 1982), pp. 89–92; Jules Witcover, *White Knight: The Rise of Spiro Agnew* (New York, 1972), pp. 75–85; *New York Times,* July 5–8, 1963.

27. J. Anthony Lukas, "Trouble on Rt. 40," *Reporter* 27 (Oct. 26, 1961); 41–43; *Sun,* Sept. 23, Oct. 10–18 and 21, Nov. 1, 3, 9, and 24, 1961; *Evening Sun,* Aug. 21, 1961; Commission on Interracial Problems and Relations, *Annual Reports* (1960–1964); J. Millard Tawes, OH 8074; David L. Glenn, OH 8112.

28. *Sun,* Nov. 9, 1961.

29. Commission on Interracial Problems and Relations, *Annual Reports* (1964–1965); *Sun,* Feb. 25, 1964; *Evening Sun,* Nov. 6, 1963; Feb. 25 and 26, 1964.

30. Commission on Interracial Problems and Relations, *Annual Reports* (1963–1967); Baltimore Commission on Human Relations, *Annual Reports* (1956–1968).

31. Commission on Interracial Problems and Relations, *Annual Reports* (1963–1965); *Cambridge Daily Banner,* Jan. 23, Feb. 2, Mar. 15, 1963; *Washington Post,* May 14, 1963.

32. Murray Kempton, "Gloria, Gloria," *New Republic* 149 (Nov. 1963): 15–17; Robert A. Liston, "Who Can We Surrender To?" *Saturday Evening Post* 236 (Oct. 1963); 78–80; Wendell P. Bradley, "Failure on Race Street," *Reporter* 29 (July 14, 1963): 20–22; L. Brent Bozell, "The Lessons of Cambridge and Salisbury," *National Review* 15 (Aug. 27, 1963): 145–47; "Gloria Richardson: Lady General of Civil Rights," *Ebony* 19 (July 1964): 23–30; J. Millard Tawes, OH 8074.

33. *Cambridge Daily Banner,* May 15–31, June 1–14, 1963; *Washington Post,* May 16–17, June 11–19, 1963.

34. *Cambridge Daily Banner,* June 11–18, 1963; *Washington Post,* June 12–19, 1963; Frank L. Williams, OH 8129; Marion C. Bascom, OH 8228.

35. *Cambridge Daily Banner,* June 16 and 17, July 12, 1963; *Washington Post,* June 19, 20, and 23, 1963; J. Millard Tawes, OH 8074.

36. *Cambridge Daily Banner,* Oct. 22, 1963.

37. Commission on Interracial Problems and Relations, *Annual Reports* (1963–1965); Ruth Ellen Wennersten, "The Historical Evolution of a Black Land-Grant College" (master's thesis, University of Maryland, 1974), pp. 97–103; Lane Berk, OH 8146; Marion C. Bascom, OH 8228; J. Parren Mitchell, OH 8170.

38. *Sun,* May 12–18 and 20, 1964; University of Maryland *Diamondback,* Feb. 12, May 6, 1964.

39. *Sun,* Sept. 2, 1964; *Evening Sun,* Sept. 2, 1964.

40. Commission on Interracial Problems and Relations, *Annual Reports* (1965–1968); Maryland Commission on Human Relations, *Annual Reports* (1969–1970); Baltimore Department of Human Relations, *Annual Reports* (1966–1974).

41. Otto Kerner et al., *Report of the National Advisory Commission on Civil Disorders* (Washington, D.C., 1968); CORE File, VF-Pratt; *Sun,* Oct. 5, 1966.

42. Wayne E. Page, "H. Rap Brown and the Cambridge Incident" (master's thesis, University of Maryland, 1970); H. Rap Brown, *Die, Nigger, Die* (New York, 1969), pp. 100–102; Senate Judiciary Committee, *Hearings on the Anti-Riot Bill,* 90th Cong., 1st sess., 1967; *Sun,* July 24–27, 1967.

43. Garry Wills, "For God So Loves Spiro Agnew That He Made Him Vice President," *Esquire* 71 (Feb. 1969): 57–61, 134–38; Evelyn T. Burrell, OH 8138; Frank L. Williams, OH 8129; Verda Welcome, OH 8145.

44. *Sun,* Mar. 31, Apr. 5 and 6, 1968.

45. Baltimore Commission on Human Relations, *Annual Report* (1968); *Sun,* Apr. 6–12, 1968; Apr. 7, 1969; Evelyn T. Burrell, OH 8138; Willie Adams, OH 8210; Verda Welcome, OH 8145; Juanita Jackson Mitchell, OH 8097, 8183.

46. *Sun,* Apr. 11–14, 1968; (Baltimore) *Afro-American,* Apr. 12, 1968; Wills, "For God So Loves Spiro Agnew," pp. 60–61; David L. Glenn, OH 8238; Verda Welcome, OH 8145; Juanita Jackson Mitchell, OH 8183.

47. Civil Rights Commission; Equal Employment Opportunity Commission; Department of Justice Civil Rights Division; Department of Justice Community Relations Service; Department of Education Civil Rights Division; Health and Urban Development Fair Housing Division; Health and Urban Development Equal Opportunity Division; Department of Labor Federal Contract Compliance Program.

48. Maryland Commission on Human Relations, *Annual Reports* (1969–1980); Baltimore Commission on Human Relations, *Annual Reports* (1968–1975); *Evening Sun,* series, Feb. 16–22, 1981.

49. Maryland Commission on Human Relations, *Annual Reports* (1968–1980); Baltimore Equal Opportunity Commission, *Annual Reports* (1968–1975); Maryland Commission on Human Relations, *Report on the Study of Weight and Size Discrimination* (1980).

50. For example, see Human Relations Commission for Baltimore, Baltimore County, Montgomery County, Prince George's County, *Annual Reports* (1966–1974); Washington Suburban Sanitary Commission, *Affirmative Action Plan for 1977–1978* (about 400 pages); Maryland Council for Higher Education, *Annual Desegregation State Report* (1975, about 600 pages, but about 100 pages shorter in each succeeding year).

51. See organizations by name, VF-Pratt; *Sun,* Apr. 4 and 16, 1967; *News American,* July 6, 1969; Willie Adams, OH 8210; Verda Welcome, OH 8145; Parren Mitchell, OH 8170; Marion Bascom, OH 8128.

52. U.S. Bureau of the Census, *Characteristics of the Population* (1940–1980); idem, *Housing Census* (1950–1980); Maryland Bureau of Vital Statistics, *Summary Reports* (1940–1980). See also Department of Economic and Community Development, *Maryland Statistical Abstracts* (1967–1984).

53. U.S. Bureau of the Census, *Characteristics of the Population* (1940–1980).

54. Ibid.; idem, *1970 Census of Population, Supplementary Report, Poverty Status;* Department of State Planning, *Maryland Family Income Characteristics* (1970); Department of Economic and Community Development, *Maryland Statistical Abstracts* (1967–1984); U.S. Bureau of the Census, *Characteristics of the Population, 1980, Maryland* (1983).

55. U.S. Bureau of the Census, *Characteristics of the Population* (1940–1980); U.S. Equal Opportunity Commission, *Minorities and Women in Private Industry* (1981).

56. John K. Garner and A. Stewart Holmes, *A Profile of Poverty in Maryland* (College Park, Md., 1973); Bradley R. Schiller, *The Economics of Poverty in Maryland* (Englewood Cliffs, N.J., 1973); Thomas Sowell, *Ethnic America: A History* (New York, 1981), pp. 122–24.

Chapter 8. The 1960s: Camelot and J. Millard Tawes

1. On Tawes's early life, see Thomas M. O'Neill, "Profile," *Sun,* June 6, 1946; obituary, *Sun,* June 26, 1979; Tawes, "Reminiscences," *Maryland Banking Quarterly* 3 (Spring 1974): 4–8; Jack Wennersten, interviews with Tawes in "History of Somerset County" (manuscript), chap. 9, pp. 11–28.

2. *Baltimore News-Post,* Sept. 6, 1938; *Sun,* Oct. 4, Feb. 22, 1937, Feb. 2, 1938, July 13, 1942.

3. *Somerset News,* Oct. 29, 1942; *Evening Sun,* Mar. 15, June 11, 1946.

4. *Somerset News,* May 27, June 3, 10, 17, and 24, 1943; *Sun,* June 7–9, 1943; *Evening Sun,* June 9–21, July 23, 1943.

5. *Sun,* Jan. 12, Feb. 14, May 8, June 9, 1946; *Evening Sun,* Mar. 1, 1946; Wennersten, "History of Somerset County," p. 19.

6. *Sun,* May 26, 1953, Jan. 17, 1956, Feb. 7, Apr. 7, 1957.

7. *Sun,* Jan. 8–10, 1958; *News American,* Jan. 9, 1958.

8. U.S. Bureau of the Census, *Statistical Abstract of the United States* (1978), p. 456.

9. Conley H. Dillon, ed., *Messages, Addresses, and Public Papers of J. Millard Tawes . . . 1959–1967,* 2 vols. (Annapolis, 1967).

10. *Sun,* Jan. 13, 1959, Apr. 1 and 10, 1961.

11. *Evening Sun,* Apr. 6, 1959; *Sun,* June 26, 1979.

12. Comptroller of the Treasury, *Annual Reports* (1959, 1967).

13. Tawes, "State of the State Message to the General Assembly," Jan. 19, 1966, in Dillon, *Messages,* 2:46.

14. The official history of the Tawes administration, reliable in statistics, is Tawes, *Governor's Report to the People, Maryland, 1959–1966* (Annapolis, 1967); see especially, pp. 5–12. Harry R. Hughes, Chairman, Committee on Taxation and Fiscal Matters, *Report* (1963); Enos S. Stockbridge, Chairman, Maryland Self-Survey Commission Relating to Education, *Report* (1959); Department of Education, *Annual Reports.*

15. Cary Kimble, "In Pursuit of Well-Being," *Wilson Quarterly* 4 (Spring 1980): 66.

16. John N. Curlett, Chairman, Commission for the Expansion of Higher Education in Maryland, *Public Higher Education in Maryland, 1961–1975* (1962), p. 12.

17. Edwin Warfield III, Chairman, Governor's Commission to Study the Problems of Expanding the University of Maryland, *A Plan for Expanding the University of Maryland* (1960); Curlett, *Public Higher Education in Maryland.*

18. Maryland Council for Higher Education, *Master Plan for Higher Education in Maryland, Phase I* (1969), pp. 2–7; catalogues of the colleges.

19. State Roads Commission, *Annual Reports* (1959–1967); Tawes, *Governor's Report,* pp. 15–18.

20. Each agency produced annual reports; see also Tawes, *Governor's Report,* pp. 21–26.

21. See agency reports; Tawes, "Address to the Governor's Conference on the Appalachian Region, May 20, 1950," in Dillon, *Messages* 1:71–74.

22. Tawes, *Governor's Report,* pp. 43–48.

23. Department of State Planning, *Future Administration of the State of Maryland Water Resources Activities* (1961); Department of Water Resources, *Water Resource Management in Maryland* (1967); Tawes, *Governor's Report,* pp. 31–34.

24. Charles L. Quittmeyer, *Report on the Chesapeake Bay Fisheries of Maryland* (Easton, Md., 1966); Tawes, "Address to the Chesapeake Bay Seafood Industries Association, November 14, 1964," in Dillon, *Messages* 2:280–83.

25. Tawes, *Governor's Report,* pp. 34–36; Maryland Economic Development Commission, "Evaluation of the Economic Impact of Private vs. Federal

Development of Assateague Island" (mimeographed, 1963), VF-Pratt; Peter Matthiessen, "Sand and Wind and Waves," *New Yorker,* Apr. 3, 1965, pp. 116–44; U.S. Department of Interior, National Park Service, *Assateague Island, National Seashore: A Proposal* (1965).

26. May Irene Copinger in *Sun,* Aug. 24, 1930.

27. Alan Z. Forman, ed., *Report of the Maryland Commission on the Status of Women* (1967); *Evening Sun,* July 29, 1974, June 2, 1975.

28. Forman, *Report of the Maryland Commission on the Status of Women;* also, "Women" and "Women's Organizations," VF-Pratt; Marianne Alexander, "Advancing the Status of Women," in *Baltimore: A Living Renaissance,* ed. Lenora Heilig Nast et al. (Baltimore, 1982), pp. 102–8.

29. Maryland Commission for Women, *Decade of Progress: Report to the Governor* (1976); *Women: A Journal of Liberation* (1969–1983).

30. League of Women Voters of Maryland, *The Maryland Experience: ERA* (1974); Governor's Commission to Study Implementation of the Equal Rights Amendment, *Report to the Governor* (1976).

31. Department of Human Resources, *Annual Planning Information Report* (1982); *Maryland Manual* (1938–1984); *Sun,* Dec. 12, 1978.

32. Joseph F. Kett, *Rites of Passage: Adolescence in America, 1790 to the Present* (New York, 1977); James Gilbert, *Another Chance: Postwar America, 1945–1968* (Philadelphia, 1981).

33. William E. Sedlack, ed., "New Student Census," 1965–1984, Counseling Center, University of Maryland, College Park.

34. *Sun,* Aug. 28, 1966, May 5, 1968, May 23, 1971.

35. Maryland Crime Investigating Committee, *Gambling Devices within the United States, With Emphasis on the Maryland Scene* (1963); *Sun,* Sept. 7, 1953, Dec. 27, 1954, June 5, 1957; Susan Hickey Shaffer, "Slot Machines in Charles County, Maryland, 1910–1968" (master's thesis, University of Maryland, 1983).

36. Maryland Slot Machine Study Commission, *Report* (1963); *Arundel Observer,* June 25, 1959; *Evening Sun,* June 9–12, 1957; *Sun,* July 23, 1957; Mar. 13, 1958.

37. Maryland Crime Investigating Commitee, *The Gambling Rackets within Maryland, 1956–1966* (1967); Anne Arundel County Citizens Committee, *Effects of Legalized Gambling in Anne Arundel County* (1959); *Sun,* July 15, 1959, Dec. 7, Mar. 13, 1960, Feb. 24, 1963, Mar. 6, 1966.

38. Maryland Gambling Study Commission, *Report* (1967); *Evening Sun,* Mar. 14, 1966; *Sun,* Dec. 10, 1967, Feb. 3, 1968, July 29, 1971; *Evening Sun,* May 15, Oct. 9, 1978, Dec. 14, 1978; see State Lottery Commission and State Racing Commission, *Annual Reports.*

39. John W. Sause, Jr., "Chronicle of the Building and Loan Industry in Maryland from 1852 to 1961," *Maryland Law Review* 22 (Winter-Spring, 1962): 1–30, 91–129; Richard W. Case, Chairman, Committee to Study the Problems Affecting . . . Savings and Loan Associations, *Report* (1963); *Sun,* Aug. 16, 1959, Apr. 30, 1962; *Evening Sun,* Feb. 10, Apr. 3, 1961, Nov. 17–24, 1965; *Baltimore News-Post,* Apr. 17, 1961.

40. Howard C. Bregel, Chairman, Governor's Permanent Commission on Municipal Courts, *Report* (1960); League of Women Voters, "Municipal Court Survey, January, 1962" (mimeographed), VF-Pratt; *Sun,* Dec. 7, 1964; *News American,* May 18, 1969.

41. Thomas B. Finan, Chairman, "Preliminary Report on the Police Department of Baltimore" (Xerox, 1962), VF-Pratt; League of Women Voters, "Report to the Board on the Police Department of Baltimore, January, 1965" (mimeograph), VF-Pratt; *Sun,* Dec. 7, 1964; *News American,* May 18, 1969.

42. John H. Michener, "History of Legislative Reapportionment in Maryland," *Maryland Law Review* 25 (Winter 1965): 1–21; *Sun,* Oct. 10, 1948,

Feb. 16, Mar. 25, May 25, July 24, 1962, Oct. 22, 28, 30, Dec. 23, 1965; *Evening Sun,* Mar. 2, 1962; *News American,* Oct. 10, 1965.

43. John P. Wheeler, Jr., and Melissa Kinsey, *Magnificent Failure: The Maryland Constitutional Convention of 1967–1968* (New York, 1970).

44. Results of all statewide elections appear in the *Maryland Manual* in the year following the election. For summaries of the campaigns, see Franklin L. Burdette, "Modern Maryland Politics and Social Change," in *Maryland: A History, 1632–1974,* ed. Richard Walsh and William Lloyd Fox (Baltimore, 1974), pp. 773–906.

Chapter 9. Poverty and the Welfare State

1. Isabel Platt Nelson, "History of Poor Law Legislation in Maryland" (master's thesis, Tulane University, 1941); Edward J. O'Brien, *Child Welfare Legislation in Maryland, 1634–1936* (Washington, D.C., 1937); Albert Goldstein, "History of Public Welfare Development in Maryland" (master's thesis, University of Chicago, 1938); Booz, Allen and Hamilton, Inc., *Public Welfare Organization and Administration in Maryland* (New York, 1964); League of Women Voters, *Public Welfare in Maryland* (1968); *Encyclopedia of Social Work,* 2 vols. (1977), 2:1503–12; James T. Patterson, *American Struggle against Poverty, 1900–1980* (Cambridge, Mass., 1981).

2. In addition to works cited in note 1, Janet E. Kemp, *Housing Conditions in Baltimore* (Baltimore, 1907); James B. Crooks, *Politics and Progress: The Rise of Urban Progressivism in Baltimore, 1896–1911* (Baton Rouge, La., 1968).

3. Dorothy M. Brown, "Maryland Between the Wars," in *Maryland: A History, 1632–1974,* ed. Richard Walsh and William Lloyd Fox (Baltimore, 1974), pp. 731–54; Donald S. Howard, *The WPA and Federal Relief Policy* (New York, 1943).

4. Brown, "Maryland Between the Wars," pp. 730–59; Board of State Aid and Charities, *Report to the Governor, 1939* (1940); Board of Welfare, *Report to the Governor, 1940* (1941).

5. Joseph Sherbow, Chairman, Maryland Commission on the Functions of Government, *Report,* 3 vols. (1975), 3:67.

6. The following publications of the Department of State Planning: *Initial Report of the Commission on Medical Care in the Counties of Maryland* (1944); *Interim Report of the Committee on Medical Care* (1947); *Hospital Survey and Plan for the State of Maryland* (1948); *A Survey of Industrial Medical Care in Maryland* (1950); *Report of the Medical Commission to Review the Medical Care Program* (1953); *Administering Health Services in Maryland* (1960).

7. Department of State Planning, *Administering Health Services in Maryland* (1960); Board of Medical Hygiene, *Annual Reports* (1940–1980); *Evening Sun,* Jan. 9, 1949.

8. Department of State Planning, *Report of the Medical Commission to Review the Medical Care Program* (1953); Maryland Department of Health, *Public Health in Maryland: Annual Reports* (1942–1980); *Maryland Health Bulletin* (monthly) (1940–1970); John P. Hivey, "Maryland Government, 1867–1956," in *The Old Line State: A History,* ed. Morris L. Radoff (Baltimore, 1971), pp. 355–87.

9. U.S. Department of Commerce, *Historical Statistics of the United States,* 2 vols. (1975), 1:340–41, 359.

10. Sherry H. Olson, *Baltimore: The Building of an American City* (Baltimore, 1980), pp. 372–78.

11. Ibid.; Baltimore City Health Department, Housing Bureau, *The Baltimore Plan of Housing and Law Enforcement* (1952); Robert K. Whelan,

"Decision-Making Process and Program Goals in Urban Renewal in the Case of Gay Street One and Inner Harbor One in Baltimore, Maryland" (Ph.D. diss., University of Maryland, 1971); Martin Millspaugh and Gurney Breckenfeld, *The Human Side of Urban Renewal* (Baltimore, 1958).

12. Roberto Brambilla and Gianni Longo, *Learning from Baltimore* (New York, 1979); Maryland Commission on the Functions of Government, *Report,* vol. 3, "Economic Development," pp. 1–31, and vol. 2, "Community Development," pp. 1–67; Louis S. Rosenberg, "The Low-Income Housing Effort in the City of Baltimore" (Ph.D. diss., Brandeis University, 1973); Regional Planning Council, *Low- and Lower-Middle Income Housing Production in the Baltimore Region* (1971); Sherry Olson, *Baltimore* (Cambridge, Mass., 1976), pp. 47–61; quotation is from Olson, *Building of an American City,* p. 377.

13. Baltimore Urban Renewal and Housing Agency, *Displacement and Relocation, Past and Future: Baltimore, Maryland* (1965); Constance L. Barker, *Relocation and the Housing Market in Metropolitan Baltimore, 1968–1975* (1968).

14. Whelan, "Decision-Making Process"; Baltimore Urban Renewal and Housing Agency, *Demonstration of Rehabilitation: Harlem Park, Baltimore, Maryland* (1965); Millspaugh and Breckenfeld, *Human Side of Urban Renewal;* Peter Bachrach and Morton S. Baratz, *Power and Poverty: Theory and Practice in Baltimore* (New York, 1970).

15. U.S. Department of Housing and Urban Development, *Statistical Yearbook, 1978* (1980), pp. 11, 311; James E. Skok, *Participation in the Community Renewal Decisions of Two Suburban Counties of Maryland* (College Park, Md., 1975); see also town and country histories.

16. U.S. Bureau of Labor Statistics, *Directory of National Unions and Employment Associations, 1977* (1978), pp. 61–63, 75.

17. Patterson, *American Struggle against Poverty,* pp. 126–41; Daniel P. Moynihan, ed., *On Understanding Poverty* (New York, 1969), pp. 3–25; Harrell D. Rodgers, *Poverty amid Plenty: A Political and Economic Analysis* (Reading, Mass., 1979); Robert D. Plotnick and Felicity Skidmore, *Progress against Poverty: A Review of the 1964–1974 Decade* (New York, 1975); U.S. Department of Commerce, *Historical Statistics,* 1:340–41; U.S. Bureau of the Census, *Statistical Abstract of the United States* (1979), p. 325.

18. Appalachian Regional Commission, *The Appalachian Experiment, 1965–1970* (1972); idem, *Appalachia, An Economic Report: Trends in Exployment, Income, and Population* (1972).

19. State Department of Welfare, *Report to the Governor* (1961–1969); State Department of Employment of Social Services, *Report to the Governor* (1970–1974); State Department of Human Resources, *Report to the Governor* (1975–1980). Also, Harry Bard, *Maryland, State and Government: Its New Dynamic* (New York, 1974), pp. 139–57; Rodgers, *Poverty amid Plenty;* Plotnick and Skidmore, *Progress against Poverty.*

20. James Leiby, *A History of Social Welfare and Social Work in the United States* (New York, 1978), p. 341; *Encyclopedia of Social Work* 2:1669; University of Maryland School of Social Work and Community Planning, *Information Bulletin* (1971), p. 17.

21. Plotnick and Skidmore, *Progress against Poverty,* pp. 2–29; Sharon Perlman Krefetz, "Urban Politics and Public Welfare: Baltimore and San Francisco" (Ph.D. diss., Brandeis University, 1976); Bachrach and Baratz, *Power and Poverty,* pp. 81–91, 140–64; Antoinette Coleman, "The Baltimore Community Action Program" (seminar paper, School of Social Work, University of Maryland, 1984).

22. Bachrach and Baratz, *Power and Poverty,* pp. 165–200; Baltimore Community Action Agency, *Progress Report* (1965); idem, *The War on Pov-*

erty [in Maryland]: A Synopsis (1966); Howard County Community Action Council, "Survey of Poverty in Howard County, with Recommendation for Its Elimination" (typescript, 1966), VF-Pratt; *Evening Sun,* Jan. 4, June 30, Dec. 9, 1965, June 26, 1968; *Sun,* Apr. 10, June 26, 1969, July 26, 1972.

23. Department of State Planning, *Deinstitutionalization: Problems and Opportunities* (1976); idem, *Inventory of State-Administered Human Service Programs* (1976).

24. Bachrach and Baratz, *Power and Poverty,* pp. 165–200; *Washington Post,* Apr. 24, 1979; Coleman, "Baltimore Community Action Program." Politicians from CAP: Parren Mitchell; Clarence Blount; Kenneth Webster; Mary Adams; Clarence DuBurns, William D. Schaefer.

25. Rodgers, *Poverty amid Plenty,* pp. 178–185; Patterson, *American Struggle against Poverty;* Department of State Planning, *Catalogue of State Assistance Programs* (1977).

26. See agencies by name, *Report to the Governor* (1900–1984); also, *Maryland Manual* (1969–1984); Bard, *Maryland, State and Government,* pp. 139–57.

27. Figures are partly estimates from U.S. Bureau of the Census, *Historical Statistics on Governmental Finances and Employment* (1979), p. 193; Department of Human Resources, *Report to the Governor* (1980); Council of State Governments, *The Book of the States, 1980–1981* (1980), pp. 402–31; Herbert Jacob and Kenneth N. Vires, *Politics in the American States: A Comparative Analysis* (Boston, 1976), pp. 368–71.

28. Department of State Planning, *Coordination in Human Services* (1978); U.S. Department of Housing and Urban Development, *Statistical Yearbook* (1980), p. 311; Eugene J. Meehan, *The Quality of Federal Policymaking: Programmed Failure in Public Housing* (Columbia, Mo., 1979).

29. Brambilla and Longo, *Learning from Baltimore;* Lawrence A. Bailey and Matthew A. Crenson, *Survey of Organized Citizen Participation in Baltimore* (Baltimore, 1971); "City on the Move," *Wall Street Journal,* Aug. 27, 1980; Charles M. Haar, *Between the Idea and Reality: A Study of the Origin, Fate, and Legacy of the Model Cities Program* (Boston, 1975); U.S. Department of Housing and Urban Development, *Statistical Yearbook* (1969–1979).

30. Patterson, *American Struggle against Poverty,* pp. 164, 171, 200.

31. U.S. Bureau of the Census, *Statistical Abstract of the United States, 1982* (1983), p. 325; idem, *Characteristics of the Population below the Poverty Level: 1982* (1984). The census provides state figures for random dates; figures for Maryland remain about 3.6 points below national figures. Mollie Orshansky, "Counting the Poor," *Social Security Bulletin* 28 (Jan. 1965): 3–29; *Encyclopedia of Social Work,* 2:1033–36.

32. See Charles Murray, *Losing Ground: American Social Policy, 1950–1980* (New York, 1984); Jonathan H. Turner and Charles E. Starnes, *Inequality: Privilege and Poverty in America* (Pacific Palisades, Calif., 1976).

33. U.S. Department of Commerce, *Historical Statistics* 1:126, 135; U.S. Bureau of the Census, *Statistical Abstract of the United States* (1984), p. 409.

34. These are national figures, not broken down by states. U.S. Bureau of the Census, *Characteristics of the Population below the Poverty Level: 1982* (1984); "Families Headed by Women Still Rise," *Wall Street Journal,* Aug. 28, 1980.

35. Maryland Department of Health and Mental Hygiene, *Vital Statistics, Annual Reports* (1960, 1977); Domestic Relations Division of the Supreme Bench of Baltimore City, *Annual Reports* (1957–1979); Sidney M. Norton and Margaret Bright, "Suicides in Baltimore City, 1950–1963," *Baltimore Health News* 42 (Dec. 1965); *Evening Sun,* May 1, 1956, Mar. 27, 1970.

36. Law Enforcement Assistance Administration, *Source Book, 1982*

(1983), table 4.19; Federal Bureau of Investigation, *Uniform Crime Reports* (1935–1982).

37. David Nurco, *Drug Abuse Study, 1969* (Baltimore, 1970); Baltimore Office of Drug Abuse, *Drug Abuse Control in Baltimore City, 1969–1974* (1974); Comptroller of the Treasury, *Alcoholic Beverage Division Reports* (1938–1984).

38. Housing Authority of Baltimore, *Baltimore's Blighted Areas: Housing Conditions and Family Characteristics, 1949* (1950); John K. Garner and A. Stewart Holmes, *A Profile of Poverty in Maryland* (College Park, Md., 1973); U.S. Bureau of the Census, *Characteristics of the Population below the Poverty Level: 1978* (1980); Oscar Lewis, "The Culture of Poverty," in *On Understanding Poverty,* ed. Moynihan, pp. 187–200.

Chapter 10. Spiro T. Agnew's Crusade for Good Government

1. Two excellent biographies provide details of Agnew's early life: Theo Lippman, Jr., *Spiro Agnew's America: The Vice President and the Politics of Suburbia* (New York, 1972), and Jules Witcover, *White Knight: The Rise of Spiro Agnew* (New York, 1972). Both are based on fine research, and I am indebted to them for the facts cited here. These facts, incidentally, often differ from facts obtained by reporters who mainly spoke to Agnew. For example, Lippman and Witcover demonstrate the prosperity of Agnew's father instead of penury, one semester at Hopkins instead of three years, and very limited success in early career instead of great success. I have also either adopted or concurred in Lippman's suburban theme; my chapter heading would have resembled his title if I had thought of it first. Also, Patrick J. Slogan in *News American,* Sept. 13–18, 1970.

2. Quoted in Carl Schoettler in *Evening Sun,* Oct. 11, 1973.

3. Lippman, *Spiro Agnew's America,* pp. 41–49; William C. Hughes, "A New Era?" chap. 10 in *A History of Baltimore County,* by Neal A. Brooks and Eric G. Rockel (Towson, Md., 1979), pp. 404–16; *Evening Sun,* Feb. 21, 1961; *Sun,* Dec. 16, 1962.

4. Lippman, *Spiro Agnew's America,* pp. 51–70; Witcover, *White Knight,* pp. 59–72; Brooks and Rockel, *Baltimore County,* pp. 380–383, 417–19; *Sun,* Nov. 4 and 5, 1966; *News American,* Sept. 2, Nov. 9, 1966.

5. Lippman, *Spiro Agnew's America,* pp. 71–85; Witcover, *White Knight,* pp. 138–49; Franklin L. Burdette, "Modern Maryland Politics and Social Change," in *Maryland: A History, 1632–1974,* ed. Richard Walsh and William Lloyd Fox (Baltimore, 1974), pp. 854–57.

6. Lippman, *Spiro Agnew's America,* pp. 86–101; Witcover, *White Knight,* pp. 150–55; William S. James, "Recollections of William S. James," 2 vols. (Hall of Records, Annapolis, used by permission), 2:85–88; Jonathan Cotten in *Sun,* Apr. 25, 1967.

7. George Stockton Wills II, "The Reorganization of the Maryland General Assembly, 1966–1968: A Study of the Politics of Reform" (Ph.D. diss., Johns Hopkins University, 1969); Robert G. Dixon, Jr., *Democratic Representation: Reapportionment in Law and Politics* (New York, 1968), pp. 217–26; Samuel B. Hopkins, *The Apportionment of the Maryland House of Delegates: An Historical View* (Baltimore, 1964); Burdette, "Modern Maryland Politics," pp. 841–42, 851–53.

8. Lippman, *Spiro Agnew's America,* pp. 86–96; Wills, "Reorganization of the Maryland General Assembly"; Burdette, "Modern Maryland Politics," pp. 866–82; Bradford Jacobs in *Sun,* Dec. 1, 1967; Gene Oishi in *Sun,* July 7, 1968; Charles G. Whiteford in *Sun,* Jan. 2, 1969; *Evening Sun,* Mar. 29, 1967.

9. John P. Wheeler, Jr., and Melissa Kinsey, *Magnificent Failure: The Maryland Constitutional Convention of 1967–1968* (New York, 1970); Marianne Ellis Alexander, "The Issues and Politics of the Maryland Constitutional Convention, 1967–1968" (Ph.D. diss., University of Maryland, 1972); Wayne R. Swanson, "The Politics of Constitution Revision: The Maryland Constitutional Convention, 1967–1968" (Ph.D. diss., Brown University, 1969). Also, if anyone should ever care, about sixty volumes of *Reports, Proceedings,* and *Journals* were published by the commission, and there are hundreds of boxes of special studies preserved in the Hall of Records, Annapolis.

10. John N. Curlett, Chairman, Commission for the Modernization of the Executive Branch, *Modernizing the Executive Branch of the Maryland Government* (1967); George S. Wills, Chairman, Citizens' Commission on the General Assembly, *Reports to the Legislature and the General Assembly* (1967); Alan Rosenthal, *Strengthening the Maryland Legislature: An Eagleton Study and Report* (New Brunswick, N.J., 1967).

11. See chapter 7. Also, Witcover, *White Knight,* pp. 11–28, 74–100, 156–79; Lippman, *Spiro Agnew's America,* pp. 102–13.

12. James, "Recollections," 2:85–88; interview, Roy N. Staten, by George H. Callcott, Feb. 10, 1983.

13. Cited in Lippman, *Spiro Agnew's America,* p. 155.

14. Witcover, *White Knight,* pp. 216–436; John R. Coyne, *The Impudent Snobs: Agnew vs. the Intellectual Establishment* (New Rochelle, N.J., 1972).

15. *New York Times,* Oct. 22, 1968. Lippman *(Spiro Agnew's America,* pp. 167–74) and Witcover *(White Knight,* pp. 128–36) clearly suspected scandal when they wrote in 1972, and they may have undertaken their books partly to uncover it. They suggest other improprieties that have never been tested in court. Without power of subpoena, these authors were unable to prove anything.

16. Lippman, *Spiro Agnew's America,* pp. 237–49.

17. The investigation and resignation were the topic of a dramatic book by Richard M. Cohen and Jules Witcover, *A Heartbeat Away: Of Vice President Spiro T. Agnew* (New York, 1974). The prosecution's case was extensively summarized in the *New York Times,* Oct. 11 and 23, 1973. A guide to the 2,685 pages of microfilm on the case is Thomas Fortune Fay's *Guide to the Microfilm Edition of the Spiro Agnew Case: The Investigation and Legal Documents* (Wilmington, Del., 1979).

18. Spiro T. Agnew, *Go Quietly . . . Or Else* (New York, 1980).

19. *Spiro T. Agnew v. State of Maryland: In the Court of Special Appeals of Maryland, September Term, 1981, no. 903,* 10 vols. (1981), filed in Maryland Law Library, Annapolis; *Sun,* July 21, 1980, Apr. 18–30, 1981, June 2, Oct. 7, 1982, Jan. 5, 1983. Clippings files exist for the trial principals in the VF-Pratt.

20. Arthur M. Schlesinger, Jr., "The Amazing Success Story of 'Spiro Who?'" *New York Times Magazine,* July 26, 1970, pp. 5–7, 52–56.

Chapter 11.
The Culture of
Bureaucracy

1. Bureau of the Census, *Historical Statistics on Governmental Finances and Employment* (1982); Department of Economic and Community Development, *Maryland Statistical Abstract* (1984); U.S. Civil Service Commission, *Annual Reports on Federal Civilian Employment* (1939–1973).

2. Frank Goodnow, Chairman, Commission on Economy and Efficiency in the State Government, *Report* (1916); Hooper S. Miles, *The Maryland Executive Budget System, A Review of Its Administration, 1916–1941* (Baltimore, 1942).

3. Walter H. Buck, *The Merit System in Maryland* (Baltimore, 1919); Charles S. Burke, Chairman, Maryland State Reorganization Commission, *Plan for the Reorganization of the Administrative Departments of the State Government* (1921); State Employment Commission, *Annual Reports* (1921–1980); Dorothy M. Brown, "Maryland Between the Wars," in *Maryland: A History, 1632–1974,* ed. Richard Walsh and William Lloyd Fox (Baltimore, 1974), p. 680.

4. Isaiah Bowman, Chairman, Committee on the Structure of the Maryland State Government, *Report* (1938); Comptroller of the Treasury, *Annual Reports* (1930–1950).

5. Simon E. Sobeloff, Chairman, Commission on the Administrative Reorganization of the State, *Reports* (1951–1953); Department of Budget and Fiscal Planning, *Maryland State Budgets . . .* (1955–1984).

6. State Planning Commission, *Annual Reports* (1933–1959); State Planning Department, miscellaneous publications, 1933–1984, especially *Activities Reports* (1961–1980) and *Maryland Manual* (1933–1984).

7. Edward Jay Miller, "Executive-Legislative Relations in Maryland: The Governor as Chief Legislator" (Ph.D. diss., University of Pittsburgh, 1973), pp. 71–79; L. Tucker Gibson, "The Role of the Governor in the Legislative Process: A Comparative Study of the Governor of Maryland and Virginia" (Ph.D. diss., University of Virginia, 1968).

8. John N. Curlett, Chairman, Governor's Commission on the Modernization of the Executive Branch of the Maryland Government, *Modernizing the Executive Branch* (1967); John G. Lauber, Director, task force, *A Management Information Program Evaluation System for the State of Maryland* (1969); John N. Curlett, Chairman, Commission on Executive Reorganization, *Executive Reorganization: A Comprehensive Plan for Maryland* (1969); Joseph Sherbow, Chairman, *Report of the Maryland Commission on the Functions of Government* (1975).

9. See Harry Bard, *Maryland, State and Government: Its New Dynamic* (New York, 1974); *Maryland Manual* (1970–1984); for an excellent series on the departments see *Sun,* Dec. 19–31, 1971, Jan. 1 and 2, 1972.

10. George A. Bell and Jean Spencer, *The Legislation Process in Maryland* (College Park, Md., 1963); Alan Rosenthal, *Strengthening the Maryland Legislature* (New Brunswick, N.J., 1967); Miller, "Executive-Legislative Relations in Maryland"; Gibson, "Role of the Governor in the Legislative Process"; William S. James, "Parliamentary Government in the Free State of Maryland" (Address to the Maryland Historical Society, 1972), William S. James Papers, Hall of Records, Annapolis.

11. Rosenthal, *Strengthening the Maryland Legislature;* Robert G. Dixon, Jr., *Democratic Representation: Reapportionment in Law and Politics* (New York, 1968), places special emphasis on reapportionment in Maryland.

12. See *Maryland State Budgets* (1965–1984); *Maryland Manual* (1965–1984); Miller, "Executive-Legislative Relations in Maryland," pp. 44–52; *Evening Sun,* Feb. 24, 1967, Apr. 13, 1971, Apr. 10, 1973; *Sun,* Mar. 7, 1971, Apr. 9, 1972, Aug. 27, 1973, Apr. 9, 1975, Apr. 13, 1976, Apr. 12, 1977.

13. Carroll T. Bond, Chairman, "Report of the Committee on the Judiciary," *Daily Record,* Oct. 22, 1942; Morris A. Soper, "Reorganizing of the Court of Appeals," *Maryland Law Review* 8 (Feb. 1944): 91–119; Elbert M. Byrd, Jr., *The Judicial Process in Maryland* (College Park, Md., 1961); Harry W. Kirwin, *The Inevitable Success: Herbert R. O'Conor* (Westminster, Md., 1962), pp. 309–14, 373–81.

14. Edward H. Burke, Chairman, Commission to Study the Judiciary of Maryland, *Report* (1953); Robert G. Dixon, Jr., "Judicial Administration in

Maryland," *Maryland Law Review* 16 (Spring–Summer 1956): 99–139, 186–221; Harry Bard, *Maryland: The State and Its Government* (New York, 1954, 1961).

15. Administrative Office of the Courts, *Annual Reports* (1955–1984).

16. Consumer Protection Division, *Annual Reports* (1967–1984); Office of the Public Defender, *Annual Reports* (1971–1984).

17. Jean Spencer, *Contemporary Local Government in Maryland* (College Park, Md., 1965); Don L. Boven and Robert S. Friedman, *Local Government in Maryland* (College Park, Md., 1955); Ray Eldon Hiebert and Richard K. MacMaster, *A Grateful Remembrance: The Story of Montgomery County, Maryland* (Rockville, Md., 1976), pp. 313–26; Neal A. Brooks and Eric G. Rockel, *A History of Baltimore County* (Towson, Md., 1979), pp. 398–409; M. Henry Eppes, *Home Rule in Maryland Counties* (College Park, Md., 1975).

18. Bard, *Maryland, State and Government* pp. 84–120; Spencer, *Contemporary Local Government,* pp. 77–84.

19. Bard, *Maryland, State and Government* pp. 117–120; Spencer, *Contemporary Local Government,* pp. 84–114; Washington Sanitary Commission, *Annual Reports* (1949–1980); Maryland-National Park and Planning Commission, *Annual Budgets* (1954–1980).

20. See note 1 to this chapter.

21. William R. Rawls, Chairman, Taxation Revision Commission, *Report* (1941); Joseph Sherbow, Chairman, Maryland Commission on the Distribution of Tax Revenues, *Report* (1946); State Fiscal Research Bureau, *Local Government Finances in Maryland* (1948); Legislative Council, Committee on Taxation and Fiscal Matters, *Report* (1955).

22. Maryland Commission on the Distribution of Tax Revenues, *Report* (1946); Comptroller of the Treasury, *Annual Reports* (1940–1980).

23. William Paul Walker, *Taxation in Maryland* (College Park, Md., 1962); University of Maryland, *Maryland Tax Study* (1965), pp. 187–88.

24. Department of Economic and Community Development, *Maryland Statistical Abstract* (1979), p. 295; University of Maryland, *Maryland Tax Study,* p. 38; U.S. Bureau of the Census, *Government Finances in 1981–1982* (1983).

25. The literature on the theory and sociology of bureaucracy is large. The following are modern treatments with full bibliographies: Ira Sharkansky, *Public Administration: Policy Making in Government Agencies* (Chicago, 1975); George E. Berkley, *The Craft of Public Administration* (Boston, 1975); Anthony Downs, *Inside Bureaucracy* (Boston, 1967).

Chapter 12.
The Fashions
of Education

1. Lawrence A. Cremin, *The Transformation of the School: Progressivism in American Education, 1876–1957* (New York, 1962), pp. 115 ff., 158–59, 280.

2. Russell Sage Foundation, *A Comparative Study of State School Systems in the Forty-Eight States* (1913); Abraham Flexner and Frank P. Bachman, *Public Education in Maryland: A Report to the Maryland Education Survey Commission* (New York, 1915).

3. Raymond S. Sweeney, "Public Education in Maryland in the Progressive Era," *Maryland Historical Magazine* 62 (1967): 28–46.

4. Maryland Department of Education, *Annual Reports* (1915–1941); National Education Association, *Education in the States: Historical Development and Outlook, Maryland* (1969), pp. 539–62; Amy C. Crewe, *No Backward Step Was Taken: Highlights in the History of Public Schools in Baltimore*

County (Baltimore, 1949), pp. 63 ff.; for an anthology of teacher recollections, see Margaret M. Casey, ed., *Our Legacy,* 2 vols. (Maryland Retired Teachers Association, 1976).

5. School Survey Commission, *The 1941 Survey of the Maryland Public Schools and Teachers Colleges* (1941), pp. 64–68 and passim.

6. All statistics in this chapter are from Maryland Department of Education, *Annual Reports,* unless otherwise noted.

7. Maryland Department of Education, *Redirection of the School Program in Wartime* (1942).

8. Maryland Department of Education, *A Decade of Progress in the Public Schools, 1939–1949* (1950); idem, *A Decade of Progress in Education in Maryland, 1949–1959* (1961).

9. Maryland Department of Education, *Decade of Progress in the Public Schools,* pp. 50–52.

10. William Dean Manifold, "A Consideration of Those Criticisms or Attacks Designed to Harm Public Education . . . in Maryland" (Ph.D. diss., University of Maryland, 1954); Maryland Department of Education, *Report of the Superintendent of Schools to Governor Lane on Charges of "Subversive Practices" in the Montgomery County Schools* (1948).

11. George H. Callcott, *A History of the University of Maryland* (Baltimore, 1966), pp. 331–33; see catalogues of particular institutions; Maryland Department of Education, *A Study of the Relationship between Subjects Taken and Other Selected Factors for the Class of 1958 . . .* (1959).

12. John H. Fischer, "The New Task of Desegregation," *Nation's Schools* 56 (Sept. 1955); 43–48; Baltimore Community Relations Commission, *Desegregation in the Baltimore Schools* (1969).

13. Commission on Interracial Problems and Relations, *Annual Reports* (1954–1965); U.S. Commission on Civil Rights, Maryland State Advisory Committee, *Report on School Desegregation in Fourteen Eastern Shore and Southern Maryland Counties* (1966); Reed Sarratt, *Ordeal of Desegregation: The First Decade* (New York, 1966), p. 310.

14. Sarratt, *Ordeal of Desegregation,* p. 114; Commission on Interracial Problems and Relations, *Annual Report* (1966).

15. Department of Education, "The Status of Ethnic and Cultural Instructional Programs and Integration in the Maryland Public Schools" (1977); U.S. Commission on Civil Rights, *Report on School Desegregation in Fourteen . . . Maryland Counties;* idem, *Long Day's Journey into Light: School Desegregation in Prince George's County, Maryland* (1976); idem, *School Desegregation in Dorchester County, Maryland* (1977).

16. U.S. Commission on Civil Rights, *Long Day's Journey;* "School Desegregation in Prince George's County: Two Views," *Civil Rights Digest* (Summer 1973), pp. 11–20; *Washington Star,* Jan. 28 and 30, 1973; *Washington Post,* Feb. 14, 1973, Nov. 18, 1976.

17. Baltimore City Schools, *Desegregation Plan for Baltimore City Schools* (1974); U.S. Commission on Civil Rights, *Long Day's Journey;* idem, *School Desegregation in Dorchester County.*

18. Governor's Task Force, *Maryland Plan for Completing the Desegregation of the Public Postsecondary Institutions in the State* (1974); Douglas Pear, "Desegregation in Higher Education in Maryland" (seminar paper, University of Maryland, 1982).

19. U.S. Commission on Civil Rights, *Long Day's Journey,* pp. 380–388; idem, *School Desegregation in Dorchester County,* pp. 13–14. These two publications contain good analyses, supported by polls of teachers and students, on the results of desegregation. Also, *Maryland Teacher* 34 (Spring 1977): 5.

20. "Forced Busing and White Flight," *Time* 112 (Sept. 25, 1979): 78.

21. Thomas G. Pullen, *Report of the Maryland Conference on Education* (Baltimore, 1955).

22. *Life,* Mar.–Apr., 1958; *U.S. News and World Report,* Nov. 1956, Jan. 1958; Enos S. Stockbridge, Chairman, Maryland Self-Survey Commission Relating to Education, *Report* (1959), pp. 9 and passim.

23. William L. Marbury, Chairman, Commission on Higher Education, *Higher Education in Maryland . . .* (1947); Edwin Warfield III, Chairman, Governor's Commission to Study the Problems of Expanding the University of Maryland, *A Plan for Expanding the University of Maryland* (1960); John N. Curlett, Chairman, Commission for the Expansion of Higher Education in Maryland, *Public Higher Education in Maryland, 1961–1975* (1962); Advisory Council on Higher Education, *Annual Reports.*

24. For example, Paul Goodman, *Growing Up Absurd: Problems of Youth in the Organized System* (New York, 1960), and Michael B. Katz, *The Irony of Early School Reform* (Cambridge, Mass., 1968).

25. "Maryland Conference on Education," *Public Education in Maryland* 16 (Feb. 1968): 1–3; *Sun,* Feb. 2, 1968; *Maryland Teacher* 25 (Apr. 1968): 67; *Maryland Teacher* 28 (Sept. 1970): 17.

26. College newspapers, 1964–1972; Commission on Interracial Problems and Relations, *Annual Reports* (1964–1972); Ruth Ellen Wennersten, "Historical Evolution of a Black Land-Grant College: The University of Maryland, Eastern Shore, 1886–1970" (master's thesis, University of Maryland, 1976); Jules Witcover, *White Knight: The Rise of Spiro Agnew* (New York, 1972), pp. 10–16.

27. University of Maryland *Diamondback,* Mar. 17–May 25, 1970; *Sun,* Mar. 23–May 20, 1970.

28. The following issues of *Public Education in Maryland:* 16 (Nov. 1967): 3; 16 (Mar. 1968): 1; 19 (Feb. 1970): 2–3; 22 (Mar. 1974): 3. Elizabeth D. Koontz, "Why Teachers Are Militant," *Maryland Teacher* 25 (Oct. 1967): 24–27; James A. Sensenbaugh, *Education in Perspective* (Baltimore, 1958); Clara P. McMahon and Samuel Strauss, *The Public Image of Education in Maryland* (Baltimore, 1967).

29. Department of Education, *One to Get Ready* (1967); idem, *The Alienation of Youth* (1972); idem, *The Schools We Want* (1970).

30. Wilson H. Elkins, *Forty Years as a College President: Memoirs of Wilson H. Elkins,* ed. George H. Callcott (College Park, Md., 1981), pp. 105–34.

31. *Public Education in Maryland* 21 (Dec. 1972); *Public Education in Maryland* 21 (May 1973); Department of Education, *Maryland Accountability Program Report, School Year 1973–1974* (1975); *Sun,* Apr. 11, 1972.

32. Terry Herndon, "Why Teachers Get Mad about Accountability," *Maryland Teacher* 31 (Spring 1974): 4–6; *Public Education in Maryland* 25 (Jan. 1977); *Public Education in Maryland* 27 (Feb. 1979); Department of Education, *Maryland Accountability Program Reports* (1973–1979); Robert A. Somerby, "Iowa Tests Are Not What They Seem to Be," *Evening Sun,* Feb. 5, 1981.

33. State Board for Higher Education, *Record* 6 (Nov. 1980); *Chronicle for Higher Education,* Oct. 6, 1980; *Washington Post,* Jan. 12, 1984.

34. Department of Education, *Maryland Accountability Report, School Year 1977–1978* (1979). For correlation of test scores with race, see table 12.1.

35. The following issues of *Public Education in Maryland:* 21 (Dec. 1972); 21 (Jan. 1973); 21 (May 1973). Department of Education, Division of Compensatory, Urban, and Supplementary Programs, *Annual Reports* (1971–1980); Department of Education, *Goals and Needs of Maryland Public*

Education (1973); Council of State Governments, *Book of the States, 1980–1981* (1980), pp. 350–57.

36. The following issues of *Public Education in Maryland:* 25 (Jan. 1977); 25 (Mar. 1977); 26 (Jan. 1978); 26 (Mar. 1978); 26 (Oct. 1978). The following issues of *School,* published by the Department of Education: 27 (Feb. 1979); 27 (June 1979); 28 (Oct. 1979); 28 (Apr. 1980). Department of Education, *Annual Evaluation Report of Programs Funded under ESEA, Title I, in Maryland . . . 1976* (1977).

37. Department of Education, *Annual Reports;* U.S. Bureau of the Census, *Money Income and Poverty* (1979), p. 2.

38. Leonard H. Rosenberg, Chairman, Commission on Structures and Governance of Education, *Final Report of the Governor's Commission on Education* (1975).

39. Elkins, *Forty Years As a College President,* pp. 153–76; David Riesman, *On Higher Education: The Academic Enterprise in an Era of Rising Student Consumerism* (San Francisco, 1980).

Chapter 13. Environment and Environmentalism

1. John R. Wennersten, "The Almighty Oyster," *Maryland Historical Magazine* 74 (Spring 1979): 80–93; idem, *The Oyster Wars of the Chesapeake Bay* (Centreville, Md., 1981); Jack Yeaman Bryan, "The Vanishing Oyster," *South Atlantic Quarterly* 48 (Oct. 1949): 546–56; Jack Kobler, "They've Been Fighting 173 Years," *Saturday Evening Post* 231 (Nov. 1, 1958): 31, 73–75; Sam Chambliss, "The Oyster Wars," *Skipper* 18 (Nov. 1958): 16–19; *Skipper* 18 (Dec. 1958): 2–21, 42–43; *Skipper* 19 (Jan. 1959): 24–26, 42–43; Board of Natural Resources, *Annual Reports* (1944–1984).

2. *Annual Reports of the Fisheries Commission* (1876–1906); *Reports of the Shellfish Commission* (1907–1916); *Reports of the Conservation Commission* (1917–1940); Board of Natural Resources, *Annual Reports* (1944–1984); Frank Henry, "Farming Invisible Fields," *Sun,* Apr. 22, 1951.

3. Wennersten, "Almighty Oyster," pp. 90–93; Rea Murdock, "Plunder on the Bay," *News American,* Mar. 30–Apr. 4, 1964; Albert C. Ritchie, "Seafood Conservation," *Maryland Conservationist* 4 (Winter 1927): 1–3; Board of Natural Resources, *Annual Reports* (1941–1984).

4. Harry W. Kirwin, *The Inevitable Success: Herbert R. O'Conor* (Westminster, Md., 1962), pp. 235–56; William H. Bayliff, "The Maryland Board of Natural Resources," *Maryland Conservationist* 20 (Winter 1943): 3–5; idem, "The Natural Resources Board," *Maryland Conservationst* 42 (July–Aug. 1965): 2–3; *Sun,* Jan. 24, July 5, Sept. 16, 1941; *Evening Sun,* May 24, 1940.

5. Board of Natural Resources, *Annual Reports* (1944–1958); *Sun,* May 2, 1947.

6. Bayliff, "Natural Resources Board"; Board of Natural Resources, *Annual Reports* (1959–1984); Department of Natural Resources, *Natural Resources Police: Ten-Year Report, 1969–1979* (1980); *Sun,* Mar. 8, Apr. 10, 1960, Aug. 20, 1968.

7. *Evening Sun,* Nov. 7, 1977; *Sun,* Jan. 10, 1979.

8. Gordon M. Cairns, Chairman, Maryland Soil Conservation Committee, *The First Twenty Years* (1958); *Sun,* Nov. 1, 1959; Maryland Association of Soil Conservation Districts, *Proceedings* (1977).

9. J. T. Singewald and T. H. Slaughter, *Shore Erosion in Tidewater Maryland* (Baltimore, 1949); Robert L. Green, Chairman, Governor's Commission, *Shore Erosion Policy for Maryland* (1961), p. 3; Energy and Coastal Zone Administration, *Maryland Coastal Zone Management Program, 1977–1980.*

10. Katherine A. Harvey, *Best-Dressed Miners: Life and Labor in the Maryland Coal Region, 1835–1910* (Ithaca, N.Y., 1969), pp. 319–71; University of Maryland, Bureau of Business and Economic Research, *Coal in Maryland's Economy* (1953); Kenneth N. Weaver et al., *Coal Reserves in Maryland* (Baltimore, 1976); Maryland Bureau of Mines, *Annual Reports 1937–1980.*

11. R. Samuel Jett, "Old Conservation Laws," *Maryland Conservationist* 15 (Summer 1938): 12–14; E. Lee LeCompte, "History of the Conservation of Natural Resources in Maryland," *Maryland Conservationist* 1 (Jan. 1924): 4–5, and *Maryland Conservationist* 1 (Fall 1924): 3–5.

12. Department of Forestry, *Annual Reports* (1906–1940); Board of Natural Resources, *Annual Reports* (1944–1980).

13. W. S. Hamill, *The Forest Resources of Maryland* (Baltimore, 1937); U.S. Forest Service, *Timber Reserves of Maryland* (1964); *Maryland Forestry* 2 (Summer 1976): 2; Department of Forestry, *Annual Reports* (1906–1940); Board of Natural Resources, *Annual Reports* (1944–1980).

14. In addition to annual reports: Department of Natural Resources, *Program Open Space: A Ten–Year Report, 1969–1979* (1979); Department of Forestry and Parks, *Maryland State Parks: A Master Plan . . . 1967–1976* (1966); Department of State Planning, *Maryland Outdoor Recreation and Open Space Plan* (1974); *Sun,* Nov. 30, 1955, July 19, 1960, Apr. 21, 1971; *Evening Sun,* Apr. 12, 1966.

15. University of Maryland, Bureau of Business and Economic Research, *Maryland Municipal Recreation Survey* (1960); Department of State Planning, *Open Space and Outdoor Recreation in Maryland* (1969); Maryland-National Capital Park and Planning Commission, *Annual Reports* (1952–1970).

16. Alfred Runte, *National Parks: The American Experience* (Lincoln, Neb., 1979); William H. Wroten, Jr., *Assateague* (Cambridge, Md., 1972).

17. Game Warden, *Annual Reports* (1938–1949); Board of Natural Resources, *Annual Reports* (1950–1980); *Maryland Conservationist* (1924–1980); Department of Natural Resources, *Wildlife Administration: Ten-Year Report, 1969–1979* (1980); *Evening Sun,* Feb. 2–8, 1951.

18. Department of Natural Resources, *Wildlife Administration: Ten-Year Report, 1969–1979; Maryland Conservationist* (1965–1980); Howard P. Brokaw, *Wildlife and America* (Washington, D.C., 1978).

19. *Evening Sun,* July 26, 1974; (Baltimore) *Daily Record,* Oct. 20, 1978; Department of Natural Resources, *Maryland Geological Survey: Ten-Year Report, 1969–1979* (1979); Board of Natural Resources, *Annual Reports* (1965–1980).

20. *Sun,* Dec. 28, 1971; *Evening Sun,* Apr. 2, 1977: Maryland Environment Trust, *Conservation Easements* (1976); *Maryland Manual* (1979), pp. 223, 451.

21. Department of Natural Resources, *Program Open Space: Ten-Year Report, 1969–1979* (1979); *Sun,* Jan. 22, 1967; Feb. 7, 1978; *Evening Sun,* Apr. 5, 1967; *Washington Post,* Jan. 24, 1972.

22. John Capper, Garrett Power, Frank R. Shivers, Jr., *Chesapeake Waters: Pollution, Public Health, and Public Opinion, 1607–1972* (Centreville, Md., 1983); Water Pollution Control Commission, *Biennial Reports* (1947–1955); Washington Suburban Sanitary Commission, *Annual Reports* (1922–1980); Board of Natural Resources, *Annual Reports* (1944–1980); *Sun,* Oct. 28, 1954.

23. Water Pollution Control Commission, *Biennial Reports* (1947–1955); Enos S. Stockbridge, Chairman, Maryland Self-Survey Commission, *First Report, Relating to the Administration of Water Pollution* (1957).

24. Douglas S. Gatlin, *State Administration of Natural Resources in Mary-*

land (College Park, Md., 1957); Department of State Planning, *Future Administration of . . . Water Resources Activities,* 2 vols. (1961); *Sun,* July 22–24, 1957; June 26, 1977.

25. Department of Natural Resources, *Annual Report* (1964), pp. 147–49; *Sun,* Feb. 17, 1963; Apr. 23, 1970; *Evening Sun,* Mar. 25, 1970; State Department of Health, *Pollution in Maryland* (1970); Nancy B. Grabler, "Baltimore's Industries Clean Up," *Baltimore Magazine* 66 (March 1973): 21–23, 58–59.

26. J. Clarence Davies and Barbara Davies, *Politics of Pollution* (Indianapolis, Ind., 1975); Charles O. Jones, "Regulating the Environment," in *Politics in the American States,* ed. Herbert Jacob and Kenneth N. Vines (Boston, 1976), pp. 388–427.

27. For activities of societies, see VF-Pratt.

28. Joseph M. Petulla, *American Environmental History* (San Francisco, 1977), pp. 239–383; Board of Natural Resources, *Annual Reports* (1960–1980).

29. Davies and Davies, *Politics of Pollution;* Jones, "Regulating the Environment"; Petulla, *American Environmental History; Book of the States, 1980–1981* (1980), pp. 497–512; *Evening Sun,* Apr. 20, 1970; *Sun,* Apr. 23, 1970.

30. *Sun,* Dec. 28, 1971, Apr. 29, 1972, July 3, 1973, Apr. 4, 1974, July 9–12, 1975, Apr. 25, 1977, Dec. 3, 1978; *Evening Sun,* Aug. 7, Nov. 14, 1974, Apr. 28, 1975, Apr. 24, Dec. 8, 1977; Mar. 4, 1978; Department of Natural Resources, *Significant Sources of Wastewater Discharge in Maryland* (1972).

31. Jones, "Regulating the Environment," pp. 411–12, and Board of Natural Resources, *Annual Reports* (1944–1984).

32. Elizabeth H. Haskell and Victoria S. Price, *State Environmental Management: Case Studies of Nine States* (New York, 1973), pp. 210–28; Department of Natural Resources, *Maryland Environmental Service: Ten-Year Report, 1969–1979* (1980); Harry Bard, *Maryland, State and Government: Its New Dynamic* (New York, 1974), pp. 231–34; *News American,* July 23, 1981.

33. Kenneth E. Perkins, "Power Plant Site Acquisition: A Status Report," *Baltimore Engineer* 48 (Dec. 1974): 4–7; Board of Natural Resources, *Annual Reports* (1970–1984). *Evening Sun,* May 7, 1976; *Sun,* June 14, 1983; Baltimore Gas and Electric, *Annual Reports* (1968–1984).

34. *Sun,* Dec. 3, 1978.

35. Cited from records of U.S. Environmental Protection Agency in Davies and Davies, *Politics of Pollution,* 157.

36. *Sun,* Feb. 15, 1972, Oct. 4, 1976, Sept. 23, 1977; *News American,* Oct. 3, 1976.

37. Extremely detailed statistics but no summaries appear in U.S. Geological Survey, *Water Resources for Maryland and Delaware,* published annually (1965–1980), and Department of Health, *Maryland Air Quality Report,* annually (1967–1980); also, *Sun,* Nov. 29, 1976, May 6, 1978.

38. *Sun,* Mar. 26, 1979; *Washington Post,* Feb. 1, 1981; Citizens' Program for the Chesapeake Bay, *Choices for the Chesapeake: An Action Agenda, 1983 Chesapeake Bay Conference Report* (1984).

Chapter 14. The 1970s Aftermath of Idealism: Richard Nixon and Marvin Mandel

1. Isaac M. Fein, *The Making of An American Jewish Community: The History of Baltimore Jewry From 1773 to 1920* (Philadelphia, 1971); Suzanne Ellery Greene, *Baltimore: An Illustrated History* (Woodland Hills, Calif., 1980), pp. 89–90, 162–64; Charles G. Whiteford in *Sun,* Oct. 29–31, 1958; *Sun,* Mar. 16 and 19, 1977.

2. Interview with Frank A. DeFilippo by George H. Callcott, Mar. 8, 1983.

3. Accounts of Mandel's youth obtained from interviews cited in *Sun,* Dec. 6, 1968, Jan. 8, 1969; *Annapolis Evening Capitol,* Dec. 28, 1968; *Washington Star,* Feb. 27, 1974; *News American,* Feb. 29, 1972, Aug. 24, 1977. Also, City College *Annual,* 1937; University of Maryland *Annuals* (1938–1941; Bradford Jacobs, *Thimbleriggers: The Law* v. *Governor Marvin Mandel* (Baltimore, 1984).

4. Michael Kernan in *Washington Post,* Jan. 8, 1969.

5. *Evening Sun,* Jan. 25, 1952, June 28, Nov. 3, 1954, May 8, 1958.

6. *Baltimore Evening News,* Nov. 7, 13–14, 1962, Feb. 20, 1963; *Sun,* Nov. 7, 1962.

7. *Sun,* Dec. 4, 1968, Aug. 24, 1977; *Annapolis Evening Capitol,* Jan. 14, 1969.

8. *Sun,* July 16, 1973; Sally Quinn in *Washington Post,* Aug. 16, 1974; *Washington Post,* Nov. 14, 1976.

9. *Sun,* Jan. 8, 1969; *Evening Sun,* Jan. 8 and 17, 1969; *News American,* Aug. 24, 1977; William S. James, "Recollections," 2 vols. (Hall of Records, Annapolis), 1:87–92.

10. Gene Oishi in *Sun,* Jan. 12, 1969; *Sun,* Jan. 21, 1971; Thomas B. Edsall in *Evening Sun,* Apr. 8, 1973; *News American,* Aug. 24, 1977.

11. *Sun,* Apr. 7, 1971; Editorial, *Sun,* Apr. 17, 1971; *Washington Star,* Aug. 23, 1977; James, "Recollections," 1:90–92.

12. *Evening Sun,* Jan. 8, 1969, Jan. 1, Apr. 3, 1970; *Sun,* Mar. 26, 1969, Mar. 24, 1970. Detailed appropriations are reported in *Maryland State Budget* (annually); detailed revenues and expenditures are reported in Comptroller of the Treasury, *Annual Report;* summary appropriations are most available in *Maryland Manual.*

13. John N. Curlett, Chairman, Governor's Commision on the Modernization of the Executive Branch of the Maryland Government, *Modernizing the Executive Branch* (1967); idem, *Executive Reorganization: A Comprehensive Plan for Maryland* (1969); Carl T. Richards, "Maryland's Administrative Reorganization" (Ph.D. diss., University of Maryland, 1972); Franklin L. Burdette, "Modern Maryland Politics and Social Change," in *Maryland: A History, 1632–1974,* ed. Richard Walsh and William Lloyd Fox (Baltimore, 1974), pp. 858–59, 882–85; *Maryland Manual* (1969–1972).

14. Edsall in *Evening Sun,* Apr. 8, 1973; *Washington Post,* Jan. 15, 1969, June 1, 1975; *Sun,* Jan. 9, Apr. 13, 1969, Nov. 26, 1975.

15. Administrative Office of the Courts, *Annual Reports* (1967–1975); James, "Recollections," 1:90–100.

16. *Sun* and *Evening Sun,* Mar. 26, 1969, Apr. 1, 1970.

17. Fred Barbash, "Mandel and the Establishment," *Washington Post,* June 2, 1975; *Sun,* Jan. 12, Mar. 26, 1969; *Evening Sun,* Apr. 3, 1970; *Washington Star,* Apr. 8, 1971.

18. *Sun,* Nov. 6, 1974; Quinn in *Washington Post,* Aug. 16, 1974.

19. Barbash in *Washington Post,* June 1, 1975; Jerome Kelly in *Evening Sun,* Aug. 23, 1971; Louis Azrael in *Baltimore News-American,* Nov. 30, 1980; *Sun,* May 12, June 20, Nov. 25, 1975, Aug. 24, 1977, Jan. 7, 1979.

20. *Sun,* Oct. 3, 1969, Sept. 16, Nov. 4, 1970; *Washington Post,* Sept. 5, 1970; Edsall in *Evening Sun,* Apr. 8, 1973.

21. *Sun,* Apr. 11, 1971, Apr. 11, 1972, Apr. 9, 1974; *Evening Sun,* Apr. 13, 1971, Apr. 10, 1973; James, "Recollections," 1:101–9.

22. *Maryland Manual* (1958–1983).

23. *Sun,* Jan. 15, Mar. 11, 1969, Sept. 25, 1970.

24. Evening Sun, May 10, May 23, 1973; *Sun,* Aug. 24 and 27, 1973, Apr. 9, 1974.

25. Barry Rascovar in *Sun,* Nov. 25, 1975; *Sun,* Jan. 9 and 22, 1972, Mar. 10, 1974, Feb. 9, 1975, Aug. 24, 1977; Barbash in *Washington Post,* June 1, 1975; *Washington Post,* Jan. 24, 1973; Edsall in *Evening Sun,* Apr. 8, 1973; *Washington Star,* Feb. 8, 1975; Interview, Bradford McE. Jacobs by George H. Callcott, Mar. 1, 1983.

26. Quinn in *Washington Post,* Aug. 16, 1974; *Washington Post,* July 4, Sept. 21, 1973, July 14, 1975, Nov. 14, 1976; *Washington Star,* July 4, 1973; *Sun,* July 6, 1973.

27. *Sun,* Dec. 6 and 7, 1970; *Washington Star,* Dec. 5, 12, and 30, 1970; *Appellants' Brief, United States of America* vs. *Marvin Mandel et al., United States Court of Appeals for the Fourth Circuit* (1978), Law Library, Court of Appeals, Annapolis, pp. 19–24.

28. *Washington Post,* June 6, 1972, Nov. 11, 1974; Quinn in *Washington Post,* Aug. 16, 1974.

29. *Sun,* July 4, 1973; *Washington Post,* Nov. 14, 1976.

30. Barbara Palmer, "Love Story," *Washington Magazine* 15 (Feb. 1980): 82–86; *Sun,* July 6, 1973, Aug. 24, 1977; Quinn in *Washington Post,* Aug. 16, 1974; *Washington Star,* Feb. 27, 1974.

31. *Evening Sun,* May 23, Sept. 1, 1973; *Sun,* Apr. 8, Dec. 16, 1973, Nov. 7, 1974, Jan. 12, 1975; *Washington Post,* July 14, 1974.

32. *Washington Post,* Nov. 14, 1976; *Sun,* Aug. 24, 1977; *Baltimore News American,* Aug. 24, 1977; Interview with Frank A. DeFilippo by George H. Callcott, Mar. 8, 1983.

33. Barry Rascovar in *Sun,* Feb. 1, 4, and 6, 1975; *Washington Post,* Nov. 14, 1976.

34. *Sun,* Jan. 16, 1975; *Washington Post,* Nov. 14, 1976.

35. *Sun,* Apr. 9, 1975, Apr. 13, 1976, Apr. 12, 1977.

36. Peter Jay in *Sun,* Feb. 27, *Sun,* Mar. 10, 1974; Barbash in *Washington Post,* June 1, 1975. The fullest and best indictment of Mandel is Jacobs, *Thimbleriggers.*

37. *Briefs* (13), *United States* vs. *Marvin Mandel et al., United States Court of Appeals for the Fourth Circuit* (1978), Maryland Law Library, Court of Appeals, Baltimore; for complete indictment see *Sun,* Nov. 25, 1975; Barbash in *Washington Post,* June 1, 1975; *Washington Post,* Nov. 14, 1976, Nov. 22, 1977.

38. Ibid. Also, *Sun,* Oct. 27, 1976; Jacobs, *Thimbleriggers.*

39. *Briefs; Sun,* Nov. 25, 1975, Sept. 21, 1976, July 24, Aug. 24, 1977, Jan. 12, 1979; *Washington Post,* Apr. 22, 1977, Nov. 7, 1979; *News American,* Aug. 24, 1977.

40. CA Md 591, F 2nd 1347; CA Md. 550 F 2nd 1001; DC Md 505 F Supp 189; DC Md 437 F Supp 262, 258; DC Md 431 F Supp 90; DC Md 415 F Supp 1079, 1033, 1025, 997; DC Md 602 F 2nd 653; "United States vs. Mandel: The Mail Fraud and En Banc Procedural Issues," *Maryland Law Review* 40 (1981): 550–89.

41. *Washington Post,* Nov. 12, 1977; *Sun,* Jan. 31, 1978, Feb. 1, Dec. 6, 1979; Jacobs, *Thimbleriggers.*

42. Newspaper coverage of each case was complete and can be followed in the clippings in VF-Pratt.

43. Charles C. Barker, *Background of the Revolution in Maryland* (New Haven, Conn., 1940), pp. 240–53.

44. Frank R. Kent, *The Story of Maryland Politics* (Baltimore, 1911); Jacobs, *Thimbleriggers,* pp. 42–43, 71–72.

45. U.S. Department of Justice, *Annual Reports* (1960–1984); Richard M. Cohen and Jules Witcover, *A Heartbeat Away: Of Vice President Spiro T. Agnew* (New York, 1974), pp. 7, 61.

46. Most of the institutions listed here issued annual reports, which pro-

vide the major source for this section. Also, see Lenora Nash et al., eds., *Baltimore: A Living Renaissance* (Baltimore, 1982).

47. Maryland Historical Trust, *Annual Reports.*

48. Department of State Planning, *Historical Survey of Capital Improvements Authorized by the General Assembly, 1969 through 1983* (1983).

49. Maryland Public Broadcasting, Maryland Arts Council, Maryland Humanities Council, Maryland Department of Economic and Community Development, *Annual Reports* (1961–1984).

50. Department of Education, "Maryland Public Libraries," *Annual Reports* (1940–1984); Baltimore Museum of Art, Walters Art Gallery, Washington County Museum of Fine Arts, *Annual Reports;* Elliott Galkin, "Recent Classical Groups," in Nash et al., *Baltimore,* p. 176.

51. See chapter 2 herein.

52. Nash et al., *Baltimore.*

53. Arthur R. Blumenthal, ed., *350 Years of Art and Architecture in Maryland* (College Park, Md., 1984).

Chapter 15.
The Respite of
Ford and Carter,
Lee and Hughes

1. U.S. Bureau of the Census, *Statistical Abstracts* (1940–1983); also, Department of Economic and Community Development, *Statistical Abstracts* (1967–1983).

2. Stephen Hess, *American Political Dynasties* (Garden City, N.Y., 1966), pp. 49–81; John Saar, "The Lees of Maryland," *Washington Post,* Nov. 23–25, 1973; *Sun,* Sept. 19, 1977.

3. Saar in *Washington Post,* Nov. 24, 1973.

4. Ibid.; also, Elections, 1954 and 1958, and General Assembly, 1955 to 1962 in VF-Pratt.

5. *Sun,* June 8, 1961, May 16, 1962; *Washington Star,* July 20 and 29, 1961, Jan. 15, 1962.

6. *Sun,* Jan. 10, 1969; *Washington Post,* Jan. 9, 1969, Nov. 24, 1973, Jan. 7, 1979; *Prince George's Sentinel,* May 13, 1971; *Washington Star,* Nov. 3, 1975.

7. *Sun,* May 19, 1971; *Washington Post,* Nov. 24, 1973, Nov. 27, 1977.

8. *Sun,* June 5 and 7, Oct. 9, 1977, Sept. 24, 1978; *Evening Sun,* Feb. 21, 1978; *Washington Post,* November 24 and 25, 1973, Aug. 7, 1977, Mar. 6, 1978; *Washington Star,* Aug. 23, 1977; *News American,* Nov. 25, 1975.

9. *Sun,* Nov. 27, 1977, Dec. 21, 1978.

10. *Washington Post,* Aug. 7, 1977, Mar. 6, 1978; *Sun,* Jan. 19, Apr. 12, Sept. 24, 1978; *News American,* Apr. 12, 1978.

11. "Harry Roe Hughes," *Maryland Reporter* 5 (Nov. 15, 1955): 3–4; *Washington Post,* Aug. 31, 1978; *Sun,* May 29, 1979; interview with Harry R. Hughes by George H. Callcott, June 14, 1984.

12. *Washington Post,* Apr. 18, 1967, Aug. 31, 1978.

13. Louis F. Peddicord, "Portage for People and Products," *Maryland Magazine* 9 (Spring 1977): 44–47; *Washington Post,* Jan. 5, 1971, Aug. 31, Nov. 1, 1978.

14. Alan M. Wilner, *The Maryland Board of Public Works* (Annapolis, 1984), pp. 113–15; *Washington Post,* May 28, June 16, 1977; *Sun,* May 28 and 29, 1977.

15. *Washington Post,* Nov. 9, 1978; *Sun,* Nov. 4, 1978; *Evening Sun,* Dec. 28, 1977.

16. Interview with Harry R. Hughes, June 14, 1984.

17. *Sun,* Jan. 20, Mar. 28, 1979, Jan. 7 and 17, Nov. 16 and 18, 1980, Oct. 17, 1982; *Evening Sun,* Aug. 31, 1978, Mar. 20, 1983; *Washington*

Post, Jan. 10, Feb. 17, 1979, Jan. 1, 1981; *Washington Star,* Jan. 8, 20, and 28, 1979; *News American,* Dec. 16, 1979.

18. Constant H. Jacquet, *Yearbook of American and Canadian Churches* (Nashville, Tenn., 1984); *Sun,* Mar. 25, Apr. 19, 1979, Apr. 8, 1980; *Washington Post,* Apr. 8, 1980, April 19, 1984; *Sun,* Apr. 18, 1981; *Evening Sun,* Apr. 14, 1981; *News American,* Apr. 19, 1981; *Evening Sun,* Apr. 13, 1982; *Sun,* Apr. 14, 1982, Apr. 11 and 13, 1983; *Evening Sun,* Apr. 12, 1983.

19. U.S. Bureau of the Census, *Statistical Abstracts* (1982–1983), p. 449. Wealth of the top 1 percent is available on a national basis only; for definition of poverty and numbers of the poor, see chapter 9 herein.

About the Author

George H. Callcott is professor of history and formerly Vice Chancellor for Academic Affairs at the University of Maryland, College Park. He is the author of *A History of the University of Maryland,* and *History in the United States, 1800–1860* (the latter also available from Johns Hopkins).

THE JOHNS HOPKINS UNIVERSITY PRESS

Maryland and America, 1940–1980

This book was composed in Sabon text and display type by
BG Composition, Inc., from a design by Chris L. Smith. It
was printed on 60 lb. Warren's Olde Style Wove Offset paper
and bound in Holliston's Payko by the Maple Press Company.